THE ROUTLEDGE HISTORY
OF THE RENAISSANCE

Drawing together the latest research in the field, *The Routledge History of the Renaissance* treats the Renaissance not as a static concept but as one of ongoing change within an international framework. It takes as its unifying theme the idea of exchange and interchange through the movement of goods, ideas, disease and people, across social, religious, political and physical boundaries.

Covering a broad range of temporal periods and geographic regions, the chapters discuss topics such as the material cultures of Renaissance societies; the increased popularity of shopping as a pastime in fourteenth-century Italy; military entrepreneurs and their networks across Europe; the emergence and development of the Ottoman empire from the early fourteenth to the late sixteenth century; and women and humanism in Renaissance Europe. The volume is interdisciplinary in nature, combining historical methodology with techniques from the fields of anthropology, sociology, psychology and literary criticism. It allows for juxtapositions of approaches that are usually segregated into traditional subfields, such as intellectual, political, gender, military and economic history.

Capturing dynamic new approaches to the study of this fascinating period and illustrated throughout with images, figures and tables, this comprehensive volume is a valuable resource for all students and scholars of the Renaissance.

William Caferro is Gertrude Conaway Vanderbilt Professor of History at Vanderbilt University. His research has focused primarily on economy and violence in medieval and Renaissance Italy, and most recently on Dante and Empire. His latest book, *Contesting the Renaissance* (2011), traces the meaning and use of the term "Renaissance" in the major debates of the historiography. He is recipient of a Guggenheim Fellowship (2010) and is foreign fellow of the Deputazione di Storia Patria di Toscana and l'Associazione di Studi Storici Elio Conti.

THE ROUTLEDGE HISTORIES

The Routledge Histories is a series of landmark books surveying some of the most important topics and themes in history today. Edited and written by an international team of world-renowned experts, they are the works against which all future books on their subjects will be judged.

THE ROUTLEDGE HISTORY OF THE RENAISSANCE

Edited by William Caferro

Routledge
Taylor & Francis Group

LONDON AND NEW YORK

First published 2017 by Routledge

2 Park Square, Milton Park, Abingdon, Oxfordshire OX14 4RN
52 Vanderbilt Avenue, New York, NY 10017

Routledge is an imprint of the Taylor & Francis Group, an informa business

First issued in paperback 2019

British Library Cataloguing-in-Publication Data
A catalogue record for this book is available from the British Library

Library of Congress Cataloguing-in-Publication Data
Names: Caferro, William editor. Title: The Routledge history of the Renaissance/
[edited by] William Caferro. Description: New York : Routledge, 2017. |
Series: The Routledge histories | Includes bibliographical references and index.
Identifiers: LCCN 2016056784 | ISBN 9781138898851 (hardback : alk. paper) |
ISBN 9781315226217 (ebook) Subjects: LCSH: Renaissance.
Classification: LCC CB361. R68 2017 | DDC 940.2/1–dc23 LC record
available at https://lccn.loc.gov/2016056784

ISBN: 978-1-138-89885-1 (hbk)
ISBN: 978-0-367-87286-1 (pbk)

Typeset in Baskerville
by Out of House Publishing

CONTENTS

CONTENTS

ILLUSTRATIONS

FIGURES

TABLES

CONTRIBUTORS

Alessandro Arcangeli is Associate Professor at the University of Verona. He is a cultural historian of early modern Europe with research interests in dance, leisure (*Recreation in the Renaissance: Attitudes towards Leisure and Pastimes in European Culture, 1425–1675* (Palgrave, 2003) and medical thought (including the history of emotions). He has studied at the Warburg Institute and has been a Fellow of Villa I Tatti. He has also worked on cultural history methodologically and historiographically (*Cultural History: A Concise Introduction*, (Routledge, 2012)). Since 2013 he has served as Chair of the International Society for Cultural History.

William Caferro is Gertrude Conaway Vanderbilt Professor of History at Vanderbilt University. His research has focused primarily on economy and violence in medieval and Renaissance Italy and most recently on Dante and empire. His latest book, *Contesting the Renaissance* (Wiley, 2011), traces the meaning and use of the term "Renaissance" in the major debates of the historiography. He is the recipient of a Guggenheim Fellowship (2010) and a Foreign Fellow of the Deputazione di Storia Patria di Toscana and l'Associazione di Studi Storici Elio Conti.

Samuel K. Cohn is Professor of Medieval History, University of Glasgow, an Honorary Fellow of the Institute for Advanced Studies in Humanities (University of Edinburgh), and a Fellow of the Royal Society of Edinburgh. Over the pass fifteen years he has focused on the history of popular unrest in late medieval and early modern Europe and on the history of disease and medicine. Among his publications are *The Black Death Transformed: Disease and Culture in Early Renaissance Europe* (Edward Arnold and Oxford University Press, 2002); *Popular Protest in Late Medieval Europe: Italy, France, and Flanders* (Medieval Sources Series, Manchester University Press, 2004); *Lust for Liberty: The Politics of Social Revolt in Medieval Europe, 1200–1425* (Harvard University Press, 2006); *Cultures of Plague: Medical Thinking at the End of the Renaissance* (Oxford University Press, 2010); and *Popular Protest in Late Medieval English Towns* (Cambridge University Press, 2012). He has published articles in referred journals such as *Studi Storici, Les Annales, American Historical Review, English Historical Review, Economic History Review*, and *Past & Present*. He is on the editorial board of *Social History* and presently on leave funded by a three-year Major Research Fellowship from the Leverhulme Trust on the Epidemics: Waves of Disease, Waves of Hate from the Plague of Athens to AIDS project.

Katherine Crawford is Professor of History and Director of the Program in Women's and Gender Studies at Vanderbilt University. She is the author of three books: *The Sexual*

Culture of the French Renaissance (Cambridge University Press, 2010); *European Sexualities, 1400–1800* (Cambridge University Press, 2007; and *Perilous Performances: Gender and Regency in Early Modern France* (Harvard University Press, 2004). She is interested in the ways that gender informs sexual practice, ideology, and identity, both in normative and non-normative formations. Her current project examines the cultural questions around gender, sexuality, and embodiment raised by castrated men in early modern Europe.

Nicholas A. Eckstein is the Cassamarca Associate Professor of Italian Renaissance History at the University of Sydney. His research and publications emphasize the social and cultural history of Renaissance and early modern Italy. Recent articles and books include a major study reconstructing the changing social context and reception of Florentine art by lay audiences in the fifteenth century, *Painted Glories: The Brancacci Chapel in Renaissance Florence* (Yale University Press, 2014). He is currently researching and publishing on several thematically interrelated projects related to the perception, utilization, and evolution of urban and rural space in early modern Italy.

Darin Hayton is Associate Professor of History of Science at Haverford College. He was originally trained as a chemist before earning his PhD in History and Philosophy of Science at the University of Notre Dame. His first book, *The Crown and the Cosmos* (University of Pittsburgh Press, 2015), investigates Emperor Maximilian I's patronage of astrology and astrologers as well as his use of that science in his many political programs. His new project seeks to recover the place of the science of the stars in early fourteenth-century Constantinople, especially around the polymath and courtier Nicephorus Gregoras.

Carina L. Johnson is Professor of History at Pitzer College and extended faculty at Claremont Graduate University. A historian of the sixteenth-century Habsburg Empire, particularly in relation to the extra-European world, she is the author of *Cultural Hierarchy in Sixteenth-Century Europe: The Ottomans and Mexicans* (Cambridge University Press, 2011) and articles on collecting, Habsburg imperial ideology, and cross-cultural exchanges. She is also co-editor, with David Luebke, Marjorie Plummer, and Jesse Spohnholz, of *Archaeologies of Confession: Writing the German Reformations, 1517–2017* (Berghahn Books, 2017). Her current research focuses on identity markers, proto-ethnography, and the home front experiences of the Habsburg–Ottoman wars.

Samantha Kelly is Professor of History at Rutgers University-New Brunswick. She is the author of two books on late-medieval southern Italy, *The New Solomon* (Brill, 2003) and an edition of the *Cronaca di Partenope* (Brill, 2011), and has received fellowships from the American Academy in Rome, Villa I Tatti, and the Mellon Foundation. Her recent work examines diplomatic and cultural exchange between Ethiopia and Europe, primarily Italy, in the fifteenth and sixteenth centuries, including articles on the European understandings of Gəˤəz, the classical language of Ethiopia (*Renaissance Quarterly*, 2015) and the relation between Ethiopian–European diplomacy and Ethiopian religious politics in the fifteenth century (*Afriques*, 2016). Her current projects center on the Ethiopian monastery of Santo Stefano degli Abissini in Rome in the sixteenth century.

Timothy Kircher studies the crossings of philosophy, literature, and religion in the writings of Renaissance humanists. He is the author of *The Poet's Wisdom: The Humanists, the Church, and the Formation of Philosophy in the Early Renaissance* (Brill, 2006) and *Living Well in Renaissance Italy: The Virtues of Humanism and the Irony of Leon Battista Alberti* (Medieval and Renaissance Texts and Studies, 2012). He is Professor of History at Guilford College and currently serves as President of the American Boccaccio Association. He is the creator and editor of *Humanities Watch* (humanitieswatch.org), a site dedicated to examining the role of the humanities in society.

Timothy McCall is Associate Professor of Art History in the History Department at Villanova University, and co-director of the Gender & Women's Studies program. Tim's research centers on Italian Renaissance art, and on visual intersections of power and gender (particularly masculinity) more broadly, in addition to histories of fashion and material culture. Forthcoming book projects include *Brilliant Bodies* – investigating the array, adornment, and bodies of men in fifteenth-century Italian courts – and *Renaissance Fashion Matters*, a critical exploration of the materiality of luxury clothing and adornment. With Sean Roberts and Giancarlo Fiorenza, McCall edited *Visual Cultures of Secrecy in Early Modern Europe* (Truman State University Press, 2013).

Paul D. McLean is Associate Professor of Sociology at Rutgers University, where he teaches courses on network analysis, social theory, and political and economic sociology. Much of his research explores the relationship between social network structure and cultural practices and schemas. His first book, *The Art of the Network* (Duke University Press, 2007), treats this relationship by examining political patronage networks and letter-writing in Renaissance Florence. His latest book, *Culture in Networks* (Polity, 2016), explores various ways in which culture and social networks intersect across sundry aspects of contemporary social life.

Germano Maifreda is Professor of Economic History at the Department of Historical Studies of the Università degli Studi di Milano (Italy). His publications include *From Oikonomia to Political Economy: Constructing Economic Knowledge from the Renaissance to the Scientific Revolution* (Ashgate, 2012) and *The Business of the Roman Inquisition in the Early Modern Era* (Routledge, 2017).

Megan Moran is an assistant professor in the History Department at Montclair State University, and her research focuses on family and gender in early modern Italy. She has published articles in the *Sixteenth Century Journal* (2013) and the *Journal of Family History* (2015). She is working on completing a book manuscript that investigates family networks and gender dynamics in early modern Florence.

Ann E. Moyer is Associate Professor of History at the University of Pennsylvania. Her current work focuses on the study of culture and the formation of cultural identity in sixteenth-century Tuscany. Her previous work has focused on musical thought, mathematics, and the relationships between the arts and the sciences in Renaissance Europe. She serves as one of the Executive Editors of the *Journal of the History of Ideas* and is past Executive Director of the Renaissance Society of America.

John F. Padgett is Professor of Political Science at the University of Chicago. He is also courtesy professor in the departments of History and Sociology at Chicago, and external professor at the Santa Fe Institute. Padgett studies the co-development of economic, political, and social networks in Renaissance Florence. Toward that end, he has assembled a relational database of such networks among approximately 62,000 people over the 150-year period in Florence of 1350–1500. He is co-author, with Walter Powell, of

The Emergence of Organizations and Markets (Princeton University Press, 2012), which places Florence in comparative perspective.

Katalin Prajda earned her PhD in 2011 from the European University Institute, Florence. Since then, she has been a postdoctoral scholar at various research institutes, among others at the Department of Political Science, University of Chicago; Institute for Advanced Study – Central European University; and Institute of History, Research Centre for the Humanities, Hungarian Academy of Sciences. She is the author of essays on trade, political, kinship, and artistic networks in early Renaissance Florence. Her forthcoming monograph, entitled *Friends of Friends. Network and Migration in Early Renaissance Florence*, explores the activity of Florentine businessmen in the court of Sigismund of Luxembourg.

Eugenio Refini is Assistant Professor of Italian at Johns Hopkins University. He was research fellow at the University of Warwick and at Villa I Tatti – The Harvard University Center for Italian Renaissance Studies, as well as the recipient of fellowships from the ENS Paris, the University of Geneva, and the Harry Ransom Research Center, Austin. He works on Renaissance poetics, rhetoric, drama, the classical tradition, and the intersections of music and literature. His publications include a monograph on Alessandro Piccolomini and articles on Ariosto, Tasso, and the early modern reception of the sublime.

Sean Roberts is Assistant Professor of Art History at Virginia Commonwealth University in Qatar and President of the Italian Art Society. His research is concerned with the interactions between Italy and the Islamic lands, the cultural history of maps, and with the place of prints in the histories of art and technology. He is the author of *Printing a Mediterranean World: Florence, Constantinople and the Renaissance of Geography* (Harvard University Press, 2013) and the co-editor with Tim McCall and Giancarlo Fiorenza of *Visual Cultures of Secrecy in Early Modern Europe* (Truman State University Press, 2013).

Sarah Gwyneth Ross is Associate Professor of History at Boston College, where she teaches courses on early modern Europe, cultural and intellectual history, and women's and gender history. Her publications include *The Birth of Feminism: Woman as Intellect in Renaissance Italy and England* (Harvard University Press, 2009), *Everyday Renaissances: The Quest for Cultural Legitimacy in Venice* (Harvard University Press, 2016), and numerous essays on women intellectuals, the literary lives of everyday people, and the *commedia dell'arte*.

Kaya Şahin is Associate Professor of History at Indiana University, Bloomington. He is the author of *Empire and Power in the Reign of Süleyman: Narrating the Sixteenth-Century Ottoman World* (Cambridge University Press, 2013; Turkish translation 2014). His other publications focus on Ottoman and Byzantine apocalypticism, Ottoman historiography, early modern Orientalism, and various aspects of Ottoman political and cultural life in the sixteenth century. He was the recipient of a Mellon Post-Doctoral Fellowship at the Newberry Library (2010–2011), an SSRC Postdoctoral Fellowship for Transregional Research (2012–2013), and an NEH Fellowship (2015–2016).

Samira Sheikh is a historian of South Asia at Vanderbilt University. She is the author of a monograph on fifteenth-century Gujarat, in western India, and co-editor of *After Timur Left: Culture and Circulation in Fifteenth-Century North India* (Oxford University Press, 2014), a collection of essays on India in the fifteenth and sixteenth centuries. She is currently working on a book on a Gujarati entrepreneur-politician of the eighteenth century.

William Stenhouse teaches history at Yeshiva University, New York. He works on the history of classical scholarship in the sixteenth century, and especially the reception of ancient material remains. His books include *Reading Inscriptions and Writing Ancient History: Historical Scholarship in the Late Renaissance* (Institute of Classical Studies, School of Advanced Study, University of London, 2005).

Susan Mosher Stuard is Professor of History Emerita at Haverford College. A medievalist interested in economic and social history, she is the author of *Women in Medieval Society* (University of Pennsylvania Press, 1976) and three further studies in the Press's Middle Ages Series. With Renate Bridenthal, Claudia Koonz, and Merry Weisner-Hanks, she edited the second and third editions of *Becoming Visible: Women in European History* (Houghton Mifflin, 1987 and 1998). More recent contributions include "Women, Gender, Family, and Sexuality," in volume 5 of *The Cambridge History of the World* (Cambridge University Press, 2015).

Suzanne Sutherland is an Assistant Professor of Early Modern European History at Middle Tennessee State University. Her research examines the meaning and impact of war on politics, society, and culture, with a special focus on seventeenth-century military contractors. She has also undertaken digital research on the letters of the Jesuit polymath Athanasius Kircher for Stanford University's collaborative, interdisciplinary Mapping the Republic of Letters project. She received her PhD from Stanford University.

Corey Tazzara is Assistant Professor of History at Scripps College. He received his PhD from Stanford University in 2011 and was a postdoctoral member of the Society of Fellows at the University of Chicago from 2011 to 2013. His forthcoming book, *The Free Port of Livorno and the Transformation of the Mediterranean World*, will be published by Oxford University Press.

Nükhet Varlık is Associate Professor of History at Rutgers University-Newark. She is a historian of the Ottoman Empire interested in disease, medicine, and public health. She is the author of *Plague and Empire in the Early Modern Mediterranean World: The Ottoman Experience, 1347–1600* (Cambridge University Press, 2015) and editor of *Plague and Contagion in the Islamic Mediterranean: New Histories of Disease in Ottoman Society* (Arc Medieval Press, forthcoming). She is currently working on a book titled *The Ottoman Healing Arts: Healers, Patients, and the State in the Early Modern Era*.

INTRODUCTION

The Renaissance question

William Caferro

The Renaissance has had a unique ability to make scholars uncomfortable. George Sarton described the period label as "a kind of weasel" on account of its uncertain geographical and temporal locus and its lack of clear applicability to the study of his subfield (history of science).[1] Mixing metaphors, Sarton declared that the Renaissance "reshuffled the cards" of a largely "old deck," while the Scientific Revolution involved a deck with mostly "new cards."[2] Nevertheless, Sarton used the Renaissance label in the title of his book on the emergence of modern science.

Sarton's reservations and ultimate acceptance of the Renaissance are representative of the broader course of the historiography. Few historical labels have produced more disagreement, but have proved more enduring than the Renaissance. In the middle years of the twentieth century, when Sarton was writing, historians spoke of a "golden age" of Renaissance studies, during which the subject was a basic and popular part of university curricula, stimulated in the anglophone academy by the work of émigré scholars such as Hans Baron, Erwin Panofsky, Paul Oskar Kristeller, Ernst Kantorowicz, Felix Gilbert, and Robert Lopez, who had fled fascism prior to World War II. Already in the 1970s, however, the Renaissance label became problematic. Scholars denounced it as the epitome of a chauvinistic "grand narrative of history with a single plot," whose purpose was to demonstrate the superiority of Western culture, most notably male Western culture. By the later years of the decade, one prominent scholar judged the discipline to be "on the point of collapse."[3]

The virulence of the rejection of the Renaissance was proportional to the enthusiasm of its prior acceptance. But in reality the field was always a contested one. When Jacob Burckhardt (1818–1897) published his seminal *Civilization of the Renaissance in Italy* in 1860, he took care to call it "ein Versuch" (an attempt/essay), underscoring its speculative nature. Burckhardt's famous contemporary John Ruskin (1819–1900) expressed dislike for the Renaissance on account of its interest in the classical past – the central feature of the period as he saw it – which substituted pagan values for Christian ones.[4] Meanwhile, Walter Pater (1839–1894) accepted the Renaissance as a "complex, many-sided movement," representing, as in Burckhardt, the "outbreak of human spirit." But in his *Studies in the History of the Renaissance* (1873) he added the very anti-Burckhardtian qualification that this spirit could "be traced far into the Middle Ages."[5] Pater's medieval component anticipated the famous assessment

1

of Charles Homer Haskins, whose *The Renaissance of the Twelfth Century* (1927) touched off the so-called "revolt of medievalists," who found – and continue to find – many of the same features in their own era and have accordingly sought a similar priority for their field.[6]

It is, I would argue, this combative past that has propelled the field forward, kept it relevant, resilient, and made it a battleground for new theories, competing interpretations, and scholarly innovation.[7] Rather than eliminate the discipline, new scholarship has broadened and enriched it.[8] The Renaissance has served as an early locus for investigation of issues relating to gender and application of anthropological and psychoanalytical theory. The cultural anthropology of Clifford Geertz and his notion of "thick description" have been employed to look at Renaissance rituals and the ways people lived – helping historians move away from a static Enlightenment view of human nature to a more contextual one. The field has brought together into conversation, if not always amicably, historian with art historian with literary critic. The Renaissance has been the site for new historicist and postmodern approaches, which have called into question some of its most basic assumptions, including the very utility of historical categories and patterns. In the hands of the literary critic Stephen Greenblatt – drawing from both Geertz and Michel Foucault – Burckhardt's modern Renaissance "individual" became "a cultural artifact."[9]

It may well be that Burckhardt is finally dead. Guido Ruggiero has recently pointed out that the enormous amount of scholarship in the field has alone "overwhelmed" the Swiss scholar.[10] But Burckhardt remains a useful *auctoritas* against which scholars situate and make relevant, implicitly and explicitly, their own ideas. As John Martin argues, the eternally disputatious nature of Burckhardt's famous concept of individualism has maintained interest in the subject over the long term, reaching a "dizzying rate" in recent years.[11] Several of the chapters in this book draw upon aspects of the Burkhardt's thesis. William Stenhouse invokes Burckhardt's notions of antiquarianism (from part three of *Civilization*, "Revival of Antiquity and the Ruins of Rome") when discussing his famous travelers, who sought to "become Roman" upon contemplation of ancient ruins. Alessandro Arcangeli draws implicitly on Burckhardtian ideas of "Renaissance play" (from part five of *Civilization*), deftly connecting the Swiss scholar to his traditional scholarly antipode, the Dutchman Johan Huizinga, author of *Homo Ludens*, but typically employed as the archetype defender of the Middle Ages. William Caferro assesses Burckhardt's notion of individualism in an Italian context, showing the ways it led to a basic divergence in study of politics and war in Renaissance Italian history. Carina L. Johnson takes the individual in a wholly different direction, looking at New World slavery and "the racialization" of identity.

But as the examples above also show, scholarly discourses necessarily change with the passage of time. Benedetto Croce, writing in the role of historical philosopher, noted the inherent necessity of "presentism" in the study of the past. "Only an interest in the life of the present can move one to investigate past fact." He asserted that "the deeds of history" must "vibrate in the soul of the historian" and concluded accordingly that the "past fact does not answer to past interest but to present interest."[12]

So it is with the Renaissance. The generation of Burckhardt and Pater, following Enlightenment and Romantic historical notions, sought to expose the "spirit" of the age. Post-WWII émigré scholars (Nicolai Rubinstein, Felix Gilbert, and Hans Baron) found special currency in the study of politics and governmental forms, reflecting their own dramatic experiences with the importance and consequences of such institutions. Demographic and social shifts of the 1960s and 1970s brought skepticism of simple historical answers and increased interest in anthropological and gender issues, neglected by earlier generations.

The historian Gabrielle Spiegel has argued that the recent "linguistic turn" owes much to a "second generation" of post-Holocaust European intellectuals on whose psyche the event was "indelibly inscribed," casting "suspicion on the ability of words to convey reality."[13] Still more recently, scholars, particularly in the anglophone academy, have taken up issues of materiality, "the life of objects," which, it may be argued, reflect in part a growing lack of interest in the efficacy of politics and human agency and with that a greater tendency to look inward, at personal possessions and commodities, which link well to Renaissance exploration and the availability of a wholly new variety of goods from the New World.

In a world dominated by the Internet and increasing availability of "big data" and new sources in digital form, scholarship has turned more forcefully to interest in globalization, positing a Renaissance that relativizes Europe in terms of the rest of the world.[14] The curators of an exhibit on the Sultan Mehmet II in Istanbul (brought to America to the Metropolitan Museum) in 1999 cast the Muslim ruler as a species of Renaissance patron and intellectual. A *New York Times* reviewer interpreted this in terms of Turkish politics, as part of ongoing attempts to integrate the country more with Europe in the hopes of becoming part of the European Union.[15]

There is in short an undeniably generational aspect to historical writing. But the point should not be overstated. Scholarship also grows organically from within, as historians extend the work of their forebears and ask new questions of old material. The most basic reality of the current state of Renaissance scholarship is that the trends are not consistent, and books such as the present one must avoid, as John Maynard Keynes warned in a wholly different context, "putting too much order into the system."[16] It is not possible to speak of a new scholarly consensus or synthesis. Historians have pointedly avoided this. The "tremendous explosion" of recent scholarship has by itself made such efforts difficult.[17] Postmodern "challenges" and other so-called "anti-Renaissance" trends appear to have helped scholars become more comfortable with contradiction. Unlike their predecessors, historians are more inclined to juxtapose categories once seen as antithetical. They deal simultaneously with secular and religious worlds, wealth and poverty, rationality and irrationality.[18] They employ Michel Foucault's notions of power and its exercise through language and symbol and its importance in human relations.[19] They have "decentered" the Renaissance in terms of the New World, Africa, and Asia. Scholars have rescued the Ottomans from the "fringe of Europe" and placed them at the center of a dynamic relationship with the West.[20] They have looked more closely at issues involving physical environment, notions of power, scientific practice, and consumer behavior. The digital age has, as Nicholas A. Eckstein notes in his chapter, aided a "spatial turn," in which scholars have begun to use modern technology to physically map out cities and regions and their relations to everyday life. There is an ongoing "sensory turn," whereby historians have looked beyond the written word at the sounds of the era. At the same time education and the "history of the book" remain vibrant fields, as scholars continue to uncover the details of what Anthony Grafton and others have called "commerce in the classics" and "an international republic of letters."[21]

The aim of the present volume is to capture some of these exciting developments by writers actively engaged with them. It treats the Renaissance not as a static concept, but as one of ongoing change.[22] The collection takes as its unifying theme the notion of "exchange" broadly defined – in terms of goods, ideas, people, language, and disease across social, temporal, religious, intellectual, political, and cultural boundaries. The theme is useful because it is inclusive, multi-dimensional, and accentuates the current trend toward inter-disciplinarity. The simple aim is to highlight current approaches that are proving fruitful, with an eye toward Europe in terms of the broader world, which has become a prominent theme of conferences and important research centers such as Villa I Tatti in Florence. The book does not offer a single new thesis, if that is possible. It presents scholarship with all its jagged edges.

The collection brings together a diverse group of scholars, both established and at early stages of their careers, including non-Europeanists, and, indeed, some whose first identification is not history at all (sociology, political science). The contributors do not all agree. For Kaya Şahin, Nükhet Varlık, and Samira Sheikh, the Eurocentric periodization has posed challenges to their work, carrying embedded and erroneous assumptions. Indeed, Sheikh notes how the traditional Western labels "medieval" and "modern" reflect chauvinistic British imperial views of India. Meanwhile, Darin Hayton argues that "forward-looking" notions implicit in the Renaissance label willy-nilly exclude consideration of the Byzantine Empire, which is seen as a wholly static entity over the centuries, whose coincidence with the Renaissance occurred only when the Empire fell in 1453 to the Ottomans, bringing Greek scholars and their language skills west. Other scholars find distinctive aspects in the Renaissance. Alessandro Arcangeli traces entirely new cultural attitudes towards exercise and leisure in the sixteenth century. Eugenio Refini sees a "turning point" in terms of language, notably the relation between Latin and vernacular languages (*questione della lingua*). Sarah Gwyneth Ross demonstrates the emergence of female humanists and intellectuals, who engaged in the famous pan-European debate, the *querelle des femmes*, on the qualities of women and whose broad-ranging skills included facility with Greek poetry. Ann Moyer examines the contemporary reception of the work of era's s most famous and unique figure, Niccolò Machiavelli, who is referenced in several chapters in this book (Tazzara, Şahin, Kircher, and Caferro).

The basic commonality is that the Renaissance label serves – as it did for George Sarton – as a point of reference for the scholars. No effort has been made to disguise disagreement, which, as noted above, reflects the tradition of the field and is the essence of a healthy scholarly discourse. The methodologies are diverse. The authors borrow techniques from the fields of anthropology, sociology, philology, and literary criticism. They use a stunningly wide array of sources, including visual, literary, and archival material taken from throughout Western Europe (Italy, France, Spain, the Holy Roman Empire, Hungary), Byzantium, the Ottoman Empire, South Asia, and the New World. Samuel K. Cohn's chapter uses archival and hagiographical material from all over Europe. The distinction between the "Renaissance" and "early modern" labels, once a point of strong contention, appears minimal in the chapters, as the authors often use the terms interchangeably. The chapters range temporarily from the fourteenth to the seventeenth century.

I have intentionally eschewed grouping the chapters under standard labels such as intellectual, legal, religious, history (etc.), in favor of broader, more inclusive categories that emphasize similarities in approaches and use of source materials across subfields. The rubrics facilitate reading the chapters in thematic ways, bringing together works that are often segregated and eliminating the recourse to categories such as "Renaissance at the margins" or "Renaissance antipodes" that are neither helpful nor fair to the scholar who wrote the chapter. Samantha Kelly's chapter may readily be fit under the category of "religion," owing to its emphasis on the church council of 1439 that attempted to unify the Latin West and Greek East churches. It may likewise fit well the rubric of intellectual history owing to its extensive use of the work of the humanist Biondo Flavio. But Kelly deals with all of these issues and – most extensively and originally – the cultural exchange between Europeans and Africans (Ethiopians) who attended the council and the "knowledge production" resulting from the encounter.

Germano Maifreda's chapter may seem most easily placed in the category of economic history. But Maifreda takes his methodology from Michel Foucault, avoiding notions of straightforward progress in historical development, and examines carefully the subliminal messages of humanists, of Christian church councils, and Reformation theologians – using source material typically fitted under the headings of intellectual history and religious history respectively.

The reality of Renaissance scholarship – and the basic ethos of this book – is that scholars, whatever their primary field of identification, work in several categories at once. The notion of "exchange" helps cut across the often artificially constructed divides of subfields. The authors in this collection use common terms such as "circularity," "networks," "artifice and deception" and "transmission" and "reception." Will Stenhouse tells of "passionately imaginative" exchanges with the classical past, whereby Italian contemporaries cloaked themselves as Romans, taking up ancient dress, creating elaborate genealogies, and even inventing fictitious Latin inscriptions to validate themselves. Conversely, Katherine Crawford shows how the Renaissance exchange with the classical past was used in negative ways. Contemporaries drew on the image of Sporus, the castrated favorite of the Roman emperor Nero, as an exemplar of social deviance, to articulate concerns about sexual comportment and the body. Similarly, Sarah Ross explores how exchange with classical past for women humanists necessarily involved overturning embedded notions of female inferiority, effectively requiring women to "throw Aristotle from the train." Susan Mosher Stuard examines exchange at the local market place, exploring consumer behavior and the intermingling of vendors and customers and of diverse social classes, transgressing traditional social boundaries. Timothy McCall and Sean Roberts stress the material nature of exchange, looking closely at the objects themselves and the dissimulation and artifice often consciously employed to make things of little value appear much more resplendent. Paul D. McLean and John F. Padgett trace exchange and "the circular flow of capital" though the major businesses of the Renaissance's most noted city, Florence, and the overlap among economic, social, and political networks in the city. Megan Moran looks at networks of exchange in the same city among patrician and *popolane* women, who were more active in the economic activities than supposed. Susan Sutherland examines the exchange networks relating to war, which brought Italian soldiers to other parts of Europe, stressing the "trans-regional" aspect of social elites that went beyond national identities. Meanwhile, Samuel K. Cohn and Nühket Varlık deal with the consequences of the deadliest form of exchange, the Black Death, from the vantage of Western Europe and the Ottoman Empire respectively. Timothy Kircher emphasizes the problematic nature of the exchange between Renaissance humanists and modern scholars, whose vocabularies do not align well and muddle interpretation of Renaissance philosophy. Corey Tazzara, among *multa alia*, traces exchange between the city and countryside in Genoa and difficulties therein.

In the hope of accentuating the connections among them, the chapters are arranged according to four general rubrics: "disciplines and boundaries"; "encounters and transformations"; "society and environment"; and "power and representation." The rubrics are imperfect and make no claim to be comprehensive.

Part I, "Disciplines and boundaries," groups together chapters that highlight the development of, and distinctions among, subject fields. Germano Maifreda traces the establishment of secular economic thought as a field of inquiry before Adam Smith and physiocrats in the eighteenth century. Samira Sheik finds aspects of a Western-style Renaissance in Northern Indian during the "long fifteenth century" (1350–1550) with regard to mobility, the rise in importance of regions, new towns, and vernacular language. Eugenio Refini picks up the notion of language in a specifically Italian context with regard to the debate about Latin versus the vernacular. William Caferro contextualizes Burckhartian notion of individualism to show how politics and warfare became separate scholarly disciplines. Timothy Kircher attempts to mediate between the divides that separate Renaissance humanism from philosophy.

Part II, "Encounters and transformations," includes chapters that deal with issues of transmission and reception of ideas and interactions and movements of people and objects. Ann Moyer assesses the reception of Niccolò Machiavelli's work in his native city. Timothy McCall and Sean Roberts examine the circulation and transformation of material objects; Will Stenhouse traces the encounters with the ancient Roman past, as does Katherine Crawford – from wholly different perspectives. Carina L. Johnson and Samantha Kelly emphasize encounters with the New World and Africa respectively: the former stressing the importance of physiognomy as an identifying feature, the latter noting the attempts at understanding foreign cultures beyond stereotypes. Meanwhile, Darin Hayton shows the importance of Byzantium as a medium for the transmission of Renaissance science. Byzantium offered a distinctive font of ancient knowledge for humanists, free from "adulteration" by Syriac and Arabic translations and commentaries of medieval Latin texts, even though Byzantine knowledge was demonstrably less advanced.

Part III, "Society and environment," deals with issues related to consumer behavior, disease and emotion, communication, education, play and leisure, and war. Samuel K. Cohn and Nühket Varlık examine very different emotions arising from the Black Death in Europe and the Ottoman Empire. Nicholas A. Eckstein looks at Florentine public sanitation related to the plague and the resulting establishment of communication networks that allow a spatial mapping of the city, particularly poorer neighborhoods. Sarah Ross emphasizes the quality of women's educations, despite their being denied university study. The chapters of Alessandro Arcangeli and Suzanne Sutherland are juxtaposed, as play and exercise for the elite often constituted a species of preparation for war.

Part IV, "Power and representation," includes chapters that touch on aspects of governance, diplomacy, and social, political and economic networks, Kaya Şahin explores the realities of Ottoman "governance" (the word Şahin prefers to "state") during the period from the fourteenth to the sixteenth century, when the Ottoman "enterprise" transformed itself from a "frontier principality" to an "early modern" empire. Şahin explores the "dynamic multi-faceted" nature of Ottoman power, extended through use of public ritual and other "networks, encounters and interactions." The Ottoman case makes a compelling comparison with Paul D. McLean and John F. Padgett's depiction of contemporary Florence, with its overlapping of economic, social, and political networks, founded on notions of trust. Corey Tazzara, conversely, stresses the incidence of customs fraud in Genoa, highlighting political and economic failures against a "myth" of the city's effective tutelage under the famous Casa di San Giorgio, a private company that administered the revenue and debt of the state. Katalin Prajda explores representation in the diplomatic sphere, in terms of Hungary, a state of great importance but too often ignored in the literature. Finally, Megan Moran explores how Florentine patrician women expressed power and agency in economic life, further complicating the "dense and multi-textured social networks" noted by McLean and Padgett in that city.

The collection has a strong economic component to it (McLean and Padgett, Maifreda, McCall and Roberts, Moran, Stuard, Tazzara, and Sutherland). This reflects my own scholarly interests and the unfortunate reality that the field is often absent from books on Renaissance historiography or reduced to the "margins" – a status quo that also reflects a tendency among economic historians to segregate themselves. Frank Nussbaum famously proclaimed (1941) that economic history did not "know a Renaissance" because it was already subsumed under the grander label of "capitalism," which has far greater scholarly currency.[23] But extant archival material relating to economic matters is immense, rivaled perhaps only by legal documentation (which are not mutually exclusive). There has in any case been much important work done in the field, by scholars with wide ranging interests.

No effort has been made to disguise the centrality of Italy and the city of Florence in the discussion of the Renaissance. Indeed, it may well be that the Renaissance belongs, as Burckhardt himself argued, solely to Italy.[24] Michael Wyatt's recent *Cambridge Companion to the Italian Renaissance* (2014) has elegantly reminded us of this. Italy possessed a distinctive quality and Florence was undeniably a center of Renaissance activity. The priority of Florence, as Paul Grendler has argued, owes also to the enthusiasm of a non-academic public and persists – and perhaps always will – in the public arena in the form of kitchen magnets emblazoned with the local *duomo* and calendars with reproductions of the paintings of Masaccio, Leonardo, and others.[25] But stressing the centrality of Italy in no way excludes other places and events. As Alessandro Arcangeli makes clear – articulating a basic theme of this collection – it was in Italy that "cultural commodities became available for re-exportation" to international markets and "where they would be further adapted and reused." And as McCall and Roberts assert, interest in material culture coincides with an emerging conception of the period as one in which the courts and merchant centers of Europe were developing ever more expansive connections with a much wider world.

The current volume purposefully avoids "state of" chapters. These are undeniably valuable, and have been done elsewhere to great effect. But one of the great challenges I found in writing *Contesting the Renaissance* (2011) was indeed finding "traditional" categories into which to place older iconic debates, which, at a distance of many years, appear more ambiguous and interdisciplinary than the scholarly caricatures of them. There is also an inevitable academic politics involved with "state of" chapters, which are sometimes tendentious and in any case have a relatively short shelf life, particularly in so volatile a field as the Renaissance.

The chapters here touch on issues involving gender, ethnicity, race, economy, politics, religion, diplomacy, philosophy, language, play, emotions, material culture, dissimulation, disease, war, and public spectacle. There is, again, no claim to completeness. As Johann Wolfgang von Goethe, a great lover of Renaissance Italy, wrote in *Wilhelm Meisters Lehrjahre*: "Das Gewebe dieser Welt ist aus Notwendigkeit und Zufall gebildet."[26] Necessity and chance are an intrinsic part of the world we live in, a point all the more applicable to scholarly books. The roster for this book has likewise been conditioned to a degree by chance and necessity: availability of scholars and their willingness to participate.

It is important to stress that the categories used here are, like all groupings, limited. The chapters deal with multiple issues and share additional and perhaps unexpected commonalities. Susan Mosher Stuard, for example, describes local market activity as a species of "performance art" played out by merchants before a passing crowd. In this respect her chapter recalls notions of artifice and dissimulation outlined by McCall and Roberts with regard to material objects, as well as notions of "reality and artifice" that Refini argues lay at the core of the Renaissance debate over vernacular and Latin. Corey Tazzara shows dissimulation and fraud in a more strictly political/economic context, while McLean and Padgett stress notions of "trust" in business.

Issues of class, movement, and language figure prominently in the chapters. Stuard's local market exchange has a strong class dimension, as does Arcangeli's "leisure," which, he notes, helped define class identity at courts, but which nevertheless moved "down" the social scale to merchants and artisans, particularly the interest in dance, some of whose "masters" were indeed Jewish. Notions of relational identity connect over to Johnson, whose traces the development of identity in racial terms, but makes clear the prior importance of language as marker, using some of the same examples as Refini and Kircher. Language figures prominently also in Sheikh, who sees "literized" vernaculars as an important feature of the "long" fifteenth century in Northern India; in Kelly, who shows how language often stood at the center of differing cultural attitudes; in Prajda, who examines the "familial" language (father and son) used in Florentine diplomacy, which makes an interesting contrast with the friendship language highlighted by McLean and Padgett in Florentine business correspondence; and in Moyer, who makes clear how Machiavelli's statements on the Tuscan vernacular were much discussed in his native city. Varlık, meanwhile, stresses the movement of people in Ottoman society as a result of plague, most notably among the Empire's non-Muslim Jewish communities, often led by their religious leader.

In a crowded field, the hope is that this volume, with its broad temporal and geographic range and diversity topics will help further the spirited discourse that has characterized the Renaissance over the centuries.

I would like to thank professors Ann Blair, Christopher Celenza, Paula Findlen, Steven Epstein, Richard Goldthwaite Anthony Grafton, and Edward Muir for their advice in putting together the list of scholars. I am grateful to Francesca Trivellato for her advice along the way. I wish also to thank my graduate student Katherine McKenna for her help in the early stages of preparing the manuscript and Mario Avaldi for helping translate Arcangeli's chapter from Italian. Above all, I am deeply indebted to J'Nese Williams for her help above and beyond the call of duty with every aspect of this book.

I dedicate the volume to my wife and life-long companion Megan Weiler, whose beauty and brilliance outshines that of any Renaissance. I thank her also for her practical help with translations.

Notes

1 George Sarton, *Six Wings: Men of Science in the Renaissance* (Bloomington: Indiana University Press, 1957), p. 2.
2 *Ibid.*, p. 4.
3 William J. Bouwsma, "The Renaissance and the Drama of European History" in *A Usable Past: Essays in European Cultural History: Essays in European Cultural History* (Berkeley and Los Angeles: University of California Press, 1990), p. 350.
4 J. B. Bullen, *The Myth of the Renaissance in Nineteenth Century Writing* (Oxford: Oxford University Press, 1994), pp. 9, 90.
5 Walter Pater, *The Renaissance*, ed. and trans. Adam Phillips (Oxford: Oxford University Press, 1986), pp. xxxi, xxxii.
6 Charles Homer Haskins, *The Renaissance of the Twelfth Century* (Cambridge, MA: Harvard University Press, 1927).
7 Paula Findlen, "Possessing the Past: The Material World of the Italian Renaissance," *American Historical Review* 103 (February 1998), pp. 83–114.
8 Randolph Starn, "A Postmodern Renaissance?" *Renaissance Quarterly* 60 (2007), p. 17.
9 Stephen Greenblatt, *Renaissance Self-Fashioning: From More to Shakespeare* (Chicago: University of Chicago Press, 1980).
10 Guido Ruggiero, *The Renaissance in Italy: A Social and Cultural History of the Rinascimento* (Cambridge: Cambridge University Press, 2014), p. 13.

11 John Martin, *The Myths of Individualism* (New York: Palgrave Macmillan, 2006), p. 209. See also John Martin, "Inventing Sincerity, Refashioning Prudence: The Discovery of the Individual in Renaissance Europe," *American Historical Review* 102 (December 1997), pp. 1309–42.

12 Benedetto Croce, *History as the Story of Liberty* (London: George Allen and Unwin Limited, 1941), pp. 19, 21.

13 Gabrielle Spiegel, "The Task of the Historian," *American Historical Review* 114 (February 2009), p. 7.

14 Lynn Hunt notes the benefits and challenges of global history. Lynn Hunt, *Writing History in a Global Age* (New York: Norton, 2014). On "big data," big idea history, and the role of history in contemporary society, see Jo Guldi and David Armitage, *The History Manifesto* (Cambridge: Cambridge University Press, 2014).

15 See Lisa Jardine and Jerry Brotton, *Global Interests: Renaissance Art between East and West* (London: Reaktion Books, 2000), p. 8.

16 John Maynard Keynes, *The General Theory of Employment, Interest and Money* (New York: Harcourt Brace, 1936), p. 3.

17 Ruggiero, *The Renaissance in Italy*, p. 13.

18 Peter Burke, *European Renaissance: Centers and Peripheries* (London: Wiley, 1998), p. 4; Alison Brown, *The Renaissance*, 2nd edn. (Harlow: Longman, 1999), p. 97; Guido Ruggiero, ed., *A Companion to the Worlds of the Renaissance* (Oxford: Oxford University Press, 2002), pp. 4–5.

19 Randolph Starn, "A Postmodern Renaissance?" *Renaissance Quarterly* 60 (2007), pp. 10–11; Peter Burke, "Renaissance Europe and the World" in *Palgrave Advances in Renaissance Historiography*, ed. Jonathan Woolfson (New York: Palgrave Macmillan, 2005), pp. 52–70.

20 See Robert Schwoebel, *The Shadow of the Crescent: The Renaissance Image of the Turk 1453–1517* (Nieuwkoop: De Graaf, 1969); Gerald MacLean, ed., *Re-Orienting the Renaissance: Cultural Exchanges with the East* (Basingstoke: Palgrave Macmillan, 2005); Margaret Meserve, *Empires of Islam in Renaissance Historical Thought* (Cambridge, MA: Harvard University Press, 2008). A review of the recent literature on Islam and the Renaissance is in Francesca Trivellato, "Renaissance Italy and the Muslim Mediterranean in Recent Historical Work," *Journal of Modern History* 82 (March 2010), pp. 127–55.

21 Anthony Grafton, *Commerce with the Classics: Ancient Books and Renaissance Readers* (Ann Arbor: University of Michigan Press, 1997).

22 I agree much with John Martin's assessment in John J. Martin, ed. *The Renaissance World* (New York: Routledge, 2007).

23 Frank Nussbaum, "The Economic History of Renaissance Europe: Problems and Solutions during the Past Generation, "*Journal of Modern History* 13, 4 (1941), p. 527; Wallace K. Ferguson, "Recent Trends in the Economic Historiography of the Renaissance," *Studies in the Renaissance* 7 (1960), p. 55. A full discussion of the vicissitudes of Renaissance economic history is in William Caferro, *Contesting the Renaissance* (Malden, MA: Wiley-Blackwell, 2011) ch. 5, pp. 138–54.

24 See also John Najemy's *Italy in the Age of the Renaissance* (Oxford: Oxford University Press, 2004). Excellent essays on Italy include Edward Muir, "The Italian Renaissance in America," *American Historical Review* 100 (October 1995), pp. 1107–8; Anthony Molho, "The Italian Renaissance, Made in the USA," in *Imagined Histories: American Historians Interpret the Past*, ed. Anthony Molho and Gordon S. Wood (Princeton, NJ: Princeton University Press, 1997), pp. 264–7 and Marcello Fantoni, ed., *Gli anglo-americani a Firenze. Idea e construzione del Rinascimento* (Rome: Bulzonu, 2002).

25 Paul Grendler, *The European Renaissance in American Life* (Westport, CT: Praeger, 2006) and in Allen J. Grieco, Michael Rocke, and Fiorella Gioffredi Superbi, eds. *The Italian Renaissance in the Twentieth Century* (Florence: I Tatti Studies, 2002).

26 Johann Wolfgang von Goethe, *Wilhelm Meisters Lehrjahre*, ch. 18. Online at http://gutenberg.spiegel.de/buch/wilhelm-meisters-lehrjahre-3669/1.

Part I

DISCIPLINES AND BOUNDARIES

1

THE 'ECONOMIC' THOUGHT
OF THE RENAISSANCE

Germano Maifreda

Recent decades have witnessed a substantial number of studies investigating the historical processes by which fields of knowledge such as economics came to claim status as a separate discipline, and how single sciences began to define and organize their own field of specialization, vocabulary and methods of study. Although the idea of continual and patient progress of scientific knowledge has been overturned by historians of science following Thomas Kuhn's famed *Structure of Scientific Revolutions*, most economists still think that this was not the case in terms of their field.[1] As a consequence, according to the traditional approach to the history of economic thought, modern economic science originates from a theoretical revolution that occurred roughly in the second half of the eighteenth century; an epoch of 'first great theoretical revolution', as for example Ernesto Screpanti and Stefano Zamagni put it, 'of great breaks with tradition ... and reached its climax with Adam Smith's *The Wealth of Nations*'.[2] Consequently, the theoretical and methodological innovations that were introduced in the period of transition to classical political economy by figures such as Petty, Hume, Galiani, Beccaria, Verri, Steuart, Anderson, Condillac, Mirabeau, Quesnay, Turgot and the whole physiocratic movement, have been well researched and described in general reference texts.

Nevertheless, the conventional approach to the history of economic thought has recently been called into question. Material, social and cultural contexts have become more central in the historical reconstructions, producing important studies specifically dedicated to the paths of construction of economic knowledge before the eighteenth century. With a few notable exceptions, such studies dwell too much upon the central years of the eighteenth century, underestimating the early modern cultural context.[3] Inquiries into economic knowledge during the Renaissance and early modern age have often implicitly been based on assumptions that are not entirely satisfactory. They are founded on the idea that there was a basic theoretic flimsiness with regard to economic information by contemporaries (before 'classical' formulations) or that information was extremely specific, and therefore incapable of generalization both in terms of later developments and in comparison with other fields of knowledge in the sixteenth and seventeenth centuries. All this makes it difficult for economic historians, historians of economic thought, political or social historians and even historians of science to discuss their ideas and experiences usefully.[4]

The relationship between Renaissance economic knowledge and the political-economic science which took shape between the eighteenth and the nineteenth centuries may best be defined, in Michel Foucault's terms, as 'archaeological'. Just as someone uncovering the remains of a Roman basilica below a Christian cathedral is led to examine the nature of the basilica, the reader of this chapter is directed back to a historical period in which the *topos* of what would become political economy slowly took on the visible traits of objects of study and observation.[5] I do not think it is rewarding today to go back in time to reconstruct a sort of continuity of economic discourse that hypothetically fell by the wayside and was forgotten. We should instead make a strenuous effort to maintain the discontinuity and the culturally fragmentary nature of the dispersion, which is historically more convincing and helpful in understanding 'why economists think as they do'.[6]

Although admitting that humanism was not specifically scientific, historians have given several reasons why humanistic Renaissance culture constitutes an essential prerequisite for the genesis of the seventeenth-century methodological revolution that permeates the ambitions of economists to be, in turn, 'scientists'. First of all, humanism was sceptical of pre-rational forms of knowledge deriving from the Middle Ages and had a positive attitude towards technology and innovation. Second, it accepted a model of debate that was internally coherent and suspicious of simple deduction from *auctoritates* (authority). Thanks to the fifteenth- and sixteenth-century redefinition of the nature and function of dialectics as a logical and rhetorical device through which knowledge affirms itself as discursive research and inter-subjective confrontation, the construction of Western knowledge spread outside of the medieval university and into the new urban society.[7]

Renaissance Neoplatonism and the construction of an economic rationality

This section briefly illuminates aspects of the Italian Platonic revival (fifteenth and early sixteenth centuries). It emphasizes the importance of the Platonic heritage through the analysis of conceptual repertoires deployed by humanists and philosophers to express their theories of economic life that would later develop into classical and post-classical theories of political economy.

We know that Renaissance Platonism was not just a hermetic and religious/mystical movement that masterfully emerged in the studies of Frances Yates; nevertheless, it is still primarily studied from strictly philosophical, religious and esoteric points of view.[8] In the last few decades, scholars have however shown that Platonism played an important role in the development of early modern political knowledge and practices, radiating from fifteenth-century Florence. Plato and his ancient followers were employed also by the Italian ruling elite to support the idea of the necessity of aristocratic government. What has been defined as 'Plato's functionalism' was employed by the Medici in order to give support to the idea of a necessary government of feudal aristocrats as well as guild-based communes.[9]

Eugenio Garin has argued that the reception of Plato in the early Renaissance should be seen as occurring in two stages, each of which reflects a political situation. The earlier phase was characterized by a fascination with the 'rational city' as laid out in the *Republic*, and lasted roughly from Petrarch to Bruni, when Florentine society was still relatively open, owing to free communal institutions. As is well known, the state in the *Republic* assures political stability by assigning a social task to all its components, following each one's natural disposition. Oligarchy and democracies are dismissed as inferior forms of government, leading

14

to tyranny. In the second stage of Plato's reception, lasting from the Council of Florence (1438–39) until the end of the century, the Medici regime replaced the free civic life of the past with an artificial court life, reducing the intellectuals to political dependency. This was the age of the revival of Plato as theologian. Garin's model, criticized as monofactorial, is useful in order to remind us of the institutional and political context in which the Florentine rediscovery of Plato took place.[10]

Cosimo de' Medici, the first *de facto* ruler of the dynasty, commissioned Marsilio Ficino to complete the translation of Plato's opus, which was concluded after his death in 1484–85. This edition was followed by Venetian editions in 1491, 1517 and 1581, Basel editions in 1546, 1551 and 1561, and a Lyons edition in 1550. The year 1492 also saw Ficino's Latin translation of Plotinus' *Enneads*, financed by Lorenzo il Magnifico, which had been completely unknown to Western European culture. Both Plato and Plotinus were translated from Greek books bought by Cosimo in 1441, and made fully available to Ficino in 1462.[11] A decisive role in inducing Cosimo to commission the translation of Plato's work was his meeting with the Byzantine philosopher Gemistus Pletho at the Council of Florence in 1439.[12] Gemistus not only started teaching Strabo's geography to the Western public, but he also popularized Platonic philosophy in Florence. Pletho had a practical and inductive approach to politics, which is reflected in the *Mémoires* he wrote for Prince Theodore Palaeologus and in his treatise *On Laws*. In the latter, he argued that laws standing out as identical throughout the diverse legislative systems of the world represented eternal principles of reason of Platonic ideas.[13]

Between the fifteenth and sixteenth centuries, Platonic ideas were widely transmitted in Florence and abroad not only through books ('without books, nothing could be done', observed Vespasiano da Bisticci in his *Vite*[14]), but also thanks to the university teaching of scholars such as Carlo Marsuppini, a great admirer of Pletho, and to public oratory, church ceremonies, sermons to lay confraternities and popular religious plays. It is often forgotten that Ficino himself was a priest, and was responsible for three parishes, writing and preaching sermons both in Latin and in the Tuscan vernacular.[15]

The growing power of the Medici in Florence, and their threat to its political and judicial institutions, was therefore a fundamental prerequisite for the rediscovery of Plato and for the development of Platonism in the early modern period. Paradoxically, Platonism gave philosophical legitimacy to the transference of power to a professional Medicean elite, despite the fact that Plato was a critic of wealth. Plato's elitism, his ideas about professionalism of government, the philosopher-ruler and the division of labour supported the rise in Florence of an administrative class of intendants and secretaries. As Alison Brown argues, 'Plato's influence is betrayed by exhortations to see the government in terms of its wisdom and flexibility, whereby men of ability would rule and allow others to protect the city and produce the necessaries of life.'[16]

We might add that Platonic inspiration led to the formulation of discourses on the 'economy' of the state, which were based on assumptions that were innovative in comparison to the medieval tradition. In fifteenth-century Florence, former political cultures, which were based on obedience to authority, were thus replaced with different, and frequently original, theories and practices regarding human intervention in the life of the community. Deepening those aspects would lead us to understand how the deductive method employed by Plato and the Neoplatonists (who find in such figures as Pico della Mirandola and Marsilio Ficino their most elegant expression) already established, during the fifteenth century, the foundations of a perception of what we now consider the 'economy' which was mechanical, model-forming and generalizable.

Several issues of intellectual discussion and political debate can be identified, over which there was disagreement between humanists, rulers and their subjects, which bear directly on the question of relations among the economy, society and the state. Since the beginning of the early modern period, Platonic inspiration led to the formulation of political-economic discourses about the state, which contained implicit allusion to theoretical models of system functioning and of good consumption. This is particularly evident with reference to the study of Plato among Milanese humanists, such as Uberto Decembrio and his son Pier Candido. Uberto Decembrio of Vigevano (*c.* 1370–1427), for example, who with his teacher Manuel Chrysoloras first translated the *Republic* into Latin by the summer of 1402, composed his own *De republica libri IV. D*iscussing the genesis of the state, Decembrio distinguished between a 'healthy' condition (human desires are simple and easily satisfied) and a 'fevered' condition, due to inflamed desires for luxuries. For Uberto, who wanted to legitimize the functions of the new bureaucratic class in the eyes of the old aristocracy and the prince, the definition of 'healthy' state is different from that of Plato. For the Greek philosopher, the healthy state has no need of foreign trade. Uberto argues that the economy of a healthy state is diversified, and needs the specialized functions of merchants, including seaports, roads, diverse additional infrastructures and trade. Plato considers war a consequence of 'fever', while Uberto maintains that a healthy state must also defend itself through mercenaries, war industries and horsebreeding. It should be recalled that arms manufacturing was a leading industry in Milan, and Uberto's translation of the *Republic* appeared in the crisis of Milan's contest with Florence for the control of central Italy.[17]

How do we decide if a state is in good health? What are the variables that should be used? What kind of relationships should be established between these variables? The discourse developed within the Platonic paradigm of knowledge addresses these questions and provides responses in ways that need to be carefully explored. The striving for generalization and extrapolation of general laws from special cases was an important contribution of the Platonic revival and the cognitive model of the development of philosophical and political knowledge, whose impact on the construction of economic knowledge still requires investigation. The work of Marsilio Ficino also presents an interesting interpretation of government. In his reading of Plato's *Sophist*, Ficino considers the superior arts of *gubernationis* as applicable in various areas of individual and social life: governing oneself and one's family, administering the state, ruling over nations and exercising global authority. Those arts imitate God's sovereignty in other ways: the soul is assuredly divine since it is God's emulator in the liberal arts and in the arts of government.[18]

Renaissance scholars enthusiastically supported the notion that the whole world can be modelled through numbers, and that mathematical structures were part of the divine figuration. The supreme ancient proponent of the view that man was a mathematician was of course Plato and, above all, *Timaeus*. All educated men were familiar with the report that the inscription in the vestibule of the Academy had forbidden anyone unskilled in geometry to cross the threshold and gain initiation into the sacred mysteries. Political life itself, according to Plato, was subject to mathematical laws, and this was one of the aspects of the ancient philosopher's thought that more attracted the interest of Marsilio Ficino. In the eighth book of the *Republic* (546Aff.), Socrates refers to a mysterious geometric/'fatal' number that explains why it is that even perfectly constituted republics nevertheless decline after the passage of many years. They declined into the first of four degenerate forms ending in a tyranny: into a 'timarchy' governed by a longing for money instead of justice and the good. 'Republics' are then, according to Plato and his fifteenth- and sixteenth-century followers, subject to some cyclical cosmic pattern. In the course of the same passage, Socrates argues for the necessity of state-planned eugenics: citizens approaching parenthood must be adjusted to each other like proportionate numbers. This way they may breed good offspring, thus ensuring the continuance of balance in the state.[19]

The major early modern intellectual who contributed to the explanation of Plato's geometric number was, once more, Marsilio Ficino, who countered Aristotle's objections to the views of Socrates and tried to explicate the passage from the *Republic*. Contemporary and later writers took into account Ficino's writings on this and other passages in Plato. Girolamo Cardano (1501–1576), in his *Opus novum de proportionibus* (1570) proposed as a solution a number occurring in Ficino's analysis, 8,128; Marin Mersenne (1588–1648), the disciple and friend of Descartes, in the second book of his *Traité de l'harmonie universelle* (1627), proposed another number that Ficino had entertained, 729. Eventually, in 1496, Ficino edited his commentary on the eighth book of the *Republic*, together with other commentaries on Platonic dialogues, in one volume dedicated to his pupil, the politician (and future ambassador to France) Niccolò Valori. His brother, Filippo Valori, had financed Ficino's monumental 1484 Plato edition. This way, the 'fatal' number and, more generally, the assumption that the evolution of fortunes, population and well-being of a state could be governed by a mathematical relationship, entered Florentine upper-class culture.[20]

Renaissance Florentine Platonism was, therefore, not a theoretical, philosophical system of thought closed in on itself. It was an exaltation of the functional specialization of the 'wise expert', understood as the creator and protagonist of qualified governance and the common good. It is not difficult to understand how this idea has aided further development of relations between knowledge, policy management and economic decisions. The idea of a link between political and moral knowledge and the works of the merchants and the life of the state permeated the Platonic philosophical paradigm, as is clear from this letter of Marsilio Ficino to the grammarian, musician and poet Cherubino Quarquagli:

> Although, as is customary for those occupied in the study of philosophy, I am perhaps sometimes less dutiful than is appropriate, I cannot now refrain from writing to the most dutiful of men something about duty ... The duty of the knight is bravery in war and noble action in peace; of the merchant, with true faith and diligence to nourish both the State and himself with good things from abroad; of the tradesman honestly to distribute the provisions received from the merchant to each member of the State. Merchants, craftsmen and others should so seek wealth that they harm no one. For whatever arises from the evil in the ends falls back into evil. Let them keep their wealth in such a way that they do not seem to have acquired it in vain, not just for the sake of keeping it. Let them so spend that they may long be able to spend, and may prove to have spent honestly and usefully.[21]

Not coincidentally, the fall of the Medici in 1494 was accompanied by strenuous attacks against Plato and 'the wise men of the world', as Savonarola said from his Florentine pulpit.[22] Brown includes the famous observations of Niccolò Machiavelli and his friend Francesco Valori, evident already in 1506 and then in their exchange of letters in 1513, on the role of fate (*fortuna*) in the government of the prince among the consequences of the sermons of Savonarola, compounded by the ineptitude demonstrated by the Medici during the first age of the 'Italian Wars'. All this rendered Platonism somewhat out of fashion in Florence between the fifteenth and sixteenth centuries, although in other Italian courts, such as Milan, Mantua, Ferrara and Urbino, Plato continued to legitimize the power of newly stabilized rulers, in terms of wisdom and culture.

The Platonic philosophical tradition, however, re-emerged in all its political significance in the Florence of the Medici dukes after the end of the turbulent first decades of the sixteenth century.[23] The institutionalization in 1542 of the Florentine Academy, whose main function was perpetuating Cosimo I de' Medici's reputation for learning, brought forth a founding father of the modern economic thought, Bernardo Davanzati, who read orations in which Plato and Platonism played an important role.[24] In the year 1588 Bernardo Davanzati wrote his *Lesson on Money* (*Lezione delle monete*), which contains the famous metaphor of the world market as a mirror, whose Platonic inspiration is evident.[25] Even outside of Tuscany, the infiltration of Platonism in the 'economic' treaties of the second half of the sixteenth century is evident. Gasparo Scaruffi, director of the mint in Reggio Emilia, in his 1579 monograph entitled *Alitinonfo* (an alchemic 'true light' directed onto the problem of monetary value[26]), warmly supported the Platonic ideal of a general return to 'real and proportionate correspondence in weights as in measures' between gold and silver, despite the fact that they 'are in movement every few years and gain some value, according to the varied disposition of appetites and men'.[27]

> That there is a lot less gold than silver has no other cause if not that one always finds the quantity of the most precious things to be scarce as compared to the less [precious] … From this it follows that, considered the real proportion among them, which is that the weight of one part of pure gold is in fact worth twelve parts of refined gold, according, I believe, to a God-given order and observed by nature and so has been declared by divine Plato in his Dialogue entitled *Ipparco* – that is in the study on profit as well as on its finality – where he made an effort with lucid reason and a solid foundation to esteem or evaluate gold and silver with fixed prices in the manner of weights, of one to twelve and twelve to one, so as to be able to make the alloys correspond proportionally, to strike coinage of various kinds which remain forever of their real values.[28]

The importance of the Platonic doctrine in the context of economic knowledge in the late Renaissance was reiterated in Scaruffi's *Breve istruzione sopra il Discorso delle monete* (*Brief Statement on the Speech of Coins*), which appeared at the same time as the *Alitinonfo*.

> Since divine Plato and other learned philosophers stated that it is natural for one part of pure gold by weight to be worth twelve parts of refined silver and twelve of silver one of gold, I believe that there will not be a single person who demurs; and when this should be denied, whoever does so must of necessity be more profound in science than Plato and the other philosophers who confirm that this is true, or else he must have made a very refined and very diligent dissection of these precious metals.[29]

The culture and practice of government inspired by the Italian Neoplatonism of the fifteenth century were an important basis for the subsequent establishment of the epistemological circularity between quantification, professional specialization of policy makers and the political and social modelling of well-being, which is the foundation of today's conception of economic science. The power of the Medici in Florence was the unavoidable introduction to the rediscovery of Plato and his ancient followers. This, in turn, gave philosophical legitimacy to the concentration of political power into the hands of professional rulers, intendants and secretaries. The intellectuals turned to this new administrative class, in order to advise them on how to govern the state and, therefore, learn to master what we would now call the economic sphere. Methods and assumptions put forward to think, organize and reform government and the society as part of new Platonic paradigms in early Renaissance Italy were founded on categories, theories and practices that contributed to the formation of a new economic rationality in the centuries to come.

Which economics?

While all this was happening, Renaissance culture maintained, on another level of discourse, the traditional vision of classical *oikonomia*. It is a paradigm which only in the eighteenth century would absorb the theoretical categories and conceptual novelties that were slowly developing in the spheres of intellectual discourse, politics and economics. The traditional concept of economics is epitomized by the representation formulated in the second edition of *Iconologia overo descrittione dell'immagini universali* by the Perugian academic Cesare Ripa.[30] This was an influential encyclopaedic repertory of human images personifying abstract concepts for artistic use, printed for the first time in Rome in 1593 and used by Jan Vermeer and the decorators of Versailles. The volume depicts economy as 'a matron of venerable aspect, crowned with an olive branch, who holds in her left hand a compass and in her right a rod, and at her side there should be a rudder'. Her aspect was like this, Ripa added, because 'happiness of political living together requires the union of many families who live under the same laws and are governed by them'. And as 'in order to maintain itself each family with good order needs laws which are more particular and specific than the universal ones', the 'private order of governing a family is denoted by our people with the Greek word *oikonomia*'.[31]

The literal familial dimension of *oikonomia* led Ripa to suggest to artists who wanted to represent her that they should work out the design of a mother 'with the rod, that signifies the rule which the head of the household has over his servants, and the rudder shows the care and discipline that the father must have over his children'. The 'olive garland' with which the woman was crowned showed, moreover, 'that the good economist must necessarily keep the peace in his house. The compass teaches that each person must measure his strength and govern himself accordingly, both in spending and other things to maintain and perpetuate his family, by means of measure'. Rule, consensus and caution: these were the traits of every good economy. By virtue of them, economy is depicted 'as a matron, belonging to the governing of the household, on account of the experience she had with things and the world'.[32]

This iconographic stereotype renders the most frequently used contemporary meaning of the term *oikonomia*. Its origins were found, as mentioned, in the eighth, ninth and tenth chapters of the first book of the *Politics* and the fifth chapter of the fifth book of the *Nicomachean Ethics* by Aristotle. Moreover the *Oeconomicus* by Xenophon also contributed to it, as well as the brief homonymous pseudo-Aristotelian treatise, the treatises on agriculture by Cato, Varro and Columella, and the *Naturalis historia* by Pliny the Elder.[33]

The cognitive status assigned by the high culture of the Renaissance to economics was thus that of a branch of 'real practical philosophy', as explained by the Florentine humanist Benedetto Varchi.

Real practical philosophy is divided principally into two parts. The first and more worthy is called 'pertaining to action', which deals not with necessary and thus incorruptible and eternal things, as does Real contemplative philosophy, but with contingent things made by men, which consequently can be and not be; and this in turn is divided into three parts: Ethics or Moral philosophy, which considers principally the customs of a single man; Economics or Domestic philosophy, which teaches how a paterfamilias should govern his household; the third and last is called Politics, i.e. Civil philosophy, which declares how states should be ruled and governed, both republics and kingdoms.[34]

The traditionally etymological meaning of the term economy (*economia*) continued to be used for a long time. The notorious *Piazza universale* by Tommaso Garzoni (1583), a ponderous *summa* of all the arts, professions and occupations of the time, explains to its reader that 'economics is nothing other than a discipline pertaining to the worthy governing of one's own family or a family taken on as one's own'. And the 'economists' are 'those who attend to the care and governing of their own household, through which they become competent for political and civil administration'.[35] The *Summa politica* of the Portuguese Sebastião Cesar, written in 1650, gave to the *Economia do Principe* a reading hinging on the pomp and liberality of the Renaissance.

> As primeiras acçoēs que daō ao Principe fama de prudente nas couses civis, saō duas, o governo de sua propria casa; que por real deve ser a primeira; e a eleiçao que fas de Ministros (come temos dito no primeiro fundamento de razaō de estado) por que elles mostram as inclinaçoēs de sua condiçaō.[36]

It is the same concept that enabled various contemporaneous treatises on domestic economy, among them *Della economica* by Giovan Battista Alessandri, to recommend prodigality to their readers, and that they should condemn those who 'in spreading' [their wealth] feel 'displeasure, as happens in the stingy or avaricious person'.[37]

Underlying the discourse was the conviction, confirmed in *Il savio industrioso nella economia* by Leone Zambelli (1635), an educational plan for the nobility dedicated to Prince Odoardo I Farnese, that the dichotomy between 'reason of State' and 'economics' in the domestic sense was merely a formal one. The same value system had to be the foundation of the prince's activity both as *paterfamilias* and as ruler. Therefore that work combined both activities, suggesting to the growing offspring the same moral comportment with regard to both spheres.

During the seventeenth century the uses of the term economy (*economia*) and its derivatives in the principal Western languages seem, however, to begin to expand, while nevertheless retaining their primarily intellectual character. The printed editions of the *Diarium europaeum*, a periodical which was a precursor to modern journalism, founded by Martin Meyer in the second half of the seventeenth century, still use the words *oeconomie* and *oeconomi*, treating them as foreign words, printing them in round characters – like Latin citations – in the context of a text printed in *Fraktur*. Their meaning is that of the state's accountancy.[38]

Another paradigm for the use during the Renaissance of the term 'economia' and its variants emerges from theological discourse. I do not intend to speak here of the formulation of economic themes by Italian and Spanish medieval theology, starting with Thomas of Aquinas and the texts of the Franciscans, about which much has already been written.[39]

I intend to concentrate instead on the fact that Christian theology, from the first centuries onward, used the word *oikonomia* in connection with one of the two paradigms dominating interpretation of political relations. The first paradigm was political in the strictest sense. It was primarily public, based on the transcendence of sovereign power in the one God. The second paradigm was economic theology, which conceived of *oikonomia* as an order intrinsic both to divine and human life. Giorgio Agamben has derived political philosophy and the modern theory of sovereignty from the first paradigm. From the second he has traced the root of a genealogical lineage of modern geopolitics, that is to say the affirmation of discourses and technologies aimed at regulating populations and at adapting, intensifying and distributing human forces.[40] I believe that we would be remiss in underestimating the revival and developments during the Renaissance of the category of *oikonomia* by Protestant theology. The re-adoption of the term contributed, in my opinion, to the consolidation of words and cultural models that we today would define as economic, in the sense that they were revived and re-launched into the contemporary world by the classical economic thought of the eighteenth century.

In the patristics of the second century CE, articulated at the councils of Nicea and Constantinople, the adoption of the word and the category of *oikonomia* formulated by Aristotle was useful to the attempt to reconcile the Trinity with monarchy and monotheism. That, too, served an antimonarchic function, affirming that the oneness of God could in no way be resolved in a plurality of divine figures. In the 'management paradigm' of *oikonomia*, Christian theology of the first centuries identified the instrument that made the reconciliation between monotheism and Trinity possible. This was done on the basis of the argument that God, who in his essence and nature is one, in his own *oikonomia*, governing his *oikos* and his divine life, can have a Son and be articulated into a triple figure. This is an *oikonomia* that is thus not science in the proper sense, since it is not tied to an internal system of discursive coherence. Rather, the decisions designated as 'economic' are those regarding, from time to time, specific problems relating to the functional order of the various parts of the *oikos*. This was the case already in Aristotle, where the term 'head of the family' (*despotes*) 'does not denote a science (*epistemen*) but a certain way of being'.[41]

When, after Nicea and the other great councils, the Christian philosophical/theological vocabulary became more sophisticated with the concept of *homoousia*, the unity of substance, the economic paradigm by which the Trinity had initially been imagined was officially abandoned, being too pragmatic for the new linguistic and conceptual schemes. This 'managerial' meaning of the theological term *oikonomia* gained renewed vigour in the mainly Protestant religious works of the fifteenth and seventeenth centuries. It occurred not only in those which, like the Lutheran theologian Justus Menius' *Oeconomia christiana* (1529), had as their subject the governing of the Christian family,[42] but also in the work of the Huguenot Jean Daillé (1594–1670), who gave the word *oikonomia* a clearly 'managerial' colouring when he declared in his sermons: 'Cette oeconomie du Seigneur dans l'oeuvre de nôtre salut, est le fundament de l'exhortation, que faisoit autrefois S. Paul aux Filippiens, et qu'il nous address auiourd'huy dans le verset que nous venons de vous lire.'[43] His fellow Huguenot Jean Claude (1519–1687), in *Traité de la composition d'un sermon*, written a few decades later, observed: 'Ces motifs se trouvent presque tous renfermez dans Jesus-Christ, et dans les mystères de son Economie: et ils sont tels qu'il n'y a point d'âme qui n'en soit touchée, à moins que d'être, je ne dis pas dure et insensible, mais morte entièrement ou possédée du démon.'[44]

An interesting English demonstration from the seventeenth century of the use of the term *oikonomia* with reference to divine ordering activity is found in the *Contemplations Moral and Divine* (1675) by the judge and natural philosopher Matthew Hale (1609–1676).[45] 'There is an *admirable Œconomy of the divine Godness and wisdom, to bring his creature Man both to his duty and happiness*',[46] wrote Hale. 'Motion, order, and divine Œconomy' are terms of which he intends to investigate 'qualities, causes and operations'.[47]

Richard Allestree (1619–1681), the provost of Eton College, also wrote of a divine 'economy' of God *vis-à-vis* human beings. 'God who is essentially happy in himself, can receive no accession to his felicity by the poor contributions of men', he wrote, using a language with financial overtones. 'He cannot therefore be suppos'd to have made them upon intuition on increasing, but communicating his happiness. And this his original design is very visible in all parts of his Economy towards them.'[48] Allestree, who not coincidentally was an able administrator of his college, was even more explicit in mentioning the divine organizational activity in another of his works, *The Causes of the Decay of Christian Piety*.

> What then are our clamorous repining, but so many loud *invectives* against Gods *decree*; a desire to subvert his fundamental *law*, and confound the *distinction* he has irreversibly set between our *earthly* and our heavenly state: and alas, what mad insolence is this, to expect that the whole *Œconomy* of the world must be chang'd only to humour us?[49]

Goerge Hickes also used the term *economy* in a biblical context and with a theological meaning, giving it a clearly 'managerial' twist: 'Hitherto I have given the reasons of altering the *Jewish Economy*, and of reforming of it into the Christian Church.'[50]

The use of the theological-managerial meaning of the word economy found particular currency in the theological 'federal' (*foedus*) paradigm. The theological theme of the pact or covenant was spread between the sixteenth and seventeenth centuries primarily in the precincts of classical Calvinism, and especially in the reformed and Presbyterian churches and in some Methodist and Baptist churches, originally in the context of biblical exegesis. By extension it became progressively chosen as the organizational principle of the whole theological science of the world and of salvation.

In general terms one can say that covenant theology reads the story of the relationship between God and humanity in terms of three great pacts:[51] the pact of redemption (*pactum salutis*), the pact of works (*foedus operum*) and the pact of mercies (*foedus gratiae*). These are defined as theological pacts, because they are not explicitly presented by the Bible as covenants between God and humanity. They are thus considered as theologically implicit and as syntheses of the entire scriptural message. In traditional Reformation thought, covenant theology is thus not treated simply as a *locus* of doctrine or as central doctrine. The *foedus* is a proper architectural principle of Scripture, an intrinsic and organizing structure, through which the biblical text finds internal coherence and a function in human history.

Insofar as the conceptual bases of covenant theology can be traced all the way back to Patristic authors, and in particular to the writings of Irenaeus and Augustine, it became necessary in the context of the Reformation, in particular with Martin Luther and Huldrych Zwingli, to renew the concept of a covenant in terms of a return to biblical interpretation as the foundation of Christian faith. The theologian Heinrich Bullinger wrote the first systematic treatise on this subject. Giovanni Calvino dedicated a large part of his work *Istituzioni della religione Cristiana* (1559) to a 'federal' reading of the Old and

New Testaments. Nonetheless, it was only in the course of the seventeenth century that covenant theology became a proper school. This school permeated Reformation thinking and practice in various areas of Europe; it was pivotal to the legal relationships within the first expansion in North America, which for this reason has recently been defined as 'a covenanted society'.[52]

The theme of the double covenant – the covenant of works stipulated by God with Adam and the covenant of mercy given as a promise in the Old Testament and fulfilled in the New one – thus became a basis for reformed theology in the seventeenth century. It appears in the 1646 Confession of Faith of Westminster, and is central in the writings of a great protagonist of seventeenth-century Protestant theology: the Dutchman Johannes Coch (1603–1669), professor of theology in the 'bastion of liberty', Leiden.[53] According to Cocceius a third covenant, that of redemption, was stipulated between Christ and God, his father, in order to expiate the sins of the elect, bringing the covenant into the inner life of the Trinity itself. It was in this phase that *oikonomia* became central in the context of covenant theology.[54] Thanks to Cocceius, the category of *œconomia* (which in his writings alternates with *dispensatio* – administration, distribution) becomes a conceptual link between the covenant and the *ordo temporum* of history. *Œconomia* and *dispensatio* would be, after Cocceius, terms to organize conceptually the complexity and the globality of the ways in which the covenant of mercies is granted, also compared to the monolithic nature of the covenant of works, given only once. The covenant of mercies, though it remains the same with regard to its *fondamentus*, finds its practical explication in relation to different historical circumstances: 'Constituto perpetuo fide justificantis et salvificae objecto', wrote Cocceius in *De differentiis prioris temporis a posteriori in dispensatione foederis gratiae*, the eleventh chapter of his *Summa doctrinae de foedere et testamento dei*, 'sequuntur differentiae, quae fidei et fidelibus ratione diversitatis dispensationum et *kairòn*, temporum accidunt'.[55]

The concept of *œconomia* thus assumed the theological function of situating revelation in the context of human events. With a changing historical context, the economy of salvation also changes. In this cultural framework, economic lemmas come therefore to designate a broad and pregnant material and historical ordering, with ambitions that are philosophically organizational, general and systematic. In the works of Cocceius' most brilliant Dutch students, these thematics assumed an ever more important role. Cocceius' successor at the University of Leiden, Herman Witsius (Herman Wits or Hermannus Witsius, 1636–1707), in his principal work, *De oeconomia foederum Dei cum hominibus* (1694), immediately translated in England under the title *The Economy of the Divine Covenants between God and Man*, distinguished nine beacons of the economy of salvation in the New Testament. Franciscus Burman (1628–1679), professor of theology at Utrecht, in turn composed a *Synopsis theologie, et speciatim Œconomia Foederum Dei*, a great summary of Cocceian dogmatic theology. It is important to observe that both students, like many Cocceians, were ardent Cartesians and thus found a vast following in the new generations of scientists throughout Northern Europe. Their opponents even went so far as to nickname them Cartesian theologians, 'Cocceio-Cartesians' or 'rationalist' theologians.[56] This is not surprising, given their propensity for general systemizations of theological knowledge about life and to the conceptual rigor on which their ordering and 'managerial' view of divine intervention in history hinged. It is emblematic of this that another student of Cocceius, Christoph Wittichius (1625–1687), author in 1682 of the expressive *Consensus Scripturae cum Cartesio* and holder of a teaching chair at Leiden, actually defended Copernicus, bringing upon himself the censure of many colleagues and problems with the local synods. Nonetheless

23

this guaranteed him a wide audience and great success among his students. Pierre Bayle at Rotterdam was informed of this, writing in a letter of 1585:

> Mr. Wittichius est fort suivi à Leyde. Il a plus d'auditeurs lui seul, que tous les autres ensembles, parce qu'il est l'appui et le rempart del Coccéius et del Cartésiens, dont le parti plait plus aux jeunes gens.[57]

The decisive influence exercised by covenant theology, and in particular by *The Economy of the Devine Covenants between God and Man* by Witsius, upon the theoretical work of Thomas Hobbes has recently been studied. It is evident in Hobbes' concept of the social contract, defined in *Leviathan* (1651) as a pact of submission (*Pactum subiectionis*) and referred to several times with the term *covenant*, by which humanity limits its own liberty, accepting rules imposed by the head of the state.[58] It should also be observed that the close bond between Cartesianism, theories of the state, new science and covenant theology was supported by the distinction, fundamental in Cocceius, between philosophy and theology: between the domain of reason, to which natural science belongs, and revelation. This drew philosophers and Cartesian and Copernican scientists to covenant theology and led them to accept its organization and vocabulary.[59]

It must be recalled that one of the fundamental conceptual elements of the evolution of modern economic thought – the metaphor of circulation of liquidity within society – found a classical formulation in Thomas Hobbes. In the dedicatory letter of *De corpore* (1655) Hobbes called the roll of what he considered the small class of real scientists, which included Galileo, Copernicus, Kepler, Marin Mersenne, Pierre Gassendi and William Harvey. The last, William Harvey, had, in his *De motu cordis et sanguinis* (1628), dedicated his discovery of the circulation of blood to King Charles I.[60] Hobbes, who was interested in autopsies, saw these performed by both Harvey and his personal secretary William Petty, one of the founders of modern economic science. From 1650 onward, Harvey was professor of anatomy at Oxford and at the same time teacher of music at Gresham College.[61] In the twenty-fourth chapter of *Leviathan* ('Of the nutrition, and procreation of a Common-wealth'), Hobbes adopted Harvey's new findings and translated them into monetary terms. The circulation of riches was represented by Hobbes as an autonomous force internal to the 'artificial man', consistent with the mechanistic Cartesian system which characterizes the whole *Leviathan*. In it, the state is a mechanical body, clock or robot.

> The conduits, and ways by which [money] is conveyed to the public use, are of two sorts; one, that conveyeth it to the publique coffers; the other, that issueth the same out again for publique payments. Of the first sort, are collectors, receivers, and treasurers; of the second are the treasurers again, and the officers appointed for payment of severall publique or private ministers. And in this also, the artificial man maintains his resemblance with the natural; whose veins receiving the blood from the several parts of the body, carry it to the heart; where being made vital, the heart by the arteries sends it out again, to enliven, and enable for motion all the members of the same.[62]

Harvey's discoveries were a cognitive dowel determining and grounding all of physiology, originally understood as an 'economic' science of nature.[63] The Englishman had obtained a doctorate at the University of Padua in the course of his sojourn in Italy between 1599 and 1603, where he spent time with Fabrizi d'Acquapendente, whose fame is linked to the discovery of venous valves (*De venarum ostiolis*, 1603). And it was precisely the reflection on the disposition of the venous valves in relation to the heart, as Harvey himself later recounted to Boyle, that led him to his insight into the circulatory system in the years leading up to 1628. Hobbes journeyed to Italy twice: the first visit, in the course of his travels of 1610–1613, he spent mostly in Venice; the second, in the period 1634–1637, took him to Florence to visit Galileo, who was confined at Arcetri. It has been recently hypothesized that it was precisely during one of these visits that Hobbes, perhaps through Paolo Sarpi, came to know the *Lezione delle monete* of Bernardo Davanzati, which identifies money with 'second blood – probably the oldest example of this analogy in monetary theory.[64]

Linguistic developments such as those we have pointed to thus far, however minute and apparently secondary, show that the declensions of *oikonomía* in the early modern era solidified semantic vibrations, metaphors and unstable rhetoric that was still in the process of evolving.

It remains to explain, by way of conclusion, how the term *oikonomia* was used in the bibliographical sector during the Renaissance. The usage anticipates the physiological/systemic meaning of economy established between the late seventeenth and early eighteenth centuries, in the fields of physiology and botany.[65] The category of 'economy' is used in the sense of a harmonious order of the parts of a work: a meaning which comes from antiquity but is at the same time present in the systematizing and harmonizing ambitions of classical economists. Quintilian in his *Institutio oratoria* recommended that young students read the Latin *veteres* with the aim of learning 'a more harmonious disposition of the [dramatic] material' (*oeconomia ... diligentior*).[66] It is in this meaning that the term was adopted in the Renaissance in titles of volumes such as *Pandectaru[m] iuris ciuilis oeconomia* by the French jurist Eguinaire Baron (François Eguinaire, baron de Kerlouan, 1495–1550)[67] or by the Lutheran jurist of Antwerp, Matthaeus Wesenbeck (1531–1586), the first to teach law at Jena, in his *Commentarius iuris oeconomia* of 1579.[68] The *Œconomia methodica concordantiarum scripturae sacrae* by the Cambridge theology professor George Bullock (*c.* 1521–1572) was a text of 1,300 pages, 40 cm high by 25 cm wide, dedicated to Gregory XIII and printed in 1572 in Antwerp by the famous Christopher Plantin, who in turn had to bear the gruelling enterprise of editorial coordination.[69] A few years earlier, in 1568, the Viennese jurist George Eder (1523–1587), known for having prepared in 1569 the fundamental catechism of the Council of Trent for scholastic use, subdividing the fundamental doctrines into sections and subsections and adding clear tables of contents with the title *Methodus Catechismi catholici*, had tested himself in his *Œconomia bibliorum*, to which he added in the same year the *Partitiones Catechismi catholici Tridentini*, which hinged on the same model of synoptic and systematizing discursive reorganization.[70]

In these and other similar cases the *oeconomia* to which the titles referred consisted of the considered and functional re-systematization of a set of statements, in a declension of the term, which perfectly complements those current at the time. The physiological and discursive meanings of *oeconomia* moreover found a perfect reconciliation in *Oeconomia Hippocratis alphabeti serie distincta* (1588) by the Metz doctor Anuce Foes (Foesius, 1528–1595).[71] The treatise was doubly 'economic': in its organization of the subject matter and in the thematic itself. The other great work of Foes, *Hippocratis opera Omnia* (1595), the first nearly complete collection of the Greek texts with Latin translation, was owned and certainly read in a seventeenth-century edition by John Locke, another philosopher with medical training and interests which today we would define as economic.[72]

Notes

1 M. Blaug, 'No History of Ideas, Please, We're Economists', *Journal of Economic Perspectives*, 1 (2001): 145–64; M. N. Rothbard, *Economic Thought before Adam Smith: An Austrian Perspective on the History of Economic Thought*, vol. 1, Cheltenham and Brookfield, VT: Edward Elgar, 1995, pp. ix–x.

2 E. Screpanti and S. Zamagni, *An Outline of the History of Economic Thought*, Oxford: Clarendon Press, 1993, p. 1.

3 See, e.g., B. Gordon, *Economic Analysis before Adam Smith: Hesiod to Lessius*, London: Macmillan, 1975; L. Dumont, *From Mandeville to Marx. The Genesis and Triumph of Economic Ideology*, Chicago: University of Chicago Press, 1977; T. Hutchinson, *Before Adam Smith: The Emergence of Political Economy 1662–1776*, Oxford: Blackwell, 1988; J.-C. Perrot, *Une historie intellectuelle de l'économie politique XVIIe–XVIIIe siècle*, Paris: Éditions de l'École des Hautes Études en Sciences Sociales, 1992; C. Larrère, *L'invention de l'économie au XVIIIe siècle, du droit naturel à la physiocratie*, Paris: Presses Universitaires de France, 1992; P. Steiner, *Sociologie de la connaissance économique: Essai sur les rationalisations de la connaissance économique (1750–1850)*, Paris: Presses Universitaires de France, 1998.

4 G. Maifreda, *From Oikonomia to Political Economy. Constructing Economic Knowledge from the Renaissance to the Scientific Revolution*, Farnham and Burlington, VT: Ashgate, 2012.

5 The reference is to M. Foucault *The Order of Things: An Archaeology of the Human Sciences*, New York: Vintage Books, 1966. For an innovative re-elaboration of this concept in the economic field see S. Todd Lowry, *Archaeology of Economic Ideas: The Classical Greek Tradition*, Durham, NC: Duke University Press, 1987; S. Todd Lowry, *Pre-Classical Economic Thought, from the Greeks to the Scottish Enlightenment*, Boston: Kluwer-Nijhoff, 1987; S. Todd Lowry, 'Are There Limits to the Past in the History of Economic Thought?', Presidential Address, History of Economics Society, *Journal of the History of Economic Thought*, 13 (1991): 134–43.

6 R. E. Backhouse, *The Ordinary Business of Life: A History of Economics from the Ancient World to the Twenty-First Century*, Princeton, NJ: Princeton University Press, 2002; R. E. Backhouse, *The Puzzle of Modern Economics: Science or Ideology?*, Cambridge: Cambridge University Press, 2010, p. 90.

7 See E. Cochrane, 'Science and Humanism in the Italian Renaissance', *American Historical Review*, 5 (1976): 1039–57, 1049; C. Vasoli, *Filosofia e religione nella cultura del Rinascimento*, Naples: Guida, 1988.

8 F. Yates, *Giordano Bruno and the Hermetic Tradition*. London and New York: Routledge, 1964. C. C. Celenza, 'The Revival of Platonic Philosophy', in J. Hankins (ed.) *The Cambridge Companion to Renaissance Philosophy*, Cambridge: Cambridge University Press, 2007, pp. 72–96.

9 A. Brown, 'Platonism in Fifteenth-Century Florence and Its Contribution to Early Modern Political Thought', *Journal of Modern History*, 58 (1986): 383–413; J. Hankins, *Plato in the Italian Renaissance*, 2 vols., Leiden, New York, Copenhagen and Cologne: Brill, 1990–1991.

10 E. Garin, *L'età nuova. Ricerche di storia della cultura dal XII al XVI secolo*, Naples: Morano, 1969, pp. 263–92.

11 E. Garin, 'Ricerche sulle traduzioni di Platone nella prima metà del sec. XV', in *Medioevo e Rinascimento. Studi in onore di Bruno Nardi*, vol. 1. Florence: Sansoni, 1955, pp. 339–74; P. O. Kristeller, 'Marsilio Ficino and His Works after Five Hundred Years', in G. Garfagnini (ed.) *Marsilio Ficino e il ritorno di Platone. Studi e documenti*, Florence: Olschki, 1986, pp. 15–195; H. D. Saffrey, 'Florence, 1492: The Reappearance of Plotinus', *Renaissance Quarterly*, 46 (1996), pp. 488–508; W. Caferro, *Contesting the Renaissance*, Chichester: Wiley-Blackwell, 2011, pp. 109–13. Marsilio Ficino wrote in a letter to Angelo Poliziano that he had produced an *œconomia*, whose structure must have been quite similar to the one proposed in Giorgio Valla's eloquently entitled *De œconomia, sive administratione domus* [*On Œconomy, or Domestic Administration*], which was part of the general encyclopedic system *De expetendis et fugiendis rebus* [*On the Things to Pursue and Avoid*]: see M. Ficino, *The Letters of Marsilio Ficino*, preface by P. O. Kristeller, vol. 1, London: Shepheard-Walwyn, 1975, p. 59. The reference is to G. Valla, *Georgii Vallae Placentini viri clariss. De expetendis, et fugiendis rebus opus, in quo haec continentur … De œconomia, siue administratione domus libri 3* [...], Venice: in aedibus Aldi Romani, 1501.

12 B. Tambrun, *Pléthon: Le retour de Platon*, Paris: Vrin, 2006.

13 F. Manetti, 'Il ritorno di un archetipo del pensiero economico: la città ideale di Gemisto Pletone', *Cheiron*, 42 (2004): 29–72; N. Siniossoglou, *Radical Platonism in Byzantium: Illumination and Utopia in Gemistos Plethon*, Cambridge: Cambridge University Press, 2011. Pletho's influence on Western Platonism, which was probably transmitted through Bessarion and his circle rather than directly, should not, however, be exaggerated: see Hankins, *Plato in the Italian Renaissance*, vol. 2, 437–40.

14 Saffrey, 'Florence, 1492', p. 488.
15 V. Rees, 'Considering Marsilio Ficino as a Preacher: Sermons and Exegesis in Fifteenth Century Florence', *Bruniana & Campanelliana* 1 (2012): 77–88.
16 A. Brown, *Bartolomeo Scala, 1430–1497, Chancellor of Florence. The Humanist as Bureaucrat*, Princeton, NJ: Princeton University Press, 1979; A. Brown, 'Platonism in Fifteenth-Century Florence and Its Contribution to Early Modern Political Thought', *Journal of Modern History*, 58 (1986): 383–413, p. 388.
17 Hankins, *Plato in the Italian Renaissance*, vol. 1, pp. 110–11; A. Gamberini, 'I piedi e le tibie dello stato: la burocrazia. Uberto Decembrio e la costruzione identitaria di un nuovo ceto politico', in A. Gamberini (ed.) *La mobilità sociale negli stati del Tre-Quattrocento: la vicenda della Lombardia*, Rome: Viella, 2016, in press.
18 M. J. B. Allen, *Icastes: Marsilio Ficino's Interpretation of Plato's Sophist*, Berkeley, Los Angeles and Oxford: University of California Press, 1989, p. 155.
19 M. J. B. Allen, *Nuptial Arithmetic. Marsilio Ficino's Commentary on the Fatal Number in Book VIII of Plato's Republic*, Berkeley, Los Angeles and London: University of California Press, 1994.
20 M. J. B. Allen, *Plato's Third Eye. Studies in Marsilio Ficino's Metaphysics and its Sources*, Aldershot and Brookfield, VT: Ashgate-Variorum, 1995, VIII (23) and X (431); P. O. Kristeller, *Il pensiero filosofico di Marsilio Ficino*, Florence: Le Lettere, 1988 (Italian edn. of *The Philosophy of Marsilio Ficino*, New York: Columbia University Press, 1943), pp. 302–3.
21 *The Letters of Marsilio Ficino*, vol. 1, pp. 64–5.
22 E. Cuttini, *Unità e pluralità nella tradizione europea della filosofia pratica di Aristotele. Girolamo Savonarola, Pietro Pomponazzi e Filippo Melantone*, Soveria Mannelli: Rubbettino, 2005, p. 51; E. Garin, 'Ricerche sugli scritti filosofici di Girolamo Savonarola. Opere inedite e smarrite', in *La cultura filosofica del Rinascimento italiano. Ricerche e documenti*, Florence: Sansoni, 1961.
23 A. Chastel, *Art et humanisme à Florence au temps de Laurent le Magnifique: études sur la Renaissance et l'humanisme platonicien*, 2nd edn., Paris: Presses Universitaires de France, 1961.
24 C. di Filippo Bareggi, 'In nota alla politica culturale di Cosimo I: l'Accademia fiorentina', *Quaderni Storici*, 23 (1973): 527–74; M. Firpo, *Gli affreschi di Pontormo a San Lorenzo: eresia, politica e cultura nella Firenze di Cosimo I*, Turin: Einaudi, 1997; C. Poncet, 'Ficino's Little Academy of Careggi', *Bruniana & Campanelliana* 1 (2012): 67–76; Maifreda, *From* Oikonomia *to Political Economy*, pp. 76–96.
25 M. Bianchini, 'The Galilean Tradition and the Origins of Economic Science in Italy', in M. Albertone and A. Masoero (eds.) *Political Economy and National Realities*, Turin: Fondazione Luigi Einaudi, 1994, pp. 17–29.
26 M. Bianchini, 'Gasparo Scaruffi. Una famiglia, una città, un visionario progetto', in A. Mazza, E. Monducci and M. Zamboni (eds.) *Palazzo Scaruffi: Storia, arte, restauri*, Parma: Grafiche Step, 2010, pp. 9–36.
27 G. Scaruffi, 'Discorso sopra le monete e della vera proporzione tra l'oro e l'argento', in *Scrittori classici italiani di economia politica*, 1st edn. 1582, repr. of the original edn. [1803–1816], Rome: Edizioni Bizzarri, 1965, vol. 2, pp. 71–264, pp. 73–4.
28 *Ibid.*, pp. 83–5.
29 G. Scaruffi, 'Breve istruzione sopra il Discorso delle monete', in *Scrittori classici*, vol. 2, pp. 265–330, p. 269.
30 C. Ripa *Iconologia overo Descrittione di diverse Imagini cavate dall'antichità et di propria inventione … Di nuovo revista et dal medesimo ampliata di 400 et più Imagini …*, 2nd edn., Rome: appresso Lepido FaciiGeorg Olms, 1603 [1st edn. 1593].
31 *Ibid.*, p. 118.
32 *Ibid.*, pp. 118–19.
33 D. Frigo, *Il padre di famiglia. Governo della casa e governo civile nella tradizione dell''economica' tra Cinque e Seicento*, Rome: Bulzoni, 1985.
34 B. Varchi, *Lezioni sul Dante e prose varie, la maggior parte inedite tratte ora in luce dagli originali della Biblioteca Rinucciniana*, ed. Giuseppe Aiazzi, Florence: Società editrice delle storie del Nardi e del Varchi, 1841, p. 763. On Varchi's neoplatonic inspiration see Firpo, *Gli affreschi di Pontormo a San Lorenzo*.
35 T. Garzoni, *La piazza universale di tutte le professioni del mondo*, ed. P. Cherchi, B. Collina, Turin: Einaudi, 1996 [1st edn. 1585], vol. 1, p. 386.

36 S. Cesar, *Summa politica, offrecida ao Principe Theodofilo de Portugal*, Amsterdam: Tipografia de Simaō Dias Soeiro Lusitano, 1650, pp. 147–8.

37 G. Guerzoni 'Novità, innovazione e imitazione: i sintomi della modernità', in P. Braunstein and L. Molà (eds.) *Il Rinascimento italiano e l'Europa*, vol. 3, *Produzione e tecniche*, Treviso-Costabissara: Fondazione Cassamarca-Angelo Colla Editore, 2007, pp. 59–87, p. 60.

38 M. Mayer, *Continuatio XXII. Diarii Europæi. Insertis variis actis publicis*, Frankfurt am Main: in Verlegung Wilhelm Serlins, 1671, p. 12.

39 C. A. Franks, *He Became Poor: The Poverty of Christ and Aquinas's Economic*, Grand Rapids, MI and Cambridge: William B. Eerdmans, 2009; G. Todeschini, *Franciscan Wealth: From Voluntary Poverty to Market Society*, Saint Bonaventure, NY: Saint Bonaventure University, 2009.

40 G. Agamben *The Kingdom and the Glory: For a Theological Genealogy of Economy and Government*, Stanford, CA: Stanford University Press, 2011.

41 *Ibid.*

42 See U. Gause and S. Scholz (eds.) *Ehe und Familie im Geist des Luthertums: Die Oeconomia Christiana (1529) des Justus Menius*, Leipzig: Evangelische Verlagsanstalt, 2012.

43 J. Daillé *Exposition sur la divine epitre de l'apotre S. Paul aux Filippiens un vingt-neuf sermons prononcés a Charenton, dans les Saintes assemblées de l'Eglise Reformér de Paris, l'an 1639-1640-1641-1642. Premiere partie*, 2nd edn., Geneve [*sic*]: pour Pierre Chouët, 1659², pp. 472–3.

44 J. Claude 'Traité de la composition d'un sermon', in *Les oeuvres posthumes*, vol. 1, Amsterdam: chez Pierre Savouret, 1688, pp. 169–492, p. 402.

45 A. Cromartie *Sir Matthew Hale, 1609–1676: Law, Religion and Natural Philosophy*, Cambridge: Cambridge University Press, 1995.

46 M. Hale, *Contemplations moral and divine*, 2nd edn., London: Thomas Leigh and D. Midwinter, 1699 [1st edn. 1675], p. 422.

47 *Ibid.*, p. 232.

48 R. Allestree, *The Art of Contentment*, Oxford: at the Theater, 1677, p. 2.

49 R. Allestree *The Causes of the Decay of Christian Piety*, London, printed by R. Norton for T. Garthwait: 1667, pp. 211–12.

50 G. Hickes *The Case of Infant-baptism in Five Questions*, London, printed for T. Basset: 1683, p. 21.

51 D. A. Weir. *The Origins of the Federal Theology in Sixteenth-Century Reformation Thought*, Oxford: Clarendon Press, 1990.

52 D. A. Weir, *Early New England: A Covenanted Society*, Grand Rapids, MI: William B. Eerdmans Publishing Company, 2005.

53 W. Otterspeer, *The Bastion of Liberty: Leiden University Today and Yesterday*, Leiden: Leiden University Press, 2008.

54 E. Busch, 'Der Beitrag end Ertrag del Föderaltheologie für ein geschichtliches Verständnis del Offenbaurung', in F. Christ (ed.) *Oikonomia: Heilsgeschicte als Thema der Theologie. Oscar Cullmann zum 65. Geburtstag gewidmet*, Hamburg-Berstedt: Herbert Reich, 1967, pp. 171–90; W. J. van Asselt, *The Federal Theology of Johannes Cocceius (1603–1669)*, Leiden: Brill, 2001.

55 Weir, *The Origins of the Federal Theology*, p. 94.

56 E. van der Wall, 'Orthodoxy and Scepticism in the Early Dutch Enlightment', in R. H. Popkin and A. Vanderjagt (eds.) *Scepticism and Irreligion in the Seventeenth and Eighteenth Centuries*, Leiden: Brill, 1993, pp. 121–41; E. van der Wall, 'Cartesianism and Cocceianism: A Natural Alliance?', in M. Magdalaine, Maria-Cristina Pitassi, Ruth Whelan and Antony McKenna (eds.) *De l'humanisme aux Lumières. Bayle et le protestantisme*, Paris and Oxford: Universitas and Voltaire Foundation, 1996, pp. 445–55.

57 van der Wall, 'Cartesianism and Cocceianism', p. 448.

58 F. Lessay, 'Hobbes's Covenant Theology and Its Political Implications', in P. Spingborg (ed.) *The Cambridge Companion to Hobbes's* Leviathan, Cambridge: Cambridge University Press, 2007, pp. 243–70.

59 R. Vermij *The Calvinist Copernicans. The Reception of the New Astronomy in the Dutch Republic*, Amsterdam: Koninklijke Nederlandse Akademie van Wetenschappen, 2002, p. 320.

60 A. P. Martinich, *Hobbes: A Biography*, Cambridge: Cambridge University Press, 1999, p. 88; T. Sorell, 'Hobbes's Uses of the History of Philosophy', in G.A.J. Rogers, T. Sorell (eds.) *Hobbes and History*, London: Routledge, 2000, pp. 82–96, p. 94.

61 J. Sawday, *The Body Emblazoned: Dissection and the Human Body in Renaissance Culture*, London: Routledge, 1995, p. 61; T. Aspromourgos, 'Political Economy, Political Arithmetic and Political Medicine in the Thought of William Petty', in P. Groenewegen (ed.) *Physicians and Political Economy. Six Studies on Doctor-Economists*, London, New York: Routledge, 2001, pp. 10–25.

62 T. Hobbes, *Leviathan*, ed. J.C. Addison Gaskin, 2nd edn., Oxford and New York: Oxford University Press, 1998, pp. 168 and 490, note 168.

63 Maifreda, *From* Oikonomia *to Political Economy*.

64 F. Boldizzoni, 'L'anatomia politica di Bernardo Davanzati: prospettive sul pensiero economico del Rinascimento', in M. Bianchini (ed.) *Il lungo Cinquecento rivisitato*, special issue of *Cheiron*, 42 (2004): 73–93; F. Boldizzoni, 'Davanzati e Hobbes: nascita e diffusione di un paradigma (XVI–XVIII secolo)', *Il pensiero economico italiano*, 1 (2005): 9–29.

65 Maifreda, *From* Oikonomia *to Political Economy*.

66 G. Aricò, 'Quintiliano e il teatro', in G. Urso (ed.) *Hispania terris omnibus felicior. Premesse ed esiti di un processo di integrazione*, Pisa: Edizioni ETS, 2002, pp. 255–70, p. 256.

67 E. Baron, *Pandectaru[m] iuris ciuilis oeconomia, per Eguinarium Baronem … olim in ordinem confecta, [et] nuper ab eodem recognita …* Pictauii: ex officina Marnesiorum fratrum, 1547.

68 M. Wesenbeck, *Commentarius iuris oeconomia iam olim dictus ex accurata authoris recognitione*, Basel: ex Officina Episcopiana per Eusebium Episcopium et Nicolai Frat. Haeredes, 1579.

69 G. Bullock, *Oeconomia methodica concordantiarum Scripturae Sacrae*, Antwerp: ex Officina Christophori Plantini, 1572. On Bullock see P. Collinson, R. Rex and G. Stanton, *Lady Margaret Beaufort and her Professors of Divinity at Cambridge 1502 to 1649*, Cambridge: Cambridge University Press, 2003.

70 G. Eder, *Oeconomia Bibliorum, siue Partitionum Theologicarum libri quinque: quibus sacrae Scripturae dispositio … exprimitur … his adiecimus etiam … Partitiones Catechismi catholici Tridentini eodem … authore*, Coloniae Agrippinae: apud Geruuinum Calenium [et] h[a]eredes Iohannis Quentelij, 1568. *For a general view, see also* E. Fulton, *Catholic Belief and Survival in Late-Sixteenth Century Vienna. The Case of Georg Eder (1523–87)*, London: Ashgate, 2007.

71 A. Foes, *Oeconomia Hippocratis, alphabeti serie distincta. In qua Dictionum apud Hippocratem omnium, praesertim obscuriorum, usus explicatur, et velut ex amplissimo penu depromitur: ita ut Lexicon Hippocrateum merito dici possit*, Frankfurt am Main: apud Andreae Wecheli heredes, Claudium Marnium & Io Aubrium, 1588.

72 J. Locke, *The Correspondence of John Locke*, ed. E. S. de Beer, vol. 8, *Letters Nos. 3287–3648*, Oxford: Clarendon Press, 1988, p. 341.

2

A MAKESHIFT RENAISSANCE

North India in the "long" fifteenth century[1]

Samira Sheikh

The notion of cultural renaissance, roughly equivalent to that in Europe, has little purchase in the historiography of South Asia except in histories explicitly informed by two ostensibly distinct but connected ideological strands: colonialism and anti-Muslim nationalism. What is more resonant is a tedious and surprisingly persistent tripartite periodization that has beset the region's historiography since colonial conquest. One manifestation of this kind of periodization is seen in the still-common characterization of India's pre-British past as "medieval." In this frame, "ancient" or "classical" India is associated with Hindu and Buddhist rule, the "medieval" period – with all its connotations of a dark age – with the rule of Muslims from the end of the twelfth century, and "modern" India dawns in the wake of the East India Company's victory in the Battle of Plassey in 1757. Stanley Lane-Poole's explanation in 1903 of the term "medieval" perfectly illustrates this thinking:

> The Mediaeval Period of Indian history, though it does not exactly correspond with the Middle Age of Europe, is not less clearly defined. It begins when the immemorial systems, rule, and customs of Ancient India were invaded, subdued, and modified by a succession of foreign conquerors who imposed a new rule and introduced an exotic creed, strange languages and a foreign art. These conquerors were Muslims, and with the arrival of the Turks under Mahmud the Iconoclast at the beginning of the eleventh century, India entered upon her Middle Age ... The Period ends when one of the last of these rulers, oppressed by the revival of Hindu ascendancy, placed himself under English protection and Modern India came into being.[2]

For British historians like Lane-Poole and generations of Indian historians who followed, the Indian medieval ended only when the British brought modernity and civilization to the Islam-oppressed natives they had come to rule.[3] For such historians, "renaissance" was generally congruent with elite colonial modernity in the nineteenth century, especially in the province of Bengal. In the first part of this chapter I will show how "renaissance" came to be defined in India by its deemed antithesis: pre-British Muslim rule, generally dubbed "medieval." I will also suggest that terms such as "renaissance" emerge from an empire-centric orientation that was natural to colonial writing but was eagerly adopted, along with the tripartite ancient-medieval-modern format, into the majority of mainstream nationalist postcolonial histories.

Once it becomes clear that arguments for a nineteenth-century renaissance derive more from the political interests and inclinations of its proponents than from the promise of historical explanation, it is worth considering whether there is any need to identify such a period in South Asian history. I am not convinced about the utility of the term for anywhere outside Europe (and of course there is a long debate about its place in European history which I will not attempt to engage or even cite here[4]) but since I have been invited to address the question in this volume, I would like to shift the emphasis away from two centuries of attempts to establish genealogies for empires and nations to smaller processes and incremental change. A generation of scholars has made the case – without, as far as I am aware, making consistent use of the term renaissance – for the intense inventiveness and vitality of South Asia in the eighteenth century as Mughal control waned and the East India Company gradually expanded its power. In the rest of this chapter, I will argue for looking even further back, for a reconsideration of the "long" fifteenth century in north India as a lower-case renaissance: a time of radically greater connectedness, new local and urban political forms, and long-lasting experiments in language, literature, and culture.

Renaissance and empire

In the eighteenth century, British administrators often cast themselves as imperial Romans, bringing civilization to the barbarian tribes.[5] As Ananya Kabir points out, British authors persistently equated their Saxon past with the Indian present of the eighteenth century, both seen as pre-Renaissance states of being. Early officials such as Sir William Jones and Warren Hastings were portrayed in Romanized form, underlining the links between "*pax Romana* and *pax Britannica*."[6] In these evolving forms of historical self-recognition, there was an unquestionable line drawn between being Roman and being modern; both were emancipatory, imperial modes that depended on the definition of South Asian (and other non-European) societies as different and inferior. As Thomas Metcalf explains, "To describe oneself as 'modern', or as 'progressive', meant that those who were not included in that definition had to be described as 'primitive' or 'backward.'"[7] One of the key aspects of India's primitiveness the British identified was "Oriental despotism," a notion that all property and law was vested in Indian rulers and was thus subject to their arbitrary whims.[8] Such arbitrariness and illiberality came to be particularly associated with the Muslim rulers who preceded the British in India. For writer-administrators such as H. M. Elliot (1808–53), Muslim rule had been corrupt, violent and brutal, and the British, as successors of the Muslim rulers of India, were benign, paternal liberators of its people. Elliot's influential eight-volume *History of India as told by its own Historians* (1853–71), completed and published by John Dowson after Elliot's death, helped drive home the consonance between Muslim India and the medieval, an era of darkness and misery, now beginning to be alleviated by a benevolent British administration.

Although this ascription of medievalism was an invention of the British, most textbooks of Indian history even today accept this chronology and ascribe "modernity" to British conquest. One reason for its tenacity may be because it maps neatly on to Indian (or, rather, Hindu) nationalist perceptions of the past, which portray a clear distinction between the glorious (Hindu, Buddhist) classical past and the subsequent "medieval" decline under Muslim rule. The attribution of medievalism to the Muslim conquest of north India was convenient for both British and nationalist writers. As Gyan Prakash remarks:

> While agreeing to the notion of an India essentialized in relation to Europe, the nationalists transformed the object of knowledge – India – from passive to active, from inert to sovereign, capable of relating to History and Reason. Nationalist historiographers accepted the patterns set for them by British scholarship. They accepted the periodization of Indian history into the Hindu, Muslim, and British periods, later addressed as the ancient, medieval, and modern eras … and reiterated the long and unchanging existence of a Sanskritic Indic civilization.[9]

Historians of a nationalist bent writing in the first half of the twentieth century usually inaugurated the medieval era in the early eleventh century (following Lane-Poole's invocation of Mahmud of Ghazni's invasions of north India in 1025–26) or in 1206 (with the establishment of a Turkic sultanate in north India). The establishment of Muslim rule was seen as the beginning of a long dark age of defeat and decline, ending only with British conquest.

It is against such powerful notions of medievalism that we must regard the two chief uses of "renaissance" in South Asian history writing. The first, and most common, usage is the Bengal Renaissance.[10] A flowering of nationalist thought among elite male, mostly Hindu, intellectuals in colonial Bengal in the mid to late nineteenth century, the Renaissance – and the consequent end of India's medievalism – is popularly thought to have been brought about as a consequence of British administrative changes and orientalists' rediscovery of the texts of a glorious Hindu past.[11] Among the key catalysts was the "enlightenment" inspired by English education introduced in Bengal from the 1830s to replace Persian, the language of education, cultivation, and government service in the preceding Mughal empire. The early nationalists of the Bengal Renaissance are popularly perceived to have begun to shake off "medieval" (read Muslim) accretions to restore Hindu civilization to its ancient Orientalist-approved glory. The British association of medievalism with Muslim rule ensured that India's renaissance meant a rejection of language and culture associated with Islam and Muslims as backward and corrupt and therefore to be discarded, an association with fateful implications for the subsequent history of South Asia.

The second, though less common, invocation of renaissance appears in descriptions of earlier religious reformism, especially between the fifteenth and seventeenth centuries, often characterized by the term *bhakti* and associated with devotional literary movements in vernacular languages.[12] When characterized as a renaissance, these movements were usually seen as manifestations of reborn Hinduism, until then suppressed by the tyranny and iconoclasm of Islamic rule. In keeping with their character as new forms of Hinduism, they were seen as influenced by Islamic practice, especially Sufism, but entirely separate from and in resistance to the activities of the Muslim state. Interestingly, there was little attempt to connect this early modern "renaissance" to humanism or scientific thought or to other values popularly associated with the Renaissance in Western Europe. Once again, this use of the term renaissance emerged out of modern Hindu nationalism.

Medievalism, Muslim rule, and the nation-state

If the use of "renaissance" in South Asia comes from Hindu nationalism, the use of "medieval" as a synonym for Muslim rule was not confined to Hindu (or British) intellectuals. For another crop of nationalist intellectuals, including some Muslims and Marxists, the medieval continued to be conflated with the Muslim, but in a more celebratory register. One of the influential writers of this kind was the historian Mohammed Habib. For him, medieval Muslim rule was itself a kind of renaissance, imbued with the "spirit" of the medieval age that pushed at the boundaries of caste and transformed the structures of Indian society.[13] Habib deemed it necessary to retrieve the true spirit of medievalism and place it in its "proper" perspective, i.e., render it in the language of a secular, progressive, and scientific India.

For the next generation of Marxist-influenced nationalist writers, led by the magisterial and prolific Irfan Habib, medieval India was still associated primarily with Muslim rule. After the creation of Pakistan as a Muslim homeland in 1947, Muslim and secular intellectuals in India were deeply concerned about the shaky and anomalous position of Muslims in India. It was politically imperative for them to assert the indigeneity of Muslim empires within India and to inscribe "medieval" Muslim rulers as predecessors, even authors, of the new, secular nation-state. Accordingly, the political domain of medieval India as they saw it was that of the centralized state: the Delhi sultanate and then the Mughals. While Habib and his colleagues were ideologically opposed to their Hindu nationalist predecessors, they shared with them an exclusive focus on empires. They too "studied ancient emperors and saw the rise of a nation-state in the creation of these ancient empires."[14] The histories they produced derived primarily from imperial records in Persian written at the glittering courts of the Mughals and the sultans of Delhi. With a few notable exceptions, they took little interest in the "intermediate" periods of decentralization or in problems of regional history, especially those of the non-Muslim states that existed coterminously with the sultanates and the Mughals.

Accordingly, India's history has been written by postcolonial historians as one of massive bureaucratic empires, ruled with a centralization that prefigured that of independent India (ironically it is lack of centralization and bureaucracies that historians of Europe see as a hallmark of the medieval period). The empire of the Mauryas (whose greatest exemplar, Ashoka, created many of the symbols that grace India's flag) was followed by the imperial Guptas, whose rule ended in the sixth century CE. After a period of "fragmentation" came the Muslim "invasion" and the establishment of the Delhi sultanate (1198–1398). And finally, in 1526, came the Mughals, who ruled a great land empire to be supplanted only by the British. Between each pair of great empires were dark ages, which schoolchildren and general readers could safely ignore. After Gupta decline, for example, was a period in which a number of major dynasties jostled for power in north India, the Pratiharas emerging dominant among them. It is telling that not a single major monograph on the Pratiharas or their southwestern contemporaries, the Rashtrakutas, has been published in the last four decades. Another dark age is that of the fifteenth century, a time between the disintegration of the "greater" sultanate of Delhi (with the *coup de grâce* delivered by Timur in 1398) and the Mughal empire, inaugurated in India by Timur's great-great-great grandson, Babur, in 1526. These were invariably portrayed as spells of decline, fragmentation, de-urbanization, and general demoralization.

It is only in the last three decades that historians have begun to dismantle the overwhelming emphasis on empires and to start looking more closely at interstitial periods and regional political formations. B. D. Chattopadhyaya's collection of essays *The Making of Early Medieval India* (1994) offered the most sustained critique of the Indian feudalism orthodoxy prevailing in early medieval studies.[15] He showed, for example, that there was little evidence of de-urbanization between the sixth and twelfth centuries. On the contrary, new towns were being built and becoming connected to each other within intensifying networks of trade and mobility. Further, there was little evidence of demonetization, another putative feature of Indian feudalism. Local currencies flourished and circulated widely, a theme explored by John Deyell's *Living without Silver: A Monetary History of Early Medieval India* (1993).[16] One of the most important interventions in dislodging the tripartite chronology and empire-centric history has been that of Sanjay Subrahmanyam. Although Subrahmanyam was not the first to dispense with the notion that the British brought modernity to India, until then languishing in a state of medievalism, he went further by arguing for modernity itself to be seen through a global lens, a "conjunctural" early modernity that was not limited to India but spanned the globe as cultures and polities encountered each other in the six-teenth century.[17] With skill and comparativist panache, Subrahmanyam "provincialized" the European renaissance, demonstrating that it was part of and informed by a connected series of global conjunctures. Elsewhere, he and his collaborators V. Narayana Rao and David Shulman suggest that all societies – not just the non-Western – live within variegated, multiple temporalities.[18]

In spite of these researches, and those of several other scholars, the neat and quite overtly imperialist and Eurocentric tripartite periodization has proved remarkably resil-ient. One cause and consequence of the persistent parallelism between periods and the religious affiliations of rulers is the question of language. Most writers in the last two hundred years have tended to look to the languages of rulers as representative of their times. This is particularly true of early periods, when the surviving records were scarce and generally derived from elite sources. Thus there has been an inbuilt predisposition to tell the story of elites and empires from their languages of power, as below, regardless of more widespread language use.

Ancient	*Medieval*	*Modern*
Hindu-Buddhist	Muslim	British/Enlightenment
Sanskrit-Prakrit-Pali	Persian, Arabic	English

Graduate training programs replicated this pattern, so that specialists of "ancient" or "classical" India – the "Indologists" – learnt only Sanskrit, Pali, or Prakrit, and those of medieval India, only Persian (and less commonly, Arabic). There are only a few scholars trained in combinations of these languages or even combinations of scripts. Thus the Indologists and medievalists have built fairly self-contained and exclusive historiographical silos, hardly breached until recently.[19]

The long fifteenth century

One of the periods that falls between the silos described above is what I shall call the long fifteenth century, a span of two centuries stretching roughly between 1350 and 1550. In a more traditional framework, the establishment of the Delhi sultanate, ca. 1200, and the invasion of Timur in 1398 are given immense transformative weight. The first marks the establishment of Muslim rule in the subcontinent, which, as we have seen, has been given enormous importance for political reasons. The other date marks the dissolution of the first great Muslim empire of north India after a devastating external invasion and has been assumed to herald a massive – and largely negative – transformation in economy and politics.

Recent work has blurred the boundaries between these assigned periods. Scholars have pointed out that economic and cultural tendencies in the early sixteenth century prefigured the great projects of the Mughals, especially those of Akbar, and that the Lodis and Surs (the last of the sultans who ruled Delhi) anticipated much of Akbar's bureaucratic ambition.[20] Similarly, Simon Digby showed that Timur's devastating invasion of Delhi in 1398 was not the transformative cataclysm that it has been portrayed as, especially if we look beyond the already attenuated court of the Delhi sultans at the time.[21] He demonstrated that the decentralization, long-distance trade networks, land clearance, and linguistic experimentation associated with the fifteenth century began in fact in the middle of the fourteenth. In the pages that follow, I will suggest that the emphasis given to both dates is misleading and that some recent research points the way to less politically freighted interpretations. In order to do so, I will point to three features that did mark the long fifteenth century in north India: mobility, a significant rise in the importance of the region and new towns, and linguistic localization and multilingualism. If a renaissance is not simply a cultural phenomenon but a historical period that paves the way for the modern world, there is a strong argument to be made that many of the fundamental institutions of modern South Asia – languages, routes, caste and land hierarchies, and regions – owe their origins to this period.

Mobility

The whole of northwestern India has long been a zone of seasonal, recurring, and occasional migration. Ever since the first century of Islam, as John Richards argued, Muslim groups had been gradually pushing eastwards along a long military frontier into north India in search of opportunity and plunder, and after the establishment of Ghurid rule in the late twelfth century, military service.[22] The establishment of the Delhi sultanate by mobile groups from the northwest might itself be considered an episode of this long-term transhumance of northwestern groups moving into the Indian plains. In 1192, the forces of Mu'izz al-Din of Ghur, in central Afghanistan, won a major battle against a confederacy of north Indian rulers. In the next two decades, the chieftains of much of north India accepted the Ghurids as their overlords and agreed to pay tribute. This acquiescence was tentative and had to be regularly enforced in the early years by Mu'izz al-Din and his generals, who made winter excursions into India to ensure compliance. After Mu'izz al-Din's efforts turned westwards towards Khurasan, he left India largely to his enslaved generals, most prominently Qutb al-Din Aybeg, who became the first "sultan" of Delhi in 1206. The Ghurids and Ghaznavids were themselves ousted from their homelands two decades later, in the face of Chingiz Khan's forces.

The "Delhi sultanate" inaugurated in the early thirteenth century has traditionally been seen as a time of centralization, especially under the rule of 'Ala al-Din Khalaji (1296–1316).[23] While all the sultans had to remain mobile in order to maintain control over their subordinates and tribute-payers, the late thirteenth century has been seen as a fairly stable time in Delhi and in much of the empire. The first phase of the sultanate – the thirteenth century – had been financed by "dethesaurization": the mobilization of large quantities of precious metal from the plunder of temples and royal lineages in India which served to build up significant military strength through local recruitment and to induce immigration from the west, thus helping the sultanate extend its authority over Bengal and further into peninsular India. The sultans' authority was shored up by immigrant Muslim groups, often "socially homogenous,"[24] who came to inhabit and defend tracts of land in north India. These included members of formerly mobile groups now sedentarizing and looking for opportunity. Some received grants of land from the sultans and were encouraged to clear and cultivate marginal and forested tracts.

Simon Digby argues that the riches derived from dethesaurization began to dry up by the 1330s. Once Muhammad b. Tughluq came to power in 1324, he faced an acute famine of specie, especially of silver, and faced difficulties in maintaining his vast army, territory, and court. New resources and administrative dodges had to be found, some of which had the effect of moving the center of power away from Delhi and towards other regions. In 1326–27 Muhammad famously started to move his entire court and many of the inhabitants of Delhi 1,200 kilometres south to Daulatabad, which was to have served as an alternative capital. Closer to the wealthy and largely self-governing western coast as well as to pockets of persistent resistance, Daulatabad would have represented a major shift of the center of power southwards if intractable logistical issues had not led Muhammad to abandon the project by the mid-1330s.[25] The move to Daulatabad also started off a period when the sultan, his entourage, and many of his courtiers had to be almost constantly on the move, traveling from one area of conflict to another to ensure compliance of subordinates while searching for resources. The sultan spent the last few years of his life chasing a rebel named Taghi in Gujarat and in the deserts of Sindh, finally dying there in 1351.[26]

Muhammad b. Tughluq's court might have been more mobile than that of his predecessors but was the mid-fourteenth century a time of accelerated mobility more generally? It has been traditional to chart the dispersal of north Indian populations *after* the invasion of Timur in 1398, when large populations fled the invading armies and others abandoned the ravaged city of Delhi and its environs in the years that followed. What I will try to suggest here is that the second half of the fourteenth century was *already* a time of greater movement, the extension of routes, and the sprouting of new towns. The dispersal in the wake of Timur's invasion was along already established routes to already established towns and settlements. The invasion was merely a tipping point. After the invasion and resultant dispersal, there was within a few decades a time of renewed sedentarization, of groups, lineages, and individuals settling down, clearing land, building forts, and turning to new kinds of authors to record their deeds.

Let us look at some of these routes and sites. Once the Ghurids established themselves in Delhi, sultanate rule expanded the evergreen market for horses that trading caravans herded along the overland route through Afghanistan and Punjab.[27] Even if previous (non-Muslim) rulers had had access to Central Asian horse sources, Delhi sultanate demand generated regular routes and horse imports continued to increase.[28] If, as Simon Digby suggests, one of the main reasons for the continued success of the Delhi sultans was their ability to regulate and control the supply of war animals, including horses, demand in the fourteenth century remained stable or increased. Muhammad b. Tughluq, for instance, is said to have distributed 10,000 Arab horses to his retinue each year.[29] The size of the horse market of north India is suggested by the fact that Mongols from the Golden Horde sent vast herds of horses from the Russian steppe to all the way to Delhi's horse markets in the fourteenth century.[30] The Moroccan traveler Ibn Battuta described the trade out of Azov, on the north shore of the Black Sea in the 1330s: "The horses in this country are exceedingly numerous and their price is negligible ... These horses are exported to India (in droves) each one numbering six thousand more or less. Each trader has one or two hundred horses or more or less."[31] The sultans and their courtiers did what they could to safeguard the supply chain of high-quality Central Asian Tatari horses, prohibiting traders from selling to rivals, but it became harder for them to maintain their monopoly as the fourteenth century wore on. Meanwhile the sultans' rivals had to work harder than ever to seek out and safeguard alternative sources of horses and other war resources. Within mainland South Asia too, cattle pastoralists, herders, horse traders, goods carriers, and mobile ascetic groups (some groups were all, or a combination, of the above) regularly moved in search of opportunity.

The importance of the overland horse route from Central Asia through Sind or Punjab to the north Indian plains kept open the long-established connections with Afghanistan, now increasingly also a source of fighting men and Sufi mystics who followed the trade routes to find fortune or influence in India. New towns mentioned in fourteenth-century texts suggest the continuing importance of a major west–east trade route that stretched from the Indus to the Ganges, and then extended further east towards Bengal. At the end of the fourteenth century, a Sufi named Ashraf Jahangir Simnani sent lavish gifts from Bengal to the Sufis of Chisht, in western Afghanistan. These included Indian textiles, golden lamps and vessels, and Bengali eunuchs, transported from the eastern end of the trade route to the west.[32]

The army of the Delhi sultanate has traditionally been characterized as dependent on military slavery. Since Dirk Kolff's important work on the military labor market, it has been clear that Timur's invasion and the subsequent rise of smaller kingdoms all over north India mobilized a vibrant market in military service from around 1450, inducing men of various classes to seek seasonal or regular military employment with the new warlords and little kings of the era.[33] Sunil Kumar has recently suggested that the distinction between military slavery (*bandagi*) and military employment (*naukari*) has been overstated.[34] In terms of how these institutions structured political relations, there was little to distinguish them, especially as former *bandas* (slaves) were manumitted and developed generational kin relationships in India. Instead of positing a dramatic shift, Kumar proposes instead that we recognize that the domain of *bandagi* shrank in the fourteenth century as the domain of *naukari* expanded. Both institutions mobilized fighting men: involuntarily for those captured as prisoners and voluntarily for *naukars*, men seeking fortune and employment with new patrons. Whether forced or voluntary, travel for military and trade reasons became increasingly common.

Sultan Muhammad's transplantation of his capital is a symptom of the accelerated mobility of the period towards areas of greater prosperity or security. This quixotic (and brutal) forced migration indicates that we should look towards the coasts, especially the coast of western India, as another zone of intense mobility, where overland trading networks intersected with the flourishing trade across the Arabian Sea and with Southeast Asia. The Indian Ocean trade world in this period has often been treated as autonomous, as a series of self-governing ports linked by regular voyages. In India, however, the seaborne economy was closely connected with, and dependent on, the land and its products, both agricultural and industrial. It cannot be understood in isolation from politics on land. In the wake of the establishment of the Delhi sultanate, the sultans made rapid moves to gain access to the goods and resources of the ports. Rapid fort-building, urbanization, and road and route development soon followed, facilitating the coastal economy while making it easier for traders and others to travel safely.

Regions and towns

The empire-centric historiography that has dominated has tended to be about what eventually became India: the India of the British Raj and then the nation-state. Through this lens, focused from above, as it were, regions are merely potential or former provinces of empire or nation; they have no importance in themselves.[35] As a result, historians have frequently failed to recognize the existence or significance of regional and local processes other than when they impinged upon "larger" entities. Similarly, networks and processes generated in the regions have often escaped notice. The consequence has been that empires and transregional agents have been given too much credit for historical change. For instance, it was often assumed that conversion to Islam in Bengal was a natural consequence of Muslim rule established in the early thirteenth century. Surely, went the assumption, Bengalis had turned to the religion of their rulers. It was not until Richard Eaton's pioneering demonstration that mass conversion to Islam in Bengal should be linked less to Muslim rule and more to local processes of agrarian expansion in the delta from the seventeenth century onwards, that it was recognized that conversion was a *local* process arising out of Bengal's specific history and geography.[36] The rule of Muslim elites, whether from Delhi or from the provincial capital, had little to do with people turning to the practice of Islam. In fact, "Muslim" rule from the twelfth century, in the so-called "medieval" period, has been the rule of Muslim elites; it has rarely, if ever, been the catalyst for major conversion movements anywhere in South Asia. While I do not wish to suggest that South Asian regions always existed or had stable boundaries, it is certainly the case that regional formations came into being as a consequence of the interplay of imperial/centralizing and local factors.

To return to the mid-fourteenth century, I suggest, following Digby, that the widespread immigration and movement along trade routes I charted in the last section resulted concurrently in the rise of new, semi-urban communities. According to Ibn Battuta, forests had been cleared and the land cultivated all the way from Delhi to the Deccan in the 1330s. Forest cover was being cleared also in the plains between the Ganga and Yamuna (the Gangetic Doab) and the Punjab, radiating out from Delhi.[37] Since the thirteenth century, the method of revenue extraction introduced by the sultans was the *'iqta* or military assignment. *'Iqta* assignments in the thirteenth and fourteenth centuries often required assignees to go out and conquer or clear assigned territory for themselves. Assignees would invite kin members or Sufis to come and settle in their lands, helping populate them and carry out the labor of land clearance, military defense, and agriculture. *'Iqta* territories were also military units, local centers for the seasonal or need-based recruitment of fighting men and resources, from war horses to swords and bows and arrows.

In the fourteenth century, *'iqta* holders and their settlements had an ambiguous relationship with the sultans and their capital of Delhi. On the one hand they relied on Delhi for the structure of the state and for their military assignments. On the other, they knew that their access to local power and resources made them vital to Delhi. The fourteenth-century Sufi poet Yusuf Gada was aware of this tension. He warned other Sufis against rising against the sultan and his authority but also warned against employment with the sultan and his officers. In his poetry, he reflected the world of semi-independent rural Muslim gentry, ready to offer service to the sultan when asked, but not to take regular employment.[38] As the Delhi rulers' ability to maintain vast standing armies declined, the second half of the fourteenth century saw them begin to make deals with chieftains, often former or current *'iqta* holders, for military support. Texts from the period urge the Muslim gentry, including rural gentry, to be armed and ready for battle equally against surrounding non-Muslims as against the sultan. By the mid-fourteenth century, many of the *'iqta* holders were dominant stakeholders of the new regions, often with multi-locational power.

Even Muhammad b. Tughluq's efforts to move his capital to South India suggest that new towns were more attractive than the old. The end of his reign saw the inauguration in 1347 of a breakaway Muslim kingdom in peninsular India (not far from Muhammad's short-lived capital Daulatabad) – that of the Bahmanis – by his own former courtiers. During his successor Firuz Shah's time (1351–88), too, several regional governors started to function with virtual autonomy. As Digby's framework shows, the beginnings of regionalism and localization should be located not in only in the wake of Timur's sack of Delhi but as a feature of the reign of one of the most powerful rulers, Muhammad b. Tughluq, as early as the 1340s.

The new settlements, along with older towns, were characteristic of the new regionalism of the long fifteenth century and gained greatly in population and importance following Timur's sack of Delhi in 1398. As in Kichhauchha, where the military commandant welcomed and assisted the Sufi Ashraf Jahangir Simnani to settle and build a *khanqah*, dozens of new settlements arose in the fourteenth century. Chanderi in central India was a junction on the route from the north to the western coast and another from the northwest to Awadh and Kalpi. At the time of Ibn Battuta's visit in 1335, it was "a large town with magnificent bazaars."[39] A key feature of the new towns was their association with Sufis, even the graves of Sufis, located along trade routes. An anecdote from the memoirs of Sayyid Muhammad Gesudaraz, traveling in north India in 1400, illustrates this perfectly.[40] Four travelers were on the road when their dog died by a pond. Distressed, they buried it under a tree, mounding the soil to make a makeshift grave, and moved on. Later, a caravan of traders reached the spot. Mistaking the dog's grave for that of a Sufi, they pledged that if their goods were sold, they would use a tenth of their proceeds to build him a shrine. Their journey was successful and on their trip back, they built not only a tomb over the grave but a mosque, a hospice, and a travelers' shelter. Soon after, a town grew around the shrine and it even acquired a king. Apocryphal as the story is, it suggests the frequency and speed with which new settlements were coming up along the trade routes, generated by a combination of lucrative trade and Sufi sanctity during the sultanate.

In spite of Sufi recommendations to avoid closeness to those in power, in practice Sufis often worked closely with rulers and officials. Ashraf Jahangir Simnani was invited by a *malik*, a mid-ranking military commandant, to establish a *khanqah* in Kichhauchha. A resident Sufi, especially one from a prestigious teacherly lineage such as that of the Chishtis, bestowed lustre on a settlement, putting it on the map, so to speak, and helping it attract more migrants. Such local officials often invited and then supported immigrant notables in their efforts to settle new neighborhoods.[41] Several new settlements grew around sites already associated with sanctity, including pre-Islamic sanctity, and often involved collaboration with non-Muslim grant-holders or locally powerful groups. As Sufis, their retainers, and kin moved to these new settlements in the Indian countryside, they began to accustom themselves to the local vocabularies and politics. Many of the tales from the period suggest that fourteenth-century Sufis, even those of immigrant background, were increasingly identifying with their Indian environment.[42]

A powerful Sufi could help convert or co-opt powerful local groups. Sufi literature of the period is full of stories of the subjection or conversion of nomadic, predatory, and professional groups, of "brigands," struck by a Sufi's superior powers, of humble curd-sellers offering thousands of gold coins to shaykhs. In other tales, Sufis humble rival religious figures, usually "jogis" or yogis, with spectacular displays of superior magical powers, and then take over their territory. By the end of the fourteenth century, Sufis were emerging as power-brokers in the emerging regionalization of the political landscape. As powerful local figures with access to complex networks of teacher–pupil relationships that could stretch from Iran and Afghanistan to Bengal or the Deccan, Sufis could make or break bids for political power. Many of the new sultans of the early fifteenth-century post-Timur regional kingdoms claimed to have received their kingdoms as "boons" from prominent Sufis, in person, or in dreams. In spite of enjoying worldly power, they had to keep propitiating the Sufis of their domains. The second sultan of Gujarat and builder of Ahmadabad recited a poem of his own composition in praise of the Sufi Qutb-i 'Alam (the Pole of the World) and, in return, asked to be rewarded with a blessing for the new city. "This city will last for ever by the favour of God, the Merciful," declared the shaykh.[43]

Sufis could with equal ease broker alliances or help negotiate between the new kingdoms of the fifteenth century. As in the fourteenth century, they continued to have ambiguous and contingent relations with the regional sultans and chieftains, maintaining their distance while being thoroughly implicated in politics. The case of the Bukhari Sufis of Ahmadabad is a case in point. Descendants of a prominent Sufi of fourteenth-century Punjab, the Sufis Qutb-i 'Alam and his son Shah 'Alam took up residence close to the sultan's palace in the Gujarat sultanate capital of Ahmadabad. While they claimed an independence from the affairs of court, several texts from the period reveal how closely their lives were intertwined with those of the sultans and how some Sufis were considered semi-royal figures. Two daughters of the ruler of Sind, Bibi Mughali and Bibi Turki, were married to Sultan Muhammad Shah of Gujarat and to the Sufi Shah 'Alam respectively. After Muhammad's death in 1451, Shah 'Alam married the sultan's widow, Bibi Mughali, and became the guardian of his son, the future ruler Mahmud Begada (r. 1458–1511). In several sultanates, the Sufi grandees became parallel centers of power and the sultans had to keep a close watch on their activities.

Following Anthony Reid, Sanjay Subrahmanyam argues that commercial cities in maritime South and Southeast Asia were the location of significant political and cultural change from 1450 to 1680. In this respect, says Reid, "the period bears comparison with its European analogue, the Renaissance, though this study has sought to make clear that neither the starting point nor the direction of change should be expected to parallel those in other parts of the world."[44] This observation may be extended, with some qualifiers, even to the new towns of north India in our period. It was in the urban centers and along the trade routes that individuals met, transacted business, turned to new mentors or religious practices, and forged new languages for religion and pleasure. As new towns proliferated, political formations grew around them, many of which came to be associated with distinct languages, literatures, and sensibilities.

Language, vernaculars, and multilinguality

Empire-centric writing privileges materials produced by elites in trans-regional languages as more historically significant and worthy of critical attention. In South Asia, such languages include Sanskrit, Prakrit, Persian, and Arabic, the languages of elite scholarship and rule, of high literature and normative religious prescription. As a result, periods when little was produced in the great trans-regional languages are seen as lacking significance in the broader scheme of history and are therefore regarded as periods of "decline." In the same vein, texts of the non-elite languages tend to be neglected as less significant. Francesca Orsini and

I have recently remarked that the long fifteenth century was not a canon-making period.[45] Those looking for major court histories, bureaucratic and legal compendia, imperial linguistic regulations, are likely to be disappointed. Instead it was a period when entrepreneurial claimants to power and influence "inscribed" themselves in a variety of evolving genres and languages. Although some authors continued to use the great transregional classical languages – Arabic, Sanskrit, Apabhramsha, and, increasingly, Persian – more and more started to compose and write in the forerunners of modern regional vernaculars. Genealogy, history, romances, plays, poetry: all flourished at this time, some circulated orally, others produced in sumptuous illustrated or illuminated manuscript form. There were more and more epigraphs and legal texts produced in the vernaculars. Multilingualism was common. By 1500, as Sheldon Pollock points out, writers in almost all parts of South Asia had turned from the transregional languages to local ones.[46]

The trade-route towns, forts, and settlements were sites for the production of new genres of texts, increasingly in local vernaculars "literized" – turned into literature – for the first time.[47] As Muslim rule eclipsed older models of Hindu kingship legitimized in Sanskrit writings by brahmins, Hindu devotionalism took new forms in vernacular languages. Warlords and chieftains who were subordinate to the sultans began to commission praise poems and plays that reflected their own times and concerns – their fascination with urban life, the sensibilities of displaced men in search of military service, the anguish of mobility and separation from lovers. Muslim Sufi poets too began to write in the north Indian vernaculars. The romance genre was particularly popular. Heroes of the new tales were not all high-status courtly or mythological figures; they now included cowherds, pastoralists, wandering ascetics, soldiers, and traders. Digby suggests that such works demonstrate "alliances of the settler-Muslim poets with groups displaying similar sensibilities, usually of a socially-disruptive and 'anti-Brahmanical kind.'"[48] Most of these compositions were deliberately local, representing not the classical geographies of pre-Islamic India or the transregional sensibilities of a unitary Muslim imagining. There was often a deliberate excision of vocabulary derived from Persian, Arabic, or Sanskrit. The new towns were fertile sites for literary experiment by Muslims, Jains, and Hindus. The new writers were determined to write as they spoke. The new authors and languages of literature represent a dramatic change in South Asian history, one that might be, as Pollock says, "the most important change in the late medieval world."[49]

While it has been long recognized that this was the period when modern languages came into being, language histories have been shadowed by the rancour of subsequent community histories. The Hindi language came to be associated with Hindus in the late nineteenth century, just as the mutually intelligible Urdu language came to be associated with Muslims, largely because the latter was written in the Arabic script. But this was not always so. In the sixteenth century, the public culture of early modernity was not split down the middle into Hindu and Muslim.[50] Without going into the question of whether a public culture existed in north India in our period, it is possible to show that from the late fifteenth century, and perhaps earlier, Persian and Arabic were available to elite Hindus from scribal groups. Conversely, Muslim writers are known to have used the Nagari script and Hindu writers used the Arabic script. There was also a common culture of bookkeeping and state accountancy that arose from the corps of scribes and bureaucrats – Hindu, Muslim, and Jain – who worked for the sultanate administration.

This was equally a time of translation: between languages and within linguistic traditions. The encounter between scribal groups from different literary and secretarial traditions provoked the production of a number of glossaries and dictionaries that helped the literati navigate the multilingual environment of their day. These were produced as much to ease the dissonance between speakers of Turki, Arabic, and Persian as to aid Persian-speakers encountering Indian languages.[51] Sanskrit and Prakrit dictionaries were also produced that glossed the unfamiliar Persian language, presumably for the benefit of those seeking sultanate service.[52]

The great transregional languages did not disappear in this period but their ubiquity was now curtailed and qualified. Land deeds and public records continued to be produced primarily in Persian, Arabic, and Sanskrit. They were often carved in stone and installed in public buildings such as city walls, gates, mosques, and wells. But a significant number of such records were in more than one language. In Gujarat, for example, there are at least fifteen surviving donative records from our period that are bi- or trilingual, featuring cognate text in Persian and/or Arabic, as well as Sanskrit and Gujarati.[53] Similar multilingual inscriptions were produced elsewhere in north India, too.[54] Visual translation was another mode of the time, as artists turned classical Persian and Indic visual vocabularies to the needs and sensibilities of new patrons, often transposing classical tales from elsewhere into characteristically Indian landscapes and palettes.

What happened next

North India famously remained oblivious to Portuguese consolidation along the coast in the sixteenth century. In the land-locked north, one major event was the toppling in 1526 of the elephant-backed army of the last of the Delhi sultans, Ibrahim Lodi, by the artillery and cavalry of one of Timur's descendants, Babur. Babur's – and Mughal – hegemony in north India was by no means assured by this victory. The military victories of Babur's short rule over north India (he died in 1530) and the unstable, intermittent control his son Humayun exercised are more of a piece with the events and processes of the "long" fifteenth century. It was only with the accession in 1556 of Akbar, the third of the Great Mughals, that we finally see the end of the period. In the succeeding decades, Akbar achieved more or less stable control over north India and launched most of the massive projects including wide-ranging land assessment, hierarchical bureaucracy, large-scale architectural projects, and a uniform official language (Persian) for which the Mughals are remembered. The great land empire of Akbar and his successors was very different from the little kingdoms and coalitions of the preceding era. The Mughal era was not one of accelerated urbanization. There was no rash of new little towns and settlements to parallel the *qasba* growth of the fourteenth and fifteenth centuries. Instead the economy became more uniformly agrarian and the state ever more dependent on agricultural revenues. As more and more regions were gathered under the imperial canopy, including much of the Deccan and South India in the 1630s, regional identities and languages were overlaid with a veneer of Mughal courtliness and a certain bureaucratic uniformity. Regional solidarities did not disappear, nor did languages wither in the face of centrally imposed Persian. Indeed, regional literatures and arts flourished. But this time they were often enriched by imperial courtliness and courtly patrons who owed their positions to Mughal hierarchy.

The Mughals were cosmopolitan rulers and their courts were worldly places, informed by and connected to the great networks of trade and commerce evolving along the fringes of their territories. Not possessing crystal balls, most of them failed to recognize that the European traders who occasionally pitched up at their courts armed with curios and asking for trade concessions would eventually come to usurp their territories. They failed also to look into the future and see that their rule would be represented as part of an era of long-term, despotic medievalism. The Mughals were secure in their sense of their place in the world; only the Safavids or the Ottomans could possibly be grander rulers or boast of better poets. They – and many of their courtiers and subjects – experienced and participated in the contingent and networked new sensibilities of global early modernity.

It could be argued that the era of the six "great" Mughals, from Babur to Aurangzeb, was one of renaissance. In my view, such an argument would revert to the top-down, empire-centric historiography with which I began this chapter. I believe there might be more justification for applying it to the preceding period, which affords us a more textured, open-ended, and polyvalent understanding of historical change. The long fifteenth century was a time of finding new homes, new connections, and new overlords. There were new literatures paid for by new patrons. The old, great languages – Sanskrit, Prakrit, Arabic – were still around, still studied, but the rapidly changing environment could only be represented, literarily and pictorially, in the young languages. The old canons were put aside as immigrants and the newly rich demanded dictionaries, works of reference, and praise poems – spiritual and temporal. In this ever-changing landscape, identities were being actively forged. If we must search for periods of renaissance, why not look at a time when profound transformations of tongue, text, and conduct were wrought by ordinary people, when power did not emanate from a single center, and when the world began to be inextricably connected?

Notes

1 I would like to thank Prashant Kidambi and Bill Caferro for their careful reading of earlier drafts and for their suggestions. All errors must, of course, be ascribed to me.
2 Stanley Lane-Poole, *The Story of the Nations: Mediaeval India under Mohammedan Rule, 712–1764*, New York: G. P. Putnam's Sons, 1903, iii, cited in Paula Sanders, "The Victorian Invention of Medieval Cairo: A Case Study of Medievalism and the Construction of the East," *Middle East Studies Association Bulletin* 37(2) (2003): 185. The ruler in question was the Mughal Shah 'Alam, who signed over the tax-collection rights of the province of Bengal to the East India Company in 1765. Sanders analyzes the closely comparable invention of medievalism in Egypt.
3 I have used the term South Asia when referring to the geographical area of the Indian subcontinent. "India" will refer either to the undivided entity prior to independence and the creation of Pakistan in 1947 or to the nation-state of India post-1947. "Indian historians" does not include Pakistanis or other South Asians.
4 For an excellent survey of the debates around the Renaissance, see the introduction to William Caferro, *Contesting the Renaissance*, Oxford: Wiley-Blackwell, 2010.
5 Thomas R. Metcalf, *Ideologies of the Raj*, Cambridge: Cambridge University Press, 12–13.
6 Ananya Jahanara Kabir, "Analogy in Translation: Imperial Rome, Medieval England, and British India," in *Postcolonial Approaches to the European Middle Ages: Translating Cultures*, ed. Ananya Jahanara Kabir and Deanne Williams, Cambridge: Cambridge University Press, 2005, 183. See also Bernard S. Cohn, "The Command of Language and the Language of Command," in *Subaltern Studies IV: Writings on South Asian History and Society*, ed. Ranajit Guha, Delhi: Oxford University Press, 1985; Gyan Prakash, "Writing Post-Orientalist Histories of the Third World: Perspectives from Indian Historiography," *Comparative Studies in Society and History* 32(2) (1990): 383–408; Harbans Mukhia, "'Medieval India': An Alien Conceptual Hegemony?" *Medieval History Journal* 1(1) (1998); and Daud Ali, "The Historiography of the Medieval in South Asia," *Journal of the Royal Asiatic Society* (3rd series) 22(1) (2012): 7–12.
7 Metcalf, *Ideologies of the Raj*, 6.
8 *Ibid.*
9 Prakash, "Writing Post-Orientalist Histories," 388.

10 Influential works include David Kopf, *British Orientalism and the Bengal Renaissance: The Dynamics of Indian Modernization, 1773–1835*, Calcutta: Firma K. L. Mukhopadhyay, 1969; Susobhan Sarkar, *On the Bengal Renaissance*, Calcutta: Papyrus, 1979.

11 Important critiques of the ascription of renaissance to this period appeared in several essays, notably those by Sumit Sarkar, Barun De, and Asok Sen in a volume brought out to commemorate the birth bicentenary of the intellectual-politician Rammohun Roy (1772–1833). See V. C. Joshi, ed. *Rammohun Roy and the Process of Modernization in India*, Delhi: Vikas Publishing House, 1975. Sarkar argued that the so-called Bengal Renaissance could be read as a period of "retreat and decline" that remained within a "Hindu-elitist and colonial framework." (p. 47) Also see Sumit Sarkar, "The Complexities of Young Bengal," *Nineteenth Century Studies* 4 (1973): 504–34; Barun De, "A Historiographical Critique of Renaissance Analogues for Nineteenth-Century India," in *Perspectives in the Social Sciences I: Historical Dimensions*, ed. Barun De, Calcutta: Oxford University Press, 1977.

12 On devotionalism as renaissance, see Asoke Kumar Majumdar, *Bhakti Renaissance*, Bombay: Bharatiya Vidya Bhavan, 1964. Interestingly, key figures of the Bengal "renaissance," such as the novelist Bankim Chandra Chattopadhyaya (1838–94), used the term to refer to the literary and philosophical achievements of the fifteenth and sixteenth centuries. See Sumit Sarkar, "Renaissance and Kaliyuga: Time, Myth, and History in Colonial Bengal," in *Between History and Histories: The Making of Silences and Commemorations*, ed. Gerald M. Sider and Gavin A. Smith, Toronto: University of Toronto Press, 1997, 108.

13 Mohammad Habib, *Politics and Society during the Early Medieval Period*, Aligarh: People's Publishing House, 1981, vol.1, 10.

14 Prakash, "Writing Post-Orientalist Histories," 388.

15 B. D. Chattopadhyaya, *The Making of Early Medieval India*, New Delhi: Oxford University Press, 1993.

16 John Deyell, *Living without Silver: The Monetary History of Early Medieval North India*, New Delhi: Oxford University Press, 1990.

17 Sanjay Subrahmanyam, "On World Historians in the Sixteenth Century," *Representations* 91(1) (2005): 99–100.

18 Velcheru Narayana Rao, David Shulman, and Sanjay Subrahmanyam, *Textures of Time: Writing History in South India 1600–1800*, New Delhi: Permanent Black, 2001.

19 See Ronald Inden, "Orientalist Constructions of India," *Modern Asian Studies* 20(3) (1986): 401–46 and Inden's introduction to Ronald Inden, Jonathan Walters, and Daud Ali, eds. *Querying the Medieval: Texts and the History of Practices in South Asia*, New York, Oxford: Oxford University Press, 2000.

20 Raziuddin Aquil, "Reconsidering Sovereignty and Governance under the Afghans: North India in the Late Fifteenth and Early Sixteenth Centuries," *South Asia: Journal of South Asian Studies* 26(1) (2003): 5–21; *Sufism, Culture, and Politics: Afghans and Islam in Medieval North India*, New Delhi: Oxford University Press, 2007.

21 Simon Digby, "Before Timur Came: Provincialization of the Delhi Sultanate Through the Fourteenth Century," *Journal of the Economic and Social History of the Orient* 47(3) (2004): 298–356.

22 J. F. Richards, "The Islamic Frontier in the East: Expansion into South Asia," *South Asia* 4 (1974): 91–109.

23 Recent works on the "greater" Delhi sultanate include Peter Jackson, *The Delhi Sultanate: A Political and Military History*, Cambridge: Cambridge University Press, 1999; Sunil Kumar, *The Emergence of the Delhi Sultanate: 1192–1286*, New Delhi: Permanent Black, 2007.

24 Digby, "Before Timur," 299.

25 Jackson, *The Delhi Sultanate*, 258–60.

26 Simon Digby, "Muhammad bin Tughluq's Last Years in Kathiavad and his Invasions of Thattha," *Hamdard Islamicus* 2(1) (1979): 79–88.

27 Simon Digby, *War Horse and Elephant in the Dehli Sultanate: A Study of Military Supplies*, Oxford: Orient Monographs, 1971, 20, 34.

28 On Indian rulers' insatiable demand for war horses, see also Ranabir Chakravarti, "Early Medieval Bengal and the Trade in Horses: A Note," *Journal of the Economic and Social History of the Orient* 42(2) (1999): 194–211; "Horse Trade and Piracy at Tana (Thana, Maharashtra, India): Gleanings from Marco Polo," *Journal of the Economic and Social History of the Orient* 34(3) (1991): 158–82.

29 Digby, *War Horse*, 25, citing al-ʿUmari, *Masalik al-absar fi mamalik al-amsar* (1961), 28.

30 Digby, *War Horse*, 35.

31 H. A. R. Gibb, trans. *Ibn Battúta: Travels in Asia and Africa, 1325–1354*, London: Routledge & Kegan Paul, 1929, vol. 2, 478–9.

32 Digby, "Before Timur," 325.

33 Dirk H. A. Kolff, *Naukar, Rajput and Sepoy: The Ethnohistory of the Military Labour Market in Hindustan, 1450–1850*, Cambridge: Cambridge University Press, 1990.

34 Sunil Kumar, "*Bandagi* and *Naukari*: Studying Transitions in Political Culture and Service under the North Indian Sultanates, Thirteenth-Sixteenth Centuries," in *After Timur Left: Culture and Circulation in Fifteenth-Century North India*, ed. Francesca Orsini and Samira Sheikh, New Delhi: Oxford University Press, 2014.

35 On regions and colonialism, see Benjamin B. Cohen, "Introducing Colonial Regionalism: The Case of India's Presidencies, the View from Madras," *India Review* 13(4) (2014): 321–36.

36 Richard M. Eaton, *The Rise of Islam and the Bengal Frontier, 1204–1760*, Berkeley: University of California Press, 1993.

37 Digby, "Before Timur," 304.

38 *Ibid.*, 306.

39 Gibb, trans., Ibn Battúta, 791.

40 *Ibid.*, 305.

41 *Ibid.*, 307, n. 12.

42 *Ibid.*, 303.

43 'Ali Muhammad Khan. *Mir'at-i Ahmadi: Supplement*, trans. Syed Nawab Ali and C. N. Seddon, Baroda: Oriental Institute, 1928, 25.

44 Anthony Reid, *Southeast Asia in the Age of Commerce, 1450–1680*, New Haven, CT: Yale University Press, 1988–93, vol. 1, 235.

45 Orsini and Sheikh, eds. *After Timur Left*, 3.

46 Sheldon Pollock, "The Cosmopolitan Vernacular," *Journal of Asian Studies* 57(1) (1998): 6.

47 Sheldon Pollock, "India in the Vernacular Millennium: Literary Culture and Polity, 1000–1500," *Daedalus* 127(3) (1998): 41–74.

48 Digby, "Before Timur," 341.

49 Pollock, "The Cosmopolitan Vernacular," 6.

50 Sanjay Subrahmanyam, "Hearing Voices: Vignettes of Early Modernity in South Asia, 1400–1750," *Daedalus* 127(3) (1998): 97.

51 See the chapters by Stefano Pello and Dilorom Karomat in Orsini and Sheikh, eds. *After Timur Left*.

52 Sreeramula Rajeswara Sarma, "Sanskrit Manuals for Learning Persian," in *Adab Shenasi*, ed. Azarmi Dukht Safavi, Aligarh: Department of Persian, Aligarh Muslim University, 1996.

53 Samira Sheikh, "Languages of Public Piety: Bilingual Inscriptions from Gujarat, c. 1390–1538," in Orsini and Sheikh, After Timur Left.

54 Pushpa Prasad, *Sanskrit Inscriptions of the Delhi Sultanate, 1191–1526*, Delhi: Oxford University Press, 1990.

3

"BY IMITATING OUR NURSES"

Latin and vernacular in the Renaissance

Eugenio Refini

As is well known, French philosopher Michel de Montaigne (1533–1592) was educated as a Latin native speaker. Or, at least, this was his father's intention. According to Montaigne's own version of the story in the essay *De l'institution des enfants* (Of the institution and education of children), until the age of six Michel was solely exposed to Latin language.[1] In fact, a German teacher who did not speak any French was hired specially to "naturally" train the child in Latin. Montaigne's father wished to spare his son the strenuous and long experience of acquiring Latin as a foreign language, in which people usually spent most of their time and energy, thus being prevented from equalling the knowledge of the ancients.[2] Put in the fortunate condition to be "naturally" conversant with Latin, Michel would be ready to fully commit himself to the acquisition of knowledge as of his very youth. By learning Latin "without art, without bookes, rules, or grammar, without whipping or whining," – which were the usual components in the study of classical languages – Montaigne's experience proved rather extraordinary.[3] Not only was he able to enjoy Ovid in the original while other children of his age would read vernacular chivalric novels, but the entire household took advantage from the situation:

> It were strange to tell how every one in the house profited therein. My Father and my Mother learned so much Latine, that for a need they could understand it, when they heard it spoken, even so did all the household servants, namely such as were neerest and most about me. To be short, we were all so Latinized, that the townes round about us had their share of it.[4]

Yet the inevitable anachronism of this experiment came to light quickly: as soon as Michel moved to boarding school, his allegedly 'natural' skills in Latin were replaced by a new proficiency in the vernacular, as if the order of nature was restored.

In its paradoxical outcome, the episode illustrates the complexity of the relationship between Latin and the vernacular in the Renaissance, particularly the dynamics between 'nature' and 'artifice' that is at the core of contemporary debates on language. Within a society that, from the Middle Ages to the modern period, has been constantly experiencing forms of multilingualism, the interaction of Latin and the European vernaculars – often described in terms of conflict – proves a very slippery field of enquiry. For centuries Latin as the language of both religious and intellectual authorities faced the concurrent development of vernacular languages as the natural expression of the many entities that made up the multifaceted cultural geography of Europe. Within such a complex process, it is undeniable that the Renaissance marked a turning point in the ways in which the relation between Latin and the vernaculars was conceived and described.[5] Yet, far from producing univocal patterns, discourses on language witness to a variety of trends, informed by both overlaps and irreconcilable views. Particularly, debates on language do convey conflicts of culture: not only Latin against the vernaculars, but also humanism (i.e. the rebirth of classical Latin) against scholasticism (i.e. the Latin medieval tradition), as well as vernaculars against each other. This chapter will not be able to answer the many questions solicited by such a manifold phenomenon. However, by exploring the ways in which the discourse on language was shaped in Italy between the age of Dante and the sixteenth century, the chapter focuses on the opposition nature–artifice as a key to understanding the cultural legitimation of the vernaculars on a larger, European scale.

Paving the way for the vernacular turn: Dante's reflection on language

In 1309 something exceptional happened in Siena, where the officers of the commune translated the Latin constitution of the city into the Italian vernacular. A copy of the so-called *Costituto volgare* would always be publicly on display: written in large-format letters, easily legible and well shaped, copied on parchment of good quality in order to ensure the durability of the codex, the constitution was meant to be available to the poor and to those people who did not have any Latin in order to let them act according to the laws.[6] The term used in the *Costituto* to refer to Latin is "grammatica." As a language built on grammatical rules, Latin stands opposite the vernaculars, commonly perceived as languages devoid of the linguistic structures that made Latin teachable and allegedly stable through time. The contrast between *grammatica* and the vulgar tongue was the theoretical premise that informed the coeval practice of translating Latin texts into the vernacular, as is suggested by several translators' prefaces to thirteenth- and fourteenth-century *volgarizzamenti*.[7] In his introduction to the *Fiore di rettorica* (Flower of rhetoric) – a loose translation of *Rhetorica ad Herennium* with excerpts from Cicero's *De inventione* – Bono Giamboni (1240–1292) explained that laymen were excluded from the study of rhetoric because they were unable to read Latin. In order to overcome this obstacle, he decided to embark on the "painful" project of providing them with bits of the discipline in the vernacular.[8] The painfulness of the endeavor was due to the difficulty of unpacking the subtleness of the topic in the vernacular, which – because of its roughness – was considered unable to express the same linguistic qualities that Latin was capable of.

Yet to translate from Latin into the vernacular meant to reach out to a wider audience, thus fostering the development of new communities of readers outside the Latinate circles of scholars in the universities and the religious schools. The ideological and political implications of a somewhat revolutionary linguistic choice – implicit in statements such as Bono Giamboni's – were crucial to the strategy deployed by the Sienese *Costituto* of 1309, which, at least in theory, would allow a wider participation in the city's jurisdictional life. Interestingly enough, those were the same years of Dante Alighieri's far-reaching reflection on the relationship between Latin and the vernacular, which – moving from similar premises – would pave the way for a veritable turn in the ways in which the status of vernacular languages *vis-à-vis* Latin was conceived and theorized.

Despite their initially modest impact on Dante's contemporaries, both the *Convivio* (The banquet) (1304–1307) and the *De vulgari eloquentia* (On vernacular eloquence) (1304–1305) played a key role in the elaboration of linguistic discourses in the Renaissance. Dante's take on the cultural and ideological conflict that informed the relationship between Latin and the vernacular differed from the most typical approaches of his time. Instead of just focusing on the assumption of an insuperable qualitative divide between Latin and the vernacular, Dante addressed the reflection on language through a double lens: on the one hand, he discussed the ethical and political role of linguistic choices within the historical context in which he was living; on the other hand, he situated his analysis within a wider reflection on the philosophy of language. What is common to both perspectives, respectively embodied by the *Convivio* and the *De vulgari eloquentia*, is the conscious claim that the vernacular *is* – as opposed to Latin – the natural option for men and women.[9] The vernacular, that is the language that we acquire "by imitating our nurses," deserves both our fullest appreciation and the commitment to enhance its beauty.[10]

As we shall see, Dante's ideas resounded widely in the Renaissance debate on the relation between Latin and the vernacular, particularly in the sixteenth century, when the debate itself influenced concurrent discussions internal to the vernacular context such as the so-called *questione della lingua* (controversy on language).[11] In fact, one conflict fed the other, and the rise of humanism in the fifteenth century did complicate things. The opposition between Latin and the vernacular that lay behind the Sienese *Costituto* and Dante's defense of the vulgar tongue turned into something even more controversial at the time of the rebirth of classical Latin. Walking in the footsteps of the ancients, most humanists would harshly criticize both medieval Latin (considered as a corruption of Cicero's language) and the vernacular (labeled as the language of the illiterates). Yet Latinate humanism paradoxically contributed to the progressive acknowledgement of the virtues of the vernacular. It was in fact by challenging common assumptions about its inferiority that advocates of the vernacular managed to legitimate its status and use. Most of their arguments were built on the same ideas that Dante championed in the early fourteenth century, particularly the notion of naturalness and the expressive potential of the vernacular.[12]

If it would be misleading to read Dante's reflection on language through the lens of later developments in the field, it is however undeniable that Dante distanced himself from contemporary approaches to the topic, particularly when the relationship between Latin and vernacular is concerned. He would have probably shared the political and ideological end that informed the Commune of Siena's decision to translate the *Costituto* (namely the idea of involving a wider public in the civic life of the city), but he would have almost certainly disapproved the means. As convincingly argued by Alison Cornish, Dante's take on the very notion of translation is problematic and challenges the ideology behind the contemporary blossoming of *volgarizzamenti* (literally, vernacular translations).[13]

Dante's harsh criticism of Taddeo Alderotti's vernacular translation of the *Summa Alexandrinorum* in the *Convivio* is emblematic of this point of view. According to Dante, Taddeo's translation of the famous compendium of Aristotle's *Ethics* from the Latin version of Hermannus Alemannus (probably completed around 1260) is a bad example of how to use the vulgar tongue.[14] Given the larger context of the passage, which focuses on the reasons why Dante has decided to write the *Convivio* in Italian rather than in Latin, the reference to Taddeo Alderotti (1210–1295) is of particular interest: in fact, despite Dante's opinion, the vernacular version of the compendium was widely read across Europe.[15] As is well known, the text reappeared in French as part of Brunetto Latini's *Tresor* (The treasure), one of the most successful encyclopedias of the later Middle Ages, written during the author's French exile between 1260 and 1266. Furthermore, the *Tresor* – soon translated from the original French into Italian – intermingled with the textual transmission of Taddeo's compendium and contributed to the vernacular spread of Aristotelian ethics that informed civic discourses in the Italian cities.[16] Within such a frame, Cornish's suggestion that targets of Dante's criticism include Brunetto Latini's choice to write the *Tresor* in French rather than in Italian, is a compelling one and contributes to a better understanding of the author's take in the *Convivio*.[17] Not only does Dante challenge the widespread phenomenon of the *volgarizzamenti*, which, in a way, mimic Latin without a real commitment to enhance the vernacular, but he also criticizes those authors who prefer other vernaculars to their own.

Dante's argument in the *Convivio* is a subtle one. While acknowledging the superiority of Latin in terms of nobility, virtue, and beauty, Dante provides a philosophical legitimation for his use of the vulgar tongue. Since the *Convivio* is a commentary on Dante's own vernacular songs, to comment on them in Latin would introduce a disproportion in the relationship between the text and the commentary (which is supposed to be subordinate to the text itself).[18] If this argument is a logical one, Dante's following remarks lead to a more profound reassessment of the cultural values of the vernacular. First, it speaks to a much larger audience than Latin does, which means that the transmission of knowledge through the vulgar tongue will have a wider impact on society, thus leading more people towards science and virtue.[19] Second – and we get here to an idea that will be key to the Renaissance defense of the vernacular – the use of the vulgar tongue is justified by the natural affection we feel for it.[20] Speaking for himself, Dante outlines a very personal experience, but his arguments lead the readers to perceive this individual account as a model which does apply to everybody: it is through their conversation in the vernacular that Dante's parents met, interacted and eventually generated him; also, it is by means of the vernacular that Dante moved his first steps down the path of science and knowledge – in fact, it is through the vernacular that he made his acquaintance with Latin, thus preparing himself for higher forms of knowledge.[21] For all these reasons, Dante feels a natural inclination to foster the growth of his mother tongue, which can be achieved by seeking the stability that is typical of "grammatical" languages such as Latin.

As shown by, among others, Gianfranco Fioravanti, Dante's manifesto goes beyond a generic discussion of language.[22] The commitment to realize the expressive potentials of the *volgare* is in fact part of an agenda that considers the transmission of knowledge as crucial to the 'architectural' function that the ruling class is supposed to embody in society. That is why the definition of the audience that Dante addresses in the *Convivio* is so important to the understanding of the work. After criticizing the numerous scholars who "do not acquire learning for its own use but only insofar as through it they may gain money or honor," Dante identifies his targeted audience as

> those who because of the world's wicked neglect of good have left literature to those who have changed it from a lady into a whore; and these noble persons comprise princes, barons, knights, and many other noble people, not only men but women, of which there are many in this language who know only the vernacular and are not learned.[23]

By focusing on the aristocracy, accused of being responsible for the cultural and political decline of Italy, Dante places his reflection on language in the reality of his own time, thus stressing the performative function that the choice of the vernacular entails.

From a slightly different perspective, the celebration of the vernacular in the *De vulgari eloquentia* adds yet another layer to Dante's discussion. If the *Convivio*, despite its innovative outcomes, shares the traditional idea of a qualitative divide between Latin and the vernacular, *De vulgari eloquentia* reassesses the relationship between the two by affirming the natural and chronological priority of the vernacular.[24] We know all too well that Dante's reconstruction of the origin of languages is faulty, particularly his idea that Latin was an artificial language created in order to cope with the progressive and unavoidable evolution of the natural ones. As we shall see, the assumption of a "diglossia" that, as early as in Roman times, would oppose grammatical Latin to a non-grammatical language, namely the vernacular, would later be used by some humanists to prove the higher value of Latin.[25] Dante's take on this issue is different, for he uses the very notion of "grammatical languages" to justify the need for the definition of a similarly stable form of vernacular. It is in fact through *art* (that is by means of rules) that a natural language can be granted the same status that the so-called *locutiones regulatae* have. Even if it is true that, by committing himself to the identification of the 'ideal' Italian vernacular, Dante moves quickly back from the natural to the artificial, his premise is revolutionary. First, he consciously applies the notion of eloquence to the vernacular, acknowledging that eloquence in the vernacular is "necessary to everyone – for not only men, but also women and children strive to acquire it, as far as nature allows."[26] As such, vernacular eloquence deserves to be enhanced, so that people can benefit from their communication skills. Second, and more importantly, Dante provides a definition of *vulgaris locutio* that, in its priority over Latin, entails the opposition between nature and art:

> I call 'vernacular language' that which infants acquire from those around them when they first begin to distinguish sounds; or, to put it more succinctly, I declare that vernacular language is that which we learn without any formal instruction, by imitating our nurses. There also exists another kind of language, at one remove from us, which the Romans called gramatica [grammar] … Few, however, achieve complete fluency in it, since knowledge of its rules and theory can only be developed through dedication to a lengthy course of study. Of these two kinds of language, the more noble is the vernacular: first, because it was the language originally used by the human race; second, because the whole world employs it, though with different pronunciations and using different words; and third because it is natural to us, while the other is, in contrast, artificial.[27]

Whereas the *gramatica* is the result of "formal instruction," hence limited to those who have a chance to study it, the vernacular is the language to which we are all naturally exposed. This makes the vernacular nobler than the *gramatica*, which partially contradicts what Dante argued in the *Convivio*. The contradiction, however, is only apparent, for the perspective of the author's discussion has changed. The nobility of the vernacular is in fact grounded in an ontological argument, which does not affect the idea of regulated languages such as Latin as a model to look at in the process of carving the literary use of the vulgar tongue. Yet Dante's argument was indeed an innovative one and – backed up by the author's own poetical experience in the *Divine Comedy* – did open a new chapter in the history of the relationship between Latin and the vernacular.

Latin humanism and the vernacular: conflict and interaction

The usual narrative about the establishment of the vernacular as a language suitable for literary purposes identifies Petrarch (1304–1374) and Giovanni Boccaccio (1313–1375) as those who, along with Dante, laid the foundations for the legitimation of the vulgar tongue. However, fully conversant with both Latin and Italian, Boccaccio and Petrarch approached their bilingualism in different ways. If Boccaccio's writings, the *Decameron* in particular, embody at its best the 'new' vernacular society of medieval Europe, Petrarch's scholarly and literary production paves the way for the humanist turn.[28] Emblematic of Petrarch's attitude towards languages is his willingness to obtain the laurel wreath as a Latin poet, to say nothing of the Latin title – *Rerum vulgarium fragmenta* (Fragments of vulgar/vernacular things) – given to the poetical achievement that, contrary to his stated plans, would make him one of the most influential poets ever. Petrarch's Latin is surely not Dante's. What distinguishes Petrarch's consciously humanist approach from Dante's relation to the classics is, among other things, the poet's commitment to restore the style of the ancients, thus introducing the opposition between medieval Latin and classical Latin that would prove crucial to the intellectual experience of humanism.[29] Petrarch's attitude towards the Latinate cultural elite represented by university professors who, despite their alleged acquaintance with the classics, are far from fully understanding the importance of eloquence, is in fact a veritable manifesto of new ideas about the epistemological potential of languages.[30] According to Petrarch, it is impossible to appropriate the teachings of the ancients without appreciating, appropriating, and, to some extent, re-enacting their use of language – an approach that differentiates him from scholasticism.

This humanist shift, which, at least in Petrarch's own terms, was not meant to denigrate the role and the legitimacy of the vernacular, had a strong impact on cultural developments of the following century. By engaging in a tenacious fight for the rebirth of classical knowledge through the rebirth of classical languages (Latin in the first place, followed by a renewed interest in Greek), humanism tended to set aside the momentum that had informed Dante's claim to the enhancement of the vernacular. Within this context, the experience of Leonardo Bruni (1370–1444) and his fellow humanists in early-fifteenth-century Florence is pivotal.[31] Bruni's ideas on classical languages are emblematically witnessed by his commitment as a translator. In particular, his translations of Aristotle – along with his treatise on the theory and practice of translation – reveal a new approach to language as a tool for knowledge. Through a harsh criticism of the medieval Latin translations of Aristotle, responsible for the barbarous linguistic shape that makes the philosopher's works unreadable and almost impossible to understand, Bruni commits himself to an entire program of new Latin translations. Imitating the style of Cicero, but also revising the interpretation of some Aristotelian passages, Bruni's versions of Aristotle generated one of the most famous controversies of the time, namely the debate with the Spanish priest Alfonso de Cartagena (1384–1456), a strong supporter of the previous Latin translations of Aristotle, which constituted the core of university curricula across Europe.[32]

If, on the one hand, Leonardo Bruni's campaign against the barbarous Latin embodied by scholasticism aimed at recovering the intellectual value of ancient eloquence, it entailed, on the other hand, a rather negative judgement of the vernacular, perceived as incapable of reaching the qualitative heights of Latin. Similar thoughts informed the 1435 debate on the origins of the vulgar tongue.[33] Whereas the humanist Biondo Flavio in his *De verbis Romanae locutionis* (On the words of the Latin language) assumed that the vernacular was the result of the progressive and historically justifiable decline of Latin, Bruni as well as other humanists shared the idea of an original "diglossia" that, in Rome, would oppose grammatical Latin to a non-grammatical vulgar tongue. As mentioned above, Dante used a similar argument in the *De vulgari eloquentia* to legitimate the notion itself of vernacular eloquence. On the contrary, Bruni employed the "diglossia" argument to focus on the restoration of classical Latin as the main condition for literary engagement.[34]

However, as shown by recent scholarship in the field, it would be misleading to think of Bruni, and of humanism more generally, as impervious to the concurrent development of the vulgar tongue as a language suitable for knowledge.[35] Bruni's own ideas on language are more articulate than has often been thought. In the *Dialogi ad Petrum Paulum Histrum* (Dialogues to Petrus Paulus Histrus) (1401), for instance, Dante is both criticized and praised. The decision to write the *Divine Comedy* in Italian (which had been already the polemical target of the proto-humanist schoolmaster Giovanni del Virgilio in Dante's own day) was, according to Niccolò Niccoli, one of the interlocutors of Bruni's dialogue, motivated by Dante's lack of Latin skills.[36] Yet in the second book of the *Dialogi*, Bruni praises Dante's vernacular poetry as an oral language. The distinction between *lingua* and *sermo*, Bruni explains, is double-sided.[37]

The ambiguous position of a humanist such as Bruni in the debate on languages is also suggested by the vernacular lives of Dante, Petrarch, and Boccaccio that he wrote late in his life and which, along with other works (including poetry), witness to the humanist's preoccupation with writing in the vernacular.[38] The multifaceted dynamics that inform the use of Latin and the vernacular in fifteenth-century Florence (but the same might be said of other places) is nonetheless confirmed by the impact that Bruni's own work in the field of Latin translation had on contemporary vernacular culture. His 'humanist' version of Aristotle's *Ethics* (1417), for instance, was soon translated into Italian by a renowned schoolteacher called Bernardo Nuti, whose professional career was indeed at the crossroads of Latinate and vernacular cultures.[39] Interestingly enough, Nuti's Italian version of the *Ethics*, which enjoyed a significant circulation among lay readers in fifteenth-century Florence, was commissioned by a Spanish humanist, Nuño de Guzman. The detail is worth mentioning because the original manuscript sent to the Spaniard – now at the Beinecke Library – played a crucial role in the vernacular dissemination of Aristotle's *Ethics* in late-fifteenth-century Spain. It was in fact the main source of a successful compendium that stands out among the works that contributed to the spread of philosophy in the vernacular.[40] The case of the Spanish afterlife of Nuti's translation shows how intricate and not mutually exclusive the paths of Latin humanism and vernacular culture were.

The ideal example to mention when discussing the humanist interaction of Latin and the vernacular is undoubtedly the literary production of Leon Battista Alberti (1404–1472). Alberti, the embodiment of what later historiography would label the "Renaissance man," was an acclaimed artist, a renowned writer in both Latin and Italian, a poet as well as a provocative thinker. He was also the figure who gathered the various threads that we have outlined so far within a single cultural program based on a multilingual notion of humanism. At the time of Bruni's assertive celebration of Latin in the *Dialogi*, Leon Battista Alberti organized an event that marked another important step in the legitimation of the vernacular: the *Certame coronario* of 1441.[41] The poetical contest, which took place in Florence, revolved around the topic of *amicitia* (friendship), a signature topic in the classical tradition, and was open to poets eager to write in Italian. Not surprisingly, the award was not assigned. The judges, chosen among the secretaries of Pope Eugenius IV, did not find any of the participants worthy. If the outcome of the *certame* tells us a lot about the widespread bias against the vernacular within the humanist milieu, it did not undermine Alberti's effort to harmonize Latinate and vernacular cultures.

The project had been a major concern of Alberti's for many years, as suggested by the various occasions on which he reflected upon it. In the preface to the third book of his philosophical dialogues *Della famiglia* (Books of the family) (1436–1437), for example, Alberti challenges the idea that Latin was an artificial language and, sharing Biondo's theory of the evolution and decline of languages, combines his passion for the classics and the legitimation of the vernacular. On the one hand, the loss of classical Latin after the fall of the Roman empire is said to be much worse than the end of the empire itself (Alberti obviously endorses the cultural value attributed by his fellow humanists to the language of the ancients); on the other hand, by introducing the notion of "language use," Alberti explains historically the origins of the vernacular and prioritizes the communicative function of language that the vulgar tongue shares with all other languages, classical Latin included.[42] Ancient writers aimed to be understood by their audiences; likewise, in order to benefit as many people as possible in modern times, the learned ones ought to commit themselves to the improvement of the vernacular.

Alberti himself offered his own contribution. Sometime around 1440, he authored the first ever Italian grammar. The so called *Grammatichetta*, which remained in manuscript and did not circulate widely, is a veritable milestone in the history of the Italian language.[43] Consistent with the author's ideas on language use, Alberti's work is not prescriptive. The vernacular, like Greek and Latin, is indeed made of grammatical structures. Its status was not inferior to that of classical languages, as Alberti argues in the prologue:

> I believe that those who argue that Latin was not common to all Latin people, but only peculiar to certain erudite scholars, as we find it in only a few people today, will acknowledge their fault by reading this booklet of ours. In it, I have gathered the use of our language in very short annotations. A similar project was pursued by ingenious scholars first among the Greeks and later among the Latins, and they called this kind of annotations – which would allow people to write and speak without making mistakes – 'grammar.' Please do read and understand what this art is in our language.[44]

By insisting on the notion of the use of language as well as its ethical duty to enhance the vernacular in order to realize its communicative potentials, Alberti updates Dante's linguistic project in the light of his humanist training. Also, by asking himself questions about which vernacular to use in his own time, Alberti touches on a topic that will be crucial to the following century's debate on language.

A fruitful compromise: Latin and the *questione della lingua*

As noted in the previous paragraph, Alberti's *Grammatichetta* did not circulate in the fifteenth century. Dante's seminal writings on language were not widely read either, at least until the appearance of the *editiones principes*: the *Convivio*, the manuscript tradition of which was limited to erudite circles, was first printed in 1490;[45] the *De vulgari eloquentia*, the original

Latin version of which would not be published until Jacopo Corbinelli's Parisian edition of 1577, first appeared in an Italian translation by Gian Giorgio Trissino (1478–1550) in 1529.[46] In fact, the translation was part of a wider project that Trissino was pursuing systematically. He not only tried to "canonize" the vernacular through the lens of the most illustrious classical genres that had newly entered the literary debate via the rediscovery of Aristotle's *Poetics* (namely tragedy and epic), but he also proposed a grammatical and orthographical codification of the Italian vernacular in both his *Grammatichetta* and in the dialogue *Il Castellano* (1529).[47] The publication of Trissino's version of Dante's *De vulgari eloquentia* could not be more timely. Only four years earlier, in 1525, Pietro Bembo had published a Ciceronian dialogue entitled *Prose della volgar lingua* (On the vernacular language), one of the most influential texts in the European Renaissance.[48] Between the two, in 1528, Baldassare Castiglione's *Libro del Cortegiano* (Book of the courtier) – another Renaissance bestseller-to-be – was also printed in Venice.[49] These works – along with which we should also recall Niccolò Machiavelli's *Discorso o dialogo intorno alla nostra lingua* (Discourse or dialogue on our language) – are the key texts in the debate traditionally known as *questione della lingua*.[50] Given the existence of many Italian vernaculars, which – as Dante had pointed out in the *De vulgari eloquentia* – vary in both space and time, what kind of "Italian" should be identified as the *volgare* par excellence? This was the question that, combining literary issues with cultural politics and linguistic ideology, was at the core of the debate.[51] Bembo's project, which would soon become a sort of cultural dictatorship, found in Petrarch and Boccaccio the two models to imitate in order to attain excellent results in vernacular writings. The idea of imposing a literary and linguistic canon from two centuries earlier was criticized by those who preferred to privilege the use of contemporary Italian: this was the case of Machiavelli's *Discorso* that, consistently with Alberti's legacy, considered the current language spoken in Florence as the best option. Less inclined to favor a specific dialect, Castiglione's "courtly" theory acknowledged the centrality of the Tuscan tradition, but suggested opening it to a broader spectrum of influences. Closer to Dante, however, was Trissino's theory, based on the idea of constructing a somewhat artificial vernacular by drawing on the various Italian vernaculars.

While there is no way to address here all the many facets of the *questione della lingua*, it will be useful to compare the reflection on the vernacular with the concurrent status of Latin. From this point of view, Bembo's *Prose* is particularly instructive. The first book of the dialogue is in fact primarily aimed at convincing one of the interlocutors, the renowned humanist Ercole Strozzi, of the legitimacy of the literary use of the *volgare*. The main argument employed by Bembo is the opposition between the vernacular as a natural language and Latin as an artificial one. The proximity of men and women to the vulgar tongue is proved by the fact that we all "drink the vernacular with the nurses' milk."[52] Furthermore, the chronological distance that separates us from Latin makes it foreign to us. The natural learning of the vernacular is thus opposed to the study of foreign languages at school, which Bembo does not hesitate to label as "non-natural."[53] Of course, this does not undermine Bembo's praise of the ancients. Trained as a humanist and well versed in both Latin and Greek, the Venetian scholar did not mean to disqualify the classical tradition. Rather, his commitment to the enhancement of the *volgare* must be read as the attempt to bring it to the same level of classical languages. By situating the relation of the Italians to their vernacular within a wider understanding of languages as historically grounded organisms, Bembo introduces a parallelism between the linguistic histories of Latin and Italian. The function that Cicero had in the evolution of Latin is taken on, within the vernacular context, by the "new" classics, namely Dante and, even more so, Petrarch and Boccaccio, who perform the role played in Latin culture by, respectively, Virgil and Cicero himself. Bembo introduces a successful compromise between the assumptions of humanists, primarily based on the authoritative connection with the ancients, and on the necessity for the new vernacular literary tradition to be legitimized.

Despite its massive influence on the linguistic culture of the time, Bembo's "humanist" compromise was not able to neutralize the conservative ideology that informed most Latinate scholars and intellectuals. In fact, if the *questione della lingua* did affect the evolution of the Italian vernacular (thus paving the way for similar developments in other European countries), the alleged superiority of Latin in many fields of knowledge (particularly those that were studied at the universities) would remain a common trope in linguistic discourses. The complex nature of the cultural conflict informed the central decades of the sixteenth century, when several authors engaged in articulate discussions of language that witness to a controversy that proved even more passionate than the one evoked by the portrayal of Ercole Strozzi in the first book of Bembo's *Prose*.

Legitimizing the vernacular as a language of knowledge

Emblematic of the cultural rivalry that characterized discourses on language in mid-sixteenth-century Italy was a series of works that focused on the legitimacy of the use of the *volgare* for purposes other than literature and poetry. In fact, if it is undeniable that Bembo did contribute to the legitimation of the vernacular for literary use, it was the employment of the *volgare* in fields such as science or philosophy that remained problematic.[54] Within a variety of concurrent trends, which the simplistic "dichotomy Latin versus vernacular" cannot properly summarize, it is crucial to distinguish those approaches that better characterized the various facets of the debate. To this end, it is useful to consider works such as those by Alessandro Citolini, Alessandro Piccolomini, and Sperone Speroni. These authors engaged in thorough discussions of the controversy between Latinate and vernacular cultures, finding in the notion of translation a possible way to harmonize the two terms of the conflict.[55]

Alessandro Citolini's *Lettera in difesa de la lingua volgare* (Letter in defense of the vulgar tongue), printed in 1540 without the author's knowledge, is a milestone in the history of the emancipation of the vulgar tongue.[56] When he wrote the letter, Citolini (1500–1582) was not new to the discussion of language. As a disciple of Giulio Camillo Delminio, whom Alessandro followed in France, the young Citolini engaged very soon in the study of literature and poetry, thus setting the stage for his later *Tipocosmia* (1561), an encyclopedic dialogue that had an important influence on similar works across Europe.[57] The letter of 1540 is a sort of premise to the major work. In fact, the defense of the vulgar tongue is twofold: on the one hand, Citolini engages in a systematic criticism of those who defend Latin, arguing that it is nobler, richer, and more common than the vernacular; on the other hand, based on the idea of the *volgare* as a living language, Citolini focuses on the ethical commitment to make it a tool for the dissemination of knowledge. As for the first point, the author situates his reflection on language within a wider consideration of cultural progress. Also, by identifying a common origin for Latin and Italian, he maintains that it is impossible to criticize one without criticizing the other. In fact, the point of Citolini's argument is not to diminish the importance of Latin, but simply to legitimize the use of the vernacular by showing that Latin is dead while the vernacular is hale and hearty. As such, the vulgar tongue is the expression of its time:

> [The vulgar tongue] is alive and grows, generates, creates, produces, gives birth, thus becoming more and more rich and abundant. This is why as soon as a new thing comes to light, among the many that every single day appear, it gets clothed by vernacular words, while lacking in Latin or Greek ones. And such things, which arise day after day, include both natural ones (that are infinite) and those related to the arts: these are so necessary and numerous as to encompass more than half our life … [E]ven if such words are not yet recorded on paper, they are not lost, as the Latin ones are … they are, instead, continuously in the mouth of the living tongue.[58]

Whereas Latin cannot be used to name all the new things that populate the modern world, the vulgar tongue is able to produce words capable of describing them. Similarly, since the various vernaculars have been diversifying one from the other, the "international" span of Latin (an argument often employed by its defenders) is also called into question: for instance, should an Italian speak to a German about military weapons for which they have created new words in their respective vernaculars, Latin would prove useless to the conversation.[59] Furthermore – and Citolini enters here the favorite battlefield of humanists – not only is the vernacular capable of expressing many concepts that Latin cannot express, but it is also able to do so in an eloquent way. By applying to the *volgare* what Cicero says about the ennoblement of Latin in both *Brutus* and *De oratore* – two of the reference texts in the study of classical eloquence – Citolini identifies language use and diachronic evolution as the two criteria that inform the progressive shaping of the vernacular. Of course, the naturalness of the vernacular is not enough to make it eloquent, and this is where the productive relation to the ancients comes in. By imitating the classics, the vernacular will indeed be able to refine itself.

However, it is not the use of a specific language that makes the speakers wise or knowledgeable. This is crucial to Citolini's argument. Rejecting a conservative approach to the humanist idea that proficiency in Latin ensures knowledge, Citolini stakes out the value of vernacular culture *per se*. Consistent with this argument, he also points out that the vulgar tongue is not only able to "speak about fables and love," but also about more serious matters, such as philosophy and astronomy.[60] The domains that should be dealt with in the vernacular, according to Citolini, include Holy Scripture, a statement that introduces another facet of the "vernacular turn." The author, known later in his life as heterodox, approaches a controversial aspect of the linguistic conflicts that informed Renaissance culture. If classicizing humanists and university professors were in fact harsh towards the literary and scholarly use of the vernacular, the Catholic Church was not more inclined to let vernacular audiences access the Bible directly.[61]

Citolini's combination of the various layers involved in the linguistic controversy finds a natural haven in the discussion of translation. It is in fact through the practice of translation that past and present interact. More specifically, by translating from classical languages into the vernacular, a double outcome can be achieved: first, vernacular readers will have a wider access to knowledge; second, by looking at the classics, the vernacular will improve its stylistic potentials. Furthermore, Citolini argues, since natural languages are better than dead ones at moving the audience, the vernacular will prove more effective than Latin in reaching the souls of men and women.[62]

Eventually, the use of the vernacular instead of Latin produces a non-negligible benefit in the general advancement of learning, for it makes people save time in their studies. Instead of years and years spent in the study of languages prior to devoting oneself to the real content of disciplines, the use of the vernacular as a language of knowledge would let people engage with learning earlier in their lives. A similar argument was at the core of Alessandro Piccolomini's defense of the *volgare*, which was a veritable *Leitmotiv* throughout his career, primarily devoted to the vernacular dissemination of classical philosophy and science.[63] In his preface to the *Filosofia naturale* (Natural philosophy) of 1551, for instance, the Sienese scholar argued that the alleged superiority of the ancients could only be challenged if all fields of knowledge were accessible in the natural languages of the moderns.[64] Since youth is the most productive part of life in terms of intellectual achievements, it is unfruitful to spend much time in the study of dead languages while postponing the acquisition of knowledge itself. Yet, while legitimizing the intellectual status of the vulgar tongue, Piccolomini agrees with Citolini on the importance of being familiar with the classics in order to make the *volgare* competitive. Indeed, even if both Citolini and Piccolomini stress the centrality of subject matter as the primary concern of learning, they do not deny the importance of eloquence as a vehicle for the acquisition and dissemination of knowledge.

Less obliging towards the humanist trend embodied by Citolini's and Piccolomini's defenses of the *volgare* was Sperone Speroni's provocative *Dialogo delle lingue* (Dialogue on languages) (1542), which inspired Joachim du Bellay's famous *Deffence et Illustration de la Langue Francoyse* (Defence and illustration of the French language) of 1549.[65] Beyond the usual arguments employed to support the use of the vernacular, Speroni's dialogue is of particular interest for the way in which it stages the cultural clash between the humanist perspective on languages and the potentially subversive implications of the vernacular turn. Within the fiction of the dialogue, an interlocutor simply called "the scholar" (possibly the voice of the author) retells a previous conversation between two iconic figures, the Italian philosopher Pietro Pomponazzi (1462–1525) and the Greek humanist Giano Lascaris (1445–1535). Whereas the humanist asserts that the study of texts in their original languages is the only path to the acquisition of knowledge, the university professor argues that the importance of ancient texts lies in what they say, and not in the way in which they say it. Two different conceptions of language are at stake here: Lascaris embodies the Platonic idea of a direct link between *res* (things) and *verba* (words), which entails that certain languages are better than others at communicating specific topics; Pomponazzi shares instead the Aristotelian notion of language as a set of arbitrary conventions, which makes all languages equally suitable for all topics. Pomponazzi's criticism of his interlocutor's elitist approach is radical: according to the philosopher, the priority assigned to the study of languages is just a way to save knowledge for the few people who are able to access it. Things, according to Pietro, are definitely more important than words, and that is why the practice of translation is more than welcome in order to let larger numbers of readers access the sources of knowledge. Furthermore – and Pomponazzi develops here the same argument as Citolini – the long time spent in studying languages keeps us from the actual acquisition of knowledge. Eventually, the philosopher goes beyond the debate on the alleged qualitative differences between classical and vernacular languages: he does not care for the refinement of the vulgar tongue, because what matters to him is the communicative function of language.

Conclusions

As noted at the outset of this chapter, the idea that the study of classical languages absorbs too many years in one's education, thus preventing one from attaining the knowledge of the ancients, was also a major concern of Montaigne's father. Sperone Speroni's argument, as mentioned above, made its way through France thanks to Joachim Du Bellay's widely successful *Deffence et Illustration de la Langue Francoyse* [Defence and illustration of the French language], which literally translated the terms of the Italian debate beyond the Alps, thus replicating the idea of a contest between the ancients and the moderns that led to the cultural affirmation of the latter. Far from representing the end of a story that would last for a few more centuries, these debates, as well as Montaigne's peculiar experience, embody the unavoidable contradictions entailed by a society in which the gradual legitimation of the vernaculars coexisted with and was shaped by the weighty legacy of the classics.

From Dante to mid-sixteenth century authors such as Citolini, Piccolomini, and Speroni, through the humanist controversies, the examples that we have examined show that attempts to reduce the relationship between Latin and the vernaculars in the Renaissance to a strict dichotomy do not work. In fact, forms of linguistic conflict involve productive interactions. First, by consciously distancing itself from Latin, the vulgar tongue acquired a new status in both cultural and grammatical terms. Second, those figures that seem to be more invested in the debate were also those who, in different ways, embodied Renaissance multilingualism at its best (just think of Leon Battista Alberti and Pietro Bembo, who wrote widely in both Latin and Italian, thus actively contributing to the mutually informing relation that characterizes the two languages in the period). Lastly, despite the differences that characterize each case, the dialectic between Latin and the vernacular found in the broad notion of translation was one of the most effective catalysts for the early modern reception of antiquity. If during the Middle Ages vernacular translations tended to be perceived as second rate products, authors such as Alessandro Piccolomini and Sperone Speroni fostered the legitimacy of the genre as a powerful means for the development and enrichment of the vernacular.

Notes

1 M. de Montaigne, *Les essais. Livre premier*, Paris: Librairie Générale Française, 2002, "De l'institution des enfants," pp. 259–313: 306–13.
2 *Ibid.*, p. 306; cf. the passage in John Florio's translation (1603): "My late father, having, by all the meanes and industrie that is possible for a man, sought amongst the wisest, and men of best understanding, to find a most exquisite and readie way of teaching, being advised of the inconveniences then in use; was given to understand that the lingring while, and best part of our youth, that we imploy in learning the tongues, which cost them nothing, is the onely cause we can never attaine to that absolute perfection of skill and knowledge of the Greekes and Romanes."
3 *Ibid.*, p. 307.
4 *Ibid.*, pp. 306–7.
5 For an overview of the topic, cf. P. Burke, *Languages and Communities in Early Modern Europe*, Cambridge: Cambridge University Press, 2004; and, with a focus on the Italian case, M. Campanelli, "Languages," in M. Wyatt (ed.) *The Cambridge Companion to the Italian Renaissance*, Cambridge: Cambridge University Press, 2014, pp. 139–63.
6 A. Lisini (ed.) *Il costituto del Comune di Siena volgarizzato nel MCCCIX–MCCCX*, Siena: Tipografia sordomuti di Lazzeri, 1903, D. I, rub. 134: "In volgare di lettera grossa, bene leggibile et bene formata, in buone carte pecorine … acciocché le povare persone et altre persone che non sanno grammatica, et li altri, e' quali vorranno, possano esso vedere et copia inde trarre et avere a loro volontà"; for an overview of the document and its context, cf. N. Giordano and G. Piccinni (eds.) *Siena nello specchio del suo costituto in volgare del 1309–1310*, Pisa: Pacini, 2013.

7   C. Segre (ed.) *Volgarizzamenti del Due e Trecento*, Turin: UTET, 1953. For a discussion of the tradition of the *volgarizzamenti*, cf. the seminal studies by C. Dionisotti, "Tradizione classica e volgarizzamenti," in C. Dionisotti, *Geografia e storia della letteratura italiana*, Turin: Einaudi, 1967, pp. 103–44; G. Folena, *Volgarizzare e tradurre*, Turin: Einaudi, 1991; and, more recently, A. Cornish, *Vernacular Translation in Dante's Italy: Illiterate Literature*, Cambridge: Cambridge University Press, 2010.

8   B. Giamboni, *Fiore di rettorica*, ed. G. Speroni, Pavia: Università degli Studi di Pavia, 1994, pp. 3–4.

9   For an overview of Dante's reflection on language, cf. S. Fortuna, M. Gragnolati, and J. Trabant (eds.) *Dante's Plurilingualism: Authority, Knowledge, Subjectivity*, London: Legenda, 2010; M. Tavoni (ed.) *Dante e la lingua italiana*, Ravenna: Longo, 2013.

10 Dante Alighieri, *De vulgari eloquentia*, trans. S. Botterill, Cambridge: Cambridge University Press, 1996, 1.2.

11 For a thorough introduction to the *questione della lingua*, cf. C. Marazzini, "Le teorie," in L. Serianni and P. Trifone (eds.) *Storia della lingua italiana*, Turin: Einaudi, 1993, vol. 1, pp. 231–329.

12 A. Mazzocco, *Linguistic Theories in Dante and the Humanists: Studies of Language and Intellectual History in Late Medieval and Early Modern Italy*, Leiden: Brill, 1993; C. Celenza, "End Game: Humanist Latin in the Late Fifteenth Century," in W. Verbaal, Y. Maes, and J. Papy (eds.) *Latinitas Perennis*, vol. 2, *Appropriation and Latin Literature*, Leiden: Brill, 2009, pp. 201–42.

13 Cornish, *Vernacular Translation*, pp. 126–57.

14 Dante Alighieri, *The Convivio*, trans. R. Lansing, New York: Garland, 1990, 1.10.10.

15 On Taddeo's translation of the *Summa Alexandrinorum*, cf. S. Gentili, *L'uomo aristotelico alle origini della letteratura italiana*, Rome: Carocci, 2005, pp. 27–55; Cornish, *Vernacular Translation*, pp. 78–9.

16 Gentili, *L'uomo aristotelico*, pp. 41–9.

17 Cornish, *Vernacular Translation*, pp. 135ff.

18 Dante, *The Convivio*, 1.5.6–7.

19 *Ibid.*, 1.9.2–5.

20 *Ibid.*, 1.10.

21 *Ibid.*, 1.12.

22 G. Fioravanti, "Introduzione," in Dante Alighieri, *Opere. Volume secondo. Convivio, Monarchia, Epistole, Egloge*, Milan: Mondadori, 2014, pp. 5–79: 53ff.

23 Dante, *The Convivio*, 1.9.3–5.

24 Dante, *De vulgari eloquentia*, 1.1.1–3; 1.9.6–11.

25 M. Tavoni, *Latino, grammatica, volgare: storia di una questione umanistica*, Padua: Antenore, 1984.

26 Dante, *De vulgari eloquentia*, 1.1.1.

27 *Ibid.*, 1.1.2–4.

28 On the role of Boccaccio as the 'father' of a new literary consciousness primarily concerned with the use of the vernacular, see F. Bruni, *Boccaccio, l'invenzione della letteratura mezzana*, Bologna: il Mulino, 1990. Cf. also M. Eisner, *Boccaccio and the Invention of Italian Literature: Dante, Petrarch, Cavalcanti, and the Authority of the Vernacular*, Cambridge: Cambridge University Press, 2015. On the intersections of Latin and vernacular in both Petrarch and Boccaccio, see V. Kirkham and A. Maggi (eds.) *Petrarch: A Critical Guide to the Complete Works*, Chicago: Chicago University Press, 2009; V. Kirkham and M. Sherberg (eds.) *Boccaccio: A Critical Guide to the Complete Works*, Chicago: Chicago University Press, 2013.

29 For a discussion of Petrarch's Latin humanism, cf. C. Celenza, "Petrarch, Latin, and Italian Renaissance Latinity," *Journal of Medieval and Early Modern Studies*, 35, 2005, 509–36.

30 Emblematic of Petrarch's position is the invective *De sui ipsius et multorum ignorantia* (On his own ignorance and that of many others, 1365–1370): cf. Petrarch, *Invectives*, trans. D. Marsh, Cambridge, MA: Harvard University Press, 2004, pp. 222–363. See also W. J. Kennedy, "The Economy of Invective and a Man in the Middle," in Kirkham and Maggi (eds.), *Petrarch*, pp. 263–73.

31 C. Grayson, *A Renaissance Controversy: Latin or Italian*, Oxford: Clarendon Press, 1960. For a recent discussion of Bruni and the humanist context in Florence with reference to debates on language, cf. the cluster of articles "Latin and Vernacular in Quattrocento Florence and Beyond," *I Tatti Studies*, 16(1/2), 2013, particularly A. Rizzi and E. Del Soldato, "Latin and Vernacular in Quattrocento Florence and Beyond: An Introduction," pp. 231–42; A. Rizzi, "Leonardo Bruni and the Shimmering Facets of Languages in Early Quattrocento Florence," pp. 243–56; B. Maxson, "'This Sort of Men': The Vernacular and the Humanist Movement in Fifteenth-Century

Florence," pp. 257–71; E. Refini, "'Aristotile in parlare materno': Vernacular Readings of the *Ethics* in the Quattrocento," pp. 311–41. See also B. Maxson, *The Humanist World of Renaissance Florence*, New York: Cambridge University Press, 2013.

32 G. Griffiths, J. Hankins, and D. Thompson, *The Humanism of Leonardo Bruni: Selected Texts*, Binghamton: Medieval & Renaissance Texts & Studies in conjunction with the Renaissance Society of America, 1987, pp. 201–8, 213–17; P. Botley, *Latin Translation in the Renaissance: The Theory and Practice of Leonardo Bruni, Giannozzo Manetti and Desiderius Erasmus*, Cambridge: Cambridge University Press, 2004, pp. 53–60; Cornish, *Vernacular Translation*, pp. 169–70.

33 Rizzi, "Leonardo Bruni," pp. 243–6.

34 Tavoni, *Latino, grammatica, volgare*; Campanelli, "Languages," pp. 141–2.

35 See the references in note 31.

36 L. Bruni, *Opere letterarie e politiche di Leonardo Bruni*, ed. P. Viti, Turin: UTET, 1996, p. 110. For a general discussion of the *Dialogi*, see D. Quint, "Humanism and Modernity: A Reconsideration of Bruni's Dialogues," *Renaissance Quarterly*, 38, 1985, pp. 423–45. On Giovanni del Virgilio's criticism of Dante's choice to write the *Divine Comedy* in Italian, see G. Albanese's introduction to the *Egloge* in Dante, *Opere. Volume secondo*, pp. 1595–621.

37 Rizzi, "Leonardo Bruni," pp. 250–1.

38 On Bruni's complex relation to the vernacular, see J. Hankins, "Humanism in the Vernacular: The Case of Leonardo Bruni," in C. S. Celenza and K. Gouwens (eds.) *Humanism and Creativity in the Renaissance: Essays in Honor of Ronald G. Witt*, Leiden: Brill, 2006, pp. 11–29.

39 Refini, "'Aristotile in parlare materno,'" p. 316.

40 J. M. Valero Moreno, "Formas del Aristotelismo Ético-Político en la Castilla del siglo xv," in D. A. Lines and E. Refini (eds.) *Aristotele fatto volgare: tradizione aristotelica e cultura volgare nel Rinascimento*, Pisa: ETS, 2014, pp. 253–310: 291–5.

41 L. Bertolini, *De vera amicitia: i testi del primo Certame Coronario*, Modena: Panini, 1993.

42 L. B. Alberti, *Libri della famiglia*, 3, prologue, in L. B. Alberti, *Opere volgari*, ed. C. Grayson, Bari: Laterza, 1960.

43 L. B. Alberti, *Grammatichetta e altri scritti sul volgare*, ed. G. Patota, Rome: Salerno, 1996.

44 *Ibid.*, prologue (translation by the present author).

45 Dante Alighieri, *Convivio*, Florence: Francesco Bonaccorsi, 1490.

46 Dante Alighieri, *De la volgare eloquenzia*, Vicenza: Tolomeo Gianicolo, 1529; for the *editio princeps* of the Latin text, cf. Dante Alighieri, *De vulgari eloquentia libri duo*, ed. J. Corbinelli, Paris: J. Corbon, 1577.

47 G. G. Trissino, *La Grammatichetta*, Vicenza: Tolomeo Gianicolo, 1529; *Dialogo del Trissino intitulato il Castellano, nel quale si tratta de la lingua italiana*, Vicenza: Tolomeo Gianicolo, 1529.

48 P. Bembo, *Prose nelle quali si ragiona della volgar lingua*, Venice: Giovanni Tacuino, 1525 (cf. the critical edition, P. Bembo, *Prose della volgar lingua*, ed. C. Vela, Bologna: CLUEB, 2001).

49 B. Castiglione, *Il libro del cortegiano*, Venice: heirs of Aldo Manuzio, 1528 (cf. the modern edition by W. Barberis, Turin: Einaudi, 1998).

50 N. Machiavelli, *Discorso intorno alla nostra lingua*, ed. by P. Trovato, Padua: Antenore, 1982; in general, on the *questione della lingua*, cf. Marazzini, "Le teorie."

51 Campanelli, "Languages," pp. 154–63.

52 Bembo, *Prose*, Book 1.

53 *Ibid.*

54 For an overview of the topic, cf. A. Calzona (ed.) *Il volgare come lingua di cultura dal Trecento al Cinquecento*, Florence: Leo S. Olschki, 2003; R. Librandi and R. Piro (eds.) *Lo scaffale della biblioteca scientifica in volgare, secoli XIII–XVI*, Florence: SISMEL, 2006.

55 For an introduction to translation in the Renaissance, see P. Burke and R. Po-chia Hsia (eds.) *Cultural Translation in Early Modern Europe*, Cambridge: Cambridge University Press, 2007; P. Burke, *Lost (and Found) in Translation: A Cultural History of Translators and Translating in Early Modern Europe*, Wassenar: NIAS, 2005; K. Newman and J. Tylus (eds.) *Early Modern Cultures of Translation*, Philadelphia: University of Pennsylvania Press, 2015.

56 A. Citolini, *Lettera in difesa de la lingua volgare*, Venice: Francesco Marcolini, 1540.

57 On Citolini's influence on English culture, cf. M. Wyatt, *The Italian Encounter with Tudor England: A Cultural Politics of Translation*, Cambridge: Cambridge University Press, pp. 203–54.

58 Citolini, *Lettera*, fol. B2r.

59 *Ibid.*, fol. [B3]r–[B4]r.

60 *Ibid.*, fol. D2v.

61 On the controversial relationship between Latin and vernacular in the field of Scripture, see at least G. Fragnito, *La Bibbia al rogo: la censura ecclesiastica e i volgarizzamenti della Scrittura, 1471–1605*, Bologna: il Mulino, 1997; and R. Griffiths (ed.) *The Bible in the Renaissance: Essays on Biblical Commentary and Translation in the Fifteenth and the Sixteenth Centuries*, Aldershot: Ashgate, 2001.

62 Citolini, *Lettera*, fols. D2v–[D4]r.

63 For a discussion of Piccolomini's ideas on language and translation, see A. Siekiera, "Riscrivere Aristotele: la formazione della prosa scientifica in italiano," in Lines and Refini (eds.), *Aristotele fatto volgare*, pp. 149–68.

64 A. Piccolomini, *La prima parte della filosofia naturals*, Rome: Vincenzo Valgrisi, 1551, prologue.

65 Speroni's text was originally published as part of his *Dialogi*, Venice: heirs of Aldo Manuzio, 1542; cf. the modern edn., S. Speroni, *Dialogo delle lingue*, ed. A. Sorella, Pescara: Libreria dell'Università, 1999. For Du Bellay and his reuse of Speroni, cf. the recent edn., J. Du Bellay, *La deffence et illustration de la langue françoyse*, ed. E. Buron, Neuilly: Atlande, 2007.

4

INDIVIDUALISM AND THE SEPARATION OF FIELDS OF STUDY

Jacob Burckhardt and Ercole Ricotti[1]

William Caferro

There is perhaps no book more influential to its field than Jacob Burckhardt's *Civilization of the Renaissance in Italy* (*Die Kultur der Renaissance in Italien*, 1860). No aspect of the book has received more attention than its emphasis of "individualism."[2] Burckhardt famously depicted individualism ("Individualismus") as the essence of the Renaissance in Italy. It created the "Renaissance man," whose "thirst for fame" allowed him to succeed "by talent not birth."[3] Burckhardt equated individualism with "unbridled egotism," which was characterized by self-reflection and illegitimacy.[4] The traits were most apparent in the careers of *condottieri*, mercenary soldiers, who by dint of their cunning and skill established the Renaissance state as a "work of art."[5] Felix Gilbert called Burckhardt's construct the "central and distinguishing aspect" of the Swiss historian's famous thesis.[6] Individualism allowed Burckhardt to make a sharp distinction between the Renaissance, which represented the "modern political spirit of Italy," and the Middle Ages, which "lay dreaming or half-awake beneath a common veil … woven of faith, illusion, childish prepossession."[7] Man was conscious of himself "only as a member of a race, people, party family or corporation, through some general category."[8]

Burckhardt's construct is so well known that there is no need to restate it here in full. For all its fame, however, scholars have devoted insufficient attention to its contemporary context. Historians have focused primarily on situating Burckhardt in terms of the German tradition of historical writing, examining him with respect to predecessors such as Leopold von Ranke or in terms of his hometown of Basel, and, more generally, with regard to his "conservative" political views and rejection of contemporary political trends.[9] The literature on Burckhardt is, in short, decidedly German or, more precisely, aimed at understanding Burckhardt in a German context.

Such endeavors are laudable and have produced exemplary scholarship. The aim of this chapter, however, is to examine Burckhardt (1818–1897) in an Italian context, in terms of an unlikely but equally prominent nineteenth-century Italian counterpart, Ercole Ricotti (1816–1883). Ricotti was a notable historian, who, like Burckhardt, occupied a prestigious university chair. He was similarly author of a magnum opus, *Storia delle compagnie di ventura in Italia*

(1844–1845), which shaped his field and continues to do so.[10] The book appeared a decade and a half *before* Burckhardt's *Civilization* and a year before Burckhardt's well-documented trip to Italy. It contains, like Burckhardt, an extended discussion of individualism in terms of *condottieri* and military men. But unlike Burckhardt, Ricotti's discussion of individualism has unfortunately gone unnoticed by scholars in the anglophone academy. The lacuna owes in large part to the fact that Ricotti's work, unlike Burckhardt's, was not translated into English or any other foreign language. The full range of his ideas and methodology has thus not received their proper due. Ricotti's influence has been restricted to the study of Italian Renaissance war, a field in which he has had a profound impact on Italian scholarship, influencing a whole generation of scholars, including his contemporary Giuseppe Canestrini (1807–1870), who expanded Ricotti's assertions, and Piero Pieri (1891–1979), who further contextualized them.[11] These works remain foundational to the study of the history of Renaissance Italian warfare. The most recent survey by Paolo Grillo (*Cavalieri e popoli in armi*, 2008) follows faithfully the general outlines laid out by Ricotti.

In any case, Burckhardt and Ricotti have not been studied together, nor indeed are they usually mentioned in the same sentence. The scholarship on Burckhardt and his nineteenth-century Italian counterparts is largely restricted to the effect of the Swiss scholar's work on Italian historians such as Pasquale Villari (1827–1917), who found aspects of Burckhardtian individualism in the lives of prominent Renaissance men such as Girolamo Savonarola and Niccolò Machiavelli. Like Burckhardt, Villari's work was widely read in the anglophone world and is available in English-language translation.[12] Nevertheless, if, as the modern umpire of Renaissance historiography Wallace K. Ferguson asserts, Burckhardt's "decisive contribution" was bringing together notions of individualism that were "in the air" among contemporaries into "a coherent system," it is all the more important to examine his *Civilization* in terms of Ricotti's *Storia*.[13] Indeed, careful comparison reveals two works that were overtly at odds with each other. It shows the distinctly Italian and political nature of Jacob Burckhardt's concept of individualism, his steadfast focus on *quattrocento condottieri*/individuals and concomitant lack of attention to their *trecento* forebears, who were often foreign soldiers of German origin. Indeed, Burckhardt systematically excludes the "German phase" of the development of the *condottieri* system and with it all trace of the German roots of individuality. Ricotti, conversely, places the *trecento condottieri* at the very core of his study, emphasizing their foreign roots, and specifically deals with contemporary opinions regarding the German tribal roots of individualism. Most importantly, the juxtaposition of the two works exposes the fault lines between the *Kulturgeschichte* advanced by Burckhardt and the "military history" advanced by Ricotti. The differences lay the groundwork for a startling disconnect between the study of Italian Renaissance political history on the one hand and Italian Renaissance warfare on the other. It is a disconnect that is unique to Italy and continues to hamper proper study of the place and the era.[14]

II

The importance of Ercole Ricotti and his work needs to be stressed from the outset. Ricotti was a famous figure in his lifetime. He began his professional career as a military engineer, became a professor at the University of Turin after writing his epochal *Storia delle compagnie di ventura in Italia*. He served as senator of the Italian republic, director of the Academy of Sciences in Turin and was the subject, just after his death, of a nine-chapter biography that was a species of secular hagiography tracing Ricotti life back to his childhood.[15] On the twenty-fifth anniversary of Ricotti's death, he was honored in his native town of Voghera by Ferdinando Gabòtto, a prominent scholar in his own right, who said of his forebear that "no one among the Italian historians of his age was more known for the severity of his investigations, sobriety of his form, and reflects better his era."[16]

Ricotti signals his interest in individualism at the very outset of his *Storia* in his note to the reader.[17] He then devotes a whole chapter (chapter 7) to carefully fleshing out the details. The chapter is conspicuous in that it deviates from the chronological narration of events of the previous chapters, which begin with the Lombard invasion of Italy. The temporal framework of Ricotti's discussion of individualism, however, mirrors that of Jacob Burckhardt. Like his Swiss counterpart, Ricotti prefaces his analysis with a recapitulation of the vicissitudes of the career of Frederick II Hohenstaufen (d. 1250) and the papal and Angevin rivalries in Italy, which is where Burckhardt famously starts his *Civilization* and the first subsection dedicated to "the state as a work of art." Burckhardt deals with individualism in the second part of his work.

Despite Ferdinando Gabòtto's praise for Ricotti's abilities as a writer, the Italian scholar's arguments are in fact diffuse and rhetorical, wholly lacking the elegance of Burckhardt's prose. Ricotti clutters his writing with repetitions and rhetorical appeals to his readers, along with vague invocations of "philosophers," who will later "work out further" the details of his assertions.

Ricotti's concept of individualism ("individualismo") nevertheless comes through forcefully. As in Burckhardt, it is the result of political and social disorder and the lack of stable institutions in Italy. Ricotti equates individualism with "uncertainty and confusion," which he in turn equates with an "absence of general principles" – an expression Ricotti uses often.[18] Political and social order is, Ricotti asserts, the foundation of properly ordered states, which possess properly ordered institutions. Properly ordered states set out "general principles" that guide men and incline them "to conform to one another" and dedicate themselves to the "public good (*ben pubblico*)."[19] Ordered states have laws, magistrates, religion, and, above all, good armies. Individualism arose where these institutions failed.[20]

Ricotti's individualism thus resembles Burckhardt's in that it reflects a basic spirit of the times. And like Burckhardt, Ricotti stresses widespread disorder throughout the Italian peninsula as its precondition. Ricotti carefully recounts the jealousies among Italian cities, the lack of internal justice, the triumph of faction, the absence of public authority and administrative and financial institutions, frequent changes in government, banishments, and "lack of public morals."[21] All these are familiar to readers of Burckhardt.

But Ricotti goes beyond Burckhardt and links individualism specifically to a "spirit of adventure (*spirito di ventura*)." This spirit is not only the result of the "confusion and weakness" of the state, but also the "external sign" of it.[22] Unable to find an assured place in a society, the individual was left to his own devises, which involved, above all, the need to defend himself. It inclined individuals toward "warlike associations" (*associazioni guerresche*), of which bands of mercenary soldiers, the so-called companies of adventure (*compagnie di ventura*) of the *trecento* – which forms the title of Ricotti work – were its most famous manifestation.[23] Thus for Ricotti individualism leads to associations, the details of which are then worked out in chapter 8, entitled "On the Spirit of the Adventure in the Middle Ages" ("Dello spirito di ventura nel medio evo"). The two chapters (the only ones that are conceptual rather than chronological) are intended to be read together.

Ricotti's construct is clearly distinct from that of Burckhardt. Burckhardt never uses the term "spirit of adventure" and he pointedly, and famously, distinguishes his brand of Renaissance individualism from the Middle Ages, which was "corporate" and "lay dreaming or half awake" under a veil – the opposite of individualism.[24] Ricotti, by contrast, links individualism directly to corporatism and "the spirit of association" of the Middle Ages, bringing Burckhardt's two antagonists together. Indeed, although the two historians deal temporally with the same years, Ricotti's uses the "medieval" period label, placing his individualism firmly under that rubric. Individualism led to corporatism and these coexisted in the Middle Ages. Burckhardt's corporate associations consisted of guilds, church and religious affiliations, all linked to the Middle Ages, but not to warlike associations of men at arms.[25] Ricotti does the same, but for him the most representative corporate form was the association of arms, "associazioni guerreschi," private military groups of men, who joined together for the sake of sustenance and protection.[26] Ricotti admits that the association of individualism with corporate forms may seem a contradiction, but both were indeed natural to man.[27]

Ricotti's argument has a decidedly Hegelian aspect to it. Individualism and corporatism are simultaneously opposing forces. They produce a synthesis in the form of mercenary companies that Ricotti then carefully compares to other corporate medieval forms. Meanwhile, Ricotti's medieval brand of individualism allows him to take a broad historical view. Ricotti stresses the importance in the first instance of the "barbarian invasions" of Italy, the advent of the Lombards and their role in damaging Italian institutions, producing "confusion" and with this the preconditions for both individualism and military associations to flourish.[28] Ricotti notes also the effect of the Crusades to the Holy Land in furthering the process, by dissolving the ties between subject and ruler and bringing men together for the purposes of arms.[29] An additional "passo," a further devolution of Italian society, was necessary in the *trecento* for the "era of the *compagnie di ventura*" to truly arrive.[30] This occurred with the "disappearance in Italy of citizen militias," which Ricotti dates to the year 1330, a formulation closely followed a century later by Piero Pieri, who dated the phenomenon to the battle of Altopascio in 1325.[31]

Ricotti follows with a long narrative of the vicissitudes of the *compagnie di ventura*, beginning with the Provençal adventurer Roger de Flor and his Catalan Company, which ravaged Sicily and Byzantium in the early fourteenth century. He follows with a detailed account of a succession of "associations of men in arms," including the great German companies of the middle and late *trecento* and a series of English and Hungarian counterparts. Ricotti pays particular attention to the German mercenaries, whose involvement in Italy was, owing to the imperial rights of the Holy Roman Emperors in Italy, long-standing. They provided him with an apposite historical precedent for modern-day Germanic oppressors of Italy in Ricotti's lifetime.

Ricotti pointedly addresses a "prevailing belief" that Italian individualism may have derived from a "German constitution" or a pre-existing German tribal "seed of liberty" and spirit of freedom, basic to the German race and first "transplanted" to Italy by the barbarians when they conquered the peninsula. Ricotti is vague here and claims to draw upon (in an ironic paraphrase of Ferguson's statement regarding Burckhardt many years later) an extant belief that is "in the air," articulated by "moderns" – presumably current scholars who share this view. Ricotti then outlines what American medievalists would call "the Teutonic germ theory," first popularized, as Patrick Geary notes, by Herbert Baxter Adams in his famous historical seminars at Johns Hopkins in the nineteenth century.[32] It portrays the "German constitution" and elective nature of tribal political structures as a distant root of American democracy. Ricotti addresses the germ theory with reluctance, expressing the opinion that it was a necessity to make room for his own view. Ricotti ultimately dismisses native German "liberty" as the first cause of individualism in Italy and argues instead for the primacy of the devolution of Italian society that was "rotta e scoinvolta" prior to the arrival of Germans. This was the true precondition for individualism.[33] It emerged because the "social order was weak." Italy had itself to blame. But, Ricotti adds, individualism can be found anywhere a society is torn asunder, including beyond Europe, with "the Tartar of the bog and the Arab of the desert." The non-European case is curiously reminiscent of Burkhardt's own example in his discussion of individualism, in which he claims that Renaissance man became a "spiritual individual and recognized himself as such. In the same way … that the Arab had felt himself an individual at a time when other Asiatics knew themselves only as a member of a race."[34]

Ricotti does not deny the reality of a "German constitution" or that there was a distinct brand of German individualism. Indeed, it is, ironically, in arguing this point that Ricotti most resembles Burckhardt. Here Ricotti places great emphasis on Italy's unique political fragmentation, the jealousies among cities, the lack of internal justice, the triumph of faction, the absence of public authority and administrative and financial institutions, frequent changes in government, banishments, and lack of public morals.[35] In short he invokes the same features as Burckhardt. Ricotti adds to his portrait the insecurity of Italian trade and transport and a lack of public hygiene.

It was in any case these "extreme circumstances" that, according to Ricotti, unleashed "un vastissimo campo" of individualism in Italy.[36] Ricotti provides four "precocious examples" of Italian individualism. Each represent men who "by themselves demonstrate the presence of the spirit of adventure that agitated individuals in Italy."[37] They are Marco Polo (1254–1324), Castruccio Castracane (1281–1328), Buonaccorso Pitti (1354–1422), and Filippo Scolari (i.e., Pippo Spano, 1369–1426). Ricotti describes them as "vagabonds and exiles," whose spirit of adventure led them ultimately to associate themselves with others for the purposes of war. Castruccio Castracane led mercenary armies that allowed him to take much of Tuscany; Pitti, a Florentine merchant and traveler, hired himself out as a mercenary soldier in the Hundred Years War; and Pippo Spano, another Florentine, served as mercenary for most of his career in Hungary. Marco Polo's connection to war is somewhat more obscure. Ricotti relates the story of how Polo fought in war for Venice and was taken prisoner, but he stresses that Polo learned, during his voyage among the "Tartars," how to make siege weapons.

Ricotti's age of the "companies of adventure" then arrived, when Italian society devolved further with "disappearance in Italy of citizen militias."[38] The companies dominated Italy for much of the next two centuries before giving way to the Italian *condottieri*, who had been taking over the states they served. Ricotti relays every detail and connects Italy's unfortunate past to present-day Italian military developments. The developments paved the way for the invasion of Italy by the French armies of Charles VIII at the end of the century. Italy became the theater for the Habsburg–Valois wars.

The construct follows closely that of Niccolò Machiavelli (1469–1527), who in several works, most notably *The Prince*, pointed to military decadence and the internecine struggles of Italian states as the cause of the unfortunate state of contemporary affairs throughout the peninsula.[39] Italian states, like ancient Rome, gave over their armies to foreign mercenaries, eschewing native citizens in the process. Political and moral weakness led, as in Rome, to subjugation by foreign powers. For Machiavelli the "sinews of war" were not money, contrary to "vulgar contemporary opinion" (chapter 10, *The Prince*), but a well-ordered native infantry, which had been responsible for Rome's greatness. This was utterly lacking in Machiavelli's day.

III

The nationalist element is writ large in Ricotti, and in this regard the contrast to Burckhardt could not be sharper. As in Machiavelli, foreigners took advantage of the confusion in Italy to oppress the peninsula. The Germans were a precocious example of this and one that continued into Ricotti's own day, making the era of the companies an apposite historical antecedent for the *Risorgimento* that was occurring in Ricotti's lifetime. Ricotti was actively involved in the *Risorgimento*. He fought for Italy against Austria in the First Italian War of Independence (1848–1849) and was member of the Italian Senate. Ricotti does not disguise his nationalism in his *Storia*. Indeed, he dedicates the book to King Carlo Alberto of Piedmont-Sardinia and tells the reader at the very outset that he seeks explicitly to serve his *patria* through his writing.[40] He wished to show how Italy had been continually victimized by foreigners and how "nostra oppresione" could best be understood by examining "the wars of the past," to find the reasons for the present circumstances.[41]

It is important to stress Ricotti's influence in this regard. Subsequent military historians – whether or not they shared Ricotti's nationalist views – have followed him closely in treating the companies of adventure as a distinct and critical phase of Italian military development, which underscored the decay of Italian military prowess and the political disunity on the peninsula. Ricotti's schema appears in the work of Giuseppe Canestrini, Piero Pieri, and the English scholar Michael Mallett. Pieri equated the decline of Italian "native militia" with the rise of the companies of adventure and traced the "tramonto" of the former to a more specific event, the battle of Altopascio in 1325.[42] In his *La crisi militare italiana* (1934), later revised as *Il Rinascimento e la crisi militare Italiana, 1494–1530* (1954), Pieri de-emphasized the "moral" dimension of Italy's military decline and stressed instead the social and political weaknesses that left Italy susceptible to foreign conquest. In *Mercenaries and Their Masters* (1974) Michael Mallett revised Ricotti's timeline, tracing the use of mercenaries by Italian states more surely to the communal period.[43] But he accepted Ricotti's depiction of the advent of companies of adventure in the *trecento* as a key phase in the devolution of Italian military organization. Mallett devoted a whole chapter to the subject and followed it, like Ricotti, with a discussion of the rise of the individual Italian *condottieri*.[44] Paolo Grillo's recent *Cavalieri e popoli in armi* (2008) follows closely Ricotti in depicting a favorable (with greater detail) communal period, succeeded by "crisi" and the emergence of "companies of adventure" in the *trecento*. Grillo then outlines the development of the "mercenary system" in the fifteenth century, the emergence of more powerful *condottieri*/tyrants, leading to the invasion and subjugation of Italy. Maria Nadia Covini's insightful recent essay on Italian warfare from 1300 to 1600 follows the same outline. She calls the *trecento* and advent of the foreign companies the "low point" in Italian military organization.[45]

The contrast with Burckhardt could not be sharper. The Swiss historian's political ideology has been the subject of much scholarly discussion. Lionel Gossman stresses Burckhardt's right-wing affinities; Richard Sigurdson prefers to call him a liberal conservative.[46] All agree that Burkhardt turned away from national movements and Sigurdson notes the frequent use of the term "unzeitgemäss" ("untimely") to describe Burckhardt's relationship with the events of his day.[47] The modernity Burckhardt equates with the Renaissance in his *Civilization* is starkly unflattering. The "modern political spirit" of the period has a "vicious nature."[48]

But distinguishing between the two authors solely according to their contemporary political attitudes is too simple. In both the *Storia* and *Civilization*, individualism arises from the same preconditions and at the same time, even if the scholars use different period labels. Both emphasize Italian political disintegration and both trace individualism to the *trecento*. It is here, as Burckhardt famously asserts, that we find men whose "thirst for fame and talent for monumental works" allowed them to succeed "by talent not birth."[49] For both Ricotti and Burckhardt, the historical past informed the present day, making the importance of their studies manifest.

Close examination of Burckhardt's depiction of the fourteenth century makes clear more subtle and fundamental distinctions with Ricotti. Burckhardt makes no mention of Ricotti's transitional figures, "the adventurers/individuals" such as Marco Polo, Buonacorso Pitti, or Pippo Spano. Burckhardt's *trecento* is filled instead with "tyrannies, great and small" and with illegitimate political leaders whose "misdeeds," Burckhardt tells us, have only been "circumstantially told" by historians.[50] Burckhardt focuses on these men and their involvement in politics: individualism told in terms of the "state" rather than war. Burckhardt links the further development of the state in the *quattrocento* directly to the development of the mercenary system, both of which, he says, became "altered in character."[51] The *condottiere* now founded "independent dynasties of their own." Petty despots entered the service of larger states, furthering still more the effect of individualism by creating a "system" founded on illegitimacy. The men acted with "greater calculation"; and the *condottiere* was the "highest and most admired form of illegitimacy."[52]

But what is so unusual in Burckhardt – and has gone curiously unnoticed by scholars – is the degree to which he ignored a whole phase in the history of Italian war and the mercenary system that is so central to his work. Burckhardt says nothing about the "companies of adventure" of the *trecento* that stood as precursors to the "calculating" and "illegitimate" Italian *condottiere* of the fifteenth century. Burckhardt's *trecento* examples are indeed entirely removed from the battlefield and their military context. And Burckhardt pointedly chooses examples that are all Italian. The *dramatis personae* of Burkhardt's *trecento* include Doge Agnello, the "upstart" ruler of Pisa, who reclined on rich draperies and showed himself "at the window of his house" as if a "relic"; Can Grande della Scala of Verona, who was the apotheosis of the ruler whose "thirst for fame" made him surround himself with poets; and the Visconti of Milan, who were "the most complete and instructive type of fourteenth-century tyranny" resembling "the worst of the Roman emperors."

Notably absent from Burckhardt's list is Castruccio Castracane, lord of Lucca and Ghibelline soldier, who stood supreme in Tuscany for a time and whose military prowess led Machiavelli to write a biography of him. Ricotti depicts Castruccio as a key figure in the evolution of the companies of adventure, as one of the first Italian rulers to rely on large numbers of German mercenary soldiers in his armies. Ricotti introduces us to Castruccio in his chapter on individualism as an "exile, merchant and lord of Tuscany," and later relays his success as a general, using German mercenaries to fight hegemonic wars.[53] Burckhardt, by contrast, mentions Castruccio Castracane only in passing, and not as part of his discussion of the *trecento*. Castruccio appears much later, described by Burckhardt as "a fancy picture of a typical despot."[54] Burckhardt mentions Machiavelli's biography of Castruccio, but says nothing of the military campaigns that made the tyrant famous and brought German mercenaries to Italy.

The differences between the two scholars are evident also in their treatment of Can Grande della Scala of Verona. Ricotti carefully narrates the details of the career of Can Grande, Dante's famous patron, immediately after speaking about Castruccio. The discussion is long and stresses how Can Grande furthered the use of companies of foreign mercenaries in Italy by means of his frequent wars and his preference for employing Germans in his armies.[55] Burckhardt's Can Grande has nothing to do with war or with mercenaries. He is portrayed as a despot, whose desire for fame expressed itself in a "passion for monumental works." Burckhardt's Can Grande kept "poets and illustrious exiles" at his famous court, men who conferred a "new legitimacy" on him.[56] Burckhardt then quotes in this context Petrarch, who was *not* in fact one of the poets or exiles who visited Can Grande's court, but who did indeed know his way around such courts from his later experiences. Burckhardt cites Petrarch as imploring lords like Can Grande to be "father to their subjects" and "love them like children."[57]

The example underscores the very careful rendering of Renaissance history by Burckhardt. By evoking Petrarch in his discussion of Can Grande, Burckhardt temporally sets him apart from Ricotti's warlike Can Grande, patron of Dante, who fought wars and employed bands of foreign mercenaries. Burckhardt treats Can Grande in a steadfastly political context, highlighted by Petrarch's wholly anachronistic remark on the proper mode of governing.

Finally, we may look closely at the figure of Ezzolino da Romano, son-in-law of the Holy Roman Emperor, Frederick II. Ezzolino appears prominently in both Ricotti, and Burckhardt. For Burckhardt, he is a transitional figure, exemplar of the "usurper," who established himself on the "throne" by "wholesale murder," an act that "once set was not forgotten."[58] For Ricotti Ezzolino is also a transitional figure, subject of a lengthy and detailed narrative,[59] which outlines his usurpation, but stresses also his use of "mercenarie stranieri" to aid him.[60] Ricotti emphasized Ezzolino's German aspect, as well as that of his family, the da Romano clan. Burckhardt treats Ezzolino as merely a precocious example of political illegitimacy in Italy.

IV

Overall, Burckhardt uses few historical examples from the *trecento*. And when speaking of the period, Burckhardt pointedly tells his readers that he will *not* provide a narrative of events. He claims that the despots of the era present us with "higher interest than mere narration."[61] The statement, which may otherwise be attributed to stylistic considerations, is more meaningful when judged in terms of Ricotti. Ricotti offers a singularly detailed narrative of the *trecento*, providing an abundance of examples. And like Burckhardt, Ricotti pointedly addresses the issue of narrative. He argues forcefully (contra Burckhardt) for its utility. He says that a chronological rendering of facts was absolutely "essential to historical certitude" (*la verità storiche*) and that without such "invincible evidence," proper reasoning is impossible.[62]

The contrast between the two authors could not be more plain. The men seem in fact to be in direct conversation with each other on the issue. Protestations notwithstanding, Burckhardt does indeed pick up a narrative in his next section on *quattrocento* despots. He speaks of the "altered character" of Italian *quattrocento* despotism, which occurred on a grander scale than in the preceding century. Burckhardt singles out as a transitional figure, the English mercenary John Hawkwood, who was, at the end of the *trecento*, given land by his employer (the Pope) in return for military service. In this way, Hawkwood served as a precursor to the "age of the Italian *condottieri*," which began with Alberigo da Barbiano and was characterized by men who obtained whole lordships "without usurpation" – the start of the political dimension of the *condottieri*. This first "Bacchanalian outbreak of military ambition," as Burckhardt called it, occurred at the same time as the disappearance, in Ricotti's more detailed rendering, of German mercenaries in Italy. To more firmly establish his thesis, Burckhardt then gives a long list of *quattrocento* Italian *condottieri*, whose "art" made states. He presents Francesco Sforza of Milan as the apotheosis of this skillful/ruthless type of ruler.[63]

It is in their accounts of *quattrocento* Italy that Burckhardt and Ricotti converge most closely. The phase was for both authors an Italian one and both men cover much of the same material and use the same examples. Ricotti likewise emphasizes the importance of Francesco Sforza, whom he similarly depicts as the embodiment of the skilled/ruthless *condottiere* turned political leader.[64]

But the distinctions are again telling. Ricotti uses the examples of the English *condottiere* John Hawkwood and the German *condottiere* Lutz von Landau to segue from discussion of the *trecento* to the *quattrocento*. Both men were transitional figures, who received land in return for their service, leading a distinctly Italian tradition of *condottieri*, who became involved in local politics. Burckhardt points out the very same transition. But he mentions only the Englishman John Hawkwood and leaves out the German Lutz von Landau. Lutz thus shares the same "silent" fate as the companies of adventure, which were filled with Lutz's German countrymen and who preceded him to Italy and play such a prominent role in Ricotti's work. In Burckhardt there is only an Englishman, and indeed Hawkwood is among the only foreign *condottieri* mentioned by Burckhardt, who has no place for the many Hungarians, Catalans, and others working on the peninsula.

Whether Burckhardt read Ricotti's work and was intentionally silent is unknown. Ricotti was a prominent professor by the time the Swiss scholar wrote his *Civilization*. It seems unlikely that Burckhardt was not aware of Ricotti. Nevertheless, our close examination of Ricotti in terms of Burckhardt suggests the substantial effort the Swiss historian made in order to cast his *Civilization* and *condottieri* in a wholly Italian context. This involved ignoring a different extant paradigm in which German antecedents played an important role, which, in turn, meant avoiding a good part of Italy's military history and a key stage of the development of the *condottieri* system that Burckhardt put so much faith in and that was already well known to contemporary scholars. Burckhardt makes clear that "individualism" existed only in Italy. He admits that one could perhaps detect "here and there" elements of a "development of free personality" outside of Italy. But Burckhardt asserts that such developments did not occur in Northern Europe and that individualism could not in any case reveal itself outside of the peninsula as it did inside. Where Ricotti attributes the involvement of German mercenaries in Italy also to the frequent incursions into Italy of Holy Roman Emperors, Burckhardt describes the descent of German emperors into Italy as "farce" and emphasizes in this regard only their ability to bestow legitimacy on pretenders to Italian rule.

Burckhardt specific discussion of a "mercenary system" is restricted to the subsection in part one dedicated to "war as a work of art." Burckhardt identifies Italy as "the first country to adopt the system of mercenary troops, which demanded a wholly different organization."[65] Elsewhere in Europe nobles directly participated in war and thus hindered military innovation. Rather than explain the distinct Italian organization, Burckhardt discusses how the introduction of firearms made war a "more democratic pursuit" and how the engineer/artillerist, a man not belonging to the noble class, played an important role in warfare.

Burckhardt says that firearms damaged the "value of the individual, which had been the soul of the small and admirably organized bands of mercenaries." The term "bands" is used here in different sense than Ricotti, referring not to "companies of adventure" but groups of men in the service of Italian cities. Burckhardt describes the hostility of the *condottieri* to firearms, but notes that the innovation was accepted in Italy and Italians became teachers of military arts to all Europe.[66] Thus the mercenary system played a role in creating what Burckhardt calls a "comprehensive science and art of military affairs," making Italian war more "rational" than elsewhere.[67]

Once again the two authors are pointedly at odds with each other. Ricotti, seemingly anticipating Burckhardt's arguments, tells us in his introduction that there are two possible ways to do examine Italian warfare. It may be done from the point of view of war as "an art" and as an "institution."[68] Ricotti asserts that war as an "art" is a "sterile" topic, particularly with regard to understanding the modern world.[69] War treated as an "institution" offered far more. It allowed scholars to see how "the story of the military is the story of the nation."[70] This alone made war worthy of serious scholarly consideration.

Burckhardt takes precisely the path that Ricotti discards. It is a path that facilitates ignoring the whole national dimension outlined by Ricotti and with it much of Italian Renaissance military history. Ricotti's "war as institution" theme leads him to individualism. Burckhardt's "war as art" reflects his brand of individualism.

V

In any case, the different approaches of the scholars has had important consequences for the study of Renaissance Italian warfare and the Renaissance more generally. Burckhardt's conceptual style and steadfastly political depiction of the *condottieri* has encouraged much of the subsequent scholarship on the Renaissance to proceed forward without proper consideration of warfare. Scholars following the Burckhardtian tradition have investigated the calculating spirit of individualism and transcendent issues of Renaissance identity and personhood. Meanwhile, Ricotti's devolutionary "stage" model of Italian warfare has relegated the subject to its own subfield, largely disconnected from the broader discourse on Renaissance Italy. Current histories of Italian war, as we have seen, continue to tell the story of a decadent Renaissance period positioned against a heroic medieval communal period. Where there has been revision, it has occurred largely in terms of Ricotti and the nineteenth-century construct of war. When Michael Mallett argued for the stirrings of a standing army in fifteenth-century Venice – hoping to bring Italian scholarship and military developments more in line with those elsewhere in Europe – he did so using evidence of longer-term contracts for service (*condotte*) of mercenaries, a notion already sketched out by Canestrini in his essay of 1851.[71] Recent research has shown, however, that the length of *condotte* and the length of actual service of soldiers were not one and the same.[72]

The entrenched narrative has limited understanding of the realities of Renaissance warfare. It hides points of continuity with the medieval past and similarities in military practice over the decades and even centuries. It masks disconcerting evidence that foreign mercenaries were often faithful soldiers, integrated into the communities they served, and that Italian "national" sentiment regarding Germans (notwithstanding Petrarch's *Italia Mia*) is not easily found in contemporary sources. Most important, the discourse has obscured the coincidence between the military and pacific activities of states, for which there was no clear line of distinction.[73]

Ricotti and Burckhardt may thus be said to represent two distinct "sides" of Machiavelli. Ricotti reflects the national implications of Machiavelli and his treatment of mercenaries as a symptom of the loss of native martial spirit and a prelude to the subjugation of the peninsula by foreigners. Burckhardt reflects the political/psychological side of Machiavelli and his treatment of the mercenary/prince as a political ruler, whose behavior was conditioned by the contrasting forces of *virtù* and *fortuna*. In any case, a true history of Renaissance Italian warfare remains to be written, one that is wholly independent of the nineteenth-century nationalist model that held the field for so long. It is striking how little the two sides have been integrated.

Notes

1 Earlier versions of this chapter were prepared for the conference on the Nineteenth Century Revival of Interest in the Trecento in Venice in 2013 and the conference on Trauma at Trieste in 2015. I thank Giacomo Todeschini, John Law, Anthony Molho, and Sam Cohn for their advice and support. A copy of the Trieste paper, "The Nineteenth Century Memory of Renaissance Italian Warfare: Ercole Ricotti and Jacob Burckhardt," is available at: www.provincia.trieste.it/opencms/…trieste/it/…/CAFERRO.pdf.

2 Jacob Burckhardt, *The Civilization of the Renaissance in Italy*, trans. S. G. C. Middlemore (New York: Modern Library, 2002).

3 *Ibid.*, p. 7.

4 *Ibid.*, p. 4.

5 *Ibid.* (section one, "War as a Work of Art"), pp. 3–90, especially pp. 70–2.

6 Felix Gilbert, *History of Politics or Culture: Reflections on Ranke or Burckhardt* (Princeton, NJ: Princeton University Press, 1990), p. 58.

7 Burckhardt, *The Civilization of the Renaissance in Italy*, pp. 4, 93.

8 *Ibid.*, p. 93.

9 Georg Iggers, *The German Conception of History: The National Tradition of Historical Thought from Herder to the Present* (Middletown, CT: Wesleyan University Press, 1968); Gilbert, *History of Politics or Culture*; Lionel Gossman, *Basel in the Age of Burckhardt: A Study in Unseasonable Ideas* (Chicago: University of Chicago Press, 2000). See also John R. Hinde, *Jacob Burckhardt and the Crisis of Modernity* (Montreal: McGill-Queen's University Press, 2000); Richard Sigurdson, *Jacob Burckhardt's Social and Political Thought* (Toronto: Toronto University Press, 2004).

10 Ercole Ricotti, *Storia delle compagnie di ventura in Italia*, 2 vols. (Turin: Giuseppe Pomba, 1844–1845).

11 Giuseppe Canestrini's long article, published in 1851, remains, along with Ricotti, the standard treatment of Italian military organization. Giuseppe Canestrini, "Documenti per servire alla storia della milizia italiana dal XIII secolo al XVI," *Archivio Storico Italiano*, 16 [1851]. Piero Pieri, who fought in World War I, wrote his classic on Renaissance Italian war, *La crisi militare italiana nel Rinascimento nelle sue relazioni con la crisi politica ed economica* in 1934, which was later revised as *Il Rinascimento e la Crisi militare Italiana, 1494–1530* (Turin: Einaudi 1954). Pieri also wrote about Machiavelli and the *Risorgimento*. See Piero Pieri, *Machiavelli e la politica del suo tempo* (Turin: Gheroni, 1953); *Storia militare del Risorgimento. Guerre e insurrezioni* (Turin: Einaudi, 1962).

12 Pasquale Villari, *The Life and Times of Girolamo Savonarola* (London: T. F. Unwin, 1899) and *The Life and Times of Niccolo Machiavelli* (London: T. F. Unwin, 1892). See Wallace K. Ferguson, *The Renaissance in Historical Thought* (Boston: Houghton Mifflin, 1948) p. 209. A fuller discussion of the historiography is in William Caferro, *Contesting the Renaissance* (Malden, MA: Wiley-Blackwell, 2011), pp. 3–7, 33.

13 Ferguson, *The Renaissance in Historical Thought*, p. 190.

14 War, armies, and state formation is a staple of study of Europe more generally at this time. See, among others, J. Russell Major, *Representative Institutions in Renaissance France, 1421–1559* (Madison: University of Wisconsin Press, 1960) and *From Renaissance Monarchy to Absolute Monarchy: French Kings, Nobles, and Estates* (Baltimore: Johns Hopkins University Press, 1994); Perry Anderson, *Lineages of the Absolute State* (London: New Left Books, 1974) and most provocatively, Charles Tilly, *Coercion, Capital and European States, A.D. 990–1992* (Cambridge, MA and Oxford: Blackwell, 1992).

15 Ermanno Ferrero, *Della vita e degli scritti di Ercole Ricotti* (Turin: Ermanno Loescher, 1888), pp. 149, 159–60. Ricotti wrote an autobiographical work published in 1886. *Ricordi di Ercole Ricotti*, ed. Antonio Manni (Turin, Naples: Roux e Favale, 1886).

16 *Commemorando Ercole Ricotti in Voghera, discorso di Ferdinando Gabotto* (Voghera, 1908), p. 5.

17 Ricotti, *Storia delle compagnie di ventura in Italia*, vol. 1, pp. xxi, xxii.

18 "mancanza di principii generali," Ricotti, *Storia delle compagnie di ventura in Italia*, vol. 1, p. 226.

19 *Ibid.*, p. 225.

20 *Ibid.*, pp. xxii, 228.

21 *Ibid.*, pp. 237–40.

22 Ricotti leaves it "to philosophers" to investigate the "origins and essence" of this spirit. *Ibid.*, p. 228 – stated also on p. xxii.

23 *Ibid.*, pp. 228, 256, 274.

24 Burckhardt, *The Civilization of the Renaissance in Italy*, p. 93 (part two, "The Development of the Individual").

25 Ricotti, *Storia delle compagnie di ventura in Italia*, vol. 1, p. 272.

26 *Ibid.*, pp. 256, 274.

27 *Ibid.*, p. 228.

28 *Ibid.*, pp. 229, 230–6.

29 *Ibid.*, pp. 261–2; Ricotti includes the crusades within Europe and Italy, pp. 263–4.

30 *Ibid.*, p. 266.

31 *Ibid.*, p. 265.

32 Patrick J. Geary, "Medieval Germany in America," *German Historical Institute*, Washington DC Annual Lecture Series 8 (1996), pp. 21–2. Online at www.ghidc.org/fileadmin/user_upload/GHI.../Medieval_Germany_in_America.pdf. See also Paul Freedman and Gabrielle M. Spiegel, "Medievalisms Old and New," *American Historical Review* 103 (1998), pp. 680–1; Robin Fleming, "Picturesque History and the Medieval in Nineteenth-Century America," *American Historical Review* 100 (October 1995), pp. 1061–94.

33 Ricotti, *Storia delle compagnie di ventura in Italia*, vol. 1, p. 230.

34 *Ibid.*, pp. 230–1. Burckhardt, *The Civilization of the Renaissance in Italy*, p. 93.

35 Ricotti, *Storia delle compagnie di ventura in Italia*, vol. 1, pp. 237–40.

36 *Ibid.*, pp. 103, 255.

37 *Ibid.*, p. 256.

38 *Ibid.*, pp. 265–6.

39 See *The Prince* (Books 12, 13), *The Art of War* (Book 1), and *The Discourses* (Book 2, discourse 20). Niccolò Machiavelli, *The Prince*, trans. and ed. David Wooten (Indianapolis: Hackett, 1995), pp. 38–45; *The Discourses*, trans. Leslie J. Walker, ed. Bernard Crick (New York: Penguin, 1970), pp. 339–41; *The Art of War*, trans. and ed. Christopher Lynch (Chicago: University of Chicago Press, 2003), pp. 13–32.

40 Ricotti, *Storia delle compagnie di ventura in Italia*, vol. 1, pp. ix–xxxii.

41 *Ibid.*, pp. xi, xiv.

42 Piero Pieri, "Alcune questioni sopra la fanterie in Italia nel periodo comunale," *Rivista storica italiana* 50 (1933), pp. 607–8.

43 Michael Mallett, *Mercenaries and Their Masters* (Totowa, NJ: Rowman and Littlefield, 1974), p. 13. Scholars have mostly reinterpreted the communal period. Daniel Waley, "The Army of the Florentine Republic from the Twelfth to the Fourteenth Century," in *Florentine Studies*, ed. Nicolai Rubinstein (Evanston: Northwestern University Press, 1968); A. A. Settia, *Communi in guerra: Armi ed eserciti nell'Italia delle citta* (Bologna: CLUEB, 1993); Jean-Claude Maire Vigueur, *Cavaliers et citoyens: Guerre et société dans l'Italie communale, XIIe–XIIIe siècles* (Paris: Éditions de l'École des Hautes Études en Sciences Sociales, 2003).

44 Mallett devoted his chapter 2 (on the era of the companies) to the companies of adventure. Mallett, *Mercenaries*, pp. 25–50.

45 Maria Nadia Covini, "Political and Military Bonds in the Italian State System, Thirteenth to Sixteenth Century," in *War and Competition between States*, ed. Philippe Contamine (Oxford: Oxford University Press, 2000), p. 14.

46 Gossman, *Basel in the Age of Burckhardt*, p. 97; Sigurdson, *Jacob Burckhardt's Social and Political Thought*, p. 7.

47 Sigurdson, *Jacob Burckhardt's Social and Political Thought*, p. 7.
48 Burckhardt, *The Civilization of the Renaissance in Italy*, p. 4.
49 *Ibid.*, p. 102.
50 *Ibid.*, p. 7.
51 *Ibid.*, p. 12.
52 *Ibid.*, p. 16.
53 Ricotti, *Storia delle compagnie di ventura in Italia*, vol. 2, pp. 12–16.
54 Burckhardt, *The Civilization of the Renaissance in Italy*, p. 67.
55 Ricotti, *Storia delle compagnie di ventura in Italia*, vol. 2, pp. 16–28.
56 Burckhardt, *The Civilization of the Renaissance in Italy*, pp. 7–8.
57 *Ibid.*, p. 8.
58 *Ibid.*, p. 6.
59 *Ibid.*, pp. 177–92.
60 Ricotti, *Storia delle compagnie di ventura in Italia*, vol. 2, p. 192.
61 Burckhardt *The Civilization of the Renaissance in Italy*, p. 7.
62 Ricotti, *Storia delle compagnie di ventura in Italia*, vol. 1, p. xvii.
63 Burckhardt, *The Civilization of the Renaissance in Italy*, p. 33.
64 Ricotti, *Storia delle compagnie di ventura in Italia*, vol. 2, p. 155.
65 Burckhardt, *The Civilization of the Renaissance in Italy*, p. 70.
66 *Ibid.*
67 *Ibid.*, p. 80.
68 "Dal lato dell'arte o dal lato del istituzioni," Ricotti, *Storia delle compagnie di ventura in Italia*, vol. 1, p. xx.
69 *Ibid.*
70 *Ibid.*
71 Michael Mallett, "Venice and Its Condottieri, 1404–1454," in *Renaissance Venice*, ed. John Hale (London: Faber and Faber, 1973), p. 139. On developments in Milan, see Maria Nadia Covini, *L'esercito del duca: Organizzazione militare e istituzioni al tempo degli Sforza* (Rome: Istituto Storico Italiano per il Medio Evo, 1998).
72 William Caferro, "Continuity, Long-Term Service and Permanent Forces: A Reassessment of the Florentine Army in the Fourteenth Century," *Journal of Modern History* 80 (2008), pp. 219–51.
73 See William Caferro, "Travel, Economy, and Identity: A Reassessment of the Mercenary System in in Fourteenth-Century Italy," in *From Florence to the Mediterranean and Beyond*, ed. D. Ramada Curto, E. R. Dursteler, J. Kirshner, and F. Trivellato (Florence: Olschki, 2009), pp. 363–80, and "Warfare and Economy in Renaissance Italy, 1350–1450," *Journal of Interdisciplinary History* 39 (2008), pp. 167–209.

5

RIDDLES OF RENAISSANCE
PHILOSOPHY AND HUMANISM[1]

Timothy Kircher

> And thought's the slave of life, and life time's fool,
> And time, that takes survey of all the world,
> Must have a stop.
>
> Shakespeare, *Henry IV part 1*

What makes up Renaissance philosophy? How is it expressed in humanist discourse? These are the guiding questions of this inquiry. One of the central riddles of this philosophy is the exchange between Renaissance humanists and modern scholars, whose vocabularies do not align and therefore demand translation and interpretation. While scholars have presented diverse viewpoints on the ways of humanist philosophy, we may appreciate them as two, often conflicting conceptions. James Hankins, Robert Black, and others have followed the lead of Ernst Cassirer and Paul Oskar Kristeller, who assessed the humanist philosophical contribution according to its systematic exposition of the fields of epistemology, ethics, and ontology or metaphysics.[2] By this measure, they have found humanists philosophically bereft. Humanists were overtly fond of rhetorical eloquence, too subjective and digressive in their writings, and unbendingly devoted to the study of classical literature. Those Renaissance authors who explicitly discuss matters of metaphysics, such as Nicholas of Cusa or Marsilio Ficino, are heralded as philosophers rather than humanists, even though they shared with humanist colleagues common ideas, books, and literary genres. For these scholars, the philosophical domain that humanists traversed was in moral philosophy, though here, too, humanists seem to wander in the pathways of earlier thinkers and seldom record anything original or profound. Renaissance humanism investigated, by this reading, a world separate from that of epistemology and metaphysics, although their orbits may occasionally intersect with one another.

Another group of scholars has sought to crown humanists with brighter philosophical laurels. Eugenio Garin, Ernesto Grassi, and more recently Nancy Struever, Christopher Celenza, and Lodi Nauta, among others, have valued the situational, unsystematic features of humanist works as part and parcel of their philosophizing; these works often speak to an historical and experiential understanding of the human condition, in which their philology and rhetoric show how humanity negotiates the meaning of things for itself, in a specific context. Humanity, according to Garin, "discovered itself [in the Renaissance] as the maker of itself and its world."[3] And yet, in the eyes of their skeptics, humanist writings still lack philosophical precision. Heidegger and Wittgenstein may have overturned systematic philosophy and metaphysics, but this occurred within the philosophical tradition and in a rigorous way. Those scholars exploring humanism's rhetorical and philological orientation, while underlining its anti-metaphysical qualities, also need to bridge the gap, and realize the exchange, between the history of ideas and history of philosophy, an exchange that also embraces the history of literature.

Until this division is dissolved, each side in the debate over humanism's role in the history of philosophy can deny the historicism of the other. The skeptics can claim that their view of both humanism and philosophy is sounder and more respectful of disciplinary distinctions that help chart historical developments; their opponents can assert that these disciplines themselves possess no *a priori* or trans-historical value, but rather have acquired modern meanings that do not easily square with humanist activities and ideas. If humanists wrote Lucianic satires of the philosophical tradition, does that make them unphilosophical?

To take on this conundrum, in all its postmodern resonance, we begin our inquiry not simply with examining concepts, but also by weighing images. For the most fruitful exchanges in humanist philosophizing occurred across the disciplines that the humanists celebrated: rhetoric, history, philosophy, grammar, and poetry. Francis Bacon, at the close of our period, wrote "poesis doctrinae tanquam somnium": "poetry is like a dream of philosophic love."[4] At this same moment, Shakespeare's Hotspur expires with the words, "Time must have a stop." *Stop* with its closed consonant has many connotations, not least that of a hold or stay, however fleeting or foolhardy one's grasp may be. Enchanted by rhetoric and poetry, humanists strove to mark the stop of time with language, whereby they resorted as much to imagery as to concepts.

The humanist imagination could therefore be simultaneously artistic and philosophical, just as Renaissance artists configured the love of wisdom in their creations. Andrea Pisano created figurations of this desire as Dialectic for the Florentine bell-tower as did Agostino di Duccio, when decorating the Franciscan church in Rimini in line with the ideas of Guarino Guarini.[5] Michelangelo expressed the humanist philosophizing most profoundly in his New Sacristy at San Lorenzo (Illustration 5.1). In marking the passing of the Medici princes, the Sacristy added mystery to the dimensions of time and space. This mystery achieves personification in the seven statues: the two Medici dukes, the four deities, and the Virgin and Child. The meaning of each of these elements is illuminated by their exchanges with the others. Duke Giuliano expresses the active life, and his sculpture faces the more contemplative Lorenzo. The deities Night and Day, female and male, recline under Giuliano, and correspond to Dawn and Dusk at the feet of Lorenzo. The female figures, Night and Dawn, are highly polished, with upraised arms, in contrast to the rougher, unfinished Day and Dusk. Night's pose is appropriately closed, while Day's lies open. Under the bent leg of Night stands an owl, whose features are reflected in the face of Day. Presenting most plainly these figures' puzzles of meaning is the mask under her left arm.

These sculptures have been viewed through a Neoplatonic lens, with the exchanges among them conveying the flow of time that is surmounted only by a turning toward the heavens and divinity.[6] Here, as in humanism, classicism meets Christianity. The Dukes, dressed in Roman garb, are turned toward the Virgin, and the visitor is constrained, by the confines of the space, to look upward above the linear pilasters and cornices toward the circular dome and its symbolic eternity. The abiding impression, however, is one of movement. The deities recline but do not rest. Night wears the crescent moon in her hair, which has waves like the

Illustration 5.1 Michelangelo, Tomb of Giuliano de' Medici, 1524–34, the New Sacristy, San Lorenzo, Florence.
Source: © Tim Kircher

sea. The alternating figurations – sleeping and waking, male and female, in various stages of polish – heighten the mystery of the masking. Are they celebrating life, or recognizing death? Heralding wisdom, or brooding over folly? What is the acuity of time-bound insight, so that it might discern truth among passing phenomena? Does the owl of wisdom only appear at night, and in the company of masks and personifications?

Like Michelangelo, humanists engaged in an exchange with the past.[7] They "revived" and adapted classical models to convey philosophical questions. The following chapter examines the humanist articulation of three key philosophical exchanges: being and seeming, virtue and fortune, and stasis and mutability. These three relations have preoccupied thinkers and poets both inside and outside the philosophical tradition, and we take our lead from Shakespeare: for we can refer the first exchange to thought ("the slave of life"), the second to life ("time's fool"), and the third to time ("that takes survey of all the world"). Or, as readers of philosophy, we can relate the humanist exchanges to matters of epistemology, ethics, and ontology, though these domains, too, are permeated by exchange. For one's thinking, Shakespeare suggests, attends one's way of living, and one's life responds to the sway of time and history.

Humanists, when grappling with these exchanges, resorted to alternative approaches. They sought to identify reality on the basis of the stability of reason, which could ground an objective view of things; or they acknowledged the transience of phenomena, which they discerned through their shifting awareness of illusion and limited vision. These two approaches confront us with a basic question: to what extent do the humanists' obvious discussions of virtue and ethical behavior have deeper dimensions, which we may explore by seeing how they understood reality, and the ways reality became manifest to them? These dimensions of epistemology and ontology, in turn, allow us to appreciate their ethical discussions in a new light.

Being and seeming (epistemology)

Cicero's *De amicitia* (*On Friendship*), a favorite humanist text, proclaims: "For only the few want *to be* endowed with virtue *rather than to seem* so [*esse quam videri*]."[8] The phrase "to be rather than to seem" became a watchword for conducting one's life in the pursuit of virtue and happiness, an alignment amenable to the humanist reading of Stoics, Epicureans, and Peripatetics. Lapo da Castiglionchio the Younger (1406–38), who recorded the humanist commonplaces in his letters, advised the young Roberto Strozzi to "choose in all things to be rather than to seem."[9] The moral mandate was not readily met, and humanists turned to confront its epistemological challenge. They viewed the world as a shadow play, full of hypocrisy and disguise. In trying to identify the covert intentions of princes and peers, the humanists often wore their own masks, using personae in their quest for sincerity and authenticity. These personifications present their philosophical puzzles, asking readers to decipher authorial meaning. Some humanist writing is relatively "closed" with respect to its hermeneutical latitude, relying on manifest statement.[10] But more frequently humanists dressed their philosophizing in dialogue, using various interlocutors, or in poetry, fables, or novels. When humanists proclaim the nature of "being" or "truth," in the sense of objectively identifying the nature of things, their readers often encounter personal features of the proclamation, exhibiting qualities of the moment, circumstance, or mood. The personality may appear transparent and direct, or else consciously feigned and more deeply disguised. The spectrum is broad.

Speaking in the first person, Leonardo Bruni (*c.* 1370–1444) composed his *Oratio in hypocritas* (*Speech against Hypocrites*) in 1418, inveighing against those who seek "not to be, but rather to seem or appear good." Hypocrites are malevolent players on the cultural stage, who, by wearing false masks (*alienas personas*), delude or play false with both God and humanity alike.[11]

In this brief speech, Bruni displays the twofold quality of humanist epistemology. First, he employs language in order to unmask hidden reality and reveal its objective nature for all the world to see. Bruni and other humanists therefore embrace a variation of the correspondence theory of truth, akin to the medieval scholastic conception of "aedequatio rei et intellectus," i.e., a statement expresses the truth of things insofar as language reflects or corresponds to reality.[12] Second, the *oratio* underlines how language itself is generated out from and speaks to personal relationships between the speaker and his audience. Bruni criticizes the hypocrites in the words of someone familiar with their treachery. For they, he writes, "deceived me, who once placed my trust in them."[13] Through a discursive context, humanist speech illuminates reality, and in fact shines a light on its concealment.

Humanist epistemology moves between these two positions. Objectively identifying reality, humanists stripped away and exposed the mask of seeming. They consistently espied the mendacity in the world around them. And by appreciating the dynamic, intersubjective conditions of knowledge, they realized how their given relation to others conditioned their perceptions of the phenomena before them. The tension within their approaches to knowledge moved them to adopt the form of dialogue in their inquiries, since this genre brought the two positions to bear on one another. The humanist adaption of classical dialogue, whether Ciceronian, Platonic, or Lucianic, is indebted to this struggle to confront, in alternate ways, the problem of being and seeming, as it pertains to knowledge.

About thirty years after Bruni's *Oratio*, his colleague Poggio Bracciolini (1380–1459) composed the dialogue *Contra hypocritas* (*Against Hypocrites*). Poggio sets the dialogue in the Florentine library of the Aretine humanist Carlo Marsuppini, in which Poggio himself is present. Marsuppini immediately agrees with Poggio's indictment of clerical dissimulation, calling the curia a "kingdom of hypocrites."[14] Girolamo Aliotti, a humanist abbot, joins the two speakers. Aliotti, similar to Bruni, turns to definitions. Hypocrites seek "to seem better than they actually are."[15] With sincerity a moral value, the humanist language also appears straightforward and sincere, contrasting and distinguishing what is from what seems to be.

If the epistemological challenge of hypocrisy first showed itself as easily resolved – by using language to identify deception and unmask the face of seeming – the dialogue reveals the deeper dimensions of the problem. Aliotti broadens the scope of hypocrisy by claiming that people "in every craft or trade [are] ready to simulate and dissimulate." In fact, he continues, "the same proclivity might be attributed to men of outstanding intelligence, and to good men: all of them seek to appear [*videri*] somewhat better than they actually are [*est*]." Furthermore, the methods of hypocrites are so diverse, so ingenious, that "it appears or seems difficult to obtain an insightful understanding of their nature, since their pretense of virtue is so deeply rooted."[16]

Aliotti's words confront Poggio's readers with a mode of discourse that is deeper than simple parody or invective. The focus shifts from unmasking deceptions practiced by others to pondering the sincerity expressed by the speaker, and examining how genuine or fraudulent his or her expression appears to be. Aliotti emphasizes how people conceal their true intentions. His assertions impress Marsuppini, who initially identified the obvious hypocrisy of the clergy, but now agrees with the truth of Aliotti's statement.[17]

This epistemological uncertainty finds its center in the humanists' phenomenological awareness. Filters of personality mask all things; there is a limit, and a finitude, to human insight into the nature of seeming that qualifies all objective assertions. The positions of the humanists are also transitory. Marsuppini changes his viewpoint over time, in the course of the conversation. The humanist dialogue, as a philosophical form of expression, showcases a mobile understanding, in which interlocutors modify their views as they continue to confront their shifting perceptions through their exchanges with others.

Humanist dialogues therefore acknowledge the fact of intersubjectivity and convey their philosophical inquiry with historical inflection.[18] Following Cicero's practice, humanists could present historical speakers in order to bestow a certain gravity on the topic under discussion. Yet they could also qualify the authority of these interlocutors through the history of the narrative: narrative time reveals the shifts and vacillations in their viewpoints, as it does with Marsuppini. Interlocutors, and by extension readers, may re-consider their perceptions as they exchange views. Here we may draw a comparison to Platonic dialogues. By inducing *aporia*, Socrates often persuades his interlocutors to abandon, or at least question, their initial positions. These reversals, however, tend to confirm Socrates' authority. Humanist dialogues, in their most open and non-didactic form, lack this stable point of reference: all interlocutors are subject to question. At polemical moments in their dialogues, Francesco Filelfo (1398–1481) or Lorenzo Valla (1407–57) made their humanist enemies uphold dubious philosophical positions.[19] Leon Battista Alberti, for his part, put forward his own persona, at various stages of life, throughout his work. Deeply engaged with the theory and practice of art, Alberti pondered the presence of appearances, for example, by outlining the system of linear perspective in his treatise on painting.

In Alberti's most famous dialogue, *Della famiglia* (*On the Family*), Alberti's uncle Lionardo speaks to "Battista," Alberti's youthful persona, about how their conversations differ from the treatises of "philosophers." These treatises pursue, he says, every implication of their "most obscure and difficult investigations," whereas the humanist household discussions do not aim for such glory.[20] Whether or not Battista, or the reader, takes Lionardo at his word strikes at the heart of the humanist's inquiry into the nature of being and seeming. The familial dialogues engage several philosophical subjects, such as friendship or the power of fortune. They include a discursive, witty commentary on Aristotle's *Nicomachean Ethics 8*, in which family members discuss the nature of friendship by focusing on the relation between being and seeing, and on ways of discerning good will from dissembling.

More fundamentally, Lionardo modifies his views intersubjectively, in response to the moment of discourse and his awareness of those present. His knowledge of their way of life affects, he says, how he expresses his point of view. Philosophical inquiry is, by these lights, a type of game, in which Lionardo, and his listeners, come to understand the orientation of others. Therefore Alberti's epistemology, like that of other humanists, does not adhere to a scholastic logical analysis, or to a strict imitation of Ciceronian *disputatio in utramque partem*. Rather it allows for intersubjective play, by accounting for the personalities involved. In this intimate exchange, the personal becomes a key modality in philosophical thinking. The characters advance their awareness by knowing one another: they carry a sense of others' history, and this history, as it changes, also shapes their shifting thoughts and impressions. Acquiring knowledge is always a problem and a test. Readers of the humanist works must negotiate the meaning of these personae as they present themselves in the course of the text, or paratext.

Alberti's Tuscan vernacular associates the verb *parere* with the neo-Latin *videri* as its counterpart. Both convey the sense of seeming and appearing or disclosure. Writing *Della pittura* prior to the Latin version *De pictura*, he states, "Know that a painted thing will never appear [*parrà/videri*] truthful where there is not a definite distance for seeing it."[21] When searching for knowledge, humanists strove to unmask what lay before them. The unmasking could entail objectifying and declaring the reality of things; it could also require patient receptivity to the way phenomena unfold over time, as one encounters them in dialogue or in observations that are conditioned by the presence of others.

This *quattrocento* epistemology has precedents in the *trecento*, with the ludic yet serious investigations of Petrarch and Boccaccio. Both humanists used various personae in their works, at times autobiographical (e.g., Petrarch's Silvius in the *Bucolicum carmen* and Franciscus in the *Secretum*). Personae appear even in their exchanges with one another, as witnessed by Boccaccio's letter to Petrarch of 1353 rebuking him for remaining in Milan. These writers established the basis for the humanist consideration of authority, whereby a speaker, no matter how distinguished, could condition or undermine his pronouncements through contradiction or vacillation. Their poetic understanding viewed the world through the prism of personality, and also remained alert for reversals of meaning on the basis of changing appearances. Although *quattrocento* humanists seldom praised their *trecento* forebears, they became a critical medium through which they understood the relation between being and seeming.

Petrarch's dialogues, as well as Boccaccio's *Decameron*, show the mutable use of personae in the search for knowledge. The *Secretum* (*The Secret*) showcases Augustinus, Petrarch's figure for his beloved St. Augustine of Hippo, guiding the troubled Franciscus through an inquisition into his psychic distress. In his *De remediis utriusque fortune* (*The Remedies for Good and Bad Fortune*), Ratio, the disembodied voice of rational certainty, tries to steady the emotions of Metus (Fear), Spes (Hope), Dolor (Sadness), and Gaudium (Joy) as they express reactions to various life situations. Both Augustinus and Ratio would speak with knowledge of moral clarity, and they reflect Petrarch's devotion to the interplay between Christian and classical traditions. This exchange, in which Petrarch engaged until his dying breath, nurtured his creative thinking. The dialogues, like his many letters, seal their authority with the impression of truth: in the *Secretum*, the figure of Veritas (Truth) introduces Augustinus to Franciscus. Yet their sovereign interlocutors are also colored by ambiguities. Augustinus is at times more Stoic than Christian, overlooking the role of grace; he also cites classical authorities when counseling Franciscus to abandon his study of literature. The entire dialogue, too, records Franciscus' own vision, and therefore relies on the memory of the imagined author, who is subject to the vagaries of time and poetic embellishment. The *De remediis* appears less problematic and more immediately didactic. But Ratio's truth-telling often resorts to rhetorical suasion, an appeal to emotion while contending with the power of the four passions. Ratio is dumbfounded at one point by Sadness's distress over severe pain, and it modulates its advice to the point of inconsistency, according to the cases it confronts, yielding to religious dogma when facing the fear of death.

With respect to Boccaccio's greatest work, the *Decameron*, humanist readers appreciated its subtle thinking on the complex relation between being and seeming. Deception is the keynote of its many tales, which often target clerical hypocrisy, and there are no fewer than five stories featuring the con artists/painters Bruno and Buffalmacco, who, like their author, enjoy playing games with people's perceptions. The reader must discern the meaning of the work, whether in whole or part, through the multiple narrative frames: of the authorial persona, of the ten storytellers, and within the stories themselves. As in other humanist dialogues, the storytellers or *brigata* highlight the fact of intersubjectivity, as they respond to one another's intentions and lessons over the course of two weeks' time. They communicate and revise their understanding of philosophical themes – virtue, friendship, fortune – during this time, shifting their perspectives as they come to know each other. Shading all their leisured conversation is their awareness of life's finitude, for the Plague has cost them kinsfolk and chased them from their native city.

Both *trecento* humanists advanced their vernacular inquiry by using the verb *parere* as the Tuscan equivalent to *videri*, and set a precedent for later humanists. Connoting illusion, *parere* repeatedly marks the scrupulous and theatrical hypocrisy of Cepparello, who deceives the pious friar confessor (*Dec.* 1.1.36). The verb expresses the work of Bruno and Buffalmacco, who, by creating false impressions, persuade the hapless Calendrino that he seems pregnant, in order to relieve him of his inheritance (*Dec.* 9.3.8–15).[22] But Pampinea in the opening of the *Decameron* also uses *parere* in addressing the mortal effects of deadly disease that move her to advise others to leave Florence: "it appears to me [*egli mi pare*] that no one has remained here except us" (*Dec.* 1.Intro.60). Thus *parere* also conveys a moment of disclosure, as when Abraam discovers the wickedness of the Roman clergy, which in turn reveals to him the greatness of the Christian religion, since it has increased its influence despite their duplicity (*Dec.* 1.2.23–6). In this vein, the reader can understand how reality may become clear, when shorn of outward simulation. New knowledge may dawn upon someone as the mists of illusion or confusion dissipate, as he or she learns, through life experience, to perceive the efforts at mystification or seeming. This path of thinking is brightened not so much by detached ratiocination as by patient apperception, often of the illogical or unexpected, as it presents itself. Abraam recognizes the illogical or unexpected on account of his historicity: the past, in recollection, extends itself into the present, shaping his apperception of his place in the world.

Petrarch's vernacular poetry also concerns itself with these epistemological issues. While his verses identify at times reason's ability to restrain the passions, in the vein of the *De remediis* (e.g., *Rvf* 97, 140, 141, 189), they continually wrestle with the presence of deception. In a sestina, the poet weeps over his lady's concealment by fog, and wishes for the sun to disperse it (*Rvf* 66.23, 39).[23] A frottola allows him to mask himself as a buffoon, and proclaim "una chiusa bellezza è più soave [a closed beauty is sweeter]" (*Rvf* 105.53); a later canzone elaborates this line, in that his *donna* showed him "pur l'ombra o 'l velo o' panni / talor di sé, ma 'l viso nascondendo [just a shadow, or veil, or garment / or her true self, while hiding her face]" (*Rvf* 119.20–1). In more Neoplatonic fashion, he states that the Po river can transport his *scorza*, his external form, but not the "spirto ch'iv' entro si nasconde [spirit that hides itself within]" [*Rvf* 180.1–3]. The turning inward, to see the essence beneath surface appearance, is also, in context of the poet's collection, a turning outward: the poet holds his conversation not merely with himself, but also with his lady, with Love, and with the world of his readers. Similar to Boccaccio and other humanists, Petrarch offers the conversation to readers' decipherment, asking them to weave the fragments together in time and over time through memory.

As inwardly directed as Petrarch's poetry tends to be, it shares with the *Decameron* an abiding intersubjectivity, an ongoing exchange with their world in their efforts to discern the real and know the truth of things. His verses locate the encounter with appearances also through the verb *parere*. Thus time seems or appears (*par*) to streak the poet's hair with age (*Rvf* 83.3). The following sonnet invents a dialogue between his heart and eyes, with the heart accusing them of false and distorted judgment: "Non son, come a voi par, le ragion pari [the reasons are not of equal standing, as it seems or appears to you]" (*Rvf* 84.9). In a renowned sonnet, "Erano i capei d'oro a l'aura sparsi," the poet himself speaks of the difficulty of seeing the truth, in this case of knowing how genuine the pity may be in Laura's demeanor: "e 'l viso di pietosi color farsi / (non so se vero o falso) mi parea [her face appeared to me, turning the color of compassion, I do not know whether false or true]" (*Rvf* 90.5–6). The poet recalls Laura in all her beauty, commemorating the ephemeral moment in its elusiveness, and marking it as singular. *Parere*, more meditative and, in this sense, more "philosophical" than in the prose of Boccaccio, attains a contemplative climax in the *Trionfi* where, from the poet's loftier vantage point, he constantly sees the passing spectacle before him. Echoing Pindar, he draws the conclusion in the *Triumphus temporis*: "Che più d'un giorno è la vita mortale? / Nubil' e brev' e freddo e pien di noia, / che po bella parer ma nulla vale [How more than a day is mortal life? Fragile and brief, cold and full of pain, it can appear beautiful, but it does not remain]."[24] Life can have its splendor, can be beautiful at its shining moment. But the moment can also be deceptive; it is fleeting and, because of memory, one and only. In Petrarch's design, time's parade is followed by the triumph of eternity, though this too is seen by earthly lights: "veder mi parve un mondo / novo, in etate immobile ed eterna [a new world appeared before my eyes, one stable and eternal]."[25]

Petrarch's final *Triumph* and his dialogues underscore the religious dimension to his inquiry into being and seeming. This dimension often disappears from view among *quattrocento* humanists, with notable exceptions such as Antonio da Rho, Ambrogio Traversari, Girolamo Aliotti, and Nicholas of Cusa. By the *cinquecento*, Niccolò Machiavelli (1469–1527) and Baldassare Castiglione (1478–1529) were understanding simulation as a more practical than moral problem. The prince should be a fox, who uses underlings to execute unpopular measures; the courtier must practice *sprezzatura*, the bearing that makes the artificial seem natural.[26]

Machiavelli's political writings are fond of overt declarations, as if trumpeting rules to follow. Thus his "new methods and approaches," announced in the *Discorsi* (*Discourses*), continue that vein of humanist thinking, which would objectively determine the truth in the world around them, and chart the features of society and politics.[27] Nonetheless these declarations are deeply indebted to the exchanges, beginning in the Rucellai Gardens, that frame his discourses. Axioms are modified or reversed, such as whether *virtù* in the affairs of state can overcome *fortuna*. His own perspective on princes, he says to Lorenzo de' Medici in *Il principe* (*The Prince*), is like that of a painter who sees the mountain-top from the valley. The reader must weigh not only the sincerity of this remark by Florence's republican *segretario* who writes a work devoted to deception, but also the state-ment's inherent epistemological limitations: from another vantage point, his portrait of princes may appear askew. In Castiglione's *Il cortegiano* (*The Courtier*), the dialogues on behavior and moral rectitude revolve time and again around comparisons with the arts. Giancristoforo Romano declares sculpture superior to painting, for painting's techniques "fool the eye"; its seeming (*il parere*) is further from the truth than its being (*l'essere*). Conte Ludovico da Canossa, who holds sway and introduces the courtier's need for *sprezzatura*, counters that painting is the more noble art, and "more capable of artifice," on account of its use of foreshortening and perspective: like the courtier, the painter is a master of appearances (1.49–54).

The courtier, the painter, and the humanist therefore "are of imagination all compact"; they express things that may not be. The humanist asks about the philosophical meaning of this seeming and masquerade. Desiderius Erasmus (1466–1536), in his *Stultitiae laus* (*Praise of Folly*), has Folly pronounce on various shades of wisdom and foolishness. If we examine these shades in the following section, we focus now on the more self-conscious conundrum that Erasmus poses in this version of the liar's paradox. At the heart of this conundrum stands the figure of Socrates, for he is represented by the Silenus who is out-ward ugly but inwardly beautiful: "you will find all things suddenly reversed," Folly states, "if you would open up a Silenus." Seeming here masks being and reality, so Folly pro-claims in her didactic oration. And yet seeming must be maintained: "What is the whole life of mortals but a type of comedy, in which various actors, disguised by various costumes and masks [*personis*], walk on and play each one his parts, until the manager waves them off the stage?"[28]

We are not far, at this point, from the more tragic conclusion of Shakespeare's Macbeth (Act V, scene 5). But Folly speaks in a comic vein, vividly captured by Pieter Bruegel's *Proverbs* (Illustration 5.2). François Rabelais (1494–1553), who wrote at least one letter to Erasmus, displays this humanist awareness with spectacular hybridity. Aware of Inquisitorial censor-ship, his play with appearances is more explicitly satirical. *Gargantua and Pantagruel* is blistering in its attack on religious hypocrisy. The novel is richly inflected, as Mikhail Bakhtin has noted, with hetero-glossic narrative, whereby the expressions of high and low culture are understood through their ongoing exchanges with one another. The prologue to *Gargantua* recalls the Silenus and Socrates, who was "always playing the fool, always dissimulating his divine wisdom." So too his ribald episodes, the author says, may disclose hidden meaning. But be wary, he adds, of those erudite scholars from Plutarch to Poliziano, who mine allegory in everything Homer

Illustration 5.2 Pieter Bruegel the Elder, *Netherlandish Proverbs*, 1559, Staatliche Museen, Berlin.
Source: © World History Archive/Alamy

and Ovid wrote. With Erasmus and Rabelais, humanist epistemology turns upon itself. Its self-parody simultaneously questions and validates its worth.[29]

Virtue and fortune (ethics)

The humanist epistemology directly conditioned their thoughts on ethics. Hypocrisy was, to their way of thinking, a moral problem. They were preoccupied by how one dwelled in the world, and one's character (*ethos*) in relation to others. Ethics therefore is at the center of exchange, as humanists pondered right courses of action, and the extent of one's moral freedom to realize them. If the hill of virtue was famously steep – an image recalled from Hesiod – one made decisions along the way (Illustration 5.3).[30] And what is of greater help in these decisions than philosophy, which "if it perhaps shines its light on us, will disperse all that gloom that disturbs us and distinguish the true way of living from the false." Thus Bruni writes in his *Isagogicon moralis philosophiae* (*Introduction to Moral Philosophy*) about countering the "blindness and darkness of humanity" so that one "may cease to live according to chance."[31] Matteo Palmieri (1406–75), composing his dialogue *Vita civile* (*Civil Life*) in the Florentine vernacular, has the leading interlocutor declare that "philosophy teaches the habits and virtues" and "the approved way of life of the virtuous."[32] Both Bruni and Palmieri place their trust in the *honestum*: the moral good, derived from Cicero and the Greek *to kalon*, that combines both inner rectitude and outward reputation. The key virtue guiding their readers' on life's way

Illustration 5.3 Pinturicchio, *The Hill of Virtue/Story of Fortune*, 1505, Siena Cathedral.
Source: © Elizabeth Leyden/Alamy

is prudence or right reason (*recta ratio*). The emphasis on rationality is hardly the province of one philosophical school, and humanists from Bruni to Giovanni Pontano (1426–1503) cheerfully combined Stoic, Neoplatonic, Peripatetic, even Cynic elements in their ethical inquiries. In Pontano's dialogue *Charon*, the infernal ferryman converses about these schools with Minos, Mercury, Diogenes, and anonymous shades in order to examine the nature of the moral good, which relies on the superiority of the mind (*animus*) over the body (*corpus*).[33]

In light of virtue's rational aspect, humanists emphasized that it could be learned, not least through exchanges with past authorities. As Pier Paolo Vergerio (1370–1444) notes: "The fruits of literature are always great, for the whole of life and for every kind of person, but it is particularly beneficial to the studious for forming a practice [of virtue]."[34] Gasparino Barzizza (*c.* 1360–1431) asks rhetorically, "Who does not realize that without these [liberal] arts that human life not only suffers dearth and deficiency, but indeed is also far worse and more degenerate than that of brutish animals?"[35] In a letter to a young Florentine, Lapo praises the literary training practiced by the ancients as the "securest basis for virtue and learning," and Alberti's dinner piece *Fatum et fortuna* (*Fate and Fortune*) shows a philosopher recounting a dream, in which shades use the liberal arts as a means of navigating the currents of fortune.[36] The optimistic credo of learning virtue continues into the sixteenth century with the treatises of Erasmus and Juan Luis Vives (1492–1540). In his *Enchridion militis christianae* (*Handbook of a Christian Soldier*), Erasmus urges the reader to follow the Platonists, and likewise his *Institutio principis Christiani* (*Education of a Christian Prince*), written three years after Machiavelli's *Il principe*, relies on Platonic precepts: "Unless you are a philosopher you cannot be a prince, only a tyrant."[37] Vives prefaces his *De tradendis disciplinis* (*On Education*) (1531) by noting that "nothing in life is more beautiful or excellent than cultivating the mind through what we call branches of learning [*disciplinae*], which separates us from the way of life and customs of beasts, restores us to humanity, and raises us toward God himself."[38]

These remarks sound the adage that reason liberates the soul from the bondage of the passions, a strain of thinking that the humanists inherited from the classical and also the medieval moral tradition. The truism surfaces in Petrarch's *De remediis*, Coluccio Salutati's *De laboribus herculis* (*The Labors of Hercules*), and in Marsilio Ficino's contemplation of the image of the charioteer in the *Phaedrus*. Plato, he writes to Giovanni Nesi, "calls reason a charioteer," and the "horses the powers of the heart and liver."[39]

The virtues may, in this respect, overcome the turbulence of the passions, and indeed, as for Ficino, harness the force of the heart's magnanimity. And so this conception provided humanists with grist for their moral mills. Their exhortations have struck many historians of humanism as stale, even with their learned leavening. For the humanists, too, virtue's greater foe was not the unruly passions or even vice, but fortune. In their imagination, she was, like the emotions, unstable, but she captured the accidents of birth and circumstance. She balanced precariously, in Pinturicchio's fresco for the Sienese *Duomo*, on the ship of life, with her arms holding a sail filled by shifting winds. Humanists therefore glimpsed fortune with a double vision: not only as one's "hap" or accidental condition, but also in the sense of life's inherent capriciousness and mutability. When translating Plutarch for Cosimo de' Medici and Nicholas V, Lapo and Niccolò Perotti (1429–80) proclaim the strength of reason and virtue in mastering fortune's whims.[40] But these turns of fortune provide opportunity or *occasio* as well. In Alberti's *Fatum et fortuna*, fortune's river brings the chance to embrace the humanities that allow an understanding of her currents; Aeneas Sylvius Piccolomini's *Somnium de fortuna*, another dream vision, celebrates Alfonso of Naples, whose virtue allows him to transfix *fortuna/occasio* by seizing her by the hair.[41] Thus the image of fortune suggests temporality and change. Petrarch explores this dimension with the shifting cases and counsel of his *De remediis*, and in his late *De sui ipsius et multorum ignorantia* (*On His Own Ignorance and That of Many Others*), he stresses how *senescunt fortune*: one's fortunes grow old, too, along with one's life.[42]

Both aspects, circumstance and change, are present in Machiavelli's treatment of fortune in *Il principe*. If the bold ruler must beat and bend *fortuna* to his will, that disturbing metaphor is mixed with a second, that of the river god. Here rulers meet with success in preventing its floods at most half the time. Rational virtue or amoral *virtù*, cunning, therefore have their limits. Poggio, more melancholy in his later works, writes in the *De varietate fortunae* (*The Varieties of Fortune*) that everyone has a role in the "theater" or "game of fortune." The work, dedicated to Pope Nicholas V, begins by decrying the ruins of Rome, and then becomes philosophical about the powerful, who so often disdain virtue: fortune "cherishes them, using them according to its rule: first casting them down, then unmasking their folly."[43]

In the ethical domain, we are brought again to the theater of illusion, with human actors misguided about the parts they play. Francesco Guicciardini (1483–1540), Machiavelli's correspondent, notes that fools often accomplish more than the wise because they rely more on fortune than on reason.[44] Erasmus' spokesperson Folly proclaims a similar view, presenting Rhamnusia or Nemesis as the "*fortunatrix* of human affairs," who favors bold fools.[45] Folly turns *psogos* or scold against the learned; for while the Stoics consider themselves wise and virtuous, they are the most deluded, and unaware of the reality of things.

The link between learning and virtue, erudition and ethics, standard in many humanist treatises, comes under critical review. This review has its own tradition within humanism, countering and in fact transforming the ethical commonplaces. Boccaccio's *Decameron* recounts comeuppances of not only the powerful, but also the educated, such as the scholar Rinieri (8.7) and Master Simone the physician (8.9), and Petrarch, in the *De ignorantia*, distinguishes between learning and wisdom: "learning for many is an instrument of mindlessness [*dementie*]"; reading Aristotle's ethical writings increased his erudition without improving his character.[46]

As indicated by Poggio's abbot Aliotti, *quattrocento* humanists heightened this skepticism toward learning, even while they reinforced erudition's ethical import: such tensions and contradictions inhere in their bifocal epistemology. Life experience challenges what is learned and accepted from books as rules for living well, and in this exchange life is thought's master. Lapo could praise the ethical teachings of the classics, but in the face of his continued misfortunes, he now finds, he tells Angelo da Recanate, that "I begin to hate my old friends, that is my books. For they have been of no value to me ... And I will not be grateful unless my circumstances change."[47]

In the later letters of his *epistolario*, Lapo regains his equilibrium and his faith in learning, just as Poggio kept his trust, despite fortune's sway, in reason's potency. Alberti continued to question erudition's ethical value, from his early *De commodis et incommodis litterarum* (*The Benefits and Troubles of Letters*), in which a student's library assails his flagging spirits, to the *Vita Sancti Potiti* (*Life of St. Potitus*), describing the martyrdom of an unlettered youth at the hands of Marcus Aurelius, and then in the *Della famiglia*, where Lionardo's learning yields to Adovardo's experience. The greatest charge is laid by his dinner piece *Defunctus* (*The Deceased*) and his novel *Momus*. In the novel, Momus, the god of fraud, mocks the way philosophers deceive others with a show of "old style morality and goodness." Jupiter, sensing Momus' own rhetorical seeming, says he first thought Momus' character admirable, being "polished by the liberal arts." He now discovers the hypocrisy of scholars: "when they strive to seem upright and most natural, that is when they are at their wickedest and most deceitful."[48] The *Defunctus* takes this learned show one step further. The title character is enveloped in learned self-deception; he cannot see, even from the standpoint of the afterlife, how his studious way of life fed his self-absorption, as well as the enmity of his kin.

Stultitia (folly), *delusio* (delusion), *dementia* (mindlessness), *insania* (deception, self-deception): these neo-Latin terms mark the shortcomings of the bookishly virtuous, who paraded their probity and prudence. Nicholas of Cusa's dialogues *De idiota* (*The Layman*) also reveal learned pretense, as the layman confounds both orator and philosopher by drawing analogies from his rustic spoon-making. At the opening of the first dialogue, he tells the orator: "Wearied by the constant reading of countless books, you are not led to humility. No doubt this is because the knowledge of this world, in which you believe you excel all others, is foolishness [*stultitia*] in the sight of God and breeds self-conceit."[49]

The anonymous layman serves as a second Socrates in Cusa's dialogue. Erasmus would hide, as we have seen, his Socratic message in Folly's oration. For appreciating this vein of humanist ethical thinking, which places the burden of insight on the individual's life experience, there is perhaps no sixteenth-century writer better suited than Michel de Montaigne (1533–92). Writing "Sur des vers de Virgile / On some verses of Virgil," he says, "Learning treats of things too subtly, in a mode too artificial and different from the common and natural one. My page makes love and understands it. Read him [the Neoplatonists] Leon Hebreo [Judah Leon Abravanel] and Ficino: they talk about him, his thoughts and actions, and yet he does not understand a thing in it. I do not recognize in Aristotle most of my ordinary actions: they have been covered up in another robe for the use of the school."[50]

We encounter again the image and metaphor of masking, one often overlooked for its philosophical significance. In his *La cultura del Rinascimento*, Garin sees this passage as a jest, and turns to stress the elite nature of Renaissance Neoplatonists and their treatises on sublime love: "without this Platonism, one cannot understand the Renaissance."[51] Montaigne is making a more fundamental philosophical point for the period: that learning has become too often life's accoutrement, if not its hindrance, instead of its guide. Virtue requires a more natural element, which one finds in one's way of life, even though, for the humanists, life is often the plaything of time.

Stasis and mutability: new visions of reality (ontology)

The term "ontology" was coined after our period, and scholars often use it interchangeably with "metaphysics," the study of that which is beyond *physis* or *natura*, in other words, its ground, the Being of beings. Few humanists speculated directly on this topic; here we may mention Ficino and Cusa, whom some scholars would isolate from humanism. Cristoforo Landino (1424–98), who exchanged letters with Ficino and presented him as a *persona* in his most famous work, speaks of "metaphysicians" and their theories of ultimate reality. But in addition to these specialists, humanists, as we have seen, wrestled with the meaning of reality, and their sense of reality conditioned their awareness of truth. Their ontological standpoint, whether explicit or implicit, informed their epistemology; and both shaped their view of ethics and the moral good. This last section of our investigation examines the ontological basis.

To recall Shakespeare's Hotspur, "time must have a stop." The question the humanists faced was how time related to being: did it rest in Being or an ultimate reality, or did it qualify reality itself, so much so as to make its origin or ground unrecognizable? With regard to the first relation, humanists often saw this "stop" in a conception of Being as stable and eternal, an idea or deity that, in its transcendence, anchored the real and the true, and thus their objective view of things. Chaucer's Theseus, speaking at the close of *The Knight's Tale*, mediates not only Boccaccio's *Teseida* but also Aristotle's *Metaphysics* when he states, "The First Moevere of the cause above, / Whan he first made the fair cheyne of love, / Greet was th'effect, and heigh was his entente" (2987–89). As the alternative exposition of the ontological "stop," humanists pondered life's ineluctable finitude, and viewed reality in the guise of temporality, change, and mortality. It is not Theseus, but his father Aegeus, who suggests this perspective: " 'Right as ther dyed nevere man', quod he, / 'That he ne lyvede in erthe in some degree, / Right so ther lyvede never man', he seyde, / 'In al this world, that som tyme he ne deyde'" (2843–6). This standpoint extended itself to any higher reality and divinity, which appeared not stable, but mutable and evanescent, and which concealed itself from view. To return to Michelangelo's Sacristy: one's view may rest the gaze on the Virgin or the circular dome; someone else may continue to look about, oscillating among the deities Night and Day, Dawn and Dusk. The Sacristy entertains both visitors, or the same one, who responds differently at different times. Humanists appreciated this diversity and vacillation of viewpoint, as they pondered the face of Being.

The humanists in the first group, who conceived of Being in its transcendent stability, often presented their conception through allegory. The poet, as *vates*, grasped these eternal truths and masked them in images for the humanist to unveil. Boccaccio, in his *De genealogia deorum*, considers Jupiter the *summum bonum* and the source of life: to the Romans, "he alone is the greatest good, because life comes from him, and because he is the helper of all … In addition, the name Jupiter in Greek is *zephs*, which means 'life.' "[52] Reading the "Pythagorean poet Aeschylus" via Cicero's *Tusculans*, as well as Ovid, Servius, Claudian, and Fulgentius, he weighs the meaning of the figure of Prometheus. Though not easy, he says, "to reveal the cortex beneath these layered fictions surrounding him," he discovers the deity to be an apt *persona* for the "true, omnipotent god."[53] For Prometheus not only creates humankind from clay, he also goes to heaven – "that is, in the place of perfection" – where "all things are animated by fire, that is, by the clarity of truth"; from there he grants humanity the flame or brightness of knowledge "from the wheel of the sun, that is, from the lap of God, whence comes all wisdom, for He is the true sun 'who illuminates every being coming into this earth.'"[54]

The exegesis is hardly systematic or consistent, since it seeks a pattern in mythological narrative. Yet Boccaccio translates the Neoplatonic allegorizing of the classical and medieval traditions, attributing to the divine being the stability, eternity, and rational light that is the source of all beings. Humanity, through rationality and education, attains its kinship with the divine, and is able to see things in the light of truth.

Coluccio Salutati (1331–1406), Boccaccio's friend and correspondent, continues this line of allegorizing in the *De laboribus Herculis* since, he claims, "poets have most closely followed the Platonists."[55] In contrast to Boccaccio, Salutati emphasizes how the myth of Prometheus employs various degrees of deception: Prometheus hides the sacrificial meat from Jupiter, who chooses the bones. But this move itself signifies, to the acute interpreter, that our spiritual life itself often remains concealed, in the bones "which by their nature lie hidden within the flesh." For "Jupiter is seen [*visus est*] to err by this decision insofar as to earthly eyes those seeking spiritual goods are seen or appear [*videntur*] to err." Jupiter, the father of the gods, oversees humanity's formation from all animate creation. It requires higher insight to unmask the true meaning behind these fictions, and this insight also requires a sublime source. Jupiter himself is the "realm of reason," which provides a transformed (*conversus*) humanity the light and fire of both reason and virtue.[56] In other words, Jupiter is the source of all created being, and as such, grounds human knowing and right action, epistemology and ethics.

Cristoforo Landino highlights other features of philosophical allegory in his *Disputationes camaldulenses* of the mid-1470s. The title indicates its humanist hybridity: a *disputatio* or debate, drawing on the transformation of medieval university tradition; one held at a friary of the Camaldolensian order, whose ranks included the humanist prior Ambrogio Traversari (1386–1429), translator of Diogenes Laertius; and not least a dialogue using *personae* of those still living, or recently deceased. These include Alberti, one of his Landino's first patrons; Lorenzo de' Medici, his current one; and Marsilio Ficino (1433–99). All these circumstances color his readers' reception of the dialogue's themes of the active and contemplative pursuit of the *summum bonum*.

The interlocutors interpret allegory, particularly in their reading of the *Aeneid*, to show how one advances in knowledge and moral virtue. This moral allegorizing also has an ontological foundation. Jupiter, Lorenzo claims, "we understand to be the world soul, according to the teachings of the Platonists," to which Alberti assents, declaring that God is the origin of everything, in fact the "architect of all things."[57] Ficino proclaims God the "best of everything," and that nature is moved toward a good as toward its end. Replying to Ficino, Alberti calls God the "good of every good," and, as a good, "by necessity it must moreover be stable."[58]

The divine good, personified by Jupiter, is inherently fixed and the source of all other beings. In the dialogue, Alberti voices the scholastic argument that "the metaphysicians have confirmed that whatever is, derives its being from God." God is both the highest good and the ground of Being. "Thus whatever is, for whatever reason it has being, is good by virtue of having being. Therefore evil has no being." Here, in a humanist dialogue, Alberti presents the logic of Thomas Aquinas, among other medieval thinkers.[59] Landino's dialogue therefore merges scholastic and humanist ontology in a way that grounds his objective understanding of knowledge and morality. Alberti consistently contrasts the biblical sisters Mary and Martha in the traditional reading of the contemplative and active virtues, and adds to this the Neoplatonic dimension of ascent. In Mary, he says, we recognize how we may gradually rise toward the knowledge of God, in which we find both our *summum bonum* and our origin. He recalls the words of his friend, the mathematician Paolo Toscanelli, who also associates knowledge with divine being, since he asserts that the divine light provides "the certainty of things."[60]

Landino carefully stages his portrait of Marsilio Ficino in order to complement those of Lorenzo and Alberti in their philosophical exchanges. In Ficino's own works, he elaborates and refines the humanist Neoplatonic principles of his predecessors and contemporaries, particularly in his *Theologia platonica* (*Platonic Theology*), which he composed in the years just prior to Landino's dialogue (1469–74). His commentary on the *Philebus*, written also at this time, interprets classical sources for ontological purposes. It notes Plato's reading of Jupiter as the "divine mind," and cites Orphic texts that declare Jupiter the source of all things. As do the other humanists, Ficino conveys the divine being through the light metaphor. Plato, in his *Republic*, states that "in the higher world, the first thing, the good itself and the one principle of things, creates with its light all the species of things." The divine intelligence, "the artificer of the world," takes its power and light from Jupiter.[61] In a later work, *De sole* (*On the Sun*), Ficino calls light "the very vision of the celestial soul," or, following Orpheus, the sun is the "eternal all-seeing eye," the "Lord of Earth, immortal Jupiter."[62] His contemporaries, Nicholas of Cusa and Alberti, offer alternatives to these conceptions of divine light and sight, which hold in view the apparent dimness rather than brilliance of divinity.

With regard to Prometheus, he becomes for Ficino part of the Godhead, the "distributor, intermediary, and preparer" of the higher powers. He intimately connects divine being and knowing, the ontological and epistemological features in Ficino's philosophizing, for he may be called the "sun cherishing the rational spirit especially."[63] This is a distinction that accords with Ficino's *Theologia platonica* and the *De sole*. In the first, he asserts that the "eye of the angelic mind" is "ruled by the divine Sun itself" and that it "seeks for and finds the light of truth," and the second commentary remarks that "Platonists posit three principles: the good itself, the divine intellect, and the world soul. The divine light, alone of its kind, openly conveys all these above all other things."[64]

Ficino is able, as an illumined "hermeneut," to unravel this allegory and discern its insights into the nature of reality and truth. The rational mind, if purged of earthly fantasy, may ascend to this more sublime understanding.[65] Pico della Mirandola (1463–94), his great colleague, set his own philosophical conceptions on these same bases, as well as on the humanist writings in this vein. Scholars have seen his *Oratio de dignitate hominum* (1486) heralding a new chapter in the philosophical thinking about human autonomy and self-fashioning.[66] Yet the very structure of the *Oratio*, announcing a *disputatio* over his 900 theses, also underlines Pico's commitment to exchanging views both with tradition and his contemporaries. "Through this rhetorical wrestling school," he says, "one's powers of mind emerge far stronger and more animated."[67] At the age of twenty-four, he asserts that he "has ranged through all masters of philosophy, investigated all books, and come to know all schools."[68] Indeed, he adds, this encyclopedic study was a custom of the ancients. Even while adding new concepts and sources, Pico shares in the humanist conventions of syncretic thinking and desire for debate. He hearkens to the humanist reading of Prometheus in his most celebrated claim, that humanity as "work of indeterminate form," which "should have joint possession of whatever had been peculiar to each of the different kinds of being."[69] Salutati had maintained that the Titan created humanity "by taking the characteristics and passions from the whole of animate nature."[70]

Like his humanist forebears and contemporaries, Pico emphasizes the need to interpret symbols and figures in order to understand the nature of Being behind surface appearances. Jacob's ladder from Genesis offers a fitting allegory of human ascent to the divine, from moral philosophy through dialectic to theological contemplation.[71] The mysteries of the Hebrews, to his mind, are kin to those of the Greeks; as did the ancient theologians, "Orpheus disguised the mysteries of his teachings with a poetic veil," requiring Pico "to draw out the meaning of this recondite philosophy from the studied knots of riddles and from the hidden recesses of stories."[72] He proposes, he says, to write a *Poetica theologia*, in order to disclose how Homer "disguised" philosophical truth "through the wanderings of Ulysses."[73] This project strikingly resembles Landino's enterprise in his *Disputationes*, of having Alberti reveal the *Aeneid*'s moral meaning.

Pico's ontology, similar to that of Ficino, Salutati, and Boccaccio, is suggested by this idea of disclosure and the symbol of light. The "true Apollo ... lights every soul as it enters this world"; the Sun, he adds, is "the father and leader" of our contemplation.[74] As it is for these other writers, the light of Being is also the light of knowing. He asks that Plato's "light of truth might dawn more brightly on our minds, like the sun rising from the deep"; we should proceed from "the still feeble light of [nature's] truth, as it were from the first rays of the rising sun" to rise "like heavenly eagles boldly enduring the most brilliant splendor of the noontime sun."[75] In this ascent of Being and truth, the mind's eye would perceive the objective nature of things.

Pico's optimism, and ambition, is to embark on the upward journey, beyond the thick shadows of earthly existence. The first sentence of his *Oratio* boldly proclaims that "nothing can be seen more admirable than humankind," a humanist variation on Anselm's "nothing can be thought greater [than God]." Pico qualifies his admiration with a figure of speech: "on this earthly stage."[76] Pico, like Ficino, claims to see behind the curtain, and discern the ontological origins of human agency. But not every humanist shared in this optimism. Poggio, we have noted, studied the "game" and "theater of fortune" in a more melancholy vein. Humanity has the potential, through virtue and reason, to challenge fortune's role as playwright and stage manager of human destiny, but few people, if any, succeed in realizing their own liberation. Not the wise man himself (*sapiens*), but only the wise man's (*sapientis*) reason and virtue are immune to fortune's sway.[77]

This concession to the theater of existence, embracing the whole person, body and mind, conditioned for many humanists the virtue of Stoicism. Both Petrarch and Lorenzo Valla, Poggio's erstwhile adversary, maintain this qualification. If Poggio sees human frailty as potentially remediable, Valla suggests that the human condition is existentially limited and benighted; humanity's ontological participation in divine being appears unrecognizable, although to God, all things are possible. His Epicurean interlocutor in the *De vero bono*, Maffeo Vegio, attacks contemplative virtue for pretending to exalt the soul above bodily sensation. He mocks the trope of contemplative ascent, for it pertains little to divinity, which already possesses perfect knowledge, and furthermore, such an effort is tiresome.[78] In the dialogue's final book, the Franciscan humanist Antonio da Rho proclaims the divine mysteries impenetrable, even to the keenest minds: "Anyone trying to examine and clarify these riddles and allegories will labor completely in vain." Moses veiled his face on Sinae, and "[o]ur face cannot be freed from its covering, which is corporeal." Humanity, like all other beings, is confined to the earthly stage, as if ontologically apart from the deity. The ways of the divine are "noncorporeal [and] of a nature not to be perceived by those who have a bodily nature," and could they be perceived, they are too sublime for our "minds shut in darkness and blindness of its earthly prison."[79] Valla therefore adopts Neoplatonic imagery, and its light-metaphor, but only to heighten the *chorismos* or separation between heaven and earth. When he employs the figure of Jupiter in other writings, as in the *De libero arbitrio* (*On Free Will*), the allegory challenges the humanist reading furthered elsewhere: his Jupiter is of a different order, who may fashion human character to goodness or to wickedness.

For this second sort of humanist, who questioned the ontological consistency between beings and their source, time "surveys the world." Their writings accent mutability and temporal change. The "world" is the arena of vision; it is where, figuratively or literally, gods and humanity encounter one another in and over time. Here truth may surface only within the flow of existence, rather than in atemporal rational certitude that the divine, as the stable, unmoved source of beings, guarantees.

Poggio wrote of the earthly theater run by fortune. To Valla, any philosophical allegorizing about ultimate Being and truth collapses under the earthliness of mortal intelligence: the divine face, or that of its Moses, remained covered. Cusa and Alberti pick up the humanist theme of metaphors and masking in order to stress divinity's disguise before human vision. "Non vien nota mai," Alberti says of the goddess Amicitia or Friendship, "ne vien composta":[ ] she does not arrive openly, but rather masked.[80] The gods, or God, also wear disguises in this time-bound theater. Ontologically, divinity can appear different from humanity; epistemologically, human vision is obscured. To humanists thinking in this vein, Being is not simply, in Neoplatonic fashion, the brilliant source of created beings; it rather shapes the world in the sense of the theater, the stage, and its temporal continuum, dimensions in which beings, including divinity and humanity, may present or conceal themselves. There is therefore no linear ascent to a higher, objective understanding. The supra-lunary vision is beyond mortal ken, which must glean its insights from the phenomena along life's way. And these phenomena present more puzzles than fixed, logical conclusions.

Cusa's *De visione dei* (*The Vision of God*) studies these riddles. Overtly a theological treatise, written to the monks of Tegernsee in 1453, it displays a number of concerns shared with other humanist works, in particular the meaning of appearances and the understanding of symbols. The author meditates on the face (*faciem*) of God, as portrayed in a painted image or icon (Illustration 5.4). He uses a traditional metaphysical vocabulary, describing God as an "absolute form" that gives existence to all things as the "one who forms heaven, earth, and everything." But the Cardinal humanist focuses on the appearance of God, his face, which he also calls, with studied ambiguity, his sight (*visus*), indicating both which sees and is seen.[81]

Humanity sees only a changing image, since by nature humanity is mutable. As Cusa writes, "and so whichever way I change my face, the face seems or appears turned toward me." God's constancy is seen, paradoxically, by human inconstancy. "For if I am moved, his face appears also to be moved, because it does not forsake me. If, while I am moving, another person looking at the face remains still, its gaze, in like manner, does not forsake him or her: on the contrary, it remains still with the one remaining still."[82]

Like other humanists, Cusa studies shifting perspectives on appearances. The verbs are critical: "the face appears to me," he writes; "his gaze appears." The divine communicates its being only through appearances, which are transitory, since "humanity can only assess things in human fashion." Those humanist thinkers who imagined the Neoplatonic notion of ascent sought a higher knowledge beyond the shadows of the cave, illumined by divine being and wisdom. Cusa however remains by the earthly veil: "the face of faces appears or is

Illustration 5.4 Copy after Van Eyck, *Vera Icon*, 1438, Alte Pinakothek, Munich.
Source: © bpk, Berlin/Gemäldegalerie, Staatliche Museen, Berlin/Jörg P. Anders/Art Resource, NY

seen in all faces in a veiled and puzzling way." Humanity only perceives things in succession, *unum post unum*.[83]

The divine, by contrast, is distinctly other. Symbol or analogy fails because it cannot access difference, only similarity, and Cusa uses analogy, as does Alberti, in order to highlight this failure, and the alterity of the divine. Eternity is neither posterior or anterior to temporal sequence, yet, he says to God, "you stand still while you are moved, and you both advance and yet are at rest," while his face "is above all rest and motion in the most simple and absolute infinity."[84] This face is only seen, or seems, unveiled (*revelate videtur*) by entering into, in his words, "a certain secret and hidden silence, where there is no knowledge or concept of a face." Here there is "gloom, fog, darkness, or ignorance" and "the very gloom moreover discloses that here is the face beyond all concealment." Thus even the "highest spirit of reason" (*spiritus altissimus rationi*), praised by Pico and Ficino, must be vanquished for this vision to become apparent: "there is no other way of coming to you," he states, "unless that one which seems or appears to all people, even the most learned philosophers, utterly inaccessible and impossible."[85]

Cusa's philosophizing, like that of Valla, marks the limits of traditional metaphysics. These "most learned philosophers," when wondering about ontology and ultimate meaning, have only mortal vision. Cusa conceives human sight as comprehending things only sequentially, in time, with before and after. God's being is like a clock, he says: it charts minutes and hours, while the clock as an image (*similitudo, conceptus*) encompasses time itself. Yet these figures fall short of granting access to a genuine insight into His nature; God is beyond human notions of being, and is hidden.[86]

Around the same time, while at the papal curia, Alberti ponders these matters of ontology and epistemology in his novel *Momus*. The work, the author declares in the Preface, is nothing but a grand allegory in the tradition of the ancient poets and philosophers: "by the names of the gods they wished their readers to understand those powers of mind by which we are moved towards one or another course of action."[87] His Jupiter should represent reason and virtue, and Alberti alludes to the interpretations of Boccaccio, Salutati, and Ficino. But this representation is *quasi per ironiam*, he adds: he is keenly focused on irony, on the playful dissimulation that not only poets and philosophers, but also divinity may employ. His allegory's center does not hold. Jupiter is no less arbitrary and meretricious than other characters, and the central figure, the god Momus, is the god of fraud and deception. The novel delights in Lucianic parodies of philosophers. Apollo eavesdrops on their erudite conversations and finds them incomprehensible: except for Socrates, he tells Jupiter, "they could not explain any obscure matters without wrapping them in the thickest blankets of words" and "long-winded quibblings." Gelastus, the soul of a philosopher wandering in the afterlife, tries to clarify the ontological nature of the universe to Charon, the infernal ferryman. He first uses Aristotelian, then Neoplatonic conceptions about causes and forms. Charon responds that "you [philosophers] know nothing except how to ... render incomprehensible the most well-known facts by the words you use."[88]

This play with verbal allegory is not simply subversive in an anti-philosophical sense, but it is deeply philosophical in its own right. Its meaning becomes clear through the exchanges that the novel undertakes with the humanist tradition. The god Momus personifies this ludic seriousness. He is an alter-Prometheus, chased from the heavens on account of his rebellious nature. Landing in Tuscany, he does not create humanity or provide them the sublime fire of intelligence, but instead teaches women to disguise themselves, and show other faces, through the use of cosmetics. In one moment of crisis, the goddess Virtue lends him her veil (*velus*), allowing him to change his appearance (*facies*) at will.[89] Returning to Olympus, he offends Juno, and she, along with other divinities, castrate and cast him from heaven and chain him, like the Titan, to a rock. Nymphs that had earlier consoled Prometheus lend him aid. Momus persuades these nymphs to spread his black cloud of sighs across the sky, and thereby conceal the earth from the vision of the gods.

The novel therefore treats with adroit gamesmanship the humanist Neoplatonic ontology. Momus is a walking, mutable allegory: deceit personified, he may present the face of virtue, while teaching others to dissemble. His divine, puckish element interferes with participation of the heavens in the earthly spectacle. At the novel's close, humanity stages a performance in the gods' honor, and rings the theatre with their statues. Jupiter and the other deities, whom Momus' cloud blocks from seeing the earthly spectacle, descend to earth – as if fools (*amentes*), the narrator says – and take the place of their own likenesses. As a result, they are abused by drunks and unruly passersby. One main performer in the spectacle is "a philosopher and also an actor," who is named Oenops (Tipsy). Held prisoner in a cave by thieves, Oenops escapes torture thanks to the statue of Stupor, because the criminals, using torches, are frightened by its sight. Seeing "that the gods were clearly present," they take flight (4.16).[90]

The cave episode, with its Platonic parody, illustrates the confusion among the mortals and the gods. This confusion extends itself to the earthly theater, which is also shrouded in darkness. Statues are mistaken for deities, and the deities, in the theater, are misunderstood as statues. Humanist allegorizing therefore only seems grounded in ontological sureties. In either domain, within or without the cave, earth or heaven, the gods remain hidden. Mortals are left in insecurity and largely focused, like the philosopher Gelastus, on their passage from this world to the next, without clear divine guidance. Apollo, the narrator states, is in love with the goddess Shadow (Umbra), the daughter of Night. Night steals Apollo's prophecies and hides them in her statue; in the nocturnal chaos, the prophecies are found by Ambiguity (Ambago), the "most mendacious of the goddesses."[91]

Night, Shadow, Ambiguity: these deities alter Apollo's insights, or at least the way he communicates them. A reader of Boccaccio, Alberti would have understood Night to be the mother of Deceit (Dolus) and Fraud (Fraus), close relations to Momus.[92] Thus does divinity, as it does for Cusa, partake in obscurity and conceal itself from view. The gods wear disguises, so that it is difficult to discern their role in shaping or founding the reality that people experience. Humanity encounters divinity in the world, which is an arena of unstable, fluctuating interchange, imbued with transience. The philosophical task for Alberti and Cusa is to illuminate this arena as a playground where masks may have meaning, if only in the fundamental sense that meaning is masked. The human experience is one of time-bound, mortal movement.

The contrasting fifteenth-century humanist ontologies left their mark in the early modern period. Cassirer and Garin have stressed how humanists such as Pico and Ficino advanced notions of proto-Cartesian ideas of subjectivity and objectivity, based on the ontological security of knowledge. The Cartesian *cogito* relies on the superiority of the *ratio*, which, for many humanists, has its foundation in the divine mind as the source of Being. With regard to the more reserved strains of Valla, Cusanus, and Alberti, both Martin Luther (1483–1546) and Montaigne elaborated them, in differing ways. Luther, like Erasmus, praises Valla's *Annotationes in Novum Testamentum*, but Luther also cites Valla's support in his 1525 polemic against Erasmus over the bondage or freedom of the will.[93] Human reason has no access to the qualities of God; it is a "little torch," he writes in 1521, compared to the divine, "burning mid-day sun." God conceals his mercy behind his anger, and his presence by his absence; he demands an experiential, rather than an intellectual engagement: "by living, indeed by dying and being damned does one become a theologian," Luther states in 1519, "not by knowing, reading, or speculating."[94] Montaigne too emphasizes the presumption of rational speculation by both theologians and philosophers in his *Apologie de Raymond Sebond*. His accent is similarly on the existential. Quoting Plutarch, he affirms that "we have no communication with being, because all human nature is always midway between birth and death, offering only a dim appearance and shadow of itself, and an uncertain and feeble opinion."[95] True, he says, philosophy is like poetry, like a veiled image. But he breaks with the hermeneutical confidence of Ficino and Pico. The image shines with "an infinite variety of false lights to exercise our conjectures." For no existing thing, either we ourselves or what we perceive, remains constant; everything flows and turns without rest. Aristotle is therefore correct to compare our vision of truth with the eye of the owl before the splendor of the sun; this light indicts mortal blindness. Our waking, he concludes, "is more asleep than sleep; our wisdom less wise than our foolishness."[96]

Conclusion

If we now return to the statue of Night with its owl and mask in the Medici tombs of Michelangelo, we can also bring these humanist philosophical offerings, these first fruits of our inquiry, into their various exchanges. Night, Boccaccio notes, is the parent of Old Age (Senectus) and Death (Mors). And Death is the "ultimate terror." Boccaccio refers to Aristotle, who states that death is frightening because "it is a limit [or end], and there seems to be nothing else for the dead, neither good nor bad."[97] In a religious setting, believers confront their fears soteriologically. They may find comfort in the sublime claims of ontological and epistemological securities, which fasten the world's wobbly transience to divine immutability and wisdom. The more concrete message of the Sacristy is that one is entering the grave of the princes. One communes with the dead, and becomes aware of their presence in their absence. Time and history connect, yet also separate, the living from the dead, present from past lives. Humanists, in their endeavor to revive the past, "awaken it from sleep," as they put it, walked through many tombs, and reconstructed communities from many ruins and remains. This imaginative enterprise was always mortal. By communing with the past, humanists could look over their own finitude. This sensibility deepened their feeling of responsibility, of being answerable in the present not only for the past, but also for the future. "Humanism" for many of these writers and thinkers was not an academic abstraction, nor a retreat from the pressures of existence. On the contrary, it was a bridge that only had meaning by arcing over the river of time. As a bridge, humanism was a place of exchange, an intersection between past and present, present and future, and not least between mortal humanity and divinity. That humanists found their freedom in this finitude, even felt joy when bidding adieu, is one of their prime philosophical accomplishments.

Notes

1 I would like to thank William Caferro, Charles Carman, and Ronald Witt for their helpful reviews of this chapter in draft.
2 Ernst Cassirer, *Individuum und Kosmos in der Philosophie der Renaissance*, Berlin: B. G. Teubner, 1927; Paul Oskar Kristeller, *Renaissance Thought and its Sources*, New York: Columbia University Press, 1979; James Hankins, ed., *The Cambridge Companion to Renaissance Humanism*, Cambridge: Cambridge University Press, 2007; Robert Black, "Humanism," in *The New Cambridge Medieval History*, ed. C. Allmand, Cambridge: Cambridge University Press, 1998, 7:243–77.
3 Eugenio Garin, "Quale 'Umanesimo'? (Divagazioni storiche)," *Giornale critico della filosofia italiana* 84 (2005): 16–26; 26: "… l'uomo si era scoperto artifice di sé e del suo mondo … faber e anche faber fortunae." Ernesto Grassi, *Rhetoric as Philosophy: The Humanist Tradition*, ed. and trans. J. M. Krois and A. Azodi, Carbondale, IL: Southern Illinois University Press, 2001; Nancy Struever, *The Language of History in the Renaissance: Rhetoric and Historical Consciousness in Florentine Humanism*, Princeton, NJ: Princeton University Press, 1970; Christopher Celenza, *The Lost Italian Renaissance: Humanists, Historians, and Latin's Legacy*, Baltimore: Johns Hopkins University Press, 2004; Lodi Nauta, *In Defense of Common Sense: Lorenzo Valla's Humanist Critique of Scholastic Philosophy*, Cambridge, MA: Harvard University Press, 2009. On the differences between these approaches, see Celenza, *Lost Italian Renaissance*, 16–57 and James Hankins, "Garin and Paul Oskar Kristeller: Existentialism,

Neo-Kantianism, and the Post-War Interpretation of Renaissance Humanism," in *Eugenio Garin: Dal Rinascimento all'Illuminismo*, ed. M. Ciliberto, Rome: Edizione di storia e letteratura, 2011, 481–505.

4 The English translation is by Johan Huizinga in his *Homo ludens: A Study of the Play Element in Culture*, Boston: Beacon Press, 1950, 119. Huizinga's reference is to Bacon's *De dignitate et augmentis scientiarum* 3.1.

5 Agostino di Duccio, figure of *Dialectic* in Chapel of the Muses and the Liberal Arts, in *Il Tempio Malatestiano a Rimini*, ed. A. Paolucci, Modena: Franco Cosimo Panini, 2010, 2:167 (image 152).

6 Ascanio Condivi, *Life of Michelangelo*, trans. A. S. Wohl, University Park, PA: The Pennsylvania State University Press, 2nd edn., 1999, 67; Charles de Tolnay, *The Art and Thought of Michelangelo*, New York: Pantheon Books, 1964, 48.

7 Kenneth Gouwens has noted that humanists and artists alike found themselves in a "discursive field" with antiquity: "Perceiving the Past: Renaissance Humanism after the 'Cognitive Turn,'" *American Historical* Review 103 (1998): 55–82; 80. See also Anthony Grafton, *Commerce with the Classics*, Ann Arbor: University of Michigan Press, 1997.

8 Cicero, *De amicitia* 26 (97): "virtute enim ipsa non tam multi praediti esse quam videri volunt." All source translations are my own, unless otherwise noted.

9 MS Biblioteca apostolica vaticana, Ott.lat. 1677, c. 227v: "cum omnibus in rebus esse quam videri malis."

10 Virginia Cox, *The Renaissance Dialogue: Literary Dialogue in its Social and Political Contexts, Castiglione to Galileo*, Cambridge: Cambridge University Press, 1992, 3; cf. Peter Burke, "The Renaissance Dialogue," *Renaissance Studies* 3 (1989): 1–12.

11 *Oratio in hypocritas* in Leonardo Bruni, *Opere letterarie e politiche*, ed. P. Viti (Turin, 1996), 307–31; 314–16: "non ... ut boni sint, sed ut boni videantur."

12 See Wolfgang Senner, "Wahrheit bei Albertus Magnus und Thomas von Aquin," in *Die Geschichte des philosophischen Begriffs der Wahrheit*, ed. M. Enders and J. Szaif, Berlin: Walter de Gruyter, 2006, 103–48; and Theo Kobusch, "*Aedequatio rei et intellectus*: Die Erläuterung der Korrespondenztheorie der Wahrheit in der Zeit nach Thomas von Aquin," *ibid.*, 149–66.

13 Bruni, *Oratio*, 310: "me olim credentem fidentemque deceperint."

14 Poggio Bracciolini, *Contra hypocritas*, ed. D. Canfora, Rome: Edizioni di storia e letteratura, 2008, 7: "regnum hypocritarum."

15 Poggio, *Hypocritas*, 10: "ut meliores quam sit videantur."

16 *Ibid.*, 12 and 19: "Nam in quolibet artificio atque exercitio reperies viros ad simulandum promptos ac dissimulandum ... Idem de prestantibus ingenio viris, idem de bonis affirmo, quorum nullus est quin cupiat paulo amplius quam sit videri"; "Multiplex igitur est hypocritarum ac varia ratio, quorum perspicua cognitio videtur difficilis, ita inest illis quedam infixa similitudo virtutis ..."

17 *Ibid.*, 32–3.

18 On intersubjectivity in humanist dialogue, see Olga Zorzi Pugliese, *Il discorso labirintico del dialogo rinascimentale*, Rome: Bulzoni, 1995.

19 In their *De exilio* (*On Exile*) and *De vero bono* / *De voluptate* (*On the True Good* / *On Pleasure*), respectively.

20 Alberti, *Della famiglia*, Book 2, in *Opere volgari* (henceforth *OV*), ed. C. Grayson, 3 vols., Bari: Laterza, 1960–73, 1:84: "... né il ragionare nostro, el quale come vedi è tra noi domestico, si richiede essere gastigato ed emendato quanto quello de' filosafi nelle loro oscurissime e difficillime questioni, e' quali disputando seguono ogni minimo membro, e della materia lasciano adrieto nulla non bene esplicato e molto aperto."

21 Leon Battista Alberti, *On Painting*, trans. J. R. Spencer, New Haven, CT: Yale University Press, 1966, 57 (rev.). *OV* 3.38–9 (1.19): "E sappi che cosa niuna dipinta mai parrà pari alle vere, dove non sia certa distanza a vederle." / "Tum etiam pictas res nulla veris rebus pares, nisi certa ratione distent, videri posse nemo doctus negabit."

22 All references to the *Decameron* are from the edition by Vittore Branca, Turin: Einaudi, 1992.

23 All references to the *Rerum vulgarium fragmenta* (*Rvf*) are from the edition of the *Canzoniere* by Mark Musa, Bloomington: Indiana University Press, 1996.

24 *Triumphus temporis* 61–3 in *Trionfi; Rime estravaganti; Codice degli abbozzi*, ed. V. Pacca and L. Paolino, Milan: Mondadori, 1996; the echo is that of Pindar, *Pythian* 8. See also *Fam.* 24.1.11.

25 *Triumphus eternitatis* 20–1.

26 Baldassare Castiglione, *Il libro del cortegiano*, ed. G. Carnazzi, Milan: Rizzoli, 1987, Book 1, chapter 26.

27 Machiavelli, *Opere scelte*, ed. G. F. Berardi, Rome: Riuniti, 1969, *Discorsi* 1. Proem: "modi e ordini nuovi."

28 *Moriae encomium*, ed. C. H. Miller, *Opera omnia* (Amsterdam and Oxford: North Holland, 1979), 4.3:104: "omnia repente versa reperies, si Silenum aperueris"; "Porro mortalium vita omnis quid aliud est, quam fabula quaepiam, in qua alii aliis obtecti personis procedunt, donec choragus educat e proscenio?" The translation is by H. H. Hudson, *The Praise of Folly*, Princeton, NJ: Princeton Universiyt Press, 1969, 36–7.

29 Revising the translation in Rabelais, *The Histories of Gargantua and Pantagruel*, trans. J. M. Cohen, Penguin: New York, 1955, 37; *Gargantua* in *Oeuvres complètes*, ed. M. Huchon and F. Moreau, Paris: Gallimard, 1994, 5: "tousjours se gaubelant, tousjours dissimulant son divin sçavoir." See M[ikhail] M[ikailovitch] Bakhtin, *The Dialogic Imagination: Four Essays*, ed. and trans. M. Holquist and C. Emerson, Austin: University of Texas Press, 1981.

30 For a study of this theme in Pinturicchio's Sienese pavement panel, see Angela Dressen, "The Marble Philosophers and the Search for *pia sapientia*," in *Representations of Philosophers*, ed. H. Langdon, in *kunsttexte.de* (2) 2011, at http://edoc.hu-berlin.de/kunsttexte/2011-2/dressen-angela-2/PDF/dressen.pdf.

31 Leonardo Bruni, *Humanistisch-philosophische Schriften*, ed. H. Baron, Wiesbaden: Martin Sändig, 1928, 21: "si forte nos dignata lumen suum admoverit, hanc omnem, quae nos turbat, caliginem dissipabit veramque vivendi viam a fallaci discernet"; "humani generis caecitatem et tenebras"; "ad casum vivere desistat."

32 Matteo Palmieri, *Vita civile*, ed. G. Belloni, Florence: Sansoni, 1982, 16 and 29: "philosophia ministra i costumi e le virtù"; "approvato vivere degli uomini virtuosi."

33 Giovanni Gioviano Pontano, *Dialogues*, vol. 1, ed. and trans. J. H. Gaisser, Cambridge, MA.: Harvard University Press, 2012, *Charon*, e.g. 13, 52–4, 58.

34 Pier Paolo Vergerio, *De ingenuis moribus et liberalibus adulescentiae studiis (The Character and Studies Befitting a Free-Born Youth)*, in *Humanist Educational Treatises*, ed. and trans. C. Kallendorf, Cambridge, MA: Harvard University Press, 2002, 50–1: "Litterarum vero magnus est semper fructus et ad omnem vitam et ad omne hominum genus; praecipue vero studiosis earum, ut … ita e ad formandum eius habitum [virtutis]"; translation revised.

35 Gasparino Barzizza, "Oratio in principio quodam artium," in *Prosatori latini del Quattrocento*, ed. E. Garin, Milan: Riccardi, [1952], 307: "Quis non sentiat hominum vitam sine his artibus, non solum desertam et destitutam, sed multis iam brutis longe inferiorem et deteriorem esse?"

36 Lapo, *Epistolae*, MS BAV Ott. lat. 1677, c. 149v: "optima … fundamenta virtutis et doctrinae."

37 Erasmus, *The Education of a Christian Prince*, trans. N. M. Cheshire and M. J. Heath (Cambridge: Cambridge University Press,1997), 15; "Ni philosophus fueris, princeps esse non potes, tyrannus potes" in *Opera omnia*, vol. 4.1, ed. O. Herding, Amsterdam: North Holland, 1974, 144.

38 Vives, *De disciplinis libri XX* (Lyon, 1551), 4v: "nihil esse in vita vel pulchrius vel praestabilius cultu ingeniorum, quae disciplinae nominantur, qui nos a ferarum ritu et more separat, humanitati restituit, et ad Deum extollit ipsum."

39 Ficino, *Letters*, vol. 3, New York: Gingko Press, 1981, 61; letter 4.27.

40 For Lapo's preface, see Marianne Pade, ed., *The Reception of Plutarch's Lives in Fifteenth-Century Italy*, Copenhagen: Museum Tusculanum Press, 2007, 2:49–53; for that of Perotti, see MS Florence BNCF II VII 125, fols. 162–164v.

41 Alberti, *Intercenales* (Latin–Italian), ed. and trans. F. Bacchelli and L. D'Ascia, Bologna: Pedragon, 2003, 41–57; Aby Warburg, *The Renewal of Pagan Antiquity: Contributions to the Cultural History of the European Renaissance*, trans. D. Britt, Los Angeles: Getty Research Institute, 1999, 452.

42 Petrarch, *Invectives*, ed. and trans. D. Marsh, Cambridge, MA: Havard University Press, 2003, 252.

43 Poggio Bracciolini, *De varietate fortunae*, ed. O. Merisalo, Helsinki: Suomalainen Tiedeakatemia, 1993, 89: "fortune ludus"; "fortune theatrum"; "Illa enim quos fovit, suo iure utens, primum deicit, tum eorum stultitiam detegit."

44 Guicciardini, *Ricordi*, ed. C. Varotti, Rome: Carocci, 2013, C. 136.

45 Erasmus, *Moriae encomium*, 4.3:176: "rerum humanarum fortunatrix."

46 Petrarch, *Invectives*, 238; 314.

47 Lapo, *Epistolae*, MS BAV Ott. lat. 1677, c. 171v: "Nam veteres amicos id est libros, quod quidem nihil mihi prodesse potuerint, odisse iam coepi … nec nisi huiusmodi temporum conditio mutetur in gratiam rediturus sum."

48 Alberti, *Momus*, ed. and trans. S. Knight and V. Brown, Cambridge, MA: Harvard University Press, 2003, 152: "veterem morem et honestatem"; 268–70: "bonis artibus excultum"; "et illic ubi se probos et simplicissimos videri student, illic maxime fallunt dolo et improbitate."

49 Cusa, *Idiota de sapientia, liber primus* in Opera omnia, Hamburg: Felix Meiner, 1983, 5.3–4: "cum continua lectione defatigeris innumerabiles libros lectitando, nondum ad humilitatem ductus sis; hoc certe ex eo, quia scientia huius mundi, in qua te ceteros praecellere putas, stultitia quaedam est apud Deum et hinc inflat." Echoes of 1 Cor. 3.19; 8.1.

50 Montaigne, *Essays*, trans. D. Frame, Stanford: Stanford University Press, 1943, 666 (Frame's translation); *Essais*, ed. A. Tournon, Paris: Imprimerie Nationale 1998, 3:146–7: "Les sciences traitent les choses trop finement, d'une mode artificielle, et différente à la commune et naturelle. Mon page fait l'amour et l'entend. Lisez-lui Léon Hébreu et Ficin: on parle de lui, de ses pensées e de ses actions, et si, n'y entend rien. Je ne reconnais pas chez Aristote la plupart de mes mouvements ordinaires: On les a couverts et revêtus d'une autre robe, pour l'usage de l'école."

51 Eugenio Garin, *La cultura del Rinascimento: Profilo storico*, Rome: Laterza, 2010, 133: "Senza questo platonismo non si intende il Rinascimento …"

52 Boccaccio, *Geneaology of the Pagan Gods*, ed. and trans. J. Solomon, Cambridge, MA: Harvard University Press, 2011, 188, 186 (2.2): "ipse solus summum sit bonum et quod ab eo vita sit et adiutorium universis … Insuper hoc nomen 'Juppiter' Grece dicitur *zephs*, quod Latine 'vita' sonat."

53 *Ibid.*, 532–4 (4.44): "Eschylus Pictagoreus poeta"; "harum fictionum involucrum … non erit leve corticem aperire"; "deus verus et omnipotens." Translation revised.

54 *Ibid.*, 538 (4.44): "id est in loco perfectionis"; "sunt omnia animata igne, id est claritate veritatis"; "a rota solis, id est e gremio Dei, a quo omnis sapientia est. Ipse enim verus est sol 'qui illuminat omnem hominem venientem in hunc mundum …'" The allusion is to John 1.9.

55 Coluccio Salutati, *De laboribus Herculis*, ed. B.L. Ullman, 2 vols., Zurich: Thesaurus mundus, 1951, 1.443 (3.43): "Platonicos, quos maxime secuti sunt poete."

56 Salutati, *De laboribus*, 1.293–6 (3.23): "que latent sui natura sub carnibus."; "Visus est autem errasse Iupiter eligendo quoniam mundanis hominibus sequentes spiritualia videntur errasse; "imperium rationis."

57 Cristoforo Landino, *Disputationes camaldulenses*, ed. P. Lohe, Florence: Sansoni, 1980, 32, 42, 88: "ex Platonicorum sententia mundi animam interpretamur"; "omnium rerum architectus."

58 *Ibid.*, 73, 75, 77–8: "omnium optimus"; "omnis boni bonum"; "bonum autem stabile esse oportet."

59 *Ibid.*, 103–14: "constat apud metaphysicos, quicquid est, id omne esse a deo"; "quicquid igitur est, quacunque ratione sit, ex eo quod est bonum est. Igitur malum nullam habet essentiam." See Thomas Aquinas, *Summa Theologiae*, PP q.5 a.3.

60 *Ibid.*, 47 and 39: "rerum certitudo."

61 Ficino, *The Philebus Commentary*, ed. and trans. M. J. B. Allen, Berkeley: University of California Press, 1975, 242–3: "divina mens"; 293; 238–9: "in mundo superno primum, hoc est, ipsum bonum et unum rerum principium species rerum mentesque omnes suo procreat lumine"; 241–5: "mundi huius artifice." Allen's translation.

62 Ficino, *De sole* in *Prosatori latini*, 972 (ch. 2): "ipse visus coelestis animae"; and 982 (ch. 6): "oculus aeternus omnia videns"; "Mundi Dominus, Juppiter immortalis."

63 Ficino, *Philebus Commentary*, 244–5: "largitor, medius … et praeparator"; "solem faventem spiritui praesertim rationali." Allen's translation.

64 Ficino, *Platonic Theology*, trans. J. M. B. Allen and ed. J. Hankins, vol. 1, Cambridge, MA: Harvard University Press, 2001, 16–17 (1.1): "Huius denique mentis oculo, qui cupit veritatis lumen et capit, solem ipsum praeesse divinum …" (Allen's translation); *De sole* in *Prosatori latini*, 1001 (ch. 11): "Tria Platonici principia ponunt. Ipsum bonum, divinum intellectum, mundi animam. Lumen unicum prae caeteris palam haec omnia refert."

65 Ficino, *Platonic Theology*, vol. 2, Cambridge, MA: Harvard University Press, 2006, 146–7 (6.2).

66 Garin, *La cultura*, 55; Stephen Greenblatt, *Renaissance Self-Fashioning: From More to Shakespeare*, Chicago: University of Chicago Press, 2005.

67 Pico della Mirandola, *Oration on the Dignity of Man: A New Translation and Commentary*, ed. F. Borghesi, M. Papio, and M. Riva, Cambridge: Cambridge University Press, 2012, §160: "in hac quasi litteraria palestra, animi vires et fortiores longe et vegetiores evadunt."

68 *Ibid.*, §180: "me per omnes philosophiae magistros funderem, omnes scedas excuterem, omnes familias agnoscerem."

69 *Ibid.*, §17: "indiscretae opus imaginis"; "commune esset quicquid privatum singulis fuerat."

70 Salutati, *De laboribus*, 1.295 (3.23): "ipsos sumptis a cunctis animantium proprietatibus seu passionibus fecerit."

71 Pico, *Oration*, §§71–81.

72 *Ibid.*, §§262–3: "Orpheus suorum dogmatum mysteria … poetico velamento dissumulavit …; ex affectatis enigmatum syrpis, ex fabularum latebris latitantes eruere secretae philosophiae sensus."

73 *Ibid.*, §224: "omnes alias sapientias, it hanc sub sui Ulixis erroribus dissimulasse."

74 *Ibid.*, §§115 and 123: "ver[us] Apoll[o] … illuminat omnem animam venientem in hunk mundum"; "pater ac dux."

75 *Ibid.*, §§192 and 135: "veritatis fulgor animis nostris quasi sol oriens ex alto clarius illucesceret"; "debile adhuc veritatis lumen, quasi nascentis solis incunabula; "quasi caelestes aquilae, meridiantis solis fulgidissimum iubar fortiter perferamus."

76 *Ibid.*, §1: "nihil spectari homine admirabilis … in hac quasi mundana scena." Anselm, *Proslogion* §2: "Et quidem credimus te esse aliquid quo nihil maius cogitari possit"; www.thelatinlibrary.com/anselmproslogion.html.

77 Poggio, *De varietate*, 104: "Ita non sapiens, sed sapientis virtus et ratio erunt extra tela fortune."

78 Lorenzo Valla, *On Pleasure / De voluptate*, ed. and trans. A. K. Hieatt and M. Lorch, New York: Abaris Books, 1977, 204 (2.28.16).

79 *Ibid.*, 288–9 (3.19.1), translation revised: "Que quidem enigmata et allegorias si quis excutere et ad liquidem perducere velit, frustra nimirum laborabit. Non potest enim facies nostra operimento detegi quod corpus est"; "extra corpus naturam non habent ut ab his qui in corpore sunt percipiantur"; "animis tenebris ac carcere ceco clausus et immersus."

80 Alberti, "De Amicitia" in *Rime / Poèmes*, ed. G. Gorni, Paris: Les belles lettres, 2002, line 7.

81 Cusa, *De visione Dei*, in *Nicholas of Cusa's Dialectical Mysticism: Text, Translation, and Interpretive Study of the "De visione Dei,"* ed. and trans. J. Hopkins, Minneapolis: Arthur J. Banning Press, 1985, 154–6 (9.35): "absoluta forma"; "formator coeli et terrae et omnium."

82 *Ibid.*, 136 (6.20): "qualitercumque faciem meam muto, videtur facies ad me conversa"; 158 (9.37): "Nam si moveor, apparet visus eius moveri quia me non deserit. Si, me movente, alius qui faciem intuetur stat, similiter eum visus non deserit, sed stet cum stante."

83 *Ibid.*, 136 (6.20): "homo non potest iudicare nisi humaniter"; 138 (6.22): "In omnibus faciebus videtur facies facierum velate et in aenigmate," alluding to 1 Cor. 13; 162 (10.40).

84 *Ibid.*, 158 (9.37): "stas simul et movens, progrederis simul et quiescis"; "est supra omnem stationem et motum in simplicissima et absolutissima infinitate."

85 *Ibid.*, 138 (6.22): "quoddam secretum et occultum silentium ubi nihil est de scientia et conceptu faciei"; "caligo, nebula, tenebra, seu ignorantia"; "ipsa autem caligo revelat ibi esse faciem supra omnia velementa"; 160 (9.39): "non est via alia ad te accedendi, nisi illa quae omnibus hominibus, etiam doctissimis philosophis, videtur penitus inaccessibilis et impossibilis."

86 *Ibid.*, 168 (11.45).

87 Alberti, *Momus*, 6: "animadverti ut deorum nominibus eas animi vires intellegi voluerint, quibus in hanc aut in alteram institutorum partem agimur."

88 *Ibid.*, 242–3: "nihil expromant rerum reconditarum nisi id sit maximis verborum involucris implictum, longis ambagibus"; 304–5: "nihil nostis nisi ita loqui ut de rebus notissimis verba facientes non intellegamini." Knight's translation.

89 *Ibid.*, 54.

90 *Ibid.*, 282–3: "philosophus idem histrio"; 284–5: "manifesto adesse deos."

91 *Ibid.*, 332–3: "Ambago, dearum mendacissima." Knight's translation.

92 Boccaccio, *Genealogy*, 134–3 (1.20–1).

93 Luther, *De servo arbitrio*, in *Werke: Kritische Gesamtausgabe*, 73 vols., Weimar: Herman Böhlau, 1883–1929, 18.640.

94 Luther, *Enarrationes epistolarum et evangelorum, quas postillas vocant*, in *Werke*, 7.496: "lux faculae" in meridie ardente sole"; *Operationes in Psalmos*, in *Werke*, 5.163: "Vivendo, immo moriendo et damnando fit theologus, non intelligendo, legendo, aut speculando."

95 Montaigne, *Essays*, 455, revised; *Essais*, 2.434: "Nous n'avons aucune communication á l'être, parce que toute humaine nature est toujours au milieu, entre le naître et le mourir, ne baillant de soi qu'une obscure apparence et umbre, et une incertaine et débile opinion"; cf. Plutarch, "On the E at Delphi" 18.

96 Montaigne, *Essays*, 401; 413–14; 427. *Essais*, 2.327: "d'une infinie varieté de faux jours à exercer nos conjectures"; 2.380: "Notre veilée est plus endormie que le dormir, nostre sagesse moins sage que la folie."

97 Boccaccio, *Genealogy*, 148 (1.28) and 162–3: "ultimum esse terribilium testatur Aristoteles." *Nicomachean Ethics*, trans. R. C. Bartlett and S. D. Collins, Chicago: University of Chicago Press, 2011, 3.6 (1115a).

Part II

ENCOUNTERS AND TRANSFORMATIONS

6

OBJECT LESSONS AND
RAW MATERIALS[1]

Timothy McCall and Sean Roberts

Not so long ago, material culture played a relatively modest role in many of the stories told about the Renaissance, and even the most artfully crafted and constructed objects were obscured in the shadow of painting, sculpture, and the remnants of classical antiquity. Over the past few decades, however, historians of all sorts have steadily, and with ever increasing momentum, embraced material and visual culture as vital forms of evidence.[2] Art historians – in concert with, and frequently at the forefront of this development – have expanded, and at times abandoned, the constraints of the canon in favor of a truly diverse range of Renaissance things. Votive plaques of little aesthetic interest, inexpensive printed saints, and glazed ceramic vessels celebrating childbirth have all anchored recent, influential studies.[3]

These examinations of ostensibly more ordinary objects have offered revealing glimpses into the lives of non-elite women and men. Simultaneously, new approaches to armor, jewelry, and all variety of sumptuous, luxury goods have substantially broadened and augmented our understanding of modes and patterns of production, consumption, and use of Renaissance art and material culture. The cultural study of clothing is one example of a previously marginal field that has flourished thanks to art history's material turn.[4] Attention to this expanding range of objects, moreover, has provided a means for scholars to re-conceptualize hierarchies of value and medium that long structured the discipline. Once routinely marginalized as merely "decorative" cousins of painting, tapestries, for instance, are now comfortably situated at the center of our understanding of Renaissance visual culture.[5]

Anthropologists and sociologists, for their part, have devoted critical attention to fundamental dichotomies that have traditionally characterized both contemporary and historical attitudes toward the very concept of materiality itself. These scholars compel us to acknowledge our conventional, indeed habitual, assumptions about the polluted, corrupt, and shallow nature of the material world, which is nearly ubiquitous in philosophical traditions ranging from Buddhism to Marxism. The Platonic opposition between form and matter is only the most familiar of the staggeringly prevalent beliefs in the essential superficiality of that which comprises our material world and lives.[6] Such oppositions were quotidian, powerful, and often threatening in Renaissance society, and they found poignant expression in confrontations between Christian ascetic traditions and a world that was conversely characterized by commerce, magnificence, and intensifying investment in naturalism. Savonarola's bonfires, Protestant image-breaking, and the elision of antiquarian interest with idolatry all materialized, at least in part, from these long-standing dichotomies.

These material tensions and antagonisms were paramount for many of the writers ushering in the Renaissance, chief among them Dante and Petrarch, who bespoke tremendous discomfort with a world they felt to be governed by proliferating demands of courtly magnificence and commercial wealth. Such moralizing appraisal of perceived economic change set the tone for and subsequently served both to engender and confirm longstanding scholarly estimations of the period as increasingly worldly, secular, and materialist, if ambivalently so.[7] Our relatively newfound appreciation for Renaissance "things" thus tends to reinforce rather than challenge an assessment of the period's economy as a fundamentally dynamic, proto-capitalist one, and the very notion of early modernity is sometimes seen as hinging upon these progressive economic developments.[8] Yet, novelty cohabited with feudal economies in large parts of both Italy and Northern Europe, with local barter economies even in the most cosmopolitan locales, and with traditions of gift exchange within and among – to name only the most prominent players – the Ottoman, Mamluk, and Hapsburg courts (and indeed, the global nature of Renaissance material culture is addressed below). The paths by which Renaissance things were produced, transported, acquired, and consumed were variegated and unpredictable.[9]

Our intention in this chapter is not to reify any particular system of exchange, but rather to focus on a few key "things" and the ways in which they were procured, produced, circulated, valued, and transformed. Such circulation was not exclusively, or even principally, one of lavishly crafted objects. Equally essential to the very fabric of Renaissance material culture, and the people entangled in these things, was the movement of many of the raw materials from which they were made. Competition for such resources was fierce and in some cases violent, as we shall see with attempts to control access to the important dye fixative alum. What follows, then, is a series of object lessons centered on finished products, the raw materials of which these were composed, and the sometimes difficult, and increasingly global paths by which material culture circulated in Renaissance Europe.

We investigate too the seemingly inherent value of materials, the problems posed by the transformation and simulation of these precious things, and the role of mimesis and deception in the values attached to objects. If the alchemist sought in vain to transform base metals into gold, the appearance of having performed such a miracle was the everyday province of Renaissance artisans. The ubiquity of such transmutations unsurprisingly introduced well-founded concerns about forgery and fraud. So too, accusations that radiant or colorful surfaces could disguise rot beneath often drew on longstanding misogynist appraisals of women's cosmetics and ornamentation.[10] Yet, we will examine a number of material fictions – imitation dyes and gold, decorated printed books simulating luxury manuscripts – which sought not to deceive, in any straightforward way, but rather to elicit responses including delight, play, and discernment. Renaissance things, it is fair to say, were often not what they seemed, and recognition of such substitutions was likewise essential to the practice and theory of art making.

Faking it? Material fictions and the play of value

Recently scholars have placed considerable emphasis on materials and their transformation, a phenomenon dubbed a "cult of materials" by Michael Cole.[11] Pamela Smith's pioneering work on artisanal knowledge has shed penetrating new light on the core Renaissance value of naturalism and alerted us to the ways in which the seeming and being of skillfully crafted objects were indelibly linked.[12] Systems of transforming raw materials were typically conventional (yet often simultaneously inventive), and artisanal knowledge of their properties was at once practical and fabulous – grounded both in practice and fiction. They ranged from the mundane to the ostensibly magical, such as the pervasive (yet seemingly functionally useless) deployment of mercury in the production of gold mosaic attributed by Smith to alchemical beliefs about the generation of gold.[13] Rather than revisit these indispensable contributions, however, we will attend to a rather different kind of transformation: the production of counterfeit goods, of simulacra that mimic precious raw materials in their more mundane cousins, of what now might be comfortably, though in some ways misleadingly, gathered under the umbrella of the fake.

The seductively glittering, golden surfaces of armor, liturgical metalwork, and brocades (cloth embroidered with metal-wrapped threads) were usually far from solid gold. Because of its relative scarcity and the near universal consensus about its intrinsic worth, gold presents a special case.[14] Artful things wrought from gold could be, and often were, melted down, liquidated as a form of currency. The goldsmith and sculptor Antonio del Pollaiuolo purportedly lamented that his name would vanish to posterity for just this reason.[15] Though these fears were ultimately unwarranted, thanks largely to his success in painting, engraving, and monumental sculpture, few of Pollaiuolo's works in precious metals survive, and some are mere fragments. The Bargello's enameled silver plaques – housed today in a sixteenth-century armature – were stripped from the artisan's monumental gold and silver cross at a moment when demand for such resources outweighed aesthetic consideration (Illustration 6.1).[16]

Sparkling surfaces, moreover, were commonly manufactured through the craft of the goldbeater (*battiloro*) who hammered and banged minuscule quantities of precious metal into sheets, far thinner than paper, for application to a wide array of finished products. Yet, both the skillful goldsmith or the tireless *battiloro* could hide the true nature of raw materials, substituting alloys for the real thing, exchanging brass for gold. In fifteenth-century Milan, for instance, a small industry arose around the production of aurichalcum (*oricalco*), an alloy of copper and calamine (a zinc oxide) similar to modern brass.[17] Even exceptionally observant viewers, let alone those who merely glimpsed liturgical vestments, jewelry, arms, or brocaded tunics, might not know the difference between *oro* and *oricalco*, or between silver and white-metallic alloys, as the lustrous materials glinted and glistened in the bright sunlight of a piazza or the flickering candles of a church interior. When confronted with the spectacle of a bishop or lord in splendid array, even knowledgeable and materially discerning viewers perhaps deemed what he wore to be the cloth of gold that literally constituted ecclesiastical and signorial authority.[18]

As was the case for gold (and gilding), a host of expensive goods could likewise activate suspicious disparities, or perhaps playful deceptions, between surfaces and what lay beneath. The "gems" adorning Renaissance popes and kings – and those with much less wealth – might instead be colored glass or paste, tinted crystal, or doublets – layered (i.e., doubled) glass or stones with colored foil placed behind or between them.[19] Gems both real and imitation, moreover, might be tinted or dyed with ingredients including various powdered or grated pigments, or heated olive oil, indigo, talc, or resin.[20] Most subjects and peers expected aristocrats to be adorned in true gems and solid gold – as befit their rank – yet we should imagine that many knew this might not be so. Proof or even claims to the contrary could impeach the authority of both ecclesiastical and secular powers. For instance, Duke Galeazzo Maria Sforza of Milan was posthumously criticized by the humanist Giovanni

Illustration 6.1 Though we tend to think of metalwork as highly durable, the fungibility of gold and silver means that comparatively few examples of the goldsmith's craft have survived intact from the Renaissance. These silver and enamel plaquettes, mounted today in later housing, are all that remains of a once monumental golden cross by Antonio del Pollauiolo, among the most famous artisans of his day.

Source: © Nicolo Orsi Battaglini / Art Resource, NY

Pontano for duplicitously exhibiting "as rare and precious many false gems that he had secretly purchased."[21] Though Galeazzo was renowned for his prodigality and vanity, the anti-Milanese position of Pontano's Neapolitan employers (plus something of a personal grudge) provided motive for such a damning slander to be levied. Typically for civic authorities, more troubling than the display, possession, or production of doublets and manufactured gems was the danger that they be mistaken for genuine items by those who bought or wore them, rather than by those who saw them worn. As we shall see below, this was similarly the case for deceptively advertised or identified dyes. Legislation served to protect the buyer, rather than eventual audiences. Indeed, throughout Europe, it was illegal for goldsmiths to set artificial jewels in gold. In 1487, to give but one example, the Senate of Venice decreed that goldsmiths or jewelers guilty of this infraction could be imprisoned, mutilated, banished, or perpetually banned from practicing their craft in Venetian territory.[22]

The simulation or substitution of costly dyes valued for the luster they provided to iridescent textiles likewise engendered highly significant material fictions in the Renaissance. It is a well-known commonplace that the most expensive pigment for painters of altarpieces was lapis lazuli or ultramarine blue, coming from, as its name suggests, beyond the sea, primarily from what is now Afghanistan.[23] For clothing, it was instead red dyes that were most precious.[24] The most valuable reds were procured from the dried bodies of, or secretions from, tiny scale insects native throughout Asia and the Mediterranean. These parasites included kermes, lac, and eventually American cochineal, and both the raw material and many of the dyes themselves were known as *grana* or grain (from which we get the English "ingrained"), because of the granular appearance of the sun-dried, desiccated bugs.[25]

Where intrinsic value was at stake, the possibility of fictive materiality – whether of textiles or metalwork – could arouse suspicion of deceit and inauthenticity. Venice, for example, strove to curb the practice of tricking buyers into purchasing textiles colored with cheaper than advertised dyes. In 1453, the Venetian senate mandated that silk brocades colored with pure red kermes be indicated differently than those tinted with combinations of dyes (Illustration 6.2).[26] Civic authorities throughout Europe, in fact, employed various methods to distinguish between red-dyed fabrics, particularly brocaded ones, and of course these restrictions – like sumptuary legislation more generally – are themselves strong indications of the contraband practices they proscribed. Yet, as we suggested above, those with the greatest purchasing power were hardly constrained or obligated to material truthfulness or authenticity. Deceiving audiences about the quality or material of dyes was one trick Renaissance lords had hidden up their brocaded sleeves, as correspondence between Galeazzo Maria Sforza, Duke of Milan, and the merchant Gottardo da Panigarola reveals.

In late 1475, Gottardo – Galeazzo's buyer, literally the court's "spender" (*spenditore*) – was instructed to provide twenty-six of the Sforza choir's singers with black velvet for doublets and dark murrey-colored cloth for additional clothing.[27] *Morello*, murrey or more precisely mulberry-colored, was a primary dynastic color of the Sforza and their adherents (who were frequently clad in murrey and white stockings); it was typically a dark red verging on brown or black, but often approaching a royal purple.[28] Multiple dyes and processes could furnish these shades, although not all wearers, let alone viewers, were equally able to discern variations in dye and material, as Galeazzo cleverly calculated. "But search out a fine enough cloth with a good, dark color," the ducal directive instructed Gottardo – "so that the singers will be persuaded that it's murrey of grain (*morello de grana*), although it's something else entirely." The lord wanted his prized singers, and no doubt those who heard but also saw them perform, to believe that their regally mulberry-colored clothing was dyed with expensive kermes *grana*, without having to pay the price.

Courtly clothing and bodily adornment comprised one highly visible locus for material fiction. Printed book illumination and its problematic relationship to manuscript sheds light on a rather different sort of apparent deception, one steeped in Renaissance attitudes toward novelty and familiarity, materials and skill, visual trickery and delight. Modern readers and viewers have long been accustomed to the appearance of black lines on the white page, an aesthetic which gradually came to vouch for authority and uniformity in early modern Europe.[29] For at least some prospective book buyers of the later fifteenth century, printed

Illustration 6.2 This small, yet sumptuous, gold-brocaded velvet fragment produced in sixteenth-century Venice is composed of crimson silk pile providing a soft, seductive texture and, together with innumerable gold-wrapped threads, alluringly charismatic and iridescent surface effects.

Source: © The Metropolitan Museum of Art

books must have seemed discomfiting shadows of the manuscripts to which they had long been accustomed.

In consequence, lavishly illuminated incipits like that of Pliny's *Natural History* (Illustration 6.3) produced in the shop of the Venice-based printer Nicholas Jenson mask the ostensibly uniform letterpress page beneath a veneer of gold foil. The skilled illuminator's brushes provide twisting *all'antica* candelabra, historiated initials, and a treasury of fictive gems.[30] Particularly revealing for our purposes, however, is the undeniable fact that hand-coloring and customization were the norm rather than exception for many early printed books and images.[31] Such modifications were prevalent among large-format, illustrated projects like the editions of Ptolemy's *Geography* (Illustration 6.4) printed in Ulm in 1482 and 1486. Translations and paraphrases of this second-century world description were ubiquitous components of Renaissance libraries and *studioli*, and were deluxe productions typically including over two dozen folio maps.[32] The addition of gold and color to a great many printed examples suggests that book buyers sought economical alternatives to manuscript that preserved as much of the basic look of their predecessors as possible.[33]

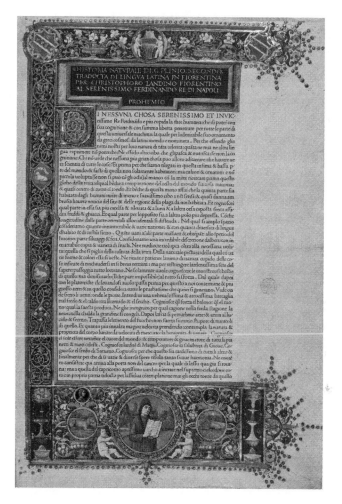

Illustration 6.3 Renaissance book buyers, accustomed to the lavish appearance of manuscripts, often demanded that printed books mimic their illuminated predecessors. Lavishly painted pages, like those found in this Venetian edition of Pliny's *Natural History*, relied upon the skill of the artist's brush to add historiated initials, author portraits, classicizing marginalia, and a host of fictive ornament. Whether printed on paper or even vellum, these hybrid products represented a liminal category between manuscript and printed book.

Source: Bodleian Library, University of Oxford

These products of the press, however, could inspire unease in some Renaissance readers and viewers. Commentators with vested interests in scribal practices and manuscript production were especially dismissive of these seemingly tawdry simulacra of true books. The Florentine book dealer Vespasiano da Bisticci famously minced no words in disparaging the novelties of print as cheap fabrications. For Vespasiano, Federico da Montefeltro's renowned library was full of books "superlatively good, and written with the pen, and had there been one printed volume it would have been ashamed in such company."[34] Moreover, the novelty

111

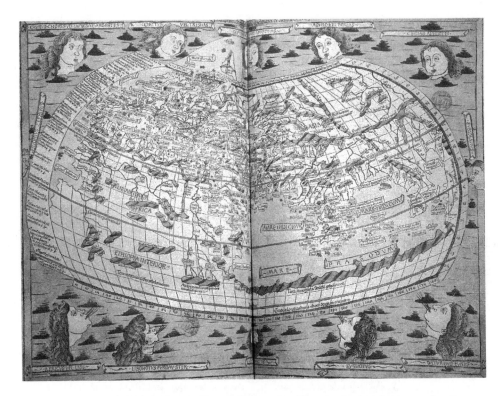

Illustration 6.4 Hand-coloring and customization were the norm rather than exception for many early printed books and images. Expensive, large-format projects like this late fifteenth-century German edition of Ptolemy's *Geography* were frequently painted and decorated with gold leaf at the point of production and demonstrate a high degree of standardization.

Source: © CCI / The Art Archive at Art Resource, NY

of these products themselves aroused suspicion in an age whose attitudes toward technological and societal change were always ambivalent. For while some like Giovanni Stradano (Jan Van der Straet) praised the "new inventions" of the day, fear of new men and their corrupting customs kept the complaints of Dante and Petrarch fresh in many Renaissance minds.[35]

As with gilded silver work, the addition of paint, gold, and other surface embellishments to the letterpress page was hardly uniformly deceptive, at least so far as value was concerned. Printed books were, assuredly, less expensive alternatives to sumptuous manuscripts. The difference in the price of vellum alone as compared to paper – upon which most books were printed – was substantial. Likewise, gold foil, pigments, and the labor costs of illuminators and scribes were hardly inconsequential. Such disparity would have been especially stark for large and complicated manuscripts, including collections of maps, choir books, and liturgical works designed to visibly impress at a distance.[36] This hierarchy of value is readily illustrated in the proliferation of geographic editions produced between the advent of printing and the mid-sixteenth century. In many cases, presentation manuscripts of these same books were simultaneously crafted for illustrious recipients and dedicatees, manifesting clear distinctions of prestige and value between printed books – however lavish – and their manuscript counterparts.

On the other hand, for authors, publishers, and printmakers these new illustrated, printed books offered much else, too. They were a means of multiplying the manuscript, a way of advertising a certain technical innovation, and provided the opportunity to carve out a distinctive craft of their own. As such, qualities that might seem at first glance to be crudely and unconvincingly dissimulative might, in another light, be seen as part of a complicated negotiation process. Indeed, early printed books were sometimes augmented in ways which made no attempt to disguise their origins on the press bed, but rather combined the technological freshness of this new art with undeniable splendor. Cristoforo Landino's *Commentary* on Dante's *Divine Comedy*, printed in Florence in 1481, supplies an example of just such an extravagant, yet conspicuously printed book. The *Commentary* was among the earliest editions to combine letterpress with engraved illustrations, a challenging (and initially frustrating) innovation for its printer to master.[37] The most lavish copy was that customized for presentation to the *Signoria* and now counted among the most precious books in Florence's Biblioteca Nazionale. The *Signoria's Commentary* is printed on vellum, the traditional stuff of manuscript, and its pages are embellished with hand-painted initials, decorative borders, and a profusion of gold leaf. Most strikingly, the tome's binding is set with silver *niello* clasps, additions likely to have been more costly than the rest of the book in total.[38] Landino, his printer, and financiers ensured that anyone inclined to judge their book by its cover would arrive at a favorable conclusion indeed.

Materiality and mimesis: Alberti's gold and pictorial naturalism

Book and art historians have struggled at times with what seems to be all too apparent imitation, so simple or obvious that it could not possibly have deceived readers and viewers. Yet, the intention was not merely to fool, but to partake in chains of associations initiated by precious materials and opulent objects, and, perhaps, to activate the delights of material deception. The study of art's economic value in the Renaissance often paints a picture in stark contrast to modern art-historical judgments. Notaries attached modest monetary worth to undisputed masterpieces of painting and even sculpture, while the same inventories recorded staggering values for tapestries, luxury cloth, and the material remains of antiquity such as cameos, vases, and coins. These discrepancies demonstrate both the continued relevance of the intrinsic value of materials including metals and textiles, and likewise the scarcity of antiquities for Renaissance patrons, buyers, and collectors.[39]

Scholars seeking redress for these economic imbalances have attached tremendous weight to the attitudes of Renaissance theorists who championed the worth of visual art as inversely rather than proportionally related to material splendor or intrinsic value. There can be little question that a great deal of the period's visual and material culture was predicated upon the mimetic or naturalistic capacities of its makers, and the authority most frequently marshaled in support of this hierarchy of value is the Florentine Leon Battista Alberti. In *On Painting*, Alberti describes and derides those painters

> who use much gold in their *istoria*. They think it gives majesty. I do not praise it. Even though one should paint Virgil's Dido whose quiver was of gold, her golden hair knotted with gold, and her purple robe girdled with pure gold, the reins of the

horse and everything of gold, I should not wish gold to be used, for there is more admiration and praise for the painter who imitates the rays of gold with colours.[40]

Art historians following these desiderata have customarily characterized the Renaissance as a period in which illusion and skill came to overtake material splendor, at least for astute viewers. This dichotomy is probably most bluntly, and persuasively, represented by Michael Baxandall's dictum that "Noticeable art draws attention to itself quite as much as noticeable material: the more modest the material, the more the skill by which it is dignified stands out. Very few artists have evaded the dilemma."[41] Moreover, if the stubborn persistence of intrinsic value is generally acknowledged, the surety of a march toward skill's triumph is rarely questioned. Thus, scholars approaching Botticelli's *Coronation of the Virgin with Saints John, Augustine, Jerome, and Eligius* and casual Uffizi visitors reading the label that accompanies the massive altarpiece learn that the panel's preponderance of gold represents an archaism dictated by its staunchly conservative patron, the guild of goldsmiths.[42] Yet such radiant displays are hardly confined to works for stodgy patrons, and gold played an undeniably central role in Botticelli's art for the entirety of his career.

Should we not then focus on the interplay rather than solely the competition between these paradigms? For there was a rather different, and equally persuasive model for mimetic dissimulation – that of play, and its (often visual) pleasures. Nor must we look far afield from the high-minded admonitions of those like Alberti to find traces of this system. Other authoritative voices, in fact, spoke of a less rigid lens for viewing deceptions. Pliny's *Natural History* exposed readers to the tale of Parrhasius' mischievous triumph over his rival Zeuxis. For though Zeuxis fooled birds into attempting to eat his fictive grapes, Parrhasius tricked Zeuxis, and the human intellect, when the latter tried to pull aside the painted curtain of his competitor.[43] These ancient tales were repeated and adapted in all manner of Renaissance sources, and they cogently demonstrate that mimesis itself worked as a trick that needed to be revealed to be appreciated.

In the Renaissance imagination, games and play were understood as a variety of simulacrum. According to the Cremonese humanist and bishop Marco Girolamo Vida, chess players, for instance, "play at war's image and feign real battles, with wooden armies and mock kingdoms."[44] Like mimetic images, games and tricks were forms of substitution. And like games, mimetic images acquired much of their value only through their ultimate dissimilarity from the materials they represented. Just as the joys of chess arise not from its substantial similarity to warfare but rather from a certain distance, the thrill of skillful victory without violence, so too did painting (at least as envisioned by Alberti) offer the glint of gold without metal, the delights of precious materials in their conspicuous absence. Parrhasius' curtain, of course, is of little value until Zeuxis recognizes its material falseness.[45] Though comparison between media is most commonly framed through the concept of *paragone*, painterly and sculptural imitations could also be understood as fundamentally mischievous, playful, and practically – rather than only theoretically – competitive.

Alberti's words are repeated, time and again, by many who have failed to recognize both the continued investment of Renaissance artisans in precious materials and the very plays of value upon which *On Painting*'s proscriptions are built. Indeed, it is the brilliant sparkle of gold that suggests the painter deployed his powers of fiction upon it – to fool the eye, but assuredly not the mind of the discerning viewer, if only for the briefest of moments. Alberti praises the artisan's deceptive powers, yet such deception is grounded in the inherent value of the material replicated. Perhaps most importantly, Alberti imagines these tricks performed not in the absence of precious gold but precisely in its contin-ued presence as an integral and constituent part of painting's material environment. For if his admonition concerning Dido's girdle is repeated *ad infinitum* in the literature on Renaissance painting, it is rarely there joined with the necessary caveat that follows. For Alberti promptly adds that he "would not censure the other ornaments joined to the paint-ing such as columns, curved bases, capitals and frontispieces even if they were of the most pure and massy [solid] gold. Even more, a well perfected *istoria* deserves ornaments of the most precious gems."[46] That is to say, he fully expected that a discriminating viewer could judge the success or failure of the painter's tricks through direct visual inspection of – and comparison with – the gold that framed and embellished such panels. Yet even this play of value was already dependent upon an ingenious yet well-understood trick; like "cloth of gold," the solid, pure gold of Alberti's columns and bases represented a sleight of hand. Writing over a century later, Vasari praised Tuscan artisans for perfecting the art of beat-ing and banging gold into leaves of nearly inconceivable thinness so that "by spreading the gold over the gesso in such a manner that the wood and other material hidden beneath it should appear a mass of gold." Far from an embarrassing counterfeit, the artisan's abil-ity to seemingly transform wood into gold represented nothing less than an "ingenious invention."[47]

A profound irony, then, sits at the core of fundamental evaluations of Renaissance arti-fice. The conspicuously skillful making of simulacra in painting and sculpture has been lauded both as a signature accomplishment of the period and as the raw material from which artisans carved out the ideal and emerging form of the artist.[48] Yet these very activi-ties, praiseworthy in Michelangelo's chisel or Holbein's brushes, are scorned as the offspring of fraud or the products of provincial anachronism within a broader material culture that includes metalwork, books, glass, and textiles. Such praise and derision surely misunder-stand the relationship of mimesis and material whose truth and falsity depended upon one another in an often playful dialectics. For many who tried to make sense of the conspicu-ously mimetic images of their day, art was both a kind of "second nature" that reconstituted the things (and materials) of the created world and a superfluous mask, obfuscating its own true nature.[49]

A world of things

The recent turn toward material culture in Renaissance studies has coincided with an emerging conception of the period as one in which the courts and merchant centers of Europe were developing ever more expansive connections with a much wider world. Art historians, cognizant of the discipline's (admittedly still aspirational) "global turn," have focused increasing attention on interactions stretching far beyond European shores. The circulation of ceramics, metalwork, and carpets throughout the Christian and Islamic Mediterranean, the blending of visual modes and materials indigenous to the Americas with those of European colonizers, and pictorial records of missionary contacts in East Asia, like Peter Paul Rubens' remarkable *Portrait of a Man in Korean Costume* (Illustration 6.5), all manifest the global nature of the early modern world.[50] So too do we find collectors developing, eventually, a taste for the exotic through accumulating rare items from new lands.[51] Of course, objects from the far-flung reaches of the world had long been amassed in Europe. Gems, which provided the luster of authority for aristocrats and church lumi-naries, were both valuable and marvelous because they came from distant lands: Arabia,

Illustration 6.5   Increasingly, scholars have focused their attention on the pivotal importance of artistic interactions between Europe and a larger world that became ever more accessible during the early modern period. Peter Paul Rubens' *Portrait of a Man in Korean Costume* provides one fascinating example of such encounters. Though he eventually used this as a model for a figure in his *Miracles of Saint Francis Xavier*, Rubens initially produced this drawing as a finished study of traditional Korean attire that he observed in Antwerp.

Source: Courtesy of the J. Paul Getty Trust

Persia, or India.[52] Pearls were transported from the Indian or Pacific Oceans, from the Red Sea and Persian Gulf, from Scottish rivers, and increasingly as the sixteenth century progressed, from the Caribbean.[53]

Iridescent silks – including velvet, satin, damask, sendal, and taffeta – were produced and traded throughout the Italian peninsula and were imported from and, later, exported to the Eastern Mediterranean, and beyond.[54] Colorful cottons often came from India, and the materials used in the production of luxury clothing – including dyes, mordants, pearls, and precious metals – originated in Africa and Asia.[55] As Marta Ajmar and Luca Molà remind us, brocaded crimson velvet fabricated in sixteenth-century Venice – for the Venetian or international market – might have incorporated Italian, Spanish, or Asian silk threads; Turkish or Italian alum; African gold; and Asian, European, or, increasingly, American dyes.[56] Indeed, expanding commerce with the Americas added another crucial conduit by which the materials of Renaissance culture reached points of manufacture. Cochineal is only the best known among a host of dyes available in Europe following the Atlantic conquests. For instance, logwood found around the Golfo de Campeche in Mexico was likewise imported in great quantities, and it revolutionized the expensive, seductive, and vibrant black fabrics of Spain (and likewise drove the economy of the British colony which would become Belize). Boiled logwood chips provided the jet-black, lustrous "crow's-wing *(ala de cuervo)*" color and light effects much preferred by fashion-forward men and women over the dull, matte "fly's wing *(ala de mosca)*" brown or black, and over other dark shades produced by combining vegetal dyes such as madder and woad.[57]

As we have suggested, mimesis and deceit, forgery and its winking recognition, offer a lens through which the value of Renaissance things might be appraised. Yet, then as today, a deadly serious logic sometimes governed the diffusion and power of goods and raw materials. Many scholars of material culture have embraced fashionable and inventive attempts to imbue the objects of their study with agency, a property once reserved for human actors. Things, long defined by their qualities as tacit and acted upon, are now routinely and profitably encountered – in historical and art historical literature that draws upon anthropology and the history of science – as agents that act upon us.[58] This shift responds, in part, to an acknowledgement of the inescapable entanglement and interconnectedness between people and things, both for us today and for the historical societies we study, and it serves as a resonant and efficacious alternative to Platonic suspicions of matter's superficiality. While these re-evaluations are most valuable for rethinking and denaturalizing assumptions and patterns of human behavior – along with fundamental social hierarchies relating to selves and things, will and agency, form and matter – those patterns yet remain stubbornly human ones.

Rivalry, envy, and the small-scale vicissitudes of fortune meant that the production and circulation of objects might generate significant uncertainty for Renaissance artisans. The economic historian Richard Goldthwaite characterized the world of the skilled artisan as one in which versatility was the order of the day, a versatility which "translates into a greater range of possibilities, freedom of choice, and greater potential" and "promotes the free exchange of ideas among occupational groups and valorizes creativity and virtuosity."[59] Such flexibility, it must be said, also had its dark side. The visual arts routinely fell between the jurisdiction of multiple guilds. Tools were an important criterion for the demarcation of crafts and therefore frequently a matter of dispute between guild and practitioner in emerging arts which employed such tools for new purposes.[60] The joiners of Strasbourg, for example, took offense that a sculptor was employing "both types of axe, plane, mallets, saws and others" for his craft.[61] Mastery of new technologies including the printing press, as well as forms of glass, ceramic, and textile production represented emerging trades, few of whose participants could fall back upon generations of family success. Moreover, many skilled crafts were characterized by a high degree of trade secrecy. Some, like the Venetian glass industry, were guarded jealously as state monopolies.[62] Artisans who ran afoul of state authorities, guilds, and even one another, could expect not merely censure or economic ruin but even violence. For this very reason, European craftsmen were increasingly granted the right to bear arms.[63] For many artists and artisans, this was a moment of thrilling but some-times frightening social mobility.

We can learn a great deal from attending to the means by which materials got from point A to point B (sometimes surprisingly circuitously so). Equally valuable is understanding the techniques and processes by which they were transformed from raw into finished products, and assessing exactly who had the expertise to perform these transmutations. In the case of lustrous, luxury clothing, the study of gold, silk, and dyes can, individually and collectively, tell us about skills, commodities, and the movement of people, and, more generally, about the connected nature of Renaissance things. So, too, can they help us to appreciate the ways in which people conceptualized materials (often in relation to wider cultural or social hierarchies), and likewise introduce us to those gradations of intrinsic value that under-wrote material cultures.[64] Thus, to conclude this chapter, we will briefly consider the origin, procurement, and control of one raw material – alum, an important dye-fixer or mordant for wool, silks, and other fabrics – to appreciate what could be at stake on both the global and local level.

The competition for scarce (or apparently scarce) raw materials could expose entire com-munities to dire risks. The savage siege and sack of Volterra in central Italy orchestrated by Lorenzo de' Medici of Florence and executed by Federico da Montefeltro of Urbino in 1472 were motivated by the Medici bank's desire to monopolize, with the Pope's support, the supply of alum.[65] Following weeks of bombardment, Volterra surrendered to Federico, and his troops subsequently raped many of the town's women and killed numerous men. The Montefeltro library in Urbino, moreover, was enlarged with dozens of Hebrew manuscripts confiscated from a Jewish merchant.[66]

Alum was particularly effective in holding fast exceedingly sought-after crimson dyes and was thus a valuable commodity exported throughout Europe. It was indispensable for the wool-centered Florentine economy, and likewise essential for the production of many of the finest, most luminous garments worn at Italian courts and in the streets of mercantile cent-ers like Bruges, Paris, and London, to where alum was shipped on Florentine galleys.[67] This mordant was thus a fundamental raw material for both the maintenance and representation of authority locally and throughout Europe. Though the merciless exercise of military might at Volterra strengthened the political power of Florence, and that of Lorenzo de' Medici, the nearby mines ultimately yielded only low-grade alum and were abandoned within a dec-ade.[68] The Medici alum "cartel," as the prominent economic historian Raymond de Roover identified it, never materialized, though for the citizens of Volterra, "ghastly" "atrocities," as de Roover called them, most certainly did.[69]

Such atrocities were tolerated as a necessary price to pay for a victory that was widely praised in Urbino and Florence alike. As Carolyn Elam and Bill Kent have recently shown, the *Signoria* commissioned views of Volterra from the mapmaker Piero del Massaio to commemorate the siege, and these rapidly took their place as standard, patriotic addi-tions to Florentine books of maps like the sumptuous copies of Ptolemy's *Geography* pro-duced by the city's illuminators for buyers and recipients up and down the peninsula, and beyond.[70] In an illuminated *Florentine History* produced in Florence and presented to Federico, moreover, the belligerent *signore* commands his steed in the foreground while his troops and their encampments menace the walled town of Volterra in the distance (Illustration 6.6). Both soldier and beast are radiantly and triumphantly adorned. Federico, crowned with laurel, ominously brandishes a heavy mace and wears both shining armor and opulent cloth; his war-horse strides confidently, draped in its dazzling golden bard.[71]

Illustration 6.6 This illuminated manuscript of Poggio Bracciolini's *Florentine History* was presented in 1472 to Federico da Montefeltro, lord of Urbino, by Poggio's son Jacopo. A few years later, Jacopo would be hanged for his involvement in the Pazzi conspiracy against the Medici, in which, we now know, Federico was also complicit.

Source: Reproduced by permission of Biblioteca Apostolica Vaticana, with all rights reserved. © Biblioteca Apostolica Vaticana

Such commemorations – and the habitual myopia of scholars eager to praise enlightened princes like Lorenzo and Federico – clash starkly with our own aspirations for a material culture that is ethical and sustainable, characterized by free and fair trade. The refined visual and sartorial culture of the Renaissance that flourished under such rulers was, in point of fact, predicated upon violent competition for resources.[72] If Lorenzo de' Medici and Federico da Montefeltro put Volterra's citizens to the point of a sword, the demand for color-fast textiles among Europe's nobility and social-climbers unquestionably set the stage for such horrors.

The case studies of this chapter might be profitably framed through histories of production and consumption, struggles for political legitimacy, and the debates of art theory. Equally though, they represent responses to the changing conditions of material cultures, to the availability and desirability of raw materials, and to disparate attitudes toward their transformation. If it remains for some, perhaps, a bridge too far to accept that material culture acts upon people, these object lessons should provide ample confirmation that the historical actions of people were always and ever bound inextricably with the properties of the things that populated and enriched their lives.

Notes

1 The authors are grateful to Bill Caferro, John Gagné, Liz Horodowich, Catherine Kovesi, Lia Markey, Christina Neilson, Jill Pederson, Meredith Ray, Andrea Rizzi, Matt Shoaf, Pat Simons, J'Nese Williams, and Kelli Wood.
2 For historians' engagement with material culture: S. Lubar and W. Kingery (eds.), *History from Things: Essays on Material Culture*, Washington, DC: Smithsonian, 1993; P. Findlen, "Possessing the Past: The Material World of the Italian Renaissance," *American Historical Review* 103, 1998, 83–114; P. Findlen (ed.), *Early Modern Things: Objects and their Histories, 1500–1800*, London: Routledge, 2013; A. Gerritsen and G. Riello (eds.), *Writing Material Culture History*, London: Bloomsbury, 2015.
3 F. Jacobs, *Votive Panels and Popular Piety in Early Modern Italy*, Cambridge: Cambridge University Press, 2013; D. Areford, *The Viewer and the Printed Image in Late Medieval Europe*, Burlington, VT: Ashgate, 2010; J. Musacchio, *The Art and Ritual of Childbirth in Renaissance Italy*, New Haven: Yale University Press, 1999.
4 This bibliography is exploding; to begin, beyond Susan Stuard's chapter in this volume, see most recently E. Welch, *Shopping in the Renaissance: Consumer Cultures in Italy 1400–1600*, New Haven: Yale University Press, 2005; U. Rublack, *Dressing Up: Cultural Identity in Renaissance Europe*, Oxford: Oxford University Press, 2010; U. Rublack, "Matter in the Material Renaissance," *Past and Present* 219, 2013, 41–85; E. Welch (ed.), *Fashioning the Early Modern: Dress, Textiles, and Innovation in Europe, 1500–1800*, Oxford: Oxford University Press, 2017; T. McCall, *Brilliant Bodies*, forthcoming; T. McCall, "Renaissance Fashion Matters," forthcoming in *Renaissance Quarterly*.
5 T. Campbell (ed.), *Tapestry in the Renaissance: Art and Magnificence*, New York, Metropolitan Museum of Art, 2002; E. Cleland (ed.), *Grand Design: Pieter Coecke van Aelst and Renaissance Tapestry*, New York: Metropolitan Museum of Art, 2014. For the increasing prominence of the decorative arts generally: L. Syson and D. Thornton, *Objects of Virtue: Art in Renaissance Italy*, London: British Museum Press, 2001; M. Ajmar and F. Dennis (eds.), *At Home in Renaissance Italy*, London: V&A Publications, 2006.
6 D. Miller, "Materiality: An Introduction," in Miller (ed.), *Materiality*, Durham, NC: Duke University Press, 2005, 1–50; J. Bennett, *Vibrant Matter: A Political Ecology of Things*, Durham, NC: Duke University Press, 2010; C. Anderson, A. Dunlop, and P. Smith, "Introduction," in Anderson, Dunlop, and Smith (eds.), *The Matter of Art: Materials, Practices, Cultural Logics c. 1250–1750*, Manchester: Manchester University Press, 2015, 1–17.
7 Findlen, "Possessing the Past"; L. Jardine, *Worldly Goods: A New History of the Renaissance*, New York: Norton, 1998; G. Guerzoni, *Apollo and Vulcan: The Art Markets in Italy 1400–1700*, East Lansing, MI: Michigan State University Press, 2011; G. Ruggiero, *The Renaissance in Italy*, Cambridge: Cambridge University Press, 2015.
8 As in R. Goldthwaite, *The Economy of Renaissance Florence*, Baltimore: Johns Hopkins University Press, 2011; J. Brown, "Economies," in M. Wyatt (ed.), *The Cambridge Companion to the Italian Renaissance*, Cambridge: Cambridge University Press, 2014, 320–37. Consider the salient responses in Welch, *Shopping in the Renaissance*, 1–15; M. O'Malley and E. Welch, "Introduction," in O'Malley and Welch (eds.), *The Material Renaissance*, Manchester: Manchester University Press, 2010, 1–8.
9 Welch, *Shopping in the Renaissance*; R. Ago, *Gusto for Things: A History of Objects in Seventeenth-Century Rome*, Chicago: University of Chicago Press, 2013; T. McCall and S. Roberts, "Art and the Material Culture of Diplomacy," in M. Azzolini and I. Lazzarini (eds.), *Italian Renaissance Diplomacy: Texts in Translation (1350–1520)*, Toronto: Pontifical Institute of Mediaeval Studies, 2017.

10 J. Lichtenstein, "Making up Representation: The Risks of Femininity," *Representations* 20, 1987, 77–87; P. Reilly, "Writing Out Color in Renaissance Theory," *Genders* 12, 1991, 77–99; P. Phillippy, *Painting Women: Cosmetics, Canvases, and Early Modern Culture*, Baltimore: Johns Hopkins University Press, 2006.

11 For appraisals of materiality's newfound popularity: M. Cole, "The Cult of Materials," in S. Clerbois and M. Droth (eds.), *Revival and Invention: Sculpture through its Material Histories*, Oxford: Peter Lang, 2011, 1–16; Anderson, Dunlop, and Smith (eds.), *The Matter of Art*.

12 P. Smith, *The Body of the Artisan*, Chicago: University of Chicago Press, 2004.

13 M. Cole, "Cellini's Blood," *Art Bulletin* 81, 1999, 215–35; P. Smith, "Vermilion, Mercury, Blood, and Lizards: Matter and Meaning in Metalworking," in U. Klein and E. Spary (eds.), *Materials and Expertise in Early Modern Europe: between Market and Laboratory*, Chicago: University of Chicago Press, 2010, 28–49; S. Dupré, D. von Kerssenbrock-Krosigk, and B. Wismer (eds.), *Art and Alchemy: The Mystery of Transformation*, Munich: Hirmer, 2014.

14 R. Zorach and M. Phillips, Jr., *Gold: Nature and Culture*, London: Reaktion, 2016.

15 A. Wright, *The Pollaiuolo Brothers*, New Haven: Yale University Press, 2005, 28.

16 *Ibid.*, 47–9; A. Galli and A. Di Lorenzo (eds.), *Antonio and Piero del Pollaiuolo: "Silver and Gold, Painting and Bronze …"* Milan: Skira, 2014.

17 Milanese *oricalco* is investigated in T. McCall, "Material Fictions of Luxury in Sforza Milan," in C. Kovesi (ed.), *Luxury and the Ethics of Greed in the Early Modern World*, forthcoming.

18 M. Miller, *Clothing the Clergy: Virtue and Power in Medieval Europe, c. 800–1200*, Ithaca, NY: Cornell University Press, 2014; McCall, *Brilliant Bodies*.

19 R. Lightbown, *Mediaeval European Jewellery: With a Catalogue of the Collection in the Victoria & Albert Museum*, London: V&A Publications, 1992, 17–22; R. Silva, "Il colore dell'inganno: gemme, perle, ambra e corallo artificiali secondo un manoscritto del XIII secolo," in *Il Colore nel Medioevo: arte, simbolo, tecnica*, Lucca: Istituto storico lucchese, 1996, 27–39; M. Zanoboni, "'Non c'é inganno a questo mondo che renda maggior guadagno.' La corporazione Milanese dei fabbricanti di pietre false," in *Rinascimento sforzesco: innovazioni, tecniche, arte, e società nella Milano del secondo Quattrocento*, Milan: CUEM, 2005, 119–32; McCall, *Brilliant Bodies*.

20 Silva, "Il colore dell'inganno," 33; P. Venturelli, *Leonardo da Vinci e le arti preziose: Milano tra xv e xvi secolo*, Venice: Marsilio, 2002, 91–104.

21 G. Pontano, *I Libri delle Virtù Sociali*, F. Tateo (ed.), Rome: Bulzoni, 1999, 228–9; E. Welch, "Public Magnificence and Private Display: Giovanni Pontano's *De Splendore* (1498) and the Domestic Arts," *Journal of Design History* 15, 2002, 223.

22 G. Giomo, "Il Lusso: leggi moderatrici – pietre e perle false," *Nuovo archivio veneto* 16, 1908, 103–14.

23 M. Baxandall, *Painting and Experience in Fifteenth-Century Italy*, Oxford: Oxford University Press, 1972, 1–27. Most enlightening is A. Dunlop, "On the Origins of European Painting Materials, Real and Imagined," in Anderson, Dunlop, and Smith (eds.), *The Matter of Art*, 76–8.

24 Of course Renaissance colors were not consistently defined, and these crimson hues ranged from orange to red to dark brown to purple: L. Monnas, "Some Medieval Colour Terms for Textiles," *Medieval Clothing and Textiles* 10, 2014, 43–57.

25 R. Donkin, "Spanish Red: An Ethnogeographical Study of Cochineal and the Opuntia Cactus," *Transactions of the American Philosophical Society* 67, 1977, 1–84; E. Phipps, "Cochineal Red: The Art History of a Color," *Metropolitan Museum of Art Bulletin* 67, 2010, 4–48. Most useful too are W. Caferro, "The Silk Business of Tommaso Spinelli, Fifteenth-Century Florentine Merchant and Papal Banker," *Renaissance Studies* 10, 1996, 417–39; L. Molà, *The Silk Industry of Renaissance Venice*, Baltimore: Johns Hopkins University Press, 2000, 108–20; J. Munro, "The Anti-Red Shift – To the Dark Side: Colour Changes in Flemish Luxury Woollens, 1300–1550," *Medieval Clothing and Textiles* 3, 2007, 55–95.

26 Molà, *The Silk Industry of Renaissance Venice*, 114.

27 This incident is further unpacked in McCall, "Material Fictions of Luxury"; for the letter, see P. Merkley and L. Merkley, *Music and Patronage in the Sforza Court*, Turnhout: Brepols, 1999, 178–9.

28 Monnas, "Some Medieval Colour Terms for Textiles," 53–7. See, additionally, S. Bowe, *Mulberry: The Material Culture of Mulberry Trees*, Liverpool: Liverpool University Press, 2016.

29 For this process, see A. Johns, *The Nature of the Book: Print and Knowledge in the Making*, Chicago: University of Chicago Press, 1999, 1–6. For discussion of the canonical view on this aesthetic in images, see

P. Parshall, "Imago Contrafacta: Images and Facts in the Northern Renaissance," *Art History* 16, 1993, 554–79.

30 On this edition see L. Armstrong, "The Hand-Illuminated Printed Book," in J. Alexander (ed.), *The Painted Page: Italian Renaissance Book Illumination 1450–1550*, Munich: Prestel, 1994, 174–6. J. Alexander, *The Painted Book in Renaissance Italy: 1450–1600*, New Haven: Yale University Press, 2016, 193.

31 S. Dackerman, *Painted Prints: The Revelation of Color*, University Park, PA: Penn State University Press, 2002. On early attempts to print in color: A. Stijnman and E. Savage (ed.), *Printing Color, 1400–1700*, Leiden: Brill, 2015.

32 P. Dalchè, "The Reception of Ptolemy's *Geography* (End of the Fourteenth to Beginning of the Sixteenth Century)," in D. Woodward (ed.), *History of Cartography*, Chicago: University of Chicago Press, 2007, vol. 3, part 1, 285–310; S. Roberts, *Printing a Mediterranean World: Florence, Constantinople, and the Renaissance of Geography*, Cambridge, MA: Harvard University Press, 2013, 20–6, 36–44.

33 R. Skelton, introduction to *Cosmographia: Ulm 1482 and 1486*, Amsterdam: Theatrum Orbis Terrarum, 1964; Roberts, *Printing a Mediterranean World*, 107–11.

34 V. da Bisticci, Renaissance Princes, Popes, and Prelates, trans. W. George and E. Waters, New York: Harper & Row, 1963, 104.

35 For the cautionary argument against novelty in the period, see Ruggiero, *The Renaissance in Italy*, 387–400. On Stradano: L. Markey "Stradano's Allegorical Invention of the Americas in Late Sixteenth-Century Florence," *Renaissance Quarterly* 65, 2012, 385–442.

36 L. Armstrong, "The Hand-Illumination of Printed Books in Italy, 1465–1515," in Alexander (ed.), *The Painted Page*, 35–47.

37 P. Dryer, "Botticelli's Series of Engravings 'of 1481,'" *Print Quarterly* 2, 1984, 111–15; P. Keller, "The Engravings in the 1481 Edition of the Divine Comedy," in H. Altcappenberg (ed.), *Sandro Botticelli: The Drawings for Dante's Divine Comedy*, London: Royal Academy of Arts, 2000, 326–33; S. Roberts, "Tricks of the Trade: The Technical Secrets of Early Engraving," in T. McCall, S. Roberts, and G. Fiorenza (eds.), *Visual Cultures of Secrecy in Early Modern Europe*, Kirksville, MO: Truman State University Press, 2013, 195–7.

38 Florence, BNC, Banco Rari 341. On its binding and illumination: S. Gentile *et al.*, *Sandro Botticelli: pittore del Divina commedia*, Milan: Skira, 2000, 326–33. On its presentation to the *Signoria*: A. Dunlop, "'El vostro poeta': The First Florentine Printing of Dante's Commedia," *Revue d'art canadienne/Canadian Art Review* 20, 1993, 29–42.

39 For a recent discussion of such relative values: R. Stapleford, *Lorenzo de' Medici at Home: The Inventory of the Palazzo Medici in 1492*, University Park, PA: Penn State University Press, 2013, 18–24. On the arts and their relative contributions to the economy: Guerzoni, *Apollo and Vulcan*.

40 L. Alberti, *On Painting*, trans. J. Spencer, New Haven: Yale University Press, 1956, 85; and see J. Białostocki, "Ars auro prior," in J. Harrell and A. Wierzbiańska (eds.), *Aesthetics in Twentieth-Century Poland: Selected Essays*, Lewisburg, PA: Bucknell University Press, 1973, 270–85.

41 M. Baxandall, *The Limewood Sculptors of Renaissance Germany*, New Haven: Yale University Press, 1980, 93. Fundamental too is Baxandall, *Painting and Experience*.

42 R. Lightbown, *Sandro Botticelli*, Berkeley: University of California Press, 1978, 108.

43 On Alberti and other fifteenth-century responses to Pliny's tale: S. McHam, *Pliny and the Artistic Culture of the Italian Renaissance*, New Haven: Yale University Press, 2013, 103–8.

44 M. Vida, *Scacchia Ludus*, Rome: Ludovico degli Arrighi, 1527, 1: "Ludimus effigie belli simulataque veris / Proelia, buxo acies fictas, et ludicra regna." We are grateful to Kelli Wood for this reference.

45 There is a voluminous literature on pictorial mimesis. To start: R. Williams, *Art Theory: An Historical Introduction*, London: Wiley-Blackwell, 2009, 57–65. On theories of mimesis deriving from ancient texts: E. Mansfield, *Too Beautiful to Picture: Zeuxis, Myth, and Mimesis*, Minneapolis: University of Minnesota Press, 2009.

46 Alberti, *On Painting*, 85.

47 G. Vasari, *Vasari on Technique*, trans. L. MacLehose, London: Dent, 1907, 248.

48 For plays and tensions between poor and rich materiality and artistic fashioning, see, importantly, M. Cole, "*Arti povere*, 1300–1650," in Anderson, Dunlop, and Smith (eds.), *The Matter of Art*, 240–62.

49 On art as a "second nature": R. Zorach, *Blood, Milk, Ink, Gold: Abundance and Excess in the French Renaissance*, Chicago: University of Chicago Press, 2006, 14.

50 Among the proliferating sources on the circulation of goods in the Mediterranean and beyond: R. Mack, *Bazaar to Piazza: Islamic Trade and Italian Art, 1300–1600*, Berkeley: University of California Press, 2002; S. Carboni (ed.), *Venice and the Islamic World*, New Haven: Yale University Press, 2007; P. Mancall and D. Bleichmar (eds.), *Collecting Across Cultures: Material Exchanges in the Early Modern Atlantic World*, Philadelphia: University of Pennsylvania Press, 2011; Findlen (ed.), *Early Modern Things*; A. Gerritsen and G. Riello (eds.), *The Global Lives of Things: The Material Culture of Connections in the Early Modern World*, London: Routledge, 2015. On the mingling of European and indigenous American styles: G. Bailey, *The Andean Hybrid Baroque: Convergent Cultures in the Churches of Colonial Peru*, Notre Dame, IN: University of Notre Dame Press, 2010. For Rubens: S. Schrader (ed.), *Looking East: Rubens's Encounter with Asia*, Los Angeles: Getty Publications, 2013.

51 On the development of exoticism: P. Schmidt, *Inventing Exoticism: Geography, Globalism, and Europe's Early Modern World*, Chicago: University of Chicago Press, 2015.

52 Lightbown, *Mediaeval European Jewellery*, 27–32; B. Buettner, "Precious Stones, Mineral Beings: Performative Materiality in Fifteenth-Century Northern Art," in Anderson, Dunlop, and Smith (eds.), *The Matter of Art*, 205–22. Of course, gems, pearls, and precious metals might be endowed with magical, talismanic, medicinal, and apotropaic qualities and powers which were intensified by astrological affinities with their wearers.

53 Lightbown, *Mediaeval European Jewellery*, 20–1; R. Donkin, *Beyond Price: Pearls and Pearl-Fishing: Origins to the Age of Discovery*, Philadelphia: American Philosophical Society, 1998.

54 For silk, see C. Zanier, "La sericoltura dell'Europa mediterranea dalla supremazia mondiale al tracollo: un capitolo della competizione economica tra Asia Orientale ed Europa," *Quaderni storici* 73, 1990, 7–53; S. Cavaciocchi (ed.), *La Seta in Europa, Sec. XIII–XX*, Florence: Le Monnier, 1993; Molà, *The Silk Industry of Renaissance Venice*; L. Monnas, "The Impact of Oriental Silks on Italian Silk Weaving in the Fourteenth Century," in L. Saurma-Jeltsch and A. Eisenbeiß (eds.), *The Power of Things and the Flow of Cultural Transformations: Art and Culture between Europe and Asia*, Berlin: Deutscher Kunstverlag, 2010, 65–89; L. Monnas, *Renaissance Velvets*, London: V&A Publications, 2012.

55 For the global exchange of gold and silver: J. Richards (ed.), *Precious Metals in the Later Medieval and Early Modern Worlds*, Durham, NC: Carolina Academic Press, 1983. For fabrics, additionally, see B. Lemire and G. Riello, "East & West: Textiles and Fashion in Early Modern Europe," *Journal of Social History* 41, 2008, 887–916; G. Riello and P. Parthasarathi (eds.), *The Spinning World: A Global History of Cotton Textiles, 1200–1850*, Oxford: Oxford University Press, 2009; S. Faroqhi, "Ottoman Textiles in European Markets," in A. Contadini and C. Norton (eds.), *The Renaissance and the Ottoman World*, Burlington, VT: Ashgate, 2013, 231–44; A. Peck (ed.), *Interwoven Globe: The Worldwide Textile Trade, 1500–1800*, New York: Metropolitan Museum of Art, 2013; G. Riello, *Cotton: The Fabric that Made the Modern World*, Cambridge: Cambridge University Press, 2013.

56 M. Ajmar-Wollheim and L. Molà, "The Global Renaissance: Cross-Cultural Objects in the Early Modern Period," in G. Adamson, G. Riello, and S. Teasley (eds.), *Global Design History*, London: Routledge, 2011, 13–14.

57 For logwood, see K. Ponting, "Logwood: An Interesting Dye," *Journal of European Economic History* 2, 1973, 109–19; W. Armstrong, "Logwood and Brazilwood: Trees that Spawned two Nations," *Pacific Horticulture* 53, 1992, 38–43; J. Colomer, "Black and the Royal Image," in J. Colomer and A. Descalzo (eds.), *Spanish Fashion at the Courts of Early Modern Europe* Madrid: CEEH, 2014, 91–4. For black clothing more generally, start with J. Harvey, *Men in Black*, Chicago: University of Chicago Press, 1995; A. Quondam, *Tutti i colori del nero: moda e cultura del gentiluomo nel Rinascimento*, Costabissara: Colla, 2007; E. Currie, "The Versatility of Black," in *Fashion and Masculinity in Renaissance Florence*, London: Bloomsbury, 2016, 93–108; McCall, *Brilliant Bodies*.

58 A. Gell, *Art and Agency: An Anthropological Theory*, Oxford: Clarendon Press, 1998; Miller, "Materiality"; D. Miller, *The Comfort of Things*, Cambridge: Polity, 2008; L. Daston (ed.), *Things That Talk: Object Lessons from Art and Science*, New York: Zone, 2008; Bennett, *Vibrant Matter*; Anderson, Dunlop, and Smith, "Introduction."

59 Goldthwaite, *The Economy of Renaissance Florence*, 351.

60 For the sometimes unexpected impact of the guilds, see S. Epstein and M. Prak, *Guilds, Innovation, and the European Economy, 1400–1800*, Cambridge: Cambridge University Press, 2008.

61 Baxandall, *The Limewood Sculptors*, 40.

62 P. Long, *Openness, Secrecy, Authorship: Technical Arts and the Culture of Knowledge from Antiquity to the Renaissance*, Baltimore: Johns Hopkins University Press, 2001.

63 L. Molà, "States and Crafts: Relocating Technical Skills in Renaissance Italy," in O'Malley and Welch (eds.), *The Material Renaissance*, 133–53.

64 Thoughtful, in relation to pigments, is Dunlop, "On the Origins of European Painting Materials."

65 Fundamental is J. Najemy, "Politics: Class and Patronage," in A. Grieco, M. Rocke, and F. Superbi (eds.), *The Italian Renaissance in the Twentieth Century*, Florence: Olschki, 2002, 120–1. For the siege and its significance for Lorenzo, see E. Fiumi, *L'Impresa di Lorenzo de' Medici contra Volterra (1472)*, Florence: Olschki, 1948.

66 M. Simonetta (ed.), *Federico da Montefeltro and His Library*, Milan: Y. Press, 2007, 22–4, 51–61.

67 R. de Roover, *The Rise and Decline of the Medici Bank 1397–1494*, New York: Norton, 1966, 152–64; F. Franceschi, "Medici Economic Policy," in R. Black and J. Law (eds.), *The Medici: Citizens and Masters*, Settignano: Villa I Tatti, 2015, 139, 149–53.

68 For Florentine and Italian politics: R. Fubini, *Quattrocento fiorentino: politica diplomazia cultura*, Ospedaletto: Pacini, 1996, 123–39.

69 de Roover, *The Rise and Decline of the Medici Bank*, 155–6. The Medici monopoly was promoted by Pope Sixtus IV, who sought to cut off the market for Turkish alum.

70 F. Kent and C. Elam, "Piero del Massaio: Painter, Mapmaker and Military Surveyor," *Mitteilungen des Kunsthistorischen Institutes in Florenz* 52, 2015, 65–90.

71 For this codex of the *Historia Florentina* written by Poggio Bracciolini and edited and enlarged by his son Jacopo, see Simonetta (ed.), *Federico da Montefeltro and His Library*, 152–61.

72 Consider a recent study's rather dubious and naïve claims that Federico and other lords, because of their "high level of civilization," preferred diplomacy over "force and violence" and practiced refined military science so as to minimize cruelty during sieges: C. Sacchetti, "La guerra nel secolo XV e la 'lista de la conducta de lo illustrissimo signor duca d'Urbino,'" in A. Falcioni and A. de Berardinis (eds.), *Federico di Montefeltro, Battista Sforza, Elisabetta Gonzaga: mostra documentaria*, Urbino: Archivio di Stato di Pesaro, Sezione di Urbino, 2010, 43–4.

7

IMAGINATION AND THE REMAINS OF ROMAN ANTIQUITY[1]

William Stenhouse

Encountering the past

In late September 1464, four middle-aged men, including a doctor, an illustrator, and two painters, took a boat out on to Lake Garda in northern Italy. They savored the local flora, which included roses, shady branches, and fruit trees. One went so far as to describe what they found as gardens of paradise.[2] So far, so unremarkable: thousands of pleasure-seekers have savored a similar late summer excursion in the years since, and reacted with similar delight. But these four men in a boat were not simply enjoying the countryside. They looked at many remains of antiquity, and took note of the Latin inscriptions that they saw. And more peculiarly, the four set off the following day having assumed Roman titles: Samuele da Tradate (d. 1466), a painter, was the emperor, the other painter Andrea Mantegna (1431–1506) and the doctor Giovanni Marcanova (1418–67) were consuls, and Felice Feliciano (1433–79), who recorded his recollections of the event, cast himself as an attendant, or procurator.[3] Da Tradate, garlanded with ivy and myrtle, played the lute as they glided across the water in their flower-strewn boat, perhaps with some sort of entourage. They noted the proximity of inscriptions in honor of the pagan emperors to contemporary Christian shrines, and finally gave praise, at a church in Sirmio, "to the Great Thunderer and his glorious Mother," thanking those deities for granting them such delights, including the various pagan antiquities that they had seen.[4]

Feliciano's account of this excursion is now fairly well known. It is of interest to students of Mantegna, as evidence for his interest in ancient remains and in the humanists who studied them. Because the party copied down inscriptions Feliciano's work is regularly cited by scholars interested in the development of a historical approach to classical antiquities, as part of what is now known as the antiquarian movement.[5] Among those scholars was the Renaissance historian Peter Burke. Around 500 years after Feliciano and friends took to Lake Garda, Burke published a short book on *The Renaissance Sense of the Past*.[6] He was interested in how the historical thought and practice of the Renaissance differed from that of the Middle Ages: he argued that it was only in the Renaissance that scholars developed a sense of anachronism, an awareness of evidence (including a skeptical attitude towards written sources), and an interest in causation that went beyond attributing events to the wills of God or individual men. Burke showed how the work of humanists like Feliciano and Marcanova, who recorded and pondered historical inscriptions, built on the insights of Petrarch, who admired the ancient Romans "as men, not as magicians … acutely aware of the difference between their age and his own."[7] It was thanks to the humanists' investigations of Roman antiquity, which included the attempt to contextualize Roman ruins and other objects, that the Renaissance sense of the past developed. Burke mentions the Lake Garda trip as part of a discussion of how "the sense of history began to affect Italian Renaissance art," showing how Mantegna adapted Roman remains for his historical tableaux.[8]

Burke demonstrated clearly and persuasively the importance of the early modern period in the development of European historical thought more generally. His work, although designed primarily for students, provided a strong rebuttal to those of his colleagues who assumed that Renaissance historical practice was largely derivative and slavishly imitative of classical models, valuing rhetorical show over investigation and reflection. His comments on source-criticism and on the development of a notion of anachronism have proved particularly fertile, although art historians and literary critics have shown how early modern viewers and readers could entertain much more flexible notions of past and present than Burke's schema allows.[9] In retrospect, we can see his book as one of many anglophone efforts in the 1960s and 1970s to reclaim the Renaissance as a period worthy of serious study, and not simply the preserve of dilettantes and connoisseurs.[10] (It is a notable feature of his text that he seems to assume his readers will have at least as much familiarity with the art of the period as with writers like Erasmus and Machiavelli, comparing Guicciardini to Titian, for example.) In his influential account, the humanist devotees of antiquity were committed and authoritative historical scholars. This is certainly true. But there is a danger that by stressing the historical implications of these antiquaries' work, we overlook the other ways in which they interacted with the classical past, such as the costumes, titles, and lute of Feliciano and friends.[11] (Not surprisingly, some scholars have suggested that Feliciano at the very least embroidered his account, but in this context what matters is his self-presentation.)[12] The antiquaries responded in a variety of ways to their encounter with antiquity, identifying with the ancients and imitating them.[13] In this chapter I will show how the very same people whose work on Roman remains led them to develop a sober sense of anachronism also enjoyed a series of passionately imaginative responses to the past. These types of commerce with the classics – to quote the title of Anthony Grafton's compelling exploration of how humanists read classical texts – in turn remind us that even as we question whether Renaissance is a good label for the period from 1400 to 1700, we cannot doubt that the classical world was a hugely fertile source of creative inspiration.[14]

Being Roman 1: Pomponio Leto and his pupils

It is difficult to know how seriously the Lake Garda participants were trying to be Roman: Feliciano's references to garlands and instruments could simply be some sort of inside joke. We are better informed about a rough contemporary of Feliciano, Pomponio Leto (1428–98), who introduces many ways in which fifteenth-century antiquaries responded to Roman antiquity, and who anticipates many of the sixteenth-century figures on whom I will concentrate in the rest of this chapter. Leto was born in Campania, south of Rome, but settled in the city from around 1450, where he became famous as an inspirational teacher, classical historian, and devotee of the city of Rome's past. He published works on Roman law, lectured on the texts of Sallust, and took his pupils and friends, members of a loose academy, around Rome, including underneath the city to the catacombs. He also wanted to recreate some ancient Roman customs and practices. He reportedly tried to garden according to the precepts of Roman agricultural writers. He put on the plays of Plautus and Terence in the courtyards of palaces in Rome, attempting to reinstate the ancient practice of theater-going, sometimes wearing the leather buskins characteristic of classical actors.[15] And he reinstated celebrations for the birthday of the city of Rome, with the result that "the offspring of Romulus [that is, Rome's fifteenth-century inhabitants] had not seen anything grander or more pleasant," in the words of Pietro Marsi's funerary oration for Leto.[16] As one of his pupils, Marcantonio Sabellico, wrote, "no one admired antiquity more, and no one did more to understand it; he was tired of his own time."[17]

On his admirers' accounts Leto seems to have been a fish out of water, a notable, sincere eccentric. But others were not so sure. In 1468 he had been imprisoned in Rome, accused of heresy, impiety, and plotting against Pope Paul II. Exactly what he had done wrong has perplexed observers and scholars since: but it is clear that Leto's very commitment to antiquity aroused hackles in the Rome of the time.[18] On the one hand, taking too close an interest in Roman history could be politically suspect. In the words of one ambassador, Leto and his followers wanted "Rome to return to its earlier form," a secular republic rather than a papal monarchy.[19] On the other hand, by forming a loose-knit academy of like-minded men, Leto seemed to be encouraging un-Christian behavior. An interest in antiquity was not necessarily problematic – see Feliciano's happy marriage of Christian devotion and Roman titles in his worship at Garda – but Leto's group of devotees invited suspicions of paganism and sodomy. It is easy to see why a casual observer might have detected pagan sympathies. Leto's interests in Roman culture included Roman religion, and he and his followers had adopted Roman nicknames in place of their baptismal Christian names. The accusation of sodomy underscores other fundamental aspects of the reception of antiquity. Renaissance humanists and artists could use classical forms and language to express erotic or sexual themes much more explicitly than they could otherwise. Humanist pedagogy was often closely associated with homoerotic attraction.[20] In particular, when Leto was accused, the study of Plato, who founded the original Academy, could already be seen as a route to same-sex love.[21] And again, Leto offered plenty of material for his detractors. Even Sabellico acknowledged that, "he loved Roman youth to the point of scandal."[22] Before his arrest in Rome, Leto had also been under investigation in Venice for sodomy. Judging by the fragment of a poem preserved in one manuscript, he seems to have compared one of his Venetian pupils favorably to Ganymede, the beautiful young man snatched up by Zeus to be his pageboy:

> I wish those early golden centuries had borne you / For you could have aroused the gods with your beauty. / A stranger would never have turned into a winged lover / Nor would a Trojan boy have shone from the sky.[23]

Leto defended himself rather ingenuously by claiming that, "I praised the Venetian boy for his beauty, nobility and dedication to me."[24] Leto's associate Filippo Buonaccorsi, who went by the nickname Callimachus, wrote explicitly homoerotic verse in Latin and escaped to Poland.[25] Texts were not the only classicizing products of this homosocial environment. We can see some fifteenth-century portrait-medals inspired by ancient coins in a similar light, not simply as celebratory records, but as intimate tokens of friendship or love. Ulrich Pfisterer has argued that we should see several all'antica medals by an artist nicknamed Lysippus, after the classical Greek sculptor, as documents of the close relationships of a group of men connected with the papal curia in the 1470s.[26] Ownership of one of the medals could signify membership of this particular circle.

Leto, fortunately, was not detained for long, and was rehabilitated in the papacy of Sixtus IV (1471–84), who was much more sympathetic to classical studies than his predecessor (nearly all of our evidence for Leto's teaching postdates the conspiracy). But his arrest is a valuable reminder of the potential consequences of a passion for the antique. It is worth comparing Leto's plight with the most famous example of donning clothes to converse with the ancients. In exile from Florence, Machiavelli wrote to his friend Francesco Vettori that in the evenings he would "put on the garments of court and palace," in order to "step inside the venerable courts of the ancients ... where I am unashamed to converse with them and to question them about the motives for their actions, and they, out of their human kindness, answer me."[27] Craig Kallendorf points out, though, while Machiavelli retreated into the past on his own, what Leto and friends had found out was that "one could set up a private club to read Latin poetry, but at the end of the day, the members of the club had to return to the world outside ... what was discussed within the club was not ideologically neutral."[28] As Leto learned, an enthusiasm for antiquity carried a considerable social and political charge.

One final aspect of Leto's admiration of Rome that should be stressed was his desire to own and preserve the material remains of its past. Leto created a "little atrium" flanked by classical inscriptions, mostly funerary epitaphs, in the house that he built on the Quirinal.[29] The majority of these inscriptions are likely to have been pieces that he discovered on his trips around the city, rather than purchases he made (he was very poor): simple inscribed stones were not yet prized by many collectors in the late fifteenth century, and were more likely to have been of interest to marble-workers, who could have burned them for lime.[30] These pieces offered a suitably reverent backdrop for meetings of the academy, redolent of the death of classical Rome as well as of the death of individual Romans.[31] Perhaps we can go further. One of the inscriptions on the wall featured an ancient Roman Pomponius (Leto copied down another example he saw with this name in his notebook collection). In addition, the courtyard included a mock epitaph for Leto himself devised by two of Leto's pupils, probably before 1471.[32] Together, these inscriptions point to Leto's metamorphosis into a relic of the ancient past.

Being Roman 2: collecting antiquities

Leto's collection served as an important model for the architectural display of inscriptions and other antiquities in the sixteenth century, and as a model of how the owners of those collections could make their own connections with the ancient Roman past. Kathleen Christian has shown how the collectors of the late fifteenth and early sixteenth centuries used their doorways and courtyards to parade their links with classical Rome, and particularly with Roman republican antiquity. For example, over the doorway of one of their houses, the Porcari family had inscribed, "I am he, Cato Porcius, author of our progeny who, with arms and diplomacy, brought his noble name to the lips [of all]."[33] This Cato Porcius was the famous ancient Roman hero Cato; the doorway survives today, and presumably it originally supported a portrait-bust. The Porcari claimed him as their ancestor on the basis of his name. Similarly, the De'Rossi displayed an ancient inscription mentioning a Gaius Roscius, perhaps recalling the first-century actor Quintus Roscius, but certainly connected to the prominent Roman *gens* (clan), and the Orsini displayed a funerary inscription of an Ulpius Ursinus.[34] The Santacroce claimed to be descended from the pioneering consul Marcus

Valerius Publicola (their family church was S. Maria in Publicolis, hence the link). Along with other antiquities, they displayed a fragment of the Roman consular list (the *Fasti Capitolini*, an inscription with a chronological list of the Roman magistrates) inscribed with the name "P. Valerius Poplicola" in the wall of their palace, proudly laying claim to another republican magistrate. Andrea de Santacroce (around 1400–73), who probably made the connection, collected records of inscriptions and coins, and was an associate of Leto's.[35] Christian argues that these displays served both to prove the antiquity of the family in question, and, by emphasizing links to a republican past, to demonstrate that it had pre-Christian roots in Rome independent of the papacy.[36] As the popes and their entourages became increasingly powerful in the city in the later fifteenth century, local families resented their influence and turned to their antiquarian knowledge for support.

By the early sixteenth century, the popes' position in the city was secure, and the ostensible republican charge of antiquities collections declined. But they still served important roles. Most famously, they provided artists with a whole range of inspiring material, particularly for the representation of bodies and clothing. The famous pieces in the papal collections, for example, like the Apollo Belvedere, the Laocoön group, and the so-called Cleopatra, were widely studied. Individual pieces in private families' collections, like the Farnese Hercules, found in 1546, won similarly high prestige. Many artists' drawings from the period document how draughtsmen copied whole statues, excerpted details, and adapted them. Soon there was a flourishing market for high-quality prints at Rome, which provided reproductions of ancient works and, sometimes, their modern settings, so that antiquities could be studied elsewhere. The collections also exuded a sensual and erotic frisson that is hard to imagine today.[37] They included full-size nude men and women, as well as antiquities like herms, male busts with genitals below. Owners were not unaware of their sexual aura. In the collection of the Cesi family, for example, a nude crouching Venus was placed next to a Cupid gripping the neck of a swan.[38] A passion for the classics, whether texts or objects, continued to be a way in which scholars could express their desires and contemplate issues connected with gender. Leonard Barkan has highlighted how ancient hermaphrodite statues in particular complicated sexual responses.[39] Jumping ahead to the seventeenth century, the most popular work of pornography in that period, the *Satyra Sotadica*, was written by Nicholas Chorier, a French antiquary whose second most famous work was a history of the antiquities in his hometown, Vienne, and was knowingly presented by Chorier as a translation made by another prominent and prolific antiquary, Johannes Meursius.[40]

The Roman antiquity collections also continued to serve political and social functions, which we miss if we simply parallel them with modern public museums.[41] For *arriviste* families whose presence in Rome was thanks to papal patronage, the opportunity to create a palace in Rome and use it generously to display antiquities to visitors was a way of showing that they belonged.[42] The Cesi, for example, had relatively modest origins in Umbria. In the sixteenth century, the family supplied three cardinals: Paolo Emilio (made cardinal in 1517), Federico (1544), and Pierdonato (1565). Paolo Emilio bought property in Rome, began to collect antiquities and support antiquarian scholars and artists. He was followed by his two younger relatives in these pursuits, and by the time Pierdonato became cardinal they had established one of the most notable collections in Rome, on the Janiculum hill near the Vatican.[43] In the Cesi garden, for example, visitors could see an Antiquario, a purpose-built pagoda, in imitation of a Roman temple, which held various free-standing statues (including the Venus and Cupid mentioned above), and could be used by the cardinal to receive guests. They also saw various antiquities designed to stress the antiquity and Romanness of the family, including a statue of triumphant Rome, flanked by images of defeated enemies, and a series of inscriptions mentioning the Caesia *gens*. The Cesi, one-time Umbrians, thus adapted on a larger scale the strategies used by indigenous Roman families a generation or two earlier to show their visitors that they were part of the city fabric. They owned a symbolic record of Rome's greatness, and were able to claim that they had a tangible place in Rome's history.

Being Roman 3: fabulous genealogies

Pierdonato Cesi did not simply allow the Caesia inscriptions to speak for themselves. To back up the connection with the *gens* of antiquity, he commissioned two humanists (first Giovanni Battista Fontei, and then, after Fontei's death, Giulio Giacoboni) to write a history of the ancient clan. They found references to Caesii in texts, coins, and inscriptions like the ones in the Cesi garden, and Giacoboni published their findings in 1583 as *De prisca Caesiorum gente commentariorum libri duo* (*Two Books of Commentaries on the Ancient Clan of the Cesi*).[44] In encouraging this genealogical research, Pierdonato was by no means a pioneer. Members of other noble families at Rome had also tried to secure their connections to the past via written accounts of their families' histories.[45] The antiquary Onofrio Panvinio, who wrote ecclesiastical history and chronological scholarship, and collected inscriptions, composed a series of these histories in the 1550s.[46] In one, for Giacomo Savelli, Panvinio simply started the story in the medieval period. But in others, he went further back. He saw the origins of the Frangipane family in the important late antique Anicia *gens*, of which Pope Gregory the Great was later a member. He tied the Massimi family to the ancient Fabia *gens*, following the tradition that Quintus Fabius Maximus (hence Massimi), the famous Roman general in the Punic wars, was a member of the family. Like Fontei and Giacoboni, Panvinio buttressed the two accounts with ancient textual and material evidence. The Anicia *gens* was well documented in inscriptions found in the center of Rome; in the account of the Massimi he mined Livy for information about early Fabii Maximi, and he referred to various inscriptions, including one from Tivoli, mentioning a Maximus who was a consul, and a famous dedication from Arezzo in honor of Quintus Fabius Maximus.[47]

These scholars were doing just the sort of historical scholarship praised by Burke, gathering evidence, and evaluating it in thoughtful and sophisticated ways. Fontei and Giacoboni, for example, pointed to a mistake in one of the ancient inscriptions that they quoted, which they attributed to a careless artisan, and tried to date another example on the basis of its letter-forms, clearly aware that the style of their artefacts varied over time. But they were putting their skills to inherently implausible projects, placing them in the service of imagined identifications: none of the ancient evidence that these scholars quoted really supported the central claim that it was supposed to make, of the continuity through the medieval period of the families involved. In addition, these scholars were happy to cite questionable sources, and, on occasion, misrepresent or falsify testimony. The best example comes from Panvinio's medieval work. He added a couple of words – "de Sabello" – to a papal bull preserved in Mantua to prove that Honorius III was a member of the Savelli family. Honorius wasn't, in fact, but thanks to Panvinio's sleight of hand, historians thought he was until someone checked the bull in 1970.[48] Fontei and Giacoboni included one funerary dedication to a distinguished law-giver from the Caesii, who supposedly lived to the age of 100; it seems to be a fairly crude forgery.[49] It is easy to mock the efforts of these scholars working so hard on behalf of aristocrats living in Rome, who wanted to be more Roman. As Roberto Bizzocchi has shown, however, their research should also be placed in the context of a much wider concern on the part of Europeans to seek their origins in the past.[50] In the same way as Julius Caesar encouraged ancient Romans to believe that he was descended from Venus, people across Europe claimed connections with ancient mythological founders. French and English scholars both claimed ancestry from Troy, for example: Francio the Trojan was supposed to have been the ancestor of the Franks, and Brutus the Trojan to have given his name to Britain.[51] By contributing material proof to these conjectures, Panvinio and others made comparatively plausible cases.

Being Roman 4: Roman citizenship

A less speculative way for non-Romans to make a link with Rome and its past was to be awarded Roman citizenship. This prerogative lay with the contemporary Roman *conservatori* as representatives of the civic government. The title seems to have been largely honorary, but it was something worth fighting for.[52] In 1519, the Flemish humanist Christophe de Longueil was nominated to receive citizenship; his angry native rivals pointed in response to an oration he had previously composed in which he argued that the Franks were the true heirs of ancient Rome. They insisted on assessing his claim publicly in a show trial on the Capitoline, in which Celso Mellini heatedly invoked the spirits of Cato, Cicero, and Livy, to reject de Longueil. De Longueil was not present – one excitable witness said that tempers rose to such an extent that he would have been killed if so – but he responded by sending an exquisitely Ciceronian speech in praise of the city to demonstrate, successfully, his suitability.[53] Julia Haig Gaisser has suggested that humanists who saw themselves as "truly Roman, whether by birth or adoption, attacked Longueil," whereas those "of broader perspective, including the German [Johannes] Goritz, tended to support him."[54] We can see the controversy as over who had the right to lay claim to Roman connections and remains. Following de Longueil's precedent, various other Northern Italians and men from the other side of the Alps also received citizenship in the sixteenth century. Most famous was Michel de Montaigne. At the end of his essay "On Vanity" (iii.9), he wrote that among Fortune's "vain favours I have none more pleasing to that silly humour in me which feeds on it than an authentic Bull of Roman Citizenship," going on to cite the decree in Latin.[55] "Not being a citizen of any city," he continued, "I am delighted to have been made one of the noblest city there ever was or ever shall be."[56] From his *Travel Journal* we learn more of the circumstances: on his visit in 1581 he found Rome "the most universal city in the world, a place where strangeness and differences of nationality are considered least."[57] So he tried by petitioning the Pope to support his attempt at citizenship, "were it only for the ancient honor and the religious memory of its authority."[58] He concluded that it was "a vain title; but at all events I received much pleasure in having obtained it."[59] Montaigne, then, was mainly attracted by the modern city's universality, but he wanted to be part of the city for its storied history, and what he calls its "ancient honor."

Citizenship seems to have been seen as particularly appropriate to those foreigners who worked with Roman remains, understood broadly. For example, Antonio Salamanca, a successful publisher whose work included prints of antique subjects, won citizenship in 1560.[60] Antiquaries responded by wanting to win citizenship and, like Montaigne, to advertise the fact. Pirro Ligorio is one example. Ligorio was a Neapolitan painter who became increasingly interested in documenting and understanding the ancient world. He compiled two vast, open-ended encyclopedias to organize what he found. This work remained unpublished, although one way we can date the first version is by looking at how Ligorio described himself at the beginning of sections: initially as a painter, then as an antiquarian, and then, after 1553, as a Roman citizen.[61] Three writers on coins, Enea Vico, Jacopo Strada, and Hubertus Goltzius, won citizenship in the 1550s and 1560s.[62] In 1566 Goltzius dedicated one of his works to "the Senate and People of Rome," following the ancient formula for the city's constitutional structure (*senatus populusque Romanus*, or SPQR). The following year, he was made a citizen. Like Montaigne, he then included the text of the decree in subsequent publications.[63] He was clearly proud of the honor in itself, and his eagerness to advertise it also suggests that he felt that the award was a confirmation both of his social standing and of his authority to write of Roman matters, despite hailing from the Low Countries.

In a letter of 1573, Antonio Agustín, who had investigated antiquities and worked in the papal judiciary before returning to Spain, nicely illustrated the combination of pride, historical identification, and practical benefits that antiquaries perceived in the title of citizen. "I want to tell you a nice dream I have," he wrote to his friend Fulvio Orsini.

> I need to make myself a Roman citizen because of a certain plan of mine, I want it to be with certain classical clauses, which recount the truth that I come from an equestrian family of Caesara Augusta, an ancient colony derived from Augusta, and that my surname seems to be that, or could be derived from it, or from Augustus … I would like to reclaim the city, and be inscribed, along with my relatives, among the noble Roman patricians, so that I should take the name Julia, or Ottavia, or Claudia, or some other ancient imperial *gens*. I'd like the privilege to apply to me, and to my brother Joan Agustín, and my relative Vincenzo Agustín, and to their sons and descendants, in perpetuity.

Agustín's tone is not unironic: he begs Orsini for help "by all the ancient Fulvii, Ursinii, and Ursicini, etc." But it is clear that he wants the title, and that this tangible connection with an ancient institution held considerable appeal and benefit at home in Spain.[64] In support of his application, he asks Orsini to remind the authorities of his legal work in Rome, but also his work on classical antiquities "in praise of Roman families," suggesting that the *conservatori* would appreciate a connection between ancient and modern.[65] He achieved his aim (Orsini was well connected, working for Cardinal Alessandro Farnese). He wrote again to thank his friend, looking forward to his nephews "being able to take part in the carnival at the Testaccio dressed *all'antica* … and being able to be *Caporioni, maestri di strade* [superintendents of the roads], and of the sewers, and of the vineyards, which are free of all those Dacians imposed as subjects of SPQR, but not of the Popes."[66] Perhaps Agustín is still being slightly sardonic as he imagines his Spanish nephews in Rome, but the opportunity to take part in contemporary Roman festivals (one set of carnival games at the Testaccio involved men on horseback dressed as Roman soldiers) and to win contemporary Roman offices (the *Caporioni* were local justices, and the *maestri di strade* were positions often held by ambitious young men) was real.[67] The reference to the Dacians, on the other hand, harks back to antiquity. The Dacians were enemies of the Romans in eastern Europe, defeated by the emperor Trajan. Various classical statues of captives, identified as Dacians, were on display at Rome, including a pair in the Palazzo Farnese where Orsini lived.[68] Most ancient statues had been found in the vineyards around Rome's walls, which the popes and prominent ecclesiastical figures were then buying up. The antiquary Agustín's image of Rome spans ancient and modern, and exemplifies the evocative historical charge, with contemporary ramifications, that citizenship carried.

Being Roman 5: the imperial triumph

Kings and princes wanted more than citizenship from Rome. Various medieval and Renaissance rulers had used images or rituals redolent of ancient Rome, and particularly of the ancient Roman emperors, to promote their power and authority. In most cases, their use was somewhat general. But in the Renaissance, antiquaries were available to help create a more precise *all'antica* spectacle, particularly in the case of triumphal entries. Early modern scholars, artists, and rulers were fascinated by the way triumphant Roman generals had paraded into the city of Rome, receiving almost superhuman honors, and displaying captives, images of conquered lands, and spoils. Humanists combined text and object to create their own descriptions of the ritual. Twenty or so years after his trip to Lake Garda, Mantegna created a huge nine-picture series of "The Triumphs of Caesar" for the ducal palace in Mantua, fairly closely based on ancient literary sources as well as some material remains.[69] And kings and their subjects tried to create a similar effect for royal entries into cities, using devices like floats and temporary arches to impress the citizens: a survey of the sixteenth-century entries of the kings of France, for example, reveals many classicizing touches, although without much attempt at consistency.[70]

When the Hapsburg Holy Roman Emperor Charles V entered Rome, however, in 1536, to celebrate the victory of imperial troops over the Ottomans at Tunis, the opportunity to recreate a triumphal entry more exactly presented itself. Pope Paul III was eager to consolidate relations with the Hapsburgs in the years following the Sack of Rome, and honoring Charles in the manner of an ancient Roman emperor served his purposes well.[71] The pope had appointed his one-time secretary and devotee of antiquities Latino Giovenale Manetti in a new role as his *Commissario alle antichità*, to protect and preserve the city's remains.[72] Manetti then also became *maestro di strade* and *conservator*, and with this assemblage of powers he prepared Charles' route into the city. Charles was to enter the Roman Forum from the southeast, and to pass under the extant triumphal arches in the manner of ancient emperors before reaching a specially created wooden arch to celebrate the new victory.[73] Manetti had the passages through classical arches cleaned and cleared (they had been buttressed by medieval buildings), and a straight route created through the ancient Forum, destroying eleven churches in the process. On the day of Charles' entry, Manetti and the other *conservatori* wrapped themselves in togas to meet the emperor, who dressed in purple but rode a white horse, rather than in the triumphal chariot of his classical predecessors. In his Roman garb, Manetti then walked alongside the emperor, pointing out classical remains to him as he and his retinue passed towards the center of the city. The following day, Manetti showed the emperor other classical sites.

The Holy Roman Emperors had long bolstered their position with reference to the concept of *translatio imperii* – "transfer of authority," the notion that power was passed from the Romans through to the Franks and on to the medieval German emperors – and Charles V's ceremony in Rome, orchestrated in part by the antiquary Manetti, gave visible proof of the connection. Other scholars, particularly ancient coin scholars, made similar arguments. Men like Panvinio and Goltzius wrote books in the 1550s that presented a chronological series of the emperors' portraits supposedly taken from coins, running from the Romans through to Charles V and beyond. The fluid sequence of images with comments that these books presented made a compelling historical impression with a wide reach; Goltzius' 1557 *Living Images of the Emperors from Julius Caesar to Charles V* appeared in Latin, German, French, and Italian. Equally pointedly, in 1557 Jacopo Strada published one of Panvinio's works entitled *Roman Fasti and Triumphs from King Romulus up to Charles V, Caesar Augustus*, which was based in part on the inscribed records of the consuls. Although the chronological list of triumphs stopped in the sixth century and did not include Charles' sixteenth-century ceremony, the "Fasti consulares" section offered an illustrated list of magistrates, emperors, and events from the beginning of Rome right through to Charles.

Problems with being Roman

We have already seen that Leto's Academy provoked political and religious criticism in the fifteenth century. Devotion to antiquity could easily be interpreted as dissatisfaction with contemporary political systems, religious beliefs, or sexual morality. Not surprisingly, such criticisms did not disappear as scholars, collectors, and rulers continued to identify themselves with aspects of the Roman world. The display of classical statues evoked fears of idolatry, especially among Catholic writers in the aftermath of the Council of Trent.[74] Thus Gabriele Paleotti was willing to tolerate images of virtuous pagans as reminders of nobility and incitements to virtue, but rejected images of pagan gods, and attacked the current craze for owning the busts of all the first twelve Caesars, which included immoral figures like Caligula and Nero alongside admirable emperors.[75] Antonio Possevino also focused on nudity, arguing that statues of satyrs, for example, destroyed piety and promoted adultery.[76] Even a more moderate voice like Federico Borromeo, who did not want to ban naked statues, reminded his readers that, "People who enjoy nudity must be warned not to imitate pagan images so eagerly that they neglect Christian piety."[77] Writing from Spain Agustín argued that, "those phallic boundary stones in the Cesi and Carpi give a bad impression, and that Hermaphrodite with a Satyr in the chapel … and the vineyard of Pope Julius III with so many Venuses and other examples of lasciviousness." He was responding to the rumors that the new Pope Pius V was extremely hostile to the display of pagan material (Pius gave some statues away, and banned women from the Belvedere).[78] Despite his antiquarian background, Agustín was not unsympathetic to Pius. He went on to say that, "although the statues are beneficial to young scholars and artists, the people from north of the Alps are ferociously scandalized, and 'the rumor of sins gains strength as it goes.'"[79] He took an elitist view: statues could be studied, but with widespread access came danger, especially when we understand that his northerners are potentially Protestant critics of the Roman Church.

As a Catholic Reformation churchman, Agustín was aware that visitors from France and Germany could be shocked that cardinals like Cesi displayed naked, sexually provocative figures. As a legal historian, he would also have been aware that reformers and Protestants were questioning some of the other consequences of the antiquaries' work. As Protestants stressed the differences between the early church and sixteenth-century Catholic Christianity, so they questioned the sort of genealogical and political scholarship of Panvinio and his colleagues. This was particularly true in France, where several anti-Italian scholars criticized fabulous genealogies and classical mythological origins (though in seeking the origins of French institutions with the pre-Roman Celts, and later Franks, they were in danger of replacing one set of myths with another) and questioned the value of continuing to use Roman legal examples in the new sixteenth-century French state.[80] In both cases, they challenged the presumed universality of Roman models, and the value of connections with classical antiquity. Many Protestants were penetrating antiquaries and very ready to investigate the classical world – one need only look at the circle of Dutch humanists around the new University of

Leiden in the later sixteenth century – but theirs was an increasingly historicized view of the past, with less personal identification, as they explored the consequences of Burke's sense of anachronism.

Conclusion: imagination and the past

Anthony Grafton has underlined a central tension in humanist engagement with the past. "One set of humanists," he writes, "seeks to make the ancient world live again, assuming its undimmed relevance and unproblematic accessibility; another set seeks to put the ancient texts back into their own time, admitting that the reconstruction of the past is difficult and that success may reveal the irrelevance of ancient experience and precept to modern problems."[81] But Grafton also reminds us that many humanists managed to be paid members of both sets and, as we have seen in this chapter, their number includes the antiquaries who both historicized the past and made it live anew. They happily embraced and challenged anachronism. Once we understand this we can come closer to understanding how the same people who studied the remains of the past also invented them: even Panvinio, for example, in his *Roman Fasti and Triumphs*, cites some inscriptions that he seems to have devised to fill in the gaps on his evidence. Historical scholarship, then and now, is a creative process, particularly when dealing with the distant and fragmentary past; Leonard Barkan talks of the process of "reimagining and restoring" as central to the Renaissance encounter with the ruins of Rome.[82] In this sense, then, as the Introduction to this volume reminds us, we are still in the debt of Jacob Burckhardt: by underlining the importance of the "poet-scholars [who] filled Italy and the world with the worship of antiquity," he identified the enormous creative power and adoration involved in the encounter with the Roman past, which inspired scholars' imagination as well as their careful reflections.[83]

Notes

1 As well as to Bill Caferro, I am very grateful to Stefan Bauer, Tanya Pollard, and John Rich for comments on this chapter.
2 For the text of Feliciano's account, see P. Kristeller, *Andrea Mantegna*, Berlin: Cosmos, 1902, pp. 523–4.
3 Da Tradate, Mantegna, and Feliciano are named; the fourth member of the party is given the pseudonym Giovanni Antenoreo, and is usually identified as Marcanova, although sometimes as Giovanni da Padua. See R. Avesani, "Felicianerie," in A. Contò and L. Quaquarelli (eds.), *L'"Antiquario" Felice Feliciano Veronese tra epigrafia antica, letteratura e arti del libro*, Padua: Editrice Antenore, 1995, pp. 3–25 (10–11).
4 Kristeller, *Mantegna*, p. 524: "Demum templum beatae virginis in garda positum ingressi sumus Laudes ingentes summo tonanti eiusque gloriose matri devotissime agentes …"
5 For the former, see, e.g. the fundamental account by A. Martindale, *The Triumphs of Caesar by Andrea Mantegna*, London: Harvey Miller, 1979, pp. 23–4; for the latter, e.g., C. R. Chiarlo, "'Gli frammenti dilla sancta antiquitate': studi antiquari e produzione delle immagini da Ciriaco d'Ancona a Francesco Colonna," in S. Settis (ed.), *Memoria dell'antico nell'arte italiana*, 3 vols., Turin: Einaudi, 1984–6, vol. 1, pp. 269–97 (280–7). For the antiquaries, R. Weiss, *The Renaissance Discovery of Classical Antiquity*, 2nd edn., Oxford: Blackwell, 1988 remains a useful survey, and note the valuable overview by A. Grafton, "The Renaissance," in R. Jenkyns (ed.), *The Legacy of Rome: A New Appraisal*, Oxford: Oxford University Press, 1992, pp. 97–123.
6 P. Burke, *The Renaissance Sense of the Past*, New York: St. Martin's Press, 1969; for subsequent reflections by the author see P. Burke, "The Renaissance Sense of the Past Revisited," *Culture and History*, 13, 1984, pp. 42–56; P. Burke, "The Sense of Anachronism from Petrarch to Poussin," in C. Humphrey and W. M. Ormrod (eds.), *Time in the Medieval World*, York: York Medieval Press, 2001, pp. 157–73.

7 Burke, *Renaissance Sense*, p. 21.

8 *Ibid.*, p. 27.

9 For a recent reaffirmation of Burke's argument for the centrality of the Renaissance, see Z. Schiffman, *The Birth of the Past*, Baltimore: Johns Hopkins University Press, 2011. Compare the responses of the art historians A. Nagel and C. Wood, *Anachronic Renaissance*, New York: Zone, 2010, who point to the temporal instability of artworks, and of the literary historian M. De Grazia, "Anachronism," in B. Cummings and J. Simpson (eds.), *Cultural Reformations: Medieval and Renaissance in Literary History*, Oxford, 2010, pp. 13–32.

10 See Burke's autobiographical comments on art history in his *The Italian Renaissance: Culture and Society in Italy*, 3rd edn., Princeton, NJ: Princeton University Press, 2014, pp. 8–9.

11 There are, of course, exceptions: for an early example see C. Mitchell, "Archaeology and Romance in Renaissance Italy," in E. F. Jacob (ed.), *Italian Renaissance Studies: A Tribute to the Late Cecilia M. Ady*, London: Faber, 1960, pp. 455–83, esp pp. 475–8. Mitchell argues that Feliciano's account of the visit to Lake Garda is heavily influenced by Cyriac of Ancona.

12 M. Billanovich, "Intorno alla 'Iubilatio' di Felice Feliciano," *Italia medioevale e umanistica*, 32, 1989, pp. 351–8.

13 For a valuable essay from a slightly different perspective examining how "the past [could] shape and even transform its students," see K. Gouwens, "Perceiving the Past: Renaissance Humanism after the 'Cognitive Turn,'" *American Historical Review*, 103, 1998, pp. 55–82 (55).

14 A. Grafton, *Commerce with the Classics: Ancient Books and Renaissance Readers*, Ann Arbor: University of Michigan Press, 1997. This chapter is indebted in numerous ways to Grafton's inspiring analyses of early modern scholars and scholarly practices: for other examples, see the papers collected as *Defenders of the Text: The Traditions of Scholarship in an Age of Science, 1450–1800*, Cambridge, MA: Harvard University Press, 1991; *Bring Out Your Dead: The Past as Revelation*, Cambridge, MA: Harvard University Press, 2001; and *Worlds Made by Words: Scholarship and Community in the Modern West*, Cambridge, MA: Harvard University Press, 2009.

15 M. Sabellico, "Lettera di Marcantonio Sabellico a Marcantonio Morosini," Emy Dell'Oro (ed.), in M. Accame, *Pomponio Leto: vita e insegnamento*, Tivoli: Edizioni TORED, 2008, p. 212: "veterem spectandi consuetudinem." Accame's book introduces Leto's life and teaching; for prosopographical details of his circle, see B. Laurioux, *Gastronomie, humanisme et société à Rome au milieu du XVe siècle. Autour du* De honesta voluptate *de Platina*, Florence: SISMEL Edizioni del Galluzzo, 2006, and the material collected in the online Repertorium Pomponianum (www.repertoriumpomponianum.it/index.html).

16 Accame, *Pomponio Leto*, p. 60.

17 *Ibid.*, p. 83.

18 For an account sympathetic to Leto, see V. Zabughin, *Giulio Pomponio Leto: saggio critico*, vol. 1, Rome: La vita letteraria, 1909, pp. 32–124.

19 See K. Christian, *Empire without End: Antiquities Collections in Renaissance Rome, c. 1350–1527*, New Haven: Yale University Press, 2010, p. 127, citing E. Motta, "Bartolomeo Platina e Papa Paolo II," *Archivio della R. Società Romana di Storia Patria*, 7, 1884, pp. 555–9: "quali per essergli forse piaciute et gustate le hystorie de Romani, et per desyderare forse che Roma torni in quelli primi stati, havevano deliberato levare questa città de la subiectione de preti ..." (p. 555).

20 For example, L. Barkan, *Transuming Passion: Ganymede and the Erotics of Humanism*, Stanford: Stanford University Press, 1991, pp. 66–74.

21 For an examination of this aspect of renaissance Platonism within a wider framework, see A. Blanshard, *Sex: Vice and Love from Antiquity to Modernity*, Chichester: Wiley-Blackwell, 2010, pp. 124–8; and D. Orrells, *Sex: Antiquity and its Legacy*, London: I. B. Tauris, 2015, pp. 41–4.

22 Sabellico, "Lettera," p. 214: "Romanam iuventutem usque ad infamiam dilexit"; trans. A. D'Elia, *A Sudden Terror: The Plot to Murder the Pope in Renaissance Rome*, Cambridge, MA: Harvard University Press, 2009, p. 93.

23 D'Elia, *A Sudden Terror*, p. 77, citing and translating J. Delz, "Ein unbekannter Brief von Pomponius Laetus," *Italia medioevale e umanistica*, 9, 1966, pp. 417–40: "Aurea te vellem vel saecula prisca tulissent,/ Nam poteras forma sollicitasse deos. / Barbarus in volucrem numquam vertisset amantem/ Nec puer e caelo ningeret Iliacus" (p. 421).

24 *Ibid.*, p. 91, citing and translating Delz, "Ein unbekannter Brief," p. 421: "Laudavi puerum Venetum in forma, nobilitate et mei observatione."

25 *Ibid.*, p. 95.

26 U. Pfisterer, *Lysippus und seine Freunde: Liebesgaben und Gedächtnis im Rom der Renaissance, oder, Das erste Jahrhundert der Medaille*, Berlin: Akademie Verlag, 2008, esp. pp. 258–86. Pfisterer identifies Lysippus as Hermes Flavio de Bonis.

27 J. Atkinson and D. Sices, *Machiavelli and His Friends: Their Personal Correspondence*, Dekalb: Northern Illinois University Press, 1996, p. 264; for the context within Machiavelli's career, see C. Celenza, *Machiavelli: A Portrait*, Cambridge, MA: Harvard University Press, 2015, pp. 57–64.

28 C. Kallendorf, "Renaissance," in C. Kallendorf (ed.), *A Companion to the Classical Tradition*, Oxford: Blackwell, 2007, p. 41.

29 Christian, *Empire without End*, p. 131.

30 S. Magister, "Pomponio Leto collezionista di antichità," *Xenia Antiqua*, 7, 1998, pp. 167–96; S. Magister, "Pomponio Leto collezionista di antichità: Addenda," in *Antiquaria a Roma. Intorno a Pomponio Leto e Paolo II*, Rome: Roma nel Rinascimento, 2003, pp. 51–121.

31 N. Petrucci, "Pomponio Leto e la rinascita dell'epitaffio antico," *Eutopia*, 3, 1994, pp. 19–44 (41–2).

32 Magister, "Pomponio Leto collezionista," pp. 173–4.

33 Christian, *Empire without End*, p. 71.

34 *Ibid.*, p. 87.

35 London, British Library, Add. MS 10100; see Pfisterer, *Lysippus*, pp. 142–9; Christian, *Empire without End*, pp. 73–4.

36 As well as Christian, *Empire without End*, see K. Christian, 'From Ancestral Cults to Art: The Santacroce Collection of Antiquities,' in W. Cupperi (ed.), *Senso delle rovine e riusi dell'Antico*, Pisa: Scuola Normale Superiore di Pisa, 2002, pp. 255–72.

37 See Kathleen Christian's useful related comments of how reproductions of antiquities could cater to male viewers' sexual fantasies: K. Christian "Antiquities," in M. Wyatt (ed.), *The Cambridge Companion to the Italian Renaissance*, Cambridge: Cambridge University Press, 2014, pp. 40–58 (p. 57).

38 K. Bentz, "Cardinal Cesi and his Garden: Antiquities, Landscape, and Social Identity in Early Modern Rome," PhD diss., The Pennsylvania State University, 2003, p. 136.

39 L. Barkan, *Unearthing the Past: Archaeology and Aesthetics in the Making of Renaissance Culture*, New Haven: Yale University Press, 1999, esp. pp. 164–7.

40 On Chorier, see Orrells, *Sex*, pp. 52–64, and J. Grantham Turner, *Schooling Sex: Libertine Literature and Erotic Education in Italy, France, and England 1534–1685*, Oxford: Oxford University Press, 2003, pp. 165–220, with previous references. For the erudite libertines of this period, see M. Mulsow, *Die unanständige Gelehrtenrepublik: Wissen, Libertinage und Kommunikation in der Frühen Neuzeit*, Stuttgart: Metzler, 2007, pp. 5–10 and 27–66. In the sixteenth century, antiquaries and libertines moved in the same circles: see, e.g., the comments on Pietro Aretino in S. Gaylard, *Hollow Men: Writing, Objects, and Public Image in Renaissance Italy*, New York: Fordham University Press, 2013, esp. pp. 123–59.

41 See the fundamental analysis of S. Settis, "Des ruines au musée. La destinée de la sculpture classique," *Annales. Économies, Sociétés, Civilisations*, 48(6), 1993, pp. 1347–80.

42 P. Falguières, "La cité fictive. Les collections de cardinaux, à Rome, au XVIe siècle," in *Les Carrache et les décors profanes. Actes du Colloque organisé par l'École française de Rome (Rome, 2–4 octobre 1986)*, Rome: École française de Rome, 1988, pp. 215–333.

43 Bentz, "Cardinal Cesi and his Garden."

44 W. Stenhouse, *Reading Inscriptions and Writing Ancient History: Historical Scholarship in the Late Renaissance*, London: Institute of Classical Studies, University of London, 2005, pp. 128–36.

45 R. Bizzocchi, "'Familiae romanae' antiche e moderne," *Rivista storica italiana*, 103, 1991, pp. 355–97.

46 On Panvinio's historical scholarship see S. Bauer, "La transizione storiografica tra Rinascimento e Controriforma: Il caso di Onofrio Panvinio (1530–1568)," in P. Pombeni and H-G. Haupt (eds.), *La transizione come problema storiografico. Le fasi critiche dello sviluppo della modernità (1494–1973)*, Bologna: Il Mulino, 2013, pp. 129–49.

47 O. Panvinio, "De gente Maxima," in A. Mai (ed.), *Spicilegium romanum*, vol. 9, Rome: Typis Collegii Romani, 1843, pp. 549–91 (pp. 577 and 569).

48 Bauer, "La transizione storiografica," pp. 141–2.

49 Stenhouse, *Reading Inscriptions*, pp. 128–9.

50 R. Bizzocchi, *Genealogie incredibili: scritti di storia nell'Europa moderna*, 2nd edn., Bologna: Il Mulino, 2009.

51 See, e.g., A. Grafton, *What was History? The Art of History in Early Modern Europe*, Cambridge: Cambridge University Press, 2007, pp. 149–65.

52 For the background and selected awardees, see F. Gregorovius, "Alcuni cenni storici sulla cittadinanza romana," *Atti della R. Accademia dei Lincei*, 274, 1876–77, *Memorie* s. III, vol. 1, pp. 314–46.

53 D. Gnoli, *Un giudizio di lesa romanità sotto Leone X*, Rome: Tipografia della Camera dei Deputati, 1891; K. Gouwens, *Remembering the Renaissance: Humanist Narratives of the Sack of Rome*, Leiden: Brill, 2008, pp. 25–6 with previous references.

54 J. H. Gaisser, *Pierio Valeriano on the Ill Fortune of Learned Men: A Renaissance Humanist and his World*, Ann Arbor: University of Michigan Press, 1999, p. 29.

55 M. de Montaigne, *The Essays*, trans. M. Screech, London: Penguin, 1991, p. 1130.

56 *Ibid.*, p. 1132.

57 M. de Montaigne, *The Complete Works*, trans. D. Frame, London: Hamish Hamilton, 1971, p. 961.

58 *Ibid.*, p. 962

59 *Ibid.* On Montaigne's responses, see M. Disselkamp, *Nichts ist, Rom, dir gleich. Topographien und Gegenbilder aus dem mittelalterlichen und frühneuzeitlichen Europa*, Wiesbaden: Harrassowitz Verlag, 2013, pp. 131–57.

60 V. Pagani, "Documents on Antonio Salamanca," *Print Quarterly*, 17, 2000, pp. 148–55; M. Crawford, "Bembo giureconsulto," in A. Lewis and D. Ibbetson (eds.), *The Roman Law Tradition*, Cambridge: Cambridge University Press, 1994, pp. 98–103.

61 C. Dionisotti, *Appunti su arti e lettere*, Milan: Jaca Book, 1995, pp. 139–40.

62 W. Stenhouse, "Agustín and the Numismatists," in A. Stahl (ed.), *The Rebirth of Antiquity: Numismatics, Archaeology and Classical Studies in the Culture of the Renaissance*, Princeton, NJ: Princeton University Library, 2008, pp. 48–65 = *Princeton University Library Chronicle* 79, 2008, pp. 262–79.

63 M. Napolitano, *Hubertus Goltzius e la Magna Graecia: Dalle Fiandre all'Italia del Cinquecento*, Naples: Luciano Editore, 2011, pp. 122–50.

64 Bizzocchi, *Genealogie incredibili*, pp. 139–40.

65 A. Agustín, *Opera omnia*, Lucca: Rocchi, 1766, vol. 7, p. 253: "Hora vi voglio dire una bella fantasia mia, che hò bisogno per certo disegno mio farmi Cittadino Romano, ma vorrei che fosse con clausule alla antiqua, narrando la verità che sono di famiglia equestre di *Cesara Augusta* Colonia antiqua deducta di *Augusta*, & che il cognome mi pare, ò potria essere che fossi di esso, ò vero altri Augusto … Dunque vorrei ricuperare la Città, & essere ascritto con i miei trà li Patricii nobili Romani, & che potessi pigliar à mia posta il nome di Julia Ottavia Claudia, ò vero altra famiglia antica di Augusti. Vorrei che servisse questo Privilegio à me, & à Joanni Augustino mio fratello, & à Vincenzo Augustino mio parente, & a suoi figli, & discendenti in *saecula saeculorum* … narrate l'essere stato in Roma XVI. anni Auditore di Rota, haver scritto in lode delle famiglie Romane … pure vi scongiuro per tutti li Fulvij, & Ursini, & Ursicini, &c."

66 *Ibid.*, p. 256: "… possano miei nepoti giuocar nella festa del Testaccio vestiti all'antiqua, & haver parte delle Bufale, & Porchette, & di qualche moggio di Sale, ò libra di Pepe, quando si dividerà nel congiario del Campidoglio, che possano essere Caporioni, & maestri di strade & delle cloache, & delle vigne, liberi di tutti Dacij imposti alli sudditi del S. P. Q. R. ma non di quelli Pontificij &c."

67 On the Festa di Testaccio, see M. Bury, *The Print in Italy 1550–1620*, London: British Museum, 2001, pp. 168–9; on the Maestri di strade, A. De Michaelis, "The Maestri di Strade: Political Strategies and Social Mobility in Farnese Rome," in P. Prebys (ed.), *Early Modern Rome 1341–1667*, Ferrara: Edisai, 2011, pp. 741–8.

68 F. Haskell and N. Penny, *Taste and the Antique: The Lure of Antique Sculpture, 1500–1900*, New Haven: Yale University Press, 1988, pp. 169–72.

69 Martindale, *The Triumphs of Caesar*; P. Tosetti Grandi, *I trionfi di Cesare di Andrea Mantegna: Fonti umanistiche e cultura antiquaria alla corte dei Gonzaga*, Mantua: Sometti, 2008.

70 R. Cooper, *Roman Antiquities in Renaissance France*, Burlington, VT: Ashgate, 2013, pp. 245–81 with previous references. Margaret McGowan points to the often heterogeneous contents of these entries in "The Renaissance Triumph and its Classical Heritage," in J. R. Mulryne and E. Goldring (eds.), *Court Festivals of the Italian Renaisssance: Art, Politics and Performance*, Burlington, VT: Ashgate, 2002, pp. 26–47.

71 For the policies of Paul III, see G. Rebecchini, "After the Medici. The New Rome of Pope Paul III Farnese," *I Tatti Studies: Essays in the Renaissance*, 11, 2007, pp. 147–200. Charles and his supporters did not limit themselves to Rome when they looked for historical and mythical forebears: see

M. Tanner, *The Last Descendant of Aeneas: The Hapsburgs and the Mythical Image of the Emperor*, New Haven: Yale University Press, 1993, esp. pp. 113–18.

72 R. Ridley, "To Protect the Monuments: The Papal Antiquarian (1534–1870)," *Xenia Antiqua*, 1, 1992, pp. 119–21; S. Feci, "Latino Giovenale Manetti," in *Dizionario biografico degli Italiani*, 2007, vol. 68 (online at www.treccani.it/enciclopedia/latino-giovenale-manetti_%28Dizionario-Biografico%29/).

73 See J. Scott, "Uses of the Past: Charles V's Roman Triumph and its Legacy," in M. Reeve (ed.), *Tributes to Pierre du Prey; Architecture and the Classical Tradition, from Pliny to Posterity*, Turnhout: Harvey Miller/ Brepols, 2014, pp. 81–97, with references to previous scholarship.

74 For the Roman context, see especially K. Bentz, "Ancient Idols, Lascivious Statues, and Sixteenth-Century Viewers in Roman Gardens," in M. Rose and A. Poe (eds.), *Receptions of Antiquity, Constructions of Gender in European Art, 1300–1650*, Leiden: Brill, 2015, pp. 418–49.

75 G. Paleotti, *Discourse on Sacred and Profane Images*, trans. W. McCuaig, Los Angeles: Getty Research Institute, 2012, pp. 183–91.

76 J. Donnelly, "Antonio Possevino, S.J. as a Counter-Reformation Critic of the Arts," *Journal of the Rocky Mountain Medieval and Renaissance Association*, 3, 1982, pp. 153–64.

77 F. Borromeo, *Sacred Painting; Museum*, trans. K. Rothwell, Cambridge, MA: Harvard University Press, 2010, p. 23.

78 On Pius' hostility, see Bentz, "Ancient Idols," pp. 423–4 and 431.

79 Agustín, *Opera omnia*, vol. 7, pp. 247–8: "certo parevano male quelli termini maschii della vigna di Cesis & di Carpi, & quel Hermafrodito col Satiro nella Capella … Et la vigna di papa Giulio Terzo con tante Veneri & alter lascivie. Che se bene alli studiosi giovano, e alli artefici, li Oltramontani si scandalizzano bestialmente, & fama malum vires acquirit eundo [a phrase adapted from Virgil, *Aeneid* iv.173–5, who refers to the dangers to Carthage caused by word of Dido's dalliance with Aeneas]." Translation adapted from J.-M. Agasse, "Girolamo Mercuriale – Humanism and Physical Culture in the Renaissance," in G. Mercuriale, *De arte gymnastica*, ed. C. Pennuto, Florence: Olschki, 2008, pp. 861–1110 (p. 1063).

80 See George Huppert, *The Idea of Perfect History: Historical Erudition and Historical Philosophy in Renaissance France*, Urbana: University of Illinois Press, 1970; and, e.g., D. Kelley, *Foundations of Modern Historical Scholarship: Language, Law, and History in the French Renaissance*, New York, Columbia University Press, 1970, esp. pp. 116–48; J. Pocock, *The Ancient Constitution and the Feudal Law: A Study of English Historical Thought in the Seventeenth Century*, 2nd edn., Cambridge: Cambridge University Press, 1987, pp. 8–29; and Z. Schiffman, *On the Threshold of Modernity: Relativism in the French Renaissance*, Baltimore: Johns Hopkins University Press, 1991.

81 Grafton, *Defenders of the Text*, pp. 26–7.

82 Barkan, *Unearthing the Past*, p. 9. See also Thomas Greene's classic, "Resurrecting Rome: The Double Task of the Humanist Imagination," in P. Ramsay (ed.), *Rome in the Renaissance: The City and the Myth: Papers of the Thirteenth Annual Conference of the Center for Medieval & Early Renaissance Studies*, Binghamton, NY: Center for Medieval & Early Renaissance Studies, 1982, pp. 41–54.

83 Jacob Burckhardt, *The Civilization of the Renaissance in Italy*, trans. S. Middlemore, 3rd edn., London: Phaidon Press, 1995, p. 174.

8

SPORUS IN THE RENAISSANCE

The eunuch as straight man

Katherine Crawford

In his *Epistle to Dr. Arbuthnot* (1735), Alexander Pope responded to his friend, John Arbuthnot, who had asked Pope to moderate his satirical venom. Masterfully explaining himself and jus-tifying his attacks with humor, Pope deftly deflected his own desire for fame while denouncing the grasping aspirants in his way. One of Pope's targets is Lord Hervey (John, second Baron Hervey, 1696–1743), called "Sporus" by Pope in his imagined conversation with Arbuthnot:

> [P.] Let Sporus tremble – A. What? that thing of silk,
> Sporus, that mere white curd of Ass's milk?
> Satire or sense, alas! can Sporus feel?
> Who breaks a butterfly upon a wheel?
> P. Yet let me flap this with gilded wings,
> This painted child of dirt, that stinks and stings;
> Whose buzz the witty and the fair annoys,
> Yet wit ne'er tastes, and beauty ne'er enjoys:
> So well-bred spaniels civilly delight
> In mumbling of the game they dare not bite.
>
> (lines 305–14)

Where "Arbuthnot" considers Hervey so inferior as to be unworthy of Pope's attention, Pope considers Hervey/Sporus to be the servile epitome of sexualized (political) corruption, but also to be effeminate in his behavior, the mark of which is his propensity to be inconsistent in ways that meld gender attributes:

> His will all seesaw, between that and this,
> Now high, now low, now master up, now miss,
> And he himself, one vile Antithesis.
> Amphibious thing! that acting either part,
> The trifling head, or the corrupted heart,
> Fop at the toilet, flatterer at the board,
> Now trips a Lady, and now struts a Lord.
>
> (lines 323–29)[1]

Although Pope did not name Hervey (one of Arbuthnot's complaints was that Pope named his targets), the poem savaged Hervey by way of Sporus, the castrated favorite of the emperor, Nero (Nero Claudius Caesar Augustus Germanicus, 15 December 37–9 June 68). When it first appeared, the poem called Hervey "Paris," but the associations of the son of Priam with beauty and even nobility led Pope to change it for his collected works, which appeared just three months after the first edition.[2] Sporus, Pope evidently felt, was a far more appropriate figure to use to disparage Hervey.

Pope assumed that his readers knew about Sporus, but what did they know? And where did that knowledge come from? The short answer to the latter question is Suetonius (*Twelve Caesars*) and Cassius Dio (*Roman History*), along with shorter references in Sextus Aurelius Victor, Dio Chrysostom, and Plutarch.[3] The longer answer involves what readers and commentators relying on those sources made of Sporus' story. Used to condemn Nero in antiquity, Sporus became a more general stand-in for gender deviance and sexual depravity. Renaissance writers upheld normative gender and sexuality through their attacks on Sporus as effeminate, sexually passive, socially depraved, and unnatural. In their hands, the story of a young man, perhaps a boy, castrated in antiquity and very publicly made to serve an emperor in provocative ways became a cultural node of gender and sexual discipline.

Sporus was known, then, in part in the old-fashioned sense that historians have used the term "Renaissance": He appeared in ancient texts that were "rediscovered" – usually meaning edited and published – by scholars with knowledge of classical languages. As an intellectual move, this "Renaissance" meant that the texts in which Sporus' story appeared were available and apparently popular within an admittedly limited reading public. Suetonius especially circulated widely in Renaissance print culture, with all subsequent manuscripts and printed editions traceable back to a manuscript (*Codex Memmianus* or Parisinus Lat. 6115) probably copied at Tours in the early ninth century.[4] Among the many manuscripts that followed, the eleventh-century copy now at Wolffenbüttel and the slightly later example in the Biblioteca Apostolica Vaticana, Vat. lat. 1904, are closely related to *Memmianus*.[5] Among the more than 200 handwritten manuscripts are one owned by Petrarch that ended up in the Visconti library,[6] and a copy in Houghton Library at Harvard from Italy in about 1450, which includes a variety of marginalia in later hands.[7] Printed editions began appearing in earnest in the 1470s, with three editions emanating from Venice, Rome, and Milan.[8] In addition to multiple editions from Italy, printers in Lyons, Paris, Strasbourg, and Antwerp produced Latin editions, followed by vernacular versions beginning in the early sixteenth century.[9] Cassius Dio Coccesianus was less popular, not least because he wrote in Greek. A manuscript in Greek but produced in Rome, vernacular versions in Italian from 1533 and French from 1542, and Latin excerpts nonetheless demonstrate Dio's availability.[10] Even this brief survey indicates that the Sporus story circulated among literate elites in Renaissance Europe.

Both Suetonius and Cassius Dio presented Sporus as part of the case against Nero. For Suetonius, Sporus was a central exhibit illustrating Nero's sexual and social depravity:

> He excised the testicles of the boy Sporus and actually tried to make a woman of him; and he married him with all the usual ceremonies, including a dowry and a bridal veil, took him to his house attended by a great throng, and treated him as his wife. And the witty jest that someone made is still current, that it would have been well for the world if Nero's father, Domitius had had that kind of wife. This Sporus, ornamented with the finery of the empresses and riding in a litter, he took with him

to the assemblies and markets of Greece and later at Rome through the Sigillaria, kissing him from time to time.

Suetonius added that Nero "married" his freedman Doryphorus as well, and emphasized that Nero was unbounded in his sexual depravity.[11] Cassius Dio provided the idea that Sporus was castrated because he resembled Sabina Poppaea, Nero's dead wife:

> Now Nero called Sporus 'Sabina' not merely because, owing to his resemblance to her he had been made a eunuch, but because the boy, like the mistress, had been solemnly married to him in Greece, Tigellinus giving the bride away, as the law ordained. All the Greeks held a celebration in honour of their marriage, uttering all the customary good wishes, even to the extent of praying that legitimate children might be born to them.

Dio names Nero's other male lover as Pythagoras, noting that Nero played the "wife" with him, while playing the "husband" with Sporus.[12] Dio later adds that the emperor Otho (r. 69) also had a same-sex relationship with Sporus.[13] In slightly different form, both Suetonius and Dio indicate that Romans were not entirely comfortable with Nero's displays of his male lovers. As in Suetonius' account, the comment about Nero's father remained, but Dio spells out the implications: "indicating that if this had been the case, Nero would not have been born, and the state would now be free of great evils." Dio also names Sporus as one of the four men who accompanied Nero on his final flight, and includes a coda in which Sporus commits suicide, rather than appear on stage playing the part of a maiden at the behest of Vitellius.[14]

Sporus was neither the only nor the only possible choice of male–male sexuality that could be deployed as a scandalous example for later centuries. There were, after all, imperial or royal favorites from which to choose from across Greek and Roman literature: Achilles and Patroclus; Alexander and Bagoas; Alexander and Haphaestion; Hadrian and Antinous, to name a few.[15] Like Sporus, Bagoas was a eunuch, and in ancient Roman culture, eunuchs were regularly employed in sensitive positions. Created by human intervention, usually lacking the need to pass on power or property to physical heirs, and unable to undermine the ruling patriline through impregnating the women they guarded or served, eunuchs were appealing on a variety of levels. The eunuch may have been tempted (although he was typically not considered sexually interested), but even if he did have sexual relations with a woman in his charge, she could not get pregnant.[16] Inverting the usual historical queasiness about eunuchs that lurks in questions about why they were utilized in administrative and ceremonial roles, Kathryn Ringrose's study of eunuchs at the Byzantine court asks why they were not more prevalent, given the advantages that they embodied.[17] Also interested in Byzantine practice, Shaun Tougher contends that the reliance on eunuchs by rulers led to castrated men becoming symbols of royalty.[18] Ancient Roman eunuchs were often the product of war, and caused periodic spasms of official disapprobation, but they never disappeared and were sometimes quite prominent public figures.[19]

Indeed, despite some negative press around self-castrating worshippers of Cybele (or Magna Mater), eunuchs were attractive as sexual partners, and Nero may have increased their popularity.[20] Juvenal's quip that women would prefer eunuchs because they could have sex without fear of unwanted pregnancy was just one of the more famous statements about eunuchs as sex objects.[21] Despite legislating against castration, Domitian (r. 81–96) had a eunuch named Earinus as a favorite.[22] Suetonius and others believed that Domitian legislated against eunuchs in reaction to Titus' (r. 79–81) fondness for them.[23] Nor did the eunuch as favorite disappear: like Nero, Heliogabalus (or Elagabalus, r. 218–222) "married" his male favorite, with Heliogabalus as the "bride," which may not seem terribly surprising, since the emperor was only fourteen at the beginning of his reign.[24] If eunuchs were associated with sexual excess and depravity by later (Christian) commentators, those same critics could point to positive examples of eunuchs as well, such as the general and *cubicularis* Narses and the Ethiopian eunuch who appeared in Acts 8: 26–40 and was widely regarded in early modern sermons as an exemplary early convert to Christianity.[25]

Even with the positive possibilities, Renaissance writers had their own ambivalent responses to eunuchs. With the use of music in its liturgy, the Catholic Church created the conditions for large-scale castration for musical purposes.[26] Through the Middle Ages and into the eighteenth century in parts of Italy, women were banned from singing in church ostensibly because of St. Paul's injunction against women speaking.[27] Boy sopranos sang the high parts, while high adult male voices created controversy. Bernard of Clairvaux (1090–1153) and the Cistercians rejected high male singing: "Viros decet virilli voce cantare, et non more femineo tinnulis." (It befits men to sing with a virile voice, and not in a womanish ringing manner.)[28] Encouraged by humanists who sought to "revive" ancient musical practices, composers and their patrons began to require a wider range of voices and more skilled singers than had been the norm a century earlier.[29] When the development of polyphony made music complex and difficult to master, the limitations on boy sopranos became apparent: Just when they developed the necessary skill level, their voices changed. One solution, turning to falsettists, proved increasingly unsatisfactory by the sixteenth century. Complaints about the quality of the falsetto voice encouraged agitation to find a different solution. Some princely courts employed female sopranos, but others sought castrated male singers.[30] The Catholic Church in the form of the Cappella Pontifica (later the Cappella Sistina) initially employed falsettists, but gradually switched over to castrati to the point that Sixtus V issued a papal bull, *Cum pro nostro pastorali munere* (1589) calling for twelve singers in Sistine Choir (four bass, four tenor, four contraltos) and "four eunuchs" to sing soprano (if eunuchs could not be found, the choir was to use six boys).[31] Castration for musical purposes was instantiated in both secular courts and Catholic choirs by 1600, and the practice of castrating for the preservation of the high male voice gained purchase with the rise of commercial opera beginning in Venice with the opening of the first public opera house in 1637.[32] Eunuchs were increasingly visible as public figures, with the physical source of their spectacular singing skills a matter of general knowledge.

The popularity of opera notwithstanding, castration made for palpable unease. Juan Huarte's (1529–1588) widely circulated *Examen de Iugenios* condemned castration for effeminizing men by removing their fundamental masculine "heat."[33] Innovative Renaissance surgeon Ambrose Paré (c. 1510–1590) described castrates as cold and moist, adding that eunuchs who had been fully ablated required a tube or funnel with which to urinate. He explained that eunuchs, like women (who lactate, menstruate, and sometimes have urinary issues after pregnancy), were physically leaky.[34] Unlike women, castrated men lost their desire. Papal physician Paolo Zacchia (1584–1659) emphasized that disabled testicles resulted in a man becoming "totally frigid" without the possibility of recovering his masculine heat.[35] According to French royal physician André du Laurens (1558–1609), "estans couppez, tournez ou refroidis, toute la virilité perit, & tout amour du congrez & copulation s'esteint & s'amortit." (Being cut or turned or made cold, all the virility perishes, and all love of sexual

143

congress and copulation extinguishes and dies.)[36] Although castration did not entirely render them as women, it effeminized men and made them rather proximate to women, perhaps uncomfortably so.

Given these multiple lines of concern about castration, Sporus could function as a marker in a variety of conversations about the sexed body in the Renaissance, but he served perhaps most obviously as shorthand for the sexual decadence of ancient Rome. Pedro Mexía's (1497–1551) historical survey *Historia imperial y Cesarea* quoted Suetonius regarding Nero's intention to turn Sporus into a woman. Leaving the crucial passage in Latin, Mexía presumed that learned readers would understand but shielded the shocking information from less reliably intellectual readers of the vernacular.[37] In his collection of *progymnasmata* or *praeexercitamina* (rhetorical practice speeches), Richard Rainolde (d. 1606) bracketed the discomfort of castration in the form of an aside, "Nero assaied to frame and fashion [Sporus] out of kinde."[38] Writers routinely branded Sporus a "Ganimede," "guelded Ganimed," "he-concubine," or simply a "concubine."[39] The deployment of a figure from antiquity to provide a moral example in a Renaissance text could be as basic as that.

But Sporus was also used in more complex critical contexts, including discussions about love and desire. Florentine Neoplatonism as posited by Marsilio Ficino (1433–1499) especially advocated a model in which male love for other men was a crucial step on the way to salvation.[40] Because of the ambiguity between love and desire, fears that male–male love was tainted with physical attraction and sex were not uncommon.[41] For several authors, Nero's love for Sporus was precisely the opposite of Ficino's salvific ideal: it was the path to damnation. For Pierre Boiastuau (c. 1517–1566), Nero was a prime example of "monstrous Love" in his illustrated collection of monsters and prodigies. After assaulting girls, married women, and Vestal Virgins, Nero "castrated a handsome young boy, who was named Sporus, thinking thereby to transform him into a woman, who he publicly married with great solemnity, assigning him a dowry and kept him as a wife as Cornelius [Tacitus] and Suetonius write." (il chastrer un beau jeune enfant, qui se nommoit Sporus, le pensant transformer en femme, lequel il espousa publiquement avec grand solemnité, luy assigna douaire et retint pour femme, comme Corneille, et Suetone écrivent.)[42] The dramatist and miscellany writer Anthony Munday (1560?–1633) was similarly troubled:

> The Tirant *Nero* ... spoyled a number of Virgins and chaste Ladyes: but also finding a beautifull Boye, more pleasaunt in his eyes then any other Virgin or woman: caused his secrets to be spoyled, thinking thereby to haue him transformed to his owne pleasure, by such a Metamorphosis as of a man to haue a woman. Not long after he married him, naming him *Sporus*, endowing him with such secret duties, as to a Wife are due by dowry.[43]

Perhaps influenced by his anti-Catholic attitude – Munday spied on Jesuits in Rome who were subsequently arrested when they went to England – Munday's Sporus was an example of love deviating from the laws of nature. For both Boiastuau and Munday, the Neoplatonic discourse of ideal love attached to the male form and exemplified in male–male friendship was hideously distorted in the case of Nero and Sporus.[44] François de Salignac de La Mothe-Fénelon offers a seemingly more generous reading of Sporus in terms of male–male love ("l'amour d' homme à homme"). Citing Ganymede, Hadrian's favorite Antinous, Achilles and Patroclus, and Hercules and Hylas among his examples, Fénelon notes different reactions to it: the Persians laugh at it; the Chinese encourage it; and the West Indians punish

144

such behavior by death.[45] The combination of historical precedent and cultural relativism allows space for male-male relationships, but the association of Sporus with Nero and situating him just after the description of the most draconian response to such relationships suggests Fénélon was damning with faint praise.

If male–male love could be idealized, part of the problem was that Nero treated Sporus like a woman, and perhaps even tried to transform a man into a woman. The author of *Anthropometamorphosis* described Sporus as "cut and made (forsooth) a woman."[46] Tomaso Garzoni (1549?–1589) included Nero in the category of "ridiculous fools" and described him as deranged for wanting to change a male into a female: "[Nero] entred into this notable follie, that he woulde needes see him of a male as hee was, turned into a woman by the Phisitions."[47] For Samuel Clarke (1599–1682), Nero's alteration of Sporus figured centrally in the example of Nero's history as an illustration of "God judgement upon Adulterers and unclean persons." Nero's faults, Clarke allows, were many, but worst of all, "Nero the Emperour kept many Catamites, and amongst the rest he caused the genitals of a boy called Sporus to be cut off, and endeavoured to transforme him into a woman, and causing him to be dressed like a woman, he was solemnly married to him."[48] Since at least Aristotle, the notion of natural hierarchy tending toward perfection meant that men were more perfect than women. Any physiological change would "naturally" be in the direction of greater perfection. Jacques Duval understood the case of Marie le Marcis, who was raised as a girl until being recognized as a man at age twenty and becoming Marin le Marcis as one of a woman "restored to a better virile state" (rendu en meilleure habitude virile).[49] The idea that a woman becoming male was the natural order of things appeared in popular literature as well. Antonio de Torquemada's *Iardin de flores curiosas* includes the tale of a woman becoming a man among its assortment of prodigies.[50]

For English anti-theatrical writers, castration might not by itself make a man into a woman, but it did make him dangerously effeminate. John Rainolds (1549–1607) warned that, when Sporus wore women's attire and was made up like a woman, it led directly to "great sparkles of lust therunto in unclean affections."[51] Rainolds' concern is that actors take on elements of the parts they play, and Sporus in his reading became feminine because Nero dressed him as his wife. For Rainolds, the inevitable result was sodomy: Nero would take Sporus for a woman and as a woman sexually although he was still a man. William Prynne (1600–1669), also an anti-theatrical polemicist, saw the responsibility for sodomy differently, but the result was largely the same. For Prynne, Sporus was among those "passive Sodomites" who dressed "sometimes, not alwayes in womans apparel." Citing "the verdict of human nature condemnes mens degenerating into women," Prynne considered effeminacy of costume to become constitutional and abhorrent because the cross-dressed male took the female role.[52] In case his readers were unclear on the dangers of cross-dressing as the inevitable road to effeminacy and sodomy, Prynne repeated his claim three times, invoking Sporus each time.[53]

As scholars have insisted "sodomy" was a catch-all category that prompted a variety of responses in early modern contexts, but the use of Sporus by Prynne and others like him was meant to render male–male homosexual sodomy as especially offensive. Michel Foucault's remark that sodomy was, "that utterly confused category" has inspired much research into the meanings of, and responses, to sodomy in early modernity.[54] Sodomy included all manners of non-reproductive sex, with significant local variation in terms of communal responses. To take just a few examples, prosecutions for male–male sodomy in Florence and Venice were a matter of public knowledge and the apparatus to deal with it was extensive, while Spanish Inquisition sources include a significant number bestiality cases.[55] Convictions in

German-speaking areas and England for sodomy were often associated with charges of heresy, while officials in Scotland had a recurrent interest in bestiality.[56] By associating Sporus with sodomy, writers could fuse multiple forms of depravity, as when Thomas Lanquet conflated Nero's predatory behaviors: "In vncleane lust of the bodye so furyously raged, that he absteined not from mother, syster ne any degree of affinitee and kinred, he toke in open mariage a bodye of excellent fauour, named Sporus and vsed him as his wife, he abandoned him selfe to filthy imbrasinges of his owne seruantes."[57] Even when authors recognized Sporus as a victim, his participation in male–male sodomy marked his personal depravity, rendered it a problem of physical desire, and linked it to moral corruption.[58]

Discomfort about Sporus' gender and its perceived sexual manifestations were at least equaled by outrage over Nero's marriage to him and its attendant social implications. John Taylor (1580–1653) described Nero taking "beastly joy" in marrying Sporus.[59] Jeremy Taylor (1613–1667) regarded Nero's same-sex marriages as both sinful and illegal: "*Nero* did marry *Sporus*, and he married *Doryphorus*, whom *Tacitus* calls *Pythagoras*: but this was no less a sin, because it was not the express vocal contradiction of a law; it was against a law that nam'd it not."[60] Male–male marriage threatened religious, legal, and civil order. For Nicolas Coeffeteau, Nero specifically castrated Sporus in order to marry him: "Nero made him a eunuch in order to marry him and to keep him as his wife." (Neron fit rendre eunuque afin de l'épouser, et de le tenir pour sa femme.) The resemblance to Poppaea is rehearsed, but Coeffeteau is far more interested in the horrific spectacle:

> The sun never saw anything so monstrous in the course of the lives of men, than the abominable nuptials that Nero would do in Greece by the intervention of Tigellinus: because he was so lost and brazen, making a marriage contract with this Sporus, assigning him a dowry, marrying him with all the usual ceremonies, and sleeping with him as with his wife. Greece deployed its eloquence to flatter such an execrable action, and there were those who rose to the heights of impudence, praying to the gods that they would give birth to a happy lineage …
>
> Le soleil ne vid jamais rien de si monstrueux au cours de la vie des hommes, que ces abominables nopces que Neron voulut faire en la Grece par l'entremise de Tigellinus: car il fut si perdu et si effronté, que de passer un contract de mariage à ce Sporus, de luy assigner un doüaire, de l'épouser avec toutes les ceremonies ordinaires, et de coucher avec luy comme avec sa femme. La Grece déploya son eloquence pour flatter une si execrable action, et mesmes il y en eut qui monterent jusques à ce comble d'impudence, *de prier les dieux qu'ils fissent naistre une heureuse lignée…*

Coeffeteau recurs to "infamous Sporus who took the place of a wife" (infame Sporus qui luy tenoit lieu de femme) in the course of recounting Nero's flight and death.[61] For Renaissance writers, two men marrying (even if one was altered by castration) was at odds with the fundamental premises of social order. Although many men did not marry, whether because they chose clerical celibacy or were not in a position to marry for financial or social reasons, the presumption was that most men married women. The further presumption was that one of the primary purposes of marriage was procreation. For writers like Coeffeteau, Nero's "marriage" to Sporus was at best absurd.

The association of Sporus with male–male marriage enabled one of those syllogistic nodes that shape the discursive and disciplinary framing of sexuality: Sporus was Nero's boy-toy, which was bad; their "marriage" illustrated the badness of their relationship; male–male marital relationships must be bad. Regardless of the availability of Sporus (in the Renaissance and now) as an example of gay marriage, in its own moment, the relationship likely meant something rather different. Taking the ancient accounts at their word and pointedly rejecting any notion that Nero was pederastically inclined, Richard Holland accepts that Sporus was chosen and castrated for his resemblance to Poppaea.[62] For Edward Champlin, the marriage was a farce, a joke for Saturnalia in which Sporus' name – Sporos in Greek means "seed" or "semen" – is part of the fun.[63] Perhaps, but the purpose of the joke remains obscure. It seems rather a long way to go for just a laugh. More moderately, Craig Williams sees Nero's actions with Sporus as at once demasculinizing and a possible threat to masculine privilege.[64] For David Woods, the threat was Sporus. Woods contends that Nero castrated him because he believed Sporus had a claim to imperial power and was a potential rival. Castration removed him from the gene pool and the marriage functioned to humiliate Sporus on an international scale. Woods specifically refutes both the "gay marriage" model and the idea that Nero and Sporus had a loving relationship. Sporus' castration and all that followed were political statements about power and access.[65] Shaun Tougher counters that contemporaries did understand Nero's relationship to Sporus in terms of love and desire. Situating Sporus in a Roman discourse of beautiful eunuchs, Tougher argues that castration was associated with preserving male beauty.[66]

As the debates among modern historians indicate, Sporus continues to provide a point of entry into matters of larger concern than one castrated boy at the court of a notorious emperor who died nearly two millennia ago. If Sporus can be a figure for gay marriage or perhaps transsexuality in the present, he allowed commentators in the Renaissance to articulate concerns about their own philosophical principles, understandings of gender, social order, sexual comportment, and the body. For them, disabling the testicles made a man something other than a man: a sodomite, a Ganymede, a wife, a woman. For Alexander Pope and his readers, Sporus was the exemplar of embodied effeminacy, sexual transgression, and social deviance because the Renaissance made him so.

Notes

1 Alexander Pope, *Epistle to Dr. Arbuthnot* (1735), in *Selected Poetry and Prose*, ed. William K. Wimsatt, 2nd edn., New York: Holt, Rinehart, 1972, 281–96.
2 Robert Halsband, *Lord Hervey, Eighteenth-Century Courtier*, Oxford: Oxford University Press, 1974, 175.
3 Plutarch, "Galba," in *Lives*, trans. Bernadotte Perrin, 11 vols., London: William Heinmann, 1915–1926, 9.1–4 (vol. 11: 222–5); Sextus Aurelius Victor, *Epitome*, in Liber de Caesaribus, ed. F. Pichlmayr and R. Gruendal, Leipzig: Teubner, 1966, 5.7 (p. 140), names Sporus as one of four present at Nero's death. Juvenal refers to Sporus in Satire 10: 306–9 by means of Nero's seduction and castration of a young boy. Sporus is not named, but Jerry Clack, "To Those Who Fell on Agrippina's Pen," *Classical World* 69(1) (September 1975): 45–63, at p. 48 suggests this reading. For Juvenal, see *Juvenal: The Sixteen Satires*, trans. and intro. Peter Green, 3rd edn., New York: Penguin, 2004: "But no misshapen stripling was ever unsexed by a tyrant in his castle,/no Nero would ever rape a clubfooted adolescent–/much less one with a hump, pot-belly, or scrofula."
4 Suetonius, *The Lives of the Caesars*, trans. J. C. Rolfe, 2 vols., Cambridge, MA: Harvard University Press, 1970, xxi–xxiv; Josiah Osgood, ed. *A Suetonius Reader: Selections from the Lives of the Caesars and the Life of Horace*, Mundelein, IL: Bolchazy-Carducci Publishers, 2011, xxvi.
5 Herzog August Bibliothek Wolfenbüttel, Cod. Guelf. 268 Gud. lat.; Katalog-Nr. 4573.
6 Anthony Hobson, *Renaissance Book Collecting: Jean Grolier and Diego Hurtado de Mendoza*, Cambridge and New York: Cambridge University Press, 1999, 13.

7 Suetonius, *Suetonii Tranquillini de vita et moribus duodecim principium Romanorum libri duodecim* (Italy, *c.* 1450), Harvard, Houghton f MS Typ 2.

8 Suetonius, *De vita Caesarum*, Venice: Nicoleos gallus, 1471; *Vita Caesarum*, Rome: Conradus Sweyheym and Arnoldus Rannartz, after 1470; *Vitae XII Caesarum*, Rome: Joh. Phil de Lignamine, 1470; *De vita Caesarum*, Milan: Filippo da Lavagna, 1475. The first three are considered *editiones principes*.

9 Suetonius, *De vita XII Caesarum*, Lyon: Balthasar de Gabiano, 1508; *Vitae duodecim Caesarim diligentissime recognitae*, Lyon: Guilhelmi Huyon, 1520; *XII. Caesares*, ed. Desiderius Erasmus, Lyon: Seb. Gryphius, 1539; *De vita Caesarum*, Paris: J. Barbier, 1508; *De vita duodecim Caesarum, Libri XII*, Strasbourg: Johann Prüss, 1520; *C. Suetonii Tranquilli XII Caesares*, Antwerp: Plantinian & Ioannem Moretum, 1591; *Des faictz et gestes des douze Cesars*, Paris: Galliot du Pre, 1520; *Vita de duodeci imperatori*, Venice: Venturino di Roffinelli, 1539; *Las vidas de los doze Cesares*, Tarragona: Phelipe Roberto, 1596; *The Historie of twelve Caesars*, London: Humphrey Lownes and George Snowdon for Matthew Lownes, 1606. There are at least forty Latin editions before 1820.

10 Harvard, Houghton MS Typ 144, *Bios kai monarchia Oktaouiou Kaisaros* (*c.* 1535–1550); Dio, *Historico delle guerre & fatti de Romani*, Venice: n. p., 1533; *Des faictz & gestes insignes des Romains, reduictz par annalles et consultez, etc. Premierement traduict de grec en italien par Nicolas Leonicene & dupuis de italien en vulgaire francois par Claude Deroziers*, Paris: A. & C. les Angeliers, 1542. For Latin, see for instance *Dionis Romanarum historiarum libri XXIII, à XXXVI ad LVIII usque*, Paris: Robert Estienne, 1548; *Dionis nicaei rerum romanarum à Pompeio Magno ed Alexandum Mamaeae epitome authore Ioanne Xiphilino*, Paris: Robert Estienne, 1551.

11 Suetonius, *Nero*, in *The Lives of the Caesars*, ch. 28 (translation modified). See ch. 29 for Doryphorus.

12 Cassius Dio, *Dio's Roman History*, ed. and trans. Earnest Cary, 9 vols., London: William Heinemann, 1914–1927, 62.28; 62[63].13.1–2. (8: 134–7; 158–9). As John Boswell notes, Dio is numbered in a confusing manner in the Loeb edition. I have followed Boswell's practice of providing the chapter headings with the marginal numbers in brackets. See John Boswell, *The Marriage of Likeness: Same-Sex Unions in Pre-Modern Europe*, London: Fontana Press, 1996, 55 (n. 7). Tactius, *The Annals*, trans. John Jackson, 4 vols., Cambridge, MA: Harvard University Press, 1937, 15.37 also called this partner Pythagoras.

13 Dio, *Roman History*, 63.8.3 (8: 208–9). For the context of sexual invective against Otho, see Michael B. Charles and Eva Anagnostou-Laoutides, "Unmanning an Emperor: Otho in the Literary Tradition," *Classical Journal* 109(2) (December 2013–January 2014): 199–222. For Dio's historiographic principles, see Adam M. Kemezis, *Greek Narratives of the Roman Empire under the Severans: Cassius Dio, Philostratus and Herodian*, Cambridge: Cambridge University Press, 2014, 90–149.

14 Dio, *Roman History*, 63.27.3–63.29.2; 64.10.1 (8:186–93; 236–7).

15 Cicero accused Marc Antony of "marriage" with Curio. See *Philippics* 2.18.44–5: "… in matrimonio stabili et certo collocavit."

16 Vern L. Bullough, "Eunuchs in History and Society," in Shaun Tougher, ed., *Eunuchs in Antiquity and Beyond*, London: Duckworth, 2002, 1–17. See p. 7; Taisuke Mitamura, *Chinese Eunuchs: The Structure of Intimate Politics*, trans. Charles A. Pomeroy, Rutland, VT: C. E. Tuttle, 1970, 10.

17 Kathryn M. Ringrose, *The Perfect Servant: Eunuchs and the Social Construction of Gender in Byzantium*, Chicago and London: University of Chicago Press, 2003.

18 Tougher, *Eunuch in Byzantine Society*, 46–53.

19 Domitian outlawed castration (see Suetonius, *Domitian*, 7.1), and additional legislation against castration forbade masters from castrating their slaves and Hadrian added punishment to castrators. See for instance *Corpus iuris civilis*, ed. Paul Krueger, Theodor Mommsen, and Rudolf Schöll, 3 vols., Hildesheim: Weidmann, 1967, 1988, *Digest* 48.8.6, 48.8.4.2, and 48.8.5 (which prohibited castration by crushing rather than excising the testicles). See Martial, *Epigrammata*, ed. and trans. D. R. Shackleton Bailey, 3 vols., Cambridge, MA: Harvard University Press, 1993, 2: 6.2 for praise of Domitian's legislation against castration. For a politically important eunuch, see Claudian Claudianus, *In Eutropium*, in *Claudian*, trans. Maurice Platnauer, London and Cambridge MA: Harvard University Press, 1963.

20 A. B. Bosworth, "Vespasian and the Slave Trade," *Classical Quarterly* 52(1) (2002): 350–7, at p. 352. On the *galli*, see especially Mary Beard, "The Roman and the Foreign: The Cult of the 'Great Mother' in Imperial Rome," in Nicholas Thomas and Caroline Humphrey, eds., *Shamanism, History and the State*, Ann Arbor: University of Michigan Press, 1996, 164–90. For ancient disapproval,

see for instance Catullus, *Catullus Poems 61–68*, ed., trans., and commentary by John Godwin, London: Aris & Philips, 1995, 63, 1–38; Lucretius, *De rerum natura*, 2: 598–643. Lynn E. Roller, *In Search of God the Mother: The Cult of Anatolian Cybele*, Berkeley: University of California Press, 1999, 297–9, understands Lucretius as highlighting Roman values in contrast with the "terrifying vision" of the rites of Cybele.

21 Juvenal, *Sixteen Satires*, 6: 366–70.

22 Despite his praise for Domitian's legislation against castration, Martial also wrote in praise of Earinus' beauty. See *Epigrammata*, 2: 9.11, 9.12, 9.13, 9.16, 9.17, and 9.36. See also Publius Papinius Statius, "Capilli flavi Earini" [The Hair of Flavius Earinus], in *Silvae*, ed. and trans. D. R. Shackleton Bailey, Cambridge, MA: Harvard University Press, 2003, 3.4 (pp. 217–25).

23 Suetonius, *Domitian*, 7.2; Cassius Dio, *Roman History*, 67.2.3 (8: 318–19).

24 Craig A. Williams, *Roman Homosexuality*, Foreword by Martha Nussbaum, 2nd edn., Oxford: Oxford University Press, 2010, 279–80, notes that courtiers who claimed to have husbands may well have been pretending in order to imitate the emperor.

25 On the Ethiopian Eunuch, see for instance Samuel Purchas, *Purchas his pilgrimage*, London: Printed by William Stansby for Henrie Fetherstone, 1613, 554–6; Pierre de La Primaudaye, *The French academie*, London: Printed [by John Legat] for Thomas Adams, 1618, 910–12; Charles Sonnibank, *The Eunuche's Conversion. A Sermon preached at Paules Crosse, the second of February. 1617*, London: Printed by H. L. for Richard Fleming, 1617. On Narses, see for instance John Martyn, "The Eunuch Narses," in *Text and Transmission in Medieval Europe*, Cambridge: Cambridge Scholarly Publishing, 2007, 46–56. For the variety of roles routinely filled by eunuchs at the Byzantine court, see Ringrose, *Perfect Servant*, 163–83.

26 Although castration was technically illegal, the Church did not prohibit it entirely. The medical exception remained in place on the grounds that losing a part of the body to save the whole was acceptable. See Canon 2354 of the Code of Canon Law.

27 1 Corinthians 14:34–35: "Let your women keep silence in the churches: for it is not permitted unto them to speak; but they are commanded to be under obedience as also saith the law. And if they will learn any thing, let them ask their husbands at home: for it is a shame for women to speak in the church" (King James Version).

28 "Statuta Ordinins Cisterciensis, 1134," ch. 123, in *Statuta Capitulorum Generalium Ordinis Cisterciensis ob anno 1116 ad annum 1786*, ed. Joseph M. Canivez, 8 vols., Louvain, 1933–1941, 1: 30. See also Idung od Prüfening, *Dialogus inter Cluniacensum monachum et Cisterciensem de diversis utriusque ordinis observcantis*, in *Thesaurus novus anecdotorum*, ed. Edmond Martène and Ursin Durand, 5 vols., Paris: Florentini Delaulne et al., 1717, 5: cols. 1585–6, which objects to high, feminine-sounding male voices. See Christopher Page and Andrew Parrott, "False Voices," *Early Music* 9(1) 1981: 71–5 for discussion of ambiguities in the medieval documents.

29 Count Giovanni de' Bardi de Vernio (1534–1612) gathered humanists, musicians, and aristocrats at his home in Florence to discuss contemporary music in relation to the ancient past. Among the central interlocutors were Girolamo Mei (1519–1594), whose *De modis musicis antiquorum* (1575) was the result of his extensive research into Greek music. Vincenzo Galilei explicated Greek monodic style that enabled the emotional expression of poetry in a single melodic line and developed Mei's insights in his polemical *Dialogo della musica antica e della moderna* (1581). See Donald Jay Grout and Hermine Weigel Williams, *A Short History of Opera*, 4th edn., New York: Columbia University Press, 2003, 34–6, for a brief account.

30 A. Bertolotti, *Musici alla Corte dei Gonzaga in Mantova dal secolo XV al XVIII. Notizie e documenti raccolti negli Archivi Mantovani*, Bologna: Forni Editore, 1969, 37, 40, 64, 66–8.

31 Anthony Miller, "The Sacred Capons," *Musical Times* 114(1561) (March 1973): 250–2. See p. 250. The bull is "Cum pro nostro pastorali munere," 27 September 1589, in *Collectionis Bullarium brevium, aliorumque diplomatum sacro sanctae Basilicae Vaticanae*, Rome: J. Maria Salvioni Typographus Pontificius Vaticanus, 1747–1752, 3: 172.

32 On Venice in Italian opera culture, see especially Hélène Leclerc, *Venise et l'avènement de l'opéra public à l'âge baroque*, Paris: Armand Colin, 1987; Ellen Rosand, *Opera in Seventeenth-Century Venice: The Creation of a Genre*, Berkeley: University of California Press, 1991.

33 Juan Huarte, *Examen de iugenios para las ciencias* appeared originally in 1575. The first English edition was *Examen de Iugenios. The Examination of mens Wits. In which, by discovering the varietie of natures, is shewed for what profession each one is apt, and how far he shall profit therein*, trans. M. Camillo Camili, London:

Adam Islip, 1594. Huarte's work was translated into Latin, French, English, Dutch, and German and appeared in multiple editions in most languages. Huarte's argument rests on a Galenic understanding of human bodies along a spectrum from male (hot/dry) to female (cold/wet). The testicles, in Huarte's understanding, are a crucial source of male heat that suffuses the entire body.

34 Ambroise Paré, *The Workes of that Famous Chirurgion Ambrose Parey translated out of Latine and compares with the French. By Th: Johnson*, London: Th: Cotes and R. Young, 1634, 27–8. Illustration at p. 877. On women as "leaky," see for instance Gail Kern Pasteur, *The Body Embarrassed: Drama and the Disciplines of Shame in Early Modern England*, Ithaca, NY: Cornell University Press, 1993, 23–63. Cathy McClive, *Menstruation and Procreation in Early Modern France*, Farnham: Ashgate, 2015, points out that men could be leaky as well.

35 Paulo Zacchia, *Quaestionum medico-legalium, tomi tres*, Lyon: G. Nanty and C. Langloys, 1674, lib. 9, tit. 10, q. 2, no. –10 (pp. 763–4). Zacchia published the first volume in 1621, and the ninth in 1650. The first complete edition was published in 1654, and Zacchia's nephew added a tenth book with eighty-five cases or "consilia." This version was printed in Lyon in 1661 and again in 1674, 1701, and 1726. See Joseph Bajada, *Sexual Impotence: The Contribution of Paolo Zacchia (1584–1659)*, Rome: Editrice Pontificia Università Gregoriana, 1988, 25, 166.

36 Du Laurens, *Toutes les oeuvres*, 326. See also p. 329: "Eunuques & chastrez ... deviennent beaucoup plus gras, & sans poil part tout, ils perdent leur couleur vermeille, la fleur de du sang se flétrissant; leurs veines s'éntrecissent: bref en eux s'éteint & amortit tout desir de copulation."

37 Pedro Mexía, *Historia imperial y Cesarea: en la qual en summa se continen las vidas y hechos de todos los Cesares empadores de Roma*, Seville: n.p., 1545, fol. 46v.

38 Richard Rainolde, *A booke called the Foundacion of Rhetorike*, London: Ihon Kingston, 1563, fol. xlv (v).

39 Garzoni, *Hospital*, 61; Mathias Prideaux, *An Easy and Compendious Introduction for Reading all sorts of Histories*, Oxford: Leonard Lichfield, 1648, 195; Richard Capel, *Tentations their Nature, Danger, Cure*, London: R. B[adger], 1633, 65; John Golbourne, *A Friendly Apology, in the Behalf of the Womans Excellency*, London: Henry Mortlock, 1674, 17; Clarke, *Mirrour or Looking-Glasse*, 380; Edmund Bolton, *Nero Caesar, or Monarchie depraved*, London: Thomas Walkley, 1624, 283.

40 Marsilio Ficino, *Commentarium Marsillii Ficini Florentini in Convivium Platonis de Amore*, in *Divini Platonis Opera Omnia Marsilio Ficino Interprete*, Lyon: Nathanaelem Vincentium, 1588, 257–99 (originally 1484 in Latin; 1544 in Italian). Among the influential commentators who took up the problem of male–male love were Leone Hebreo, *Dialoghi di Amore*, Venice: Aldo, 1545; Pietro Bembo, *Gli Asolani di messer Pietro Bembo*, Venice: Aldo Romano, 1505; Baldassare Castiglione, *Il libro del cortegiano del conte Baldesar Castiglione*, Florence: Per il heredi di Philippo du Giunta, 1528; and Loys Le Roy, *Le Sympose de Platon, ou de l'amour et de beauté traduit de grec en François*, Paris: Jehan Longis & Robert le Mangnyer, 1558.

41 For some of the complications encountered with Ficino's model, see Katherine Crawford, "Marsilio Ficino, Neoplatonism, and the Problem of Sex," *Renaissance and Reformation; Renaissance et réforme* 28(2) (Spring 2004): 3–35.

42 Pierre Boaistuau, *Histoires Prodigieuses (édition de 1561). Édition critique*, intro. Stephan Bamforth, ed. Stephan Bamforth and Jean Céard, Geneva: Librairie Droz, 2010, 531. Tacitus does not write about Sporus. Boaistiau is probably repeating the error of Ravisius Textor [Jean Tixier de Ravisi], *Officinae Ioannis Ravisii Textoris epitome*, Lyon: Seb. Gryphium, 1551.

43 Anthony Munday, *A courtly controuersie, betweene looue and learning Pleasauntlie passed in disputation*, London: Iohn Charlewood, 1581, sig. Div(v). Others attributed the transformation into a woman to marriage. See for instance John Speed, *The history of Great Britaine under the conquests of ye Romans, Saxons, Danes and Normans*, London: William Hall and John Beale, 1611, 201 (marginal note): "*Nero* solemnely maried one of his youths called *Doriphorus*, and kept him as his wife: so likewise did he with *Sporus*, whom he endeauoured to transforme into a woman."

44 On Neoplatonism's sometimes vexed relationship to friendship and love, see Todd W. Reeser, "Redeeming Desire: Symphorien Champier's *La nef des dames vertueuses*," in *Men and Women Making Friends in Early Modern France*, ed. Lewis Seifert and Rebecca Wilkin, Farnham: Ashgate, 2015, 81–98.

45 François de Salignac de La Mothe-Fénélon, *Cinq dialogues faits à l'imitation des anciens*, 1631; ARTFL Electronic Edition, 2009, 27.

46 J. B., *Anthropometamorphosis: Man Transform'd: Or, The Artificial Changling Historically presented*, London: William Hunt, 1653, 407. See also Hieronymus Magomastrix, *The Strange Witch at Greenwich*, London: Thomas Harper, 1650, 17 for similar language.

47 Tomaso Garzoni, *The Hospitall of Incurable Fooles*, London: Edm. Bollifant for Edward Blount, 1600, 61. Originally *L'hospidale de' pazzi incurabili*, Venice: Gio Battista Somascho, 1586.

48 Samuel Clarke, *A Mirrour or Looking-Glasse Both for Saints, and Sinners, Held forth in about two thousand examples*, London: Tho. Newberry, 1654, 111.

49 Jacques Duval, *Traité des Hermaphrodits parties génitales, accouchemens des femmes*, Paris: Isidore Liseux, 1880, 10 (originally Rouen, 1612). Duval's interest in the case is discussed in Kathleen Long, "Jacques Duval on Hermaphrodites," in *High Anxiety: Masculinity in Crisis in Early Modern France*, ed. Kathleen Long, Kirksville, MO: Truman State University Press, 2002, 107–38. Marie/Marin is also analyzed in Katharine Park and Lorraine Daston, "The Hermaphrodite and the Orders of Nature: Sexual Ambiguity in Early Modern France," *Gay and Lesbian Quarterly* 1 (1995): 419–38.

50 Antonio de Torquemada, *Iardin de Flores curiosas, enque se tratan algunas materias de humanidad, philosophia, theologia y geographia*, Salamance: Iuan Baptista de Terronova, 1570. The book was translated into French (1579), Italian (1590), English (1600), and German (1626).

51 John Rainoldes, *Th'overthrow of stage-playes*, Middleburg: Richard Schilders, 1599, 32. See also p. 101

52 William Prynne, *Histrio-mastix. The Players Sourge, or, Actors Tragaedie*, London: for Michael Sparke, 1633, 199–200.

53 *Ibid.*, 206, 208–9, 213.

54 Michel Foucault, *The History of Sexuality: An Introduction*, trans. Robert Hurley, New York: Pantheon, 1978, 43.

55 Michael Rocke, *Forbidden Friendships: Homosexuality and Male Culture in Renaissance Florence*, Oxford and New York: Oxford University Press, 1996; Guido Ruggiero, *The Boundaries of Eros: Sex, Crime and Sexuality in Renaissance Venice*, Oxford and New York: Oxford University Press, 1985; William Monter, *The Frontiers of Heresy: The Spanish Inquisition from the Basque Lands to Sicily*, Cambridge: Cambridge University Press, 1990.

56 Marie R. Boes, "On Trial in Early Modern Germany," in *Sodomy in Early Modern Europe*, ed. Tom Betteridge, Manchester: Manchester University Press, 2002, 27–45; Helmut Puff, *Sodomy in Reformation Germany and Switzerland, 1400–1600*, Chicago: University of Chicago Press, 2003; Alan Bray, *Homosexuality in Renaissance England*, New York: Columbia University Press, 1995.

57 Thomas Lanquet, *An epitome of chronicles Conteyninge the whole discourse of the histories as well of this realme of England*, London: William Seres, 1559, 99r.

58 Among those who emphasize Nero's blame and Sporus' victimization are Ioannis Ravisii Textoris Niverensis [Jean Tixier de Ravisy] *Officina*, Basel: Nikolaus Brylinger, 1552, 493; Lodowick Lloyd, *The marrow of history, or, The pilgrimmage of kings and princes truly representing the variety of dangers inhaerent to their crowns*, London: E. Alsop, 1653, 197; Richard Grafton, *A Chronicle at Large and Meere History of the Affayres of Englande*, London: Henry Dedham for Richarde Tottle and Humffrey Toye, 1569, 79, although Grafton says Nero "caused himself to be gelded," which is not quite right.

59 John Taylor, *All the Workes of Iohn Taylor The Water Poet*, London: Iames Boler, 1630, 108.

60 Jeremy Taylor, *Ductor Dubitatium, or The Rule of Conscience in all her Generall Measures*, London: James Flesher for Richard Royston, 1660, 397. See also William Howell, *An Institution of General History from the Beginning of the World to the Monarchy of Constantine the Great*, London: Henry Herringman, 1661, 808, who similarly condemns the marriages to both Pythagoras and Sporus.

61 Nicolas Coeffeteau, *Histoire romaine*, Paris: G. Loyson, 1646, 411, 418. Emphasis in the original. Coeffeteau died in 1623, and his *Histoire Romaine* was first published the same year.

62 Richard Holland, *Nero: The Man behind the Myth*, Stroud: Sutton Publishing, 2000, 157, 205. Holland also argues that Nero was boldly attempting to create "a living work of art, symbolizing the ultimate divine power to defeat death itself" (p. 204).

63 Edward Champlin, *Nero*, Cambridge MA: Belknap Press, 2003, 149–50. Champlin later suggests that the relationship with Sporus could have been, "at best, a simultaneously romantic and ironic homage to Poppea, and, at worst, a joke" (p. 165).

64 Williams, *Roman Homosexuality*, 286.

65 David Woods, "Nero and Sporus," *Latomus: revue d'études latine* 68(1) (2009): 73–82. For Woods, the resemblance to Poppaea is not an accident: she and Sporus were related, and Poppaea had convinced Nero that she was of imperial blood. Wood counters Champlin's reading of "Sporus" meaning "semen" with it perhaps meaning instead "Spurius." See pp. 79–80.

66 Shaun Tougher, "The Aesthetics of Castration: Roman Eunuchs," in *Castration and Culture in the Middle Ages*, ed. Larissa Tracy, Cambridge: D. S. Brewer, 2013, 48–72. See pp. 63–6.

9

HERITABLE IDENTITY MARKERS, NATIONS, AND PHYSIOGNOMY[1]

Carina L. Johnson

In 1536, an Indian named Martyn testified before a Castilian court that "I am a free person by my nation and inherent quality, a son of free people."[2] To unravel this statement requires understanding not only the history of indigenous enslavement in sixteenth-century Castile and the Spanish Empire, but also the meaning of "nation" as collective identity. In early modern Europe, the concept of *natio* or nation framed discourses of distinct identity and difference between peoples. To belong to an early modern nation, in contrast to later political nation-states, denoted belonging to a people, variously called a *gens, natio, populus, ethnos,* or stock.[3] Membership in such a group could be based on self-assertion or might be visibly evident to observers. Place of origin, native language, territory, and costume could all mark and establish one's identity as part of a particular nation. Some of these identity markers were heritable and passed from parents to children. The term heritable rather than hereditary underscores that these transmissions, whether complete or imperfect, were not biological or genetic in a post-Enlightenment sense; in twenty-first-century terms, some of these heritable identity markers were cultural or religious.

In the history of racialization and racisms, the co-evolution of racialization and forced labor in the Americas culminated in eighteenth- and nineteenth-century plantation slavery and contemporaneous ideas of biological race.[4] These ideas were preceded by the seventeenth- and eighteenth-century Spanish American *casta* hierarchy of racialized difference.[5] Yet a gap remains between these colonial histories and the fifteenth-century "genealogical turn" undergone by collective Jewish and Christian religious identities in Iberia.[6] Bridging the gap between those two sets of structuring ideas and social frameworks calls for careful attention to practices that shaped collective identities in the sixteenth century.[7]

This chapter examines one possible bridge, a set of judicial practices in Castile from the 1530s to the 1570s. In judicial hearings of the Council of the Indies,[8] Indians and crown prosecutors sought to confirm the status of individual Indians as free rather than enslaved, by establishing their identities as people born in the viceroyalties of New Spain and Peru who could not be enslaved legally. Early modern natio's fluid and multivalent meanings allowed several familiar identity markers to be deployed in that process. In the face of limits to those markers' successful applications, it also allowed for innovation through a new emphasis on physical appearance that expanded the working definition of physiognomy (*filosomia*).

The sixteenth-century flexibility of identity based on natio drew on medieval precedents. In Isidore of Seville's *Etymologiae*, gens referred to a people defined by a shared origin (including familial descent) and natio, a people holding themselves distinct from others as a group. Gens derived from *gignendo* (begetting) and natio from *nascendo* (being born). Language lay at the heart of the identity of gens because, according to the Old Testament, the proliferation of language had preceded the proliferation of peoples.[9] Grounded in the influential *Etymologiae*, medieval protoethnographers often described the subjects of their studies as peoples defined by a common homeland, by shared language, or by genealogical descent.[10] Yet natio's use would not remain exclusively ethnographic in subsequent centuries.

In the thirteenth and fourteenth centuries, the word nation began to be commonly used at universities to describe self-defined groups of scholars. Students or masters formed corporations based on natio that denoted a common tie of birthplace, cultural region, language, or geographic proximity. As universities increasingly depended on the institution of nations for their organization and representative governance, membership in a corporate nation often became required. A scholar would select the nation with the closest connection to his own place of origin or language and make his oath of affiliation to it. A scholar's word and oath, his own self-identification, were sufficient to determine his nation. The number of nations varied from university to university, reflecting the examples of Bologna and Paris as rivals for the title of oldest university. At Bologna, where a scholar's place of birth was the crucial determinant of nation, the nations were numerous, ranging from twenty to over thirty (for example, the French, Poitevin, Tourainian, and Gascon were all separate nations). At Paris, the number of nations shrank to a formalized group of four: French, Norman, Picard, and English. When limited to four, university nations could be quite expansive; Paris' English nation included a swathe of scholars from the northeast: the Germanys, Flanders, Finland, Hungary, as well as the British Isles. University nations in the Holy Roman Empire followed the Paris model of four umbrella or general nations, as did the regionally focused University of Salamanca. Salamanca, where the majority of sixteenth-century Castilian crown officials would be trained, housed four nations corresponding to Iberian ecclesiastical provinces. At Aragonese Lérida, in contrast, law students were divided into twelve nations, six representing geographic regions of Iberia and six populated by students originating beyond the Pyrenees.[11] In the course of their studies, students and scholars of the universities would all have affirmed their natio as a participatory act.

By the beginning of the fifteenth century, the term nation had gained another institutional definition and usage at the general church councils called in the face of a papal schism and pressing threats of heresy from Bohemia. The general councils involved thousands of clerical participants, a large majority of whom had been educated in the universities. In order to allow for decision-making with such a populous body, the participants of general church councils developed a theory and practice of conciliar representative authority grounded in nations, modeled after those of the universities. The Council of Pisa (1409) caucused and voted through four nations, sometimes conceptualized as representing the four quarters of the world. When the Council of Constance (1414–1418) convened, a contemporary observer commented that custom dictated the existence of four nations: the Italian, German, French, and Spanish. Due to the Iberians' initial refusal to participate in the council, an alternate fourth nation was created.[12] The English nation was separated from the German nation and the four nations of the Italians, Germans, French, and English began the work of the council. The criteria for these nations' constituencies remained flexible and broad, centered on geography and ecclesiastical organization, yet stretching beyond those categories and the limits of linguistic cognates. The German nation, for example, encompassed Hungary, Croatia, Poland, Lithuania, the various Russias, and the kingdoms of Scandinavia, while the French nation included territories claimed by the kingdom of France.[13]

The conceptualization of conciliar nations as four in number did not survive the politics of Constance. Two years into the council's sessions, an Iberian delegation appeared and demanded that they, as the Spanish nation, should have priority over the upstart English nation. In the ensuing debate over who properly constituted a nation, the continuing malleability and multivalency of the concept of nation was evident. The French argued that there should only be four general nations and the English nation should be demoted in favor of the Spanish. The English responded by listing the multiple definitions of nation and explaining how the English met each criterion. They agreed, with their opponents, that a nation should not correspond to a kingdom alone, noting that the English nation encompassed multiple kingdoms. A nation or gens, they argued, could be formed by family descent, long-accepted unity of identity, difference of languages, or territorial affiliation. Although the English acknowledged that language was the preferred determinant of a nation, their discussion closed by promoting natio as a geographic area. After much debate, the Council of Constance accepted a new organization of five caucusing nations.[14]

In the decades following the Council of Constance, the term natio was also applied to merchants from specific geographic locations who conducted trade in distant cities. These nations were constituted as corporate groups with chartered legal and administrative rights and responsibilities, such as the Portuguese in Flanders.[15] The emphasis on self-determination in the definition of natio, as well as the fluidity of its meaning, can be traced in medieval lexicographic texts that began to circulate more widely with the advent of print. In the second half of the fifteenth century, editions of Papias' eleventh-century *Vocabularium* and Giovanni Balbi's thirteenth-century *Catholicon* followed Isidore of Seville closely, discussing natio briefly as a self-delimited group and repeating Isidore's examples of Greek and Asian nations. Papias maintained Isidore's sense of a natio determined by birth because of its etymology from nascendo, as well as Isidore's link between the seventy-two languages and subsequent seventy-two peoples that resulted from the collapse of the Tower of Babel. Balbi diverged from Isidore to offer examples of more contemporary nations as distinct peoples: Greeks, Italians, or Franks.[16] At the end of the fifteenth century, new print lexicons appeared alongside these older texts, although Antonio de Nebrija's 1492 brief-entry Latin–Castilian *Vocabulario* did not innovate upon its predecessors.[17] In contrast, former royal chronicler Alfonso de Palencia's 1490 *Universal vocabulario en Latin y en Romance* expanded the older definitions of natio. His exemplary nations were the German, Italian, and French, mirroring the nations of the conciliar debates. Explaining the difference between gens and natio, he noted that gens referred to blood relationship or common descent, while the definition of natio extended beyond affiliations determined by kinship or language. Members of a natio shared a *patria* or native soil. He supported this interpretation by citing Sextus Pompeius Festus, who identified the necessity of local origin in his abridgement of Marcus Verrius Flaccus' *De verborum significatione*.[18]

Natio's expanding use as a term for corporate identities defined by place of origin was accompanied by an expanding European attention to the extra-European world. At the beginning of the sixteenth century, ethnographic texts applied the term to peoples of the continents of Europe, Asia, Africa, as well as the New World. Castilians and other Habsburg subjects encountered, and sometimes conquered, new territories and peoples that were designated nations. In his 1522 letter to Emperor Charles V, Hernán Cortés identified the Mexica as one of the "nations of reason."[19] Niclaus Federmann's *Indianische Historia* (1557) recounted his travels during the 1530s through many Indian nations in what is present-day Venezuela. For Federmann, each *natio* was distinguished from the others by a combination of language, customs, territory, and long-recognized enmities.[20] These ethnographic applications of the term gained additional legal and political significance when the Indians of specific *natios* became "good subjects and vassals" of the Castilian crown.[21]

In the dynamic colonial Iberian world, the question of collective identity was no longer simply descriptive or a means of gaining corporate representation in universities, trade, or church council. Because *natio* determined legal status and rights in the Spanish Empire, it became linked to the economic pressures of slavery. A complicated and fluctuating Castilian crown position on Indian slavery resulted in the enslavement of hundreds of thousands of indigenous people during the first half-century of Iberian conquest. In the first decade of the sixteenth century, Indians could be legally enslaved on several grounds: seizure in just war, purchase or trade after being enslaved by other Indians as slaves of *rescate*, and the perceived moral failings of Indians such as the Caribs.[22] Indians in permanent personal servitude, *naborias*, could not be bought and sold or branded as slaves.[23] As early as November 1526, the Castilian crown sought to curtail wrongful post-conquest enslavements in New Spain, initially with only limited success.[24] In the 1530s and first years of the 1540s, the crown issued multiple edicts in its effort to limit exploitative and abusive treatment of Indians, as well as the exportation of slaves to Spain.[25] In 1542, the crown sought to unambiguously confirm the liberty of Indians with the New Laws of the Indies. Indians were vassals of the crown of Castile, and thus slavery as a result of just war, rebellion, or rescate was forbidden, as was involuntary naboria servitude. All slaves whose owners did not possess a clear title of their legal slavery were to be freed.[26] Spanish colonists resisted the crown's authority, accepting the New Laws unevenly in the subsequent decade; Vasco de Puga's collection of law codes from 1525 to the date of publication in 1563 included a 1550 edict rather than the 1542 laws.[27] The abolition of Indian slavery during the sixteenth century would take decades to resolve, both in New Spain, where there was a significant wave of emancipation from 1549 to 1552,[28] and in Iberia.

In Castile during the 1540s, crown officials Gregorio López and Hernán Pérez engaged in focused efforts to free wrongfully enslaved Indians. The 1542 laws' intent was not directly challenged in the Iberian peninsula and these *visitadores* worked to resolve many straightforward cases of Indians whose enslavement had been declared illegal.[29] By the 1550s, Indians who sought freedom before the judges of the Council of the Indies often lived in complicated circumstances requiring multiple witnesses to testify to the claims of plaintiff and defendant. In these cases, crown prosecutors continued to enforce edicts and worked to confirm the freedom of Indians. Yet how to establish which enslavements were wrongful?

Indian plaintiffs' rights to freedom depended on their and the crown prosecutor's success in demonstrating that the plaintiff had the right to liberty. Most of these rights were based on *natio*, on being a *natural* of a province where Indians possessed freedom under crown law.[30] Perhaps the most significant barrier to liberty was being born in the Portuguese Indies of Brazil. Those Indians with a Brazilian *natio* would have been enslaved under Portuguese law and did not have to be emancipated when brought into Castile. Other legal grey areas of servitude for conditions established prior to 1542 had to be clarified. Some slaves had been captured during wars of indigenous resistance to Spanish encroachments on the circum-Caribbean frontiers of Castilian control.[31] Children born of slave mothers were also at risk of enslavement by their owners, and the status of naborias continued to be regarded as ambiguous by masters and mistresses.[32] The court generally sought to enforce crown law. So, in the 1552–53 case of four sons (a Perico and three Franciscos) of Indian women who had been slaves since the conquest, the decision was emphatic in its pronouncement that such children should not be branded or treated and traded as slaves.[33]

The crown prosecutor worked to argue for the freedom of these Indian plaintiffs whenever possible, mobilizing long-standing self-determined criteria for establishing natio and identity in Europe. In his 1536–37 case, Martyn narrated his own and his family's history, testifying to his birthplace, his natio, as well as his family's status before and after the conquest. As a free Indian he had followed his master Gonzalo de Salazar from his hometown in New Spain to Castile. To Martyn's dismay, once they had arrived in Castile, his master began to claim that Martyn was a slave. Martyn explained that he and his family had never been unfree, rejecting a claim that he was a slave of rescate as evidenced by a royal brand.[34] Martyn's assertions were accepted and he was found to be free. In 1544–48, the sailor Francisco de Pañuco claimed New Spain as his natio in language similar to Martyn's.[35] And in the 1554–55 case of Gonzalo, he could state unequivocally that he was born in Tlaxcala, a city that had been a key ally of the Spaniards and certainly not engaged in rebellion or war against the crown.[36]

As crown decrees defined growing numbers of Indian subjects to be legally free, natio as self-declared affiliation could not always suffice. In the 1550s and early 1560s, non-Indian slaves sought their freedom by claiming that they too were Indians from New Spain or Peru and thus had been wrongfully enslaved. Court proceedings identified some plaintiffs to be mulattos, berbers, or of the "nation of Moors," all peoples who could legally be enslaved in sixteenth-century Iberia and did not fall under the jurisdiction of the Council of the Indies.[37] Because successful claims of false natio would be highly advantageous for plaintiffs, the court needed to proceed carefully in determining true natios.

In these conditions, identity markers that could be verified by observers became increasingly important to establish membership in a natio. Slaves could be visibly marked with brandings, but the brand as proof of slave status was suspect by mid-century. Branding by private parties had technically become illegal after 1532 even as compliance with the royal edict left much to be desired. The crown called repeatedly for an end to illegal branding of free Indians, attempting to limit and control branding. The repetition of this effort recognized branding's unreliability as an identity marker. While brands were regularly brought into evidence, as they were in Martyn's case, they were not perceived as reliable markers for establishing slave or free identity.[38] Other forms of verifiable evidence were sought to determine membership in a natio.

Judicial cases before the Council of the Indies between the 1550s and 1570s reveal patterns in petitions of liberty. An Indian would be born into a natio as a natural of New Spain or Peru and then serve a Spaniard as a recognized dependent. After some length of time had passed, the master or mistress would begin to assert that the dependant had never been free, that their legal status was that of a slave rather than, in some cases, a naboria. Thus they could be sold to another owner. The Indian would then seek a judgment from the Council of the Indies in order to confirm their freedom. The example of Pedro of Mexico is illustrative: Pedro had served Nuño de Guzman for twenty-five years since the initial days of the conquest. In 1549, he and his fellow Indian and wife Luisa decided that they wished to return to their land (*tierra*), but Nuño de Guzman claimed that they did not possess the liberty to do so. The former governor then tried to define Pedro and Luisa as Indians from the province of Panuco who had been taken captive in war, enslaved by other Indians. Nuño de Guzman's defense was resoundingly rejected and he was required to pay the couple twenty ducados of gold for their decade of labor.[39]

These cases were relatively unconstrained by the social rank of the defendant master or mistress. Some defendants were relatively well placed, holding positions such as court attendant of the regent Princess Juana of Portugal, court bureaucrat, or grandee's son. Others were cathedral canons or widows and other heirs of conquistadors.[40] Defendants employed a variety of tactics to argue for the right to restrict their Indian servants' liberty. Losing these cases could be expensive, sometimes resulting in fines intended to reimburse workers for the years of labor during which they had toiled without remuneration.[41] In cases where the defendants realized they were losing, their arguments might shift in the middle of the case. Many claims and counter-claims for the validity of specific identity markers were presented and defendants routinely proffered evidence supporting the claim that a plaintiff was a natural of Brazil or Portuguese India.[42] As the crown worked to eliminate the vestiges of Indian slavery in its dominions, the court sought to establish whether or not these claims were disingenuous. During the 1550s, court prosecutors employed a set of persuasive proofs for natio. Lists of witness questions in individual cases reveal the crown's understanding of verifiable and applicable evidence for belonging, as a true member, to a free natio. The resulting testimonies more fully reveal the shifting standards of evidence by all participants in the proceedings.

Two prominent heritable identity markers in the histories of racialization, blood and color, played little part in these inquiries of liberty before the Council of the Indies. Beginning in the mid-fifteenth century, pure and impure blood had become first a rhetorical mechanism and then a practice to define and exclude converted Jews from civic membership,[43] yet untransformed blood itself did not factor into these proceedings as evidence of heritable identity. Similarly, the role of skin color as an identifying marker was minimal. In the sixteenth century, skin color was often understood as an accident of climate or other external forces. The capacity of an individual's body color to reveal the balance of their humors was more significant.[44] Although slaves could be sold with accompanying information about skin color, it was not a dominant or useful descriptor in these cases of unjust servitude. As Francisco López de Gómara noted in the *Primera y Segunda parte dela historia general de las Indias* (1553), skin color whether black, white, or red was a marvel of God. More pragmatically, skin color was difficult to use as an identity marker because the gradations of color among humans, including those among Indians, were manifold.[45]

Costume, a popular means to determine or at least conceptualize natio elsewhere in Europe during the sixteenth century,[46] could not serve as credible proof in these cases, either. Slaves and servants were separated from their natios for lengthy stretches of their lives, and by the time they appeared before the court they were clothed by their masters and mistresses. Social appearance did factor into the trials as evidence of the common understanding of a plaintiff's legal status and well-being. Defendants presented evidence that plaintiffs were well maintained in an effort, presumably, to avoid financial penalties. Witnesses might offer evaluations of the social appearance of the plaintiffs, noting that the Indians were fed, clothed, and cared for as if they were free. So in the case of Ynes from the island of Cubagua in the Viceroyalty of Peru, petitioning for the freedom of herself and her children in 1556, evidence was proffered that her master Juan de Salamanca provided for her as if she were his daughter.[47] The failure of visible social status, as marked by dress, to determine free status was evident in the 1551–52 case of Catalina. Several of the witnesses noted that Catalina had been given gifts and delicacies, treated by doctors (along with paying for medicine) when she was ill, and clothed as if she were a sister. This testimony about her treatment as a cared-for member of the household was only the preliminary to further investigations into the evidence of Catalina's natio. Several other cultural and physical identity markers were more important in determining identity and thus liberty.

Catalina claimed that she was a free Indian woman of New Spain, from the pueblo of Nonoalco in Cuzcatan. Her master Juan Pantiel de Salinas claimed instead that he had been told that she was a captive of war from the province of Nicaragua, noting that she had been part of his household in Castile for approximately eight years. Both plaintiff and defendant agreed that she had been taken into servitude as a young girl and many witnesses estimated that Catalina was now approximately forty years old.[48] In order to resolve the conflicting claims of natio, additional proofs of identity were applied.

The first additional proof was evidence of native language or mother tongue. Many of the Indian plaintiffs appearing before the court declared that they had been taken as little children from their homelands.[49] Because the test of language was based on theories of language transmission to infants, the young age of the children when taken from their natios was not considered a meaningful barrier to the application of this test and the expectation that the plaintiff would possess this identity marker. Youth should have in itself provided another legal justification for freedom; after 1534, the crown decreed that that no women or children under the age of fourteen could be enslaved as a captive of just war. Women and children could serve in households as naborias, but not as slaves.[50] Yet in these hearings, prosecutors built a case for liberty on the grounds of natio.

By basing identity on language, the crown prosecutors drew on a long-standing and broadly employed marker of natio, one previously utilized in universities, general councils, and lexicons. The idea that language proliferated through the construction of the Tower of Babel had been the starting point for Dante Alighieri's influential reflections on vernacular language in *De vulgari eloquentia*. For Dante, a mother tongue was a language transferred between mother or wet nurse and child. Its nurturing source made it natural, given from birth. The only exception to this was Adam, who was a "man without mother or milk."[51] For thirteenth-century Iberian authors and their sixteenth-century followers, breast milk and nursing transmitted cultural or religious knowledge and virtues or moral failings. In the *Doctrina pueril* (ca. 1275), Ramon Llull emphasized that milk was important not only for the health of the body, but also for inculcating morals. Virtue passed from breast to baby through this medium. This stance was echoed in Juan de Pineda's 1589 statement that milk was responsible for the goodness of the soul.[52] The heritable capacity of milk to transmit qualities from nurse to child was contained in a proverb collected by Sebastián Horozco during the sixteenth century – what is formed in the milk stays until death.[53] Ideas of transmission between nurse and infant encouraged prohibitions against employing wet-nurses of other faiths in Alfonso X's thirteenth-century Castilian legal code, the *Siete Partidas*. These connections were strengthened over time; by the late sixteenth century José de Acosta argued that idolatry was heritable through mother's milk.[54] Whether the transmission of culture, religion, or virtue was literally physical or only metaphorically so, it occurred in the context of nursing.

Milk's capacity to transmit idolatry paralleled the genealogical transmission of religion via blood, reflecting contemporaneous ideas about the relationship between blood and milk. Medical theories of lactation had understood milk to be whitened blood. A pregnant woman nurtured her fetus with the blood that would otherwise be removed from her body through menstruation. When nursing began after a child was born, the woman's body transformed this blood into milk, and she continued to provide nutrition for the infant.[55] Humanist Juan de Valdés brought together Dantean and Alfonsine ideas regarding milk transmission in his *Diálogo de la Lengua* (ca. 1535). He described native language as that which people acquire through suckling at their mother's breasts.[56] The link between maternal language and natio was also affirmed by el Inca Garcilaso de la Vega in *La Florida del Inca* (ca.1571–1591). He argued that his status as a native of Peru, with particular authority in matters of Andean history, was demonstrated persuasively by his "natural and maternal language."[57]

In the judicial cases before the Council of the Indies, knowledge of a relevant natio's mother tongue was considered evidence of belonging to that group. Plaintiffs asserting a natio of New Spain were tested first in the *lengua mexicana*, or Nahuatl.[58] In these tests, the plaintiff was expected to understand and ideally answer questions spoken in the dominant language of New Spain, which they had learned in their childhood. In Francisca's case (1551–1553), the regidor of villa de Pontevedra offered detailed circumstantial evidence of her Brazilian origin. She had been purchased from a Portuguese ship stocked with merchandise from the land of Brazil and converted to Christianity by her master Lorenzo Salcedo. The crown prosecutor pursued linguistic evidence of her natio and, responding to her performance on two language tests, witnesses noted that Francisca did not speak Nahuatl, or, in one case, the *lengua guatimaltesca*. Another noted that when asked her place of origin in Nahuatl, she answered in Castilian that she was from Brazil. Francisca both had the reputation of being a natural of Brazil and was known to speak the Brazilian language. Geography was also brought to bear on the issue: one witness argued for her liberty based on his knowledge and understanding of her language and where it was spoken.[59]

For other liberty cases of Indians taken into servitude as young children, mother tongue often proved insufficient as the only proof of natio. Some plaintiffs claiming a natio of New Spain did not speak Nahuatl; unsurprising since New Spain encompassed parts of the circum-Caribbean where Nahuatl was not the dominant language. Wrongful enslavement hearings took place decades after plaintiffs had been removed from their homelands, and thus some stated that they had forgotten their mother tongues in captivity.[60] In the face of the inadequacy of self-testified place of origin, memory, and language, several cases from the early 1550s illustrate the crown prosecutors' turn to an alternate form of evidence, physical appearance.

Returning to Catalina's 1551–52 case, the test of language was applied in an effort to establish her natio. She was questioned in Nahuatl and answered in Castilian. While multiple witnesses accepted this reply demonstrating her comprehension of Nahuatl, her lack of substantive knowledge about this language produced some uncertainty. At least one witness probed the question of whether or not she spoke the language of Guatemala as an alternate mother tongue. These responses were ambiguous and the trial turned to another evidentiary test for additional support: Catalina's physical appearance. Along with her arguable comprehension of Nahuatl, the appearance "of her face and physiognomy" served as proof of her natio and her freedom was affirmed.[61]

In 1552–53, Francisco Manuel also succeeded in establishing his claim to be a natural of New Spain, born in Colima. Thirty-three witnesses testifying for and against his liberty emphasized the evidence of his mother tongue. Francisco Manuel was questioned in Nahuatl and, like Catalina, responded in Spanish. His explanation for his inability to speak his mother tongue was the very young age at which he had been taken from the city of his birth, Colima. Other witnesses noted that he spoke some words of Nahuatl. The fifteen witnesses who testified in favor of a natio of New Spain drew on Francisco's language comprehension but also his appearance and physiognomy. Over half the witnesses cited the physiognomy of his face ("filosomia de rostro") in their identifications and several added a mix of additional physical features: *forma*, body, head. Many of the eighteen witnesses for the defendant Sebastian de Aguilar countered that Francisco Manuel's lack of command over Nahuatl revealed that his claim was false, pressing the point repeatedly as support for their belief that he was a natural of Portuguese India. Only a few of the eighteen read his physical appearance as evidence of a Portuguese India natio: two noted his physiognomy without additional details, two based identification on his face, and another argued that not only his manner but his color was that of the Portuguese Indies.[62]

The turn to physiognomy freed prosecutors from having to establish the veracity of other claims such as self-asserted place of origin or the test of the mother tongue. Instead, the knowledgeable witness could simply look at a plaintiff and know his or her natio from physical signs. At the beginning of the sixteenth century, physiognomy focused on the semiotics of the individual body. Closely connected to medicine, physiognomy drew on the evidence or symptoms of an individual's color, movement, shape, texture, and temperature to diagnose their condition. The art or science of physiognomy had developed from the pseudo-Aristotelian text *Physiognomonics*, which understood the body and soul to be linked.[63] The *Physiognomonics* listed three methods of practicing physiognomy, which Pseudo-Aristotle described as reading the soul or character in the body. The first method compared individual humans with animal genera. The second method distinguished between different groups of humans, such as Egyptians, Thracians, or Scythians, through differences of appearance and character. The third method, which he described as defective, was to read individual facial expressions.[64] Three thirteenth-century scholars working with the pseudo-Aristotelian text and associated Arabic commentators had promoted the usability of the physiognomic study of individuals.[65] In the following centuries, physiognomy as a method of reading appearance was consistently applied to individual dispositions rather than the characteristics of nations. Physiognomic texts focused on the form and shape of an individual's features and complexion. The physiognomy of individual complexion even provided advice on how to select a good wet-nurse. A woman's individual complexion determined the quality of her milk, "milk of a black or brown woman is always better than that of a white or red woman."[66] This better milk reflected the medieval medical understandings of differently complected women's heat, menses, and consequently differing milk production.[67] At the beginning of the sixteenth century, physiognomic manuals were printed with texts explaining the physical systems of the body or offering different methods of divination that revealed knowledge about an individual based on the astrological and other signs of their body.[68]

In the most popular physiognomy texts of the early sixteenth century, people's astrological signs and individual natures determined their appearance, not their natio. The priest Johannes Indagine's *Introductiones Apotelesmaticae elegantes* was published with Charles V's privilege in 1522. Circulating widely throughout the sixteenth century and translated into multiple vernacular languages, the text offered no readings of physiognomy beyond that of the individual. Instead, Indagine argued that individual body color was linked to the four humors: an individual with a red complexion was sanguine, white phlegmatic, swarthy (*fusca*) choleric, and black melancholy. The text provided extensive illustrations of the physiognomy of the forehead, face, lips, eyes, brow, and head to explain the positive and negative qualities indicated by these signs.[69] Bartolommeo della Rocca Cocles, whose physiognomic text

Chyromantie ac Physionomie Anastasis was first published in Bologna in 1504, similarly explained the individual meanings revealed by body parts, forehead, face, brow, and head. Cocles' text was published in many Latin and vernacular editions during the sixteenth century, with meaningful changes introduced by different printers. Some early versions explained that a knowledge of physiognomy allowed sellers and buyers in the Ottoman slave trade to select the best slaves. A 1519 Strasbourg edition of Cocles' text added material that proposed a climatic explanation for skin color and in one case hair. People in warm lands had skin that was brown or red mixed with a little white and frizzy coarse hair, while people in cold lands were very white.[70] Although Pseudo-Aristotle's second method had proposed the possibility of studying the physiognomy of a natio, with the exception of these climactic commonalities in some editions of Cocles, it had no place in manuals of physiognomy.

In contrast, physiognomy of a natio was not only applied to cases of liberty before the Council of the Indies, it became a regular component of hearings. In standard formulas, witnesses were asked to assess the plaintiff's "appearance and physiognomy" or their "physiognomy of face, body, head, and speech"[71] to determine an individual's membership in a particular natio. Witness testimonies regularly utilized the concept of a physiognomy shared by a natio to identify Indians. "Physiognomy of the face" was a commonly mentioned point of evidence.

In some cases, a reliance on filosomia (physiognomy of a natio) allowed the court to ignore the ambiguities of the language test and rule in favor of the Indian plaintiff's freedom. In 1558, Martin Quintin successfully claimed his liberty as a natural of New Spain, taken as a boy from his homeland. His master Francisco Bravo asserted that he had a bill of sale for Martin Quintin, proving that he was, instead, from Brazil, where Indians could be enslaved as captives of just war. Responding to the crown's question about whether Martin Quintin appeared to be a natural of New Spain, according to the "physiognomy of the face, head and speech," seven witnesses testified in favor of Martin Quintin's freedom. The majority focused on various aspects of the plaintiff's physical appearance or filosomia to justify their opinions. Two witnesses, including Bartolome de las Casas and one who thought Martin Quintin was from the province of Guatemala, added that Martin's color demonstrated his origin. Another noted his understanding of Mexican words. Bravo's witnesses, in contrast, emphasized the legality of enslaving Brazilian Indians and affirmed that Martin Quintin spoke the language of Brazil as his mother tongue, and not Nahuatl.[72]

The theory of a physiognomic link between spirit and bodily signs of difference was most evident in the case of Juan, a mestizo who came before the court in 1557–58 and proved his case through filosomia or physical appearance. He was the son of the deceased Juan Carretero and the Indian woman Margarita from the city of Mexico. Margarita had served Carretero's patron Gaspar de Rotulo for many years. After Gaspar's death, his heirs tried to sell Juan as a slave. Juan, already married to a Castilian woman, sought legal confirmation of his free status, to resolve his potentially ambiguous position between voluntary personal service and slavery. All the witnesses testifying to his mestizo status based their assertions on mestizo filosomia, although the physical characteristics that they highlighted were not always the same. Their knowledge of mestizos, whether in the Indies or Spain, was carefully detailed in the court proceedings. Baltasar Garcia from the Santo Domingo testified that, based on his experience of seeing mestizos in the Indies, Juan's filosomia and the appearance of his head and hair were that of a mestizo. Juan Barba de Vallezales of Honduras concurred that mestizo sons of Indians had very recognizable filosomia of hair and forehead, while Pedro de Vergara from Asuncion in Rio de la Plata relied on the numerous mestizos and mestizas he had seen in the Indies and in Spain to single out the quality of Juan's speech as well as his head and hair. Andres de Montalno, also from Asuncion, noted Juan's mestizo "color" in his evaluation of Juan's appearance, filosomia, head, and hair. Francisco Lopez Tenorio, regidor of Antequera in New Spain offered the most detail. Like Pedro de Vergara, he based his testimony on the many mestizos he knew in the Indies and in Spain. Lopez Tenorio was the only witness other than Montalno to mention color; he listed head, hair, color, speech, and filosomia. He continued with an assessment of mestizo character, asserting that they were not as simple as Indians, and their greater courage of spirit was inherited from their Spanish fathers.[73]

Filosomia played an important role in some petitions of liberty. In 1556, Francisco was judged to be from Mexico, based on his bearing, filosomia, and speech. Testifying witnesses cited their familiarity with the "filosomia, appearance, speech, and bodies" of other Indians of New Spain. One explained that if he compared Francisco to other Indians of New Spain known to him, Francisco looked sufficiently similar for the witness to conclude that he must have been born in New Spain.[74] Evidence of appearance and physiognomy was invoked during Ginesa's case in 1566–1568.[75] And even with the proof of physical appearance, the 1567 petition of another Catalina, supervised by the pastry-maker Gil Perez, was not initially successful. Catalina and the crown prosecutor persisted, gaining her freedom in 1574 with new evidence regarding Catalina's filosomia of face, head, and speech, which established she was a natural of New Spain.[76]

By the 1570s, the court's reliance on physical markers might also involve bringing expert witnesses to testify about the physiognomic evidence. The 1572–73 case of Nicolas included the standard witness question about his filosomia of face, gesture, body, head and speech. Nicolas asserted that he was a natural of New Spain, taken as a young child to the kingdom of Portugal and enslaved in bad faith and without title. His master countered that he was a black rescate slave, rescued from a brutal and savage life. Doctor Sancho Sanchez de Muñon, a *maestre escuela* of Mexico, offered an analysis of Nicolas' head shape. Although some aspects of the form of the head were those found among Brazilian Indians, the back of the head more strongly conformed to the head-shaping that the people of New Spain practiced on their children.[77]

When Antonia Mia of Lima sought liberty for herself and her four children, the prosecutor based his case not on royal edicts forbidding the enslavement of women and children under the age of fifteen or on the prohibition on involuntary naborias, but on filosomia. Antonia Mia was approximately twenty-five in 1574 and, despite being under age at the time, had been sold as a slave a dozen years previously. The fiscal focused his effort on calling witnesses to testify that her "physiognomy of face, expression, body, head, and speech" all revealed her natio of Lima, Peru. By this date, even other Indians embraced the rhetoric and proof of physiognomy as a physical marker for natio determination. Antonia Mia's highest-ranking witness was a noble Andean Indian, Don Sebastian Pomalaquila of Cuzco. He affirmed that key aspects of Antonia Mia's physiognomy were familiar to him as a member of that natio.[78] Physical appearance had become a determinant of natio, above place of origin, family, memory, or language. By employing the physical marker of physiognomy to determine membership in natios, the court of the Council of the Indies laid the ground for increasingly physically defined or 'racialized' shared identities for Indians.[79]

This set of legal cases suggests that the developing legal discourse about determining cultural *natio* might be considered a counter-history of the state. Regardless or perhaps in spite of the crown prosecutors' efforts to improve the condition and status of peoples from the

New World in Castile, the same sixteenth-century imperial policies that confirmed the freedom of unjustly enslaved Indians also promoted ideas of physical distinctness and confirmed the use of group physiognomy as legal evidence. To free its subjects from the cruelties of an unjust enslavement, the crown reshaped the definition of nation by adding the physiognomy of physical shape to the list of identity markers of language, geographic proximity, custom, shared blood, and self-declaration of affiliation or origin. Physiognomy would continue to serve as a method to read an individual's character in Europe,[80] but also as a bridge in the history of racialization – a heritable rubric of shared identity based on natio.

Notes

1 The research for this chapter was supported by a grant from the Program for Cultural Cooperation between Spain's Ministry of Culture and US Universities. Earlier versions of this chapter were presented at the Rereading the Black Legend conference at Duke University in April 2003, the University of Oregon's Early Modern Studies Group in March 2004, the History Department of Queen's University in November 2006, and the April 2013 Renaissance Studies Association Conference. I would like to thank those participants for their comments and suggestions. A note on terminology: I use the word 'Indian' throughout to refer to the indigenous peoples of the Americas, following sixteenth-century usage by both Castilians/Spaniards and the Hispanized indigenous.

2 "soi onbre libre de mi nasçion e yngenio hijo de onbres libres," Seville, Archivo General de Indias (AGI), Justicia 1007. The thirty-four judicial cases of this study date from the 1530s to the 1570s, with the majority from the 1550s. They are drawn from Indian petitions of liberty in the AGI, Justicia. Esteban Mira Caballos' rich social history draws on an overlapping subset of these cases, *Indios y mestizos americanos en la España del siglo XVI*, Madrid: Iberoamericana, 2000.

3 Scholarship on the relationships between ethnicity and nationalism is generally impressionistic for the early modern period. Often-cited examples of theorizing the late modern nation are B. Anderson, *Imagined Communities*, London: Verso, 1983; A. Hastings, *The Construction of Nationhood*, Cambridge: Cambridge University Press, 1997; E. Gellner, *Nations and Nationalism*, Ithaca, NY: Cornell University Press, 1983; and multiple works by David T. Goldberg and Anthony D. Smith.

4 P. Wolfe, "Land, Labor, and Difference," *American Historical Review*, 106, 2001, pp. 866–905, offers a thoughtful introduction to the scholarship of plantation slavery.

5 For the Viceroyalty of Peru, I. Silverblatt, *Modern Inquisitions: Peru and the Colonial Origins of the Civilized World*, Durham, NC: Duke University Press, 2004 and R. S. O'Toole, *Bound Lives: Africans, Indians, and the Making of Race in Colonial Peru*, Pittsburgh: University of Pittsburgh Press, 2012; for the Viceroyalty of Mexico, M. E. Martínez, *Genealogical Fictions: Limpieza de Sangre, Religion, and Gender in Colonial Mexico*, Stanford: Stanford University Press, 2008.

6 F. Bethencourt, *Racisms*, Princeton, NJ: Princeton University Press, 2013 and D. Nirenberg, *Neighboring Faiths: Christianity, Islam, and Judaism in the Middle Ages and Today*, Chicago: University of Chicago Press, 2014.

7 "Practice theory" is also emphasized in A. B. Fisher and M. D. O'Hara (eds.), *Imperial Subjects: Race and Identity in Colonial Latin America*, Durham, NC: Duke University Press, 2009, while discursive practice is explored in M.R. Greer, W.D. Mignolo, and M. Quilligan (eds.), *Rereading the Black Legend: The Discourses of Religious and Racial Difference in the Renaissance Empires*, Chicago: University of Chicago Press, 2007.

8 In sixteenth-century Iberia, slaves originated from sub-Saharan Africa, North Africa, Iberia (primarily morisco slaves), the Canary Islands, and the Indies. William D. Phillips, Jr. surveys Iberian slavery in *Slavery in Medieval and Early Modern Iberia*, Philadelphia: University of Pennsylvania Press, 2014.

9 Isidore of Seville, *Etymologiae* 9.1–4.

10 R. Bartlett, "Medieval and Modern Concepts of Race and Ethnicity," *Journal of Medieval and Early Modern Studies*, 31, 2001, pp. 39–56 and H.-D. Kahl, "Einige Beobachtungen zum Sprachgebrauch von *natio* im mittelalterlichen Latein mit Ausblicken auf das neuhochdeutsche Fremdwort 'Nation'" in H. Beumann and W. Schröder (eds.), *Aspekte der Nationenbildung im Mittelalter*, Sigmaringen: Thorbecke, 1978, pp. 63–108.

11 P. Kibre, *The Nations in the Medieval Universities*, Cambridge, MA: Medieval Academy of America, 1948; see also G. C. Boyce, *The English-German Nation in the University of Paris*, Bruges: St. Catherine Press, 1927; H. de Ridder-Symoens (ed.), *A History of the University in Europe*, vol. 1, Cambridge: Cambridge University Press, 1992; and R. L. Kagan, *Students and Society in Early Modern Spain*, Baltimore: Johns Hopkins University Press, 1974.

12 Ulrich Richental, *Chronik des Konstanzer Konzils, 1414–1418*, fac., Constance: Friedrich Bahn, 1965, fols. 1r, 29v–31r.

13 L. R. Loomis, "Nationality at the Council of Constance," *American Historical Review*, 44, 1939, pp. 508–27. For a recent synthetic discussion of the council, W. Brandmüller, *Das Konzil von Konstanz 1414–1418*, vols. 1–2, Paderborn: Schöningh, 1999.

14 "sive sumatur natio ut gens secundum cognationem et collectionem ab alia distincta, sive secundum diversitatem linguarum, que maximam et verissimam probant nationem et ipsius essentiam, jure divino pariter et humano, ut infra dicetur; sive etiam sumatur natio pro provincia aequali etiam nationi Gallicanae, sicut sumi deberet." Loomis, "Nationality at the Council of Constance," p. 525. Loomis also provides an English translation of the debate compiled from an edition of Guillaume Fillastre's *Gesta* and several seventeenth-century sources in *The Council of Constance*, New York: Columbia University Press, 1961, pp. 315–47.

15 In Flanders, corporate Portuguese legal status as "marchans du Royaulme et nation de Portugal" was confirmed in a 1438 charter, A. Braamcamp Freire, "Maria Brandoa," *Archivo Historico Portuguez*, 6, 1908, p. 423 and I. Elbl, "Nation, Bolsa, and Factory: Three Institutions of Late-Medieval Portuguese Trade with Flanders," *International History Review*, 14, 1992, pp. 1–2; for the Portuguese merchant nation more widely, D. Studnicki-Gizbert, *A Nation upon the Ocean Sea*, Oxford: Oxford University Press, 2007; and for a discussion of other fifteenth-century merchant nations, Sheilagh Ogilvie, *Institutions and European Trade: Merchant Guilds, 1000–1800*, Cambridge: Cambridge University Press, 2011.

16 Papias, *Vocabularium*, Venice: Pincius, 1496, fols. I iii recto, O iiii verso; Johannes Balbus, *Catholicon*, Mainz, 1460. Steven A. Epstein, *Speaking of Slavery: Color, Ethnicity, and Human Bondage in Italy*, Ithaca, NY: Cornell University Press, 2001, discusses Papias' and Balbi's definitions of *gens*, "black," "white," and "slave," pp. 19–24.

17 E. A. de Nebrija, *Diccionario Latino-Español (Salamanca 1492)*, fac., Barcelona: Puvill, 1979.

18 A. de Palencia, *Universal vocabulario en Latin y en Romance*, Seville, 1490, fols. clxxviii verso, cclxxxxvi recto.

19 "naciones de rayzon," in *Carta de la relacion enbiada a su S. majestad del emperador nuestro señor por el capitan general de la nueva spaña: llamado fernando cortez*, Seville: Cromberger, 1522, fol. b8r.

20 *Indianische Historia* was written in Castilian at Charles V's command and later translated into German, Hagenau: Sigmund Bund, 1557, fol. Aii verso.

21 The crown declares Indians of Caribbean islands to be "nuestros buenos súbditos y vasallos" in 1501, R. Konetzke, *Colección de Documentos para la Historia de la Formación Social de Hispanoamérica 1493–1810*, vol. 1, Madrid: CSIC, 1953, p. 5; Cortés reports on the willing submission of peoples to Castilian authority in *Carta de la relacion*.

22 Konetzke, *Colección de Documentos*, pp. 14–18, 31–3; Mira Caballos, *Indios y mestizos*, pp. 19–29.

23 W. L. Sherman, *Forced Native Labor in Sixteenth-Century Central America*, Lincoln: University of Nebraska Press, 1979, pp. 33–8.

24 Konetzke, *Colección de Documentos*, pp. 87–8; Vasco de Puga, *Provisiones, cedulas, instrucciones para el gobierno de la Nueva España*, Mexico: Pedro Ocharte, 1563, fac., Madrid: Ediciones Cultura Hispanica, 1945, fols. 16v–17r.

25 Konetzke, *Colección de Documentos*, pp. 134–6, 153–9, 197–9; Mira Caballos, *Indios y mestizos*, pp. 55–6; and for an example of these 1530s decrees relevance in practice, AGI Justicia 1028.4.3.

26 *Leyes y ordenanças nuevamente hechas por su Magestad / para la governacion de las Indias y buen tratamiento y conservacion de los Indios*, Barcelona, 1543, fols. vi recto–vii recto; Konetzke, *Colección de Documentos*, pp. 216–20.

27 16 April 1550, Valladolid, in Vasco de Puga, *Provisiones*, fols. 178v–179r.

28 L. B. Simpson, *The Encomienda in New Spain*, Berkeley: University of California Press, 1950, p. 176.

29 J. Gil-Bermejo García, "Indígenas americanos en Andalucía," in *Andalucía y América en el siglo XVI*, Seville: Escuela de Estudios Hispano-Americanos, 1983, pp. 548–50; Mira Caballos, *Indios y mestizos*, pp. 158–60.

30 For a discussion of *personas naturales* and law regarding all subjects of Charles V, *Las cortes de Valladolid de año de M.d.xxiii. años*, Burgos, 1535, fol. aiii verso.

31 AGI Justicia 1022.3.2.

32 For a later example of the ongoing difficulty with naborias, see Konetzke, *Colección de Documentos*, pp. 197–9.

33 AGI Justicia 1022.1.4.

34 AGI Justicia 1007.

35 "natural de la nueva españa es onbre libre e yngenio de su nascimiento," AGI Justicia 1019.5.1.

36 AGI Justicia 1022.2.3.

37 AGI Justicia 1025.1.2 (Gaspar 1561), 1025.3.2 (Ysabel 1563), 202.3 (Sebastian and Francisco 1553).

38 Vasco de Puga's 1563 volume *Provisiones* published a decree dating from 24 August 1529, fols. 71r–71v; compare with Konetzke, *Colección de Documentos*, pp. 109–11, 130–1, and 138–9; in practice, see AGI Justicia 1007, 1022.1.4, 1022.3.2., 202.3.

39 AGI Justicia 1021.1.2.

40 AGI Justicia 1077, 1028.4.1, 1019.5.1, 1013. Comparative data on slaves and slaveowners is found in Alfonso Franco Silva, *La esclavitud en Sevilla y su tierra a fines de la Edad Media*, Seville: Diputación Provincial de Sevilla, 1979, pp. 275–331; Aurelia Martín Casares, *La esclavitud en la Granada del siglo XVI: género, raza y religión*, Granada: Universidad de Granada, 2000, pp. 293–327.

41 For example, AGI Justicia 1021.1.2, 1028.4.1, 1028.4.3, and Mira Caballo, *Indios y mestizos*, pp. 77–8.

42 For example, AGI Justicia 1022.1.1, 1022.1.2, 1022.1.5, 1022.5.1, 1023.2.2, 1024.5, 1025.3.2, 1026.2.2, 1028.4.1, 1028.4.3.

43 Albert Sicroff, *Los estatutos de Limpieza de Sangre*, Madrid: Taurus, 1985; Linda Martz, "Converso Families in Fifteenth- and Sixteenth-Century Toledo: The Significance of Lineage," *Sefarad*, 48, 1988, pp. 117–96 and "Pure Blood Statues in Sixteenth Century Toledo: Implementation as Opposed to Adoption," *Sefarad*, 54, 1994, pp. 83–107.

44 V. Groebner, *Who Are You? Identification, Deception, and Surveillance in Early Modern Europe*, trans. M. Kyburz and J. Peck, New York: Zone Books, 2007, pp. 129–40.

45 Francisco López de Gómara, *Primera y Segunda parte dela historia general de las Indias*, Zaragoza: Agustin Millan, 1553, fols. xii recto and cxvii recto-verso.

46 Christoph Weiditz's *Trachtenbuch*, based on his travels through Iberia ca. 1529, is one of the earliest manuscript versions of a successful print phenomenon in the 1570s. Ulinka Rublack surveys this trend in *Dressing Up*, Oxford: Oxford University Press, 2010.

47 AGI Justicia 1075.2.4.

48 AGI Justicia 1021.3.1.

49 For example, AGI Justicia 1013 (Christobal), 1021.2.1 (Catalina), 1022.2.2 (Gonzalo), 1022.3.2 (Sancho), 1022.4.1 (Francisco), 1023.1.1 (Esteban), 1024.5 (Francisco), 1025.5.2 (Maria), 1026.2.2 (Ginesa), 1028.4.3 (Catalina).

50 Toledo, 20 February, 1534, in Konetzke, *Colección de Documentos*, pp. 153–9.

51 Writing ca. 1303–5, Dante continued with the belief that all languages descended from an originating one and that vernacular languages were most worthy of esteem, *De vulgari eloquentia*, S. Botterill (ed.), Cambridge: Cambridge University Press, 1996, section I.1 and "vir sine matre, vir sine lacte" in I.6.

52 R. L. Winer, "Conscripting the Breast: Lactation, Slavery and Salvation in the Realms of Aragon and Kingdom of Majorca, c. 1250–1300," *Journal of Medieval History*, 34, 2008, pp. 165–6; "sino y aun para las buenas costumbres del alma," Diálogo XV chapter XXI, Juan de Pineda, *Los Treynta y Cinco diálogos familiares de la agricultura christiana*, Salamanca: Pedro de Adurça and Diego Lopez, 1589, p. 103.

53 Martínez, *Genealogical Fictions*, pp. 55–6; S. Horozco, *Teatro Universal de Proverbios*, Salamanca: University of Salamanca, 2005, p. 342.

54 Jose de Acosta, *De procuranda indorum salute* (1592) V:9.

55 Christiane Klapisch-Zuber, "Blood Parents and Milk Parents: Wet Nursing in Florence, 1300–1530," in *Women, Family, and Ritual in Renaissance Italy*, Chicago: University of Chicago Press, 1985, p. 161; for Iberia, E. Bergmann, "Language and 'Mothers' Milk': Maternal Roles and the Nurturing Body in Early Modern Spanish Texts," in N. J. Miller and N. Yavneh (eds.), *Maternal*

Measures, Aldershot: Ashgate, 2000, pp. 105–20; in M. Horstmanshoff, H. King, and C. Zittel (eds.), *Blood, Sweat, and Tears: The Changing Concepts of Physiology from Antiquity into Early Modern Europe*, Leiden: Brill, 2012, K. van 't Land discusses blood and milk's relationship to male and female sperm, "Sperm and Blood, Form and Food," pp. 382–5 and B. Orland describes the post-1650 move away from the theory of milk as blood in "White Blood and Red Milk," pp. 443–78.

56 "la lengua que nos es natural y que mamamos en las tetas de nuestras madres," Juan de Valdes, *Dialogo de la Lengua*, Madrid: Clásicos Castalia, 1969, p. 44.

57 Here, "lengua natural y maternal" and "soy natural de aquella tierra." El Inca Garcilaso de la Vega's emphasis on his natio of Peru, and birthplace of Cuzco, is important to his broader claims about knowledge, Margarita Zamora, *Language, Authority, and Indigenous History in the Comentarios Reales de los Incas*, Cambridge: Cambridge University Press, 1988, pp. 48–61.

58 Perhaps the earliest Castilian–Nahuatl dictionary is Alonso de Molina, *Aqui comiença vn vocabulario en lengua castellana y mexicana*, Mexico: Juan Pablos, 1555.

59 AGI Justicia 1022.1.1.

60 AGI Justicia 1022.1.2, 1023.2.2, 1021.3.1.

61 "por su rrostro y filosomia," AGI Justicia 1021.3.1.

62 "aspeto y filosomia," AGI Justicia 1022.1.2.

63 Joseph Ziegler, "Philosophers and Physicians on the Scientific Validity of Latin Physiognomy, 1200–1500," *Early Science and Medicine*, 12, 2007, pp. 285–312; Martin Porter, *Windows of the Soul: The Art of Physiognomy in European Culture, 1470–1780*, Oxford: Clarendon Press, 2005.

64 Aristotle, *Physiognomonics* 805a1–805b9.

65 For a discussion of Michael Scot, Albertus Magnus, and Pietro d'Abano, see Porter, *Windows of the Soul*, pp. 68–73.

66 "Lac mulieris nigrae & brunae est melius semper illo mulieris albae & rubaeae," Michael Scotus, *Liber physiognomiae*, chapter 13, fols. b viii verso–c i recto.

67 Pseudo-Albertus Magnus, *De secretis mulierum et virorum*, Commentary, Liptz: Lotter, 1505, fol. Aiv recto. Steven Epstein attributes this, instead, to associations of such women to caprids in *Purity Lost*, Baltimore: Johns Hopkins University Press, 2006, p. 216.

68 Michael Scot, *Liber physiognomiae* [Treviso, 1483]; a closely related text in Castilian, "de la phisonomia," is the eighth tract of the *Compendio dela salud humana*, Zaragoza, 1494, fols. xlviii verso–l recto.

69 Johannes Indagine, *Introductiones Apotelesmaticae elegantes, in Chyromantiam, Physiognomiam, Astrologiam naturalem, Complexiones hominum, Naturas planetarum*, Strasbourg: 1522, fols. 3r–7v. For its vernacular popularity, see Porter, *Windows of the Soul*, p. 123.

70 Bartolommeo della Rocca Cocles, *In disem biechlein wirt erfunden von complexion der mensch[e]n*, Augsburg, 1512, fol. ai verso; Bartolommeo della Rocca Cocles, *In disem büechlin wirt erfunden von Complexion der Menschen*, Strasbourg: Flach, 1519, fol. aiv verso.

71 "aspecto y filosomia" and "filosomia de rrostro, cuerpo, cabeza y habla": AGI Justicia 1028.4.3.

72 "filosomya de rrostro caveça e habla": AGI Justicia 1023.2.2.

73 AGI Justicia 1023.1.2.

74 "filosomia aspecto habla y cuerpo": AGI Justicia 1022.4.1.

75 AGI Justicia 1026.2.

76 AGI Justicia 1028.4.3.

77 AGI Justicia 1028.4.1.

78 "filosomia de rrostro, gesto, cuerpo, y cabeça y habla": AGI Justicia 446.2.7.

79 Concepts of group identity determined by common appearance continued in later practices of racialization, particularly in eighteenth-century casta paintings. Casta divisions subdivided the peoples of the colonial Spanish Empire into categories of familial descent from Spaniards, Indians, and Africans; the paintings asserted the visibility of those ancestors in the bodies of their descendants.

80 Bronwen Wilson, "The 'confusion of faces': The Politics of Physiognomy, Concealed Hearts, and Public Visibility," in B. Wilson and P. Yachnin (eds.), *Making Publics in Early Modern Europe: People, Things, Forms of Knowledge*, New York: Routledge, 2010, pp. 177–92.

10

BIONDO FLAVIO ON ETHIOPIA

Processes of knowledge production in the Renaissance[1]

Samantha Kelly

The *Historiarum ab inclinatione Romanorum imperii decades* of Biondo Flavio (1392–1463) was the work of a lifetime: a history of Italy from antiquity to the present, whose third decade especially, covering events of the fifteenth century, Biondo constantly revised, expanded into a fourth decade, and left unfinished at his death.[2] Among the noteworthy contemporary events here recorded were the various stages of the Council of Ferrara-Florence, wherein Pope Eugenius IV sought an ecumenical union of the world's Christian communities. By spring 1442 Biondo had completed his account of the historic union of the Greek and Latin churches, achieved in 1439. He then turned to events that promised an even broader ecumenical union: namely, the arrival in late summer 1441 of representatives of the Ethiopian Orthodox Church and their subsequent interview by a papal committee, which both Biondo and his fellow humanist and papal secretary, Poggio Bracciolini, attended.[3]

Though a brief set piece in the context of the *Decades*, Biondo's account of the Ethiopian delegation's visit is of considerable interest to historians. The council's importance to contemporary Europeans and the significant dossier regarding Ethiopia that it produced make it arguably the most important event in Ethiopian–European relations before the sixteenth century. Ethiopianists have carefully reconstructed the series of events leading up to and including the delegation's visit, reflected on its role in the pope's political and religious strategies, and translated and analyzed many of the relevant documents resulting from it.[4] Curiously, Biondo's account has not been scrutinized to the same degree, though it is the most comprehensive account of the Ethiopian delegation to issue from the council. Scholars of Renaissance humanism, for their part, have mined Biondo's comments on the council to explore his views on the papacy in the context of his overall historical and political thought, though rarely with particular attention to the Ethiopians' participation.[5]

One way to approach Biondo's account is as a witness to the much more accurate knowledge of Ethiopia Europeans gained from this encounter, as Salvatore Tedeschi has done for the description penned by Poggio Bracciolini. Indeed, so accurate was the Ethiopian delegates' testimony that Tedeschi has been able to identify, via Poggio's rendering, the Ethiopian geographical landmarks described by the delegates and such plants and animals as the "false banana," African civet, zebu, dikdik, and ibex.[6] In terms of the history of Italian humanism, on the other hand, it is impossible to ignore Biondo's role in reworking that testimony and the ways he framed the delegation's presence within his larger vision of history. But Biondo's viewpoint was not the only factor mediating the transmission of information about Ethiopia at the council. General European presumptions about Ethiopia, shaped by inherited traditions and by contemporary European priorities, dictated both the questions that the European interviewers asked of the delegates and their interpretation of the responses. The Ethiopians themselves made their own choices about what to relate and how to relate it. Finally, though its effects are difficult to pinpoint, one cannot overlook the potential distortions accruing from translation across multiple languages.[7] Given the total ignorance of Ethiopian languages in Europe, the delegates must have spoken in Arabic, a language doubtless familiar to them from their time in Jerusalem but which was neither their native vernacular nor even the literary and ecclesiastical *lingua franca* of Ethiopia, Gəʿəz.[8] That testimony then passed (as the Europeans' questions also passed) through two anonymous translators, one *Arabs*, the other *Latinus*, who were tasked with rendering often technical scientific and religious terminology and whose ignorance Biondo lamented.[9]

In sum, the actual state of Ethiopia in 1441, and the account of it rendered by Biondo in the context of his *Decades*, were merely the terminal poles in a complex process of transmission. Biondo's text certainly reflects an increasingly accurate apprehension of Ethiopian realities capable of supplanting largely legendary medieval descriptions of the country. It also bears the stamp of Biondo's own opinions and perspective. In a fuller sense, however, it is an artifact shaped by all the factors conditioning the Ethiopians' report and its reception. The analysis offered here treats it as a witness to this process of transmission: as a case study, that is, in the contingencies surrounding the Renaissance production of knowledge about the past and about the wider world.

Ethiopia and crusade: the Prester John legend

As is well known, Eugenius IV convened the Council of Ferrara-Florence in response to two principal threats: the conciliar movement, which challenged papal sovereignty over the Church and had been conducting a council of its own in Basel since 1431, and the steady advance of the Turks into Byzantine territory. Eugenius' efforts to achieve an ecumenical union were a direct answer to the first threat, illustrating international recognition of the pope as the true head of the Latin Church. Ecumenical union, in turn, was expected to pave the way for effective response to the second threat, in facilitating coordinated military action to stem Turkish territorial advance and to achieve the much older goal of Christian recovery of the Holy Land. The union of the Latin and Greek churches, symbolically the most important, was achieved in July 1439, and was followed four months later by the addition of the Armenians.[10]

For crusade against the Muslims, however, little could be expected of either the Greeks or the Armenians. Ethiopia, by contrast, promised much. Ever since Otto of Freising had reported the existence of Prester John in 1145, the Prester had been hailed by Europeans as a crucial potential ally for recovery of the Holy Land. Piously Christian and militarily powerful, the Prester had already, according to Otto, launched his own attack on the Muslims from his homeland in the east, but had found his way obstructed.[11] In Otto's time, admittedly, the Prester was assumed to reside somewhere in Asia. But European travelers' repeated failure to find him there, and increasing reports of just such a powerful Christian king south of Egypt, led to the firm identification of the Prester with the Ethiopian *nəguś* (ruler) by the turn of the fifteenth century. The Prester's perceived utility for crusade was unchanged by this geographical transfer. Since a single power, the Mamluk sultanate, controlled Syria and Palestine as well as Egypt, an African Prester was still strategically located to attack it, not from the east now, but from the south. So Marino Sanudo and William Adam had argued in the fourteenth century.[12] So Alfonso of Aragon had proposed to the Ethiopian envoys he received in 1427 and again in 1450.[13] And so, certainly, expected Eugenius IV. The papal committee charged with interviewing the Ethiopians posed a series of probing questions about Ethiopia's military capacity, and in the final, climactic moment of the interview asked the delegates point blank if their ruler would, at the pope's command, expel the Muslims from the Holy Land.

The Ethiopians' answers were doubtless dictated by their own desire to paint their realm in the best possible light. One hundred kings were subject to their ruler, they claimed, each of whom possessed a kingdom larger than those of Europe. As for the army, it comprised 500 generals, each commanding 50,000 cavalry. Their armor was as splendid as that of Europe, their archers more expert than those of Syria.[14] On the final, crucial question of the nəguś's willingness to launch an attack on the Muslims, however, the delegates were in a delicate position. They were not, in fact, official representatives of the nəguś, whom Ethiopians recognized as the true head of their Church. Rather, they were monks culled from the Ethiopian monastery in Jerusalem when the papal envoy tasked with fetching Ethiopian delegates had realized that the Coptic Patriarch in Alexandria could not speak for Ethiopia and that a journey to the nəguś himself in Ethiopia was unfeasible. These monks had arrived bearing a letter (in Gəʿəz) from their abbot in Jerusalem that underlined their unofficial status.[15] They nonetheless replied that if their king were asked to expel the Saracens from the Holy Land, he certainly would.[16] Or perhaps this was Biondo's interpretation, and the delegates had actually said merely that he *could*. Their acknowledged inability to make such commitments, underscored by their own monastic superior, argues against their making such a claim. So does the somewhat odd proof of the nəguś's crusade enthusiasm the delegates then supplied, which, as will be discussed below, concerned neither the current ruler of Ethiopia nor a war against Muslims. There is reason to suspect that on this point, so important to Biondo and to European crusade proponents generally, the Europeans heard what they wanted to hear. The Ethiopians' answers nevertheless met European expectations on the central issue: they confirmed the military might of the nəguś in a way that matched the Prester's reputation and fulfilled the committee's hopes.

Biondo certainly shared those hopes. He continued to believe in the urgency of a Christian crusade against the Turks, exhorting Emperor Sigismond and Alfonso of Aragon to lead one together in 1452, and repeating the plea to Alfonso alone in 1453.[17] He also seems to have shared his fellow Europeans' attachment to the identification of the nəguś as Prester John. The Ethiopian delegates, as Biondo noted in the *Decades*, protested this appellation as "absurd and unworthy" of their exalted ruler, and informed the committee of his true personal name, Zärʾa Yaʿəqob, as well as his throne name Qʷäsṭänṭinos (Constantine).[18] Even this information, however, failed to dislodge the traditional appellation of Prester John or expose it as a medieval European fabrication. Biondo instead treated it as an acceptable alternate title, one widely used outside if not within Ethiopia. The Ethiopian king, he wrote, "is called Prester John among us, *and in Syria and Egypt*" – a false assertion, and one whose most plausible explanation is Biondo's unwillingness to discard a tradition so firmly established in the European imagination.[19] In terms of the military goals of the Council of Florence, there is no doubt that the European legend of

169

Prester John played an influential role in the committee's questions to the Ethiopians and their understanding of the answers.

Ecumenical union and Biondo's view of history

While military alliance was a pressing political goal of the Council, ecumenical union was the council's primary and official aim, and one Biondo fully endorsed.[20] Indeed, ecumenical union had a special significance for Biondo, as comments found throughout his works attest: it was the means by which the current age could match, in a different register, the glorious dominion of the ancient Roman Empire. As Biondo claimed in the conclusion of his *Roma instaurata*, "The perpetual dictator is now not Caesar, but the successor of Peter the fisherman, the highest pontiff, vicar of the emperor [Jesus Christ], whom the princes of the world adore and revere."[21] The college of cardinals, by extension, was the modern version of the Roman senate, revered only slightly less than the pope-cum-emperor. These comments were written shortly after the conclusion of the Council of Florence and were certainly inspired by it. In another passage of *Roma instaurata* Biondo addressed Eugenius directly, crediting him with beginning the process of ecumenical union that would soon comprise all the Christians of Europe, Asia, and Africa. He also reiterated his similitude of the pope to the perpetual dictator and of the college of cardinals to the ancient senate in his *Roma triumphans*, again with particular emphasis on the efforts of the reigning pope (now Pius II) to unite Christian powers against the Turks.[22]

Such ideas owed much to the medieval tradition of papal supremacy. Unlike medieval apologists, however, Biondo did not extend his claims to the pope's jurisdiction in temporal affairs: as a political actor Eugenius, like other popes, was viewed by Biondo in a wholly secular light.[23] Nor did Biondo's enthusiasm for the contemporary papacy's potential dim his admiration for ancient Rome. Especially in his *Roma triumphans*, written at a greater distance from the Council of Florence, Biondo made clear his view that "contemporary Rome falls short in both power and grandeur from its ancient counterpart."[24] We might call Biondo's view a particularly humanist interpretation of papal triumphalism: one deeply admiring of antiquity and cognizant of the limits within which the current age could match it, but also inspired by Biondo's piety, and by his role as client and employee of the pope, to claim a spiritual means by which the present could reincarnate ancient greatness.

Biondo's comments on the Ethiopian delegation must be seen in this larger interpretive framework. The union with the Greek Church had historic resonance: it had been sought by the popes for centuries and would restore to the popes' spiritual dominion much of the territory of the ancient empire. But the possibility of adding Ethiopia to that sphere of dominion held a special excitement, for here, as Biondo noted, was a country that had escaped even the long arm of ancient Roman rule.[25] Indeed, for late-antique and subsequent Christian writers "Ethiopia" was sometimes understood as a shorthand for "the ends of the earth," and its inclusion in the Christian fold a sign of Christianity's universal destiny. So Augustine, a writer familiar to Biondo, had commented in a reflection on the psalm verse "Before him the Ethiopians shall fall down."[26] Unity with the Greek Church achieved a certain parity with regard to antiquity. Unity with the Ethiopian Church would surpass ancient boundaries, approaching that truly universal Christian dominion foretold in the Bible.

Petros, the chief spokesman for the Ethiopian delegation, reinforced such ideas in his opening oration to the Roman curia. In a striking adoption of the European perspective, he described his homeland as located "not only at the very edge of the world, but almost beyond the edge of the world itself."[27] To the Europeans, such a description doubtless underscored the momentousness of union with the Ethiopian Church and the potential extension of papal authority to the distant corners of the globe. There is no reason to assume this was not part of Petros' purpose. Diplomacy recommended that he both praise the council's initiatives and emphasize the importance of his own delegation's role. It is clear, nonetheless, that Petros had additional motives for his comment. He proffered Ethiopia's great distance from Europe as one reason Ethiopia had for so long lacked communication with the pope. Another reason was the "negligence of the Roman pontiffs, your predecessors, since among our people there is no memory of any previous pastor visiting or showing concern for [us], so many sheep of Christ. Some say that 800, others that 900 years have passed during which not even one pope has cared to greet us with a single word."[28] Petros' line of argument was therefore one of Ethiopian self-justification: it was not "faithlessness or fickleness" that had led the Ethiopian Church to diverge from the Latin and lose contact with it, but rather geography and Roman indifference. All told, Petros' comments were a careful balance of praise and criticism, of voicing a European perspective and affirming an Ethiopian one. But his conclusion regarding Eugenius' undertaking perfectly matched Biondo's own: "Our highest praise for you [Eugenius] and the increase of our joy lies in this: that you were the first and only pope to desire to unite our emperor and our people with the Catholic faith."[29]

Ptolemy and Ethiopia: surpassing antiquity

For Biondo, then, ecumenical union promised a new incarnation of ancient Rome's universal dominion, not through force but through faith. With the inclusion of countries like Ethiopia, Christian Rome might even surpass the geographical limits of the ancient empire. But the very presence of the Ethiopian delegates in Florence had already allowed the current age to surpass antiquity in one respect: with regard, that is, to geographical knowledge.

Geography was a subject of considerable interest in early fifteenth-century Europe, as merchants, prelates, and princes alike eagerly sought new and more accurate geographical information to facilitate their commercial, evangelical and political designs on distant locations. It is no accident, for instance, that two Ethiopian embassies that preceded the Council of Florence – to Venice in 1402 and to Alfonso of Aragon in 1427 – both produced new geographical texts based on the testimony of the Ethiopian ambassadors.[30] For humanists, geography was also the field that virtually inaugurated Latin Europe's deeper engagement with ancient Greek science. Manuel Chrysoloras, the first great teacher of Greek in Renaissance Europe, brought a copy of Ptolemy's second-century *Geographia* with him to Florence in 1397, and thereby introduced Western Europeans to the original text of the greatest ancient authority on world geography. It is not surprising, therefore, that the two humanists attending the interview of the Ethiopian delegation in 1441 both reported on the delegates' geographical testimony, and did so with Ptolemy in mind. Poggio Bracciolini's account, indeed, concerns itself almost entirely with the Ethiopians' geographical and natural-scientific comments. He himself asked the delegates (through an interpreter) about the location and source of the Nile, and when two of them responded that its source lay near their homeland, "my desire was piqued to learn those things which seem to have been unknown to ancient writers and philosophers, and to Ptolemy, who was the first to write about the source of the Nile."[31]

Biondo, too, was struck by the way the Ethiopians' report expanded and revised Ptolemy. After summarizing their description of Ethiopian geography, Biondo observed, "we responded to them what Ptolemy, the most learned surveyor of the sky and earth with the most authority among the Greeks and among ourselves, passed down … They said that we were deceived."[32] Two paragraphs later he returned to the question of Ptolemy's authority, pausing in his report to offer a long defense of the superiority of the Ethiopians' information compared to ancient knowledge. Here it was no longer "we" who cited Ptolemy, but skeptics unwilling to believe that the ancient writer's authority could be surpassed. "Many who are experienced in Roman and Greek history contend that these things [reported by the Ethiopians], which have never before been written or made known, must be considered false and fabricated, and they oppose to them Ptolemy, the most skillful surveyor of the world," Biondo observed.

> But we know and understand that Ptolemy was wrong about many things regarding the northern regions, regions that are very well known to men of our time and to us. Beyond the British ocean, where [Ptolemy] marks the land and sea as 'unknown,' we have information of five hundred islands populated by Christian peoples … Just so Ptolemy, who knew only that first and smallest part of Ethiopia bordering Egypt, could not know of the regions and kingdoms beyond.[33]

For Biondo, the delegates' reliability was confirmed by the reputation of the papal envoy, Alberto da Sarteano, who had been sent to fetch them, "certainly a man as learned and pious as he is wise in secular matters," and by the prelates of Egypt and Jerusalem, "men of great authority and reputation," who had selected the delegates.[34] In short, Biondo was persuaded of the veracity of the Ethiopians' testimony, in part because the delegates were eyewitnesses whose credibility was backed by authorities of their society and of Europe's, and in part, no doubt, because their comments corresponded to his sense of the council as a historic event through which the current age could match or even surpass the achievements of antiquity.

Eyewitness status, however, was a double-edged sword. Though considered the gold standard of narrative reliability from antiquity forward, it carried with it the constraints of the eyewitnesses' personal experience and the potential bias of their understanding of that experience. When eyewitness testimony was transmitted across cultures, there was the further possible complication of terminological shift: a word or concept's meaning in one cultural tradition was not necessarily identical with its meaning in another.

The Ethiopian delegates' description of the source of the Nile is a case in point. According to Poggio's more detailed account of this subject, the delegates stated that the Nile originated on the slopes of high mountains; its waters were clear and sweet until mixing with those of its many tributaries, and its source was not far from their home city of Warwar.[35] As Salvatore Tedeschi has observed, this is a very accurate description of the Täkkäze River, which does indeed begin in the mountains near Warwar (i.e. Lalibela) in the province of Lasta, and whose sweet waters are praised in Ethiopian literature.[36] For a fifteenth-century Ethiopian, and especially a native of Lasta, it was perfectly logical to identify the Täkkäze as the Nile. *Täkkäze*, which can also mean simply "river," is the word used in the Gǝʿǝz Bible for the "waters" of Egypt (the term "Nile" does not appear in the Bible).[37] Further, the river in Ethiopia for which *Täkkäze* became the proper name was indeed a major affluent of the Nile. It was still common in the later fifteenth and early sixteenth centuries for Ethiopians, when asked (by Europeans) about the Nile, to describe the Täkkäze.[38] That said, the Ethiopian river identified by Europeans in the sixteenth century as the source of the Nile, and today called the Blue Nile, is the Abbay, which originates well to the south of the Täkkäze, not in mountains but in Lake Ṭana. As Christian Ethiopians settled more heavily south of Lake Ṭana in the fifteenth century they, too, sometimes identified the Nile with the Abbay, and had the delegates hailed from a more southerly region they might have offered this different – from a European perspective, more accurate – identification. But the limits of their personal experience prevented this: they could only refer to a body of water fifteen days' journey from their home region that they had never seen.[39]

Similar observations can be made about delegates' claim that "the borders of their own province stretched to India." When the papal committee protested, citing Ptolemy on the several countries and seas separating Ethiopia from India, the Ethiopians replied, as noted above, that the Europeans were deceived, "or else that there was another India bordering the eastern shore. This India was a nation of so many peoples that they hindered the power of [the Ethiopian] king with nearly unending wars." The delegates' description suggests they were referring to the Muslim sultanates of the eastern Horn of Africa, with which the rulers of Christian Ethiopia did indeed wage frequent wars. That region, however, was certainly not called "India" in Ethiopia.

The most likely explanation is that the European interviewers introduced the term "India" and asked the delegates about its location relative to their own kingdom. In antiquity and medieval Europe "India" could designate the southeastern and southwestern shores of the Red Sea as well as the Indian subcontinent, sometimes with distinguishing modifiers.[40] The papal committee surely perceived the Ethiopian delegates as useful informants on this geographical question. As for the delegates' response, it does not appear that they, or indeed medieval Ethiopians generally, were familiar with the European tradition designating a part of the Horn of Africa as India.[41] Furthermore, the Arabic term that the interpreters would have relayed to them was "Hind," which, if the delegates were aware of Arabic geographical usage, they would certainly have understood as the Indian subcontinent. Their reply suggests that they were not familiar with the terms India or Hind but, understanding the Europeans to be interested in the Red Sea coast or more southerly shores of the Horn, duly reported what they knew of that region. As with the Nile, the disjunctures between European and Ethiopian geographical terminology, combined with the horizons of the delegates' personal experience, resulted in the transmission of knowledge that by later centuries' standards would be deemed incorrect.

Ethiopian Christianity

While the papal committee was clearly curious about Ethiopian geography, their primary task was to ascertain the Ethiopians' religious beliefs and practices for the purposes of ecumenical union. Biondo reported on this subject in considerable detail. His account makes clear that papal authorities acquired a good deal of knowledge of Ethiopian Christianity already in the first half of the fifteenth century. It also suggests, however, that this knowledge reflected the particular views of the delegates, which were not identical with those of Ethiopian Church authorities.

Most notable in this regard is the delegates' statement that Ethiopian Christians observed Saturday as well as Sunday as the Lord's days.[42] In 1441, observance of the "first Sabbath" or Saturday was not a universally accepted feature of the Ethiopian Orthodox Church. Indeed, it was so controversial in the late fourteenth and early fifteenth centuries that it threatened to split the Ethiopian Church in two. Pro-Sabbath or "Ewosṭatean" monastic communities, condemned as heretics and persecuted throughout the fourteenth century, had nevertheless come to dominate the northern provinces of the kingdom, while traditionalist monasteries, backed by the *nägäst* (rulers) and by Ethiopia's sole metropolitan, dominated the south. In an effort at conciliation, the *nəguś* Dawit permitted the Ewosṭateans to observe the Sabbath in 1404, thus removing from them the ranks of heretics. Sabbath observance was still forbidden to all other Ethiopian Christians, however, and the Ewosṭateans continued to face much hostility from Ethiopia's rulers, metropolitans, and other monastic orders in the first half of the fifteenth century. Only in 1450 did the *nəguś* Zär'a Ya'eqob (1434–68) make Sabbath observance an official and requisite feature of Ethiopian Church practice, an about-face apparently greeted with reluctance by traditionalist elements.[43]

When the delegates identified Sabbath observance as a feature of the Ethiopian Church in 1441, therefore, they were not merely simplifying a complex political and religious issue. They were expressing a deeply partisan position. This statement in itself proves that the delegates were Ewosṭateans: before 1450 they and only they were permitted to observe the Sabbath. As with their comments on the location of India and the source of the Nile, the delegates' representation of their home country was predicated on their personal experience. In this case, however, it was not the limits of their firsthand knowledge, nor terminological differences with Europe, that produced information one might adjudge false. Ewosṭateans knew perfectly well that Sabbath observance still lacked the official imprimatur of the *nəguś* and metropolitan and was denied by many of their coreligionists. They chose to portray the Ethiopian Church not as Ethiopian authorities defined it, but as they themselves practiced it and believed it should be.

On a second topic, too, the delegates' testimony contradicted the state of affairs in Ethiopia. Regarding the sacrament of marriage, the delegates claimed that "even the ruler is permitted only one wife, though if she dies he is permitted a second, and a third – but no more."[44] Ironically, marriage laws were a point on which Biondo particularly praised the Ethiopians as holding to a higher moral standard than Europeans – ironic, because regarding monogamy the delegates' statement was simply untrue.[45] Until the sixteenth century it was common for Ethiopian *nägäst* to have multiple wives. Polygyny was indeed enshrined in the structure of the royal court, where the "queen of the left" and the "queen of the right" were official titles.[46] Implied in the delegates' statement was a critique of royal marriage practice, and indeed such critique was common to Ewosṭateans and other reform-minded monastic movements, especially in the fourteenth century.[47] On this subject, too, the delegates portrayed Ethiopia not as it was, but as they believed it ought to be.

The papal committee was interested in questions of Christian doctrine quite as much as practice. Its members were aware that the Ethiopian Church was non-Chalcedonian: that is, that along with the Syrian, Coptic, and other "Oriental" churches it had withdrawn from the Council of Chalcedon in 451 over that council's formulation of Christ's dual nature, human and divine. The committee members thus posed the question explicitly, and "when asked, [the Ethiopians] replied that the Lord Jesus was truly God and truly man, and that in him were two natures."[48] The statement is somewhat surprising, especially coming from Ewosṭatean monks.[49] It could, however, be considered an acceptable (if particularly conciliatory) expression of Ethiopian Orthodox theology, according to which Christ possessed two natures, human and divine, in one nature (*mia physis*).[50] The answer nonetheless contradicted European understanding of the Oriental churches, whence the committee returned to the issue with a question intended, apparently, to catch the Ethiopians in their lie. They asked the Ethiopians about their views on two protagonists of the fifth-century Council of

Chalcedon, Eutyches and Dioscorus. The Ethiopians replied that "they venerated Dioscorus as a saint, but that they did not recognize Eutyches." The committee evidently found this answer outrageous, protesting that "if Eutyches were not recognized, it was impossible to recognize Dioscorus, who was condemned for following the errors of Eutyches."[51]

Here it was the limits of European understanding that distorted the transmission of information about Ethiopia. The Ethiopian Orthodox Church followed (and follows) Dioscorus' more moderate Christological stance rather than the extreme monophysite position of Eutyches. The Catholic Church would eventually (in modern times) acknowledge that miaphysitism was compatible with its own view.[52] Perhaps, in affirming Christ's dual nature, the delegates sought to stress an essential agreement between their own and the Latin Church's views without delving into the theological distinctions between them. Perhaps they attempted a more fine-grained discourse and the translators were incapable of rendering it. Their distinction between Eutyches and Dioscorus was certainly correct. Their discourse, in any case, was incapable of dislodging the European presumption that all non-Chalcedonian churches were monophysite and was therefore rejected.

That Biondo recorded all this is a testament to the even-handedness of his exposition. We know, however, that he was deeply committed to the prospect of ecumenical union, and it is not surprising that he tended to present differences in theology and practice without commentary, while emphasizing wherever possible the similarities between Latin and Ethiopian Christianity. He had done the same with regard to Ethiopian botanical and zoological information: where Poggio stressed the exotic, unknown species described by the Ethiopians, Biondo focused on their relative likeness to European ones: "they produced the same or even a greater amount of grain, oil and fruits [compared to Europe]; they raised cows and horses larger and, in their opinion stronger than ours; the same beasts both wild and tame that they saw among us had [there] a different, unfamiliar appearance."[53] Just so with Christianity, Biondo carefully enumerated the convergences. They recognized the same books of the Bible.[54] They knew many Greek and Latin Fathers. They had the same ecclesiastical hierarchy. They baptized with water and the Holy Spirit, recited the same canonical hours, even initiated Christian warriors by a similar rite.[55] Whether Ethiopian Christianity was fundamentally compatible with Latin Christianity or comprised of "the worst heretics" (in the words of another fifteenth-century European) was in the eye of the beholder, and Biondo's own convictions and aspirations certainly played a role in the portrait he painted.[56]

Ethiopia and antiquity

On the topics thus far discussed, antiquity figured principally in Biondo's narration as a standard of comparison for the achievements of the present. Ecumenical union was desirable in part for reconstituting, in the spiritual realm, the global primacy of ancient Rome; the Ethiopians' report of northeast African geography permitted present-day Europeans to surpass even the greatest ancient expert of the subject. A few clues, however, suggest that Biondo also saw Ethiopia as a source of information on antiquity itself: that is, as a country whose longtime isolation (as perceived by Europeans) had permitted it to preserve certain aspects of ancient culture.

The Ethiopians' testimony certainly encouraged such a perspective. From late antiquity forward, and particularly from the late thirteenth century, Ethiopian *nägäst* and the clerics in their service had placed great emphasis on their links to ancient Israel.[57] The most famous expression of this vision was the fourteenth-century *Kəbrä Nägäśt* ("Glory of the Kings"), which recounted the origins of the Ethiopian royal dynasty in the union of King Solomon and the Queen of the South (generally identified in later tradition with the biblical Queen of Sheba). The son born of this union not only perpetuated the Solomonic royal line in Ethiopia but brought back from Jerusalem the Ark of the Covenant, making Ethiopia the new Promised Land and the Ethiopians the especial chosen of God.[58] Ethiopia's Christian origins were equally ancient: the apostle Philip's conversion of the eunuch in Candace's service, recounted in the Acts of the Apostles, was generally taken (in Europe as in Ethiopia) as the beginning of Ethiopia's turn to Christianity, which was solidified in late antiquity by the formal conversion of the monarch and by the introduction of monasticism by the Nine Saints.[59]

In recounting these historical traditions, the Ethiopian delegates focused only on figures attested in the Bible who would be most familiar to their audience. Even so, they invoked Ethiopia's deep roots in the Judeo-Christian tradition. As Petros, the head delegate, related in his opening oration, "not the least part of our glory is the Queen of Sheba who, inspired by the fame of Solomon's wisdom, betook herself to Jerusalem just as we, though much less great than the Queen of Sheba, have come to you, who are even greater than Solomon. Also sprung from our people were Queen Candace and the eunuch, whom Philip the apostle of the Lord baptized."[60] And though neither Petros nor the other delegates seem to have mentioned the Ark's voyage to Ethiopia, they did note Ethiopia's apparently unique preservation of another artifact of Solomon's time. When listing the books of the Ethiopian Bible, the delegates mentioned "the books of Solomon, of which they said they had more than we. Indeed, they said they had all the books written by Solomon."[61] The Ethiopian Bible did in fact have five, rather than the Vulgate's four, Solomonic books. The titles differed, and doubtless textual comparison was not undertaken; it thus escaped notice that the Ethiopian Bible had an extra book as a result of dividing the contents of Proverbs in two.[62] But to the humanists and book hunters who heard the delegates' testimony, the prospect of hitherto unknown Solomonic texts must have been captivating. The news clearly spread from the council's attendees to like-minded bibliophiles. In 1459 Francesco Sforza, Duke of Milan, was introduced to an Ethiopian known as Giorgio Michele who agreed to serve as the duke's envoy to the Ethiopian nəguś. Among the things Sforza requested was precisely the "books of Solomonic wisdom" to be found in Ethiopia, ideally in a Latin translation.[63]

Through other comments, meanwhile, the delegates conveyed a sense that the ancient past remained immediate and relevant in Ethiopia. As noted above, Petros claimed that Ethiopian communal memory stretched back eight or nine centuries when mentioning the popes' historic neglect of Ethiopia. And, strikingly, it was again an ancient event that the Ethiopians cited to prove their current ruler's ability to oust the Muslims from the Holy Land. One might expect the delegates to have mentioned the many Christian Ethiopian victories won over the previous century against the Muslim sultanates of the eastern Horn, which were against the same enemy of interest to Europeans and would presumably better reflect current Ethiopian power. Instead they offered the example of a war fought against Himyar, a Jewish kingdom, some nine centuries before.[64]

In terms of Ethiopian–European diplomacy, this choice had much to recommend it. Himyar, in the Yemen, controlled a strategic region for Red Sea trade in late antiquity, and the Byzantine and Persian empires both sought influence there in their territorial and commercial rivalry with each other. But it was the rulers of ancient Aksum (predecessor of the medieval kingdom of Ethiopia) who first occupied Himyar on their own initiative, and who undertook a full conquest of the kingdom in 525 for which the Byzantine emperor offered naval reinforcements.[65] The parallels with fifteenth-century conditions were not hard to make out. Once again rival empires – the Dar al-Islam and Christian Europe – were battling for strategic territory, and Ethiopia's location and capacity to conquer that territory made it an ally that the pope, like the Byzantine emperor before him, would do well to cultivate. Biondo, who called the anecdote "one of which we had already heard," seems to have understood the reference. To do so, however, Biondo, like the Ethiopian delegates, had to collapse the passage of 900 years and view contemporary Ethiopia as more or less equivalent to its sixth-century forebear.

Certainly Biondo followed the Ethiopians' lead when he invoked ancient authority to prove the Ethiopians' reliability. Naysayers, he noted, "believe that there are no peoples beyond the Ethiopia known to Ptolemy against which the enormous army of Zär'a Ya'əqob could be opposed, and therefore maintain that these claims about [the army's] size and magnitude are false."[66] To prove that fifteenth-century Ethiopia could indeed have such a large army, Biondo cited a "certain and very reliable authority": the Old Testament. "In the Book of Chronicles, it is said that Zerah the Ethiopian came with ten hundred thousand men against Asa, king of Judea. Though Asa had three hundred thousand men from Judas and two hundred and eighty [thousand] from Benjamin, he feared the large number of Ethiopians and, having no faith in his own army, begged for help from God."[67] Biondo's logic was precisely that of the delegates: ancient evidence was wholly applicable to the current conditions of Ethiopia, as if the kingdom's territorial limits, population, and military capacity had been preserved unchanged across more than a millennium. In a sense Biondo combined two threads of the Ethiopians' discourse – the country's biblical link to ancient Israel and the evocation of antiquity with regard to military capacity – to offer his own argument in the Ethiopians' defense. It is worth noting that in his treatment of European history Biondo displayed a keen sensitivity to chronological change. His bracketing of diachronic considerations here clearly had something to do with Ethiopia specifically: with his investment in the Ethiopians' arguments, and perhaps also with his willingness to view Ethiopia as a land out of time.

In Biondo's account, the notion that Ethiopia preserved aspects of ancient culture remained a suggestion more than an argument. We have observed it in Biondo's method of argumentation and in his mention, later taken up by other Renaissance bibliophiles, of Ethiopia possessing otherwise lost Solomonic books. At the turn of the sixteenth century the notion resurfaced in a more emphatic form, when Johannes Potken, co-editor of the first printed book in Gə'əz, claimed – and claimed to have learned from Ethiopian authorities – that sacred language of Ethiopia was none other than ancient Chaldean, the original language of Heber and Abraham and perhaps, therefore, the original language of mankind.[68]

The specific context and content of Potken's and Biondo's portraits of course differ, but both episodes testify to the complex processes underpinning the Renaissance production of knowledge. In the case of Biondo's *Decades* (and much the same could be said of Potken's comments), contemporary testimony was compared and sometimes conflated with ancient source texts, in a fascinating, unspoken negotiation of the relationship between the past and the wider world and of their relative claims on Renaissance scholars' attention. In both too, and most clearly in Biondo's *Decades*, eyewitness report was showcased as a proof of reliability, and yet proves, on closer inspection, its own slipperiness. Actual Ethiopians – educated, multilingual, and able to answer questions in person – were as good an authority on Ethiopia as Europeans could hope to find. The information produced by their dialogue was nonetheless mediated by the personal experience and strategic choices of the speakers, by the inherited traditions, current priorities, and individual predilections of the listeners, and by the potentially distorting effects of translation through multiple languages. By attending to the individuality of the non-European as well as European actors in these exchanges, and to the cultural traditions each brought to their encounter, we may be better able to recapture a sense of the freshness, instability, and contingency of the knowledge thereby established.

Notes

1 My sincere thanks to Alessandro Bausi, Marie-Laure Derat, Getatchew Haile, and Angelo Mazzocco for their valuable comments on earlier versions of this chapter.

2 Biondo Flavio, *Historiarum ab inclinatione Romanorum imperii decades*, Venice, 1483 *Decades*. On Biondo's continual work on the third decade (which expanded to twelve books, and hence includes two books of a fourth *decas*) see Bartolomeo Nogara, ed., *Scritti inediti e rari di Biondo Flavio*, Rome, 1927, lxxxii–cvi.

3 The first eleven books of the third decade, finished by spring 1442, became the basis for most subsequent editions. The twelfth book, which covers the Ethiopian delegation and other events of 1441, was written later that year, but as Biondo intended to continue expanding it and left it unfinished, it did not appear in print until Nogara's edition of 1927, where it occupies pages 19–27: see Nogara, ed., *Scritti inediti*, lxxxiv–lxxxviii.

4 Enrico Cerulli, "Eugenio IV e gli etiopi al Concilio di Firenze nel 1441," *Rendiconti della reale accademia nazionale dei Lincei*, ser. 6, 9 (1933), 347–68; Salvatore Tedeschi, "Etiopi e Copti al Concilio di Firenze," *Annuarium historiae conciliorum* 21 (1989), 380–407; Benjamin Weber, "La bulle *Cantate Domino* (4 février 1442) et les enjeux éthiopiens du concile de Florence," *Mélanges de l'École française de Rome: Moyen Age* 122 (2010), 441–9; Benjamin Weber, "Vrais et faux Éthiopiens au XVe siècle en Occident? Du bon usage des connexions," *Annales d'Éthiopie* 27 (2012), 118–20. Documents have been edited or translated in Franco Cardini, "Una versione volgare del discorso degli 'ambasciatori' etiopici al concilio di Firenze," *Archivio storico italiano* 130 (1972), 269–76, at 274–6; Cerulli, "L'Etiopia del secolo XV in nuovi documenti storici," *Africa italiana* 5 (1933), 63–6; G. Hofmann, ed., *Epistolae pontificiae ad concilium florentinum spectantes*, vol. 2, Rome, 1944, 38–40, 98–101, 108–9; G. Hofmann, ed., *Orientalium documenta minora*, Rome, 1953, 59–66; H. Justinianus, *Acta Sacri Oecumenici Concilii florentini*, Rome, 1637, 379; Salvatore Tedeschi, "L'Etiopia di Poggio Bracciolini," *Africa: Rivista trimestrale di studi e documentazione dell'Istituto italiano per l'Africa e l'Oriente* 48 (1993): 333–58, at 343–7; and Natalie Bouloux, "Du nouveau au sud de l'Égypte: une ambassade éthiopienne au concile de Florence," in P. Gautier Dalché, ed., *La Terre. Connaissance, représentations, mesure au Moyen Âge*, Turnhout, 2013, 420–8, at 422–4.

5 E. Marino, "Eugenio e la storiografia di Flavio Biondo," *Memorie domenicane* 4 (1973), 241–87; L. Onofri, "A proposito di un recente studio su Eugenio IV e Biondo Flavio," *Archivio della società romana di storia patria* 99 (1976), 349–56; Denys Hay, "Flavio Biondo and the Middle Ages," *Proceedings of the British Academy* 45 (1959), 102–27; Riccardo Fubini, "Biondo Flavio," in *Dizionario biografico degli italiani*, vol. 10, Rome, 1968, 536–59, esp. 541. Angelo Mazzocco is rare in discussing the Ethiopian delegation's role in Biondo's overall views of the council: see "A Glorification of Ancient Rome or an Apology of Papal Policies: A Reappraisal of Biondo Flavio's *Roma Instaurata* III: 83–114," in Anna Modigliani, ed., *Roma e il Papato nel medioevo. Studi in onore di Massimo Miglio*, vol. 2, Rome, 2012, 73–88, at 77–9.

6 Tedeschi, "L'Etiopia di Poggio," 343–52.

7 Cerulli, for instance, has observed some notable differences between the original Gəʿəz letter of Nicodemus and the Latin translation of it effected at the council: "L'Etiopia del secolo XV," 68–9.

8 Tedeschi, "Etiopi e Copti," 392–3. For Ethiopian names and terms I follow the transliteration system advocated by the editors of the *Encyclopaedia Aethiopica* (hereafter *EA*), 5 vols., Wiesbaden, 2003–14.

9 "[M]andata ... binis interpretibus, quorum unus esset Arabs alter Latinus, alternis referentibus, in hanc sententiam exposuere": Nogara, ed., *Scritti inediti*, 20. Biondo is here speaking of Petros' opening oration, but the interpreters were also of course used in the subsequent interview, when Biondo noted that "ea vero in re maximo fuit incommodo interpretum imperitia, quod eorum nullus doctrina vel mediocriter tinctus erat": *ibid.*, 22.

10 Joseph Gill, *The Council of Florence*, Cambridge, 1959; Tedeschi, "Etiopi e Copti."

11 Otto of Friesing, *The Two Cities: A Chronicle of Universal History to the Year 1146 AD*, ed. C. Mierow, C. Knapp, and A. Evans, New York, 1928, 443–4.

12 Enrico Cerulli, *Etiopi in Palestina*, 2 vols., Rome, 1943–7, at vol. 1, 91–101. The medieval authors tend to use the terms "Nubia" and "Ethiopia" as interchangeable or overlapping, but Cerulli believes the Ethiopian kingdom, then expanding against Muslims, was intended, rather than the adjoining Nubian kingdom which was in its final decline.

13 Peter Garretson, "A Note on Relations between Ethiopia and the Kingdom of Aragon in the Fifteenth Century," *Rassegna di studi etiopici* 37 (1993), 37–44; Constanin Marinescu, *La politique orientale d'Alfonse V d'Aragon, roi de Naples (1416–1458)*, Barcelona, 1994, 18–20; Alfonso Cerone, "La politica orientale di Alfonso di Aragona," *Archivio storico per le province napoletane* 27 (1902), 64–6.

14 Nogara, ed., *Scritti inediti*, 23.

15 The letter was translated at the council (clearly with the delegates' help) into Italian and Latin: see Cerulli, "L'Etiopia del secoli XV," and Cardini, "Une versione volgare."

16 "Interrogati an rex eorum, requisitus a summo pontifice tamquam Christi vicario, immissa exercituum quos habet tantos parte, Saracenos Hierosolyma et Sacrae Telluris civitatibus atque locis … pelleret, responderunt: eum procul dubio quicquid pontifex iusserit effecturum": Nogara, ed., *Scritti inediti*, 26–7.

17 *Oratio coram serenissimo imperatore Frederico et Alphonso Aragonum rege inclito* (1452), in Nogara, ed., *Scritti inediti*, 107–14; *De expeditione in Turchos* (1453), *ibid.*, 31–51.

18 "[R]esponderunt: eum qui indigne ferat hanc absurdam sibi natam [*sic:* datam] appellationem, nomine proprio Zareiacob, quod interpretari volunt Iacob prophetae soboles, sed cognomine et simul dignitate Constantinum dici, tamquam virtute et potentia illi similem qui primus Romani imperii sedem transtulit Byzantium, Flavio Constantino": *ibid.*, 23. On Constantine in the Ethiopian tradition see Paola Buzi and Alessandro Bausi, "Tradizioni ecclesiastiche e letterarie copte ed etiopiche," in Alberto Melloni *et al.*, eds., *Costantino I. Enciclopedia costantiniana sulla figura e l'immagine dell'imperatore del cosiddetto editto di Milano 313–2013*, vol. 2, Rome, 2013, 401–23, at 412–18.

19 "De rege interrogati, cui apud nos et in Syria ac Aegypto presbytero Iohanni est appellatio …": Nogara, ed., *Scritti inediti*, 23.

20 Biondo had been deeply involved in the council since its beginnings (Fubini, "Biondo Flavio," 541) and, in addition to narrating its achievements in the *Decades*, reproduced in full the bull of union of 1439 (*Decades*, 550ff.).

21 *Roma instaurata* III. 88, cited by Mazzocco, "Glorification of Ancient Rome," 78.

22 Mazzocco, "Glorification of Ancient Rome," 85. The work was written over the years 1457–60: see Nogara, ed., *Scritti inediti*, cxlix–cli.

23 Hay, "Flavio Biondo," 120–1.

24 Mazzocco, "Glorification of Ancient Rome," 84.

25 Biondo noted that the Ethiopians "aut Romanorum rebus olim florentibus fuerint intacti, aut a maioribus nostris incogniti": Nogara, ed., *Scritti inediti*, 22.

26 "Per Aethiopes, a parte totum, omnes gentes significavit; eam eligens gentem … quae in finibus terrae est … [C]atholica Ecclesia praenuntiata est, non in aliqua parte terrarum futura … sed in universo mundo fructificando atque crescendo, usque ad ipsos Aethiopes": Augustine, *Enarratio in Psalmum*, in *Patrologia Latina*, vol. 36, col. 909, cited in Paul Kaplan, *The Rise of the Black Magus in Western Art*, Ann Arbor, 1985, 233.

27 "Neminem credimus remotiori ab orbis parte huc se conferre quam nos, qui non extremam modo orbis partem, sed paene extra ipsum orbem positam, incolimus Aethiopiam": Nogara, ed., *Scritti inediti*, 20.

28 "[N]ostra autem intermissio et elongatio a sede tua … processit … a praedecessorum tuorum Romanorum pontificum negligentia, cum nulla apud nostros homines sit memoria visitationis factae aut curae tot Christi ovium, quam pastorum quispiam ante te voluerit suscipere. Nam fert opinio nostra octogintos et, ut plures dicunt, nongentos effluxisse annos, ex quo nullus pontifex Romanus nos vel levi et unico verbo curavit salutare": *ibid.*, 21.

29 "In hoc itaque summa laus tua et nostri gaudii magnitudo consistit, quod tu solus ac primus imperatorem nostrum et nostram gentem catholicae fidei et tibi ipsi studeas unire": *ibid.*, 21.

30 Renato Lefevre, "Riflessi etiopici della cultura europea," *Annali lateranensi* 9 (1945), 378–81; Raymond Thomassy, "De Guillaume Fillastre considéré comme géographe," *Bulletin de la société géographique (de Paris)*, 2nd ser., 17 (1842), 144–55.

31 Poggio Bracciolini, *Historia de varietate fortunae*, Paris, 1723 (hereafter *De varietate*), 149. On Poggio's use of ancient authorities see Didier Marcotte, "Diodoro Siculo e Poggio Bracciolini, dall'India all'Ethiopia," *Sileno* 40 (2014), 135–51.

32 "Et cum eis responderetur quod tradit Ptolemaeus, caeli terrarumque dimensor peritissimus maximae apud Graecos nostrosque auctoritatis ... dixerunt ... nos falli": Nogara, ed., *Scritti inediti*, 22.

33 "Contendunt vero multi Romanae et Graecae historiae peritiores, haec ipsa, quae nulla ex parte aut scribant aut indicent scriptores, pro falsis commentitiisque habenda, et Ptolemaeum opponunt peritissimum orbis terrarum descriptorem ... Sed Ptolemaeum scimus pervidemusque multa sub arcto ignorasse, nostris hominibus nunc nobisque notissima, quando quidem ultra oceanum Britannicum, ubi mare et terram ponit incognitam, quinquaginta insulas christianis populis frequentatas adeo habemus notas ... Qui itaque minimam et primam Aethiopiae partem, quae continet Aegypto, solam cognovit Ptolemaeus, non potuit quae ultra sunt regiones et regna non ignorare": *ibid.*, 23–4.

34 "[S]ed velim mecum considerent [opponentes] quis est Albertus Sarthianensis, homo certe cum doctus religiosissimusque, tum etiam in rebus saeculi prudentissimus; qui, cum a viris magnae auctoritatis et famae patriarcha et abbate eadem audita referat, cum monachos deduxerit selectissimos": *ibid.*, 23.

35 "Oriri Nilum circa aequinoctialium plagam, in radicibus altissimorum montium ... testantur ... Aquam Nili, antequam aliquis immisceatur, dulcissimam, sapidissimamque esse ... dicunt ... Juxta Nili ortum, civitatem, ex qua orti essent, nomine Varvariam": Bracciolini, *De varietate*, 149.

36 Tedeschi, "L'Etiopia di Poggio," 347–9.

37 Wolbert Smidt, "Nile," in *EA*, vol. 3 (2007), 1178.

38 O. G. S. Crawford, *Ethiopian itineraries circa 1400–1524*, Cambridge, 1958, 93, 112–13, 165 (Täkkäze as Nile), 153, 179 (Abbay as Nile).

39 "Ultra Nili fontes, XV dierum spatio, regiones fertiles habitari, colique & in eis plurimas egregias urbes; extra ea loca mare dicit esse, quod tamen ipsi nunquam vidissent": Bracciolini, *De varietate*, 149. This "sea" is certainly Lake Ṭana, but the Gəʿəz word used by the delegates was doubtless *baḥr*, which can denote a sea, lake, or any large body of water. I thank Getatchew Haile for this observation.

40 Gianfranco Fiaccadori, "'India' as a name for Ethiopia," in *EA*, vol. 3 (2007), 145–7.

41 Ancient and European usage usually made "India" a synonym for Aksum/Ethiopia, and not a territory neighboring Ethiopia as the delegates suggested. One exception is the early-Christian writer Rufinus, who treated Ethiopia and India as separate but neighboring territories in the Horn of Africa, and whose work was a major source for a Gəʿəz text (the *Sälama* or Frumentius) known in fifteenth-century Ethiopia. His geographical distinction was effaced in the Gəʿəz translation, however, which therefore could not have transmitted the idea of "India" as a non-Ethiopian part of the Horn. See Philip Mayerson, "A Confusion of Indias: Asian India and African India in the Byzantine Sources," *Journal of the American Oriental Society* 133 (1993), 169–74, at 171; Françoise Thelamon, *Paiens et chrétiens au IVe siècle. L'apport de l'"Histoire ecclesiastique" de Rufin d'Aquilée*, Paris, 1981, 49–60; *The Book of the Saints of the Ethiopian Church*, trans. E. A. Wallis Budge, Hildesheim and New York, 1976, 669–70. I thank François-Xavier Fauvelle for the references and Yikunnoamlak Mezgebu for checking the Gəʿəz text on Frumentius.

42 For a fuller discussion and more extensive bibliography on the delegates' testimony regarding the Sabbath and Ethiopian marriage practices, see Samantha Kelly, "Ewosṭateans at the Council of Florence (1441): Diplomatic Implications between Ethiopia, Europe, Jerusalem and Cairo," *Afriques. Débats, méthodes et terrains d'histoire* (online), Varia, May 2016, at http://afriques.revues.org/1858.

43 Gianfranco Fiaccadori, "Ewosṭateans," in *EA*, vol. 2 (2005), 464–9; Taddese Tamrat, *Church and State in Ethiopia, 1270–1527*, Oxford, 1972, 209–31; Pierluigi Piovanelli, "Les controverses théologiques sous le roi Zarʾa Yaʿeqob (1434–68) et la mise en place du monophysitisme éthiopien," in Alain Le Boulluec, ed., *La controverse religieuse et ses formes*, Paris, 1995, 189–228; Robert Beylot, "La controverse sur le sabbat dans l'Église éthiopienne," in *La controverse religieuse*, 165–87; Marie-Laure Derat, *Le domaine des rois éthiopiens (1270–1527). Espace, pouvoir, et monachisme*, Paris, 2003, 170–1, 181–2.

44 "[C]um unica [sponsa] tantum etiam regi habere permittatur, ea mortua, alteram et tertiam nec plures habere permitti": Nogara, ed., *Scritti inediti*, 26.

45 Biondo praised the Ethiopians' marriage law as "melius quam nostri" because of its greater strictness: *ibid.*, 26.

46 Margaux Herman, "Les reines d'Éthiopie du XVe au XVIIe siècle. Épouses, mères de roi, 'mères du royaume'" (doctoral thesis, Université Paris I Panthéon-Sorbonne, 2012), 15–19, 96–103; Steven Kaplan and Marie-Laure Derat, "Zärʾa Yaʿǝqob," in *EA*, vol. 5 (2014), 146–50, at 149.

47 Fiaccadori, "Ewosṭateans," 468; Tamrat, *Church and State*, 116–18.

48 "Dominum Iesum, interrogati, dixerunt verum Deum et verum hominem fuisse, et in eo duas fuisse naturas": Nogara, ed., *Scritti inediti*, 25.

49 The early Ewosṭatean leader Absadi instructed his followers on the matter of Christ's nature in explicit contrast to Chalcedonian views. See Gianfranco Lusini, *Il "Gadla Absadi,"* vol. 104 of *Corpus Scriptorum Christianorum Orientalium, Scriptores Aethiopici*, Louvain, 1996, 32–3.

50 The debate at Chalcedon centered on the relationship of *physis* (nature) to *hypostasis* (person). Whereas the Council, and following it the Latin Church, held that Christ was one person in two natures, the anti-Chalcedonians held that in Christ *hypostasis* and *physis* were identical: Christ was two natures in one nature (*mia physis*). Theresia Hainthaler, "Monophysitism," in *EA*, vol. 3 (2007), 1006–9, at 1007.

51 "[Q]uaesitum est de Dioscoro et Eutyche quid sentirent. Qui, cum fassi fuerint se Dioscorum ut sanctum colere, dixerunt Eutychem ignorare. Tunc responderunt nostri, si ignoraretur Eutyches, non posse sciri Dioscorum, qui vel ea ratione damnatus sit, quod illius secutus errores …": Nogara, ed., *Scritti inediti*, 26.

52 Hainthaler, "Monophysitism," 1006–9.

53 "[D]ixerunt gignique eandem vel maiorem frumenti vini olei et frugum vim: ali boves equosque nostris maiores et, ut aestimant, fortiores; ferarum cicurumque easdem quas apud nos viderint et alias nobis incognitas species habere": Nogara, ed., *Scritti inediti*, 22.

54 Europeans were as yet unaware that the Gǝʿǝz Bible included the Book of Enoch and Jubilees, texts absent from the Vulgate and considered apocrypha by the Catholic Church.

55 The comments are all found on p. 25 in the edition of Nogara.

56 The phrase "worst heretics" belongs to Francesco Suriano, who described the Ethiopians in an account of his four years in Jerusalem written in 1485: Francesco Suriano, *Trattato di Terra Santa e dell'Oriente*, ed. Girolamo Golubovich, Milan, 1900, 77.

57 Paolo Marrassini, *Storia e leggenda dell'Etiopia tardoantica. Le iscrizioni reali aksumite*, Brescia, 2014; G. W. Bowersock, *The Throne of Adulis: Red Sea Wars on the Eve of Islam*, Oxford, 2013, 87–8, 102; Marie-Laure Derat, "Enquête sur les rois Zagwe, Royaume chrétien d'Éthiopie, XIe–XIIIe siècle" (unpublished manuscript, 2013), 87, 138–41.

58 Paolo Marrassini, "Kǝbrä Nägäśt," in *EA*, vol. 3 (2007), 364–8; an English translation of the text is E. A. Wallis Budge, trans., *The Queen of Sheba and her Only Son Menyelek*, London, 1922.

59 Antonella Brita, "Nine Saints," in *EA*, vol. 3 (2007), 1188–91; Stuart Munro-Hay, "Abǝha and Aṣbǝha," in *EA*, vol. 1 (2003), 45–6; Derat, *Le domaine des rois*, 155–6.

60 "Est etiam gloriae nostrae pars non minima regina Saba, quae excita fama sapientiae Salomonis ita se contulit Hierosolymam, quemadmodum nos qui, licet multo minores simus Saba regina, ad te venimus, qui es etiam plus quam Salomon; ex gente item nostra fuerunt Candacis regina et eunuchus, quos Philippus Domini apostolus baptizavit." Nogara, ed., *Scritti inediti*, 20–1.

61 "[U]tuntur … libris Salomonis, quos plures quam nos, immo omnes a Salomone scriptos, habere dixerunt": *ibid.*, 25.

62 These are the *Tägśaṣä Sälomon* and the *Mǝssale*: Steven Kaplan, "Solomon," in *EA*, vol. 4 (2010), 687–8.

63 Pietro Ghinzoni, "Un'ambasciata del Prete Gianni a Roma nel 1481," *Archivio storico lombardo* 16 (1889), 149; Weber, "Vrais et faux Éthiopiens," 108–11.

64 Ethiopian memory of the Himyarite wars was not, however, continuous from antiquity forward, but rather re-established from the thirteenth century via translation into Gǝʿǝz of the "Martydom of Arethas" and other texts. Alessandro Bausi, "The Massacre of Najran: The Ethiopic Sources," in Joëlle Beauchamp, Françoise Briquel-Chatonnet, and Christian Julien Robin, eds., *Juifs et chrétiens en Arabie aux V et VI siècles. Regards croisés sur les sources*, Paris, 2010, 241–54.

65 Marrassini, *Storia e leggende*, 141–78; Iwona Gajda, *Le royaume de Himyar à l'époque monothéiste*, Paris, 2009, 97–109; Bowersock, *Throne of Adulis*, 87–105.
66 "Hinc, cum nullos aestiment populos ultra cognitam Ptolemaeo Aethiopiam esse, quibus Zareiacob Constantini maximus ille opponatur exercitus, false esse arguunt quae de ipsius multitudine apparatibusque dicuntur": Nogara, ed., *Scritti inediti*, 24.
67 "[S]ecundo libro Paralipomenon habetur Zare Aethiopem cum decies centenis millibus venisse contra Asa Iudaeae regem, qui, licet de Iuda haberet trecenta millia et de Beniamin ducenta et octogenta, tantam timens Aethiopum multitudinem, suo diffisus exercitu, Dei auxilium implorabat": *ibid.*
68 Samantha Kelly, "The Curious Case of Ethiopic Chaldean: Fraud, Philology, and Cultural (Mis)Understanding in European Conceptions of Ethiopia," *Renaissance Quarterly* 68 (2015), 1227–64.

11

TRADITIONS OF BYZANTINE ASTROLABES IN RENAISSANCE EUROPE

Darin Hayton

History of science remains dominated by narratives of progress and innovation that relegate practices and knowledge that fail to advance our understanding of the world to the dustbin of history or, worse, to the domain of antiquarians. Such narratives often find reinforcement in histories of Renaissance or early modern Europe with their explicit and implicit forward-looking historiographies. A casualty of such scholarship is the textual output of the Byzantine Empire and especially Byzantine science. A recent assessment of Byzantine science illustrates the general problem:

> Despite efforts of pioneering scholars, Byzantine science remains both marginal to mainstream Byzantine history and poorly integrated into history of science surveys. Science in Byzantium is often portrayed as akin to a repository awaiting later use, whether by Islamic civilizations or Latin Europe. One recognizes at once, in lightly edited form, the familiar narrative structure that once framed early accounts of Latin and Islamic science, back when historians could more plausibly claim to know nothing about them.[1]

If we value Byzantine science only insofar as it contributed to the progress of modern science, then perhaps its dismissal is valid. Such a dismissal, however, assumes that scientific knowledge is and was meaningful only when it seems, retrospectively, to have contributed to our current understandings of the natural world. But if we consider the production of scientific knowledge as a culturally meaningful activity, Byzantine science becomes interesting because it lacked our comfortable criteria of, for example, technological innovation or increased numerical precision. And if we broaden our criteria, we can begin to recover a wide range of scholars in Renaissance Europe who struggled to locate, translate, and interpret Byzantine science and who contributed to a general conception of science in the period. I want to examine Nikephorus Gregoras and his text on the astrolabe as a case study that that draws our attention to the place of Byzantine science in Renaissance Europe.

Nikephorus Gregoras in the astronomy canon

In 1675 Edward Sherburne published an English translation of Marcus Manilius' *Astronomicon*. He appended to his translation a list of important astronomers from antiquity to the seventeenth century:

> I have therefore chosen for the better Information (and it may be Delectation) of the more Inquisitive and Ingenious Lovers of these studies, to collect a Catalogue of the most Eminent Astronomers, as well Ancient as Modern, their Works and Writings, according to the Succession of Time from the first Birth of Astronomy to this present, whereby the Curious Reader may perceive, when, how, and by whom it hath been improved to that Degree of Perfection wherein it now stands.[2]

Through his canon of astronomers Sherburne represented contemporary astronomy as the realization of a tradition that stretched back through classical antiquity to biblical times. He included religious figures such as Adam and Zoroaster alongside the mythical astronomers Atlas and Hermes. Historical astronomers like Anaxagoras and Eudoxus stand along with Roman emperors. Julius Caesar, he claimed, "left several not unlearned books on the motions of the Stars."[3] Sherburne sought to promote the study of astronomy in seventeenth-century Scotland and, in particular, to encourage his readers to support the new observatory at the University of St. Andrews.[4]

Sherburne was merely the latest author to construct a canon of astronomers. As his notes reveal, he compiled his list from more than a century of earlier authors who had assembled lists of great astronomers. He relied on Conrad Gesner's *Bibliotheca universalis* as well as Josias Simler's edition of Gesner's *Epitome*. He also turned to more specific bibliographies and histories of astronomy in his search for canonical figures. Giovanni Battista Riccioli's various catalogs of astronomers in his *Almagestum novum*, his *Astronomiae reformatae*, or his *Chronologiae reformatae* were favorite sources, as was Andreas Cellarius' *Harmonica macrocosmica*. The point is that Sherburne's canon of astronomers was not aberrant. It was, instead, a reflection of a broader set of ideas about the history of astronomy that were scattered through general and specific bibliographies circulating in the sixteenth and seventeenth centuries. The canonical figures listed in Sherburne's text, then, give us a sense of the broader contours of the history of astronomy as understood in that period.

Among the names so familiar to us, such as Hipparchus, Ptolemy, Firmicus, Abumasar, Alkindi, Sacrobosco, Regiomontanus, and Copernicus, is a thread of Byzantine astronomers that weaves from the sixth to the fifteenth century. Johannes Philoponus, we read, "deserves here to be recorded for his Comment *in Astrolabium planum, sive de usu Astrolabio*, written in *Greek*, yet extant in New College, *Oxford*, and (as Simler in *Bibl. Gesner.* adds) in the *French King's Library*."[5]

A dozen or so Greek scholars and astronomers, including Michael Psellos, Johannes Kamateros, Nikephorus Gregoras, and George Plethon, populate Sherburne's canon. Some, such as Theodore Meliteniotes, deserved a place in the canon because they wrote learned commentaries on Ptolemy: others, such as George Chrysokokkes, composed original texts on astronomy. Of Gregoras, Sherburne noted:

> Nicephorus Gregoras, writ *De astrolabio*, extant in the King's Library at St. James's. Gesner mentions another Piece of his, *De Calumniatoribus Astronomiae & De Astronomia*.

Andreas Cellarius, in *Praeloquio Harmon. Macrocosm.* reports that in the 27th year of his Age he applied himself to *Andronicus Palaeologus*, Emperor of *Constantinople*, offering to him Reasons for the Emendation of the *Roman* Calendar.[6]

Gregoras and the other Byzantine astronomers appear in Sherburne's "Catalogue of most eminent astronomers" less for the content of their work and more because of the social and intellectual ideals at play in Renaissance Europe, ideals that stretched back to the late fifteenth century. For sixteenth-century scholars, Byzantium represented a font of scientific knowledge and information distinct from classical Greek sources. Renaissance thinkers sought, read, translated, and published Byzantine texts because they offered a linguistically pure tradition and because they provided a means to assert and reinforce their own identity.

Despite Sherburne's passing reference to an extant copy of Gregoras' *De astrolabio* in the King's Library at St. James', his reliance on existing bibliographies and canonical lists suggests that he did not know Gregoras' work except through others' references to it.[7] Sherburne's sources slowly construct an image of Gregoras by attributing to him more and increasingly specific texts. In 1545 Conrad Gesner had already identified Gregoras' work as worthy of inclusion in his *Bibliotheca universalis*. He lists Gregoras' historical work, his orations, and his commentary on Synesius. He also mentioned a commentary on Aristotle supposedly written by Gregoras, but then dismissed it as unlikely because he has not been able to find any such work: "But I have found nothing written on Aristotle by any author by this name, but by a Nicephorus Blemmida."[8] Gesner mentioned two astronomical texts by Gregoras, a "De illis qui calumniantur astronomiam" and "Ad eundem adhortatoria de astronomia."[9] Ten years later, when Josias Simler produced the *Epitome* of Gesner's work, he truncated the entry on Gregoras but still included the two astronomical works.[10]

In books on astronomy published in the middle of the seventeenth century Sherburne found scattered references to Gregoras' contributions to the development and spread of astronomy. Sherburne mined Giovanni Battista Riccioli's various astronomical works. In 1669 this Jesuit astronomer had published his *Chronologiae reformatae* in which he cited Gregoras' work on chronology, which often relied on astronomy to correlate reigns and other significant events with celestial events.[11] A few years earlier, when Andreas Cellarius had composed his magisterial *Harmonia cosmographica*, he compiled his own history of astronomy, replete with its cast of famous astronomers. Cellarius' explicit goal in offering his canon was to provide a glorification of the Republic of Letters, which was first found within the borders of Greece and then migrated to Italy. Later, after the collapse of the Roman Empire, it was finally resurrected and spread throughout Europe, flourishing in Germany, France, and Italy.[12]

Like Sherburne, Cellarius crafted a history of astronomy that established simultaneously its antiquity and its progress to his present. He grounded modern astronomy in its celebrated practitioners of the past. In the prose history of astronomy he wrote for his *Harmonia cosmographica*, Cellarius implicitly praised Gregoras for having advanced astronomy at Emperor Andronicus' court in Constantinople through advising the emperor on the question of calendar reform.[13]

By the middle of the seventeenth century, a general image of Gregoras the astronomer had come to occupy a space in the canon of astronomers. Ptolemaic Jesuits in Rome, Protestant cartographers in the Low Countries, and naturalists in Switzerland, as well as poet-dilettantes in England, among others, cited Gregoras. Canons create and maintain the identity of particular groups by providing members with a shared set of cultural and intellectual values and useful markers of inclusion and exclusion. In Renaissance Europe a culture of astronomy was built on a foundation of Byzantine astronomers and their works. Citing Byzantine astronomical texts indicated an author's eligibility for and membership in that culture of letters and aided in its construction. In this context, familiarity with distinctly Byzantine forms of knowledge became an important marker.

Giorgio Valla and Byzantine scientific texts

Another entry in Sherburne's list points to how Gregoras came to occupy a place in the canon: the fifteenth-century Italian humanist and university professor Giorgio Valla had identified Gregoras and had celebrated his work. Valla had, according to Sherburne, composed a work on astrology and another on using astrolabes. Valla had also translated various works from Greek into Latin, including works by Proclus and Cleomedes.[14] Through the 1480s and 1490s Valla had translated and published a number of Greek scientific texts, including texts on astrology and astronomy, logic, mathematics, medicine, and music.[15] In 1498 he published his *Collectio*, a compendium of two dozen translations of various ancient and Byzantine scientific texts, and one Arabic work. To some of these he added his own interpretation and explanation. About the time he published his *Collectio*, Valla boasted that through his efforts he had recovered wrongly neglected work from the most outstanding amongst the Greek authors.[16] Nicephorus Gregoras and his text on the astrolabe was one of the outstanding but neglected Greek authors.

By the 1490s Valla had amassed an impressive collection of Greek codices containing classical and Byzantine manuscripts, including many scientific texts.[17] Among them was a codex that included two anonymous texts on the astrolabe, which Valla suspected had been written by Gregoras and Philoponus, or perhaps Proclus.[18] By the time he published his translations, he had determined that Gregoras and Proclus were the authors of these two short texts. They appeared as "Nicephorus de Astrolabo" and "Proclus de Astrolabo," the fifth and sixth texts in his *Collectio*.

In translating Gregoras' work Valla followed both the structure and the language of the original closely. He offered little explanation or elaboration and did nothing to update Gregoras' text. The first pages offer only a small assortment of loosely related uses, including instructions on how to find the latitude of a place, the time of day, the time of sunset and sunrise, ruling planets, and the time after nightfall.[19] Valla's Greek original and his translation then shift abruptly to discuss the various lines engraved on the astrolabe's plates, such as the hour lines, the tropics of Capricorn and Cancer, and the stars on the rete (i.e., map of bright stars that rotates on the top of the astrolabe).[20] When Gregoras composed his text it resembled in content and form much older Greek texts on astrolabes. Valla was not the only scholar to think Gregoras' text might, in fact, be by Philoponus.[21] It was no accident that Gregoras' text looked like a sixth-century text. Gregoras himself seems to have eschewed a millennium's worth of development on the astrolabe, its design, and its uses, in an effort to compose a work that celebrated Greek contributions to the instrument.

In addition to the content of the text, Valla also stayed close to the illustrations in his manuscript, simply translating the words on the illustrations, though sometimes without apparently understanding how the label identified a particular part of the instrument.[22] His adherence to Gregoras' illustrations is most notable in the illustration of the rete. The illustration in his Greek manuscript included merely six stars, far fewer than any useful astrolabe would have contained. Moreover, those six stars were indicated by simple, antiquated star pointers that had ceased to be used on astrolabes centuries before Valla's translation.[23] Nevertheless, Valla reproduced the diagram without making any revisions. He labeled only the star, *cor leonis*, which was also the only star clearly labeled in his manuscript. He misleadingly labeled the edges of the rete, the east and west cardinal points, "polus" and "boreus," whereas the diagram in his manuscript correctly labeled the center of the rete "βόρευς πόλυς" (north pole).[24]

Like Gregoras' original, Valla's translation was out of date when he published it. Valla's preference for Gregoras' text reflects his commitment to Greek scientific knowledge. He must have known of the much more sophisticated texts on astrolabes in circulation by his time. Manuals on constructing and using astrolabes had undergone considerable development over the previous few centuries, especially from scholars writing in Arabic. These Arabic texts, sometimes stretching to a hundred pages or more, examined in considerable detail the construction of the instrument and provided canons for every possible use of an astrolabe. As early as the twelfth century these texts were being translated into Latin and soon found a place in the university curriculum throughout Europe, where they underwent further development. In the fourteenth century Chaucer translated into English a Latin version of Messahalla's text on the astrolabe, probably the most commonly used text on the astrolabe throughout the Middle Ages and Renaissance. Chaucer claimed to give the text to his young son as he went off to Oxford to study.[25]

In the late fifteenth century, Gregoras' text did not contribute materially to the construction or use of astrolabes, as Valla surely recognized. His decision to translate and publish it must, therefore, be grounded on something besides innovation. Instead, the value of Gregoras' text must rest on a balance of cultural identity and content. Valla seemed to appreciate Byzantine science because it was linked to his understanding of language's role in the formation of knowledge. Similarly, he preferred original Greek medical texts because they had not been degraded through the process of translation into Arabic and then Latin. Consequently, he preferred Byzantine medical texts even when they were demonstrably less advanced than Latin translations of Arabic texts then circulating.[26] The same system of values seems to have prompted Valla to translate and publish Gregoras' text.

In 1501, shortly after Valla died, his massive *De expetendis et fugiendis rebus opus* appeared. He had composed more than a dozen works on topics ranging from arithmetic, geometry, and music to grammar, poetry, and moral philosophy. It also included a text on astrology that included a section on the construction and use of the astrolabe.[27] Although Valla had produced an expanded and more sophisticated text, he still praised Gregoras along with Ammonius, Proclus, and Philoponus, all Byzantine authors, for their contributions to the development of the astrolabe.[28] Like Gregoras before him, Valla seems to eschew Arabic authors. Also notably absent are other recent authors, either Greek or Latin. Although Valla had expanded his work on astrolabes, echoes of his translation reverberate through his new text. In at least one place, "On the latitude of any climate or region," he quotes his own translation.[29]

Valla's translation in the sixteenth century

Valla's list of eminent Byzantine scholars who wrote on the construction and use of the astrolabe found an eager audience in Johannes Stöffler, the German astrologer, instrument maker, and professor of mathematics at Tübingen. In 1513 Stöffler published his *Elucidatio fabricae ususque astrolabii*. Over the next century, Stöffler's work went through more than a dozen editions in Latin, French, and German, and became the standard work on the construction and use of astrolabes. In the opening pages, Stöffler echoed Valla in singling out Ammonius, Proclus, Philoponus, and Gregoras, along with Ptolemy for praise for their works on astrolabes.[30] When he cited Gregoras in the body of his work, he praised Gregoras' solution to a problem and then used it as an opportunity to present a more general approach to that particular operation. So, for example, he cited Gregoras in his proposition on finding the latitude of any location. He commended Gregoras' method but then worried that it was too limited because it relied on an event that occurred only twice a year.[31] Stöffler then presented a method that could be used to determine the latitude any day of the year.[32] Stöffler's *Elucidatio* introduced Gregoras to a much wider readership. Stöffler was, however, just one of various sixteenth-century authors who elevated Gregoras to a position of authority.

Another scholar who relied on and extended Gregoras' authority was Juan Martinez Población. Población first published his *De usu astrolabi compendium* in 1519 in Paris.[33] Unlike Stöffler, Población said little about the construction of an astrolabe and concentrated instead on how to use one. Población identified Gregoras as a source for a number of his operations throughout the text, often citing which proposition in Gregoras' text treated similar operations. So, when explaining how to find the seasonal hours, Población pointed out to his reader that Gregoras covered this method in his fourth proposition in his text on the astrolabe.[34] Readers of Población's *De usu astrolabi* could follow his references to Gregoras' text simply by turning to the back of the book, where Población had reprinted the first half of Valla's translation, that is, the seven propositions that cover using an astrolabe.[35] Over the next thirty years Población's text was reprinted at least five times.[36] By the late seventeenth century, Población's fame was linked to his *De usu astrolabi* and, in that way, to Gregoras' text on the astrolabe.[37]

Echoes of Byzantine science

Renaissance scholars' interest in Byzantine science was not confined to astrolabes and astronomy. Valla's translations of medical texts, such as his translation of Michael Psellos' *De victu humano*, found eager readers in the sixteenth century. Psellos' *De victu* along with Valla's translation of Rhazes' text on epidemics was reprinted in 1529.[38] Psellos' text on demons, his *De daemonibus*, offers another example. It was originally translated into Latin by Marsilio Ficino and published in 1495. It enjoyed a wide readership for nearly two centuries across Renaissance Europe. Scholars as diverse as Heinrich Cornelius Agrippa, Pierre de Ronsard, the *Pléiade* poet, Ben Johnson and John Milton, and Johann Weyer all read and incorporated Psellos' work into their own texts. The most detailed commentary and analysis of Psellos' work occurred in Girolamo Cardano's *De rerum variete*. Even as late as the 1670s the Cambridge Neoplatonist Ralph Cudworth considered Psellos' work an important source on demons.[39]

When we scratch the surface of Renaissance science, we find tendrils of Byzantine knowledge reaching into almost every corner. Valla and his contemporaries sought Byzantine Greek scientific knowledge because it had not been adulterated by Arabic translations and commentaries, even when that Byzantine knowledge was demonstrably less advanced than the Latin translations of Islamic texts. Byzantine science offered a linguistically pure knowledge, one that had not been corrupted by translations through Syriac and Arabic, and into medieval Latin. Such transmission risked introducing errors through linguistic confusion and corruption.[40] Knowledge of Greek allowed scholars to distinguish between medieval accretions and the Greek foundations on which those accretions were based. In this context, familiarity with Byzantine knowledge became evidence of intellectual authority and a mechanism for those scholars to assert and reinforce their own identity. For Valla and his contemporaries, Byzantine Greek texts had values inhering in them precisely because they were identified as Byzantine.

Valla's elevation of Byzantine materials reflected his strategic understanding of his cultural milieu. He and other scholars eagerly sought, translated, printed, and read Byzantine scientific texts in such diverse disciplines as astrology and astronomy, botany, demonology, mathematics, medicine, and oracles.[41] Knowledge of distinctly Byzantine forms of science became a characteristic of early modern scientific canons. This process of recovering Byzantine scientific texts reveals that in Renaissance Europe what might look to us as philology and antiquarianism were not distinct from valid scientific knowledge.

Notes

1 David C. Lindberg and Michael Shank, "Introduction," in *The Cambridge History of Science*, vol. 2, *Medieval Science*, ed. David C. Lindberg and Michael Shank, Cambridge: Cambridge University Press, 2013, 25. Anne Tihon corroborates Lindberg's opinion in her contribution to the new Cambridge volume, where she writes: "we can say that the scientific efforts of Byzantium have been underestimated by modern historians of science." Anne Tihon, "Science in the Byzantine Empire," *ibid.*, 206.

2 Edward Sherburne, *The Sphere of Marcus Manilius Made an English Poem: With Annotations and an Astronomical Appendix*, London: Nathanael Brooke, 1675, 5.

3 *Ibid.*, 15.

4 At the end of his catalog, Sherburne thanks donors to the observatory who by "Heroick Example we hope may animate those of like Condition and Abilities in this Nation to incourage the promoting of the same Laudible Design amongst us." *Ibid.*, 126.

5 *Ibid.*, 25.

6 *Ibid.*, 37.

7 Sherburne's references to manuscripts are tantalizing. In some cases he identifies copies of texts that are still extant, as is the case with his reference to Philoponus' text on the astrolabe that survives in the New College Library, Oxford. However, I have not been able to identify the copy of Gregoras' text in the "King's Library at St. James."

8 "Ego nihil invenio in Aristotleem ab aliquo huius nominis scriptum, sed Nicephoruo Blemmida." Conrad Gesner, *Bibliotheca vniuersalis, siue catalogus omnium scriptorum locupletissimus: in tribus linguis, Latina, Graeca, & Hebraica*, Tigurum: Christophorus Froschauer, 1545, 516v. Blemmida in this quotation is Nikephorus Blemmydes, a thirteenth-century Byzantine scholar who wrote a work on logic, an epitome of physics, and various other literary texts.

9 *Ibid.*

10 Conrad Gesner and Josias Simmler, *Epitome bibliothecae Conradi Gesneri*, Tigurum: Christophorus Froschauer, 1555, 134v–135r.

11 Giovanni Battista Riccioli, *Chronologiae reformatae et ad certas conclusiones redactae*, Bologna: Dominicus Barberius, 1669, 211 and *passim*. On Riccioli, see the excellent study by Christopher M. Graney, *Setting Aside All Authority. Giovanni Battista Riccioli and the Science against Copernicus in the Age of Galileo*, Notre Dame, IN: University of Notre Dame Press, 2015.

12 "Atque hic est usque ad hæc nostra tempora decursus Reipublicae Literariae, quae primum exiguis Graeciae limitibus coërcita, inde in Italiam migrans, posteà cum Imperio Romano collapsa, tandem resurrexit, & per totam Europam se diffundens in Germania, Gallia, & Italia adeò effloruit." Andreas Cellarius, *Harmonia macrocosmica seu atlas universalis et novus, totius universi creati cosmographiam generalem, et novam exhibens*, Amsterdam: Johannes Janssonius, 1661, 125.

13 *Ibid.*, 115.

14 Sherburne, *The Sphere of Marcus Manilius*, 50.

15 *Giogrio Valla: tra scienza e sapienza* includes a partial bibliography of Valla's work. See Gianna Gardenal, Patrizia Landucci Ruffo, and Cesare Vasoli, *Giorgio Valla: tra scienza e sapienza*, Florence: Olschki, 1981, 93–6.

16 In a letter to Johannes Maria Ruzinentus, Valla wrote: "Recondita siquidem et abstrusa de Graecis eminentissimis sumpta autoribus ibi spectaveris …" J. L. Heiberg, *Beiträge zur Geschichte Georg Vallas und Seiner Bibliothek*, Leipzig: Otto Harrassowitz, 1896, 90.

17 See Giovanni Mercati, "L'inventario dei codici greci Pio trovati dopo la morte del Card. Rodolfo nel 1564," *Studi e testi* 75 (1938), 223–33.

18 The first folio of the codex includes a note: "De usu Astrolabi Autores duo Anonymi puto esse Nicephori et Philoponi vel Procli" Nicephorus Gregoras, "Τοῦ Γρηγορᾶ Κυροῦ Νικηφόρου Τοῦ Φιλοσόφου Πόνημα Περὶ Κατασκευῆς Καὶ Γενέσεως Ἀστρολάβου," Bibliotheca Estense, Modena, fol. 1v.

19 Giorgio Valla, *Collectio*, Venice: Simon Bevilaqua, 1498, d8r–e1v.

20 Early astrolabes had fifteen to twenty bright stars on the rete. Later astrolabes might include as many as forty stars.

21 Even modern bibliographers occasionally catalog Gregoras' text as a Philoponus text.

22 Not all of Gregoras' texts are illustrated, but the copy that Valla had did contain three illustrations: one side of a tympan or plate; one set of circles showing the tropics, the celestial equator, and the ecliptic; one showing the rete or star map.

23 The one surviving Byzantine astrolabe, from the eleventh century, has similar, simple star pointers that were commonly used on astrolabes as early as the late ninth century. Surviving astrolabes suggest that the simple star pointer had been replaced by the eleventh or twelfth century. Nevertheless, diagrams of retes in later copies of Gregoras' text all show the same, antiquated star pointer.

24 The two diagrams are found in Gregoras, "Τοῦ Γρηγορᾶ Κυροῦ Νικηφόρου," fol. 21v; Valla, *Collectio*, fol. 184v. The other two diagrams in Valla's translation are nearly identical to those in his copy of Gregoras' text.

25 Geoffrey Chaucer, *A Treatise on the Astrolabe*, ed. Sigmund Eisner, Norman, OK: University of Oklahoma Press, 2002. A family of astrolabes is generally called "Chaucer astrolabes" because they resemble the diagrams in manuscripts of Chaucer's text. For a critical evaluation of these instruments, see Catherine Eagleton, "'Chaucer's Own Astrolabe': Text, Image and Object," *Studies in History and Philosophy of Science* 38 (2007), 303–26.

26 Vivian Nutton, "'Prisci Dissectionum Professores': Greek Texts and Renaissance Anatomists," in *The Uses of Greek and Latin: Historical Essays*, ed. A. C. Dionisotti, Anthony Grafton, and Jill Kraye, London: The Warburg Institute, 1988, 111–26.

27 Sherburne referred to this text when he mentioned Valla.

28 Giorgio Valla, *De expetendis et fugiendis rebus opus*, Venice: Manutius, 1501, gg2r.

29 Valla, *Collectio*, d8v; Valla, *De Expetendis Et Fugiendis Rebus Opus*, gg6r.

30 Unlike Valla, Stöffler included three late medieval Latin authors. Johannes Stöffler, *Elucidatio fabricae ususque astrolabii. A Ioanne Stoflerino iustingensi viro germano: atque totius spherice doctissimo nuper ingeniose concinnata atque in lucem edita* (1513), 1r. In the body of his text, Stöffler cites other authors, including medieval Arabic and Latin authors.

31 Gregoras' solution to finding the latitude of any location depended on finding the elevation of the sun at its zenith when the sun entered Aries or Libra. This operation was the second one in Valla's translation of Gregoras' text. Valla reproduced it nearly verbatim in his own text on the astrolabe in his *De expetendis et fugiendis rebus opus*.

32 Stöffler, *Elucidatio fabricae ususque astrolabii*, 45r.

33 We know little about Población. He had previously published a text on critical days and another on arithmetic. His text on the astrolabe, however, seems to have been his most successful.

34 Johannes Martinus Pobalción, *De usu astrolabi. Compendium, schematibus commodissimis illustratum*, Paris: Joannes Barbaeus, 1546, 18r.

35 He was uninterested in constructing astrolabes and so ignored the latter portion of Gregoras' text. Población, *De usu astrolabi*, 59r–64r. Población had also reprinted Valla's translation of a text on the astrolabe attributed to Proclus.

36 Población's *De usu astrolabi* was reprinted almost immediately in 1520 and then at least four more times by 1560.

37 Sherburne identified Población as the author who "put forth a small Treatise entituled [*sic*] *Compendium de Usu Astrolabii Schematibus commodissimis illustratum.*" Sherburne, *The Sphere of Marcus Manilius*, 216.

38 Michael Psellos, *Pselli De victus ratione ad Constantium imperatorem II. Rhazae, Cognomento experimentatoris, De pestilentia liber*, Basel: Andreæ Cratandri, 1529.

39 On the widespread reading and use of Psellos' *De daemonibus* in Renaissance Europe, see Darin Hayton, "Michael Psellos' *De Daemonibus* in the Renaissance," in *Reading Michael Psellos*, ed. Charles Barber and David Jenkins, Leiden: Brill, 2006, 193–215. While most modern scholars doubt the authenticity of this text, such doubts were absent in Renaissance Europe. On Psellos' authorship, see: Paul Gautier, "Le *De daemonibus* du pseudo-Psellos" *Revue des études Byzantines* 38 (1980), 105–94; Paul Gautier, "Pseudo-Psellos: Graecorum opiniones de daemonibus," *Revue des études Byzantine* 46 (1988), 85–107; Mariarosa Cortesi and Enrico V. Maltese, "Per la fortuna della demonologia pselliana in ambiente umanistico," in *Dotti bizantini e libri greci nell'Italia del secolo xv*, ed. Mariarosa Cortesi and Enrico V. Maltese, Naples: M. D'Auria Editore, 1992, 129–92, and Enrico V. Maltese, "'Natura daemonum … habet corpus et versatur circa corpora': una lezione di demonologia dal medioevo greco," in *Il demonio e i suoi comlici. Dottrine e credenze demologiche nella Tarda Antichità*, ed. Salvatore Pricoco, Messina: Rubbettino, 1995, 265–84.

40 Vivian Nutton has argued a similar point for medicine. Valla seems to have expressed a similar preference for Byzantine astronomical knowledge. See Nutton, "Prisci Dissectionum Professores."

41 Even such luminaries as Copernicus read and quoted Valla's translations of Byzantine texts. See Edward Rosen, "Nicholas Copernicus and Giorgio Valla," *Physis* 23 (1981), 449–57.

12

READING MACHIAVELLI IN SIXTEENTH-CENTURY FLORENCE

Ann E. Moyer

In 1577 the Florentine physician Paolo Mini, then resident in Lyon, took up his pen against a wave of anti-Florentine criticism. The massacre of St. Bartholomew's Day was being blamed on the influence of Florentines, both the queen mother, Catherine de Medici, and even more on Niccolò Machiavelli. The Huguenot author Innocent Gentillet had published the previous year his *Discours contre Machievel*; his was hardly the sole voice.[1] Florentines stood accused collectively of immorality and atheism. Lyon's substantial Florentine community included a number of anti-Medici exiles, to whom the charges must have seemed particularly unfair. Mini quickly published his *Difesa della città di Firenze, et de i Fiorentini*.[2] In it, he argued at some length not only that Florence was certainly not a nest of atheists, but that Florentines were not actually reading Machiavelli at all because he was on the Index.

Index or not, readers elsewhere were reading Machiavelli, and especially the *Prince*. The reception of Machiavelli's work across Europe in the decades after his death has received its fair share of scholarly attention in recent years.[3] But what about his readership and image in his native city as these colorful claims developed and spread? Europeans might know Machiavelli only by his writings or by reputation; yet in Florence he had been very much a real person and a noted citizen. Florentines had known him as a career diplomat and member of the chancery, one of many ousted by the new Medici government of 1512, who had worked gradually to regain political standing as he wrote the texts for which he is now so famous. Well before the development of Machiavelli's outsize image and reputation, his fellow citizens read his works and composed their own on related topics. As the years after his death stretched to decades, his name remained current in the city and his descendants continued to live there.

Perhaps it is not surprising that the readings of Machiavelli in Florence came to vary in some distinct ways from the image taking shape across the rest of the continent. Florentines shared the general fascination with the *Prince*, especially in the years before and after Machiavelli's death. In the decades that followed, it continued to find some detractors.[4] Yet engagement with the *Prince* was not at the heart of their interest in his writings; other works gained and kept a greater role. The *Florentine Histories*, the *Discourses*, and even the *Art of War* figured prominently for them, though some readers differed with his arguments about religion and morality. They also valued his contributions as a man of letters: the author of comedies, a respected stylist, and a devoted promoter of the vernacular language. Subsequently

192

they experienced a collective blow when Machiavelli's name, along with those of a number of other prominent Florentine authors, appeared on the Index of Forbidden Books. Thus fifty years after Machiavelli's death, Paolo Mini and other Florentines were dismayed not only at being depicted collectively in ways they found unfair and inaccurate, but also at finding depictions of Machiavelli significantly different from his reputation in Florence itself, and certainly much more one-dimensional. Consistent with his claim that Florentines respected the limitations of the Index, Mini went on to defend his fellow citizens without further discussion of the banned author. In fact, Machiavelli continued to find Florentine readers during these years as well.

A closer look at these Florentine readers and writers is not only instructive in its own terms, but also sharpens our understanding of Machiavelli's image among other early modern Europeans. Francesco Guicciardini, Filippo Nerli, Benedetto Varchi, Jacopo Nardi, Donato Giannotti, and others wrote on a range of related topics. Although many of them are not household names to anglophone readers, they shared a reading audience with Machiavelli across Europe and beyond through the eighteenth century. Remigio Nannini's *Considerazioni civili*, for example, circulated in both French and English as well as its original Italian.[5] Several major works by these sixteenth-century Florentines were first published outside of Italy in the eighteenth century, both separately and as part of large collections, by editors and publishers who assumed they would find an interested audience.[6] Some of these had been circulating in manuscript during the intervening years, among them Varchi's history. Others, such as that of Bernardo Segni, had been previously unknown.

The far-flung readership of these authors may be exemplified by American president John Adams. Adams read and wrote extensively on history, politics, and society, and owned works by Giovanni Battista Adriani, Leonardo Bruni, Domenico Buoninsegni, Francesco Guicciardini, and Giovanni and Matteo Villani as well as Machiavelli.[7] In *A Defence of the Constitutions of Government of the United States of America* he made extensive use of Nerli, Segni, Nardi, and Varchi as well as Machiavelli and Guicciardini.[8] To many later readers, as for Adams, these Florentine authors maintained an identity and relevance as a scholarly circle connected not only by the city that was the focus of their narratives, but also by common interests and questions.

Especially prominent was the interest in history, above all modern history and the history of their city, along with a historically informed approach to the study of society and politics. A number shared Machiavelli's interest in the behavior of social groups, particularly the roles and natures of factions and the connection between the behaviors of such groups and the morality of individual historical actors. A few employed comparative approaches that combined a discussion of current events with historical ones, as Machiavelli did in his *Discourses*. Remigio Nannini carried such modeling to an extreme in a work based very clearly on that of Machiavelli. Cosimo Bartoli and Scipione Ammirato also composed works modeled on the *Discourses*. Given these interests, it is not surprising that Florentines made more use of the *Discourses* and *Florentine Histories*, and even of the *Art of War*, than they did of the *Prince*.

Florentines also saw Machiavelli as a Florentine man of letters as well as a citizen. People read and performed his plays, and ornamented their own works with references and quotations from his literary writings. Not only was Machiavelli held in esteem as a stylist, but his opinions on literary and spoken vernacular were cited and repeated. His heirs put into manuscript circulation the *Dialogue on the Florentine Language*. These facets of Machiavelli's local image were perhaps those farthest from the caricature that Mini encountered, and probably least accessible to those who read Machiavelli elsewhere and in translation.

I

Florentine intellectual life in Machiavelli's era is much better understood now than just a few decades ago. The deaths of such luminaries as Pico della Mirandola, Angelo Poliziano, and Marsilio Ficino in the last decade of the fifteenth century once seemed to leave something of a void, and the rapid pace of political change in the city contributed to a difficulty in identifying intellectual centers. Peter Godman, Alison Brown, Lorenzo Polizzotto, Jonathan Davies, and many others have added considerably to the work begun by Felix Gilbert.[9] Scholarship on Machiavelli's writings continues at a rapid pace, and Robert Black, Corrado Vivanti, and others have returned to his biography.[10]

Machiavelli composed his works during the years of Medici control of the city between 1512 and 1527, during which time he was kept from participation in the city's government. His death in his late fifties after a brief illness was portrayed among his fellow citizens as untimely, not least because he left so much unfinished writing; his political and historical writings except the *Art of War* (Florence, 1521) remained in manuscript in various stages of completion. Some had circulated in manuscript during his lifetime.[11] *The Prince* (composed 1513–14) was already well known among Florentines.[12] Godman suggests that others had kept it out of print after its composition: first Marcello Virgilio Adriani in his role as censor; later because Giulio de' Medici allowed Agostino Nifo, then professor of philosophy at Pisa, to use it as the basis for his own *De regnandi peritia* (1523), for presentation to the newly elected Charles V.[13] Nifo's work, not published again until 1645,[14] appears in fact not to have competed seriously with writings of Machiavelli. Brian Richardson suggests, conversely, that Machiavelli had preferred manuscript circulation for both the *Prince* and *Discorsi*.[15] In any case, the longer works remained unfinished at his death.

Giambattista Busini's later memories of Machiavelli (1550) focused on the local reputation caused by the *Prince* in his late years:

> Everyone despised him because of the *Prince*: to the rich it seemed that the *Prince* was a document to teach the duke to take away all their goods; to the poor all their liberty. To the Piagnoni it seemed he was a heretic; to the good, dishonorable; to the bad, he seemed either more so or more capable than they; so everybody disliked him.[16]

Busini also noted that Machiavelli had remained a lover of liberty to the end, and regretted his association with Giulio de' Medici (Clement VII). He claimed further that Machiavelli's character suffered late in life, from greed, but most of his words about Machiavelli's local unpopularity blame not his character but the local circulation of his writings, the *Prince* in particular.

Within a few years of Machiavelli's death, his unpublished works, finished or not, were prepared for the press.[17] Publication of the *Discourses*, the *Prince*, and the *Florentine Histories* began in Rome in 1531–32, followed immediately by Florentine editions, and already in 1532 the *Discourses* were picked up by presses in Venice, the heart of the print industry.[18] By mid-century, the *Discourses* had gone through some eleven editions and the *Florentine Histories* seven, two of them Florentine in each case. At least eight editions of Machiavelli's collected works came out thereafter, until his inclusion on the Index of 1559 disrupted further production. Some nineteen editions of the *Prince* were produced in Italy during these years, eight of them by 1540. A closely related work also did well, a vernacular translation by Jacopo

Nardi of the first ten books of Livy that had been the basis of the *Discourses*. First published by Giunti in Venice, 1540, it was reissued numerous times throughout the century.[19]

Most editions are unadorned versions clearly intended for use rather than collection, with little beyond the author's original dedications in the way of paratext to help assess reception. The first Florentine edition of the *Florentine Histories* includes a one-page dedication by Bernardo Giunta to Duke Alessandro de' Medici, dated March 1532; it precedes Machiavelli's own dedication to Clement VII (Giulio de' Medici) and offers a brief praise of the author. He laments that God had willed death to snatch him away too soon, leaving his works to be brought out posthumously. Giunta avoids the potential problem of praising such a republican figure in Alessandro's Florence by emphasizing instead Machiavelli's Medici connections. Alessandro and Clement shared the distinguished ancestors Cosimo and Lorenzo, and Giunta notes that Machiavelli had discussed in depth their great deeds. In an allusion to the end of the *Prince*, Giunta expresses the wish that someday poor and mistreated Italy might take up again its ancient valor. Giunta thus portrays Machiavelli as an illustrious Florentine, a patriot and supporter of Italian renewal at the end of the wars, as well as an author who had glorified the Medici name.

With so many editions and thus so many readers, it is safe to say that most of Machiavelli's Florentine readers were exactly that. They were not writers and left no record of their opinions. After his works were placed on the Index many Florentine owners seem nonetheless to have kept their copies, given the large number that survive. Yet they would have been understandably wary of leaving new marks of ownership or readership or keeping copies that already held such marks; thus surviving volumes offer fewer insights into reading habits and reactions than do other less controversial books. Authors who published books before that date, or whose works were published much later, had no reason not to mention him or make use of his works. A number of Florentine publications from the 1530s through the 1550s thus refer to Machiavelli. Some are simply brief allusions. For example, Bernardo Segni mentioned the *Prince* in his translations of Aristotle's *Politics* and *Ethics* in 1549 and 1550, as Victoria Kahn has noted.[20]

More substantial references appeared especially in historical writings. Florentines were avid readers as well as writers of history both before and after Machiavelli's lifetime.[21] Most wrote not with public commissions but as private citizens, in a tradition that dated back to the fourteenth-century banker Giovanni Villani, and before. Many Florentines living at the time of the Italian wars recognized it as an era of great significance that merited recording for posterity. A number of personal jottings developed into full-fledged diaries or chronicles. Some were eventually published; others remained in manuscript until recently. Domenico Moreni identified a number of them in the early nineteenth century; Felix Gilbert and Eric Cochrane later identified more. More than a dozen Florentine historical accounts survive from the late fifteenth century through the first years of the sixteenth.[22]

Machiavelli's own historical writings bridged the years between these writers and those of the ducal era. So too did those of Francesco Guicciardini and of several others. Francesco Vettori composed a historical summary of the years 1511–27.[23] A diary kept by Francesco Baldovinetti runs through 1528; Mariano Cecchi wrote a chronicle that extends through 1530;[24] Jacopo Pitti wrote a history for the years 1527–30.[25] Moreni identified other anonymous works as well.[26] Benedetto Varchi used several diaries from these years when he was working on his own history of the city.[27]

Production of such works continued after the transition from republic to duchy. Indeed, the period has been referred to as a golden age for historical writing.[28] Moreni identified over thirty diaries, histories, and similar writings by Florentines about Florence from the middle and later sixteenth century, in addition to their histories of religious institutions, lives of individuals, or other such works. Many now enjoy modern editions.[29] Gilbert and Cochrane identified several surviving examples of these as well.[30] Some diarists expressed a hope that someday they might expand this record into a history of their times. Machiavelli's grandson Giuliano de' Ricci acknowledged in one of his own later diary entries that he would surely never get around to revising these jottings into a full history, as indeed he did not.

The more formal histories of the city often had a complex path to publication. In most cases the authors clearly intended to publish during their lifetime, yet many died with the unfinished manuscript still in process. Several factors contributed to the large number of such incomplete historical projects. The stability of Cosimo's regime followed by orderly succession presented no obvious terminus. And Florentines took history writing seriously; they were harsh judges of one another's work, which led many to endless perfectionist rounds of tinkering or to authorial paralysis, even as they critiqued the efforts of others. Their competitive interests helped produce a high standard for historical writings. Filippo Nerli (1485–1556) and Donato Giannotti (1492–1573) wrote at mid-century. Giovanni Michele Bruto's (1517–92) history of Florence might be noted as well given its readership, though he was Venetian. Jacopo Nardi (1476–1563), Benedetto Varchi (1503–65), and Bernardo Segni (1504–58) were followed by Giovanni Battista Adriani (1511–79); Scipione Ammirato (1531–1601) wrote during the century's last decades.[31] Though not a native Florentine, Ammirato lived and worked there many years.

These authors generally relied on Machiavelli as a principal narrative source for the events in Florence after the eras treated by Bruni and Poggio Bracciolini, that is, the second half of the fifteenth century. The *Discourses* included some subsequent events as well. An exception is Adriani, whose history begins with the accession of Alessandro. And following Cosimo de' Medici's request, he continued his narrative from the point at which Varchi had left off, so he had little reason to make use of Machiavelli's historical writings.[32] In several works Machiavelli also figures at relevant points as a character in the historical narrative itself.

Donato Giannotti's treatise on the Florentine republic was the earliest written, though he kept careful control of its circulation until his death. Thereafter it was read widely in manuscript until its eighteenth-century publication.[33] Giannotti had served in the city's last republican government, and suffered imprisonment and exile after the rise of Alessandro; he eventually settled in Rome. He composed the work during the 1530s, presenting the strengths and the weaknesses of the earlier republican governments.[34] He followed it with another on Venice. Like Machiavelli in the *Discourses*, Giannotti bases his discussion of forms of government on Polybius, and uses similar terminology to describe Florentine society. His textual references to Machiavelli are found in Book 4, where he mentions the *Art of War* and his writings on the militia. Machiavelli's name appears there in a very different context as well, as the author of dramatic comedies. When discussing problems of young people and public order, Giannotti gives an example of a dinner party. To render the occasion more festive, the host had arranged that dinner be followed by a comedy of Machiavelli's, since it was well known and people wanted to see it.[35]

Giannotti had known the older Machiavelli, perhaps from their time together at the Rucellai Gardens.[36] Their careers had numerous parallels, and their intellectual circles shared common points as well. Randolph Starn has noted that rather than seeing Giannotti simply as a follower of Machiavelli, the two are better understood as part of the same intellectual environment; the similarities extend well beyond the use of a given text or a reference by one writer to another.[37] This observation also holds true for the Florentines of the subsequent decades. They met regularly in formal and informal settings, conversed often, and were familiar with one another's work. The intellectual and social networks continued, though by the later sixteenth century, Florentine men of letters would have had a personal acquaintance not with Machiavelli but with his grandson.

Filippo Nerli had been a supporter of Medici causes for many years.[38] He was part of a group (also including Guicciardini) that discussed with the Pope in 1531 how best to organize the city's government after its surrender following the siege of 1529–30, and was named a senator of the city the next year. He wrote his *Commentari* just before and after 1550. It remained unpublished at his death and circulated only in manuscript until the eighteenth century. Nerli considered himself a friend of Machiavelli's; he notes this relationship as part of his discussion of the events of 1521, while Cosimo Rucellai was still alive, and a group of young men of letters gathered in the gardens:

> [A]mong them was Niccolò Machiavelli, who frequented them constantly (and I was extremely friendly with Niccolò and all of them, and conversed with him very often) and they worked together on letters, on readings of histories and so on, and at their instance Machiavelli composed his book of discourses on Titus Livius, and also those treatises and arguments about the militia.[39]

A few pages earlier he had noted Machiavelli's imprisonment in 1513 as well as his release. At several points during his narrative of these years, Nerli also quotes lines from Machiavelli's *Decennali*.[40] Alessandro Montevecchi has observed the frequent echoes of Machiavelli's phrases, concepts, and methods in Nerli's work. Nerli agreed with Machiavelli that one of the significant features driving Florentine history was the city's chronic problem with factions and divisions. Nerli began his work with the conquest of Fiesole in 1125 and moved quickly to the origins of the divisions into Guelfs and Ghibellines. That rift played into others, old and new, both within and among the city's major social groups. He noted, as Nardi would later, that each attempt at a resolution simply produced a new cluster of winners who acted with insolence and pride, and of losers who plotted to turn the tables. Like Varchi, Bernardo Segni, and others, he uses the term "sect" (*setta*) for the factional groups in the city.

Only a major political change could rid the city of this chronic dysfunction, a change that he had witnessed himself. Already by the end of Book 1 Nerli observed that "it was decreed by the heavens that this city of ours would never rest or find peace except under the government of a single prince, as finally has happened."[41] He ended Book 2 with similar reflections on the peaceful period under the control of Cosimo il Vecchio, who had kept the factions quiet, an argument that echoed Machiavelli. Those who had been exiled upon Cosimo's return to the city, however, had continued to plot and to negotiate with the other peninsular powers, so factional strife remained part of the narrative. He repeated these sentiments about factions and their destructive power at the end of Book 8 (1529), and again at the end of Book 11 and the death of Clement VII (1534); that is, the continuing dissatisfactions of these groups contributed to the city's ongoing instability.

The years in which he completed the work, and in which the work's narrative concludes, marked for Nerli a distinct change and a new era in Florentine history. Duke Cosimo's victory and the defeat of the exiles at Montemurlo, he argued, finally put an end to the ancient and modern discords of the citizens. At the same time they ended his own need as author to record them. One might certainly consider such a conclusion to be high praise for Cosimo in ending such long-standing and destructive internal strife, but Nerli sounds more disparaging of the weakness and pettiness of his fellow Florentines.

Jacopo Nardi had both a distinguished lineage and a respected career in public life through the 1520s; indeed, the other historians of the era wrote with great praise about his conduct during those years.[42] From the events of 1529–30 that brought Alessandro into power until his death in 1563, Nardi remained a committed republican and an exile, first involuntarily, later by choice. He spent most of that time in Venice, a leader in the community of Florentine exiles.[43] His involvement with publishing in Venice included his translation of the first ten books of Livy, the books Machiavelli had used in his *Discourses*.[44]

Nardi composed his history in exile and hence without access to Florentine archival records. He did, however, have access to other exiles and to their own records and papers and could make use of his own memories, papers, and experience as a former member of the Florentine government. Given his familiarity with print and publishing, he could refer readers easily to other European histories of the era such as that of Philippe de Commines on France. He and Varchi remained in touch for many years about their respective projects, in letters and in person.[45] Publication was slowed first by his own death and then by that of the publisher, Tommaso Giunta, in 1566. Nannini claimed in his 1567 Guicciardini edition that Nardi's book was forthcoming, but it appeared only in 1582, by the Giuntini in Lyon, followed by the Florentine edition in 1584.

Nerli and Nardi may have disagreed about how best to run the city, but they both agreed with Machiavelli that one of the significant features driving Florentine history was the city's chronic problem with factions and divisions. Social divisions, their attributes, and their labels are at the center of Nardi's history from the very first sentence: "The city of Florence (like almost every city) had three types of inhabitants, that is, the nobility, the *popolo grasso* and the *popolo minuto*."[46] The first group, subdivided still further by some analysts, he notes, was long hostile to republican governments, and the *popolo minuto* or plebeians had not been involved in government except the single moment of the Ciompi revolt. Those too might be subdivided into those who owned real estate and those with no property. It is the middle group, states Nardi, which is generally best suited to republican government.[47] Nardi's main narrative begins with the events of 1494, but he precedes it with essential background information on these divisions. He presents first the Ciompi revolt of 1378, then the Medici control of the city in the fifteenth century. Factional dominance and control had figured large in both cases, and both had attracted Machiavelli's attention as well. Most of Nardi's history follows individual actors through the major public events of these years. Yet throughout the work, he returns to the opinions, behaviors, and tendencies of these large social groups, and their role in historical change.

The groups and the labels used by Nardi and Nerli as well as Machiavelli were well known to Florentines. The divisions between *popolo grasso* (professionals and guild members) and *popolo minuto* (workers and craftsmen) were traditional, and labels for political parties such as the *arrabbiati, piagnoni,* or the *ottimati,* were also in general use. These authors' innovations lay rather in the level of attention they offered to these social groups and their behaviors, and the causal roles they gave them in explaining historical events and change. And like Machiavelli, their interests in society extended beyond Florence; they sought not simply to understand Florentine events better, but also to use information about the past behavior of Florentines to understand political behavior more generally. Nerli and Nardi made slightly different points. Nerli argued that faction-ridden populations like Florentines could maintain stability only with an autocratic ruler such as Duke Cosimo, though he did not claim that such a state was ideal. Nardi believed that a republican government, which he favored in general, required a mercantile population. He was especially interested in the interactions of this group with those at both higher and lower social levels. For both, historical writing offered a way to extract and examine general principles of public action of all sorts, as it had for Machiavelli.

Varchi began his own history with the Medici; chased from the city three times in some ninety-four years, they had returned from each one stronger than before. Hence, he notes, though he intends to focus on the third and final instance, the story must begin with the first two. A brief summary in Book 1, including the years covered by Machiavelli's own history, takes him to the death of Pope Adrian VI and the election of Clement VII (1523), at which point his own main narrative begins. Machiavelli also appears in Varchi's work as a historical actor. Varchi offered mixed assessments of many or most of his figures, and Machiavelli was no exception; some of it echoes Busini's letter, as Villari noted long ago.[48] Varchi acknowledged his great understanding of politics and matters of state; given Machiavelli's expertise in government and practical matters, he observes, had this only been matched by sincerity of habit and gravity of life, he would have been on par with the ancients who are held in esteem over moderns.[49]

Later he presents an anecdote about Machiavelli's death that he says was in general circulation: that Francesco Tarugi, named as secretary to the Ten in the last republic, had died suddenly and Machiavelli had been hoping for the position. The post had been given instead to Giannotti and Machiavelli died of disappointment. Varchi then repeats a variation of Busini's claim about Machiavelli's unpopularity among various sectors of the population. Yet he follows this with more positive assessments: Machiavelli had been pleasant in speech, generous to his friends, friend to virtuous men, and both he and Giannotti should be considered among the rarest of men in matters political not just of the city, but of their time. Further, he notes, the anecdote could not possibly be true because Machiavelli's death had preceded that of Tarugi. Varchi closes with a general remark about reputation and flawed character: just as there is no greater reward for virtues than praise and honor, so too the worst punishment for one's vices is a reputation that persists into death. Like many of Varchi's historical characters, Machiavelli receives a very mixed portrait.[50]

In Book 9 Varchi digresses from his narrative to discuss the city's origins. He begins with the story offered by Giovanni Villani in his fourteenth-century chronicle, and notes the low level of historical knowledge actually possessed by Villani and other early historians and chroniclers. He moves on to Bruni and Poggio and adds opinions by Raffaele Maffei and Lorenzo Valla. He then turns to Machiavelli, who had also taken up this topic as a digression, and to Poliziano; from there he launches into a comparison of sources and arguments. Machiavelli's account, he concludes, has some merit, as do parts of the other modern historians.[51] A few pages later Varchi takes on the controversial question of whether the Goths had really destroyed the city; again, Machiavelli's authority has weight in his final opinion. While Varchi concludes that the city had not been completely abandoned (the side Machiavelli had taken), it must have been badly damaged and partially depopulated.[52]

Varchi was also among the authors at mid-century who noted Machiavelli's reputation as a stylist.[53] His dialogue on language, the *Ercolano*, was published posthumously (1570), though with far less delay than his history. It had been inspired by a dispute over language and literature, but grew into a much broader discussion. Partway through the dialogue the interlocutors turned to the ways one might compare the qualities of different languages, and specifically to comparisons of Greek, Latin, and vernacular. Boccaccio, it was generally agreed, had been a vernacular prose author of major importance. Some modern authorities had questioned whether he was a good model for prose on serious subjects, since he had produced mainly narratives, particularly narrative fiction. Gabriele Cesano and Bartolomeo Cavalcanti had agreed with Paolo Giovio that Machiavelli had a more lively style than Boccaccio. The Varchi character differed; nonetheless Varchi as author has attributed the opinion to important arbiters of language and style.[54]

Carlo Lenzoni (1501–50) invoked Machiavelli for his opinions on the Florentine language. His posthumously published *In difesa della lingua Fiorentina, et di Dante con le regole da far bella et numerosa la prosa* by Torrentino in 1556,[55] consisted of three dialogues left at his death in various stages of completion. Cosimo Bartoli completed the task, begun by Pierfrancesco Giambullari, of editing the volume (and was cast among the interlocutors). In the first dialogue, Giovambattista Gelli (who comes the closest to Lenzoni's voice) relates to a Venetian Bembist a conversation that had occurred after the publication of Bembo's *Prose della volgar lingua* (1525) involving Machiavelli, Giunti the printer, and a Venetian. Gelli and the Bembist agree that Machiavelli had always been aggressive at chasing down arguments and lively in speech, pressing the point at hand to its conclusions, and so his voice was worth hearing.

Bembo had advocated a literary standard based on the great early Florentine writers, and argued that with study, anyone could learn to write well; like Latin, one did not need to be a native speaker. Machiavelli had pursued this topic with his Venetian interlocutor. He asked the Venetian to imagine a Florentine man of letters who decided to learn Venetian outside of Venice; they agreed that he would wind up writing and speaking in many ways that would vary from actual spoken Venetian. Machiavelli continued the imagined scenario as a parallel to Bembo's model of an idealized literary Florentine based on the best earlier authors. Now suppose, he asks the Venetian, this Florentine decided to use one or another Venetian poet as his model for rules and vocabulary. Then he asked pointedly whether such a speaker would ever be seen as better at Venetian than a native, leaving his Venetian interlocutor speechless. In this case, Lenzoni has presented Machiavelli as an advocate of spoken Florentine, an author with a considered position in the ongoing language debate, and one whose opinion commanded interest and respect.

II

Lenzoni's writings were published well before the existence of the Index of Forbidden Books. Varchi had listed his sources and discussed them by name in the manuscripts of the *Ercolano* as well as the history, both unfinished and unpublished at his death in 1565. The Roman Index of 1557 and the fuller one of 1559 banned all of Machiavelli's writings, a position only reinforced in subsequent versions of the Index.[56] Godman's discussion of the Index and the haphazard development of its implementation is especially helpful in following the case of Machiavelli. The opaque process has bedeviled historians nearly as much as it infuriated authors, editors, and publishers at the time.[57] The Index caused significant changes in the use of Machiavelli's texts. The volumes did not disappear from the bookshelves or libraries of readers despite the ban, as the many surviving copies attest. Nonetheless, they could not be printed or sold in regions of Europe that recognized the Index's authority. Florentines as well as other Italians avoided citing him by name in print, nor would they refer to his works in a manner sufficiently obvious as to bring trouble to themselves and those publishing their works. Some skirted the issue by replacing his name with a vague and banal reference like "storico fiorentino." Sydney Anglo has identified a number of such disguised citations, by Florentines and others.[58] Victoria Kahn has noted Giovanni Botero's frequent circumlocutions.[59]

Others, where appropriate, substituted both the name and the works of Francesco Guicciardini. For at this point, his *History of Italy* finally became available. Guicciardini's nephew Agnolo had held control of the unfinished manuscript but long delayed publication.[60] He restricted access to the manuscript, but a few readers saw at least sections of the work in that form, among them Paolo Giovio, Filippo Nerli, and Benedetto Varchi.[61] Eventually Agnolo turned it over to Vincenzio Borghini and the ducal secretary Bartolomeo Concini. They edited both for style and to tone down anti-papal and anti-clerical remarks to avoid papal wrath and the Index. In 1561 Torrentino brought out two editions at once of the sixteen books Agnolo had released: one in folio, the other in a more portable octavo.

The abundance of editions and apparatus that followed testifies to the work's popularity. Brian Richardson has described its "snowball-like accumulation of editorial matter."[62] Two Venetian editions soon appeared; one by Sansovino with a brief biography, one by Bonelli including an index, marginal indicators, and summaries by Remigio Nannini. Bevilaqua copied it in three additional printings. More editions, summaries, and related texts continued to pour from the presses, including the incomplete books Agnolo had refused to release. Thus a new publishing phenomenon captured the attention of the history-reading public; it helped to replace, in its way, the loss of Machiavelli.

Nannini used his editorial experience and his familiarity with Guicciardini's text to compose a work of his own. It exemplifies the close connection Guicciardini's writings had with those of Machiavelli: *Consideratione ciuili sopra l'historie di M. Francesco Guicciardini e d'altri historici: trattate per modo di discorso.*[63] Published posthumously, the volume also includes Guicciardini's *Maxims and Reflections* and some of Nannini's letters, a mix that may reflect the publisher's marketing interests more than the author's intentions.

The choice of genre shows Nannini's continued engagement with Machiavelli, to whom he was alluding in the title phrase "altri historici." He employed Guicciardini's text as Machiavelli had used that of Livy to compose a set of free-form reflections and comments on the work and the events described in it. The topics he chose for a number of these "Considerations" (*Considerazioni*) also recall Machiavelli's *Discourses*; they make it clear that Nannini had in mind not only Machiavelli's title and genre, but the work's contents as well. *Consideratione* 11 (14r–15r) addresses a subject Machiavelli treated in *Discourses* 1.45: "He is a bad example who makes a law in a Republic that then is not observed, especially by those who made it, nor defended against those who wish to break it."[64] Machiavelli's discourse begins with the example of Appius and Virginius, moves from there to Florence's government during the Savonarola years, and back to Rome after the fall of the Decemviri. Nannini uses only the Savonarola example (citing Guicciardini Book 3); he states at the end that those who have written a discourse on the matter gave the example of Appius and Virginius, but so as not to multiply examples, that has been omitted.

Consideratione 32 is based on Discourse 1.27 and discusses how men are seldom able to be entirely evil. Nannini has changed the title slightly, but Machiavelli's heading appears in the margin. Our author as well as other writers have already noted the resolve of Julius II and the abstinence of Giampaolo Baglioni, begins Nannini, and he retells the famous story related by Machiavelli of the evildoer who failed to kill the Pope when he had the chance. *Consideratione* 39 (53v–54v), entitled, "That one should not trust a great error that one sees the enemy commit; rather, one should believe it was done deliberately and that there be some trickery behind it,"[65] is perhaps even more closely modeled on Machiavelli, in this case his penultimate discourse (3.48). Machiavelli's discourse begins with the example of the Roman general Fulvius, who recognizes a trap set for him by the Etruscans; it continues with the Gauls' caution about entering an apparently abandoned Rome; and then moves on to the 1508 Florentine siege of Pisa. Nannini merely adds a couple of introductory sentences to summarize the point that a prudent military captain should never trust an apparently large mistake committed by the enemy. Otherwise he goes through the same examples in the same order and draws the same conclusions as Machiavelli.

Yet the work is not simply a paraphrase. Many other *considerationi* are modeled more loosely on the *Discourses*, and a number of topics significant for Machiavelli's work do not appear in that of Nannini. Yet in a number of places it is apparent, as in 11, that references to Guicciardini serve as substitutes for Machiavelli, and examples from Livy appear frequently. The *Considerationi* might be dubbed a partial plagiarism, though its posthumous publication brought the author no personal benefit. Yet it could also be understood as an effort to return some of Machiavelli's ideas to circulation despite the Index, an early example of the efforts to circumvent the censors.

Nannini was not alone in his imitation; nor was he the first. Francesco Guicciardini had composed a set of "Considerations on Machiavelli's Discourses," but they remained unpublished and unknown until the nineteenth century.[66] The Considerations begun by his younger brother Bongiovanni Guicciardini have remained in manuscript.[67] Cosimo Bartoli (1503–72) began in the 1550s a set of forty *Discorsi historici universali* (1569, 1582) modeled on Machiavelli's *Discourses*. Judith Bryce, who has discussed the work at some length, has noted that the two surviving manuscript drafts mention Machiavelli by name, but in the later version his name was subsequently struck out and replaced with "nostro historico Fiorentino," which is how he appears in the printed work.[68] Both the format and the topics themselves are heavily indebted to Machiavelli. Bartoli chose not to base his discourses on a single historical text or author, but rather a broad range of both ancients and moderns; they are noted regularly in the text, but more often by marginal references. Among the former are Plutarch and Tacitus as well as Livy. Moderns include Paolo Giovio as well as Guicciardini, both of whom are cited frequently, in addition to Poggio, Bruni, Machiavelli, and a number of others.

The reference above comes from Discourse 13, which begins with Bartoli alluding directly to Machiavelli's Discourse 2.10, on the role of wealth in waging war. Our Florentine historian, he notes, discussed the matter of wealth and argued that good soldiers rather than money were the sinews of war.[69] Bartoli takes his own historical examples in this discourse mainly from Paolo Giovio. Here as elsewhere, he proceeds almost in a response to Machiavelli, setting out his own opinions on topics he seems to assume his readers will find familiar as well as relevant. In general, as Bryce has observed, Bartoli's views are much more conventional than those of Machiavelli. In many cases Bartoli's examples follow the relevant historians so closely that they are at times almost paraphrases. Especially with current and widely read authors such as Giovio and Guicciardini, these would appear to be deliberate efforts to follow closely works with which readers were already familiar or wanted to become familiar with quickly.

Over two decades later, Scipione Ammirato wrote a set of discourses modeled on those of Machiavelli.[70] In this case the author chose deliberately to compose a work set not just in dialogue form, but in opposition to that of his predecessor. Ammirato seems to have become interested in the topic in the mid-1580s, at which time he drafted some discourses that took issue with Machiavelli's position on the role of the Church in Italy[71] He composed the greater part of the work around 1590. Ammirato found much to commend in the rule of a virtuous prince, and he supported the institutional role of the Church on the Italian penin-sula and elsewhere. Accordingly, he found much to disagree with in Machiavelli. Ammirato deliberately chose Tacitus rather than Livy as the basis for his own discourses, so as to refer to the era of the Caesars rather than the republic. Divided into twenty-one books, his dis-courses follow the order of Tacitus' *Annals* and then of the *Histories*. They were reprinted several times after their initial 1598 publication, and enjoyed a French translation as well.

Ammirato took on a broad range of topics and issues prominently associated with Machiavelli, from the role of religion in society, to military matters, to personal traits and moral behavior of princes and others, often in obvious disagreement. Like his predecessors, Ammirato seldom referred to Machiavelli by name, preferring allusions, circumlocutions, or other oblique references as needed. Yet Machiavelli's discourses seldom seem far away, and as Rudolfo de Mattei has noted in his study of Ammirato, his accent can be heard throughout.[72]

Sydney Anglo has identified a number of other Italian writers, mostly outside Florence, who also used the *Discourses* in their works.[73] The Venetian Interdict Crisis of 1606–7 increased interest in Machiavelli, and saw the production of anthologies under false cov-ers as well as more popular versions of his ideas.[74] By the seventeenth century, pseudony-mous publications of his works appeared; The *Discourses* were printed in Venice in 1630 (and again in 1648) under the name "Amadio Niecollucci."[75] Giovanni Maria Pichi published in Florence (1641) a version of the *Prince* edited into aphorisms that cleared the censors, who were perhaps less vigilant at that point.[76]

Other colleagues of Nannini made more direct efforts to get Machiavelli back into print in Italy, even as editions and translations multiplied in other European regions. The goal was to produce editions that would somehow pass the review of the censors. Godman has narrated the events of both the censorship and the extensive but unsuccessful efforts to produce an edition.[77] All writings by Machiavelli were banned in the Roman Indexes of 1557 and 1559, as well as that of 1564. In the many revisions of the Index and the related debates over the decades that followed, Machiavelli's works continued to be reviewed and revisited, but with-out a positive result; indeed, in 1579 it was proclaimed that no exemptions could be issued to allow the reading of Machiavelli even by individuals with compelling reasons.

A number of other noted Florentine authors had joined Machiavelli on the Index, among them Giovanni Boccaccio. Boccaccio was held in high esteem as a prose stylist, as seen above in Varchi's reference. Given the growing interest in both modern and early Florentine lan-guage by the city's sixteenth-century men of letters, this ban on major authors was particu-larly offensive. The efforts to rehabilitate Machiavelli's works were part of this wider interest in restoring access to the city's great writers. Some of Florence's leading scholars embarked upon a series of efforts to produce versions of these texts that would allow them to be pub-lished and read, and their authors cited once again. Among them were two of Machiavelli's grandsons. One bore his grandfather's name; the other, Giuliano de' Ricci (noted above for his diary), was also an editor of the fourteenth-century Florentine chronicler Matteo Villani and other works.

While some of these efforts were effective for other authors, none succeeded for Machiavelli. In some instances the parties disagreed on issues such as whether Machiavelli could be named as author of his own works on the title-pages. In others, potential editors like Vincenzio Borghini, exhausted from completing the expurgated *Decameron*, simply declined in the end to take on another such project. As each effort failed in turn at one or another crucial point for the remainder of the century and beyond, new editions and translations proliferated across northern Europe, attracting the readers that so upset Gentillet. Perhaps the most substantial result was that given so many unsuccessful efforts that involved so many of Florence's men of letters, a significant number of Florentines apparently remained famil-iar with Machiavelli's writings. The ban, then, succeeded at keeping Machiavelli's name and writings mostly out of print in those places where enforcement was a concern; those places included Florence and the rest of Italy in the later sixteenth century. That success was the source of Mini's claim. Yet these editorial projects, though they failed to meet their goals, certainly subverted any hope by papal bureaucrats that his texts would remain out of the hands of the city's learned community.[78]

It was also de' Ricci who found a manuscript of the *Dialogo della lingua* and first attrib-uted it to Machiavelli. That attribution has seen significant controversy.[79] The work would date from about 1514–15. Giangiorgio Trissino had discovered in 1513 a manuscript of Dante's *De vulgari eloquentia*, previously unknown, and discussed it in Florence at the Rucellai Gardens. Many Florentines rejected the attribution to Dante, and the *Dialogo* includes a debate between Dante and Machiavelli in which Machiavelli argues for Florentine, as opposed to Dante's advocacy of a more general courtly vernacular. De' Ricci claims in an introductory note that he had not found the work among Machiavelli's papers but received it from the hands of others. He believed it to be genuine despite some stylistic issues because of the opinions expressed and because Machiavelli's son Bernardo (still alive as he wrote) remembered hearing about it and seeing him with the text. This work seems not to have circulated widely; neither Lenzoni nor Varchi referred to it or seemed familiar with it, for example, despite their interest in Machiavelli's opinions on language. Thus despite the inter-est it would have held for Florentine readers, it had little or no effect on them.

III

Even without this little work in circulation, it seems clear that Machiavelli as known by sixteenth-century Florentines had a singularly Florentine inflection. His writings and inter-ests were consistent with a significant corpus of works composed and read by Florentines both during his lifetime and in the decades that followed. A number of topics that engaged him were topics of longstanding Florentine attention, such as the role of factions. A num-ber of innovative features in his work also came increasingly to be found in the writings of Florentines, particularly comparative approaches to the study of society, including compari-sons not only across regions but over time.

Given the degree to which Machiavelli's European notoriety was shaped by the *Prince*, it is notable that in his hometown, this work was less used or cited than the *Florentine Histories* or the *Discourses* or the *Art of War*. Perhaps this was due in part to the *Prince*'s notoriety, but more significant was the continuing importance of his other themes and texts to the Florentines of the generations that followed. Although they may have been less than fully successful at keep-ing his own works out before local readers in the tumultuous decades of the later sixteenth century, nonetheless they carried on to develop the studies of society to which he made such a famous contribution.

And even Mini did his part for Machiavelli's name and achievements during these years as well. Back in Florence, Mini published in 1593 another version of his little work, reti-tled as *Discorso della nobiltà di Firenze*.[80] Gone was the defensive tone along with the con-cerns about atheism, a charge Florentines did not much use against one another. In it he presented lists of Florentines who had achieved great things in fields such as painting, medicine, and more. Machiavelli's name appears among the diplomats, due to his efforts to address issues raised by the Pisan war.[81] And although Mini may not have been able to quote Machiavelli's works, he did nonetheless name him as an author. Mini places him with Benedetto Varchi, Giovanni Villani, Guicciardini, Jacopo Nardi, and many others, as a writer of Florentine history.[82]

Notes

1 Innocent Gentillet, *Discours svr les moyens de bien govverner et maintenir en bonne paix vn royaume ou autre principauté ...*, Geneva: Jacob Stoer, 1576.

2 Paolo Mini, *Difesa della città di Firenze, et de i Fiorentini, contra le calunnie & maledicentie de maligni*, Lyon: F. Tinghi, 1577.

3 See, e.g., Sydney Anglo, *Machiavelli: The First Century. Studies in Enthusiasm, Hostility, and Irrelevance*, Oxford and New York: Oxford University Press, 2005; Jacob Soll, *Publishing "The Prince": History, Reading, and the Birth of Political Criticism*, Ann Arbor: University of Michigan Press, 2005; Patricia Vilches and Gerald Seaman, eds., *Seeking Real Truths: Multidisciplinary Perspectives on Machiavelli*, Leiden and Boston: Brill, 2007. On early editions see Sergio Bertelli and Piero Innocenti, *Bibliografia machiavelliana*, Verona: Edizioni Valdonega, 1979, xli–lxxxvi.

4 For a discussion of reception in Florence of the *Prince* see Gregory Murry, *The Medicean Succession: Monarchy and Sacral Politics in Duke Cosimo dei Medici's Florence*, Cambridge, MA: Harvard University Press, 2014, 104–32.

5 Remigio Nannini, *Consideratoni ciuili sopra l'historie di M. Francesco Guicciardini e d'altri historici: trattate per modo di discorso ...*, Venice: Damiano Zenaro, 1582; Remigio Nannini, *Civill considerations vpon many and sundrie histories, as well ancient as moderne, and principallie vpun those of Guicciardin ... out of the French into English by W.T.*, London: Imprinted by F.K. for Matthew Lownes, 1601; Remigio Nannini, *Considerations civiles, sur plusieurs et diverses histoires tant anciennes que modernes, & principallement sur celles de Guicciardin ...*, Paris: Abel L'Angelier, 1585; Remigio Nannini, *Consideratoni civili, sopra l'historie di M. Francesco Guicciardini, e d'altri historici*, Venice: Zenaro, 1603.

6 Bernardo Rucellai, *Bernardi Oricellarii de bello italico commentarius, ex authentici manuscripti apographo nunc primùm in lucem editus*, London: Bowyer, 1724; Filippo de' Nerli, *Commentari de' fatti civili occorsi dentro la città di Firenze dall'anno 1215 al 1537*, Augsburg: Mertz & Majer, 1728; Benedetto Varchi, *Storia fiorentina*, Cologne: P. Martello, 1721; Ildefonso di San Luigi, *Delizie degli eruditi toscani*, 25 vols., Florence: Gaetano Cambiagi, 1770.

7 www.johnadamslibrary.org/search/books/?category=European history.

8 John Adams, *A Defence of the Constitutions of Government of the United States of America*, Philadelphia: Printed for Hall and Sellers; J. Crukshank; and Young and M'Culloch, 1787.

9 Felix Gilbert, *Machiavelli and Guicciardini: Politics and History in Sixteenth-Century Florence*, Princeton, NJ: Princeton University Press, 1965; Peter Godman, *From Poliziano to Machiavelli: Florentine Humanism in the High Renaissance*, Princeton, NJ: Princeton University Press, 1998; Alison Brown, *The Return of Lucretius to Renaissance Florence*, Cambridge, MA: Harvard University Press, 2010; Lorenzo Polizzotto, *Children of the Promise: The Confraternity of the Purification and the Socialization of Youths in Florence, 1427–1785*, Oxford and New York: Oxford University Press, 2004; Jonathan Davies, *Florence and its University during the Early Renaissance*, Leiden and Boston: Brill, 1998.

10 Corrado Vivanti, *Niccolò Machiavelli: An Intellectual Biography*, trans. Simon MacMichael, Princeton, NJ: Princeton University Press, 2013 (first published as *Niccolò Machiavelli: i tempi della politica*, Rome: Donzelli, 2008); Robert Black, *Machiavelli*, London and New York: Routledge, 2013. For a valuable overview see Robert Black, "Machiavelli: Some Recent Biographies and Studies," *English Historical Review* 127(524) (2012): 110–25.

11 Brian Richardson, *Manuscript Culture in Renaissance Italy*, Cambridge and New York: Cambridge University Press, 2009, 18–19; Victoria Kahn, "Machiavelli's Afterlife and Reputation to the Eighteenth Century," in *The Cambridge Companion to Machiavelli*, ed. John M. Najemy, Cambridge and New York: Cambridge University Press, 2010, 239–55, at 241–2.

12 Brian Richardson, "*The Prince* and its Early Italian Readers," in *Niccolò Machiavelli's "The Prince": New Interdisciplinary Essays*, ed. Martin Coyle, Manchester: Manchester University Press; New York: St. Martin's Press, 1995, 18–39.

13 Godman, *From Poliziano to Machiavelli*, 237, 253; Agostino Nifo, *Augustini Niphi Medice philosophi suessani De regnandi peritia ad Carolum.VI. [i.e. V] Imper. Caesarem semper augustum*, Naples: In aedibus Dominae Catherine de Siluestro, 1523. For a facsimile edition with French translation, see Agostino Nifo, *Une réécriture du Prince de Machiavel: le "De regnandi peritia" de Agostino Nifo*, trans. Simone Pernet-Beau, ed. Paul Larivaille, Paris: Université Paris X Nanterre, 1987. See also Adolph Gerber, *Niccolò Machiavelli, die Handschriften, Ausgaben und Übersetzungen seiner Werke im 16. und 17. Jahrhundert: eine kritisch-bibliographische Untersuchung*, 3 vols., Gotha: F. A. Perthes, 1912, 3.7–12.

14 Agostino Nifo, *Augustini Niphi sua tempestate philosophi omnium celeberrimi Opuscula moralia et politica*, ed. Gabriel Naudé, Paris: Sumptibus Roleti Le Duc, 1645.

15 *Ibid.*

16 "e l'universale per conto del Principe l'odiava: ai ricchi pareva che quel suo Principe fosse stato un documento da insegnare al duca tòr loro tutta la roba, a' poveri tutta la libertà. Ai Piagnoni pareva che e' fosse eretico, ai buoni disonesto, ai tristi più tristo o più valente di loro; talchè ognuno l'odiava." Giambattista Busini, Letter of 23 January 1549 (i.e. 1550), in Giovanni Battista Busini, *Lettere di Giovambattista Busini a Benedetto Varchi sopra l'assedio di Firenze*, ed. Gaetano Milanesi, Florence: Felice Le Monnier, 1860, 84. On circulation of *The Prince* in manuscript, see Brian Richardson, *Printing, Writers, and Readers in Renaissance Italy*, Cambridge and New York: Cambridge University Press, 1999, 84–5; see also Gerber, *Niccolò Machiavelli*, vols. 1 and 3.

17 On Machiaveli's early readership across Europe, see Anglo, *Machiavelli: The First Century*. For a critical evaluation of the *Florentine Histories*, including criticism by sixteenth-century readers, see Eric W. Cochrane, *Historians and Historiography in the Italian Renaissance*, Chicago: University of Chicago Press, 1981, 265–70.

18 On early editions see Bertelli and Innocenti, *Bibliografia machiavelliana*, xxviii–xxxvi, 3–80; Gerber, *Niccolò Machiavelli*, 2.7–21.

19 1547, 1554, 1562, 1567, 1574, 1575, 1581, and 1586.

20 Victoria Ann Kahn, *Machiavellian Rhetoric: From the Counter-Reformation to Milton*, Princeton, NJ: Princeton University Press, 1994, 64.

21 On history writing in Florence see Emanuele Cutinelli Rèndina, Jean Jacques Marchand, and Matteo Melera-Morettini, *Dalla storia alla politica nella Toscana del Rinascimento*, Rome: Salerno, 2005.

22 Domenico Moreni, *Bibliografia storico-ragionata della Toscana o sia Catalogo degli scrittori che hanno illustrata la storia dell città, luoghi, e persone della medesima*, Florence: Ciardetti, 1805. Anonymous (1435–1522: Florence, Archivo di stato di Firenze [ASF] Manoscritti 117). Moreni identifies two additional anonymous chronicles from this period, one at the Biblioteca Riccardiana (Cod. R. n. 44), the other at the Seminario Fiorentino: Biagio Buonaccorsi, *Diario dall'anno 1498 all'anno 1512 e altri scritti*, Rome: Istituto storico italiano per il Medio Evo, 1999; Giovanni Cambi, *Istorie fiorentine*, in *Delizie degli eruditi toscani*, ed. Ildefonso di San Luigi, vols. 20–3, p. 143, Florence: Cambiagi, 1786; Bartolomeo Cerretani, *Dialogo della mutatione di Firenze*, ed. Raul Mordenti, Rome: Edizioni di storia e letteratura, 1990; Francesco Gaddi, *Ricordi*, in C. Bologna, *Inventario di mobili di F. di Angelo G*, Florence, 1883; Tommaso Ginori, in *Quellen und forschungen zur geschichte Savonarolas*, ed. Joseph Schnitzer, Veröffentlichungen aus dem Kirchenhistorischen Seminar München, 3 vols., Munich: J. J. Lentner, 1902, 1.94–104; Francesco Guicciardini, *Storie fiorentine dal 1378 al 1509*, Milan: Biblioteca universale Rizzoli, 1998; Luca Landucci, *Diario fiorentino*, Florence Sansoni, 1985; Piero di Marco Parenti, *Storia fiorentina*, ed. Andrea Matucci, 2 vols., Florence: L. S. Olschki, 1994–2005; Filippo, Alamanno, and Neri Rinuccini, *Ricordi storici ... * Florence: Stamperia Piatti, 1840; Tribaldo de' Rossi, *Ricordanze*, in *Delizie degli eruditi toscani ... * vol. 23, 236–303; Gherardo Bartolini Salimbeni, "Del magnifico Lorenzo de Medici, Chronica," in *Delizie degli eruditi toscani*, vol. 23 app., 1–80; Bernardo Rucellai, *De Bello Italico Commentarius*, London, 1724. For references to a number of unpublished or partially published diaries, see Cochrane, *Historians and Historiography*, 538, n. 30. A number of these authors are discussed by Jean Jacques Marchand and Jean-Claude Zancarini, eds., *Storiografia repubblicana fiorentina: 1494–1570*, Florence: F. Cesati, 2003, 175–85.

23 Francesco Vettori, *Scritti storici e politici*, Bari: Laterza, 1972.

24 Moreni identifies Baldovinetti's Chronicle as being in the hands of descendants; Mariano Cecchi's Annals were reportedly in a private collection.

25 Florence, Biblioteca Nazionale Centrale di Firenze (BNCF) Magl. XXV.349.

26 "Ragguaglio succinto istorica della Città di Firenze, e del suo Stato da"lanno 1100 all'anno 1532." Florence, Biblioteca Medicea Laurenziana.

27 Lupo Gentile, Sulle fonti, 61–75, Studi 99–100. Baccio Carnesecchi, BNCF Magl. XXV.555; "L. Mar.", probably Lorenzo Martelli, diary 1529–31; Michele Ruberti, diary; Anon. diary, 1524–30, BNCF Magl. XXV.570, copy Magl XXV.555.

28 Nicholas Scott Baker, "The Remembrance of Politics Past: Memory and Melancholia in Jacopo Nardi's *Istorie della città di Firenze*," in *After Civic Humanism: Learning and Politics in Renaissance Italy*, ed. Nicholas Scott Baker and Brian Maxson, Toronto: Centre for Reformation and Renaissance Studies, 2015, 259–72, at 259–72; Cochrane, *Historians and Historiography*, 277–82.

29 Bastiano Arditi (*Diario*, Florence: INSR, 1970); Piero Buondelmonti, "Vita d'Alessandro dei Medici" (Moreni, *Bibliografia*, 1.190; in a private collection); Francesco di Andrea Buonsignori (*Memorie*, Florence: Chiari, 2000); Giovanni Battista Busini, "Letters to Benedetto Varchi" (Giovanni Battista Busini, *Lettere ... a Benedetto Varchi sugli avvenimenti dell'assedio di Firenze*, Florence: Le Monnier, 1822); Migliore di Lorenzo Cresci (*Istoria Fiorentina*, Turin: Paravia, 1905); Francesco d'Abramo ("Diario," Moretti, *Bibliografia*, 1.396, formerly Strozziana 314); Agostino Lapini (*Diario fiorentino*, Florence: Sansoni, 1900); "Marucelli" (*Diario*, ed. Enrico Coppi, Florence: Olschki, 2000); Giuliano Ughi della Cavallina ("Cronica," ASI 1.7 app.); Piero di Banco di Frosino Verrazzano ("Cronica 1507–53"; Moretti, *Bibliografia*, 2.447, "Ms. originale presso la famiglia").

30 For references to a number of unpublished or partially published diaries, see Cochrane, *Historians and Historiography*, 538, n. 30. In addition to those that follow may be added: ASF, Manoscritti 117, anon. "Diario istorico di quello, ch'e' seguito nella Città di Firenze cominciando l'anno 1435 a tutto il'1522." A number of these authors are discussed by Jean-Jacques Marchand, "Componenti formali del discorso politico nella storiografia toscana minore del primo Cinquecento," in Marchand and Zancarini, *Storiografia repubblicana fiorentina*, 175–85.

31 Giovanni Battista Adriani, *Istoria de' suoi tempi*, Florence: Giunti, 1583; Scipione Ammirato, *Dell'istorie Fiorentine*, Florence: Giunti, 1600; Donato Giannotti, *Della repubblica fiorentina*, Venice: Hertz, 1722; Francesco Giocondo, *Istoria fiorentina* (Ricc. Ms. S.II, N. 4); Jacopo Nardi, *Le Historie della Città di Firenze*, Lyon, 1582; Nerli, *Commentari*; Varchi, *Storia fiorentina*; Giovanni Michele Bruto, *Florentinae historiae libri octo priores*, Lyon: Giunti, 1562.

32 On Adriani see Giovanni Miccoli, "Adriani, Giovanni Battista," *Dizionario biografico degli italiani*, ed. Alberto Ghisalberti, Rome: Istituto della Enciclopedia italiana, 1960–), hereafter DBI; Cochrane, *Historians and Historiography*, 282–3.

33 On Giannotti see Stefano Marconi, "Giannotti, Donato," DBI; Randolph Starn, *Donato Giannotti and his Epistolae, Biblioteca Universitaria Alessandrina, Rome, Ms. 107*, Geneva: Librairie Droz, 1968; Donato Giannotti, *Republica Fiorentina*, ed. Giovanni Silvano, Travaux d'humanisme et renaissance, Geneva: Droz, 1990. On Giannotti's limits on circulation, see *ibid.*, 60–7.

34 For a useful summary see Starn, *Donato Giannotti and his Epistolae*, 36–8.

35 Giannotti, *Republica Fiorentina*, 208–9.

36 Starn, *Donato Giannotti and his Epistolae*, 14–15, 16–17.

37 *Ibid.*, 39. Starn echoes Felix Gilbert in turn: Felix Gilbert, "Florentine Political Assumptions in the Period of Savonarola and Soderini," *Journal of the Warburg and Courtauld Institutes* 20(3/4) (1957): 187–214.

38 On Nerli, see Vanna Arrighi, "Nerli, Filippo de'," DBI; Alessandro Montevecchi, *Storici di Firenze: studi su Nardi, Nerli e Varchi*, Bologna: Pàatron, 1989, 71–104; Michele Lupo Gentile, *Studi sulla storiografia fiorentina alla corte di Cosimo I de' Medici*, Pisa: Tipografia Successori Fratelli Nistri, 1905, 26.62, 69.

39 "infra' quali praticava continuamente Niccolò Machiavelli (e io eo di Niccolò, e di tutti loro amicissimo, e molto spesso con loro conversavo) s'esercitavano costoro assai, mediante le lettere, nelle lezioni dell'istorie, e sopra di esse, ed a loro istanza compose il Machiavello quell suo libro de' discorsi sopra Tito Livio, e anco il libro di que' trattati, e ragionamenti sopra la milizia." Nerli, *Commentari*, 138.

40 On the Decennali see Bertelli and Innocenti, *Bibliografia machiavelliana*, IX–XIII, 3.

41 "perchè era disposto da' cieli, che questa nostra città non dovesse mai posare, nè quietarsi, se non sotto il governo d'un solo Principe, come finalmente ha fatto," Nerli, *Commentari*, 37.

42 On Nardi, see Stefano Dall'Aglio, "Nardi, Jacopo," DBI.

43 On Nardi in Venice, see Paolo Simoncelli, "The Turbulent Life of the Florentine Community in Venice," in *Heresy, Culture, and Religion in Early Modern Italy: Contexts and Contestations*, ed. Ronald

K. Delph, Michelle Fontaine, and John Jeffries Martin, Kirksville, MO: Truman State University Press, 2006, 113–33, and "Su Jacopo Nardi, i Giunti e la 'Nazione fiorentina' di Venezia," in *Studi in onore di Arnaldo D'Addario*, ed. L. Borgia, F. de Luca, P. Viti, and R. M. Zaccaria, Lecce: Conte, 1995, 937–49.

44 Brian Richardson, *Print Culture in Renaissance Italy: The Editor and the Vernacular Text, 1470–1600*, Cambridge and New York: Cambridge University Press, 1994, esp. 127.

45 For the letters from Nardi to Varchi in the 1540s and 1550s, see Salvatore Lo Re, *La crisi della libertà fiorentina: alle origini della formazione politica e intellettuale di Benedetto Varchi e Piero Vettori*, Rome: Edizioni di storia e letteratura, 2006, 212–57.

46 Jacopo Nardi, *Istorie della città di Firenze*, 2 vols., Florence: Società editrice delle storie del Nardi e del Varchi, 1838, 1.1. "Aveva la città di Firenze (come quasi tutte l'altre città) il popolo suo di tre generazioni di abitatori, ciò è la nobiltà, il popolo grasso, e il popolo minuto."

47 On politics and Nardi's history see Montevecchi, *Storici di Firenze*, 23–69.

48 Pasquale Villari, *The Life and Times of Niccolò Machiavelli*, 2nd edn., 2 vols., New York: Scribner, 1891, vol. 2, 202.

49 Benedetto Varchi, *Storia fiorentina*, Milan: Società tipografica de' classici italiani, 1803, vol. 1, 58–9.

50 *Ibid.*, vol. 1, 209–12.

51 *Ibid.*, vol. 3, 56–68.

52 *Ibid.*, vol. 3, 70–6.

53 See also Christopher F. Black, *The Italian Inquisition*, New Haven: Yale University Press, 2009, 160, 165, 172.

54 Benedetto Varchi, *L'ercolano: dialogo*, Florence: Stamperia di S.A.R. per gli Tartini, e Franchi, 1730, 327–8.

55 Carlo Lenzoni, *In difesa della lingua Fiorentina, et di Dante: con le regole da far bella et numerosa la prosa*, Florence: Torrentino, 1556.

56 Jesús Martínez de Bujanda, *Index de Rome, 1557, 1559, 1564: les premiers index romains et l'index du Concile de Trente*, Index des livres interdits 8, Sherbrooke, Québec and Geneva: Centre d'études de la Renaissance, Droz, 1984.

57 Peter Godman, *The Saint as Censor: Robert Bellarmine between Inquisition and Index*, Leiden and Boston: Brill, 2000, 3–99; Peter Godman, *From Poliziano to Machiavelli*, 303–33.

58 Anglo, *Machiavelli: The First Century*, 164–5, 180–2, 438–9, 459, 486, 655–7, 662.

59 Kahn, "Machiavelli's Afterlife."

60 Roberto Ridolfi, "Documenti sulle prime stampe della Storia d'Italia," in *Studi guicciardiniani*, Florence: Olschki, 1978, 197–223.

61 *Ibid.* See also Donato Giannotti, *Opere politiche*, ed. Furio Diaz, 2 vols., Milan: Marzorati, 1974, vol. 2, letter 23, 422, says he read it in manuscript: "io la lessi tutta quanta l'anno 46 in Bagnaia col cardinale Ridolfi." Vincent Luciani, "Francesco Guicciardini and his European Reputation," PhD thesis, Columbia University, New York, 1936, 402 n. 38.

62 Richardson, *Print Culture*, 150–1, 174–5.

63 Remigio Nannini, *Considerationi civili sopra l'historie di M. Francesco Guicciardini e d'altri historici: trattate per modo di discorso ...*, Venice: Damiano Zenaro, 1582.

64 "Chil far una legge in una Rep. & poi non l'osservare, e massimamente da quei che l'han fatta, nè difenderla contra chi la vuol rompere, è cosa di mal essempio."

65 "Che non si deue dar fede ad un error grande che si ueda fare al nimico, anzi si deue credere che lo faccia a posta, e che ui sia sotto qualche inganno," Nannini, *Considerationi civili*, fols. 53v–54v.

66 Francesco Guicciardini, *Opere inedite*, Florence: Barbera Bianchi, 1857.

67 Florence, BNCF, Magl. VIII, 1493, fols. 287r–289v. See Randolph Starn, "Francesco Guicciardini and his Brothers," in *Renaissance Studies in Honor of Hans Baron*, ed. Anthony Molho and John A. Tedeschi, Dekalb, IL: Northern Illinois University Press, 1971, 409–44, at 437.

68 Cosimo Bartoli, *Conseils militaires, fort vtiles et necessaires a tovs generaulx, colonnels, capitaines & soldats ...*, Paris: Lucas Breyer, 1586. See Judith Bryce, *Cosimo Bartoli (1503–1572): The Career of a Florentine Polymath*, Travaux d'humanisme et Renaissance, Geneva: Droz, 1983, 281–303. See also Cesare Vasoli, "Osservazioni sui 'Discorsi historici universali' di Cosimo Bartoli," in *Firenze e la Toscana dei Medici nell'Europa del '500*, Florence: Olschki, 1983, 727–38.

69 Cosimo Bartoli, *Discorsi historici universali*, Venice: Francesco de Francheschi Senese, 1569, 85.

70 On Ammirato see Rodolfo De Mattei, "Ammirato, Scipione," DBI. On the *Discourses* see Umberto Congedo, *La vita e le opere di Scipione Ammirato (notizie e ricerche)*, Trani: V. Vecchi, 1901, 341–72; Rodolfo De Mattei, "L'Ammirato e il Machiavelli," *Studi Salentini* 5–6 (1958): 99–142, and *Il pensiero politico di Scipione Ammirato*, Milan: Giuffrè, 1963.

71 Congedo, *Vita e le opere di Scipione Ammirato*, 252–7.

72 De Mattei, *Il pensiero politico di Scipione Ammirato*, 114–17.

73 Aureliano Cicuta (1566), Francesco Bocchi (1573), Pier' Maria Contarini (1601), Lorenzo Capelloni (1576), and Imperiale Cinuzzi (1604); Anglo, *Machiavelli: The First Century*, 181.

74 Black, *Italian Inquisition*, 196; Filippo de Vivo, *Information and Communication in Venice: Rethinking Early Modern Politics*, Oxford and New York: Oxford University Press, 2007, 207, 214, 216, 235–6; Paul F. Grendler, "The Roman Inquisition and the Venetian Press, 1540–1605," *Journal of Modern History* 47(1) (1975): 48–65.

75 Amadio Niecollucci, *De' discorsi politici, e militari libri tre, scielti fra grauissimi scrittori da Amadio Niecollvcci Toscano*, Venice: Marco Ginammi, 1630; Amadio Niecollucci, *De' discorsi politici, e militari libri tre*, Venice: Marco Ginammi, 1648. On clandestine circulation in Venice see Bertelli and Innocenti, *Bibliografia machiavelliana*, lv.

76 Giovanni Maria Pichi, *Avvertimenti politici*, Florence: A. Massi e L. Laud, 1641; Anglo, *Machiavelli: The First Century*, 671–8.

77 Godman, *From Poliziano to Machiavelli*, 303–33.

78 On Machiavelli's readership among Florentine religious dissidents, see Maurizio Viroli, *Machiavelli's God*, trans. Antony Shugaar, Princeton, NJ: Princeton University Press, 2010, 212–13.

79 On the debate, see among others Cecil Grayson, "Machiavelli e Dante: per la data e l'attribuzione del 'Dialogo intorno alla lingua'," *Studi e problemi di critica testuale* 2 (1971): 5–28; Mario Martelli, *Una giarda fiorentina: il Dialogo della lingua attribuito a Niccolò Machiavelli*, Rome: Salerno editrice, 1978; Ornella Castellani Pollidori and Niccolò Machiavelli, *Nuove riflessioni sul Discorso, o, Dialogo intorno alla nostra lingua di Niccolò Machiavelli, con una edizione critica del testo*, Quaderni di "Filologia e critica," Rome: Salerno editrice, 1981. For text plus discussion see Ornella Castellani Pollidori, *Niccolò Machiavelli e il Dialogo intorno alla nostra lingua*, Biblioteca di Lettere italiane 22: Studi e testi, Florence: Olschki, 1978; Niccolò Machiavelli, *Discorso o Dialogo intorno alla nostra lingua*, Turin: Einaudi, 1976.

80 Paolo Mini, *Discorso della nobiltà di Firenze, e de Fiorentini*, Florence: D. Manzani, 1593, followed by Paolo Mini, *Avvertimenti e digressioni sopra 'l Discorso della nobiltà di Firenze e de' Fiorentini*, Florence: D. Manzani, 1594.

81 Mini, *Discorso*, 126.

82 *Ibid.*, 101.

Part III

SOCIETY AND ENVIRONMENT

13

WHY VISIT THE SHOPS?

Taking up shopping as a pastime

Susan Mosher Stuard

Why the sudden interest in attending the noisy, sometimes foul, and often rank open market that provisioned a town when convention dictated sending a servant for necessaries, even for indulgences? Town markets had been around a long time without attracting people with the discretionary cash to spend for pleasure. On the grounds that markets were known for raucous folk bawling their wares a person could find a more pleasant part of town for a stroll:

> There never was so noble a garden
> As the Mercato Vecchio at that time …
> Every morning the street is filled
> With cartloads of Goods, and so great is the
> Throng that many stand waiting to pass.
> Noblemen and ladies stand to one side
> And often see the costerwomen and
> The gambling hucksters come to blows.

So Antonio Pucci (1310–1388), the versifying town crier of Florence, declared.[1] For the well-born and wealthy to stand aside for hawkers may have been unseemly but fourteenth-century folk were willing enough to put up with indignities in the interest of shopping – and being seen doing so. This was something of a new pastime and it had to do with the immediate pleasures of spying out goods, buying them on the spot, and satisfying appetites.

Open markets had emerged in Italian cities much earlier, witness efforts to prevent market wares from exiting Verona: "no one who transports … to the city market in order to sell … should dare or presume to carry any part of it out of the market" the statute read.[2] This was not new but a reiteration of old laws from a time when governments had worried more about supplying local consumers' needs than regulating business exchanges. Statutes that supervised long-distance trade were sharply differentiated from those governing local shopping, and Cicero's (106 BCE–40 BCE) distinction between great merchants and small tradespeople in *De officiis* still determined social attitudes by assigning prestige to the former while petty retailers who hawked and haggled garnered little. "Trade if it is on a small scale is to be considered vulgar; but if wholesale and on a large scale, importing large quantities from all parts of the world, and distributing to many without misrepresentation, it is not to be greatly disparaged. Nay, it even seems to deserve the highest respect," Cicero pronounced.[3]

Italians had long applauded their towns, and markets received some share of adulation. Bonvesin de la Riva's *On the Marvels of Milan*, 1288, saw an abundance of goods and foodstuffs as signs of Milan's greatness.[4] In the 1330s Giovanni Villani, the Florentine enumerator of all things great in his city, counted out the wool shops and money changers, livestock, and farm produce from the countryside supplying the Mercato Vecchio.[5] Opicino de Canistris praised his city of Pavia in 1330, especially the outdoor market where one could buy skins and furs or purses and gloves as well as cooked foods and wax candles.[6] Ambrogio Lorenzetti (1290–1348) merely changed the medium when celebrating the glories of Siena in *The Allegory of Good Government* painted for the Palazzo Publico; it featured shops frequented by passersby (see Illustration 13.5).

Antonio Pucci's "Proprietà di Mercato Vecchio" quoted above captures the color and sound of a Florentine market in progress in 1380 but it explains little other than that uninhibited rubbing shoulders when shopping transgressed distinctions of class, of wealth, and of affiliation.[7] It does not explain the draw of the marketplace for the great or why privileged persons were willing to tolerate assaults on their sensibilities and endure the inevitable jostling by crowds. Pucci's verse does indicate that wealthy Florentines visited the Old Market habitually thus identifying new cultural preferences that demand attention because the best people in town indulged in them. Then where are the social critics, the pundits, and commentators who spotted the market as a space that had developed sudden allure? Why is there a paucity of written comments about people who had started visiting shops? In 1304 in a sermon preached at Florence the Dominican friar Giordano da Pisa used the market place as analogy comparing Mary to a merchant who gave up material pleasures in favor of eternal ones.[8] This was certainly an apt contrast understood by a people who frequented markets but it scarcely answers the question why fourteenth-century people sought out pleasures through shopping, since this behavior is taken as a given.

In retrospect it appears that businesses in shops and booths meant opportunities where consuming itself, sometimes regardless of the product consumed, took on consequence. Consumption as a meaningful activity affected sales largely through enhancing simple, long-established provisioning with what may be regarded as embellishments and extra services. This was particularly true in the decades after the Black Death (1347–1350) during the "fat years" in Northern Italy when workmen's wages rose and urban folk had more discretionary cash to spend. Added to this luxury goods were available in far greater abundance than in earlier times. Sometimes luxury goods were sold in their own artisanal neighborhoods but often they were available in open markets as well. A market place presenting expensive wares would not be judged as especially "vulgar" since only a few could afford luxury goods.

At the same time the balance in social prestige between great and petty traders was growing more imprecise and "vulgar" was becoming somewhat less pejorative as the fourteenth century progressed. The diversity and number of consumables in urban markets, portrayed so attractively in the popular *Tacuinum sanitatis, c.* 1380–1400, marked a remarkable enlargement of interest in visiting shops.[9] It depicted shopping in a manner captivating for the public while it signaled to its viewers that provisioning local consumers was ripe for a rise in social status, dragging shop owners, hawkers, and salespeople, even raucous costermongers, along in its wake. Regulations for guilds like those in Perugia expanded beyond supervising corn and vegetable markets to inspecting guilds of mercers, second-hand cloth dealers, bag makers, goldsmiths, and even the local guild of miniaturists, all of whom had shops or set up stalls in the market.[10]

And it is not just that a miniaturist might set up shop in the town market, but traditional provisioners changed their ways of doing business. Between 1380 and 1400 several copies of an illustrated version of Ibn Butlan's *Tacuinum sanitatis* (actually a new pictorial device that combined words and images) appeared that featured vignettes that for information about the markets of Italy cannot be matched by written texts of the day. These picture books – three full versions and some partial texts survive from the dei Grassi workshop in Milan – featured charming idealized images of everyday life sketched into a book one could hold in one hand. It might well prompt its possessor to query, with a shrug of the shoulders, "and why shouldn't the shop selling pheasants serve a meal to a customer?". As a traditional service a shop of this kind cooked and sold fowl, and the smell might well attract a hungry man, so why not feed him in a logical extension of takeaway, the original function of the shop? The immediate gratification of a meal enhanced the shopping experience, encouraging sales. In this instance

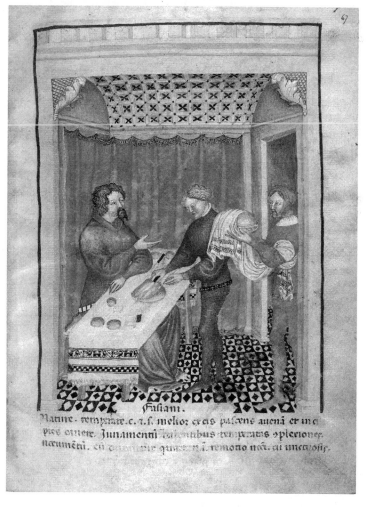

Illustration 13.1 Pheasant shop, *Tacuinum sanitatis*, Paris, BNF MS f. 67, 1380–1390.
Source: © Bibliothèque Nationale de France

215

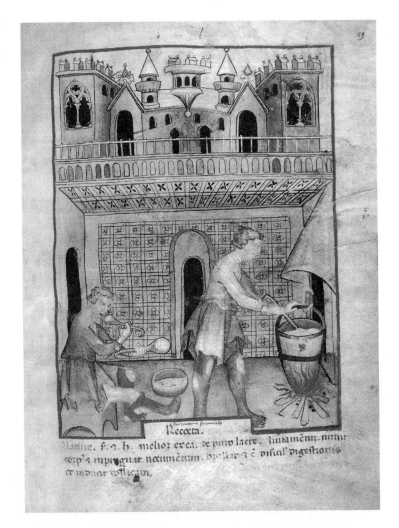

Illustration 13.2 Ricotta shop, *Tacuinum sanitatis*, Paris, BNF MS f. 59, 1380–1390.
Source: © Bibliothèque Nationale de France

a shop moved from merely provisioning to dining: the quick meal became an extension of service to customers, one visible to all. Likely as not passersby would see the well-dressed customer, with satisfaction written on his face, as he partook of a hot meal on the spot. An open shop functioned much like a stage and it turned out to be advantageous to shopkeepers to have spenders wandering the marketplace looking for a meal, that is, quick gratification; it encouraged the sale of pheasant.[11]

The *Tacuinum sanitatis* in its various illustrated editions differentiated shoppers into the prosperous, less prosperous, and the poor. If the pheasant shop fed the well-dressed customer, the ricotta shop, complete with boiling cauldron, did the same for a man so poor he lacks a robe and his hose is tattered and torn. The poor man eats with a large wooden spoon, most likely the same spoon used to stir a cauldron, but even his presence as a customer might

Illustration 13.3 Wine shop, *Tacuinum sanitatis*, Vienna, ONB MS f. 87v, fourteenth/fifteenth century.

Source: © Album / Art Resource, NY

garner some sales from passersby: here was nourishment that even the poor can afford, so get some ricotta today when you shop.[12]

At the other end of the provisioning scale stood the wine shop. A small crowd of wine tasters has gathered at a shop and the table before them is covered with cups, pitchers, and carafes. All imbibe; the crowd appears voluble and jolly. In this illustration the public was invited to watch the well-heeled at their pleasure, in a way that a tavern with its stout walls could not do. Opinions of the product might be overheard and less wealthy folks might learn which vineyards and vintages have caught the attention of local big spenders. The setting was accessible to all because shops encourage onlookers while at the same time creating a discernible social barrier between customers within the shop enjoying themselves and those outside left to envy people with cash on hand who have entered. At the most onlookers learned what was popular among wines and worth the expenditure even though their own funds were limited. Markets encouraged spending at descending levels; they were only democratic in access to shops; in terms of purchasing power that aroused new wants and desires, markets sharply differentiated shoppers according to their ability to spend.

In a certain sense shopping was transformed from the bottom up, beginning with foodstuffs. But if food purveyors could enhance sales by offering new features and services, so could others, like retailers of clothing, provide amenities and better services. With clothing shops visits to the market place became theatre. When it came to fine goods like silk fashioned into garments, the artist's gaze into the shop stood for the casual, but curious onlookers outside. Passersby became a spontaneous audience for transactions inside: negotiations on quality of cloth, on style, on fit, and on payment. Promoting the sale of ready-made, or partially constructed garments, that could be tailored to each customer, who then modeled the outfit on the spot, was a retailing stroke of genius. It was encouraged by the intimacy of the booth, which just happened to open onto a frequented passageway, in other words served as an instantaneous stage.

In the depiction of the silk shop in the Paris manuscript of the *Tacuinum sanitatis* a woman customer is not completely at ease in performing before curious onlookers: the apprehension on her face suggests shopping might test the limits of decorous behavior. The master of the shop fingers the silk of her sleeve, leaving the impression that shopping for silk could border on intimacy and was therefore somewhat audacious in a public venue. The customer's shopping experience, and the bespoke garment that will be her prize, may be worth pushing the boundaries of ladylike behavior: this customer has taken that risk.

The instrument of display on which textile shops often relied was a pole hung from the ceiling with garments shown off for all to see. This pole had a venerable history as a traditional peddler's pole at market fairs or brandished along roadways before it was brought indoors to the shops. It had a bright future as well because it may be seen today as a favored device mounted in shop windows. A convenience for the small space of a shop or stall, it also functioned as a valuable display space for the work carried out in the shop. At once observable yet safe from customer's hands, the pole became a staple of merchandizing by the fourteenth century.

Clusters of competing *bottege* in the market (clothes, hats, accessories in proximity to each other, likely somewhat removed from butcher shops) became an important feature of merchandising. Retailers competed in a fashion arcade with a variety of commodities roughly gathered by category. Grouped together, ready-made import shops located near the textile stalls competed effectively for the fashion penny with the bespoke clothing tailored there. Hats and headdresses were in demand since both new clothes and new hats could turn out a fashionable figure. It is possible to imagine a substitution curve of sorts where customers might choose dashing hats over new fine robes because either enhanced a wardrobe and the hat might be a good deal cheaper than the robe (although not always, careful reckoning on the part of the customer was in order in the case of a beaver hat). Shops provided a range in available wares, cost, and a heightened capacity for enhancement, which in turn tested an individual customer's ability to assess the whim of fashion, carry it all off, and in turn attract imitators.

The choices were many: *berrette di bevero (castoro) di Venezia, berrette di lana colorate di Parigi, berrette di pesce di Milano, berrette di lana fatte ad ago, cappelli di bevero dell'Inghilterra, di Bruges, cappelli di paglia di Parigi e di Cremona* (Datini company of traders, fourteenth century). Berets

Illustration 13.4 Silk shop, *Tacuinum sanitatis*, Paris, BNF MS f. 95, 1380–1390.
Source: © Kharbine-Tapabor / The Art Archive at Art Resource, NY

(visorless caps) of beaver from Venice, berets of colored wool from Paris, berets of beaver from Milan, berets of knitted wool, hats (with brims) from England and Bruges, and hats of straw from Paris and Cremona.[13] The market was deep and varied because suppliers like Francesco Datini of Prato and his partners saw to it that a range of luxury goods were available.[14] Wholesale, ready-to-wear hats were a specialty trade provided to townspeople by knowledgeable traders. Those beaver hats mentioned above suggest that Europe's supply of aquatic animals had yet to be exhausted, even if the public failed to distinguish aquatic animals like beavers from fish, as in *"berrette de pesce* [of fish] *da Milano."* These were beaver, like the beaver hats from Venice.

Each luxury category of goods had its suppliers, and each category competed in the open market with other luxury wares. Most precious of all were accessories of silver and gilded silver studded with gems. Traditionally these had been provided to the aristocracy and royalty, who could expect merchants to come to them with the finest wares. *Bottoni d'ottone dorati e argentati di Milano, Firenze, Lucca* (Datini company of traders, fourteenth century); *maspillas et planetas et alios arzenteos deauratos in saculla ponderis unciarum XXVII* (Doge Lorenzo Celsi inventory, 1365); *buctonos de argento undecim, buctonos quatuor de curallo, buctones de argento decem cum petris clavatos* (inventory of the Queen of Sicily, 1393).[15] Buttons of brass, gilded and silvered, from Milan, Florence, and Lucca, buttons and plaques and other gilded silver pieces in a sack weighing 27 ounces; eleven buttons of silver, four buttons of coral, ten silver buttons with embedded stones. Supply routes had been thoroughly rationalized over the previous century, so in direct competition to hats, retailers supplied the market with brass buttons, gilded or silvered, and also cheaper buttons of brass, and some of iron. It is important to note that many editions of similar items, or cheaper imitations that could pass for the real thing, were for sale in town marketplaces. Rather than buy new clothes, a customer might merely add buttons for a new look and tight fit, providing a retailer of bespoke garments further competition.

To imagine a substitution curve for fashionable goods – the three noted above: ready-made clothing, imported beaver hats, and accessories like decorative buttons ranging from cheap brass to gilded and embossed buttons – multiple products competed in the market allowing retailers to tempt shoppers with alternatives. Fabric, costly in better grades, represented inelastic cost to be passed through to consumers but ready-made garments abated the sting somewhat through the instant gratification of a fitting on the spot, very likely before an admiring audience of passersby. A well-run clothing shop had staff on hand to finish a garment promptly. Nonetheless items of clothing needed clever selling stratagems to compete with imported hats and well-crafted buttons in markets influenced by fashion. Since second-hand outlets functioned nearby, the ingenious shopper could find the same or similar products in used and refurbished condition. Choice favored the consumer.

The high end of the market proved to be even more innovative than provisioning food and clothing once luxury shopping established itself in fourteenth-century Italian towns. For high-end shopping premises were often stationary and clustered together in a street devoted to their trade, with safety of the inventory a consideration.[16] Since painters were disposed to paint *orafi* or goldsmiths, who were their associates and fellow craftsmen, cityscapes in religious as well as genre painting featured goldsmiths' luxury wares with some frequency; this was especially the case when painters were called upon to depict the life of popular St. Eligius, the seventh-century patron saint of goldsmiths. How was it that artists captured the selling stratagems of high-end retailers in images so effectively when prose descriptions remained rare and uninformative? Artists painted the devices for selling objects of precious metal with an acute eye as characteristically urban behaviors, bearing witness to the prosperity of the community. Their works of art were commissioned and completed at about the same moment that customers first encountered new stratagems in retailing, so images relate up-to-the-minute information on how retailing markets functioned. The artist, whether in the dei Grassi workshop that produced the *Tacuinum Sanitatis* manuscripts, or one who individually fulfilled commissions for religious or civic painting, adopted a buyer's gaze mimicking a customer's vantage point.

As a result artists are an unmatched source of information about the new pastime of high-end shopping in fourteenth-century Italian towns. They painted to inspire, to elucidate, to educate, or in the case of the *Tacuinum sanitatis* to explain how one lives a healthful life. They employed towns as settings because townscapes helped to create an important explanatory

Illustration 13.5 Section from Ambrogio Lorenzetti, *The Allegory of Good Government*, fourteenth century, Siena.

Source: © Scala / Art Resource, NY

space for their chosen subjects. Artists were keen observers not disposed to ignore daily routines and the material conditions of urban life. As a result their art explained behaviors that were no more than alluded to elsewhere.[17]

By contrast fourteenth-century textual evidence tells about supply networks, seldom does it provide description or analysis of market behaviors. Historians search for useful evidence about customer demand, and how retailers encouraged it, but they may search in vain if authors of the day failed to find retailing activity a fitting topic for comment or study. Were the devices employed in marketing too mundane, shallow, or crass to warrant the attention of literate men? Marketing today relies on comparable ploys, and advertisers argue over an ounce difference in sizing to achieve a competitive edge or insist about white in packaging for instant recognition for a product or a product line.[18] In the modern world market behaviors are worthy of serious study, but in the late medieval world artists were among the few dependable observers. They understood that what may appear trifling can add up to significant innovation. Since production and selling were closely associated, and often practiced in the same venue, artisans, like goldsmiths, tailors, and gem cutters participated in learning the skills of merchandizing. They did not disdain the simple, but effective, tools that were the tricks of the trade.

Illustration 13.6 Master of the Madonna of Mercies, *St. Eligius Fashioning a Gold Saddle for King Chlothar*, fourteenth century, Prado Museum, Madrid.
Source: © The Art Archive / Museo del Prado Madrid / Collection Dagli Orti

St. Eligius (*c.* 588–660), patron saint of goldsmiths, was a popular subject in late medieval painting and his legend allowed for numerous genre scenes to commemorate piety. Even more popular than his depiction as a bishop, counselor, or healer was St. Eligius as craftsman in a contemporary goldsmith's shop where both production and retailing take place. The market scene, now on view in the Prado diptych painted by the Master of the Madonna of Mercy, shows the saint at his bench with the tools of his trade flanked by his two assistants. He fashions a gold saddle for King Clothar on a glamorous work counter covered by a fine Turkish carpet. An imported oriental carpet signified wealth and only the finest shops in town could afford such a display.[19] To use one as a cover on which one hammered metal was an ostentatious touch intended to amaze customers. The gathered crowd is duly impressed and perhaps intrigued as well by the artisanal work carried on in the rear of the shop, yet clearly visible to the public. Here one workman pumps bellows and another one hammers metal. Behind them hangs a pole used for the display of shop wares, in this case, gold belts, or more likely silver belts gilded to mimic gold. Considering the gold saddle on the counter, the gold religious objects worked by the saint's two seated assistants, and gold coins on the counter, a full display of what a goldsmith will supply to the public confronts the viewer; a comprehensive inventory of a goldsmith's goods is on view. This was advertising at an exalted level celebrating a saint through an exhibition of the goldsmith's range of wares. Gold saddles were certainly beyond the reach of customers but gilded silver belts might not be.

There is a further question worth raising: at the top of the hierarchy of retailing activity, that is, the gem shops and purveyors of gold and silver wares, great importance was attached to the site itself – often a setting determined retail success. What a man selected and bought there would be widely noted and important purchases furnished topics for local gossip. When the agents of King John I of Portugal (1357–1433) negotiated Venetian government bonds at Rialto, then purchased luxury wares nearby, the world took note.[20] Venice was particularly accommodating to luxury shopping because steps away from Rialto, in nearby S. Silvestri, gem and goldsmith shops lined the *fondamenta* and nearby passageways. Jewelers and goldsmiths, recognized elites among retailers, were situated so they could be observed by fellow artists, visitors, and local magnates; these clusterings indicated important merchandizing development although it would take a good century for written commentary to catch up to what images reveal about innovation in high-end shopping venues.

When a writer finally did so, Benedetto Cotrugli Raguseo (1410–1469) in *Il Libro dell'arte della mercatura*, about 1458 – Odd Langholm describes this merchant manual as the first recognizable textbook of business – it marks a moment when writerly prose finally supplants painterly acuity in describing retail markets. The work contains systematic analysis of retail activity: location, choice of merchandise, forms of exchange, resource allocation, partnership, insurance, correspondence, record-keeping, and accounting.[21] It antedates Luca Pacioli (*c.* 1447–1517) in descriptions of double entry bookkeeping. Cotrugli, a practical man, analyzes retail activity and translates it into embryonic economic theory producing a *practicum*, or medieval merchant manual that recognizes the consequence of selling to the urban public. Cotrugli collapses the Ciceronian distance in social status between the great and the petty merchant by elevating the man who sells in the marketplace to *gentleman* of the first order. Such a man may with confidence consort with the most exalted customers on equal terms because his calling is honorable and he is himself a gentleman, Cotrugli informs his readers.

"He [the merchant] also has to be eloquent and amiable so that he can almost continuously converse in the same manner with men, ladies, and gentlemen. And this is surely a polite art and every gentleman should be versed in it," Cotrugli stated.[22] Resource allocation, partnerships, insurance, and record-keeping will not alone bring success, the retailer must add sure social capabilities to his repertoire of skills.

"The dignity and office of the merchant is grand and sublime," Cotrugli proclaimed, partly because of his wealth and lifestyle, and partly because of his contribution to the common good.[23] The merchant supplies the community with commodities, as well as with money, fine gems, and precious metals. He causes its various crafts to flourish, the earth to be cultivated, animal husbandry to prosper, he secures employment for the poor, increases public revenue through taxes and duties and thus fills the public treasury.[24] Eloquent and affable, his place of business is as worthy of frequenting as the council chamber or halls of justice. The noblest of men may meet in such a fine shop and converse, but certainly the Master of the Madonna of Mercy, had seen, and highlighted, all this a century earlier. Cotrugli began his analysis with the crucial question of the social distance between great or long-distance merchants on the one hand and retailers in the market place on the other. He then mounted a bold defense for the gentlemanly status of the latter. In this way he signaled to his reader that he understood that selling turns on social status, with wealth as the arbiter. Yet what follows in each of his chosen topics is comment on the economic consequences of merchant activity, and Cotrugli should not be interpreted as a simple snob, he is merely aware of how social standing determines retailing success.

Yet Cotrugli often fails to excite readers to the true significance of his insights into selling because he was prolix, tendentious, pompous, and much given to over-citing a parade of classical authorities.[25] Furthermore his text appeared in corrupted form until Ugo Tucci edited Cotrugli from the recovered Strozzi manuscript of his work in 1990. Today Cotrugli remains difficult to appreciate compared to his contemporaries, the spritely humanist word-smiths of Tuscany. Cotrugli is liable to be dismissed out of hand for bad prose, but pompous commentary has its virtues for his message. Fine manners and social pretensions are neces-sary to sell at the top of the retail market and blend that with business sense and a good Classical education and a merchant becomes the equal of any gentleman in Italy. Thus the merchant's finest product is himself, and Cotrugli celebrated this with his insights steeped in sonorous phrases. In doing so he minimized any distinction between great or small mer-chants, long distance or local commerce. All mercantile activity warrants respect and the gentlemen who follow trade attain the highest respectability. Cotrugli goes so far as to assert that a great merchant falling on hard times should not disdain engaging in brokerage or even lending horses. Erudition, business acumen, and gentility determine status, not the scale of the endeavor or selling to the public.

In certain instances, like the goldsmith's shop or the jeweler's shop, selling to the public ascended to the heights of great social distinction; sales were treated as exclusive interviews and personal encounters, yet their drama also played out before an audience in the street. The Venetian 1573 printed text of Cotrugli's work, much amended and titled *Della mercatura et del mercante perfecto* (shortened today to *The Perfect Merchant*) revealed how selling at the best shops had raised the social standing of certain retailers. It reads "[Our] own people of Ragusa are very skilled in this management. I should praise them ... because they employ wares which are quickly sold, such as silver, gold, lead, copper, wax, crimson, and leather, and because of the dexterity of mind they have."[26]

With this in mind let us return to the workshop of St. Eligius for a lesson in how a retailer at the high-end of trade succeeded. St. Eligius, a celebrated seventh-century saint who had achieved cult status in Italy by the fourteenth century as patron saint of goldsmiths, sits between his apprentices, who fashion a crucifix and an icon (Virgin Mary?). Solemnity and gravity envelop the scene, which lends cachet to the products displayed in the nether reaches of the workshop. To the back of the shop and on a pole gilded artifacts are carefully, if casually, displayed; these are *not* sacramental objects but rather ready-made high-priced con-sumer goods that for instant gratification would be hard to beat. Responding to this scene of saintly veneration, purchasing luxury wares to enhance one's appearance might just be passed off as a pious endeavor.

To return to Verona, where earlier town statutes governing the marketplace had been con-cerned with provisioning townspeople with necessities, much had changed by the late years of the fourteenth century. By an account in Franco Sacchetti's *Trecentonovelle*, when three young swells walk out in Verona to be admired by the ladies, and are instead mocked for their "Florentine" fashion of wearing gorgets (neck armor) as casual dress, Sacchetti remarked of them in 1385: "Now we have our fashion of wearing these gorgets, within which our necks are held so stiffly that we cannot even look upon our feet."[27]

The author of *Trecentonovelle* tells little about the vain young men, but the reader learns that men may obtain pieces of military armor in the Verona market place (or any other local market for that matter) and dress up to impress the ladies.[28] Giovanni and Piero ditch their gorgets, but their friend Salvestro keeps his on, spills his supper of hot beans down his neck inside his gorget (eating in one was difficult) and burns himself. All this nonsense is possible in a busy marketplace so, of course, expect a moral. "O vanagloria dell'umane posse, che per te si perde la vera Gloria," which translates "O vainglory of human powers, true glory is lost through you."[29]

I would argue that "true" glory was increasingly difficult to achieve in the face of markets' lures, their vain glories. In a town market one might find a bean supper around a turn of the corner from the armorer's shop. And that armorer had new or "lightly used" gorgets that could be bought and donned on the spot. In this staged setting the enticement of desirable goods was performance art played out before the passing crowd, that is, the casual market frequenter. A customer might stroll by the grisly abattoir and then move further on toward the hushed interior of the jeweler's luxurious premises. A range of products, cheap to dear, homely to exotic, with a drama played out before crowds, characterized shopping. This pleasurable pastime in turn relied on heightened awareness of appearances, of fashion, and the many new wares available for displays of oneself. Selling might mean greater social status for some local merchants, especially those who knew how to freight snob appeal onto their retail acumen and do it up right. The appeal to self-enhancement that could cut through a customer's reservations about spending his or her cash on hand developed into a reputable technique at the high end of retail markets. In time the world would come to Italy to visit fabled premises like these fine shops and they would spend their money. Material goods revealed an enhanced capacity for expressing wants, desires, preferences, and status, even veneration of holy saints.

Notes

1 Antonio Pucci, "Proprietà di Mercanto Vecchio," in *Poeti minori del Trecento*, ed. Natalino Sapegno, Milan: F. Villardi, 1934, p. 403–7. See also Franco Sacchetti, *Treventonovelle*, ed. Vincenzo Pernicone, Florence, Sansoni, 1946, Novella CLXXV, pp. 432–5, which tells about Antonio Pucci; see also Sacchetti's Novella CLIX about a mule in the Mercato Vecchio, pp. 387–94.

2 *Statuti di Verona del 1327*, ed. S. A. Bianchi and R. Granuzzo, Rome: Jouvence, 1992, pp. 546–7. Texts in notes 1 through 3 have been translated into English in Trevor Dean, trans. and ed., *The Towns of Italy in the Later Middle Ages*, Manchester: Manchester University Press, 2000, pp. 121–8.

3 Cicero, *De officiis*, trans. and ed. Walter Miller, New York: Macmillan, 1913, Book I, xlii, pp. 154–5 for facing translation.

4 Bonvesin de la Riva, *De magnalibus Mediolani*, 1288, ed. Maria Corti, Milan: Bompiani, 1974.

5 Giovanni Villani, *Cronica di Giovanni Villani*, repr., 8 vols., Rome: Multigrafica Editrice, 1980.

6 Opicino de Canistris, *Il libro delle lodi della città di Pavia*, trans. and ed. Delfino Ambaglio, Pavia: Logos International, 1984.

7 Pucci, "Proprietà di Mercanto Vecchio," pp. 403–7.

8 Giordano da Pisa, *Avventuale fiorentino 1304*, ed. Silvia Serventi, Bologna: Il Mulino, 2006, p. 591. On Italian markets see Dennis Romano, *Markets and Marketplaces in Medieval Italy c. 1100 to c. 1440*, New Haven: Yale University Press, 2005, and Evelyn Welch, *Shopping in the Renaissance*, New Haven: Yale University Press, 2005.

9 Cathleen Hoeniger, "The Illuminated *Tacuinum sanitatis* Manuscripts from Northern Italy (ca. 1380–1400): Sources, Patrons, and the Creation of a New Pictorial Genre," in *Visualizing Medieval Medicine and Natural History, 1200–1550*, ed. Jean A. Givens, Karen M. Reeds, and Alain Touwaide, Aldershot: Ashgate, 2006, pp. 51–91. See Luisa Cogliati Arano, *The Medieval Health*

Handbook: Tacuinum sanitatis, New York: George Braziller, 1976, for the illustrations. See also F. Moly Mariotti, "Contribution à la connaissance des '*Tacuina sanitatis*,'" *Arte Lombarda* 104 (1993): 32–9, and Brucia Witthoft, "The *Tacuinum sanitatis*, a Lombard Panorama," *Gesta* 17 (1978): 49–60, on the relationship of the various manuscripts to each other. Much of the literature on the manuscripts has to do with how to live a healthful life or depictions of plant life.

10 *Statuti de Perugia* (1342), vol. 1, corrected and interpreted according to the 1596 Latin printed version in Dean, *Towns of Italy*, p. 127, and F. Agostino, "Il volgare Perugino negli 'Statuti del 1342,'" *Studi di filogogio italiana* 26 (1968): 91–199.

11 The *Tacuinum sanitatis* illustrated pleasures including courtly love, fashion, mild eroticism, comedy, the hunt, gardening, agriculture, managing the estate, cooking, new foods, and shopping. Hoeniger, "The Illuminated *Tacuinum sanitatis* Manuscripts," p. 76. The illustrations overwhelm the brief lines of text on a healthful life found at the bottom of each page. They derive from Ibn Butlan's writing and stress harmony and balance for health. See selected translations in Arano, *The Medieval Health Handbook*, color plates I–XLVIII, e.g., a translation for ricotta (*recoccta*) in illustration 2: "*Nature*: Cold and humid. *Optimum*: That obtained from pure milk. *Usefulness*: It nourishes the body and fattens it. *Dangers*: It causes occlusions, is difficult to digest, and favors colic. Paris, fol 59." Arano, plate XXXI. See also note 12.

12 An ancient Italian recipe, ricotta was a whey-based product made from sheep, goat, or water buffalo milk. As a by-product from making sharp cheese, which was often used for grating by the wealthy, ricotta only required boiling and it could be eaten without aging. Ricotta has low protein content. It was relatively inexpensive and therefore it attracted the poor in need of sustenance.

13 "*berrete di bevero (castor) di Venezia, berrette di lana colorate di Parigi, berrette di lana fatte ad ago*," Luciana Frangioni, *Chiedere e ottenere: L'approvvigionamento di prodotti di successo della bottega Datini di Avignone nel XIV secolo*, Florence: Opus Libri, 2002, p. 14.

14 Francesco Datini of Prato (1335–1410) joined a company of Florentine traders at a young age and supplied arms to Avignon. Later he provided local cardinals with luxury wares. With time his growing company of traders expanded their territory to supply luxuries to cities throughout north Italy. In 1870 his 500 account books and over 150,000 business papers were discovered in his residence in Prato, which had been gifted to the town.

15 "*bottoni d'ottone dorati e argentati di Milano, Firenza, Lucca*," Frangioni, *Chiedere e ottenere*, p. 14. Bartolomeo Cecchetti, *La vita dei Veneziani*, Venice: Emiliana, 1886, p. 123, "Le gemme del Doge Lorenzo Celsi," citing Venetian State Archives, Procuratori di s. Marco, Misti, vol. 120. Daniela Santoro, "Il tesoro recuperato. L'inventario dei beni delle regine di Sicilia confiscate a Manfredi Alagona nel 1393," *Anuario de Estudios Medievales* 37 (2007): 71–106, see p. 105.

16 In Dubrovnik (medieval Ragusa) the street of the goldsmiths still exists. In Venice goldsmith shops were clustered near Rialto and still are. See Susan Mosher Stuard, *Gilding the Market*, Philadelphia: University of Pennsylvania Press, 2006, pp. 146–81.

17 For comparison see Giovanni da Taranto, *c.* 1305, *San Domenico vende i suoi libri per darne il ricavato ai poveri di Palencia*. Naples: Pinacoteca nazionale di Capodimente, in Ferdinando Bologna, *I pittori alla corte Angiona di Napoli*, Rome: Ugo Bozzi, 1969, pp. 1–34, fig. 70

18 Today coffee is prone to changes in container weight as a selling stratagem. Brands like Pepperidge Farms grew to prominence employing white in packaging.

19 See *Treatise on the Seven Vices*, Genoa, fourteenth century. British Library, MS Add. 27695. The goldsmith shop illustrates the vice of greed. No goldsmithing work is in progress, so the Turkey carpet shown here is simply a backdrop for displaying the goldsmith's art to customers.

20 Reinhold Mueller, "Foreign Investment in Venetian Government Bonds and the Case of Paolo Guinigi, Lord of Lucca, Early 15th Century," in *Cities of Finance*, ed. Herman Dierderiks and David A. Reeder, Amsterdam: North-Holland, 1996, pp. 69–90.

21 Odd Langholm, *The Merchant in the Confessional*, Leiden: Brill, 2003, pp. 266–7, 280. See also Gunnar Dahl, *Trade, Trust, and Networks: Commercial Culture in Late Medieval Italy*, Lund: Nordic Academic Press, 1998, pp. 253–62.

22 "Debbe anche essere eloquente et affabile, perché al continuo quasi conversino simili consignori, signore et gentilomini. Et questa per certo è gentile arte, et ogni gentilomo se ne doverria intendere," Benedetto Cotrugli Raguseo, *Il libro dell'arte di mercatura* [*c.* 1458], ed. Ugo Tucci, Venice: Arsenale, 1990, "De gioiellieri," pp. 176–7.

23 Cotrugli, *Il Libro dell'arte di mercatura*, p. 177. See Pierre Jouanique, "Three Medieval Merchants: Francesco di Marco Datini, Jacques Coeur, and Benedetto Cotrugli," *Accounting, Business and Financial History* 6(3) (1996): 261–75, K. P. Kheil, *Benedetto Cotrugli Raguseo: Ein Beitrag zur Geschichte der Buchhaltung*, Vienna, 1906, and Basil S. Yamey, "Benedetto Cotrugli on Bookkeeping (1458)," *Accounting, Business and Financial History* 4(1) (1994): 43–50.

24 *The Merchant in the Confessional*, p. 268. Cotrugli, *Il Libro dell'arte di mercatura*, pp. 206–8.

25 See Ugo Tucci, "Introduction," in *Il libro dell'arte di mercatura*, pp. 3–128, especially p. 36. Cotrugli salted his pages with references to the Bible and church fathers as well. For examples see p. 171 for reference to Pliny's *Natural History*, p. 177, to St. Augustine, p. 180, to Boethius, and invoking the names of all the Roman gods, p. 185.

26 Benedetto Cotrugli, *Della mercatura et del mercante perfetto*, ed. Francesco Patrizi, Venice, 1573, Book I, fols. 35–8 and 25v–29r. Robert S. Lopez translated excerpts from this version in *Medieval Trade in the Mediterranean World*, New York: Columbia University Press, 1955, pp. 375–7, 413–19, noting in footnote 10, p. 416, that Cotrugli was verbose.

27 Franco Sacchetti, *Il Trecentonovelle*, ed. Vincenzo Pernicone, Florence: Sansoni, 1945, Novella CLXXVIII, pp. 443–6. See also *Tales from Sacchetti*, trans. Mary Steegman, New York: Dent, 1908, Tale 178, p. 199, for the quotation. After the introduction of plate armor about 1350 the gorget that covered the space between helmet and breastplate became attractive to civilians as a military affectation and fashion. The gorget was to enjoy many centuries of popularity and it often served as a mark of military rank. Charles Wilson Peale painted General Washington wearing a gorget in 1772. Officers of the Swedish army favored the gorget and Hitler reintroduced the gorget to Europe in the mid-twentieth century. See Herbert Norris, *Medieval Costume and Fashion*, Mineola, NY: Dover, 1999, and Elizabeth Lewandowski, *Complete Costume Dictionary*, Lanham, MD: Scarecrow, Press, 2011.

28 Sacchetti, *Il Trecentonovelle*, Novella CLXXVIII, pp. 443–6; Tale 178.

29 *Ibid.*, p. 446.

14

THROWING ARISTOTLE
FROM THE TRAIN
Women and humanism

Sarah Gwyneth Ross

In dedicating her erudite *Lettere* (1617) to Carlo Emmanuele II, Duke of Savoy, the celebrated actor, poet and playwright Isabella Andreini asserted her membership in the humanist republic of letters. After rehearsing Anaxagoras' claim that the purpose of human life is to study the heavens and the order of the universe, and on her way to ventriloquizing the complaint of Scipio Africanus that he was never less at leisure than when he was at leisure, she paused to present herself as a new Socrates. "Now I," she explained, "having been by the generosity of the Supreme Maker sent to be a Citizen of the World, and the desire for knowledge by chance arising in me more passionately than in many other women of our age ... I have wished with all my power to nurture it."[1] Andreini was in good company. She was correct that many women of the Renaissance era did not pursue higher learning, but a substantive number of others did engage in the *studia humanitatis*. If Joan Kelly decided in the late 1970s that women did not have a Renaissance (during the Renaissance), research in the ensuing decades has revealed hundreds of women engaging Renaissance literary culture as Andreini did.[2] Considering only Latin poets known to contemporaries, as Jane Stevenson has done, still yields over a hundred women humanists writing between the years 1400 and 1650, strong concentrations of whom were in Italy, England, Germany, France, and the Netherlands.[3] When we include women who were Latin readers, like Andreini, or who made ancient culture and literature, encountered in the vernacular, their principal intellectual commitment, that hundred increases by at least an order of magnitude. Women's sustained encounters with the liberal arts through the Renaissance centuries and the positive celebrity that their work often received indicate that they were not exceptional or marginal figures, as we once claimed.[4] Instead, early modern intellectual women are best understood as active members of the communities of knowledge stretching from Italy, France, and Spain to England and Germany.[5]

Most often born into prosperous families within the patrician and mercantile elites, educated at home and sometimes in convents, women from the fifteenth through the seventeenth centuries went on to publish in all of the major genres of humanistic writing: epistles, treatises, translations, oration, dialogues, poetry, and drama. In the course of their work, women humanists made numerous contributions to Renaissance thought, but in the aggregate their most innovative contributions centered on arguments for the intellectual equality of the sexes.[6] The pan-European *querelle des femmes* (debate on women), within which we find a substantive proportion of women humanists' literary production, attracted numerous male writers. Yet, from its inception in the late fourteenth century with Christine de Pizan's war against the misogynistic *Romance of the Rose*, the debate was initiated, renewed, and transformed by women writers who deployed the classical canon to redefine female capability and the boundaries of normative female endeavor.

Women's literary work, together with that of their male supporters and colleagues, threw Aristotelian misogyny some distance from Renaissance Europe's principal train of thought. Especially in the *Physics* and *Generation of Animals*, Aristotle situated the female consistently on the negative side of his characteristic binaries. If men were active, courageous, strong, and rational, women were passive, timid, weak, and irrational. Claiming that nature always aimed at perfection, in this case the creation of males, the existence of females proved that reproduction did not always go according to plan. By the time Andreini passed to a better life in 1604, one could not call women "nature's mistakes" and expect agreement in literary circles; that position now required argument. Contributors to the *querelle* had proved to a broad sector of the educated public that women's intellectual capabilities could equal or even surpass men's.

Surveying this shift and some of its most creative participants, we will begin by examining the contexts that nurtured women's minds. Without the benefit of the educational system many young men followed from grammar school to university, women's education happened at home or in convents. The educations gleaned in these settings were not necessarily inferior to those obtained by men in dedicated pedagogical institutions; indeed, they could be far superior depending on the quality of the instructors. Still, it remains true that women's access to educational resources throughout the early modern period depended on parental goodwill more than was the case for men. Once educated, many learned women had a great deal to say on that point, and on women's intellectual equality more generally, as we will see when we turn to their writings as such in the second half of this chapter.

Patterns of education

The most famous Italian women humanists of the fifteenth century all received a good portion of their instruction at home. This was the case for the Florentine Hellenist Alessandra Scala no less than Latinist celebrities of the Veneto, including Isotta and Ginevra Nogarola, Cassandra Fedele, and Laura Cereta.[7] Scala and Fedele were taught principally by their humanist fathers, though Angelo Fedele, being more of an aspirant to than a master of Latin letters, arranged for his daughter to continue her studies beyond his own range of competence with the learned monk Gasparino Borro. Bianca Borromeo, mother of Isotta and Ginevra Nogarola, provided her daughters with an excellent tutor, Martino Rizzoni, who was at the time fresh from his own studies with the illustrious pedagogue Guarino Guarini da Verona. Laura Cereta speaks at length in one of her autobiographical letters about the early instruction she received from a learned nun, but the legal terminology that appears throughout her letterbook also attests to significant instruction from her lawyer father, Silvestro.[8]

Humanism also began at home for learned sixteenth-century women, including Moderata Fonte (Modesta da Pozzo) and Lucrezia Marinella. Fonte spent some time at the convent of Santa Marta, but got more substantive training in Latin from her grandfather, the poet

Prospero Saraceni.[9] Marinella's writings suggest exclusive tutoring from her father, Giovanni, who was a physician and humanist.[10]

Women's classical education elsewhere in Europe followed similar patterns. Sixteenth-century England boasted its own roster of women humanists, paradigmatically Margaret More Roper.[11] Roper and her siblings were taught directly by their father, Sir Thomas More, through a Latin correspondence course with him, as well as by tutors whom More had hired, including William Gonnell and John Clement. Roper's own children, including Mary Roper Bassett (a translator of Eusebius), were schooled both by Roper herself and by tutors whom she enlisted. The four daughters of the Cooke family also enjoyed paternal support, but tutors undertook their instruction. Sir Anthony Cooke, while certainly a man of learning (and represented by contemporaries as a reformist version of Thomas More), came to the study of Latin and Greek comparatively late in life and probably learned some of the finer points alongside his children.[12] Jane and Mary Fitzalan, together with their brother, represented their father, Henry Fitzalan (Earl of Arundel), as their "headmaster," but they, too, were taught the classics by tutors, among them most likely the Italian Protestant exile Francesco Ubaldini who was a longtime client of their father.

In France and the Low Countries, we find similar household enclaves of humanist endeavor. The Morel family, for instance, headed by the diplomat and royal tutor Jean de Morel (d. 1581) and the poet Antoinette de Loynes, boasted three brilliant women Latinists: Lucrèce, Diane, and the famous Camille, all of whom received instruction from their learned parents, but also extensive tutoring from the Dutch polyglot Carolus (Karel) Utenhove (b. 1536).[13] Similarly, the Franco-British calligrapher and linguist Esther Inglis benefited from the instruction from her mother, the calligrapher Marie Presot, and her father, Nicolas, a schoolmaster in France and later master of the French School in Edinburgh, where he moved his Huguenot family in the wake of St. Bartholomew's Day. The seventeenth-century celebrity Anna Maria van Schurman seems to have begun her education by eavesdropping on her father as he was teaching Latin to her brothers; later, when it was clear she derived as much (if not more) benefit from the lessons, she became an "official" student in the household school, perfecting her Latin and going on to learn Greek, Hebrew, Syriac, and Coptic.[14]

Similar stories abound concerning women's advanced education in Spain, as we are learning from Anne Cruz, Rosalie Hernández, and Elizabeth Howe.[15] The Spanish scholars Luisa Sigea (d. 1560) and Ana Francisca Abarca de Bolea (d. 1686), both skilled Latinists, were daughters of humanists and enjoyed considerable tutoring at home – in de Bolea's case, probably in large part from her mother.[16] Humanist tools built notable careers. Sigea's erudition brought her service as lady-in-waiting and tutor at the Portuguese royal court. De Bolea, benefitting also from her natal family's nobility, became an abbess.

The role of convents in bringing women into contact with classical languages and literature in the first place is more difficult to assess. Many women no doubt owed their knowledge of Latin at least in part to convent schooling. As we have seen, Laura Cereta and Moderata Fonte received some convent education, though Fonte, unlike Cereta, never speaks of convents as sources of intellectual opportunity for women.

The quality of instruction in European convents varied wildly. Some elite convents, for example the Vergini in Venice, housed nuns who both wrote and delivered orations in Latin.[17] Before she took her vows, Teresa of Ávila read Cicero and Virgil in her convent library.[18] Other prosperous convents fostered the vernacular literary and theatrical talents of their inhabitants, as Elissa Weaver has shown.[19] Yet often one cannot determine how much instruction took place in convent schools and how much the nuns had brought with them from earlier studies at home. The learned Charitas Pirkheimer (d. 1532), for instance, abbess of St. Clara in Nuremberg and best known for her correspondence with Conrad Celtis, had completed her humanistic education before taking the veil.

The European Reformations complicated the landscape of women's education, as they did to so much else. Latin education in convents, no less than the institution as such, drew fire from reformers throughout the sixteenth century. Indeed, one condition of Pirkheimer's election as abbess was that she cease to correspond in Latin – albeit she ignored this injunction, and also continued to run the convent's Latin school for girls.[20] And convents of all varieties ceased to be an option for women's education in reformist regions by the middle of the sixteenth century.

Even in Catholic territories, ambitious educators of this new era often watched their institutional programs founder – though not, it must be stressed, on account of pedagogical deficiencies. Mary Ward, for instance, directed much of the energy of her Institute of the Blessed Virgin Mary toward instructing girls in the humanities. Ward's schools gained popularity among urban families, a testament in itself to the fact that a considerable number of parents were ready to invest in the education of their daughters. This promising development, however, was nullified by papal decree.

All the same, some of the most powerful defenses of women in this later period came from nuns. Sor Juana Inés de la Cruz (d. 1695) would from her convent in New Spain make brilliant pleas for women's education. Another paradigmatic case is Suor Arcangela Tarabotti (d. 1652), whose *Paternal Tyranny* as well as her voluminous collection of letters have recently inspired critical editions and astute analysis by Letizia Panizza, Meredith Ray, and Lynn Westwater.[21] Tarabotti engaged with contemporary academies, intervened in polemics and controversies, and circulated her writings all from behind convent walls. Still, even if we read Tarabotti's rages against the meager library of her convent, Sant'Anna in Castello, for limiting her intellectual range of motion less as a description of immediate reality than as evidence crafted to strengthen her feminist point about the injustice of women's forced monachation, her frustrations were hardly baseless.

On balance, then, before the advent of girls' schools with classical curricula, the most reliable site for women's advanced education remained the household. And contemporary observers viewed the household academy as at least equivalent to institutional schooling. Nicholas Harpsfield, for one, celebrated the More household as a new "Plato's Academy – nay, what say I, Plato's? Not in Plato's, but in some Christian well-ordered academy and university."[22] Indeed, the image of the household academy resonated so much in the Renaissance imaginary that ambitious women appropriated it. Marie de Gournay, for instance, made a father-patron of Michel de Montaigne, portraying herself as his *fille d'alliance* (adoptive daughter).[23]

Writing and fighting

The contributions of women humanists exhibit the same diversity as those of their male counterparts. We have numerous examples of women's Latin verse, from occasional poems in a funerary mode – for instance, the Latin epitaph penned by Elizabeth Cooke Hoby in 1570 for her daughters, or Camille de Morel's elegy on the death of Henri II – to multilingual collections, such as the 1616 *Musa Virginia Graeco-Latina-Gallica* of Bathsua Reginald (later Makin). Repositories from Lisbon to Stockholm yield myriad editions of women's Latin spiritual poetry. Italian women humanists, especially of the fifteenth century, have also left us complete letterbooks that display their mastery of epistolary discourse, their wide circles of colleagues and admirers, and orations on topics as wide-ranging as the crusades against the Turks, the beauties of the liberal arts, and the death of a donkey. Women humanists were also collectors, editors and translators. Ginevra Nogarola made her own copy of Justinus in the late fifteenth century, and Lucy Hutchinson (née Apsley) made the first complete translation of Lucretius' *De rerum natura* in the 1650s.[24] Much as no single essay can summarize the activities of male humanists, the pursuits and publications of women humanists defy survey.

There was a genre, however, within which women made consistently innovative interventions, the so-called "debate on women" (*querelle des femmes*). Christine de Pizan's *City of Ladies* (1405) led the way, offering a synthetic exploration of women's positive contributions to society and culture from antiquity to her own day. Over the next 300 years, her successors would direct their compositions, in Latin and in the vernacular, to reshaping conceptions of women inherited from the Bible and Aristotle, and the problem of women's education.

Isotta Nogarola's *Dialogue on Adam and Eve* (1451) used a skillful exegesis of the Book of Genesis to argue that Eve was less culpable than Adam in original sin. *Querelle* texts of subsequent centuries borrowed heavily from Nogarola. Among the works that incorporate Nogarola's line of reasoning are Henricus Cornelius Agrippa's 1529 *Declamation on the Nobility and Preeminence of the Female Sex* and Lucrezia Marinella's treatise *On the Dignity and Nobility of Women and on the Defects and Vices of Men* (1601).

Working along similar lines, Marie le Jars de Gournay's *Egalité des hommes et des femmes* (1622, revised 1641) used the Book of Genesis to argue for the original equality of the sexes. But Gournay went further, contending that men and women share not only the same spiritual and intellectual capacities but also the same physical substance. In her formulation, sexual characteristics are accidentals, not essentials.

Other learned women of the Renaissance targeted the problem of women's education, arguing that daughters should receive the same education as sons. In a delicious Latin invective of the late fifteenth century directed against a fictional antagonist dubbed "Bibolo Semproni" (Always Tipsy), Laura Cereta defined education as a freedom or even a "right" (*licentia*) possessed equally by women and men. While not all advocates adopted her legalistic stance, Cereta's claim found a steady stream of adherents. An important later example is Anna Maria van Schurman's 1632 *Dissertatio logica* (commonly entitled *Whether a Christian Woman Should be Educated*), which emerged through her debate with the Leiden theologian Andre Rivet and engaged the conservative syllabus articulated by Juan Luis Vives in his *On Education of a Christian Woman* (1524).

Still others spoke directly to their contemporaries, urging them to wield the pen in addition to, and sometimes instead of, the needle. In France, Louise Labé and Catherine and Madeline des Roches (mother and daughter) used this image. The Ferrarese humanist and Protestant convert Olympia Morata (d. 1555) celebrated her own actions in a Greek poem:

> I, a woman, have dropped the symbols of my sex,
> Yarn, shuttle, basket, thread,
> I love but the flowered Parnassus with the choirs of joy,
> Other women seek after what they choose
> These are my pride and my delight.[25]

Moderata Fonte took it upon herself to solve, so far as any one publication could do, the problem of women's access to knowledge. Fonte's dialogue, *Il merito delle donne* (*The Worth of*

Women, 1600), presents a gathering of erudite women whose conversation, rich in classical allusions and glosses, explores essential topics from ancient and contemporary literature, moral philosophy, history and science – all interwoven as support for her critique of the patriarchal order, but useful in themselves as primers for female audiences. By teaching her readers how to become "Renaissance women" through the voices of women speakers, Fonte also revolutionized the masculine dialogic model of Baldassare Castiglione's *Courtier*. Female interrogatories nudge the discussion forward in Castiglione's dialogue; women speakers take center stage in Fonte's.[26]

Women humanists in northern Europe, above all in England, have received less modern attention than they deserve, because they most often worked in the genre of translation. Accordingly, their work can seem less exciting or innovative, and we can miss the contributions they made to the *querelle*.

Margaret More Roper became synonymous with erudite piety for her translation of Erasmus' *Treatise on the Pater Noster*. While attesting to her skill in sorting out the original author's thorny Latin, this production also contributed in its own way to the European *querelle*. Roper's editor, William Rastell, took the opportunity to write an eight-page prefatory disquisition on the suitability (if not indeed the necessity) of teaching women Latin, an argument substantiated beyond refutation, so Rastell reasoned, by Roper's translation. Anne Cooke Bacon's English rendering of John Jewell's Latin *Apologie on the Church of England* (1564, shortly thereafter available in all English parish churches), garnered similar praise from Matthew Parker, Archbishop of Canterbury. Parker termed the translation "publicly beneficial" for having safely delivered the author's meaning "from the perils of ambiguous and doubtful constructions" and urged contemporaries (male and female) to follow her example of putting their own learned piety to public use.[27]

And if we engage manuscript evidence as well, we find fascinating cases of English women creatively working against Aristotelian binaries. "Friendship is the nearest union which distinct Souls are capable of," announced a prolific portraitist and humanist named Mary Beale in her 1666 treatise "On Friendship."[28] This topic served as Beale's point of departure for an elegant and erudite exploration of sexual equality in thirteen folios, a bravura "scribal publication." Beale argued for women's equality in marriage, an institution which she redefined as ideal friendship, but she also emphasized friendship between women by dedicating the work to Elizabeth Tillotson, wife of John Tillotson, Archbishop of Canterbury. Beale represented Tillotson as the ideal friend and herself as the ardent protégée, situating their relationship as exemplary. Beale thus turned ancient philosophy on its head. No longer a male political relationship that excluded women, in Beale's argument friendship only enjoyed full expression when women entered into it – with their husbands, of course, but also with each other.

Beale suggests wider boundaries for egalitarian thinking than we have quite appreciated. Jacques Derrida influentially claimed that the European hermeneutic of friendship, from Aristotle to Alexander Pope, rested upon a strict discourse of brotherhood founded upon a "double exclusion" of friendship between men and women, and between women.[29] Alan Bray shifted our attention to sixteenth- and seventeenth-century conceptions of "noninstrumental" friendship, an emotional affinity that did not entail practical, reciprocal obligations and might therefore coexist with the demands of work and family.[30] When we turn to women, some historians and literary critics looking specifically at friendship in early modern Britain argue that women served (at best) as currency to be exchanged in male kinship and friendship economies.[31] Others, focused on women's friendships with other women, have begun to recover a variety of relationships, from the formal bonds of mistresses and servants to the most passionate expressions of same-sex love.[32]

Literary critics are also revealing how intellectual women in different social contexts rewrote classical definitions of friendship as a foundation for egalitarian social thinking.[33] Matthew Wyszynski and Monica Leoni, for instance, have shown the creativity with which the playwright María de Zayas (d. 1661) at once rejected the definitions of friendship as a male political relationship and situated female friendship *as* political.[34]

While de Zayas wrote and performed, British writers were significantly revising the paradigm, even reimagining marriage as friendship. One revisionist was John Milton. As Gregory Chaplain has taught us, Milton's writings on marriage and divorce in the 1640s fused the discourses of Renaissance friendship and Christian marriage and redefined marriage as a union of friends.[35] But, as Chaplain points out, Milton's subject did remain the universal male. He considered neither the benefits of friendship for women, nor the subject of female friendships.

The enigmatic latitudinarian divine Jeremy Taylor followed Milton in his *Discourse on the Nature and Offices of Friendship* (1657), which would serve, in turn, as Mary Beale's model. Taylor framed his treatise as a letter to the celebrated poet, Katherine Philips, the fulcrum around which an extensive literary circle, her "Society of Friendship," pivoted. Taylor presents Philips as an ideal and virtuous friend. And he extended this generosity to women as a category, in his words "admitting your sex into the community of noble friendship" since women, too, were capable of participating in "the nearest love and the nearest society of which persons are capable."[36] Yet Taylor, too, skirted friendships between women and even the social implications of his own theoretical inclusivity.

Milton and Taylor served Beale well as precedents for dispensing with Aristotle enough to situate marriage as an ideal form of friendship, rather than a baser fusion of utility and pleasure. But their works hardly prefigured her vision of the female self *as* a friend – let alone as a friend to another woman. Fortunately, three centuries of the *querelle* had introduced such ideas. Women writers, in particular, had also formulated new visions of female community. For instance, the prolific sixteenth-century Venetian poet and feminist Moderata Fonte (Modesta da Pozzo) took the *querelle* directly to the field of friendship. Fonte's dialogue, *Il merito delle donne* (*The Worth of Women*, 1600), while modeled on Castiglione's *Courtier* and Pietro Bembo's *Gli Asolani*, recast the *dramatis personae* as a "women only" group, who convene to enjoy each other's conversation. One of the central arguments that her speakers advance is that women, superior to men in every sense, form friendships with each other that are superior to those formed between men.[37] Mary Beale probably had not read Fonte's dialogue, but *Il merito* nonetheless serves as a gauge of the boundaries of the thinkable by the seventeenth century. Fonte idealized female friendship on its own terms and in its own literary space, but she did not quite contend that women served better than men *as men's friends*. Beale took up this argument.

Mary Beale's treatise redirected the ongoing *querelle* and the provisional models for inclusivity that Milton and Taylor offered. She envisioned friendship in marriage as a catalyst for sexual equality. Turning from Aristotle's contention that man is a social animal, naturally suited to friendship, to the story of the creation of Eve, Beale argues that God gave Adam "a wife and Friend, but not a slave. For we find [Eve] not in the beginning made subject to Adam, but always of equal dignity and honor with him." Humanists writing long before Beale, including the firebrand Henricus Cornelius Agrippa, had made a similar point about "original equality," but had been unable to extend this to "contemporary equality" because of Eve's punishments for her transgression, chiefly subjection to her husband. Beale contends that this paradigm has shifted in her own time. She points to "a small number, who by Friendship's interposition, have restored the marriage bond to its first institution."[38] Friendship, for Beale, provided a new dispensation for women: marriage as a union of equals.

Her egalitarian thinking pushed even further in constructing the female self *as* friend. In dedicating the work to Elizabeth Tillotson, Beale offered their friendship as a model. So did Beale's famous contemporary, the learned poet Katherine Philips (d. 1664). Throughout her collection of poems and letters Philips made women subjects in fused discourses of friendship and egalitarianism.[39] The vast majority of the poems in Philips' posthumous anthology concern friendship, especially friendships between women and paradigmatically her close and passionate friendship with Anne Owen, dubbed "Lucasia" in the pastoral nomenclature adopted by Philips' literary circle. Philips even justified the inclusion of women in the discourse of friendship in a decidedly Renaissance feminist register. In Poem 64, "A Friend," Philips reflects on the Aristotelian and Ciceronian topic of friendship in marriage, declaring that "the Marriage-tie / Hath much of Honor and Divinity / But Lust, Design, or some unworthy ends/ May mingle there, which are despis'd by Friends" (Poem 57). Philips deploys the classical hierarchy not to exclude women, as they did, but rather to exalt female friendship outside the married state.

Reception

Intellectual women of the Renaissance sometimes complained of having to work in a hostile climate. Christine de Pizan lamented in her *City of Ladies* that male writers commonly urged fathers to keep their daughters from literary education, lest the girls' morals be corrupted, even if her own father had ignored such prescription.[40] Centuries later, Bathsua Makin still anticipated a negative response to the curriculum that she outlined in her *Essay to Revive the Antient Education of Gentlewomen* (1673). One could not say that they oversold the risks of their endeavors. Renaissance literature furnishes plenty of anti-woman sentiment, and Renaissance society had its persecuting spirit. Yet it is rare to catch anyone denigrating women humanists.

To be sure, the cultural type of the educated woman did not enjoy universal acclaim. Some elite prescriptive texts, paradigmatically Francesco Barbaro's *On Wifely Duties*, advocated only vernacular education for women. Barbaro did not forbid daughters to study the liberal arts, and he saw to it that his own daughter received a thorough education in Latin that aligned with contemporary humanist works on pedagogy such as Leonardo Bruni's *On Studies and Letters* (ca. 1423).[41] Still, Barbaro's treatise did nothing to ensure that women as a group would enjoy the training his daughter did. And some diatribes scourged female encroachment on male prerogative; for the latter period, a classic example is the infamous *Hic Mulier* (*Man-Woman*, London, 1620). In seventeenth-century Italy, as Virginia Cox has illustrated, a baroque fascination with the salacious and the ludic also brought with it satires of the learned woman as a figure, even if only a handful of works made this their principal aim.[42]

Reactions to particular women humanists, however, provide little evidence of systemic hostility. There is the fifteenth-century case of an invective directed at Isotta Nogarola, in which an anonymous pamphleteer accused her of committing incest with her brother. But supporters and encomiasts diffused these claims with fulsome praise of her erudition and chastity.[43] And invective was a common if unpleasant reality in the tough literary marketplace. Few male humanists escaped unscathed, and attacks on them used a similar lexicon of sexual insult.[44]

All the same, one struggles to find systematic criticism of women's advanced education, less still of particular educated women. Even Boccaccio's *De mulieribus claris* (*On Famous Women*, 1362), a foundational text for praising and blaming female achievement, exempted learned women such as the orator Hortensia and the poet Cornificia from the coupling of accomplishment and moral turpitude characteristic of biographies treating women in politics.

What we find instead is a considerable body of texts, both in print and in manuscript, praising learned women. Italian biographical encyclopedias are the most accessible, but by no means the only, evidence of this positive reception. Giuseppe Betussi's revision and expansion of Boccaccio, *Delle donne illustri*, which enjoyed four printings and further additions from 1545 to 1596, erased its model's connection between talent and sexual appetite, positing instead a fusion of virtue and accomplishment in the lives of all its protagonists. Pietro Paolo di Ribera and Francesco Agostino della Chiesa, among others, brought this celebratory model into the seventeenth century, though Chiesa refined the paradigm by focusing on women writers.[45] By the mid-seventeenth century, critical editions of women humanists' writings appear, complete with biographical essays. Classic examples of this phenomenon are Giacomo Filippo Tomasini's editions of Cereta (1636) and Fedele (1640).

Italian biographers and editors taught their readers that learned women were virtuous in all senses of the term and assets to family and civic honor. Tomasini's Latin *vitae* reproduce what had become the standard laudatory tropes. Cereta brought further honor to her native city of Brescia, notable "not only for its preeminent men, who have ornamented various European cities with their speech and writings" but also "for its women of surpassing piety and doctrine."[46] His biography of Fedele emphasized her wish to enhance the intellectual honor of her immediate family. "I apply myself to studying the noble arts," Tomasini has her explain, "lest I seem unworthy of my great-great grandfather, my great-grandfather and all of our most famous ancestors."[47] Modern readers find these categories of praise formulaic, if not condescending, but discourses of civic and domestic honor did crucial cultural work in making women intellectuals plausible and attractive figures to contemporary readers.

Women humanists proved the central tenets of the humanist enterprise, chiefly that a classical education ennobled its recipients, compensating for "natural" defects. Being born female constituted just such a defect, as far as Aristotle and his imitators were concerned. Humanists also strove to prove that their own age could surpass excellence of pagan antiquity. The ancient world provided examples of learned women, including not only Hortensia and Cornelia, but also Tullia, the daughter of Cicero, and Sappho, termed "the Tenth Muse" from Plato to Plutarch.[48] But these figures were few, little or nothing of their own compositions remained, and they were not Christian. By contrast, Renaissance biographers could point to hundreds of contemporary women poets, orators, and writers, who bested the ancients for erudition and piety. The cleric Tomaso Garzoni alluded to "thousands" of such women as he added his own voice to the chorus.[49] Ribera, more conservatively, posited the number 845.

Texts devoted to commemorating women's scholarly achievements proliferated in France by the mid-seventeenth century and gave new force to arguments concerning the intellectual equality of the sexes. Jean de la Forge's *Cercle des femmes savantes* (1663, reprinted 1667), for instance, provided much fodder for François Poulain de la Barre's claim that "the mind has no sex."[50] In England, one of the earliest examples of an encyclopedia of women writers was George Ballard's 1751 *Memoirs of Several Ladies of Great Britain*, which explicitly cited Betussi,

Ribera, and Chiesa as models – even if Ballard's eighteenth-century encyclopedia evinces more careful attention to the scholarly apparatus.[51]

The same program of preservation and celebration appears much earlier, however, in a more heterogeneous collection of sources, including treatises on pedagogical theory, letters, and biographies. One example from sixteenth-century England is Richard Mulcaster's *Positions wherein Those Primitive Circumstances Be Examined Which Are Necessary for the Training Up of Children* (1581). Mulcaster characterized English women humanists as "so excellently well trained, and so rarely qualified, either for the tongues themselves or for the matter in the tongues, as they may be opposed by comparison, if not preferred as beyond comparison, even to the best Roman or Greekish paragons, be they never so much praised; to the German or French gentlewomen, by late writers so well liked; to the Italian ladies who dare write themselves, and deserve fame for so doing."[52] In a perhaps less exalted but no less important register, the English divine and poet Samuel Woodford (d. 1700) in his publications celebrated Mary Beale as the embodiment of all virtues, and represented her household as a learned salon and a godly retreat.[53]

This is not to say that intellectual women encountered no resistance, and even that compliments sometimes stung. As Lisa Jardine noted long ago, one form of compliment emphasized the learned woman's exceptionality; she became for some a "phoenix" or a new "tenth Muse."[54] Such emphasis on intellectual women's rarity, stretched from Europe's heartlands to its colonies. Sor Juana Inés de la Cruz, nurtured in her grandfather's remarkable library, aimed to extend her good fortune to others. Elizabeth Howe aptly characterizes Sor Juana as an "apogee for women writing in defense of the education of their own in the sixteenth- and seventeenth-century Hispanic world."[55] Yet this writer, too, found herself frequently dissociated from other women by being characterized as unique.

At the same time, however, the churning out of biographical encyclopedias in the sixteenth and seventeenth centuries continued to erode the image of the solitary female prodigy. Women writers also emphasized their membership in communities of knowledge, sometimes led by or including other women, a phenomenon studied in the Italian context by Diana Robin and in the northern European republic of letters by Carol Pal.[56] A testament to the success of women writers and their biographers in challenging exceptionality tropes, Mulcaster, while stressing the unusual brilliance of English women humanists with respect to their peers on the continent, still praised in the plural.

Conclusion

Humanist credentials brought confidence, a sense of scholarly entitlement that funded bold interventions. Christine de Pizan had stripes in all of the liberal arts and accordingly felt comfortable taking on even Aristotle, "the Prince of Philosophers," in her *City of Ladies*. Laura Cereta's robust Latin served her well as a weapon against detractors of women. While Gournay was (and is) best known for her contributions to French literature, including her role as Montaigne's literary executor and editor of the later editions of his *Essays*, she was first a humanist in the stricter sense of the term; her earlier publications include a collection of translations from Virgil, Tacitus, Sallust, Ovid, and Cicero.[57] Similarly, Bathsua Makin's *Essay* has enjoyed consistent attention from scholars, in part because she offered a blueprint of a secular girls' school with a classical curriculum. But Makin's career, too, began with a volume of poems in Latin, Greek, French, Hebrew, and Italian. So, too, Sor Juana Inés de la Cruz worked from a strong foundation in Latin.

Classical studies also introduced scholars to ancient models that could prove very useful for criticizing women's subordinate condition in their own time. On gender parity in the fullest sense, they had recourse to Plato's female guardians in the Republic, together with a veritable library on the Amazons from Greek and Latin poetry.[58] On women's excellence in matters literary and spiritual, antiquity offered precedents from the ubiquitously cited Hortensia to the most obscure female prophets. Above all, commerce with the ancients helped ambitious women to place themselves in a worthy tradition. "I am impelled to show," Cereta announced, "what great glory that noble lineage which I carry in my own breast has won for virtue and literature – a lineage that knowledge, the bearer of honors, has exalted in every age."[59] Many other women of Cereta's era and subsequent centuries would join that lineage.

When we imagine the Renaissance woman scholar, then, we should imagine not a recluse, but an active participant in an ancient tradition that took new shape in the humanist *res publica litterarum*. And while not all women humanists used their erudite pens to rewrite gender categories, many contributed to the process of throwing negative Aristotelian conceptions of women as kin and friends from European trains of thought.

Notes

1 Isabella Andreini, *Lettere della Signora Isabella Andreini Padovana*, Venice: G. B.Combi, 1617, sig. A2v. Translations are my own unless otherwise indicated.
2 Of all the bibliographic and digital repositories that house the myriad new cases scholars unearthed every year, the leader remains the book series "The Other Voice in Early Modern Europe" (University of Chicago Press).
3 See the "Checklist of Women Latin Poets" in Jane Stevenson's magisterial *Women Latin Poets: Gender, Language and Authority from Antiquity to the Eighteenth Century*, Oxford: Oxford University Press, 2005, pp. 428–595. Stevenson's book is a first port of call for the topic of women humanists.
4 Patricia Labalme, ed., *Beyond their Sex: Learned Women of the European Past*, New York: New York University Press, 1980; Margaret King, "Book Lined Cells: Women and Humanism in the Early Italian Renaissance," in Labalme, ed., *Beyond Their Sex*, pp. 66–90, and "Religious Retreat of Isotta Nogarola (1418–1466): Sexism and its Consequences in the Fifteenth-Century," *Signs* 3 (1978): 807–22; Lisa Jardine, "'O Decus Italiae Virgo' or the Myth of the Learned Lady in the Renaissance," *Historical Journal* 28 (1985): 799–819; Stephanie Jed "The Tenth Muse: Gender, Rationality and the Marketing of Knowledge," in Margo Hendricks and Patricia Parker, eds., *Women, "Race," and Writing in the Early Modern Period*, London and New York: Routledge, 1994, pp. 195–208. These older interpretive models, despite much recent work to the contrary, continue to inform work not immediately in this vein. Douglas Biow, for instance, claims flatly that "humanism excluded women," in *Doctors, Ambassadors, Secretaries: Humanism and the Professions in Renaissance Italy*, Chicago and London: University of Chicago Press, 2002, p. xiii.
5 The new consensus receives emphasis in two recent pan-European surveys of intellectual women by Diana Robin, "Women Intellectuals in Early Modern Europe," in Allyson M. Poksa, Jane Couchman, and Katherine A. McIver, eds., *The Ashgate Research Companion to Women and Gender in Early Modern Europe*, Aldershot: Ashgate, 2013, pp. 381–406, as well as Robin's essay on "Gender" in Sarah Knight and Stefan Tilg, eds., *The Oxford Handbook of Neo-Latin*, Oxford: Oxford University Press, 2015, pp. 363–78.
6 Patricia Labalme, "Venetian Women on Women: Three Early Modern Feminists," *Archivio Veneto*, 5th series, 117 (1981): 81–109; Diana Robin, ed. and trans., *Laura Cereta: Collected Letters of a Renaissance Feminist*, Chicago: University of Chicago Press, 1997; Margaret King, *Women of the Renaissance*, Chicago: University of Chicago Press, 1991; Julie Campbell, *Literary Circles and Gender in Early Modern Europe*, Aldershot: Ashgate Publishing, 2006; Virginia Cox, *Women's Writing in Italy, 1400–1650*, Baltimore: Johns Hopkins University Press, 2008; Sarah Gwyneth Ross, *The Birth of Feminism: Woman as Intellect in Renaissance Italy and England*, Cambridge, MA and London: Harvard University Press, 2009; and Carol Pal, *Republic of Women: Rethinking the Republic of Letters in the Seventeenth Century*, Cambridge: Cambridge University Press, 2012.

7 For the training of Italian women humanists, see King, *Women of the Renaissance*, pp. 184–5; for father-teachers and the household school more broadly as a model, Ross, *Birth of Feminism*, chs. 1 and 2; for particulars of the education of Fedele, Cereta and Nogarola, see the introductions in Diana Robin, ed. and trans., *Cassandra Fedele: Letters and Orations*, Chicago: University of Chicago Press, 2000, *Laura Cereta: Collected Letters of a Renaissance Feminist*, and Margaret King and Diana Robin, eds. and trans., *Isotta Nogarola: Complete Writings: Letterbook, Dialogue on Adam and Eve, Orations*, Chicago: University of Chicago Press, 2004.

8 Robin, *Laura Cereta*, p. 25; Ross, *Birth of Feminism*, pp. 48–9.

9 This is the view propounded in the *vita* penned by her biographer, Niccolò Doglioni, which prefaces Moderata Fonte, *Il merito delle donne*, Venice: Domenico Imberti, 1600, sigs. A1v–A2r.

10 Lucrezia Marinella, *La nobiltà et l'eccellenza delle donne et mancamenti de gli huomini*, Venice, 1601, pp. 33–44. See also L. Panizza's introduction in A. Dunhill's translation of this text, *The Nobility and Excellence of Women and the Vices of Men*, Chicago: University of Chicago Press, 1999, p. 3.

11 For particulars on the education of women humanists of the More, Cooke, and Fitzalan families, see Ross, *Birth of Feminism*, pp. 69–87.

12 Marjorie McIntosh, "Sir Anthony Cooke: Tudor Humanist, Educator and Religious Reformer," *Proceedings of the American Philosophical Society* 119(3) (1975): 233–50.

13 Stevenson, *Women Latin Poets*, pp. 188–93.

14 *Ibid.*, pp. 348–54; Ingrid de Smet, "'In the Name of the Father': Feminist Voices in the Republic of Letters," in Michel Bastiaensen, ed., *Lettered Women in the Renaissance*, Brussels: Peeters, 1997, pp. 177–96. On Schurman's career more broadly see Pal, *Republic of Women*.

15 Anne Cruz and Rosilie Hernández, eds., *Women's Literacy in Early Modern Spain and the New World*, Farnham: Ashgate, 2011; Elizabeth Howe, *Education and Women in the Early Modern Hispanic World*, Farnham: Ashgate, 2008.

16 A good introduction to Sigea with a sample of her writings is Edward George, "Luisa Sigea (1522–1560) Iberian Scholar-Poet," in Laurie Churchill, ed., *Women Writing in Latin: from Roman Antiquity to Early Modern Europe*, vol. 3, New York: Routledge, 2002, pp. 167–87. On de Bolea's maternal tutoring, and the phenomenon of mothers as tutors more general in the Iberian context, Cruz and Hernández, *Women's Literacy*, pp. 2–4, and 4–6, respectively.

17 K. J. P. Lowe, *Nuns' Chronicles and Convent Culture in Renaissance and Counter-Reformation Italy*, Cambridge: Cambridge University Press, 2003.

18 Robin, "Gender," 371.

19 Elissa Weaver, *Convent Theater in Early Modern Italy: Spiritual Fun and Learning for Women*, Cambridge: Cambridge University Press, 2002; Sharon Strocchia, *Nuns and Nunneries in Renaissance Florence*, Baltimore: Johns Hopkins University Press, 2009, pp. 144–51.

20 Stevenson, *Women Latin Poets*, p. 226, and King, *Women of the Renaissance*, p. 99.

21 Arcangela Tarabotti, *Paternal Tyranny*, ed. and trans. Letizia Panizza, Chicago and London: University of Chicago Press, 2004; Meredith Ray, "The Pen for the Sword: Arcangela Tarabotti's *Lettere familiari e di complimento*," in *Writing Gender in Women's Letter Collections of the Italian Renaissance*, Toronto: University of Toronto Press, 2009, pp. 184–213; Elissa Weaver, ed., *Arcangela Tarabotti: A Literary Nun in Baroque Venice*, Ravenna: Longo, 2006; Meredith Ray and Lynn Westwater, eds., *Lettere familiari e di complimento della sign. Arcangela Tarabotti*, Turin: Rosenberg & Seller, 2004.

22 Nicholas Harpsfield, *The Life and Death of St. Thomas More, Knight*, ed. E. V. Hitchcock, London: Oxford University Press, 1932, p. 92.

23 Tilde Sankovitch, *French Women Writers and the Book: Myths of Access and Desire*, New York: Syracuse University Press, 1988, p. 76; for Gournay's own use of the term, see Richard Hillman and Colette Quesnel, eds., *Preface to the Essays of Michel de Montaigne*, Tempe, AZ: Medieval and Renaissance Texts and Studies, 1998, p. 21. On discursive daughterhood, de Smet, "In the Name of the Father"; Ross, *Birth of Feminism*, especially pp. 11–14, 42–50 and 209–12.

24 On collecting in the Nogarola family, see Stevenson, *Women Latin Poets*, p. 145; for Lucy Hutchinson, see David Norbrook's critical edition of her epic poem on the Book of Genesis, *Order and Disorder*, Oxford: Blackwell, 2001.

25 Quoted in King, *Women of the Renaissance*, p. 181.

26 Introduction by Virginia Cox to her edition of Fonte's *The Worth of Women*, Chicago: University of Chicago Press, 1997, p. 10.

27 Matthew Parker, unpaginated prefatory letter in Anne Cooke Bacon, trans., [John Jewell,] *Apologie or Answer in Defence of the Churche of Englande*, London: Reginald Woolfe, 1564.

28 Mary Beale, "On Friendship," British Library, MS Harley 6828, fol. 510v. An excellent treatment of Beale's life and oeuvre appears in Tabitha Barber *et al.*, eds., *Mary Beale (1632/3–1699): Portrait of a Seventeenth-Century Painter, Her Family and her Studio*, London: Geffrye Museum Trust, 1999.

29 Jacques Derrida, "The Politics of Friendship," *Journal of Philosophy* 85(11) (November 1988): 632–44; for the "double exclusion," p. 642; Eve Sedgwick, *Between Men: English Literature and Male Homosocial Desire*, New York: Columbia University Press, 1985; and Tom MacFaul, *Male Friendship in Shakespeare and His Contemporaries*, Cambridge: Cambridge University Press, 2007, pp. 3–5, 48–64 and 78–9.

30 Alan Bray, *The Friend*, Chicago: University of Chicago Press, 2003, esp. p. 41.

31 Lorna Hutson, *The Usurer's Daughter: Male Friendship and Fictions of Women in Sixteenth Century England*, London: Routledge, 1994.

32 An excellent collection of essays that lays out the problem is Susan Frye and Karen Robertson, eds., *Maids and Mistresses, Cousins and Queens: Women's Alliance in Early Modern England*, Oxford: Oxford University Press, 1999. For an earlier treatment of early modern women's ambiguous feelings about the concept of "community" (in light of the patriarchal organization of society), see Elizabeth Janeway, *Man's World, Woman's Place: A Study in Social Mythology*, New York: Morrow, 1971.

33 For these conceptions, Aristotle, *Nicomachean Ethics*, VIII.xii.7. On Aristotle and the "woman question," see especially Cynthia A. Freeland, ed., *Feminist Interpretations of Aristotle*, University Park, PA: Pennsylvania State University Press, 1998, and Leah Bradshaw, "Prudence and the 'Woman Question,' in Aristotle," *Canadian Journal of Political Science/Revue canadienne de science politique* 24(3) (September 1991): 557–73. For a useful synthetic treatment of Aristotle's definitions from fourth-century Greece to seventeenth-century Britain (especially in the work of Francis Bacon), see Lorraine Smith Pangle, *Aristotle and the Philosophy of Friendship*, Cambridge: Cambridge University Press, 2003. See also Aristotle, *Ethics*, VIII.x.5, as well as Cicero, *De amicitia*, X.34, XIII.46 and XX.74 for categorical exclusions of women.

34 As Matthew A. Wyszynski, "Friendship in María de Zayas's *La traición en la amistad*," *Bulletin of the Commediantes* 50(1) (1998): 21–33; quotation at p. 28. See also Monica Leoni, "María de Zayas's *La traición en la amistad*: Female Friendship Politicized?" *South Atlantic Review* 68(4) (Autumn, 2003): 62–84.

35 Gregory Chaplain, "'One Flesh, One Heart, One Soul,': Renaissance Friendship and Miltonic Marriage," *Modern Philology* 99(2) (November 2001): 266–92.

36 Jeremy Taylor, *Discourse on the Nature and Offices of Friendship*, London, 1678 [repr.], pp. 63 and 14.

37 For a fuller treatment of friendship in Fonte's dialogue, see Ross, *The Birth of Feminism*, 282–4. See also Moderata Fonte, *The Worth of Women*, ed. and trans. Virginia Cox, Chicago: University of Chicago Press, 1997, p. 123, n. 4.

38 Beale, "On Friendship," fol. 510v.

39 An excellent first port of call for Philips is Paula Loscocco, ed., *Katherine Philips (1631/2–1664): Printed Publications, 1651–1664*, Aldershot: Ashgate, 2007.

40 Christine de Pizan, *Le livre de la cité des dames*, ed. Eric Hicks and Therese Moreau, Paris: Editions Stock, 1986, pp. 178–9.

41 Leonardo Bruni, "De studiis et litteris," in Craig Kallendorf, ed. and trans., *Humanist Educational Treatises*, Cambridge, MA: Harvard University Press, 2002, pp. 47–64.

42 Cox, *Women's Writing in Italy*, pp. 195–204.

43 King and Robin, eds., *Isotta Nogarola*, p. 6; see also Arnaldo Segarizzi, "Niccolò Barbo patrizio veneziano del secolo XV e le accuse contro Isotta Nogarola," *Giornale storico della letteratura italiana* 43 (1904): 39–54.

44 Cecil Clough, "The Cult of Antiquity: Letters and Letter Collections," in Cecil Clough, ed., *Cultural Aspects of the Italian Renaissance: Essays in Honour of Paul Oskar Kristeller*, Manchester: Manchester University Press; New York: Alfred F. Zambelli, 1976, pp. 33–67; Stevenson, *Women Latin Poets*, pp. 144–5; Lauro Martines, *Strong Words: Writing and Social Strain in the Italian Renaissance*, Baltimore: Johns Hopkins University Press, 2001, pp. 14–15 and 24–36.

45 Pietro Paolo di Ribera, *Le glorie immortali de'trionfi et heroiche imprese d'ottocento quarantacinque donne illustri antiche e modern*, Venice: Evangelista Deuchino, 1609; Francesco Agostino della Chiesa, *Theatro delle*

donne letterate, con un breve discorso della Preminenza, e perfettione del sesso donnesco, Mondovi: Giovanni Gislandi e Giovanni Tomaso Rossi, 1620.

46 Giacomo Filippo Tomasini, ed., *Laura Cereta Brixiensis Feminae Clarissimae Epistolae iam primum e MS in lucem productae*, Padua: Sebastiano Sardi, 1640, sigs. 3v–4r.

47 Giacomo Filippo Tomasini, ed., *Clarissimae Feminae Cassandra Fidelis, Venetae: Epistolae et Orationes*, Padua: Francesco Bolzetta, 1636, p. 12.

48 On Sappho's sobriquet, see Judith Hallett, "Sappho in Her Social Context: Sense and Sensuality," in E. Greene, ed., *Reading Sappho: Contemporary Approaches*, Berkeley: University of California Press, 1996, pp. 125–6.

49 Tomaso Garzoni, "Discorso … sopra la nobiltà delle donne," in *Le vite delle donne illustri nella scrittura sacra*, Venice: Domenico Imberti, 1586, p. 171.

50 Siep Stuurman, "Social Cartesianism: François Poulain de la Barre and the Origins of the Enlightenment, *Journal of the History of Ideas* 58(4) (1997), p. 627. See also Stuurman, *François Poulain de la Barre and the Origins of Modern Equality*, Cambridge, MA: Harvard University Press, 2004.

51 George Ballard, *Memoirs of Several Ladies of Great Britain Who Have Been Celebrated for their Writings or Skill in the Learned Languages, Arts and Sciences*, Oxford: W. Jackson, 1752, p. vi.

52 Richard Mulcaster, *Positions*, ed. R. de Molen, New York: Columbia Teacher's College Press, 1971, p. 127.

53 Ross, *Birth of Feminism*, pp. 267–9.

54 Jardine, "O Decus Italiae Virgo."

55 Howe, *Education and Women*, p. 185.

56 Robin, *Publishing Women*; Pal, *Republic of Women*.

57 Stevenson, *Women Latin Poets*, p. 197.

58 *Republic*, 453e–457c.

59 Translation in Robin, *Laura Cereta*, pp. 76–7.

15

MECHANISMS FOR UNITY

Plagues and saints

Samuel K. Cohn

The Black Death of 1347–51 has cast a long shadow over our expectations on how big epidemics have conditioned social and psychological reactions, not only for plague and the Renaissance, but for epidemics across time and place. This is especially true when epidemics were new and mysterious, leaving priests, medical professionals, and the state helpless in controlling, preventing, or curing them.[1] To be sure, the Black Death unleashed waves of persecution against beggars and priests in regions such as Narbonne in Spain,[2] Carcassonne and Grasse in Southern France,[3] against pilgrims in Catalonia, Catalans in Sicily, and most viciously against Jews across German-speaking regions of Central Europe, the Rhineland and in Spain, France, and the Low Countries. From the volumes of the *Germania Judaica*, painstakingly amassed from German archives, mass persecution and annihilation of Jewish communities can be estimated in at least 235 places during the Black Death.[4]

Yet in other regions of Europe, no evidence of massacres occurred as in England, where Jews had been earlier expelled, or in Italy, which still contained ancient Jewish settlements in cities such as Rome and Spoleto.[5] Besides, not all inhabitants, even in the worst affected regions – cities and castellans of the Rhineland – partook in this mass hysteria, if it were in fact "mass hysteria." As I have argued previously, the primary sources defy the standard story that artisans, labourers, and peasants concocted the myths of Jews creating the plague "through poisons of frogs and spiders" put in streams and wells to destroy Christendom during the years 1348 to 1350, or that lower classes perpetrated the massacres.[6] Rather, the impetus came from above, patrician oligarchies, castellans, regional rulers such as Duke Albrecht of Austria, Count Amadéo VI of Savoy, and the Holy Roman Emperor Charles IV of Bohemia. As for the Holy Roman Emperor, he arranged for the disposal of Jewish wealth before the massacres began and encouraged leading burghers, bishops, and knights at Nuremberg, Regensburg, Augsburg, and Frankfurt to murder Jews, granting them immunity in advance from punishment, and afterwards cancelling all debts owed by local elites to Jews in several towns across German-speaking lands.[7]

While the Black Death may not have unleashed pogroms everywhere in Europe or across social classes during its first appearance, it provoked other divisive behaviour, perhaps less dramatic but more pervasive according to the sources. These reactions stretched across Europe and across social classes but have received far less attention than the Black

Death flagellants or burning of Jews. Although the supposed vicious deeds of Jews to end Christendom and the punishments meted out to them were central planks of Black Death chronicles in German-speaking regions, this was not the case outside these regions. Of 128 chronicles covering the Black Death written through the Italian peninsula, not one reported Jews poisoning wells or their fate at the hands of German or French authorities. Of forty-two chronicles, authors of letters, and poems by contemporary French authors on 1348, only two – the chronicle of the Carmelite friar Jean de Venette and the royal chronicle by Richard Lescot – referred to the accusations against Jews or the atrocities that followed.[8] Of fifty-eight British and Irish chronicles, none reported these atrocities, and only three of twelve did so from the Low Countries.[9]

The more widespread message of cruelty in the sources was a direct consequence of the Black Death's rapid spread, considered unprecedented by contemporary chroniclers and physicians. Fear of contagion and almost certain death ruptured societies down to their foundations. Most famously Giovanni Boccaccio elaborated on this cruelty in his Introduction to Day One of the *Decameron*, most likely completed around 1355:

> This unheard of contagion caused various fears and fantasies to take root in the minds of those who were still alive and well. And almost without exception, they took a single and very inhuman precaution, namely to avoid or run away from the sick and their belongings.

More than most, Boccaccio elaborated on the theme of fear, flight, and abandonment of friends and family, and refusal by physicians, notaries, and clergy to render essential services to the dying. He was, however, hardly the first and the *Decameron* was certainly not the *Urtext* of these Black Death observations as some have assumed.[10] Already with the plague's first landing in Western Europe at Messina in October 1347, the Franciscan friar Michele da Piazza observed this pattern of behaviour: "Neither priests nor sons, nor fathers nor any other kinsmen dared enter [to bury them]. The living did not enter these houses of the dead even to collect their goods, money, or treasures."[11] A wide variety of authors in letters, histories, chronicles, and monastic Annals cried out against the abandonment of loved ones. The Florentine chronicler Matteo Villani exclaimed that such "barbarism" was not of human nature, and should be dispised by the fairthful.[12] For the poet Antonio Pucci, not even the Jew, infidel, or apostate deserved such cruelty.[13] With different words, phrases, and examples written within months of each another, these sentiments filled chronicles across Europe from as far east as Salona on the Dalmatian coast,[14] Krakow,[15] and an Olivetan monastery in Poland,[16] to northwestern Europe with the Oxfordshire clerk Geofrey le Baker,[17] the Dublin friar John Clyn,[18] and the Scottish writer of the *Gesta Annalia*.[19]

The evidence does not derive solely from chronicles. In January 1349, following instructions from the Pope, the Bishop of Bath and Wells addressed his congregation not with fiery exclamations but with practical advice:

> because priests cannot be found for love or money to take on the responsibility of those places [many parish churches and other benefices in our diocese] and visit the sick or administer the sacraments … perhaps because they fear that they will catch the disease themselves, we understand that many people are dying without the sacrament of penance … Therefore, desirous as we must be to provide for the salvation of souls … that if … they cannot secure the services of a properly

ordained priest, they should make confession of their sins ... to any lay person, even to a woman if a man is not available.[20]

In addition to differences of expression from one writer to the next – variations in language, examples, and explanations for the abandonment and neglect[21] – an abrupt change occurred after 1348. With numerous waves of plague lasting into the modern period and hundreds of accounts of them, I have found only five stories of abandonment that have seeped into these later accounts and none filled page-plus descriptions as seen for 1348.[22] Furthermore, one of these claims lasted only for a moment. Ser Luca Dominici's initial picture of the 'terrible plague' of 1399–1400 recalls the Black Death horrors:

> [T]hey locked their houses and shops, and fled here and there. The dead and afflicted could find no assistance and remained behind. A more astounishing thing had never been seen.[23]

Yet clearly this chronicler, living less than 40 kilometres from Florence, knew nothing of the abandonment tales of 1348, not even those of Boccaccio's *Decameron*. But Dominici's message soon changed. His central focus became fixed on a social movement that paralleled the 1399–1400 plague, the Bianchi processions. These cut across age groups, gender, city and countryside, and most strikingly, social classes. They brought crowds together with songs of praise and cries of 'misericordia e pace' to end current wars between bickering city-states and squabbles among neighbours from civil litigation to generations of vendettas involving rape, murder, and destruction. During this two-year history of pestilence, no more is heard from Dominici about abandonment. Instead, unity, charity, and peace were the overriding sentiments heard of these plague years. If the 1348 descriptions of abandonment and neglected duties were empty "literary constructions"[24] without relevance to realities, as some have alleged, then why had authors suddenly ceased repeating them with successive plagues, when copying Boccaccio or others would have been all the easier?

Further evidence from archival sources points to other ways in which the Black Death divided societies, sparking blame and violence, raising controversies over dowries and inheritance and increasing criminality. Best studied for these changes remains William Bowsky's for Siena published over forty years ago.[25] In addition, new legislation restricting prices and wages and curtailing the movement of labour immediately after the Black Death has attracted much attention. The laws blamed certain sectors of the population and pried open civic divisions. Best known are England's Ordinance and Statue of Labourers enacted in 1349 and 1351, but similar laws appeared in cities, regions, and kingdoms across Europe. Overwhelmingly, these decrees blamed artisans and labourers for the economic disasters that followed the plague, and their preambles sounded condemnations similar to those heard in contemporary texts by Boccaccio, William Langland, Matteo Villani, Agnolo di Tura, Marchionne di Coppo Stefani, Henry Knighton, and others. They scorned labourers for their sloth, dissolute behaviour, arrogance, lack of obedience, and, above all, greed.[26] Most of these laws, as in Provence and the Ile de France, quickly disappeared, but others changed fundamentally, as with new labour decrees in Italian city-states as early as the second plague of 1361–3.[27] These recognized and accepted the new market realities. Instead of blaming and penalizing labourers with heavy fines and attempts to prohibit their movement, governing elites now competed among themselves for the scarce labour with new laws encouraging movement into their territories. At Florence, for instance, labour legislation shifted abruptly from the stick to the carrot, granting peasants tax exemptions of up to fifteen years to settle and work within their territory.[28] England was the exception. In 1360–1, 1388, and 1406, new amendments and statutes became more draconian, adding flogging and branding foreheads to fines.[29] Yet even here a shift away from blaming labourers is evident: violations coming to court declined sharply after 1352.[30] A *modus vivendi* developed: to ensure labour stability and rising nominal wages, labourers and lords agreed to pay the state low fines. As a result, by 1357, riots against these laws disappeared.[31]

Saints and the Black Death

Creation of saints and blessed ones (*beati/ae*) marks another change with plagues post 1348. In the vast literature of saints' lives, and in marked contrast with contemporaneous chronicles, the Black Death hardly existed. No martyrs or even acknowledgement of the sacrifices made by those who risked their lives aiding those spiritually or corporeally afflicted by the plague appear in the saints' lives during the Black Death. Yet as the historians Richard Emery, William Bowsky, Daniel Smail, and Shona Kelly Wray have emphasized, not everybody ran, despite their immediate realization of this disease's dangerous contagion. Societies continued to function and quickly reinstated institutions of government, even if many were suspended during the worst of the summer months. Everyday religious and civic practices such as making wills, notarizing contracts, baptisms, and funerals continued, even if many priests, notaries, and physicians fled, and the legal requirements of witnesses had to be curtailed.[32] While chroniclers charged that prelates abandoned their flocks, others like Michele da Piazza pointed to his fellow Franciscans who stayed, visited the infected, administered the sacraments, and, as a consequence, perished. The abbot of Tournai claimed the same for his curates, even though, as the abbot said, fulfilling their duties led almost certainly to sudden death.

Without using the word, both authors sketch pictures of martyrdom of those following religious and humanitarian convictions. But unlike newspapers and public ceremonies with commissions of monuments in late nineteenth-century America to 'martyrs' (and called as such), who sacrificed their lives to comfort the Yellow Fever afflicted,[33] neither Michele, Gilles, nor any other commentator used the term or named any of the thousands they claimed had lost their lives while attending to plague victims. The massive compilation of saints' lives in the Bollandists' *Acta Sanctorum*, stories of thousands of holy men and women from the earliest Roman martyrs to the early eighteenth century, sketched for hagiographic glory in over sixty weighty volumes, goes a step further: it fails to mention, even in passing, the Franciscans at Messina, curates at Tournai, or thousands of others who faithfully continued performing their duties: not a single name emerges from the Great Plague massacres, and no one has commented on this blackening out of the Black Death from the Saints' Lives' pages.

With later plagues of the fourteenth and into the fifteenth century, hagiographic attention begins to shift, albeit more slowly and subtly than seen in chronicles or secular literature. Later plague stories of saints risking their lives to save the plague afflicted remain rare. As we shall see, saintly intercessions to save those dying of plague increase, especially in the seventeenth century, but overwhelmingly these were risk-free works of saints long dead before the Black Death or the plagues in which they miraculously interceded. Moreover, when blessed ones and saints begin to appear, who during their lifetimes attended to the plague-stricken, their acts fail to emerge as the essential biographical traits for their canonization or later cults of remembrance.

The first example of a blessed one or saint caring for the plague afflicted during his or her lifetime did not happen until the fourth wave of pestilence in 1374. The figure was Siena's St. Catherine, but her acts were of no importance to her later cult. Looking back from 1390, ten years after her death, her confessor, teacher, and follower, Raymond of Capua, recollected her miraculous plague deeds. She intervened on four occasions in 1374, first, for the rector of Siena's Misericordia hospital. Matteo di Cenni di Fazio, a Sienese nobleman and close friend of Raymond's, was more than an administrator removed from the mundane but dangerous chores of caring for the sick. During this plague he worked the wards, attended to pilgrims, the poor and afflicted, and in so doing caught "the contagion in the groin." When carried by his lay brothers to his room, "like one dead," Catherine heard the news and raced to his bedside but did not nurse or even touch him. Instead, she uttered an angry incantation against the plague that cured the nobleman, who rose to his feet, enjoyed a quick festive meal with his brothers, and immediately returned to attend Misericordia's plague afflicted.[34]

Her other two interventions followed similar magical suits. Another friend of Raymond, the hermit, Santi, who led an exemplary life of poverty, was stricken. Catherine arrived at his deathbed accompanied by her unnamed companions and whispered that he would recover. Words again worked the miracle. No nursing, no toil, emptying of bedpans, or acts of abnegation were required: "Nature had obeyed God through the mouth of the virgin."[35] Another of her miraculous plague performances saved a Sienese friar, Bartolommeo di Domenico, from death's throes.[36] Finally, Catherine miraculously cured Raymond, after he had been attending plague victims for weeks, "always leaving the monastery, hardly with any time to eat and sleep or even to breathe."[37] Finally, this time, the virgin touched a plague victim: putting her hand on Raymond's forehead, she prayed silently, but words again worked the miracle. Once he had recovered, she commanded him to return to his non-miraculous-risk-prone chores, working the plague wards,[38] and Catherine returned home.

As for the care of the sick, Catherine's hagiography pays far greater attention to her non-plague experiences. Treatment of her lay sisters for chronic illnesses illustrates Catherine's tireless energy, self-sacrifice, hands-on nursing, but especially her heroic feats of self-humiliation. Unlike her four interventions of 1374, these derived from sweat and toil and were not infection-free incantations. Such was her daily journey to care for her fellow Sister of Penance, Andrea, whose nose streamed nauseous mucous, and a cancerous wound between her breasts seeped pus and stank. Catherine bandaged and un-bandaged, wiped, and washed it, while enduring an internal battle within herself, seeing her disgust with Andrea's horrid appearance and fetid stench as the devil's work. To defeat her instincts, she sank her mouth and nose into the sore between the breasts, and sucked out the "horrible filthy pus."[39]

In contrast to Catherine's plague experience, Raymond's biography of her becomes for 1374 more his autobiography, heralding his own sacrifices, working to exhaustion until succumbing to the plague. He was fully cognizant of the risks he ran, but from duty, with many dying "left without spiritual advice or help," he exposed himself to death, "obliged to love his neighbours' souls more than his own body." He "made a firm decision … to visit as many of the sick" as he could.[40] Raymond, not Catherine, first cared for their friends. He nursed them, took their pulses, bottled their urine samples, and exposed himself to contagion. Yet, in his life and process for beatitude, this courage and sacrifice played no part. Instead, his fame was won for this world and the next as Catherine's confessor and hagiographer.

The next holy one whose hagiography signals any lifetime activity during a plague again comes from Siena, but not until that city's sixth plague of 1400. Chroniclers as far north as

Flanders and burial statistics from Florence suggest that this plague was particularly virulent, reversing the steady downward trend in plague mortalities since 1348. According to the life of Bernardino da Siena, the governor of Siena's principal hospital, Santa Maria della Scala, almost single-handedly was attending to the growing numbers of pilgrims, fuelled by the papal jubilee, and to Siena's population falling victim to plague. Bernardino, aged nineteen, heard the governor's pleas for assistance and arrived with twelve companions of his confraternity, who, however, were never named. Unlike St. Catherine's, Bernardino's plague interventions were this-worldly and practical. Immediately, he took the keys and responsibilities for running the hospital, relieving its over-worked, now sickly director. Bernardino organized the workloads of caring for the sick, accepted and rejected pilgrims, and distributed alms. He procured vinegar and strong fumigations to purify the air and cover the stench. He made sure priests were called in time to administer sacraments to the dying and that all were given decent burials. As death tolls mounted, he recruited more from his confraternity (who remained unnamed) to join the original band, several of whom had died in the performance of their charity. His contribution was not limited to possibly safe administration; rather, he assisted the sick "day and night," giving them food and medicine, applying plasters, cleansing wounds, washing feet, preparing beds, and weeping with them as he listened to their troubles. With "delight" he assumed any task no matter "how loathsome or vile."[41] His ardour and seeming carelessness for his own life raised suspicions from the patients' relatives, who called him mad.[42]

But as with Catherine's work in 1374, Bernardino was not alone in his plague self-abnegation. Before his arrival, the aristocratic rector had worked himself to exhaustion, becoming a plague victim. Nor was Bernardino the first to heed the rector's call. Instead, he followed the footsteps of his cousin Tobia – "sequens vestigia Tobiæ consobrinæ" – who had served as one of his two pious mentors when he arrived at Siena as an orphan, aged six, and was fostered in his aunt's household.[43] Yet, neither the rector nor Tobia received any recognition from the Church other than a brief mention in Bernardino's life. The same was true for Bernardino's many companions who devoted their lives to the plague-stricken, many of whom paid a higher price than Bernardino: they became infected and died, but the Church did not record their names.

Yet even Bernardino's one narrated plague experience (he lived through several others) made little impact on his cult and hence on Church ideology. Of the vast pictorial representations of his life – preaching to the masses in front of churches, chasing demons, and especially his figure haggardly posed before his "IHS" insignia – none illustrates his risks at Santa Maria della Scala. Further, modern surveys of saints, such as the Italian *Bibliotheca Sanctorum* and various editions of *Butler's Lives of the Saints*, devote at most a phrase to this plague experience.[44]

The third saint active in the day-to-day treatment and salvation of plague victims became the most important plague saint by the Renaissance – San Rocco (Roch). He is also historically the most problematic. According to the revised *Butler's Lives of the Saints* and André Vauchez, the various versions of his life "consist of legends entirely without ascertainable basis in fact."[45] The account that contributed most to his cult dates his birth to 1290 and death to 1327. Vauchez questions these dates because no signs of his cult appear until the fifteenth century. More to the point, by these narratives he died before the Black Death, and in the interval, 1290–1327, no trans-regional epidemics of any sort spread through central and northern Italy, where Roch worked his plague miracles. Further, the most detail of any plague described in Roch's life struck Acquapendente, Cesena, Rome, Rimini, and Novara severely, while major cities and ports – Florence, Siena, Messina, Genoa, Pisa, and Venice – so hammered in 1348, appear unscathed, suggesting that this plague could not have been the Black Death or any other major plague of the second half of the fourteenth century. In addition, Roch visited the Pope at Rome during this plague but no post-plague pope resided there until 1367.[46] According to Vauchez, speculation presently points to Roch's plague either as one of 1414 or a plague at Ferrara in 1439. But why then and not with the more widespread plague of the previous year, and why have historians not sought to check when fifteenth-century plagues struck places such as Acquapendente, Cesena, Rome, Rimini, and Novara with particular force but not major cities?[47] Of course, as with other aspects of Roch's ragged chronology, perhaps this picture of plague was a collage of multiple epidemics. Given the narrative sequence of events, Roch is converted to treating plague victims later during his life at Piacenza, inspired by patrician Gottardo Pallastrelli's labours in the city's hospital. Roch's conversion thus appears after he had travelled from Rome to Novara, already having sacrificed for the plague afflicted.

At any rate, Roch's lifetime interventions were more direct and risky than Catherine's but not the equal of young Bernardino's changing bedpans, washing victims, and administering medicines to them. Roch cured his patients mostly miraculously but by more than whispered incantations. At least he touched them and at Piacenza worked in the hospital alongside Pallastrelli. Moreover, unlike either Sienese saint, Roch caught the plague and retired to the wilderness to die until cured by a dog licking his pestilential wounds. No matter how vague or absurd Roch's story may seem, finally with the curing cur by his side and suppurating bubo down his thigh, a graphic iconography of plague and a saint fixed to it by a sign and symptom arrives in Western art, but only by the late fifteenth century. Yet as with the rectors of Siena's hospitals, Bernardino's cousin Tobia, and his many companions, who paid with their lives, Pallastrelli, Roch's exemplar and teacher, goes without holy recognition.

Francesca Romana (Francesca Bussa dei Ponziani [1384–1440]) unites various strains seen with plague saints who, while alive, sacrificed for the spiritual and physical health of plague victims. Unlike Roch, her life is well grounded in political facts, precise chronologies, and specific institutions of social welfare, which she founded and which have left lasting marks.[48] Unlike Catherine, her intervention was not even partially miraculous. Unlike Catherine and Bernardino, she paid the price for her care in 1414 by becoming infected, and unlike them, plague finally figured in her future cult and was recognized by painters and scholars. From a wealthy background, she married into the Ponziani family, one of late medieval Rome's most powerful dynasties. With the Great Schism and civil war between the Roman *Comune* and papacy, ending in the *Comune*'s defeat in 1398, after several invasions and occupation by Ladislao di Durazzo, King of Naples, combined with famine and plague, Rome reached its late medieval nadir in the first decade of the fifteenth century. With these disasters, the Ponziani paid dearly with their fortunes and lives.[49] During the famines and plagues from 1402 to 1414, Francesca worked in Rome's hospitals of Santa Cecilia, Santo Spirito in Sassia, and above all Santa Maria in Cappello in her neighbourhood of Trastevere. Further, she converted her husband's palace into an additional hospital and foraged his estates for firewood and food to comfort her patients. Yet, as in the stories above, the saint was not alone or even extraordinary in her endeavours. For thirty-eight years, her sister-in-law, Vanozza, worked alongside her; yet Vanozza received no blessed status.[50] In the fifteenth century, others can be added, who achieved holy recognition for real-life charitable activity in plagues, such as St. Columba Reatina of the Franciscan tertiaries (1467–1501). Her saintly model was Catherine of Siena, and she persuaded Perugia's magistrates to combat the plague of

1494 by instituting penitential processions. She also healed the afflicted by her touch and paid for her interventions by catching plague.[51] Such plague saints, even ones like Columba who relied more on miraculous acts than on treatment, nonetheless, remain rare.

More extraordinary is the complete absence of anyone in Europe who obtained holy status for sacrifices or charity performed during the Black Death, or any saint engaged in hands-on care of the plague stricken before Bernardino and the plague of 1400, and any holy one represented caring for plague victims until Blessed Francesca in the mid-fifteenth century, who was not elevated to sanctity until Pope Paul V's canonization in 1608.[52] Furthermore, Francesca may have been the high point of such holy recognition for real-life sacrifice in combating plague. Although many followed in her footsteps caring for plague victims in homes and hospitals across Europe, few received saintly awards for these deeds. St. Aloysius might be counted as an exception. He died at twenty-three, after months of dedicating himself to the physical and spiritual needs of the indigent and ill in Rome's streets and hospitals, sweeping floors and cleaning the filth from beds during the famine and plague ("lues") of 1591 – the century's worst food shortage or even the worst ever faced by the Italian people.[53] That "plague," however, was not the bubonic one. Perhaps it was typhus or dysentery combined with other ailments associated with starvation, even though it spread to members of the papal court and included the Pope himself, Sixtus V.[54]

The intervention of San Carlo during the pan-Italian plague of 1574–7, named after him, was different from Bernardino's and Francesca's. It focused largely on administration, drafting statutes to protect his clergy, inventing new communal forms of prayer for Milanese citizens still under strict quarantine, and his close cooperation with the city's Health Board to achieve spiritual and physical wellbeing for his city. While Borromeo may have visited the sick, he was careful to keep them at a safe distance. Not even his most sympathetic supporters or his later iconography pictured him emptying bedpans or touching the sick.[55] In addition, before the seventeenth century, plague saints actively intervening in their lifetimes appear exclusively from Italy. Even the largely legendary Roch, who by accounts was born in Montpellier and returned there to die, after being imprisoned as a foreign spy, was in effect an Italian saint: his plague endeavours occurred exclusively on Italian soil. Such was not the case with Europe's most prominent contagious disease (at least culturally) before the plague, leprosy. Except for St. Francis of Assisi, its most prominent saints came beyond the Alps – St. Elizabeth of Hungary and Thuringia, St. Louis IX, King of France (1214–70), and St. Martin of Tours (d. 397). More strikingly, along with Italian leper saints such as the Florentine Philip Benizi (1233–85), they appear in their own lifetimes and their later iconography engaged in charitable acts for lepers, by donating their cloaks, holding the lepers' hands, washing their feet, administering medicines, and nursing them in leprosy hospitals.[56]

Nonetheless, with the Renaissance and increasingly during plagues of the sixteenth and seventeenth centuries, plague intercessors increased exponentially. These saints and blessed ones differed from the leper ones or the few plague saints examined above. They had died often centuries before the Black Death, and many of them show no evidence in their lifetimes as healers, no matter what the disease, chronic or epidemic. The plots of their pestilential miracle tales remain mostly the same from their earliest appearances in the mid-fourteenth to the eighteenth century as during Italy's last major plague at Messina in 1743. After physicians had tried all their remedies, with all hope lost and the plague patient ready for last rites, a relative, usually the mother, went to the grave of a local saint, prayed, and often made a votive offering – a candle, wax figure, or occasionally a painting. The earliest to succeed in one of these post-mortem intercessions was Blessed Giovanna da Signa (1266–9 November 1307), at Signa, 12 kilometres west of Florence. As a young girl she herded sheep and cows for her father. She learnt to cherish solitude and became a hermit in Signa's foothills, where she performed miracles and at the end of her life walled herself into a gate. She was the only holy person, dead or alive, miraculously to save any plague victim in 1348, and she did it only once that year, rescuing a farm labourer afflicted with an "evil round swelling ("mala bulla") on his chest." Yet through the fourteenth century, despite great numbers continuing to be felled by plague across Europe, even these post-mortem interventions were rare, and they occurred exclusively in Italy. For the next plague again only one plague miracle surfaces from thousands recorded in the *Acta Sanctorum*. Again, Signa's young shepherdess, now dead for fifty-six years, appears. Her miracle again concerns a victim from this rural community, this time a woman with a pestilential swelling under her left breast. By the fifteenth century, however, these interventions with detailed descriptions of plague cases increase. The mid-thirteenth-century saint Rosa of the Franciscan tertiaries at Viterbo became active in the plague of 1449 to 1451, miraculously curing seventeen individuals after relatives made votive offerings.[57] In the late sixteenth and seventeenth centuries, post-mortem plague miracles finally fan widely across Europe from Ireland to Poland and into the New World.

The interventions, moreover, begin to show new trends, which were more communal than earlier saintly intercessions and unified societies as opposed to dividing them as plague had so sorrowfully achieved in 1348. These trends appear much earlier in chronicles from the second or third plague (depending on the region) and become the norm for protecting against and ending plagues as early as 1362.[58] With one exception, evidence of such future saints or *beati/ae* faced with plague uniting cities by inspiring community-wide processions appears only at the end of the fifteenth century. Such was the call of the to-be-Blessed Columba of Rieti at Perugia during the pestilence of 1494. On receiving advice from long-dead saints Catherine and Bernardino, she encouraged the church and Perugia's municipal government to organize public processions and create a fund for the poor and afflicted during the plague. At the holy altar in one of Perugia's churches, perhaps the cathedral, she made known to the community that she would be present to cure any who became infected, and "many" came to receive her miracles. She travelled to Perugia's outlying villages, again beseeching Catherine to end the plague, and as in Perugia, had monasteries and convents open their doors to the afflicted, where she erected a bed to perform her hands-on miracle cures.[59] From her advice, the University of Perugia built a monastery from their own and public funds and commissioned a banner to be painted and kept in the city's archives, ready to lead the populace in processions to end future plagues.[60] During a "big plague" in Monza in 1521, citizens processed with paintings of Roman martyrs and commissioned a painting of St. Gerard the dyer, their twelfth-century patron and founder of the town's hospital. Afterwards, not a single Monzesi died in this plague. To protect the town from future plagues, the procession, as though a communal vaccine, was instituted annually on Gerard's anniversary, ending in his church with songs, masses, and offerings of wax and money.[61] St. Torpes, a courtier of Nero, beheaded for his conversion during Nero's persecution in 68 CE, may have been the earliest saint to intercede in a later plague. At Pisa, during its last devastating plague of 1630, the city organized various processions, but the plague could only be calmed and the afflicted cured when a Pisan magistrate presented the head of the martyr to lead a procession throughout all the squares and streets of the city.[62]

Such community-wide actions in the *Acta Sanctorum* can also be detected beyond the Alps. In fact, I have found one from a plague at Perpignan in 1384, which supposedly killed 8,000 between November and March. Only with a procession, organized by a local monastery, carrying the relics of the ninth-century Occitan peasant Gualdericus (Guaderico), was it finally calmed.[63] Within the *Acta Sanctorum*, the next collective enterprise outside Italy to end a plague appears almost two centuries later. This miraculous protection of a community in rural Portugal near Várzea was more elaborate and had a clearer sense of saintly interces- sion. Shepherds tending their flocks came upon a painting of the fifth-century virgin martyr St. Quiteria, which they happily handed over to a local monastery, and the monks built a church around it. After the church had fallen into ruin "for many years," and plague began to rage through Portugal in 1568, the community restored the church. In return, Quiteria interceded; afterwards no one in the village became infected.[64] At the end of the sixteenth to the eighteenth century, such communal acts and general processions with paintings and promises of shrines and construction of churches and hospitals to end plagues or protect communities from being infected in the first place, multiplied. The thirteenth-century Polish saint and queen, the virgin Kinga (Kunga, Cunegundis, or Cunegonda[65]) performed sixty- seven post-mortem miracles. Several were collective endeavours that bound communities together during or immediately after a plague, first to process and make votive offerings beseeching Kinga's intercession, then with festivities of gratitude and making good their promises. In 1624 plague hit Newmarcht [Novum forum] in Silesia. Twice its inhabitants were prompted to process to Kinga's grave, where they offered prayers, beseeching her to deliver them from the plague. They carried a silver-framed icon of the saint bearing the inscription: "the inhabitants of the royal city of Newmarcht because of the plague devote themselves to Beata Cunegundis with their prayers."[66] Two years later they assembled again to process and commemorate Cunegundis' liberation of their town.

Sicily, however, was the region *par excellence* of communal rituals for plague protection. In 1525, 1575, and 1625, inhabitants of Licata on Sicily's southern coast marched barefoot in multiple processions with relics of their thirteenth-century patron saint, the martyr Angelo, who three centuries earlier had combated the Cathars. While nothing in his hagiography suggests any involvement with any disease in his lifetime, suddenly in the second half of the seventeenth century, he arose to protect his city from plague and now with a new wrinkle: no plagues then were present in Sicily or Italy.[67] Nonetheless, in 1662, Licata's citizens exhumed their patron to rebury him in a new votive church, constructed in gratitude for protecting them from pestilence over the past thirty-nine years.[68]

Santa Rosalia

The most prolific of miracle makers, at least as regards plague, was another Sicilian, Rosalia, born of a mid-twelfth-century Norman aristocratic family resident at Palermo. Her moment of glory did not come, however, until much later, during Palermo's last plague in 1624, when a peasant woman supposedly discovered her bones in a cavern ("spelunca") atop Monte Pellegrino, a peak, 606 metres above Palermo and 12 kilometres north of the city. For this plague alone she interceded over 200 times as recorded in the *Actum Sanctorum*, miraculously curing at least 101 persons individually of plague (40 men, 37 women and 23 infants, undis- tinguished by sex). Most often, her cure was the waters taken from her grotto, her sup- posed thirteenth-century cell and place of burial. In addition to sex, these victims were often identified by age, place, and occasionally profession. The course of their illness was sometimes noted, along with the date of their recovery, whether the waters were mixed with stones or her bones at the shrine, and how or where the solution was applied. For instance, a thirty-year-old fisherman from Palermo, attacked by plague in 1624, suffered from a high fever and horrendous tumours, one of which formed in his armpit. The doctors gave up hope, "having never heard of any in his condition surviving." When priests were called to perform last rights, a Capuchin suggested beseeching Santa Rosalia. Water from her grotto was brought down for him to drink and bathe his pestilential wounds. His fever subsided, the swellings healed, he recovered.[69]

Her plague miracles, however, point to trends rarely seen, if at all, earlier in the *Acta Sanctorum*. First, she cured not only young innocents whose mothers or guardians happened to call on long-dead saints; several of Rosalia's intercessions recognized the services and self-sacrifice of those working in hospitals or outside them, as with the Jesuit Francesco Marino, who became infected while administering to the plague stricken.[70] As the hagiographer expressed it when Rosalia interceded to cure Girolamo Canina while he was attending to plague victims at Palermo's hospital, Francesco "was damned because of the services he paid to the plague-infected." After his doctors gave up ("a medicis esset derelictus"), he accepted Rosalia's waters and within twenty-four hours recovered.[71] Another, Domenico of Messina, caught the plague while caring for victims in Palermo's hospital. Once recovered, he returned to his duties and caught it a second time and was left to die, when Rosalia with her waters interceded.[72] While these plague miracles celebrated the virgin, they also recognized for the first time the charitable deeds of the non-saintly plague workers: seven men and two women – nurses, doctors, and surgeons – who while working the wards of Palermo's *valetudinarium* had become infected. Saved by Rosalia's waters, they returned to their posts during this, Palermo's last plague.[73]

Unlike previous plague saints whose intercessions were overwhelmingly addressed to individual plague sufferers, almost two-thirds of Rosalia's were collective. Several were multiple cures for groups of plague afflicted as during the 1625 plague in Corleone, when with votive gifts the town's inhabitants implored Rosalia to save "many from the plague" of whom four men and one woman were named along with their "two or three" children and another thirteen unnamed infants.[74] Much more numerous, however, were her intercessions that brought communities into collective acts of veneration with processions, communal prayers, and contributions for votive gifts, ranging from shrines, paintings and statues to elaborate artistic ephemera and construction of new churches to celebrate a plague's end. From the plague of 1624 on, Rosalia became a turbine of artistic production. Among others, these included a painting of the virgin Rosalia commissioned by Palermo's senate during the plague in 1624.[75] At that plague's end, Palermo's senate then organized much more, spending at least 15,000 gold coins ("aureorum"). The city also received contributions from Palermo's principal nations (gens) of foreign bankers and merchants – the Catalans, Florentines, Genoese, and Neapolitans – to build four well-buttressed triumphal arches, decorated "at the highest expense (maximo sumptu)" with paintings, insignia, epigrams, poetic verses, forty-eight columns draped with painted silk interwoven with gold and silver and other decorations, a large building, richly attired with long curtains, four new open spaces in the city ("aere"), thirty-three altars, decorated with insignia and vases "ingeniously crafted in gold and silver" and erected at each of the city's major street crossings, and innumerable other ornaments, "exciting the highest admiration" to celebrate this plague's cessation and to give thanks to the virgin. According to her life, the collective giving and communal thanksgiving turned "the entire city into a gigantic temple to her honour."[76] Collective gifts spread to smaller Sicilian towns. The following year at Bivona its people commissioned a church and shrine with a painting of Rosalia,[77] and at Noto an ex-voto painting of the saint.[78] In 1626, the hilltop town of Modica

(Motucae) constructed a new church next to its hospital in the saint's honour.[79] In 1630, a monumental marble tomb ("Arca marmoreal") for Rosalia was erected at her grotto, Monte Pellegrino.[80] With no declared plague deaths on 4 September 1743, after Messina's most disastrous plague since 1347–8, "all its citizens" in gratitude adopted Rosalia as their patron and promised to build a temple to her.[81] Several days earlier, with the plague on the wane, the city's senate had already commissioned a painting of the saint for a chapel in their chambers.[82]

While these works of art, paintings, shrines, and churches clustered in Sicily and primarily in Palermo, promised gifts to end plague were being made to her in other parts of Italy, as at Cremona in 1633 and Sezza, near Rome, in 1716.[83] Moreover, such gifts, commemorations, and celebrations fanned across Europe to places as far away as Paris in 1628,[84] Gau (Molinenses) in Germany in 1631,[85] and for the construction of a church in her name at Cilley (Celia) in Austria, where her saint's life maintained 60,000 had perished from plague in 1649.[86] Her fame extended still further to Portuguese Goa, where "an elegant votive church" was built in her name during or immediately after a plague in 1666.[87]

More extensive than these votive commissions for concrete works of art were other means by which Rosalia brought communities together. These were processions through streets of cities, towns, and villages with inhabitants often carrying her relics. Within Sicily, these often came on loan from Palermo, extending that community's networks of solidarity across Sicily. Her cult and anti-plague protection reached beyond Italy. In the late seventeenth century she was active at Mela in Brabant and Antwerp, where she became its patron saint. With commissioned paintings and a shrine during the plagues of 1668 and 1678, citizens of Antwerp collectively invoked her intercession at least seven times during the plagues of 1629, 1665, 1668, and 1678.[88] Her cult travelled west to Nice in 1633,[89] south to Malta in 1676,[90] east to Warsaw in 1630,[91] southeast to Transylvania in 1737–8,[92] and across the ocean to provinces in the New World, "to all of Brazil" and Peru ("Peruvia") at unspecified dates, Durango, Mexico ("Nova Biscaia"] in 1716,[93] Lima in 1746, California in 1701, although the disease now was smallpox,[94] and to Tunisia ("in regno Tunetano") in the early 1700s.[95]

During the second half of the seventeenth and early eighteenth century, she operated not only when plagues struck but, like Licata's martyr, to keep communities plague-free. To ensure her protection, citizens processed with her relics, engaged in collective prayers and litanies, made votive gifts, and when the danger passed, celebrated her success with city-wide festivals. In 1645, a second shrine was promised in fields outside Bivona,[96] where no plague had struck (or for that matter anywhere else I know of in Italy). In 1649, a plague case arose in Palermo's hospital but developed no further. The city's mayor ("praetor") attributed his city's immunity to Rosalia's intercession and ordered a public festival.[97] When Italy's last plague pandemic in 1656–7 struck Genoa and Naples at levels not seen since 1348, a Florentine merchant smuggled goods into Palermo, breaking its quarantine. The goods, however, failed to ignite the pandemic in Palermo or elsewhere in Sicily: in return for Rosalia's protection, Palermo's citizens processed in thanksgiving, and its senate voted to erect a monument and a statue "in her likeness" with the inscription: "To the divine Rosalia servant of her country, 1656, S.P.Q.P."[98] Nonetheless, plagues continued to threaten Palermo, from Coversano ("Conversanum"), near Bari in 1691,[99] Marseille in 1720,[100] Messina in 1743,[101] as well as by ones from unnamed places in 1710[102] and 1744.[103] Despite contraband goods slipping through Palermo's docks, the city miraculously escaped them all, thanks they thought to their votive gifts, processions, fasts, and barefoot treks to Rosalia's cave. Instead of stirring blame and hatred that divided classes and targeted minorities, these acts, despite the epidemiological dangers they posed, unified inhabitants across social classes and city walls into the countryside. With the expansion of her cult and exchanges of her relics, Rosalia's supposed post-mortem intercessions via the Jesuits extended Palermo's connections, good will, and fame beyond Sicily, Italy, even Europe.

In conclusion, the Black Death sparked conflict, hatred, and violence from 1347 to 1351, and not just with the well-studied incidents of burning Jews and flagellants. More widespread, at least from chronicles' reportage across Europe, was the cruelty of abandoning loved ones and refusal of trusted professionals to perform their essential duties. In addition, laws fixing prices and wages also inflicted blame and violence on artisans and peasants, pinned as the ones greedily exploiting new market realities. What the current historiography has failed to notice, however, is just how short-lived these initial Black Death reactions were. Successive plagues ceased to spur pogroms against Jews or any other "Others"; claims of abandoning afflicted loved ones all but disappeared and plague decrees regulating wages turned about-face to reward rather than punish those who moved.

Another indication of post-plague mentality is more enigmatic. The Church failed to recognize the thousands who did not run but faced the violent contagion and in so doing lost their lives comforting their plague-afflicted neighbours. The Church honoured no Black Death martyrs who risked their lives succouring the plague afflicted until 1400, and thereafter did so only rarely and with the cults illustrated only faintly – a fact that neither religious nor art historians have confronted. With successive plagues, the Church slowly began to remember a few who in their own lifetimes assisted the plague stricken. Yet overwhelmingly, the increasing numbers of plague saints were long-dead figures resurrected to save the afflicted miraculously and risk-free, when votive gifts were on offer. Nonetheless, by the plagues of the seventeenth century, these miraculous deeds began to mount and shifted from ones pertaining to individual supplicants to ones that unified communities through collective acts of penance, fasting, singing litanies, processions, pooled contributions, and festivals of thanksgiving. These collective gifts to saints to end plagues and protect communities from future ones resulted in public works, from ephemeral objects and simple roadside shrines to major constructions of churches and hospitals with charitable offerings to the poor and infirm. Our understanding of the immediate socio-psychological reactions, not only to the Black Death, but to epidemic disease across time, has emphasized the negative, highlighting violence and blame and the splintering of communities, while remaining blind to epidemics' force in unifying and strengthening societies in past times.[104]

Notes

1 For this historiography, see my *Epidemics: Hate and Compassion from Antiquity to the Great Influenza* (forthcoming).

2 Rosemary Horrox, ed. and trans., *The Black Death*, Manchester Medieval Sources, Manchester, 1994, p. 223.

3 Jean-Noël Biraben, *Les Hommes et la Peste en France et dans les pays europééns et méditerranéens*, 2 vols., Paris, 1975–6, vol. 1, p. 59.

4 Nico Voitgländer and Hans-Joachim Voth. "Persecution Perpetuated: The Medieval Origins of Anti-Semitic Violence in Nazi Germany." *Quarterly Journal of Economics* 127, no. 3 (2012), 1348.

5 Cecil Roth, *The History of the Jews of Italy*, Philadelphia, 1946, p. 142, charged that anti-Semitic attacks occurred in Mantua and Parma during the Black Death, but he did not cite his sources, and I know of no historians to corroborate them.

6 Samuel Cohn, Jr., 'The Black Death and the burning of Jews', *Past & Present*, no. 196 (August, 2007): 3–36; for the citation, *Die Weltchronik des Mönchs Albert, 1273/77–1454/56*, ed. Rolf Sprandel, MGH, Scriptores rerum Germanicarum in usum scholarum, new ser., xvii, Munich, 1994, p. 109.

7 On Charles IV's pivotal role in the massacres see Alfred Haverkamp, " Die Judenverfolgungen zur Zeit des Schwarzen Todes im Gesellschaftsgefüge deutscher Städte', in *Zur Geschichte der Juden im Deutschland des späten Mittelalters und der frühen Neuzeit*, ed. Alfred Haverkamp, Stuttgart, 1981, p. 65; and Jörge Müller, "*Erez gererah* – 'Land of Persecution': Pogroms against the Jews in the *regnum Teutonicum* from c. 1280 to 1350," in, *The Jews of Europe in the Middle Ages (Tenth to Fifteenth Centuries): Proceedings of the International Symposium held at Speyer, 20–25 October 2002*, ed. Christoph Cluse, Turnhout, 2004, pp. 245–60, p. 257; for earlier works and sources, see Cohn, "The Black Death and the Burning of Jews," p. 15, n. 32.

8 *Chronique de Richard Lescot religieux de Saint-Denis (1328–1344) suivi de la continuation de cette chronique (1344–1364)*, ed. Jean Lemoine, Société de l'histoire de France, Paris, 1896, p. 83. Jean de Venette, in *Chronique latine de Guillaume de Nangis de 1113 à 1300 avec les continuations de cette chronique de 1300 à 1368*, ed. H. Géraud, Paris, 1843, vo. 2, pp. 213–14. Several other French chroniclers reported the processions of the flagellants across Europe such as *Les Grandes Chroniques de France*, ed. Jules Viard, vol. 9, *Charles IV Le Bel, Philippe VI de Valois*, Paris, 1937, p. 323; and *Chronique de Jean le Bel*, ed. Jules Viard and Eugène Déprez, 2 vols., Paris, 1904–5, vol. 1, pp. 222 and 224.

9 Andries Welkenhuysen, "La peste en Avignon (1348) décrite … Louis Sanctus de Beringen …" in *Pascua Mediaevalia: Studies voor Prof. J. M. De Smet*, ed. R. Lievens, E. Van Mingroot, and W. Verbeke, Leuven, 1983, pp. 452–92 (text, pp. 465–9); and *Breve Chronicon Clerici Anonymi*, pp. 5–30, in *Recueil des Chroniques de Flandre publié sous la direction de la Commission Royale d'histoire*, ed. J.-J. de Smet, III, Brussels, 1856. *Chronique et annales de Gilles le Muisit (1272–1352)*, ed. Henri Lemaître, Paris, 1906, *Annales*, pp. 222–3. *Chroniques des Ducs de Brabant, par Edmond de Dynter*, ed. P. F. X. de Ram, 2 vols., Brussels, 1854, vol. 2, p. 683. These tallies have been taken from my earlier survey of chronicles listed in Appendix II of Cohn, *The Black Death Transformed: Disease and Culture in Early Renaissance Europe*, London, 2002, pp. 251–73.

10 I elaborate on these criticisms in my *Epidemics*, ch. 2.

11 Michele da Piazza, *Cronica*, ed. Antonino Giuffrida, Palermo, 1980, p. 82.

12 Matteo Villani, *Cronica con la continuazione di Filippo Villani*, ed. Giuseppe Porta, 2 vols., Parma, 1995, vol. 1, p. 11.

13 *Annales seu Cronicae incliti Regni Poloniae opera venerabilis domini Joannis Dlugossii canonici Cracoviensis*, ed. I. Dabrowski, 10 vols., Warsaw, 1964–85, vol. 9, p. 301.

14 *Ecclesia Spalatensis*, in *Illyrici sacri*, III, Venice, 1765, p. 324.

15 *Annales seu Cronicae*, ed. Dabrowski, vol. 9, p. 301.

16 *Chronica Olivensis auctore Stanislao, abbate Olivensi*, in *Monumenta Poloniae Historica* I ser. VI (1893), pp. 310–50.

17 *Chronicon Galfridi le Baker de Swynebroke*, ed. E. M. Thompson, Oxford, 1889, p. 99.

18 *Annalium Hiberniae Chronicon ad annum MCCCXLIX*, ed. Richard Butler, Irish Archaeological Society, Dublin, 1849, pp. 1–39, p. 37.

19 *Johannis de fordun Chronica Gentis Scotorum*, ed. William F. Skene, The Historians of Scotland, Edinburgh, 1871, vol. 1, p. 369; and largely copied in Walter Bower, *Scotichronicon*, ed. D. E. R Watt, 9 vols., Aberdeen, 1989–98, vol. 7, pp. 272–3.

20 Horrox, *The Black Death*, pp. 271–2. By comparing many more contemporaneous texts across Europe from the period of the Black Death, my *Epidemics*, ch. 2, challenges the present consensus on abandonment – that it was simply a literary *topos*; see Richard Emery, "The Black Death of 1348 in Perpignan," *Speculum*, 42, 4 (1967): 611–23; Daniel Smail, "Accommodating Plague in Medieval Marseille," *Continuity and Change*, 11 (1996): 11–41; and Shona Kelly Wray, *Communities and Crisis: Bologna during the Black Death*, Leiden, 2009.

21 These differences are illustrated in greater detail in *Epidemics*, ch. 4.

22 Elites and others leaving cities during plague time persisted to the last epidemics of the eighteenth century, but these became regularized and accepted events, unlike the abandonment of the sick and family members or the stripping of cities of vital services as chroniclers decried in 1348. Even during the disastrous plagues of London in 1603, 1625, and 1665, when authors such as Thomas Dekker, John Taylor, Thomas Brewer, and Daniel Defoe crafted vignettes of cruelty, they also had to praise mayors, aldermen, councillors, and their deputies, who remained at their posts with many dying as a consequence; see Charles Creighton, *History of Epidemics in Britain*, ed. D. E. C. Eversley, 2 vols., London, 1965 [Cambridge, 1894], vol. 1, pp. 481–4, 512, 517, 666–7. For the Ottoman Empire, by contrast, I do not find any claims of abandonment in 1347–8, but later during the 1467

plague in Istanbul it surfaces with all the condemnation of Western Black Death chroniclers from the Greek historian Kritovoulos, *History of Mehmed the Conqueror*, trans. Charles Riggs, Princeton, 1954, pp. 220–1; also cited in Nükhet Varlik, *Plague and Empire in the Early Modern World: The Ottoman Experience, 1347–1600*, Cambridge, 2015, p. 136. For threats of butchers and bakers leaving Aix-en-Provence, because of surrounding towns blocking their supplies, and almost all notables fleeing town during the plague of 1580, see Claire Dolan, *La notaire, la famille et la ville (Aix-en-Provence à la fin du XVIe siècle)*, Toulouse, 1998, pp. 25–35. However, these impulses did not revive the horrors of 1348. Soldiers and young artisan and merchant volunteers guarded the city; notaries stayed, shifting their business to meet the demand for testaments; churchmen continued with their services, and families, afraid of catching the plague from the pall-bearers, carried their children or parents to the cemeteries themselves. In fact, this "exceptional situation" revived family solidarity (p. 34).

23 *Cronache di Ser Luca Dominici*, ed. Giovan Carlo Gigliotti, vol. 1, *Cronaca della venuta dei Bianchi e della Moria 1399–1400*, Pistoia, 1933, p. 232.

24 Smail, "Accommodating Plague," p. 22.

25 William Bowsky, "The Impact upon Sienese Government and Society," *Speculum*, 39 (1964): 1–34.

26 Giovanni Boccaccio, *The Decameron*, trans. G. H. McWilliam, Penguin Classics, Harmondsworth, 1972, pp. 15–16; William Langland, *Piers the Ploughman*, trans. J. F. Goodridge, Harmondsworth, 1959, pp. 127–8; Villani, *Cronica*, I, pp. 15–17 and 392; Stefani, *Cronica fiorentina*, p. 232.

27 See Robert Braid, "'Et non ultra': politiques royales du travail en Europe Occidentale au XIVe siècle," *Bibliothèque de l'École des Chartes*, 161 (2003): 437–91; and Robert Braid, "Peste, prolétaires et politiques: la législation du travail et les politiques économiques en angleterre aux XIIIeme et XIVeme siècles," PhD thesis, Université Paris (Paris 7), 2008, and its exhaustive bibliography.

28 For post-plague labour legislation in central and northern Italy, see Samuel Cohn, "After the Black Death: Labour Legislation and Attitudes towards Labour in Late-Medieval Western Europe," *Economic History Review*, 60(3) (2007): 457–85. Siena anticipated these trends; see Bowsky, "The Impact of the Black Death," p. 32. Other Italian regions such as Milan, changed their policies later (Cohn, "Labour Legislation").

29 For these references, see Cohn, "After the Black Death."

30 For this evidence, see Lawrence Poos, "The Social Context of Statute of Labourers Enforcement," *Law & History Review*, 27 (1983): 27–52, p. 48; Simon Penn and Christopher Dyer, "Wages and Earnings in Late Medieval England: Evidence from the Enforcement of the Labour Laws," *Economic History Review*, 2nd ser., 43 (1990): 356–76, p. 359; and Cohn, "After the Black Death," p. 461

31 See Samuel Cohn, *Popular Protest in Late Medieval English Towns*, Cambridge, 2013, pp. 126–8.

32 See for instance the funerary restriction passed and revised during the Black Death at Pistoia; A. Chiappelli, "Gli ordinamenti sanitari del commune di Pistoia contro la pestilenza del 1348," *Archivio Storico Italiano*, ser. 4, 20 (1887): 3–21.

33 See Cohn, *Epidemics*, ch. 18.

34 Raymond of Capua, *The Life of St Catherine of Siena*, trans. George Lamb, London, 1960, pp. 222–4; and *Acta Sanctorum* (hereafter *AS*).

35 *Ibid.*, pp. 224 and 228.

36 *Ibid.*, p. 231.

37 *Ibid.*, p. 230.

38 *Ibid.*, p. 231.

39 *Ibid.*, pp. 140–1.

40 *Ibid.*, pp. 229–31.

41 *The Life of S. Bernardine of Siena, Minor Observantine*, London, 1873, pp. 21–6.

42 *Ibid.*, p. 26.

43 *AS*, Maii V, pp. 287, 290, 305–6; Also see Iris Origo, *The World of San Bernardino*, New York, 1962, pp. 15–16, and 68.

44 *Butler's Lives of the Saints* (hereafter *BLS*), revised by Paul Burns *et al.*, 12 vols., Tunbridge Wells, 1995–2000, vol. May (revised by David Hugh Farmer), pp. 107–8, states only: "During the plague of 1400 he and some other companions took over the local hospital because the regular staff had died." It is moreover, misleading: some of the original brothers were still around and, most importantly, Bernardino's cousin had arrived there earlier and had organized plague relief in the women's ward. Bruno Korosak's entry in *Bibliotheca Sanctorum*, Rome, 1961–87 (hereafter *BS*), vol.

2, pp. 1294–321, is equally brief and incorrect: "Mentre curava gli appestati nell'ospedale di Santa Maria della Scala, Bernardino si ammalò." Instead, he became ill after leaving the hospital and not of plague. Origo, *The World of San Bernardino*, p. 18, spends less than a paragraph on the saint's four months at Santa Maria della Scala. Given her valiant hospital care during World War II on her estates, I find this near omission striking; see her *War in Val d'Orcia*, London, 1947.

45 *BLS*, rev. John Cumming, Tunbridge Wells, 1998, pp. 162–4; André Vauchez, "San Rocco," *BS*, XI, cols. 264–73.

46 Vauchez, "San Rocco."

47 Also, see detailed descriptions of Saint Roch's life and its sources in Louise Marshall, "Manipulating the Sacred: Image and Plague in Renaissance Italy," *Renaissance Quarterly*, 47(3) (1994): 485–532, pp. 502–4; and Thomas Worcester, "Saint Roch vs. Plague, Famine, and Fear," in *Hope and Healing: Painting in Italy in a Time of Plague, 1500–1800*, ed. Gauvin Bailey, Pamela M. Jones, Franco Mormando, and Thomas W. Worcester, Worcester, MA, 2005, pp. 153–75. But they do not speculate on Roch's period of activity or on what plague or plagues he may have confronted.

48 It is not true that saints' lives were universally so indifferent to precise dates and events as apologists for Roch's life insist; see for instance Allie Terry-Fritsch, "Introduction," in *Beholding Violence in Medieval and Early Modern Europe*, ed. Allie Terry-Fritsch, Farnham, 2012, pp. 24–6.

49 Arnold Esch, "Processi medioevali per la cononizzazione di Santa Francesca Romana (1440–1451)," in *La canonizzazione di Santa Francesca Romana: Santità, cultura e istituzioni a Roma tra medioevo ed età moderna. Atti del Convegno internazionale, Roma, 19–21 novembre 2009*, ed. Alessandra Bartolomei Romagnoli and Giorgio Picasso, Florence, 2013, pp. 39–51, at pp. 39–40.

50 *AS*, Emnziana Vaccaro, "Francesca Anna-Francesca Romana," *BS*, V, pp. 1011–28; *BSL*, rev., March, "St Frances of Rome, Foundress (1384–1440)," pp. 79–82.

51 *AS*, Maii V, Dies 20, B. Columba Reatina, Virgo tertii Ordin. S. Dominici Perusii in Vmbria; *BLS*, May, pp. 110–11; Antonio Blasucci, "Colomba, da Rieti, beata, 1467–1501," *BS*, IV, cols. 101–3.

52 Giorgio Picasso, "Introduzione," in *La canonizzazione di Santa Francesca Romana*.

53 See Guido Alfani, "The Famine of the 1590s in Northern Italy: The Analysis of the Greatest 'System Shock' in the Sixteenth Century," *Histoire & Mesure*, 26 (2011): 17–50, p. 34. On the climatic, economic, and psychological factors of this three-year plague, across the Italian peninsula and Europe, see Guido Alfani, *Il Grand Tour dei Cavalieri dell'Apocalisse: L'Italia del "lungo Cinquecento" (1494–1629)*, Venice, 2010, pp. 96–109.

54 *AS*, Jun. IV, cols. 1009–10 and 1018. Not only are there no descriptions of buboes and quick death with the diseases of 1591, it took the already sickly Aloysius fifty days to die of the disease, 3 March to 21 June. Despite the attention given to this famine, I know of no work to examine the signs, symptoms, or courses of its accompanying diseases.

55 Among other places, see my *Cultures of Plague: Medical Thinking at the End of the Renaissance*, Oxford, 2010; and Pamela Jones, "San Carlo Borromeo and the Plague Imagery in Milan and Rome," in Bailey *et al.*, eds., *Hope and Healing*, pp. 65–96.

56 Christine M. Boeckl, *Images of Leprosy: Disease, Religion, and Politics in European Art*, Kirkville, MO, 2011, pp. 45, 52, 81, 83–90.

57 *AS*, Sep. II, Dies 4, Rosa virgo tertii Ordinis S. Francisci, Viterbii in Italia, 4 September.

58 This change in plague action and mentality is explored in detail in my *Epidemics*, ch. 2.

59 *AS*, Maii V, Dies 20, B. Columba Reatina, Virgo tertii Ordin. S. Dominici Perusii in Vmbria,

60 *Ibid.*, another life of Beata Columba.

61 *AS*, Jun. I, Dies 6, S. Gerardus Tinctorius, Modoetiae apud Insubres in Italia, miracles 20 and 21.

62 *AS*, 1.Maii IV, Dies 17, De S. Torpes Martyr, Pisae in Hetruria, p. 18.

63 *AS*, Oct. VII, Dies 16, S. Gualdericus agricola in Occitania, p. 1116.

64 *AS*, Maii V, Dies 22, S. Quiteria Virgo, Martyr in Adurensi Vasconiae dioecesi.

65 Pietro Naruszewicz, "Cunegonda (Kinga, Kunga)," *BS*, IV, pp. 460–1.

66 *AS*, 252.Jul. V, Dies 24, S. Kinga seu Cunegundis virgo, Poloniae ducissa, Ord. S. Clarae, apud antiquam Sandecz, in palatinatu Cracoviensi.

67 *AS*, Maii II, Dies 5, S. Angelus, Presbyter Ordinis Carmelitani, Martyr Leocatae in Sicilia, miracles, 6, 7, 9.

68 Giuseppe Morabito, "Angelo da Gerusalemme o da Licata, sant," *BS*, I, pp. 1240–3.

69 *AS*, Sep. V: 2, Dies 4, S. Rosalia, Appendix Miraculorum ac Beneficorum, no. 19.

70 *Ibid.*, cap. II: Prosecutio eorundem miraculorum ex Cascino cap. 12, no. 40.

71 *Ibid.*, no. 46. The hospital is not identified but was probably the Lazaretto of Palermo.

72 *Ibid.*, no. 49.

73 *Ibid.*, nos. 34, 36, 40, 42, 43–6, 49.

74 *Ibid.*, cap. XXXIV. no. 361.

75 *Ibid.*, XX. Cura archiepiscopi: Vota Panormi contra pestem, no. 208.

76 *Ibid.*, XXII. Corpus S. Rosaliae solemni pompa per urbem circumlatum finis pestilentiae ejus beneficio impetratus, no. 235.

77 *Ibid.*, Vita Brevis, Octavio Caietano S.J., no. 2.

78 *Ibid.*, XXXVII, Cultus, reliquiae & miracula in diocesibus Catanensi & Syracusana, no. 398.

79 *Ibid.*, no. 397

80 *Ibid.*, Vita Altera, Jordano Cascini S.J.: II. Miracula post corpus inventum; no. 22.

81 *Ibid.*, Appendix: Miraculorum ac beneficiorum, no. 152.

82 *Ibid.*, no. 151.

83 *Ibid.*, Commentarius Praevius: XXXIX. Cultus, reliquiae & beneficia S. Rosalia in Italia, nos. 420 and 422.

84 *Ibid.*, XL. Gallia, Hispania, Germania, & Hungaria, no. 429.

85 *Ibid.*, no. 431.

86 *Ibid.*, no. 437.

87 *Ibid.*, XLI. Cultus, reliquiae & beneficia S. Rosaliae in Belgio & praesertim Antverpiae: item Polonia &in insula Melitensi, no. 468.

88 *Ibid.*, XLI. nos. 445, 478, 450–3.

89 *Ibid.*, no. 427.

90 *Ibid.*, nos. 456–7.

91 *Ibid.*, no. 455.

92 *Ibid.*, XL. Gallia, Hispania, Germania & Hungaria; post votum S. Rosalia, no. 441.

93 *Ibid.*, XLIII. America & Africa: variola, no. 472.

94 *Ibid.*, XLIII. America & Africa, nos. 472–6; and XXXI. Missa propria pro regno Siciliae, no. 326.

95 *Ibid.*, XLIII, nos. 447–8.

96 *Ibid.*, Vita Brevis, Octavio Caietano S.J., no. 2.

97 *Ibid.*, Appendix III. Alia miracula,relata a Cascino, no. 138.

98 *Ibid.*, Appendix Miraculorum ac Benediciorum, XXXIX. Cultus, reliquiae & beneficia S Rosalia in Italia, no. 138; and Appendix: Miraculorum ac beneficiorum, no. 168.

99 *Ibid.*, no. 139.

100 *Ibid.*, no. 141.

101 *Ibid.*, no. 142.

102 *Ibid.*, no. 140.

103 *Ibid.*, no. 139.

104 Recent work by art historians – Marshall, "Manipulating the Sacred"; Boeckl, *Images of Leprosy*; and Bailey *et al.*, eds., *Hope and Healing* – has changed an earlier picture of plagues shrouding Europe in fear and doom from 1347 to the Enlightenment. While plague as a manifestation of God's punishment persisted through the early modern period, painting and religious culture of the Counter-Reformation also encouraged reassurance and hope. Yet this literature has not addressed the theme of this chapter, a dichotomy between hate, blame, and division on the one hand and forces for unity on the other, or that a major shift from the first to the second began after the Black Death of 1348.

16

DEAD(LY) UNCERTAINTIES

Plague and Ottoman society in the age of the Renaissance[1]

Nükhet Varlık

While recounting the events of the summer of 1584, the Ottoman chronicler Selaniki Mustafa Efendi (d. after 1600) mentions the following incident. Hüseyin Agha, the Equerry-in-Chief, contracted the plague as the epidemic was ravaging Istanbul. While he was sick and enduring the pains of disease, another man from the court, also named Hüseyin Agha, approached the Grand Vizier to plead for the post held by the sick man. The Grand Vizier dismissed the request, saying that the post could not be re-assigned while the office-holder was still alive. He was baffled to hear this demand, for he did not understand how the post could be granted to someone else before the death of the current office-holder. He was right to be taken aback by this request, since according to Ottoman bureaucratic custom a post became vacant only through the death of the office-holder or by his dismissal. Neither was at issue here. Upon hearing the Grand Vizier's refusal, the ambitious Hüseyin Agha exclaimed: "I doubt that he will recover!" When the Grand Vizier heard this, he replied in exasperation: "It is possible that you [will] die before him." Indeed, according to our chronicler, the latter Hüseyin Agha soon contracted the plague and passed away four days before his namesake.[2]

This curious anecdote encapsulates the widespread uncertainties felt at the Ottoman court at a time when the plague was taking a heavy toll on the empire. An acute observer of his society, Selaniki was remarkably astute in recording urban disasters, such as plagues, fires, and earthquakes, as much as he was in giving a voice to the gloomy emotions of the Ottoman people suffering from these catastrophic events. In referring to this outbreak in Istanbul, he writes that plague was so agonizing that the loud sighs and mourning of the people reached the sky; there was no one in the city whose heart was not burning with the pain of separation brought by death and no one who was not crying.[3] In fact, this particular outbreak was only one among many that the empire suffered. Since the Black Death of the mid-fourteenth century, recurrent epidemics continued periodically across the Ottoman lands, as they did elsewhere in the Mediterranean world.[4]

Plague was an unsettling fact of life in the early modern Ottoman Empire. The seemingly indiscriminate patterns of plague mortality (young and old, women and men, rich and poor), the swiftness of death, the unsightliness of its symptoms, and the difficulty of making predictions about its prognosis triggered widespread anxieties at all levels of society. It brought

259

political and economic instability, unrest and upheaval, and rapid social change. The widespread uncertainties of the times, especially when coupled with a sense of urgency caused by imminent and unpredictable death, invoked sentiments about the volatility of human life and even the future of the empire itself. Ottoman society was not alone in experiencing the emotional burden of devastating plague outbreaks. In fact, it was more or less a shared experience across the Mediterranean world (and beyond) throughout the late medieval and early modern eras. Even though the historical scholarship has thoroughly examined the impact of plague in economic, political, religious, cultural domains, little has yet been done to explore the plague's impact on the *emotional* landscape of early modern Mediterranean societies.[5]

This chapter seeks to map out the emotional burden plague placed on Ottoman society, and to make its effects more visible to the historical gaze. To do so, it will address the widespread uncertainties that were expressed, including those felt at the level of individuals (e.g., about their future, fortunes, and death), communities (e.g., about administrators, spiritual leaders), and imperial structures (e.g., about the continuity of the dynastic family, the state, and its institutions). Hence, the chapter attempts to put these uncertainties at the center of historical inquiry, and to better understand the behavior of individuals who experienced them. In doing so, it will unpack both the burden felt at a moment of crisis and its repercussions on individuals, institutions, and conventions. Exploring this aspect of the plague experience does not require us to search out new historical sources; rather, it requires that we ask different questions of our sources. If we were to imagine the plague as a dust veil that shrouded the emotional state in which people responded to crisis, shedding light on the dust veil could help us to detect the configurations of uncertainty that lay beneath it. This historical exercise, in turn, may afford us a better understanding of the complex interplay between emotions, agency, and disease in an early modern society.

Approaching emotions and agency in a pre-modern society from a modern vantage point can be misleading. It is tempting to conceive of past plagues in modern epidemiological terms, i.e., as epidemics, the effects of which could be measured in terms of mortality rates that reflect certain epidemiological models of increase and decrease.[6] However, by imagining past plagues as merely quantifiable outbreaks, we are likely to underestimate the full impact of the phenomena for the historical actors that experienced them. We also risk missing one of the most important building blocks of the plague experience: uncertainty. We can better comprehend the experiences of historical actors at times of plague, by studying their responses in the face of prevailing uncertainties.

To clarify, the goal here is not to treat plague as the sole cause of the myriad uncertainties of early modern Ottoman society. On the contrary, it is essential to recognize that plague was one of the many factors that contributed to the uncertainties of the empire in the late sixteenth and early seventeenth centuries. Indeed, there was a perfect storm of climate and ecological crisis, rebellions, ongoing wars in east and west, and fear of dynastic extinction.[7] The uncertainties, real and imagined, were equally frightening, as this was also an age of apocalyptic expectations and anxieties, not only in the Ottoman Empire but across the Mediterranean world.[8]

Plague in the age of the Renaissance

Plague was ubiquitous in early modern Ottoman society. Since its re-introduction to the Mediterranean world in 1347, the disease had established itself in both urban and rural reservoirs that kept it alive through a succession of epidemic outbursts followed by periods of relative inactivity. Even though it varied vastly in its epidemiological manifestations around the Mediterranean basin, the plague came and went in waves, sometimes lasting for months or even years, only to recede and come back again in the next cycle. In a world of repeated plagues, an adult member of Ottoman society would have experienced multiple outbreaks both growing up and into his or her adult years. Hence, plague and knowledge of what to do when the disease hit was part of the common lived experience of early modern Ottomans.

Notwithstanding its regularity and pervasiveness, or perhaps because of it, plague was a destabilizing factor in early modern societies. High mortality meant a huge blow to precarious economic and political structures, and was difficult to recover from. To make matters worse, mortality did not seem to have recognizable demographic patterns; the young died alongside the old, locals alongside foreigners, rich alongside the poor; they all suffered the same fate. Hence, every new visitation of the plague left behind a heavy death toll that furthered social and economic re-configurations – changes which meant disaster for some, opportunity for others. For example, widespread mortality and increased wages in the aftermath of sweeping plagues typically led to a surge of immigration to major Ottoman cities. Economic historians stress multiple changes in pre-modern urban economies, such as "higher per capita wealth and incomes and changes in the distribution of income" in the aftermath of major plague epidemics.[9] In a climate of rapid social and economic change, individuals could face quick change in fortunes in an unpredictable and uncertain future, which often elicited an increase in risk-taking behavior.

Historians have studied many aspects of plague and responses to them, since the inception of plague historiography in the nineteenth century. Europeanist historiography has unmistakably taken the lead. The effects of plague in Europe have been thoroughly studied with respect to their political, social, economic, religious, legal, military, scientific, cultural, and artistic ramifications. The resulting output is immense, creating an illusion that the Black Death was an iconic moment in European history. Recent works take issue with the narrow scope of historical inquiry and open up discussions of the Black Death to different historical contexts.[10]

Not only has Europeanist plague scholarship sought answers to major questions in the historiography, it has also shaped the field of inquiry itself. In other words, Europeanist plague studies influence the scholarship beyond their immediate area of inquiry. Arguments made from within this body of scholarship are often recycled into a non-European context. No matter whether the focus is plague in the Eurasian steppes or in the deserts of the Arabian Peninsula, the study of the plague typically has been approached with questions that supported the prevailing debates in the Europeanist historiography. When historians study the history of plague in other parts of the world, they are often expected to relate the histories of local occurrences of plague and their effects to the European experience.[11]

Notwithstanding the breadth and depth of plague historiography, the scholarship to date has paid little attention to the level of uncertainty induced by plague. The swift appearance and spread of the disease and the high mortality it caused produced rapid but profound changes in the societies that encountered it. As such, it was an unsettling force to which societies had to respond. Indeed, plague was all about uncertainty – incomprehensibility of the present and unpredictability of the future. These moments of uncertainty, however, have been erased from history. A historical imagination of past plagues that does not recognize the high level of anxiety and uncertainty involved cannot do justice to historical realities. How do we study such moments of uncertainty in history?[12] How do we reinstate uncertainty into plague historiography? How do we historicize the anxiety that resulted from repeated widespread mortality? And how does studying the uncertainties of plague help us to understand the experience of the society in question?

These questions are especially perplexing in the context of the Renaissance – an era imagined by some Europeanists as a watershed moment of cultural achievement and intellectual self-confidence. Despite all its glory, the Renaissance era entailed deeply entrenched anxieties and uncertainties. As Renaissance historian William J. Bouwsma notes, this was a time of heightened anxiety in European society, sustained by "uncertainty inherent in time itself," "untrustworthiness of the future," and ultimately "the uncertainty surrounding death."[13] How, then, can the Renaissance be understood apart from the shaky scaffolding of uncertainty that sustained it? As a matter of fact, the historical imagination of the plague and that of the Renaissance, skewed in different ways, can be productively questioned one against the other, especially given their temporal and spatial overlap (i.e., the Eurocentric emphasis). Not unlike the historiography of plague, the scholarship on the Renaissance has also suffered from the handicap of Eurocentrism. Throughout the nineteenth and twentieth centuries, Renaissance historiography was dominated by a vision that the Renaissance was unique to European history alone. A new generation of historians has developed a broader approach to the Renaissance, one that explores the phenomenon in different historical contexts and that seeks to establish its connections, including with Ottoman society.[14]

Fickle fortunes: uncertainties of plague in Ottoman society

Plague entailed myriad uncertainties at various levels. Oftentimes, the disease itself and its prognosis was the very source of uncertainty. An infectious disease caused by the bacterium *Yersinia pestis*, plague has an incubation period that ranges from a few hours to five or six days (or sometimes longer). But its sudden and severe onset – which manifested itself in high fever (reaching 40°C), rapid pulse, and a range of varying symptoms – must have been disturbing enough to the afflicted individual and those around him/her to stir high levels of anxiety. In most cases, the condition of the patient worsened quickly, followed by death within three to five days. In its bubonic form, plague typically causes inflammation in the lymph nodes and painful swellings (buboes) appear in the neck, armpits, or the groin area. In 40 to 70 percent of bubonic cases, death follows after the bacteria are disseminated via the blood vessels, causing organ failure, shock, and septicemia.[15]

Despite the high mortality levels caused by bubonic plague, it was understood that some could recover from the infection. Especially when buboes spontaneously suppurated, the afflicted often recovered. Members of early modern Ottoman society must have developed a certain wisdom drawn from their first-hand experience with plague. Indeed, both scholarly and popular sources from the Ottoman era elaborated on the clinical symptoms of the disease and its prognosis.[16] Since buboes were the most visible symptom of the disease, they were oftentimes associated with the disease itself. It is no coincidence that most therapeutic effort focused on treating the buboes, including cupping, bleeding, branding, and applying leeches or medicine on the buboes. Sometimes, medical texts recommended experimental treatments, such as applying live chickens or pigeons on a plague bubo.[17]

In the absence of a conceptual difference between the symptoms and the disease itself – typical in pre-modern medicine – there was a heavy emphasis on buboes. It is no coincidence that the condition of the buboes was taken as an indication for the prognosis of the disease and whether a patient was likely to recover. For example, the early sixteenth-century plague treatise by İlyas bin İbrahim, a Sephardic convert physician, noted that when the plague bubo is black, the infected individual was most likely to die.[18] Another example comes from the fifteenth-century Anatolian physician İbn Şerif, who reported a curious method practiced in the Mamluk region. According to this, an "adequate number of worms" would be placed over the patients' buboes, which would be kept covered for an hour or two. When the covering was opened, if the worms had died then it was believed that the patient would recover. If the worms were still alive, then it was likely that the patient would expire eventually.[19]

Even though medical texts pointed out the signs needed to make predictions about prognosis, this information might have been limited to physicians and those who had intimate knowledge about the patient's body. Popular sources also emphasized the unpredictability of the disease, since it was often difficult to know whether the patient would recover. In the Ottoman sources, we can find instances of cases in which the stricken individual recovered. Among the most famous of such cases was the recovery of the renowned sixteenth-century Ottoman poet Aşık Çelebi (d. 1572). While he was afflicted with plague in 1543–44 and in bed suffering in pain, the poet's friends came to visit him. Upon feeling his pulse and deciding that he was soon to die, they started to cry about their friend's imminent death. The news of the poet's death soon started to spread. However, the poet recovered from the plague. Upon hearing the rumors about his own death, he composed a poem in which he expressed the anguish of imminent death and celebrated his recovery.[20]

Another example is the case of Melek Ahmed Pasha (d. 1662), a great statesman of the seventeenth century and the patron of the renowned Ottoman traveler Evliya Çelebi. In the year 1652, when the pasha was appointed to a new administrative position in Sofia, plague broke out in the city. According to Evliya Çelebi, the epidemic was so severe that 500 people died every day, including seventy-seven of the pasha's retinue. Eventually the pasha himself contracted the disease, whereupon "his head swelled up like an Adana squash, his tongue was scorched and turned black, his ears oozed with pus. More than once he was on the verge of death."[21] According to the testimony of our traveler, the pasha's condition worsened rapidly and his physicians and members of household feared his death. This time, the pasha's recovery was heralded in a dream that Evliya Çelebi had. The next morning, when he recounted his dream to the pasha, the latter interpreted it as a sign that he was soon to recover. And indeed, he did gradually recuperate.[22]

In yet another example, the daughter of a prominent eighteenth-century religious dignitary, İsa Efendi, was suffering from plague. Her parents feared her death and in much despair, they sought the intercession of Muhammad Nasuhi (d. 1718), a well-known Ottoman mystic. Nasuhi comforted the couple, saying they should not grieve. Indeed, their daughter started feeling better shortly thereafter, and eventually recovered. Elated to see their daughter's full recovery, the couple soon heard the sad news of the mystic's own teenaged daughter who had contracted the plague and died soon after. It was understood that the mystic sacrificed the life of his own daughter in return for that of the dignitary's.[23]

As we see in each of these examples, the unpredictability of the disease's prognosis reflected the uncertainty of life and death. Family and friends of plague-stricken individuals coped with the uncertainty by praying, mourning, and seeking help from physicians and mystics. Yet sometimes uncertainties about plague extended well beyond the death of individuals. Just as it was difficult to judge the prognosis of the illness when an individual was infected, there were sometimes uncertainties about whether someone's death was even caused by plague. Especially at times of heavy plague mortality, other diseases or even violent crimes could potentially be concealed in this manner. In one such instance, a certain Sinan who lived in the Thracian town of Vize reported that the death of his son was not caused by the plague outbreak that was raging in the town in early 1576. According to Sinan's testimony, his son was stabbed to death by one of his brothers who subsequently registered the death as caused by plague. In despair, Sinan appealed to the authorities to investigate the matter, including requesting the interrogation of those who had washed the body of the deceased and buried him about signs of stabbing.[24] A similar example comes from the court records of the Anatolian city of Ankara dating from the year 1583–84. In this case, it is said that a certain Akkoca was registered as having died of plague. However, a petition requesting an investigation of the latter's cause of death suggested the possibility of physical aggression. It is understood that the petitioner had an ongoing legal case with the deceased and that the cause of death was expected to have an impact on how the case was decided.[25] Unfortunately, we lack the necessary information to follow up the results of the investigations in both cases. However, what is clear is that uncertainties generated by plague outbreaks could sometimes motivate people to pursue posthumous investigations to determine the cause of death of loved ones (or even rivals).

Sometimes the anxieties caused by plague and the sudden death it entailed went beyond conducting posthumous investigations. In such cases, we see that the body of the deceased could be subjected to additional procedures to eliminate any trace of uncertainties. One such case concerns a fourteen-year-old boy, Constantine of Moldavia, who died of plague in Istanbul in the mid-sixteenth century. While the body of the deceased was being prepared for burial according to the customs of the Orthodox creed (confession, consecration with bread and wine), some Muslims found out about this and instead performed Muslim burial rites. In doing so, they circumcised the body posthumously, and then made testimonies heard by witnesses that the deceased had wanted to convert to Islam before he died. They carried the body to the burial ground in a coffin with Muslim headgear placed on top, according to custom.[26] Performing the right funerary rites according to confessional identity was deemed essential, as it meant restoring the peace of the deceased in the afterlife. However, uncertainty about whether the deceased had to be treated as a Muslim or as a Christian could cause controversies.

The uncertainty stirred by plague epidemics and the possibility of imminent death must have affected people's decisions in myriad ways.[27] For one, it would have had an impact on what individuals decided to do about their property. Death usually came quickly, without leaving individuals sufficient time to make difficult financial decisions and to take legal action to implement them. However, in some cases, doing so was necessary, especially when decision-making involved the inheritance of individuals who were considered to be part of the sultan's household, serving either in the immediate palace or in the capital or the provinces. When such high-status individuals died, a portion of their inheritance was returned to the imperial treasury. Hence, when plague hit, the uncertainty between life and death could compel those individuals to seek legal action. In one such example, Belkıs Hatun, who formerly served in the Ottoman palace, had to make arrangements in the face of plague that devastated Egypt in the spring of 1587. Were she to die from plague, she requested that all of her property be kept under the control of her confidant Dilaver Hatun. If they were both to die, then a former palace employee was to arrange to send her property back to Istanbul.[28]

Uncertainties brought by plague affected decisions in many other ways as well, perhaps more visibly in the economic domain. In modern societies, it is generally accepted that high levels of uncertainty can lead to reduced spending by individuals and businesses, decline in investments, and an overall slowing of the economy.[29] In pre-modern societies, uncertainty also had immense impact on the decisions of economic agents.[30] The unpredictability of financial prospects affected the decision of individuals, businesses, and even of the Ottoman state. Those decisions could be simple and temporary, such as diverting business away from places where there was plague. Sources often mention examples of how merchant ships changed their destination away from ports upon hearing news of plague. For example, an Ottoman document from August 1586 noted that ships bringing provisions to Istanbul headed toward other Black Sea ports on account of plague in the city. Such ships were ordered to bring their cargo to Istanbul to prevent possible provisioning problems in the capital.[31] One of the greatest anxieties of the Ottoman central administration at times of plague was provisioning the capital and ensuring a steady flow of foodstuffs and other staple items. In another example, we hear about the case of Marino, a contractor to whom collection of Atlantic bonito was farmed by the Ottoman administration; he had to send the fish to Venice on account of a plague outbreak raging in the Morea.[32]

In a precarious economic environment, businesses could be adversely affected. At such times, severe plague could cause shop-owners to lose business or even to close down entirely.[33] In one such documented instance, we hear that shops selling fermented millet beer (*boza*) in the Anatolian city of Bursa suffered a considerable loss in their business during a plague epidemic in 1491. Given that these shops were also important places of socialization, it is understood that their clientele stopped going there on account of the raging plague.[34] Another example was the case of bathhouses in Trabzon, on the southern coast of the Black Sea, which lost business during a major plague epidemic in 1565. According to local court registers, when a majority of the town's population fled "on account of fear of plague," the bathhouses lost their customers.[35] Like shops selling millet beer, bathhouses were important venues for socialization in early modern Ottoman society, in addition to their function of supporting cleanliness and bodily hygiene.[36]

Perhaps one of the most important decisions individuals had to make when faced with the uncertainty generated by plague was how to protect themselves and their loved ones. Ottoman archival and narrative sources suggest that urban populations sometimes fled towns and cities. It is difficult to know what percentage of the population could or did follow this path, as the evidence at hand is anecdotal rather than statistical. Nevertheless, we know that at least some of the Ottoman urban population fled plagues.[37] If a handful of Ottoman documents are anything to go by, it should be possible to argue that high mortality and flight may have left behind less than half the population in some places. For example, in one document we read that the number of households in the village of Lapseki, on the Anatolian shores of the Dardanelles, was reduced from forty-five to nineteen, as a result of deaths and flight.[38] In another instance, heavy plague mortality and flight in Aleppo's district of Üzeyir is documented in the year 1574. The number of pass-guard households who were responsible for maintaining the safety of the roads (this place was located on the pilgrimage route) was reduced dramatically. Only 60 households were left out of a total of 236, which is a mere quarter of the entire population.[39]

Both documentary and narrative evidence seems to suggest that flight was one means of protection for early modern Ottoman urban populations, though it seemed to be more or less limited to those who could afford it, that is, the elite. I discuss elsewhere at length the flight dilemma (or the question of flee or not to flee) of the Ottoman Muslim urban population.[40] Here I would like to explore how such flights are related to uncertainties. How did people decide to leave? When did they reach the decision? Did they wait until mortality figures climb up to a certain level? Or did they rely on their local knowledge about plague's seasonal patterns, which would be familiar to urban populations in the sixteenth century? It is difficult to answer these questions with confidence, as we lack narrative evidence detailing these points. However, archival evidence sheds some light on the issue. For example, a document issued by the Ottoman central administration in late May 1573 stated that the residents of the villages around Edirne had fled on account of plague and that the villages now harbored bandits. It was ordered that the village populations be brought back to their residences.[41] Under the circumstances, it should be possible to surmise that the residents had fled early spring of that year, if not much earlier, which would typically correspond to increasing plague activity on account of favorable weather conditions.[42] When plague struck, those who could leave generally did so early on.

Whatever the rationale and motivations behind the decision to flee may have been, the individual (or the household) should have had some prior familiarity with and connections in the flight destination. Advance arrangements may have been necessary for an entire family to relocate, even if temporarily. Better-documented cases from the seventeenth century onwards suggest that families maintained countryside residences outside of towns for this purpose.[43] For example, the villages north of Istanbul, especially the village of Belgrad (Belgradcık) became especially popular destinations. Eventually, it became customary among the French and British ambassadorial missions in Istanbul to maintain summer residences outside of the city where they could take refuge at times of plague or other such crises. Similarly, the Jewish residents of Thessaloniki mostly took refuge in nearby villages, such as Livadi, at times of plague.

The Ottomans had to tackle various uncertainties while considering fleeing from epidemics. Individuals had to make decisions about which places were considered to be free from plague, when travel was deemed safe for the purpose of avoiding diseased areas, and how long it would be safe to stay out in the flight destinations. However, these questions did not always have precise answers. At least in one particular case, the uncertainty regarding the locality (or boundaries) of the epidemic was clearly expressed. During a plague epidemic in the late sixteenth century, a female member of the Ottoman dynastic family was staying in a village not too far from the capital. Anxious to get away from the diseased area, she sent a letter to the Topkapı Palace, inquiring about the state of the epidemic and requesting to be moved to a safe place. In response to her inquiry, she was informed that "no place was free from that blessed disease," and was advised to stay put.[44] As we see in this example, it was not always easy to determine the locality of the epidemic with a degree of certainty, which made decisions to flee plagues even more risky.

Regardless, it is difficult to comment on whether this was a decision that individuals or households made independently or whether it was more of a communal decision. In the case of the empire's non-Muslim population, religious leaders may have advised and even regulated leaving urban areas at times of plague. For example, the flight of the Jewish community of Thessaloniki is well documented in Ottoman sources owing to a conflict of interest that arose with the Ottoman central administration regarding the production of broadcloth used for the janissaries. Yet there is no clear indication as to whether each congregation tried to save its own members or collaborated with each other in the event of flight.[45] As for the Muslim population of the empire, it could turn to the religious elite for advice. In fact, the legal opinion (*fatwa*) issued by one of the most renowned men of religion of the sixteenth century, Chief Jurisconsult Ebussuud Efendi (d. 1574), is telling for this purpose, showing us that the population sought advice from religious scholars about whether to leave diseased areas, and under what conditions this was permissible.

Evidently, not everybody left. Those who stayed developed ways of dealing with the misfortune and the uncertainties it entailed. One form of response must have been to help one's community and those in need. This may have involved tending to the sick, helping families in need, and perhaps helping bury the plague victims in one's own family or community. There is some evidence that physicians and other health professionals continued their services in Ottoman cities at times of plague, though their clientele must have been limited to the elite.[46] Every now and then sources mention people who deteriorated very quickly and died of plague in plain sight. The English traveler Fynes Moryson noted dead bodies that were left lying on the streets during a plague outbreak in Istanbul in 1597.[47] Plague-stricken individuals were sometimes helped by strangers. In one such case, we hear about the sad story of the sixteenth-century Venetian *bailo*, Andrea di Priuli, who died of plague in Istanbul in the summer of 1523.[48] According to the Venetian sources, after helping a sick man left on the street and carrying him to his own residence, Priuli contracted the plague and died shortly afterwards.[49] Even though some may have avoided contact with those afflicted with plague and those who died from it, there are ample examples that suggest that close contacts did take place, from tending to the sick to washing and even circumcising the body of the plague victim posthumously, as mentioned above.

By the same token, those who stayed in the cities during plague outbreaks sometimes engaged in penitential activities to help save their communities, while reducing prevailing anxieties. Ottoman chronicles mention how large communal prayers and processions were organized, where people gathered to pray for the lifting of plague. Selaniki recounts such communal prayers and processions organized in late sixteenth-century Istanbul. According to him, men of religion and Sufi leaders attended these events in which animals were sacrificed and distributed to the needy as alms. Prisoners were let free in the hope that God would accept and respond to their prayers.[50] Such processions at times of plague were organized in both the Christian and Muslim worlds in the medieval and early modern eras.[51] Even though religious contexts and practices varied, it was important to organize processions in a manner that would maximize their impact. For this reason, the timing of the procession typically coincided with religious holidays, and its strength was solidified with additional penitential activities such as fasting, animal sacrifice, reading of the Qur'an, and the like.[52] Beyond communal engagements, there is evidence for a plethora of individual pursuits. Individuals could engage in spiritual methods not only to protect themselves from plague but also from the anxiety that it caused. Plague treatises constantly reminded their audiences of the power of spiritual methods of protection by means of reciting prayers, wearing amulets, or other sundry techniques recommended.[53] All of these undertakings were in some way designed to help manage the anxieties of Ottoman urban populations at times of plague.

In one way or another, the uncertainties brought by plague touched the lives of Ottomans from all walks of life. Generally speaking, it is more difficult to speculate about how such uncertainties directly affected the decisions individuals made. Documentation is especially scarce for tracing the decisions made by taxpayers (*reaya*), the majority of the empire's population. Overall, we are better informed about the members of the tax-exempt (*askeri*) classes who constituted the military, administrative, and religious elite of the Ottoman state. The bodies of the elite were monitored much more closely than were those of the rest of the taxpaying population, and there is much better documentation for every stage of their professional careers. The corpus of documentation enables us to see more closely how their bodies were governed in health and in sickness by the Ottoman administration.[54] Despite their official duty, members of the elite often left plague-infested cities to protect themselves and their families, as testified by the sources.[55]

When it came to state affairs, the uncertainties triggered by plague proved to be more significant. As we read in the opening story told by the chronicler Selaniki, the appointment of state functionaries to posts and other similar decisions were doubly difficult during the fiery days of plague. As a meritocracy, the Ottoman bureaucracy and administration offered abundant opportunities for professional movement by individuals. One could be promoted to the top-ranking office of the Grand Vizier overnight, or executed by mute dwarfs in the palace, as was the case of the very controversial lightning promotion and subsequent execution of İbrahim Pasha (d. 1536). A tragic figure of Ottoman history in the age of the Renaissance, İbrahim Pasha's example illustrates the quickly changing scene of the inner politics of the Ottoman court.[56] Plague thus only accentuated the fickle fortunes of the members of Ottoman administrators.

Such uncertainties did not only affect members of the Ottoman court. Even the sultan was not immune to those uncertainties.[57] In the sixteenth century, when the daily death toll increased to several hundred, the court was closed to outside contact. Neither could the sultan leave the palace nor could audiences be granted to ambassadors. Sometimes the sultan did not make a public appearance for several days or weeks at a stretch. At such times, it was not unusual for rumors of the sultan's death to spread in the city. In one such case, when Sultan Süleyman (r. 1520–66) did not leave the palace on account of an ongoing epidemic in early 1527, rumors spread that he had died of plague, as testified by Venetian sources.[58]

The fickle fortunes did not only apply to the fate of individuals. Sometimes, it could affect the fate of the dynasty. Plague and the uncertainties caused by it sometimes threatened the very *raison d'être* of the Ottoman state – the continuation of the dynastic lineage. Historian Günhan Börekçi has argued that epidemic diseases like plague and smallpox played an important role in the already precarious nature of dynastic continuity in the Ottoman Empire in the early seventeenth century. When a succession of underage and/or childless sultans came to the Ottoman throne in the first half of the seventeenth century, there were already widespread uncertainties about the continuation of the dynastic lineage. Soon after his enthronement, Ahmed I (r. 1603–17), a thirteen-year old childless new sultan, and his younger brother Mustafa (the future Mustafa I, r. 1617–18; 1622–23) both contracted smallpox. The condition of the sultan remained grave, which kept anxieties about the extinction of dynastic lineage climbing, until his eventual full recovery.[59] Even though this moment represents a dramatic example of the near-extinction of the Ottoman royal family, uncertainty about the state's future was almost an integral part of the imagination of state. Ottoman political theory embraced the notion of uncertainty and unpredictability of the future, perhaps best embodied in the very concept of the state as fortune – subject to change.

In a prevailing climate of uncertainty, individuals, communities, and the state tried to manage uncertainties by making predictions. It is tempting to believe that prediction is one of the building blocks of the modern age. And so is certainty. However, the need to make informed and accurate predictions was based on societal needs that were clearly formulated in the early modern era. Weather forecasting, for example, did not become a "scientific" effort until the modern age, even though it has a longer history.[60] Similarly, the insurance industry, though much older in its inception, heavily relied on making accurate estimates of risk and uncertainty through its spectacular rise in the modern era.[61] In effect, early modern societies were as busy trying to clear uncertainties as they were making predictions about the future. Prophecies, astrological predictions, and geomancy were all prestigious avenues of knowledge in early modern Ottoman society.[62] If not based on empirical evidence, measurement, and statistical patterns, making the right predictions was still vital for the survival of individuals, communities, and states. It should not come as a surprise that the Ottoman court astrologers and timekeepers served this very purpose, i.e., making predictions. These experts were consulted regarding the timing of critical decisions or before launching new initiatives. Even though forecasts entailed a more general pool of predictions and a degree of uncertainty, they guided decision-making processes.

When it came to plague, one can surmise that experience brought knowledge and familiarity, and allowed room to develop insights and make predictions. Sources tell us that knowledge drawn from familiarity could be used to make predictions about how a certain epidemic would progress, depending on weather conditions, for example. Often times we find in the early modern sources predictions regarding how weather would affect plague. It should be possible to assume that merchants and businessmen made important financial decisions on the basis of predictions about how people would respond to plague. By the same token, it only follows that taking plague tolls also had to be serving this very purpose: clearing out some uncertainty about the epidemiological behavior of the disease and making predictions using numbers served to quell unrest and unease.[63]

As we seek to restore materiality into historical inquiry, it may be necessary to invite past experiences that have hitherto remained invisible. Often these experiences are discernible only in the face of shared traumatic historical experiences, as much in the East as in the West. Studying the plague reminds us of the inconstancy of the human condition in a pre-modern society in which human life expectancy was about half of what is accepted in today's developed countries, even at the best of times. The vagaries of plague served both to make life more tenuous and to significantly increase the level of individual and social anxiety about the apparent ambiguity of life and death. The age of the Renaissance was a time of discovery and rediscovery, of reform and renewal, and of science and reasoning; it was also "plagued" by deadly uncertainties.

Notes

1 An earlier version of this chapter was presented at the 2016 meeting of the American Association for the History of Medicine. I am grateful for the feedback I received from the audience there. I would like to express my gratitude to William Caferro for his editorial interventions; to Lori Jones for her very helpful suggestions and edits; to Ann Carmichael for her insightful questions and comments; and to Monica Green, Michelle Ziegler, and the other members of the Plague Working Group for their invaluable suggestions.
2 Selaniki Mustafa Efendi, *Tarih-i Selaniki*, ed. Mehmet İpşirli, Istanbul: İstanbul Üniversitesi, 1989, 148.
3 *Ibid.*
4 Nükhet Varlık, *Plague and Empire in the Early Modern Mediterranean World: The Ottoman Experience, 1347–1600*, Cambridge: Cambridge University Press, 2015.
5 For a study of plague images in Renaissance Italy as reflecting lived experiences of and emotions about the disease, see Louise Marshall, "Manipulating the Sacred: Image and Plague in Renaissance Italy," *Renaissance Quarterly* 47, 3 (1994): 485–532; for a study that integrates the emotions of those who suffered from plague and sought healing in the fourteenth century, see Nicole Archambeau, "Healing Options during the Plague: Survivor Stories from a Fourteenth-Century Canonization Inquest," *Bulletin of the History of Medicine* 85, 4 (2011): 531–59; for a discussion of "plague psychology" in sixteenth-century Italy, see Samuel K. Cohn, *Cultures of Plague: Medical Thinking at the End of the Renaissance*, Oxford: Oxford University Press, 2010, ch. 9. For an exceptional narrative that brings to life the experiences and emotions of ordinary villagers in rural England during the Black Death, see John Hatcher, *The Black Death: A Personal History*, Cambridge, MA: Da Capo Press, 2008.

6 Social scientists tend to emphasize the vulnerability of societies in the face of macro-level trau-
mas, such as those brought by heavy epidemic mortality. For an approach that stresses resilience
instead, see, e.g., Peter Suedfeld, "Reactions to Societal Trauma: Distress and/or Eustress,"
Political Psychology 18, 4 (1997): 849–61; Fran H. Norris, Susan P. Stevens, Betty Pfefferbaum,
Karen F. Wyche, and Rose L. Pfefferbaum, "Community Resilience as a Metaphor, Theory, Set of
Capacities, and Strategy for Disaster Readiness," *American Journal of Community Psychology* 41, 1–2
(2008): 127–50.

7 Sam White, *The Climate of Rebellion in the Early Modern Ottoman Empire*, Cambridge: Cambridge
University Press, 2011; Oktay Özel, "The Reign of Violence: The *celâlis*, c.1550–1700," in *The
Ottoman World*, ed. Christine Woodhead, London: Routledge, 2012, 184–202; Günhan Börekçi,
"Smallpox in the Harem: Communicable Diseases and the Ottoman Fear of Dynastic Extinction
during the Early Sultanate of Ahmed I (r. 1603–17)," in *Plague and Contagion in the Islamic
Mediterranean: New Histories of Disease in Ottoman Society*, ed. Nükhet Varlık (forthcoming).

8 Cornell H. Fleischer, "The Lawgiver as Messiah: The Making of the Imperial Image in the Reign
of Süleymân," in *Soliman le magnifique et son temps*, ed. Gilles Veinstein, Paris: La Documentation
française, 1992, 159–77; Cornell H. Fleischer, "From al-Bistami (d. 1454) in Bursa to Postel (d.
1581) in Paris: The Trajectory of Apocalyptic in the Early Modern Mediterranean," in *Speaking the
End Times: Prophecy and Messianism from Iberia to Central Asia* (special issue of the *Journal of the Economic
and Social History of the Orient*), ed. Mayte Green-Mercado (forthcoming). For connections between
plague and apocalyptic ideas in European society, see Robert E. Lerner, "The Black Death and
Western European Eschatological Mentalities," *American Historical Review* 86, 3 (1981): 533–52;
Faye Marie Getz, "Black Death and the Silver Lining: Meaning, Continuity, and Revolutionary
Change in Histories of Medieval Plague," *Journal of the History of Biology* 24, 2 (1991): 265–89;
Laura A. Smoller, "Of Earthquakes, Hail, Frogs, and Geography: Plague and the Investigation
of the Apocalypse in the Later Middle Ages," in *Last Things: Death and the Apocalypse in the Middle
Ages*, ed. Caroline Walker Bynum and Paul Freedman, Philadelphia: University of Pennsylvania
Press, 2000, 156–87. For the Ottoman case, see Nükhet Varlık, "From '*Bête Noire*' to '*le Mal de
Constantinople*': Plagues, Medicine, and the Early Modern Ottoman State," *Journal of World
History* 24, 4 (2013): 741–70.

9 Şevket Pamuk and Maya Shatzmiller, "Plagues, Wages, and Economic Change in the Islamic
Middle East, 700–1500," *Journal of Economic History* 74, 1 (2014): 196–229, at 210; Süleyman
Özmucur and Şevket Pamuk, "Real Wages and Standards of Living in the Ottoman Empire,
1489–1914," *Journal of Economic History* 62, 2 (2002): 293–321. For a discussion of the relationship
between plague, immigration, and urbanization in three Ottoman cities during the fifteenth and
sixteenth centuries, see Varlık, *Plague and Empire*, 153–8.

10 See, e.g., Monica H. Green, ed., *Pandemic Disease in the Medieval World: Rethinking the Black Death*,
Kalamazoo, MI: Arc Medieval Press, 2014. For a discussion of the historical scholarship on the
Black Death being heavily Eurocentric, see my "New Science and Old Sources: Why the Ottoman
Experience of Plague Matters," *Medieval Globe* 1 (2014): 193–227.

11 Even though there is a fairly large body of scholarship devoted to the discussion of plague in non-
European contexts, the underlying questions seem to have been drawn from prevailing discussions
in the Europeanist plague historiography. Here I shall limit the citations only to those studies that
have spatial or temporal affinity to the Ottoman case. See, e.g., David Neustadt [Ayalon], "The
Plague and Its Effects upon the Mamluk Army," *Journal of the Royal Asiatic Society* 66 (1946): 67–
73; Jean-Noël Biraben, *Les hommes et la peste en France et dans les pays européens et méditerranéens*,
Paris: Mouton, 1975; Michael Dols, *The Black Death in the Middle East*, Princeton, NJ: Princeton
University Press, 1977; J. Norris, "East or West? The Geographic Origin of the Black Death,"
Bulletin of the History of Medicine 51, 1 (1977): 1–24; John T. Alexander, *Bubonic Plague in Early Modern
Russia: Public Health and Urban Disaster*, Baltimore: Johns Hopkins University Press, 1980; Daniel
Panzac, *La peste dans l'empire ottoman, 1700–1850*, Leuven: Éditions Peeters, 1985; Uli Schamiloglu,
"Preliminary Remarks on the Role of Disease in the History of the Golden Horde," *Central Asian
Survey* 12, 4 (1993): 447–57; Uli Schamiloglu, "The Rise of the Ottoman Empire: The Black Death
in Medieval Anatolia and Its Impact on Turkish Civilization," in *Views from the Edge: Essays in Honor
of Richard W. Bulliet*, ed. Neguin Yavari, Lawrence G. Potter, and Jean-Marc Ran Oppenheim,
New York: Columbia University Press, 2004, 255–79; Ole Jørgen Benedictow, *The Black Death,
1346–1353: The Complete History*, Woodbridge: Boydell Press, 2004; Stuart J. Borsch, *The Black*

Death in Egypt and England: A Comparative Study, Austin: University of Texas Press, 2005. Economic historian Şevket Pamuk situated the Black Death as an important moment in the history of the global economic changes, as a marker of what became the "great divergence." See Şevket Pamuk, "The Black Death and the Origins of the 'Great Divergence' across Europe, 1300–1600," *European Review of Economic History* 11 (2007): 289–317.

12   The concept of uncertainty has been studied mostly in the contexts of economic history, the history of insurance, shipping, and trade, as well as the history of science and medicine. For the "measurement" of uncertainty, see, e.g., Stephen M. Stigler, *The History of Statistics: The Measurement of Uncertainty before 1900*, Cambridge, MA: Harvard University Press, 1986; Theodore M. Porter, *The Rise of Statistical Thinking, 1820–1900*, Princeton, NJ: Princeton University Press, 1986; Lorraine Daston, *Classical Probability in the Enlightenment*, Princeton, NJ: Princeton University Press, 1988. For uncertainty in early modern oceanic trade and ways of managing it, see, e.g., Peter Musgrave, "The Economics of Uncertainty: The Structural Revolution in the Spice Trade, 1480–1640," in *Spices in the Indian Ocean World*, ed. M. N. Pearson, Aldershot: Variorum, 1996, 337–50; Xabier Lamikiz, *Trade and Trust in the Eighteenth-Century Atlantic World: Spanish Merchants and Their Overseas Networks*, Rochester, NY: Boydell and Brewer, 2010; Jeremy Baskes, *Staying Afloat: Risk and Uncertainty in Spanish Atlantic World Trade, 1760–1820*, Stanford, CA: Stanford University Press, 2013; Emily Erikson and Sampsa Samila, "Social Networks and Port Traffic in Early Modern Overseas Trade," *Social Science History* 39, 2 (2015): 151–73. On economic uncertainty, also see note 29 below. For medical (un)certainty, see, e.g., Renée C. Fox, "The Evolution of Medical Uncertainty," *Milbank Memorial Fund Quarterly: Health and Society* 58, 1 (1980): 1–49; Renée C. Fox, "Medical Uncertainty Revisited," in *Handbook of Social Studies in Health and Medicine*, ed. Albrecht R. Fitzpatrick and S. D. Scrimshaw, London: Sage, 2000, 407–25; Michael R. McVaugh, "The Nature and Limits of Medical Certitude at Early Fourteenth-Century Montpellier," *Osiris* 6 (1990): 62–84; Thomas Schlich, "Objectifying Uncertainty: History of Risk Concepts in Medicine," *Topoi* 23, 2 (September 2004): 211–19. On uncertainty in meteorology and weather forecasting, see note 60 below.

13   William J. Bouwsma, "Anxiety and the Formation of Early Modern Culture," in *A Usable Past: Essays in European Cultural History*, Berkeley: University of California Press, 1990, 157–89, at 161–2. For a discussion of Bouwsma's interpretation of the period in conjunction with plague, see Ann G. Carmichael, "Infectious Disease and Human Agency: An Historical Overview," in *Interactions between Global Change and Human Health 31 October–2 November 2004*, The Pontifical Academy of Sciences, Scripta Varia 106, Vatican City: Pontificia Academia Scientiarum, 2006, 3–46, especially 19–20. For historical discussions of fear and anxiety, see Arne Öhman, "Fear and Anxiety: Overlaps and Dissociations," in *Handbook of Emotions*, ed. Michael Lewis, Jeannette M. Haviland-Jones, and Lisa Feldman Barrett, New York: Guilford Press, 2008, 709–29; Jean Delumeau, *Sin and Fear: The Emergence of a Western Guilt Culture, 13th–18th Centuries*, New York: St. Martin's Press, 1990; Joanna Bourke, "Fear and Anxiety: Writing about Emotion in Modern History," *History Workshop Journal* 55, 1 (2003): 111–33; Joanna Bourke, *Fear: A Cultural History*, London: Virago, 2005; Michael Laffan and Max Weiss, eds., *Facing Fear: The History of an Emotion in Global Perspective*, Princeton, NJ: Princeton University Press, 2012. More specifically, in early modern societies, see Eric R. Dursteler, "Fearing the 'Turk' and Feeling the Spirit: Emotion and Conversion in the Early Modern Mediterranean," *Journal of Religious History* 39, 4 (2015): 484–505; the essays in William G. Naphy and Penny Roberts, eds., *Fear in Early Modern Society*, Manchester: Manchester University Press, 1997, especially William G. Naphy, "Plague-Spreading and a Magisterially Controlled Fear," 28–43; Andrew Wear, "Fear, Anxiety, and the Plague in Early Modern England: Religious and Medical Responses," in *Religion, Health, and Suffering*, ed. J. Hinnels and Roy Porter, London: Routledge and Kegan Paul, 1999, 339–63; Margaret Healy, "Anxious and Fatal Contacts: Taming the Contagious Touch," in *Sensible Flesh: On Touch in Early Modern Culture*, ed. Elizabeth D. Harvey, Philadelphia: University of Pennsylvania Press, 2003, 22–38. For sorrow and consolation in Italian humanism, see George W. McClure, *Sorrow and Consolation in Italian Humanism*, Princeton, NJ: Princeton University Press, 1991.

14   For examples of scholarship of "global Renaissance," especially pertaining to the eastern Mediterranean world, see Julian Raby, *Venice, Dürer, and the Oriental Mode*, [London]: Islamic Art Publications, 1982; Lisa Jardine, *Worldly Goods: A New History of the Renaissance*, New York: W. W. Norton, 1998; Anna Contadini and Charles Burnett, eds., *Islam and the Italian Renaissance*, London: The Warburg Institute, University of London, 1999; Deborah Howard, *Venice and the East: The*

Impact of the Islamic World on Venetian Architecture, 1100–1500, New Haven: Yale University Press, 2000; Lisa Jardine and Jerry Brotton, *Global Interests: Renaissance Art between East and West*, Ithaca, NY: Cornell University Press, 2000; Jerry Brotton, *The Renaissance Bazaar: From the Silk Road to Michelangelo*, Oxford: Oxford University Press, 2002; Linda Darling, "The Renaissance and the Middle East," in *A Companion to the Worlds of the Renaissance*, ed. Guido Ruggiero, Oxford: Blackwell, 2002, 55–69; Nancy Bisaha, *Creating East and West: Renaissance Humanists and the Ottoman Turks*, Philadelphia: University of Pennsylvania Press, 2004; Gerald M. MacLean, *Re-Orienting the Renaissance: Cultural Exchanges with the East*, New York: Palgrave Macmillan, 2005; Gülru Necipoğlu, *The Age of Sinan: Architectural Culture in the Ottoman Empire*, Princeton, NJ: Princeton University Press, 2005; Margaret Meserve, *Empires of Islam in Renaissance Historical Thought*, Cambridge, MA: Harvard University Press, 2008.

15 Elisabeth Carniel, "Plague Today," in *Pestilential Complexities: Understanding Medieval Plague*, ed. Vivian Nutton, London: Wellcome Trust for the History of Medicine at UCL, 2008, 115–22, at 118–19.

16 For a discussion of the symptoms, prognosis, and treatment of plague in Ottoman medical texts, see Varlık, *Plague and Empire*, 224–34.

17 *Ibid.*, 233; İbn Şerif, *Yâdigâr: 15. Yüzyıl Türkçe Tıp Kitabı*, ed. Ayten Altıntaş, *et al.*, 2 vols., Istanbul: Merkez Efendi ve Halk Hekimliği Derneği, 2003–4, vol. 2, 152–3. On live chicken treatment, see Erik A. Heinrichs, "The Live Chicken Treatment for Buboes: Trying a Plague Cure in Medieval and Early Modern Europe," *Bulletin of the History of Medicine* (Special Issue: *Testing Drugs and Trying Cures*), forthcoming.

18 İlyas ibn İbrahim, *Tevfikâtü'l-hamidiyye fi def i'l-emrâzi'l-vebâ'iyye*, trans. Ahmedü'ş-Şami Ömeri, MS, Istanbul University Cerrahpaşa History of Medicine Library, 105, 16–17.

19 İbn Şerif, *Yâdigâr*, vol. 2, 321–2.

20 The poet mentions his recovery from plague on two different occasions. See Hatice Aynur, "Kurgusu ve Vurgusuyla Kendi Kaleminden Âşık Çelebi'nin Yaşamöyküsü," in *Âşık Çelebi ve Şairler Tezkiresi Üzerine Yazılar*, ed. Hatice Aynur and Aslı Niyazioğlu, Istanbul: Koç Üniversitesi Yayınları, 2011, 52–3.

21 Evliya Çelebi, *The Intimate Life of an Ottoman Statesman: Melek Ahmed Pasha (1588–1662)*, trans. Robert Dankoff, Albany: State University of New York Press, 1991, 99.

22 *Ibid.*, 99–104.

23 John J. Curry, "Scholars, Sufis, and Disease: Can Muslim Religious Works Offer Us Novel Insights on Plagues and Epidemics in the Medieval and Early Modern World?" in *Plague and Contagion in the Islamic Mediterranean*, ed. Varlık.

24 Istanbul, Prime Ministry Ottoman Archives (BOA), Mühimme Defteri [Register of Important Affairs] 27, 261/612: 12 February 1576.

25 Halit Ongan, ed., *Ankara'nın 1 Numaralı Şeriye Sicili*, Ankara: Türk Tarih Kurumu, 1958, 115.

26 Hans Dernschwam, *İstanbul ve Anadolu'ya Seyahat Günlüğü*, trans. Yaşar Önen, Ankara: Kültür ve Turizm Bakanlığı, 1987, 104–5.

27 For a recent study of how the Black Death affected people's decisions and how this is reflected in the notarial records in Bologna, see Shona Kelly Wray, *Communities and Crisis: Bologna During the Black Death*, Leiden: Brill, 2009. For a more comprehensive study based on testaments from six Italian towns (Arezzo, Assisi, Florence, Perugia, Pisa, and Siena) during and after the Black Death, see Samuel K. Cohn, *The Cult of Remembrance and the Black Death: Six Renaissance Cities in Central Italy*, Baltimore: Johns Hopkins University Press, 1992. For the case of Cyprus during and after the Black Death, see Aysu Dincer, "Disease in a Sunny Climate: Effects of the Plague on Family and Wealth in Cyprus in the 1360s," in *Le interazioni fra economia eambiente biologico nell'Europa preindustriale. secc. XIII–XVIII / Economic and Biological Interactions in Pre-Industrial Europe from the 13th to the 18th Centuries*, ed. Simonetta Cavaciocchi, Florence: Firenze University Press, 2010, 531–40.

28 BOA, Mühimme Defteri, 62, 59/135: 24 April 1587.

29 One of the classic studies that explored the effects of uncertainty on business investments is Ben Bernanke's (1983) article in which he studied the effects of the financial crisis of the Great Depression. See Ben S. Bernanke, "Nonmonetary Effects of the Financial Crisis in Propagation of the Great Depression," *American Economic Review* 73, 3 (1983): 257–76. Since then, economists have published many works on the question. See, e.g., Michael J. Brennan and Eduardo S. Schwartz, "Evaluating Natural Resource Investments," *Journal of Business* 58, 2 (1985): 135–57; Rob McDonald and Daniel Siegel, "The Value of Waiting to Invest," *Quarterly Journal of Economics*

101, 4 (1986): 707–28. For a more recent study that questions uncertainty and economic effects, see Nicholas Bloom, "Fluctuations in Uncertainty," *Journal of Economic Perspectives* 28, 2 (2014): 153–76.

30 Like plague, warfare created similar economic uncertainties. William Caferro complicates a moment of crisis in post-Black Death Florence, by demonstrating the fluctuating character of the economy of war. See William Caferro, "Petrarch's War: Florentine Wages and the Black Death," *Speculum* 88, 1 (2013): 144–65.

31 BOA, Mühimme Defteri 61, 67/176: 18 August 1586.

32 BOA, Mühimme Defteri 48, 88/238: 22 August 1582. For the types of fish and fishing in early modern Istanbul, see Suraiya Faroqhi, "Fish and Fishermen in Ottoman Istanbul," in *Water on Sand: Environmental Histories of the Middle East and North Africa*, ed. Alan Mikhail, Oxford: Oxford University Press, 2013, 91–109.

33 Historical scholarship has examined many aspects of plague's effects on businesses in Europe, including the disruption of financial businesses owing to the death of debtors and the inability of landlords and credit lenders to collect them, along with changed business techniques that benefitted certain entrepreneurs. See, e.g., Edwin S. Hunt and James M. Murray, *A History of Business in Medieval Europe, 1200–1550*, Cambridge: Cambridge University Press, 1999.

34 Granted that they could demonstrate their loss of business, the shop owners were partially subsidized for losses incurred owing to plague. See Varlık, *Plague and Empire*, 146, table 2. For shops selling *boza* as important venues of socialization in Ottoman society, see Ebru Boyar and Kate Fleet, *A Social History of Ottoman Istanbul*, Cambridge: Cambridge University Press, 2010, 189–90.

35 Ronald C. Jennings, "Plague in Trabzon and Reactions to It According to Local Judicial Registers," in *Humanist and Scholar: Essays in Honor of Andreas Tietze*, ed. Heath W. Lowry and Donald Quataert, Istanbul: Isis Press, 1993, 27–36, at 30–1.

36 On bathhouses in Ottoman social life, see Boyar and Fleet, *A Social History of Ottoman Istanbul*, 249–70; Nina Cichocki, "Continuity and Change in Turkish Bathing Culture in Istanbul: The Life Story of the Çemberlitaş Hamam," *Turkish Studies* 6, 1 (2005): 93–112.

37 Flight from plague in early modern Ottoman society is a controversial issue in the scholarship. For further discussion, see Heath W. Lowry, "Pushing the Stone Uphill: The Impact of Bubonic Plague on Ottoman Urban Society in the Fifteenth and Sixteenth Centuries," *Osmanlı Araştırmaları* 23 (2003): 93–132; Sam White, "Rethinking Disease in Ottoman History," *International Journal of Middle East Studies* 42, 4 (2010): 549–67; Yaron Ayalon, *Natural Disasters in the Ottoman Empire: Plague, Famine, and Other Misfortunes*, Cambridge: Cambridge University Press, 2014, 135–51; Nükhet Varlık, "Plague, Conflict, and Negotiation: The Jewish Broadcloth Weavers of Salonica and the Ottoman Central Administration in the Late Sixteenth Century," *Jewish History* 28, 3–4 (2014), 261–88; Varlık, *Plague and Empire*, 72–88.

38 BOA, Mühimme Defteri 14/2, 628/904: 5 December 1570.

39 BOA, Mühimme Defteri 24, 96/262: 6 April 1574.

40 Varlık, *Plague and Empire*, 240–6.

41 BOA, Mühimme Defteri 22, 38/82: 25 May 1573.

42 For a discussion of plague's seasonality, see Varlık, *Plague and Empire*, 18 and the references therein, 221–3.

43 Eremia Kömürcüyan, *İstanbul Tarihi: XVII. Asırda İstanbul*, trans. Hrand D Andreasyan, Istanbul: Eren, 1988, 31; Nigel Webb and Caroline Webb, *The Earl and His Butler in Constantinople: The Secret Diary of an English Servant among the Ottomans*, London: I. B. Tauris, 2009, 19–26.

44 Letter (second half of the sixteenth century), Istanbul, Topkapı Palace Museum Archives, E. 4214.

45 Varlık, "Plague, Conflict, and Negotiation."

46 Varlık, *Plague and Empire*, 239–40. For a discussion of how Italian health professionals continued to serve their patients during the Black Death, see Shona Kelly Wray, "Boccaccio and the Doctors: Medicine and Compassion in the Face of Plague," *Journal of Medieval History* 30, 3 (2004): 301–22.

47 Fynes Moryson, *An Itinerary: Containing His Ten Yeeres Travell through the Twelve Dominions of Germany, Bohmerland, Sweitzerland, Netherland, Denmarke, Poland, Italy, Turky, France, England, Scotland and Ireland*, Glasgow: J. MacLehose and Sons, 1907, vol. 2, 100–1.

48 Marino Sanudo, *I diarii di Marino Sanuto (MCCCCXCVI–MDXXXIII) dall' autografo Marciano ital. cl. VII codd. CDXIX–CDLXXVII*, 58 vols., Venice: F. Visentini, 1879–1903, vol. 34, 384.

49 *Ibid.*, vol. 35, 257.

50 Selaniki, *Tarih*, 285–7.

51 See, e.g., Dols, *Black Death in the Middle East*, 246–54; Michael Dols, "The Comparative Communal Responses to the Black Death in Muslim and Christian Societies," *Viator* 5 (1974): 269–87; Justin Stearns, "New Directions in the Study of Religious Responses to the Black Death," *History Compass* 7, 5 (2009): 1363–75; Jussi Hanska, *Strategies of Sanity and Survival: Religious Responses to Natural Disasters in the Middle Ages*, Helsinki: Finnish Literature Society, 2002, 48–100.

52 For similar efforts to maximize the effect of processions in the Christian world, cf. Hanska, *Strategies of Sanity and Survival*, 52–5.

53 For further discussion of early modern Ottoman plague treatises and the methods of protection recommended, see Varlık, *Plague and Empire*, 228–40.

54 *Ibid.*, ch. 8.

55 *Ibid.*, 241–2.

56 On İbrahim Pasha, see Ebru Turan, "The Sultan's Favorite: İbrahim Pasha and the Making of the Ottoman Universal Sovereignty in the Reign of Sultan Süleyman (1516–1526)," PhD diss., University of Chicago, 2007.

57 Cf. Lowry, "Pushing the Stone Uphill."

58 Sanudo, *I diarii*, vol. 44, 263.

59 Börekçi, "Smallpox in the Harem."

60 On the element of uncertainty in weather forecasting, see Phaedra Daipha, *Masters of Uncertainty: Weather Forecasters and the Quest for Ground Truth*, Chicago: University of Chicago Press, 2015. On the science of meteorology in Victorian-era Britain, see Katharine Anderson, *Predicting the Weather: Victorians and the Science of Meteorology*, Chicago: University of Chicago Press, 2005. For efforts to make long-range weather forecasting "scientific" in the US, see Jamie L. Pietruska, "US Weather Bureau Chief Willis Moore and the Reimagination of Uncertainty in Long-Range Forecasting," *Environment and History* 17, 1 (2011): 79–105.

61 On the history of insurance in the modern era, see, e.g., Viviana A. Rotman Zelizer, *Morals and Markets: The Development of Life Insurance in the United States*, New York: Columbia University Press, 1979; Timothy L. Alborn, *Regulated Lives: Life Insurance and British Society, 1800–1914*, Toronto: University of Toronto Press, 2009; Geoffrey Clark, *The Appeal of Insurance*, Toronto: University of Toronto Press, 2010; Jonathan Levy, *Freaks of Fortune: The Emerging World of Capitalism and Risk in America*, Cambridge, MA: Harvard University Press, 2012; Sharon Ann Murphy, *Investing in Life: Insurance in Antebellum America*, Baltimore: Johns Hopkins University Press, 2010; Harold James, Peter Borscheid, David Gugerli, and Tobias Straumann, eds., *The Value of Risk: Swiss Re and the History of Reinsurance*, Oxford: Oxford University Press, 2013.

62 See, e.g., Cornell H. Fleischer, "Seer to the Sultan: Haydar-ı Remmal and Sultan Süleyman," in *Cultural Horizons: A Festschrift in Honor of Talat S. Halman*, ed. Jayne Warner, Syracuse, NY: Syracuse University Press, 2001, 290–9; Cornell H. Fleischer, "Shadows of Shadows: Prophecy and Politics in 1530s Istanbul," *International Journal of Turkish Studies* 13, 1–2 (2007): 51–62.

63 For a discussion of taking death tolls during plague epidemics in sixteenth-century Ottoman cities and the function of this practice, see Varlık, *Plague and Empire*, 253–62.

17

MAPPING FLORENCE AND TUSCANY

Nicholas A. Eckstein

In the 1970s the historiography of the Italian Renaissance city was revolutionized by approaches and methods imported from the fields of anthropology and sociology. As a result, historians questioned central elements of Jacob Burckhardt's epochal nineteenth-century essay, which presented the Italian Renaissance as the historical moment when modern man – and the Swiss historian meant men, not women – first became conscious of himself as an individual. As an idealized antecedent of the nineteenth-century liberal European male, Burckhardt's Renaissance man was an autonomous historical actor unencumbered by medieval corporations like the church and the medieval clan.[1]

Focus on issues like kinship and family structure, affective relations, ritual and gender caused scholars to realize that Italian citizens of the fourteenth, fifteenth and sixteenth centuries – at least those among them who left a written record of their thoughts and actions – did not think of themselves in this way at all. Instead, they habitually defined and expressed themselves in terms of their association with an array of groups and corporations. They were particularly loquacious about a trio of relationships with married relations (*parenti*), friends (*amici*) and neighbours (*vicini*). The impact of the scholarship produced since the 1970s on these and other varieties of group experience has been profound, and it is too far-reaching to comment on here.[2] It can simply be noted that one of its effects was to knock Burckhardt's heroic, modernizing Renaissance individual off his perch, never to be reinstated. In fact, one of the few generalizations that can confidently be made about this elusive and multifarious society is that personal status was defined less by freedom to act as an autonomous individual than by people's inescapable involvement in numerous overlapping groups, some complementary, others in competition with each other. To adapt an assertion made by Richard Trexler, in the urban centres of late medieval, Renaissance and early modern Italy, one either had friends, relatives, colleagues and rivals in the neighbourhood or one was nothing at all.[3]

Of the three primary bonds referred to above, the last, *vicini*, emphasizes the crucial importance of the urban terrain of the neighbourhood. In 1982, D. V. and F. W. Kent published a case-study of the *gonfalone* of the Red Lion, one of the sixteen districts into which the late medieval communal government had divided Florence for the purposes of apportioning taxes and electing officials to the highest political offices of the commune. The authors made clear that although the local power structure of the Red Lion was dominated by a small group of patrician males from exactly the powerful lineages that one would have expected to find in charge, these elite citizens did not act as individuals in the Burckhardtian sense. Instead, they relied on networks of informal, personal relationships that proliferated most densely at the local level.[4] In the same year Ronald Weissman described Florence as a society in which the experience of neighbourhood was a fact of everyday life, especially for artisans, shopkeepers and the lower classes in general.[5]

What the Kents dubbed "the atmosphere of neighbourhood" was effectively established as a given in all subsequent inquiry into early Renaissance Italian urban society and culture. This early work, however, tended not to pay direct attention to the urban space in which social interaction took place. Most of the attention was given to official forms of neighbourhood: the sixth (*sesto*), the quarter and the *gonfalone*, all of which were subdivisions of the commune, and to a much lesser extent the church parish. This is an approach that treats neighbourhood sociability as a phenomenon contained within clearly identifiable boundaries.[6] More problematically, it assumes, at least implicitly, a relationship – even a causal link – between the existence of a division like the Florentine *gonfalone* and the social life that takes place within it.

More recent scholarship has addressed this lacuna by identifying and analysing factors responsible for generating neighbourhood sociability. One fruitful development has been the so-called spatial turn made by historians who have taken as their subject the relationship between renaissance citizens and the urban environment itself. As the term 'spatial turn' suggests, these scholars treat urban space itself as a dynamic element, which both acts upon and is conditioned by social behaviour and contemporary perception of the city.[7] A generation of feminist historians has taught us both that places and spaces in the city were gendered, and that their gendered state altered at different moments in relation to the purposes to which they were being put and the sections of the population who used them.[8] Public ceremonial and ritual life, not all of which was sanctioned by government, overlaid the official geographical divisions already referred to, and in some cases subverted them.[9] Taking the spatial turn often means embracing a 'sensory turn' as well, a corollary that leads to the questioning of historians' traditional love affair with the written word. Scholars interested in the senses explore the role of sight, sound, touch and even smell for their potential to bring us closer to actual contemporary experience of the pre-modern urban environment.[10]

Florentines envisioned their city by mentally mapping built space in terms that both informed and reflected the patterns of their everyday behaviour.[11] One of many examples of the spatial ordering that such thinking could produce can be found in the chronicle of the fifteenth-century commentator, Benedetto Dei. Benedetto alternates catalogues of political figures and events with passages of patriotic boasting in an account that maps Florence as an opulent environment crowded with magnificent buildings and busy workshops, and ordered by graceful piazzas and noble thoroughfares.[12] At times Benedetto's chronicle reads like a guidebook for a walking tour, as he reels off lists that conflate prominent citizens with the built environment. One of these describes the "fifty named piazzas inside the walls (*drento alla città*)" on every one of which there are "churches with palaces and houses all around belonging to the leading citizens of the ruling group." In typical fashion he then goes on laboriously to list forty of the said piazzas.[13] Benedetto's purpose is to aggrandize Florence, but the technique he often employs, of fashioning his cultural identity in relation to the physical setting of his city, was not always or necessarily celebratory. Such patterns of thinking were fluid, and they were strongly influenced by context and prevailing circumstances. Depending on the frame of reference in which they were operating and the

276

events or concerns that were pressing in on them, citizens were capable of thinking in more than one way about their urban environment. At other times and in various ways, they conjured a very different Florence in the mind's eye.

In August 1630, officials of the Magistrato della Sanità, Florence's permanent health office, responded to the menace of an approaching plague by ordering a walking survey of the city's poorest households.[14] Forty-eight lay members of an aristocratic charitable confraternity, dedicated to the Archangel St. Michael, were instructed to inspect every Florentine household where dirt, putrefaction or bad odours were suspected of posing a threat to public health. They were then to report their findings to the Sanità, which would arrange for the nominated premises to be cleaned up. As the brothers walked in pairs from house to house through their appointed sectors, they compiled detailed lists of what they discovered, which have survived among the company's records in the State Archives of Florence (ASF). No strangers to the sight of poverty and deprivation, the brothers were nevertheless shocked by the widespread squalor and human suffering that they witnessed. Their lists express a troubling collective vision of the city and its inhabitants, a mental map of human suffering whose major features are the city's poorest neighbourhoods and the paupers who inhabited them.[15]

In what follows I extend the logic of this analysis to a repository of documents that belonged to the Sanità itself, namely, the correspondence by means of which the magistrates carried out their duties throughout the sixteenth and the early decades of the seventeenth century. Tens of thousands of the letters that comprise this correspondence survive today in the ASF, bound into volumes that range from a few dozen folios to as many as 1,500 or more. The letters are of several different kinds. They include inbound correspondence, sent to the Sanità from other places by a variety of authors, as well as by the office's own agents and delegates and the staff of health offices in other major cities. These letters typically report on outbreaks of disease about which the authors felt the Florentine magistrates needed to be informed, so that the latter could implement appropriate measures. A second category includes outgoing correspondence: this is identical to the letters in the first category in every way, except that it comprises accounts written by Florentine magistrates to inform their official counterparts in other Italian urban centres. A third group consists of information and instructions sent by the Florentine magistrates to their representatives in subject towns and agents in the field throughout the Grand Duchy of Tuscany. The fourth category may be described as internal correspondence. These are letters written by the magistrates to the Grand Duke of Tuscany, combining summaries or digests of the most up-to-date information with policy advice and recommendations as to necessary actions, usually requiring the Grand Duke's formal approval.

These letters are not arranged separately, but are bound together in chronological order. Reading them in sequence, therefore, creates the effect of an unfolding narrative from which one gains insight into the process by which the magistrates learned about events in other places, the criteria by which they compared, weighed and assessed the many reports that they received, and how they attempted to distinguish fact from unsubstantiated rumour and gossip as they determined the best course of action. So detailed are the letters that it becomes clear that they constituted a journal of record of the Sanità's collective knowledge about the extent and seriousness of the plague threat at every moment. Each missive was an active element in the Florentine government's systematic attempt to deal with the threat posed by epidemic. Irrespective of year, decade or generation, one sees the same process at work: as days, weeks and months passed, currents of information from near and far generated a geographically keyed institutional vision of the risk to the Florentine population posed by outbreaks of plague and other infectious diseases. The letters document a process of collective mental mapping comparable to that revealed by the city survey of August 1630. But where the brothers of the Archangel St. Michael looked inward at the squalid reality of Florence's darkest precincts, the horizons of the Sanità's magistrates were vast. They and their colleagues looked outward to the city's surrounding territories and regions beyond, mapping them as a hostile and dangerously porous environment, forever on the brink of disorder and constantly refashioned by the arrival of new information.

Managing the stream of incoming intelligence made busy men of the Sanità's magistrates. At times they were forced to manage a veritable tide of information, and while the influx might slow at times, it never actually stopped. Even during quiet periods the magistrates could not afford to lower their guard, given the potential gravity of information emanating from abroad. News was exchanged with places as close to home as Borgo San Sepolcro, Colle di Val d'Elsa, Pisa and Volterra. It also came from Italian cities in other regions, such as Ancona, Bologna, Genoa, Messina, Milan, Naples, Rome and Venice. Perhaps most striking from the point of view of a twenty-first-century reader, however, is the frequency of letters reporting developments in *ultramontane* Europe and distant places spanning the length and breadth of the Mediterranean basin. Opening the latest correspondence, the magistrates might expect almost equally to read news of an emergency brewing in northern Africa as to hear from the town of Prato less than 20 kilometres up the road. As is clear in what follows, the speed and efficiency of contemporary communications means that intelligence about faraway places would in no way have been considered out of the ordinary, let alone remarkable.

In mid-June 1591, for example, reports arrived of a disease in Methoni on the west coast of the Peloponnese. In a worrying departure from the normal course of events, this outbreak was killing citizens of substance rather than paupers: "in that city more nobles than common citizens are dying ... in one stroke two of that city's leading doctors have died, as well as five or six honourable knights and other citizens, and in some of these cases they have discovered carbuncles [*carboncelli*]."[16] About a month later, on 23 July, news arrived of plague in Perpignan.[17] Three days after that the magistrates learned of a "malady" (*male*) gripping Crete (identified as "Candia," the name given to the city of Herakleion, and by extension to the whole island), Constantinople, Alexandria in the Peloponnese, Smyrna on the Anatolian coast and various islands in the Aegean archipelago, including Milos, Patmos and Scio.[18] In the same month the Sanità found itself dealing with rumours, as yet unsubstantiated, that plague had arrived in the Sicilian port of Messina and on the island of Malta.[19] Reports such as these, which are prevalent wherever one searches in the Sanità's records, demonstrate that generations of Sanità officials faced a more or less constant barrage of information from the cities and regions with which the Florentine government was in contact or had formal relations. Reading them, one quickly develops a picture of the Florentine Sanità as a central convergence point for incoming information, a headquarters where busy officers discussed and reconciled the multitude of disparate reports delivered from the field, thereafter devising policy, advising and seeking approval for their favoured course of action and implementing specific measures once they had obtained the Grand Ducal imprimatur. Such a picture would not be inaccurate, but in fact it understates the complexity, fluidity and flexibility of the Sanità's communications with the outside world.

To understand exactly how this system worked, it is necessary to look closely at the structure of the letters themselves and their place in the network of communications of which the Sanità was part. Reading sequences of these letters today, conveniently bound as they are, initial impressions easily mask an important fact. It is immediately apparent that the officials, secretaries and other assorted correspondents who wrote to the Florentine Sanità never failed to report the latest developments that had occurred in the places from which they were writing. The Florentine magistrates replied in kind. Binary exchanges such as this, however, were just one strand of a far more complicated system. Certainly, the Sanità's informants always sent local news; but they also, and habitually, gathered and mediated the latest reports that had arrived in from other places. Information about a particular place, therefore, did not necessarily come to Florence from that place. The magistrates did not learn of the plague in Methoni from a correspondent in that city but by way of a contact in Bologna who relayed the news; they were told about the *male* spreading over Crete and the Aegean by one of their counterparts in the health office at Ferrara. It was an official of the Genoese Sanità who wrote to Florence about the plague in Perpignan, and he explained moreover that he had not learned of that crisis from Perpignan, but by a roundabout route in a letter from Barcelona, which referred in addition to other outbreaks in the environs of Tarragona in Catalonia.

It was by means of such letters – which passed on information from earlier reports whose authors had previously gone through the same process with still other sources – that officials in government offices were able to maintain a watching brief on places very far away. For obvious reasons, the authors of these letters sent information to as many recipients as possible, in the process creating interlocking chains of correspondence. The vast geographical panorama that this practice opened up for the magistrates frequently emerges in a single letter. One spectacular, though by no means unusual, example is a terse message of fewer than 200 words dispatched from Genoa on 20 December 1591. Its opening sentence includes a reference to letters written a fortnight earlier from Lyon, in which the Genoese learned that officials in the city of Arles had blocked traffic with areas of Languedoc, including Carcassonne, to defend the population from plague that was spreading in that region. In the following sentence the correspondent refers to other recently arrived letters from Tunisia, which described an outbreak of pestilence moving through north African villages along the Barbary coast (*Barberia*) and the Tunisian hinterland.[20]

Cited in isolation, such notifications may appear anecdotal. In fact, however, tens of thousands of them survive in the Sanità's archive, and it is in this context, as parts in an unceasing, geographically extended polyphonic conversation, that their true significance is to be found. Adopting a current metaphor, one may think of each letter as an individual signal, or packet of data, in a massive web of live communications, crisscrossing the physical spaces between the many health offices with which the Florentine Sanità was constantly in touch, and the more distant regions and centres to which news was sent and from which it constantly arrived. As with twenty-first-century social media, this web was multi-polar. News did not travel uni-directionally from point of origin to a single destination. Carried outward by many couriers to multiple destinations, it proliferated in ever more complex and indirect patterns so that, as the brief letter just cited so eloquently demonstrates, it could arrive by the most circuitous and indirect of routes. The polycentricity and consequent unpredictability of this network – both features of the twenty-first-century Internet – heightened the likelihood that a major centre like Florence would receive important intelligence because information emanated simultaneously from many directions at once. If for any reason news ceased to flow through a single region, chances were high that it would arrive by an alternative route. The impact of such communication on the magistrates' perception of geographical space was profound.

Several months after receiving the Genoese message of 20 December 1591, the Florentine magistrates summarized some news recently culled from this network. Based on letters that had arrived from Venice on 4 April 1592, it is even shorter than the letter from Genoa (less than half the length) and may be quoted in full:

> Confirmed reports have arrived that a small outbreak of pestilence [*un poco di peste*] has arisen in Candia [Herakleion]. It is believed that it was carried there by a ship which has brought it to that island, and it is hoped therefore, there being no infection of the air, that it may be quickly resolved through the due diligence that will be used. These gentlemen are going about spreading this information as widely as possible, and yet one sees how greatly it weighs upon them, given the many [negative] consequences that this implies if their fears are realized.[21]

As brief as it is, this paragraph encompasses both possible extremes of the dilemma that it evoked. At one end of the scale was the devoutly wished for possibility that the "poco di peste" in distant Crete, apparently not yet accompanied by the lethal miasmic corruption of the air that heralded an epidemic, would die down as quickly as it arose. At the other end lay a fear that was already preying on the minds of local officials, of the runaway devastation wrought by a fully-fledged emergency. It would have mattered little to the Florentines that these events were happening far away because of the deadly fact, known to all and therefore unarticulated, that plague could travel as swiftly as the correspondence that reported it. Distance, no matter how great, was never a guarantee of safety, because it followed axiomatically that if one were reading news of pestilence in a far-off place then it might already be too late to take preventative action. This chilling awareness accounts for the sense of urgency that suffuses every one of the thousands of letters of the Sanità's correspondence. It explains why the magistrates took minor reports from distant places so seriously, why the geographical space evoked by the Sanità's correspondence was so great, and why this space was never a theoretical abstraction but stood always at the forefront of the magistrates' attention as an active field of operations. Psychologically and emotionally speaking, the same awareness may also be understood to have produced a shrinking effect on the Mediterranean basin, not to mention the Italian peninsula. In absolute terms the areas involved were huge, but knowing that plague represented a genuine threat even when it arose as far away from Florence as Spain, northern Africa, Crete or Anatolia would have brought these locations much closer to home in the collective consciousness. At times the Mediterranean would have seemed alarmingly small.

Inhabitants of Venice, where the news about Candia came from, may have experienced a heightened sense of this risk, given that plague could enter the city on any one of the many ships that docked every day in the Mediterranean's busiest port. But one did not need to be a Venetian to be fearful. The letters of the Sanità make it clear that Florentines were perennially anxious on the same account. Because plague could spread so rapidly once it made landfall, they perceived Mediterranean shipping as a general threat. Florentines were especially concerned about the proximate danger posed by ships plying routes between the many Tyrrhenian ports that were sprinkled all up and down the western coast of Italy. Their apprehension is evident during one putative emergency caused by yet another constant and potentially devastating background threat: human error. A letter of 11 June 1592 refers to "two great Turkish vessels, full of cargo" which had been plundered by Florentine galleys between Sicily and Tunisia, near the island of Pantelleria. Reading the opening sentences one immediately senses a deadly irony: the victorious Florentine mariners had treated the crews of these ships as part of the booty, taking 150 prisoners and exultantly towing the captives – humiliatingly imprisoned on their own ships – back to Portoferraio on the island of Elba with the intention of selling them into slavery. Unfortunately, enthusiasm seems to have overtaken common sense during this escapade, because none of the captors had second thoughts when some of the prisoners developed symptoms of plague, even allowing a number of them to disembark on reaching the port. On learning what had happened the magistrates in Florence were less complacent. In addition to ordering an immediate maritime blockade of Portoferraio and the entire island of Elba, they intensified surveillance and ordered an armed patrol to stop all traffic between Elba and the mainland Tuscan ports, including Piombino, Scarlino, Grosseto, Porto Ercole, Talamone "and other places in the area."[22]

Geographical nervousness produced what one might very well call a fortress mentality on the part of the Sanità and the government for which the magistrates acted. Their ideal scenario was always to act early – as soon as they had received news of plague spreading in a distant location – by enacting blocking measures designed to isolate entire regions and thereby prevent plague from entering Tuscan territory in the first place. One characteristic response appears in a letter sent to the Sanità on 30 July 1592. Writing from Pratolino near Florence, where the Grand Duke was currently residing, a secretary informed the magistrates that he had received letters from Naples. These referred to rumours of a plague on Malta, and stated that the Neapolitans had taken the early precaution of reinforcing their city guard. The secretary added that security in Rome had also been increased, and that travellers from Naples were being denied entry unless they could display a clean bill of health (*bullettino*). The clear, albeit unstated, implication is that the Roman authorities were concerned that the Maltese disease might already have breached Neapolitan defences and that as a result they needed to stop traffic from that quarter. The secretary in Pratolino also reported that he had read, or learned the contents of, letters that had arrived that very day (that is, on 30 July) from Malta itself, confirming that the outbreak that was the original cause for all these measures was indeed true plague. "Pestilence" was being openly discussed on the island, and it was said to be spreading day by day. Acknowledging that the epidemic was real and that news could no longer be contained, the Maltese "plague commissioners" (*commessarij sopra la peste*) had ordered more than thirty houses to be locked. In conclusion the secretary explained that the Grand Duke, having taken all of this news into account, had ordered him to advise the Florentine magistrates to ban all Maltese traffic and to instruct the authorities at Livorno and in Siena to block all ships from the island.[23]

Every time the magistrates received credible reports of a threat from outside Tuscan territory, they followed the same procedure. Assembling as much reliable and up-to-date information as they could obtain, they directed their response where the threat seemed most serious. In the early stages of a crisis their stated objective was always twofold: block and exclude anyone who might transmit or already have contracted plague; allow entrance only to people who carried an official bill of health issued in their place of origin (called a *bulletta* or a *fede di sanità*). One cannot fault the Sanità's reasoning. Early modern Europeans did not understand the real causes of infection, but they knew for a fact that plague was spread by human contact and they acted accordingly. Preventing an influx of people who might bring the disease with them was therefore a logical response, and if such measures could be effectively implemented, they could actually make a difference.

The plague that finally arrived in Florence in August 1630 had been brought across the Alps into Italy by French and Imperial troops in 1628 and 1629. In the first half of 1630 the Sanità assiduously monitored the progress of the disease as it descended with increasing speed through the northern part of the peninsula. In a report sent to the Grand Duke on 11 June, the Sanità informed His Highness that despite local protestations to the contrary, people in Bologna had begun dying of plague. The magistrates had sent their Provveditore to Bologna to assess the situation on the ground, and while they expected to hear from him either on the evening of the 11th or the following day, they felt that the situation was so urgent that they should bring the Grand Duke up to date immediately – hence the present letter. They advised that the government should strictly monitor all traffic emanating from Bologna. Orders were to be sent north to the outpost of Pietramala on Tuscany's mountainous border with Bolognese territory, as well as to guards patrolling the Apennine passes, to the effect that

> until they receive orders to the contrary they are not to admit or to let pass either people or merchandise that originated from that city [Bologna] or its state. And in the event that the disease continues to spread and suspects [*sospetti*] continue to arrive so that it becomes necessary to ban or suspend traffic with the said city and state, the Magistracy recommends that these measures should be reinforced so as to maintain the security of Your Highness's borders.[24]

Seventy-five years before this emergency it had been the same story. On 8 September 1555 the Florentine magistrates then in office sprang into action on learning from their counterparts in Bologna and Lucca that plague had been detected in the Val Padana in the towns of Padua, Modena and Gazzuolo and their surrounding territories.[25] Communicating this intelligence to Filippo de' Nerli, the Sanità's man in Pistoia, they articulated their apprehension about the risk to Tuscany now posed by the large commercial traffic between Gazzuolo and Modena, and by the latter's proximity to the mountains lying between Modena and Pistoia. Knowing that even this rugged barrier could not prevent plague from penetrating Tuscan territory, they urged Filippo to remain vigilant. More importantly, they instructed him to discourage citizens under Pistoian jurisdiction from transacting business or having anything else to do with anyone from the Modenese *contado*. In enforcing these restrictions the agents were authorized to impose

> whatever punishments and sanctions you as a prudent judge deem appropriate. And if anything should happen, you are to report it without fail to the Captain of the Mountains, who has been written to at length and advised similarly. And you are to keep yourself informed daily of everything that does or might happen, to which end you must deploy the forces under your control to your best advantage. This matter is of the greatest importance, therefore apply the usual diligence in such a way that, as in all of your other operations, you merit commendation. Farewell.[26]

Volleys of letters issued from the Sanità's office over the following days, warning citizens in every corner of the Tuscan Grand Duchy to deny entry to anyone from the affected regions who could not display a verifiable bill of health.[27] On 15 September, the magistrates thanked their colleagues in Lucca for sending a wax impression of their seal, so that Florentine guards would not be deceived by anyone who attempted to counterfeit the Lucchese device. Adamantly reaffirming their determination that "here no person will enter who comes from outside the dominion without a *fede di sanità*," the Florentine magistrates reciprocated by sending an impression of their own seal.[28]

It is impossible to peruse the correspondence of the Sanità without being impressed by the clarity of the magistrates' purpose and the efficiency with which they implemented their policy. In addition, however, beneath the surface of the office's businesslike approach there ran an undercurrent of genuine fear. Often manifesting itself as authoritarian harshness, this emotion surfaced whenever standard measures failed. On 22 September 1555, the magistrates wrote again to Filippo de' Nerli in Pistoia, this time with sobering news that the bodies of three or four plague victims had been discovered at Serra Villa di Castel Bolognese, southeast of Bologna, and that a similar number of villagers were infected. More worrying than the deaths themselves were reports suggesting that the disease had been brought to Serra Villa by two peasants who, either inadvertently or by design, had slipped undetected past the Bolognese Sanità's security officers on their way home from a visit to Bagni di Padova to the north. After praising Nerli for his work so far, the magistrates informed him that the events at Serra Villa had impelled them to intensify Florentine surveillance of nearby borders and mountain passes. While betraying the anxiety aroused by this reminder of the inherent fallibility of their policies, they expressed hope that their letter would fortify Nerli in his resolve and that he would: "be vigilant so that this fire does not ignite in our territory, for this would be our ultimate ruin."[29] They were also angered by what they clearly regarded as the laxity of the Bolognese guards in allowing this "mishap" (*accidente*) to occur.[30] With reports mounting of plague taking hold in Cremona, Ferrara, Parma, Bologna and in Venice's Lombard territories, the magistrates sent a barrage of letters urging their representatives in Tuscany's border towns, and especially their agents in the field, to maintain the highest levels of vigilance: by admitting only travellers who could display a valid *fede di sanità*; and by monitoring minor rights of way along which those seeking to flout the rules might try to pass.

In fact the magistrates knew that no matter how well they implemented their policies, the best that they could hope for was to slow the plague's advance. Awareness of their ultimate impotence may be one factor responsible for the harsh edge of much of the Sanità's language, and their readiness to resort to extreme measures. There is no need to read between the lines in the correspondence of 1630 – the magistrates conceived and overtly characterized this situation as a military campaign. On 11 June they recommended immediate action on Tuscany's borders because, in their words, "we are without *antemurali*." A military term, *antemurale* denoted not only actual fortifications but also the strategy of defence adopted by an army. Absence of the former was what caused the Sanità to insist on the alertness of all officials and guards working in the field. And it was because of the enormous difficulties of implementing the latter that the magistrates resorted to a more ominous usage of military terminology. Given the inherent insecurity of Tuscany's mountainous northern frontier, the Sanità advised His Highness that:

> It would be wise – beginning from Terra del Sole and Romagna, and arriving in the mountains of Pistoia as far as Pescia – to mount a continuous assault on those borders, employing numerous squads of soldiers of those militias and units so as to interrupt and provoke terror among wayfarers [*dar terrore a' viandanti*] who by paths or circuitous routes seek to penetrate these territories, giving [the soldiers] the orders and advisories that seem most appropriate. Resourcing should not be a

consideration. An aggressive campaign of enforcement would begin immediately and last as long as necessary without paying any heed to cost.[31]

This chilling reference to "terror," which was anything but windy hyperbole, can be explained in the spatial terms that are the subject of the present chapter. The magistrates were proposing nothing less than to run a *cordon sanitaire* through wild, mountainous terrain stretching the entire width of the Apennines, over 100 kilometres as the crow flies, and they must have known before they started that they could not succeed. Less than three weeks later they were forced to write to the Grand Duke to inform him that security was failing, that "despite the numerous measures being taken at the borders, there are always some people from banned or suspect areas who find a way to sneak through."[32] Harsh punishments, clearly intended to act as a deterrent, had already been introduced. Travellers without a *fede di sanità* faced the threat of execution, and the magistrates now recommended that anyone who offered shelter to such fugitives – as they now would be – should suffer the same punishment or be imprisoned.[33] When even these deterrents failed, the magistrates resorted unhesitatingly to a genuinely brutal measure, which they explained to the Grand Duke: "severe orders have been issued against those people coming from villages and locations that are banned or under suspicion, including that they may be killed with impunity if they are discovered away from the main roads." Unauthorized travellers would forfeit their right to exist merely by wandering away from one of the principal routes that the Florentine state was attempting to police.[34]

The extremity of this law reveals it for what it was: a desperate measure. It suggests also that in the end, the spatial ideal to which the magistrates aspired – of a hermetically sealed, rigorously patrolled and effectively defended Tuscany, impervious to foreign incursion – was a pipe dream. Instead, the magistrates' collective consciousness was haunted by the ineradicable vision of a territory torn open and exposed, its borders punctured by so many points of entry that there was no hope of policing all of them. Within those borders was a spider-web of minor roads, tracks, byways and watercourses that rendered the Florentine territory unpatrollable and uncontrollable. Plague, a lightning-quick enemy that could arise suddenly at one end of the Mediterranean and be discovered at the next moment ravaging one's closest neighbours, effortlessly infiltrated this sieve-like landscape, corroding and disordering the political integrity of the Tuscan Grand Ducal state.

Many letters in the Sanità's correspondence suggest that this spatial disintegration signified a moral as well as an existential threat. One of the most hair-raisingly chaotic possibilities was of a landscape across which potentially disruptive elements, driven by starvation and the threat of infection, would begin to move from their villages in the *contado* and, in a worst-case scenario, descend on Florence itself in search of physical security and food. In this way, long-standing suspicions of the poor and the lower classes mapped themselves on to perceptions and interactions with Florentine territorial space. In September 1555 the Sanità attempted to slow the plague's advance by exhorting its officers to be especially vigilant in their rural jurisdictions, not simply because of intruders from outside, but because, "as you know, in these times many poor people seek to come here to the city [that is, to Florence], bringing their families from various and diverse locations in our *contado* and region, in order to beg."[35] Starving and weakened, they were especially vulnerable to plague. Local officials, therefore, were admonished to spread the word "in all public places of our jurisdiction, and especially in the markets and churches" where people were accustomed to gather, that if they arrived at the gates of Florence, they would be denied entry. In attempting to prevent unauthorized human movement across the physical space of the Florentine territorial state, the Sanità was primarily concerned to prevent the human and demographic catastrophe that only plague could cause.

Notes

1 Jacob Burckhardt, *The Civilization of the Renaissance in Italy*, London: Phaidon, 1995. For a recent, lucid, critique of Burckhardt's individualizing protagonist see John Jeffries Martin, *Myths of Renaissance Individualism*, New York: Palgrave Macmillan, 2004.

2 The following is a sample of the pioneering work referred to here: F. W. Kent, *Household and Lineage in Renaissance Florence: The Family Life of the Capponi, Ginori, and Rucellai*, Princeton, NJ: Princeton University Press, 1977; D. V. Kent, *The Rise of the Medici: Faction in Florence, 1426–1434*, Oxford: Oxford University Press, 1978; Richard C. Trexler, *Public Life in Renaissance Florence*, New York: Academic Press, 1980; Edward Muir, *Civic Ritual in Renaissance Venice*, Princeton, NJ: Princeton University Press, 1981; Ronald F. E. Weissman, *Ritual Brotherhood in Renaissance Florence*, New York: Academic Press, 1982; Christiane Klapisch-Zuber, *Women, Family, and Ritual in Renaissance Italy*, Chicago: University of Chicago Press, 1985.

3 Trexler, *Public Life*, p. 14.

4 D. V. Kent and F. W. Kent, *Neighbours and Neighbourhood in Renaissance Florence: The District of the Red Lion in the Fifteenth Century*, Locust Valley, NY: J. J. Augustin, 1982, p. 48.

5 Weissman, *Ritual Brotherhood*, ch. 1.

6 I have referred to this danger elsewhere. Nicholas A. Eckstein, *The District of the Green Dragon: Neighbourhood Life and Social Change in Renaissance Florence*, Florence: Olschki, 1995.

7 See, e.g., the recent essays assembled by contributing editors Georgia Clarke and Fabrizio Nevola on "The Experience of the Street in Early Modern Italy," special issue of *I Tatti Studies in the Italian Renaissance*, 16, 1/2 (2013).

8 For example, Natalie Tomas, *"A Positive Novelty": Women and Public Life in Renaissance Florence*, Clayton: Monash Publication in History, 1992; Stefanie B. Siegmund, "Gendered Self-Government in Early Modern Jewish History: The Florentine Ghetto and Beyond," in *Gendering the Jewish Past*, Marc Lee Raphael, ed., Williamsburg: The College of William and Mary, 2002, pp. 137–55; Elizabeth S. Cohen, "Seen and Known: Prostitutes in the Cityscape of Late-Sixteenth-Century Rome," *Renaissance Studies* 12, 3 (1998): 392–409; Elizabeth S. Cohen, "To Pray, to Work, to Hear, to Speak: Women in Roman Streets C. 1600," in *Cultural History of Early Modern European Streets*, ed. Riitta Laitinen and Thomas V. Cohen, Leiden and Boston: Brill, 2009, 95–117; Tessa Storey, *Carnal Commerce in Counter-Reformation Rome*, Cambridge and New York: Cambridge University Press, 2008, *passim*.

9 David Rosenthal, *Kings of the Street: Power, Community, and Ritual in Renaissance Florence*, Turnhout: Brepols, 2015.

10 On sound see Niall Atkinson, "The Republic of Sound: Listening to Florence at the Threshold of the Renaissance," *I Tatti Studies in the Italian Renaissance* 16, 1/2 (2013): 57–84; and now the same author's *The Noisy Renaissance*, University Park, PA: Penn State University Press, 2016; Kate Colleran, "*Scampanata* at the Widows' Windows: A Case-Study of Sound and Ritual Insult in Cinquecento Florence," *Urban History* 36, 3 (2009): 359–78; Flora Dennis, "Sound and Domestic Space in Fifteenth- and Sixteenth-Century Italy, *Studies in the Decorative Arts* 16, 1 (Fall/Winter 2008–2009): 7–19; Stephen Milner, "'Fanno bandire, notificare et expressamente comandare': Town Criers and the Information Economy of Renaissance Florence," *I Tatti Studies in the Italian Renaissance* 16, 1/2 (2013): 107–51; Blake Wilson, "Dominion of the Ear: Singing the Vernacular in Piazza San Martino," *I Tatti Studies in the Italian Renaissance* 16, 1/2 (2013): 273–87.

11 I have used the metaphor of the mental map in a recent article: Nicholas A. Eckstein, "Florence on Foot: An Eye-Level Mapping of the Early Modern City in Time of Plague," *Renaissance Studies* 30, 2 (2016): 273–97.

12 Dei, *Cronica*. For examples see pp. 82–4, 86, 91–2.

13 *Ibid.*, p. 79. On the construing of the city as a network of overlapping itineraries, see my *Painted Glories: The Brancacci Chapel in Renaissance Florence*, New Haven: Yale University Press, 2014, pp. 52–3.

14 In this chapter it is necessary to distinguish between the Florentine Sanità and the health offices of other cities. From this point, therefore, I will refer to the Florentine office simply as "the Sanità." Wherever the health office of another city is mentioned I will specify that city. I follow the same practice for the officials themselves. From this point the officials of the Florentine Sanità will be referred to simply as "the magistrates." References to officials in other cities will be specifically identified.

15 Eckstein, "Florence on Foot."

16 Florence, Archivio di Stato di Firenze (ASF), Sanità 134, fol. 4r. *Carboncello* is one of several terms for a swelling, pustule or bubo and its presence was regarded as an indicator of pestilence. See Cohn, *Cultures of Plague*, p. 45.

17 ASF, Sanità 134, fol. 39r.

18 *Ibid.*, fol. 40r.

19 *Ibid.*, folio following 43r.

20 *Ibid.*, fol. 6r.

21 *Ibid.*, fol. 23r.

22 *Ibid.*, fols. 24, 25.

23 *Ibid.*, fol. 434.

24 ASF, Sanità 37, fol. 42r. I have cited this letter in a related context in "Mapping Fear: Plague and Perception in Florence and Tuscany," in *Mapping Space, Sense, and Movement in Florence: Historical GIS and the Early Modern City*, ed. Nicholas Terpstra and Colin Rose, London and New York: Routledge, 2016, pp. 169–86.

25 ASF, Sanità 45, fols. 1r–2r.

26 *Ibid.*, fols. 1v–2r. Filippo de' Nerli is not named as the recipient of this letter. He is, however, named in another letter that the Sanità sent to Pistoia on 20 September (ASF, Sanità 45, fol. 5r). Both letters are written in the same familiar mode of address, and both were almost certainly sent to him.

27 See, for instance, the text of the letter sent to twenty-one Tuscan towns on 14 September. ASF, Sanità 45, fol. 3v

28 *Ibid.*, fol. 4v. "… et nelle presente [letters] sarà l'impronta del nostro sigillo col quale saranno sigillatj e nostri bullettinj a causa che quelle non sieno defraudate."

29 *Ibid.*, fol. 5r.

30 *Ibid.*, fol. 5v. In letters to the Bolognese Sanità, also written on 22 September, the Florentine magistrates expressed the "greatest displeasure" at the events described.

31 ASF, Sanità 37, fols. 42v–43r. The harsh measures were to be implemented "notwithstanding that this resolution would involve thirty squads of five soldiers per squad to the number of 150, paid one *Giulio* each per day and to the corporals one *lira*, requiring approximately fifteen *scudi* per day, that is, 450 *scudi* every month. Given the nature and importance of the case, the Magistracy is of the opinion that [the campaign] should continue for as long as is necessary." The *giulio* was a silver coin used by the Florentines, named for a Roman coin commemorating Pope Julius II. Richard A. Goldthwaite, *The Economy of Renaissance Florence*, Baltimore: Johns Hopkins University Press, 2009, p. 56.

32 ASF, Sanità 37, fol. 83r.

33 *Ibid.*, fol. 83v. By contrast, loyal subjects who exposed transgressors were to be offered a financial reward.

34 *Ibid.*

35 ASF, Sanità 45, fol. 3v.

18

EXERCISE AND LEISURE

Sport, dance, and games[1]

Alessandro Arcangeli

It was Johan Huizinga's famous essay in the late thirties of the last century that program-matically and systematically attracted the attention of historical studies to play as an impor-tant sphere of human action and a meaningful element in the realm of culture in its many manifestations and forms. The Dutch scholar portrayed the period to us in a very special light: "The whole mental attitude of the Renaissance is one of play. This striving, at once sophisticated and spontaneous, for beauty and nobility of form is an instance of culture at play."[2]

To the Italian Renaissance belongs in effect a ludic dimension that, while it presents clear European parallels, does not lack specificity. It is a set of practices accompanied by moments of theoretical reflection of notable respite with implications that range from ethics to aes-thetics. In the anthropological system of the era, it invests both the physical and psychic aspects of human beings: in the culture of play, therefore, the fields of knowledge pertaining to the body and to the mind were implicated, from the medical level onwards. The Western medical discourse inherited from the Hippocratic–Galenic tradition – and reworked by the intermediary of Arab and medieval Mediterranean scientific culture – a notion of exercise that had among its most indispensable implications the binomial *otium/negotium*. According to its own nature, in fact, it is something other than anyone's ordinary occupation: it can assume the form of recreation which relaxes, but also, and almost oppositely, represents a logic not far removed from the techniques of postmodern fitness, which seek to restore bodies weighed down by activities altogether too sedentary. The practices that take hold in this ambit acquired, in the symbolic universe of the Renaissance, a variety of meanings and implications that go beyond the cyclical alternation of motion and rest. The collective and leisurely participation in dances or ball games at different levels of the social hierar-chy – without excluding interaction between the levels – performs specific tasks in defining class identity, in the sedimentation of forms of sociability among the most diverse and most characteristic, in the public exhibition of power and in the representation and transmission of its particular messages and facets. Free time was not a residual space that housed what was superfluous and irrelevant, but a strategic intersection for the definition of social relations in a complex universe subject to dramatic changes.

Exercise

The conceptual framework and background of bodily practices into which physical exercise is best fitted is the system that traditional Greek medicine called 'hygiene.' Hygiene must not be understood as cleanliness. It was, instead, a prophylaxis interpreted not as a safeguard from specific health threats, but rather as self-care that maintained the various humors in harmonic balance and thus precluded the onset of a crisis resulting from an imbalance. As such, the doctrine essentially provided a surveillance of what entered and exited the body. But this should be understood in a rather broad sense and, while having at the center a cycle of nutrition, also regiments the rhythmical alternation of physical activity and rest, as well as sexual intercourse, baths and massages.[3] It is in this context that the medical literature considered, without disdain for details, ludic-sporting activities as forms of exercise.

The most famous example of the Renaissance revival of the themes is the work of physician Girolamo Mercuriale of Forlì, one of the most important figures in European medical culture during the second half of the sixteenth century. His influence is due in large part to his long career as a lecturer at the universities of Padova, Bologna, and Pisa. Mercuriale's *De arte gymnastica* (1569) – among his first publications – is regarded as the beginning of the modern study of gymnastics. The work, consisting of six books, resulted from an antiquarian interest cultivated during Mercuriale's presence in the Roman circle of Cardinal Farnese, and was thus a specific and inimitable yield of the humanistic environment in which it was produced. As has been suggested, the orientation of *De arte gymnastica* is mainly classical, in line with the erudition of the era and the curiosity of an educated public, seeking to reconstruct an aspect insufficiently explored by the author's predecessors. There is no lack of references to current practices, and the interest shown in Mercuriale's continuation of his work, which grew in subsequent editions and throughout the course of his career, serves as testimony to his 'militant' credo of realistic and possible usage and the healthful efficacy of exercise. As required by systematic treatment, the themes range from the most general (i.e., the origins of medicine, components of hygiene, a definition and division of gymnastics), to the reconstruction of ancient practice and context (gymnasia, bathrooms), to the proposal (after a discussion of the previous literature) of a definition of exercise that illustrates its varieties, results, and properties for individuals of different complexions. The woodcuts that accompanied the second edition (1573) are even more renowned than the text, which does not lend itself to an easy or entertaining read. The woodcuts are the result of an iconographic project by the prominent antiquarian Pirro Ligorio. In turn, they offered to the collective imagination a visual shortcut to a world of the ancient games, which survived only in fragmentary figurative evidence. Even today, ancient fighting or boxing recalls Ligorio's drawings.[4]

Nevertheless, to limit Renaissance exercise, or even its documentation in treatises, to Mercuriale's books would be reductive. It is time to resettle them in a context that is not restricted only to Italy, and is not dependent on well-known sources or linked to issues and skills described therein that are marginal to the historiographical vernacular. An important non-canonical text, known only esoterically and lacking essential details such as the nationality of its author, is the Latin work *Exercitiorum atque artis militaris collectanea*, consisting of three books. They are a collection of military exercises by Pietro (or Pero) Monti (del Monte). They were published in Milan in 1509 together with a treatise written by the same author on dueling. They appear to mark a change in the status quo and a new interest in the world of exercise at the opening of the sixteenth century. The date of the work is notable not so much for its composition, but for its printing. As we will see, the fifteenth century saw the composition and circulation, in various places in Italy and elsewhere in Europe, of a series of expositions on the art of the fencing and horsemanship, as well as on dance. Most of these, however, retained their status as manuscripts, and were published only in the twentieth century.

Information concerning "Pietro Monti" is not certain. Two renowned specialists, Marie Madeleine Fontaine and Sydney Anglo, were split in their opinions, believing the author alternately to be an Italian commander or a Spanish nobleman. What is known for certain only augments the fascination surrounding his persona and his reasons for writing. Monti was among the most experienced and sought-after men of arms of the era. He is mentioned by no less than Baldassare Castiglione in the *Book of the Courtier* (*Libro del Cortegiano*, I, 25) as the instructor of Galeazzo da Sanseverino "in wrastling, in vawting, and in learning to handle sundry kinde of weapons." In his depiction of the ideal courtier. Ludovico da Canossa lauded him as "the true and only maister of al artificiall force and slight." Monti was known even to Leonardo, who takes note to remember to talk to him and ask for clarifications regarding the trajectory of javelins. In the same year as the publication of the collection, Monti appears to have taken part in the Battle of Agnadello on the side of the defeated Venetian troops.

Monti's career and the publication history of his treatise were, if not anything else, Italian. His work had been preceded in 1492 by a treatise devoted to combat, printed likewise in Milan in Latin translation of a Spanish original – one of the strongest pieces of evidence produced by Anglo in favor of the author's supposed Iberian origin. It was the first printed work on the topic. The different fighting techniques in use in a wide range of European countries were not discussed from a sporting perspective, but as martial arts in warfare.[5]

After defining his terms, Pietro Monti goes on to describe again the fight and the various forms of armed combat and other physical exercise such as running, which should also be used in military training. The discussion includes the general practices of sporting competitions, including races between two contenders. This is followed by a section illustrating the basics of the medical doctrine of humors, commenting for each of the four complexions (the sanguine, the choleric, the melancholic, and the phlegmatic) on their physical predisposition and on the greater or lesser utility of exercise. Monti's work moves on to survey other characteristics that affect the usefulness of gymnastics for different people, including their stature. It then examines the variety of European nations, adding Asia and Africa, noting the physical implications of a person's ethnic and geographic origins. In this section, Monti did little more than follow an ancient medical tradition that had an authoritative foundation in Hippocratic writings (in particular *De aeris aquis locis*), which considered environment a decisive determinant of one's physical constitution, and, as a result, of one's overall health and susceptibility to particular diseases. The greatest cause for disparity is differences between the climates of cold and warm regions. The second book further develops the theme of the gymnasium. It subsequently returns to consider, in detail, armed exercises on foot and on horseback. The third book, alluded to in the second part of the title, addresses military art. It renews considerations of complexion and exercise that must be considered by army leaders.

Beyond the examples taken from ancient military literature and the scholarly apparatus employed in the text (by an author who elsewhere commented even on theology), Monti's work takes on particular importance in its publication at a time of genuine revolution in the art of war, with the decline of feudal cavalry and affirmation of the role of infantry. In this era, the discussion and emphasis on training of troops was not a purely literary exercise. The physical description and instruction for use of the various weapons provided by a professional specialist opens an important viewpoint into an aspect of the Renaissance that remains relatively overlooked, but had considerable influence and dramatic effect on everyday lives of contemporaries (in the era of the "Italian wars"). All this is situated firmly at the center of a historical phase characterized by the eclipse of the socio-cultural model of the medieval knight.

Upon closer inspection, however, Monti's writing remains a rather isolated case. It does not seem to have found wide readership or to have solicited contemporary discussion. It probably remained confined to the discourse on military art. This was likely because it is a large and complex Latin text, which hindered its wider circulation. It is no coincidence, therefore, that fifty years later it was thanks to the publication of some vernacular texts that the thematic on exercise was revitalized and opened to new developments and audiences.

Two books published in close temporal proximity to each other – in 1553 in Spain and 1555 in Italy – indicate a turning point in sixteenth-century European cultural attitudes toward sport and exercise. The works, the *Libro del ejercicio corporal y de sus provechos, per el qual cadauno podrà entender que exercicio le sea necessario para conservar la salud* by Cristóbal Méndez and the *Trattato del giuoco della palla* by Antonio Scaino, appeared a generation before the work of Mercuriale. Compared to Monti, the first is better known, at least among the historians of medical thought. The author, Cristóbal Méndez, was an Andalusian physician and the text may have been conceived while he was in Mexico (thus giving our discussion an internationality or, rather, an inter-continentality). The *Libro del ejercicio corporal* was written from a purely medical perspective, with emphasis on the physiological dimension of exercise, treating motion as beneficial to health by its production of heat. Like Monti, Méndez distinguishes exercise for individuals embodying each of the four complexions. He also includes a definition of exercise, enumerating the advantages that result from its practice, and providing instructions for its execution. Méndez assigns the prize for the best individual exercise for a particular part of the body to walking. The special status is bestowed in part because walking gives pleasure and joy. This psychophysical dimension is not indeed absent from humoral medicine: joy affects one's balance and thus contributes to one's well-being.

The type of exercise that Méndez deems common (involving more than one body part) is ascribed differently to individual social groups. To the nobility belong the arts of hunting, dancing, and the game of *pelota*. The last, a Spanish variety of ball game, is a theme on which the author lingers for more than a chapter. The discussion takes up the argument first exposed by Galen, who in a short treatise recommended games involving a small ball as the best form of exercise. It worked the various parts of the body in a most balanced way. In addition, it presented the practical advantage – almost 'democratic' in bearing – of not requiring, like hunting, a good deal of equipment and great expense. What little it did require was portable, thereby making it useful even in travel.[6] On the whole, the work is deeply rooted in ancient medical literature. It had the benefit, however, of reviving for the Renaissance reader a detailed examination of exercise that was intended to be up-to-date to the requirements of the time, and was, in its breadth and specificity, unprecedented. Méndez's work does not seem, however, to have circulated widely and did not have the resonance throughout Europe of Girolamo Mercuriale's later *De arte gymnastica*.

Masters and treaties

The first printed treatise dedicated to a specific sector of activity in recreational sports belongs to the same humanistic culture of the Italian Renaissance that nurtured Mercuriale. The *Trattato del giuoco della palla*, an early work by the Brescian Antonio Scaino, published in Venice in 1555, is one of the most systematic writings of this or any age. The shortest part of Scaino's treatise is the third section that has a medical perspective comparable to that of Méndez. But the section is preceded by two longer ones dedicated to an explanation of the technical details of the game. They provide a comprehensive establishment of identity and its variants, and propose a choice of the noblest kind. Scaino, who was later distinguished primarily as a commentator on Aristotle, dedicated his work to Alfonso II d'Este, the young Duke of Ferrara, four years before his assumption to the principality. Ferrara is an important geographic context for understanding the meaning of the work and the reality of social practice represented therein. The Este court, particularly under Alfonso II, offered unique hospitality to gymnastics and sport that allowed a re-evaluation of the corporeal dimension of man and the pedagogical value of physical education. These facets are commonly traced back to fifteenth-century humanism – to the work of Guarino (again, active in Ferrara) that clearly provides a common pan-Italian and European background to this set of practices, which were located at the interface between bodily health and recreational aristocratic sociability. They do not, however, find parallels elsewhere in Italy and Europe, but remained reflections of the exclusive passion the Prince of Ferrara had for physical play which, twenty years after Scaino's writing, found expression in the iconographic work designs by Pirro Ligorio for the hall and the small chamber of games in the castle of Este.[7]

Moreover, the Duke of Ferrara is in good company in his preference for ball games. The *jeu de paume* – owing to the eponymous oath taken by the deputies of the National Assembly held in the hall to which that *loisir* was in fact dedicated at Versailles (20 June 1789) – has an exquisitely French history in the collective historical memory. But the role played by the Italian court system in promoting real tennis in the form of elite sociability should not be neglected. It must also be noted via merit as an environment of elaboration of cultural models with wider European resonance, not the least – as for a wider range of disciplines – through the diffusion of texts and motifs and the circulation of equipment and of specialized personnel.[8]

Scaino's treatise represents, in hindsight, a rather rare case of its kind. Historians of sport praise it as the only textual reference belonging to a span of a few centuries, on a European scale, concerning rules of ball games. The same judgment may also offer insight into its possible failure. The book was not the subject of reprints or translations into other languages, and its effectiveness in regulating the measures that should have been respected in building the rooms dedicated to these games, as well as in determining the manner of execution, seems to have been somewhat limited.[9]

Scaino's work carries us back to Italy, but it also brings us to a context of social practices of specific physical disciplines and to the intersection between direct and literary experience in their transmission. In this regard, it is important that we deal not only with written works: the function of the treatises drafted in these years provides a point of departure to discuss issues beyond the texts themselves. The authors – whether or not masters of the arts of which they record knowledge – were aware that bodily techniques require direct learning for which written instructions were an unsatisfactory substitute. The works sometimes address these issues explicitly and provide information on the actual operation of the schools where their subjects were taught. These developments were not all Italian, but Italian masters and writers played a leading role. At stake, however, was how to represent effectively movement graphically – a challenge in which artists were simultaneously engaged.

The solutions first adopted for visually representing martial arts later found application to a variety of different but related activities, especially choreography.[10] It is important to point out that this survey of a series of texts and practices does not necessarily yield a clear distinction between the dimension of gymnastics (also in medical use), military exercise, and leisure. It has been said that Monti began with purely military skills and interests. This is also true of other works that will be mentioned. This does not mean, however, that brief consideration alongside materials of a different nature is not opportune. It is indeed perhaps necessary, given that the most technical material associated with the exercise of arms – as expressly lamented by the intellectual historian, Sydney Anglo, who dealt with it most systematically – has suffered from a certain *damnatio memoriae*, and is rarely put into the social and cultural context in which it properly belongs.

The first work produced by the Italian school of fencing, *Flos duellatorum* or *Fior di battaglia* (Battle flower) by Fiore dei Liberi, presents a number of notable features. The author was a Friulian *maestro* with personal contacts in German lands, which already had an established school and a tradition of manuscripts on fencing and combat, works partially by Jewish teachers. In this respect, Fiore plays the role of mediator of cultural transfers, even in the practice of effectively combining a text with some illustrations. *Flos duellatorum* was composed in 1410 in Ferrara at the request of Niccolò III d'Este. The location and time places him between the realm of the art of war and medieval *condottieri* and the rituals of Renaissance courts. It is particularly rich in the variety of fighting techniques that it illustrates. It gives a typology of military guards, from those with a wide variety of weapons (with preference for the art of managing a two-handed sword), to combat with bare hands, to combat on horseback.[11] The number of Italian fencing treatises continued to grow between the sixteenth and seventeenth centuries, but this is not the place to discuss it in detail. It will suffice to recall the well-known and unusual case of Camillo Agrippa, an intellectual who wrote as an amateur on the topic of fencing and offered the most ambitious "mathematization" of the discipline. The discussion is evocative but did not have a great impact in the field.[12] That a number of masters and treatises had significant success abroad represents something characteristic of the international reception of the *ante-litteram* culture of sport in the Italian Renaissance. A representative of this culture, Vincenzo Saviolo, is believed to have been the first Italian author to publish a work in English, in any discipline. Saviolo, a denizen of Padua who succeeded in the management of his school by another Italian master, Rocco Bonetti, was a well-known figure in Elizabethan London. He was mentioned in one of the dialogues of John Florio, who may have played a major role in the translation of the text and in the entire editorial enterprise, and was the target of a bitter polemic of the first English writer on the aforementioned matter, George Silver.[13]

A Renaissance field of experience elaborated in Italy in which theory and practice constitute an obvious international reference point is dance. Dance was in the second half of the fifteenth century the subject of a series of treatises predominantly understood as mnemonic devices for aristocratic readers. The treatises take for granted understanding of such particulars as steps and style that had evidently been entrusted to teaching that was not based on books. Instead, the treatises contain theoretical sections devoted to the cultural aggrandizement of art and notation (by verbal description) of the choreography of specific dances.[14] Italians and Franco-Flemings stood at the forefront of developments in this era. The two languages use the same term for ballroom dance, the low dance (*bassadanza*), the most widespread of the day. Apart from the same name, however, there are upon close inspection notable differences. While the repertoire used elsewhere is of a traditional type and consists essentially of a series of ballroom dance forms, the change that takes hold in the Italian fifteenth century is directed toward the development of dance in an artistic sense, with the composition of specific choreographies normally associated with the names of their inventors, even if others transcribed them. This is precisely the case with the low dances documented in the manuscripts of the period, and with the *balli* (in a narrower or technical sense): the latter was another form of composition that is rooted in Italy, and is structured in different measures of variable musical meter and time (inspired, therefore, by an aesthetic principle that enhances rhythmic change). The variety of styles does not imply that interconnection in a broader European context is not possible: it was in fact very strong, both in the form of a vocabulary at least partially shared, or in the international familiarity with – and in the recognition of – distinct national or regional styles. One can know how to dance in the fashion of Lombardy or France even if one is not native to that area, and it may be an important strategy for public relations to become familiar with like customs of different countries.[15] The letters sent by music pedagogue Johannes Cochläus from Bologna at the beginning of the sixteenth century to the Nuremburg humanist Willibald Pirckheimer, containing (for the benefit of the recipient's daughters) a detailed description of the choreography of eight dances which the writer had seen, have been interpreted to mean different things. They certainly signal the popularity of Italian dances among the social and cultural elite of Europe, both from the point of view of the *langue* (the ensemble of rules: posture, spatial arrangement, steps and their sequence, modes of execution and stylistic idiolects) and from that of *parole* (specific choreographies and the accompanying music, known as successful pieces in any type of performance).[16]

Here again there was no lack of physical circulation among skilled personnel. Two Italian dance masters/writers offer valuable testimony, a century apart from each other. At the end of the fifteenth century Guglielmo Ebreo of Pesaro, in an appendix to one of the manuscript versions of his treatise that has been appropriately labeled an "artistic autobiography," mentions a variety of places and instances in which he choreographed festivities and danced. He thus gives testimony to the cultural ties that connected different Italian states. At the end of the sixteenth century the Milanese Cesare Negri drew up in the introduction to his work a detailed list of fifty Italian masters (in skills that included the art of tumbling), who had worked during the last generations in a wide range of locales across Europe, including France, Savoy, Flanders, Spain, the Holy Roman Empire, and Poland.[17]

The relationship established between Italian dance and Europe has to do, on the one hand, with a wide circulation of cultural models and personnel used in the realization of a variety of forms of spectacle. It also naturally has a specificity which in terms of the historical record and historiographical reconstruction makes the Italian case intertwined with the French model – which, downstream of the temporal period considered here, in the age frequently labeled 'Baroque' became culturally dominant. It has been authoritatively argued, however, that the lack of presence and influence of Italian dance in the Baroque period is at least partially the product of a nominalist squint, insofar as an Italian style different from that of the fifteenth century established itself from the middle of the sixteenth century and persisted through the seventeenth century. This finds expression in a large number of treatises (a second season, this time involving the press) and other forms of written documentation.

These are commonly classified as late Renaissance, implying that Baroque – and implicitly the whole seventeenth century – was an age and style depending on the art of dance in vogue across the Alps.[18]

The role played in Italy by Jewish dance masters opens a window for a specific ethno-cultural component (for which the documentation so far available allows only a glimpse), which might have contributed more than others in the designing of a style. It would be paradoxical but not entirely unlikely that a minority just like that of Judaism – which Nazi barbarism would purport to be recognizable even by a supposedly distinct way of walking (an examination actually practiced to identify Jews) – significantly contributed to teaching European nobility the rules of etiquette and the most refined and socially exclusive gestural forms.[19]

Within that anthropological universe which the theory and praxis of Renaissance dance realize more distinctly than in other disciplines, a dimension that cannot go unnoticed pertains to the relational identity of gender. The ballroom space established an essential repertoire of figures that converge in distinctive ways to define the image of the woman in early modern Europe. This does not mean that the era did not value the masculine expertise of dance. Indeed, the male dancer and professional dilettante are unmistakable characters on the social scene. Moreover, in the ballroom the separation of roles is not so clearly defined: while the recommendations to women to maintain a certain modesty and behavior appropriate to their condition – taken from the classical and Christian traditions – echo the moralists of the time and find their way into the text of dance treatises, they do not, in fact, shape an explicit characterization in gestures distinctly associated with man or woman.

Exchange and acceptance of models

The ludic system that developed in Renaissance Italy resulted from the combination of a lifestyle and a system of values, along with the presence of a highly qualified class of professionals, and an even greater number of dilettantes, dedicated to these activities. The professionals were not necessarily of Italian origin. Italy attracted a creative elite who, although their training may have been different, converged in an environment that, more so than elsewhere in Europe, stimulated the production, trade, and circulation of ideas and cultural artifacts. In this unique environment, cultural commodities became available for re-exportation to an international market, where they would be further adapted and reused. The immigration to Italy of Franco-Flemish musicians over generations is the most glaring evidence of the pattern, which is too simplistically explained purely in terms of patronage and the availability of financial resources.

Italy quite naturally saw the influx of foreigners impelled by a variety of motives, not necessarily linked to the activities under discussion here. Nevertheless, Italy welcomed them and gave them the opportunity to develop and publicize the skills for which they have come to be remembered. Religious persecution constituted one of the most frequent and characteristic causes of emigration. An example of this is Pedro Damião of Odemira, a Jewish pharmacist expelled from Portugal at the end of the fifteenth century. He emigrated to Rome, where he published, in 1512, an Italian–Spanish book on chess, later rendered in several editions, including translations in French and English. The work contains, as is customary, a description of the origins of the game. It outlines the rules and potential openings. It offers suggestions and answers problems, which the author calls 'subtleties.' The scope of table and parlor games – recreations viewed as more spiritual than physical – constituted a point of Italian culture in a Europe context, in ways closely intertwined with the development of the art of conversation.[20]

The converse – Italians abroad – represents perhaps the best-known form of circulation. Cultural models traveled on the legs of people who crossed political and linguistic boundaries: the Italian aristocrat who settled often permanently in foreign monarchies (for marriage, or court service), the ones with entrepreneurial undertakings, or even (like the foreigners in Italy) prompted by other reasons. We have already mentioned the case of the movement across Europe of Italian choreographers and dancers, as well as the presence in London of weaponry masters from the Italian peninsula. The latter has been painted in very vibrant colors in the fresco on the Italian Renaissance in England created at the beginning of the twentieth century by Lewis Einstein:

> It is curious to think that England, which today claims superiority in sport, should have submitted in the sixteenth century to Italian methods and instruction. The accomplishments and pleasures of the courtly life had, however, first been systematized in Italy, and in sport, as well, its guidance was supreme.[21]

This, the American scholar says, is valid for horsemanship. Edward VI had at his disposal an Italian instructor and the first treatise published in English, which is nothing more than Thomas Blundeville's translation (1560) of the *Ordini di cavalcare* by the Neapolitan gentleman Federico Grisone. It was the same for hunting and falconry. "It was in fencing, however, then so essential a part of the gentleman's education, that the skill of the Italian showed itself to the greatest advantage." The result was both a presence of teachers and a circulation of treatises: in addition to that of Saviolo, Giacomo Grassi's *Ragione di adoprar sicuramente l'arme* was also translated into English (1594).[22]

Between the mid-sixteenth and mid-seventeenth centuries, masters-at-arms together with masters of horsemanship became familiar figures in France – first in their service at court, later also finding their way into the capital city. Between 1551 and 1663 some thirty masters-at-arms and Italian squires became naturalized French citizens. In Paris, the masters-at-arms were well known to one another. They lived in the same locale (the Faubourg Saint-Germain) and worked together, adding to the Italian color of the profession. As for horsemanship, Italian superiority existed since the fourteenth century, and the French aristocracy in the sixteenth century, regardless of religious affiliations, made use of the services of Italian squires. In France, Italians also managed activities related to breeding and training horses – themes that are traditionally treated in the treatises in the field of horsemanship.[23]

A particularly interesting case, if only for the relative rarity of the expertise to which it testifies, is that of Arcangelo Tuccaro, a gymnast from Abruzzo who published in Paris the first treatise on acrobatics at the end of the sixteenth century. Tuccaro had been a member of the court of Maximilian II of Austria. In 1570 he accompanied Maximilian's daughter Isabella to France when she married King Charles IX, a sovereign who was fond of physical exercise. Tuccaro remained in the service of the French court as master of ceremonies and a choreographer under the succeeding reigns of Henry III and Henry IV. His dialogues are not lacking in classical erudition and boast of exercise's medical benefits. It has been suggested that one must read and appreciate especially "that engagement and refinement and ennoblement of the exercises performed in squares by tightrope walkers, jugglers, acrobats, etc., to finally raise them to the rank of art and entertainment, well able to interest more than just the common classes."[24] This angle opens interesting perspectives of interpretation of what was going on in terms of the athletic expertise in different environments and at different levels in the social hierarchy of the time; while, more generally, it holds well with the strategy of writing as a technique (or tentative) aiming toward the ennoblement of a corporeal skill, which also agrees well with the contemporary treatises on dance (with which, in any case, Tuccaro's dialogues are closely related).[25]

This series of cultural exchanges has left many linguistic traces. The first Italian manual of combat, an anonymous manuscript from the second half of the fifteenth century, was inspired by the Spanish technical vocabulary, at some points including the invention of new words and, in other cases, limiting itself to minimal adaptations or even pure and simple adoptions; meanwhile, in the sixteenth century the Italian vocabulary of horsemanship, in turn, lent a number of terms to French (such as in *terre à terre, pésade, pirouette, groupade, capriole,* or *pas et saut,* which appear in transalpine manuals starting with *Maneige royal* of Pluvinel in 1623).[26] The same is true of English in the sixteenth century with regard to fencing and again, horsemanship: the need to understand its technical language offers Florio a justification for publishing his Italian–English dictionary.[27]

Performance versus audience

The game of real tennis, with the added attracting element of betting on the outcome of matches, was at least in part a spectator sport, wherein wealthy patrons hired professional players. This tendency is well known and encompasses the entire realm of Renaissance entertainment from theater to music. It thus also interests the spectacular aspects (both theater and music) of dance. The increasing distinction between specialists of more sophisticated physical techniques and audience naturally had older roots, and to some extent the throws or the most daring contortions constitute a gestural repertoire apart from that of the dominant social classes (as well as of the common individual), associated with a liminal professionalism reserved for athletes and circus exhibitions (thus also to a social status of public entertainer which was anything but flattering). To some extent, therefore, this is the age in which a path of long-term social differentiation in the arts reached a consummation – or at least an advanced level of maturity, to an epochal stay: the one marked, in any case, by the advent of academies and other specific institutions and by the emergence of performances for a paying audience. A society that was gradually surtaxed with – and that correspondingly went on to introject – measures of distinction and discipline could do nothing but proceed, even in this area, in the direction of a growing separation of roles.

Nevertheless, this would be too brief and obvious a lesson to draw from the whole experience that we have here tried to examine. Professional dancers, horsemen, fencers, or tennis players certainly set the stage in various forms of performance, themselves with a story that is rich and intertwined. But it is equally true that in those same disciplines, and at levels barely recognizable as inferior from the point of view of their technical and athletic requirements, as well as the aesthetic quality of the results, generations of royals, gentlemen and ladies, did not evade exhausting bouts of training and improvement, and apparently had more than one reason (personal ones or those of state and rank, such as the need to stand out from plebeians) for wanting to appear proficient and elegant in public. The attention devoted by members of Italian noble dynasties like the Este to obtaining this quality, and the skill with which one knew how to utilize it as a diplomatic tool in the preparation of parties and shows, offer clear testimony.[28] There was indeed upon close inspection a true climax with regard to this matter. The last chronological stage considered here corresponds, in terms of the historical development of Italian and European dance, to the "age of the galliard," where techniques and fashionable aesthetic models required vigor and an uncommon physical agility, even for the dilettante.[29] From this point of view, the Renaissance is perhaps the last period in which the dominant cultural models allow a degree of confusion between the lifestyle of the elite and a showmanship at its histrionic limits, or athletic programs for professional gymnasts.[30]

Play and civilization

What has been said so far should suggest that the stakes of the ludic system developed in Renaissance Italy, in close and fruitful communication and mutual exchange with other cultural centers in Europe and the Mediterranean, had implications that go far beyond the recreational use of the skills learned and exhibited. The treatises that have been taken into account here, and social practices that have been represented, confronted openly, and often with original solutions, the problems of intermingling orality and writing, of mental learning and the embodiment of technical skills. They did so in a period that, from art to science, produced a breakthrough in the West in terms of geometrizing space: the ground of dance and the exercise of fencing significantly contributed to define this evolution in sensibility, in perceptual systems, in the bodily experience of individuals, and in their mutual interaction.[31]

Presenting the case of the dance in the early modern Dutch Republic, Herman Roodenburg has confronted the paradox of distinctive features in posture, in poise and in gesture, and more generally in the behavior of the ruling classes, largely presented as innate and un-teachable by those same authors who, by discussing them in their works, to some extent at least assumed the task of transferring them. That the models developed primarily in aristocratic environments were one of the main vehicles of the social climb of bourgeois groups provides further evidence of their relative transmissibility. Yet a paradox existed; and the Dutch historian suggests that the way out of the potential impasse was in a *corporeal memory*, which could have resulted in *habitus* by means of demanding but informal training, outside of the academic training circuits: "a world of family tradition and parental advice, of private tutors, of making a grand tour or even serving at court."[32] If the fate of these patterns of behavior was undoubtedly European, the time and place of their ultimate and most sophisticated elaboration is not hard to identify:

> [T]he first users of this *je ne sais quoi* are found in Renaissance Italy. It denoted an indefinable grace, an elusive quality that Cicero already described as *venustas* or *suavitas*, and Quintilian as *gratia*. But it is a grace, according to Agnolo Firenzuola, "which is not in our books" and which is, "as one says of things that we do not know how to express, *un non so che*." ... As Cesare Gonzaga, one of the characters in Castiglione's famous dialogue, put it, it is a grace or seasoning that should accompany all the courtier's actions, gestures and habits – in short, his every movement.[33]

It is not extraordinary, then, if the exercise of the dance itself supplies Castiglione one of the most appropriate purviews to illustrate the concept of *sprezzatura*, or nonchalance (*Cortegiano*, I, 28: "Lykewyse in daunsinge, one measure, one mocion of a bodye that hath a good grace, not being forced, doeth by and by declare the knowledge of him that daunseth"). On the other hand, the 'Baroque' Italian treatises (like that of Fabrizio Caroso, whose illustrations by Giacomo Franco are also famous as a source that informs us on the dazzling attire of the era) faced the issue of good manners head-on, assuming also, specifically and in detail, the task of providing the rules of etiquette on behavior at parties during which people danced. That the learning of dance (as well as of a variety of other skills with a physical dimension, from real tennis to fencing and horsemanship, while observing the respective properties of one kind or another) represented a crucial source of encouragement for the learning of these fields of bodily knowledge, clarifies the decision to conclude an essay on the ludic by talking about *civilité*; and it documents best how this dimension of early modern society was anything but marginal – as already underlined by Roodenburg's famous Dutch counterpart and predecessor Johan Huizinga.

It would yet be too simplistic to close the discussion here without expounding some of the social implications, which have repeatedly emerged. In a sense, this chapter has focused in good measure on treatises, testimonies in a certain way indirect with respect to the documentation of actual practices – regulative sources, which typically express intentions rather than reality. Additionally – and the two limitations are correlated – the discussion has prioritized the ludic culture of the elite, above that of other groups (that is, the majority) of the population. This fact should not surprise, since it belongs to rather common and obvious distortions, which have largely to do with the nature of the documents available. The thread that connects these two problems is the nature of Renaissance tracts on sport and games that have been discussed here. They are often tied to the court environment or anyway to that of the dominant aristocracy. Sometimes such social connection is evident in the mere occasional circumstances of publications (dedications and other paratexts), other times in more structural terms, when the instruction of noble patrons in the subjects concerned is the *raison d'être* for the production of a work, handwritten or printed. This sociologically disproportionate representation has historical and cultural roots that account also for the weight that powerful minorities exerted on the system of values and way of life of the rest of the population. This acknowledgement is not, however, the result of an ideological or epistemological choice that implicitly considered members of the powerful minority as the only ones worthy of consideration, or those who decided tastes in a unidirectional manner.

The signs to the contrary – namely, that the interrelationships between the different levels were complex and exchanges multidirectional – are manifold. In the preceding remarks, the 'learning paradox' (Roodenburg) was mentioned, for which social distinction, ideologically given as a precondition to excel over others, was in fact something else: a habitus which required a process of acquisition, and as such could escape the monopoly that some have purported it would function to help preserve. The historiography of the twentieth century has spoken, for Renaissance dance, of "noble dance." But the same choreography that was composed for court settings also thrived in urban environments; furthermore, in Italian cities artisans and merchants had available numerous dance schools in which to learn the same dance forms that were practiced in high society. In fact, to mark their distinction, the aristocracy was forced to resort to more effectively exclusive status symbols such as conspicuous waste and the ostentation of clothing, jewelry or other objects, instead of an inherent recognition of a heritage of gestural and corporeal practices. Not to mention the custom of cultural elements that climb, rather than descend, the hierarchical ladder (in the opposite direction, therefore, to the supposed "civilizing process"), a case which was invoked in the example of subsuming the acrobatic culture of Tuccaro. In addition, the masters, schools, and treatises represent, in hindsight, a difficult world to liken *sic et simpliciter* to that of the elite: they were the custodians of a practical knowledge that is first transmitted in oral form; they were engaged in a battle to improve their status and see the artistic content of their profession (which for them is exactly such, and not free time) recognized and valued; they may have depended on the patronage of their lords, but with that world they could hardly aspire to identify.[34] A multiplicity of cultures was inevitably at play.

Notes

1 Federico Barbierato and Barbara Sparti offered valuable comments and suggestions to an earlier draft of this contribution. Sadly, the intervening passing away of Barbara leaves me in the condition of only being able to thank Federico.

2 J. Huizinga, *Homo ludens*, London, 1949 [1938], p. 180. For general surveys of related matter: J. McClelland, *Body and Mind: Sport in Europe from the Roman Empire to the Renaissance*, London, 2007; L. Turcot, *Histoire des loisirs et des sports*, Paris, 2016 (forthcoming).

3 For this theme I refer to A. Arcangeli, *Recreation in the Renaissance: Attitudes towards Leisure and Pastimes in European Culture, 1425–1675*, Basingstoke, 2003, ch. 3 (Italian trans.: *Passatempi rinascimentali: storia culturale del divertimento in Europa (secoli XV–XVII)*, Rome, 2004, ch. 4).

4 On the author and his work see *Girolamo Mercuriale: medicina e cultura nell'Europa del Cinquecento*, A. Arcangeli and V. Nutton, eds., Florence, 2008; for the text and illustrations: G. Mercuriale, *De arte gymnastica*, ed. C. Pennuto, trans. V. Nutton, with an essay by J.-M. Agasse, Florence, 2008.

5 P. Montis, *De dignoscendis hominibus*, Milan, 1492; P. Montis, *Exercitiorum atque artis militaris collectanea*, Milan, 1509. Cf. S. Anglo, "The Man Who Taught Leonardo Darts. Pietro Monte and His 'Lost' Fencing Book," *Antiquaries Journal*, 69 (1989), pp. 261–78; S. Anglo, *The Martial Arts of Renaissance Europe*, New Haven, 2000, pp. 317–18 and *ad indicem*; M. M. Fontaine, *Le condottiere Pietro del Monte, philosophe et écrivain de la Renaissance (1457–1509)*, Geneva, 1991 (continued in a series of subsequent contributions), which includes four pages (pp. 73–7) of extracts from the diaries of Marino Sanudo. The passage of the *Courtier* is: "And of men whom we know nowadayes, mark how wel and with what a good grace Sir Galiazzo Sanseverino, M. of the horse to the Frenche king, doth all exercises of the body: and that because, besyde the naturall disposition of person that is in him, he hath applyed all his study to learne of cunning men, and to have continually excellent men about hym, and of every one to chuse the best of that they have skill in. For as in wrastling, in vawting, and in learning to handle sundry kinde of weapons he hath taken for his guide oure M. Peter Mount, who (as you know) is the true and only maister of al artificiall force and slight: so in ridyng, in justyng, and everye other feate, he hath alwayes had before his eyes the most perfectest that hath ben knowen to be in those professions." The text is that of Thomas Hoby's sixteenth-century translation, used throughout this chapter.

6 C. Méndez, *Libro del ejercicio corporal y de sus provechos*, ed. E. Álvarez del Palacio, León, 1996.

7 Cf. L. Caporossi, "Gioco e tempo nell'*Appartamento dello Specchio* del castello estense di Ferrara. Ipotesi per il programma iconografico di Pirro Ligorio," *Ludica*, 8 (2002), pp. 98–114.

8 Cf. C. de Bondt, *Royal Tennis in Renaissance Italy*, Turnhout, 2006.

9 *Ibid.*, p. 202.

10 Cf. Anglo, *The Martial Arts*.

11 Cf. *Sport e giuochi: trattati e scritti dal XV al XVIII secolo*, ed. C. Bascetta, Milan, 1978, vol. 2, pp. 125–44; Anglo, *The Martial Arts, ad indicem*.

12 Cf. *Sport e giuochi*, vol. 2, p. 186; Anglo, *The Martial Arts, ad indicem*.

13 *Vincentio Saviolo, his practise, in two bookes*, London 1595; the second book is largely a translation of *Duello* by Girolamo Muzio. Cf. S. Rossi, "*Vincentio Saviolo his Practise* (1595): A Problem of Authorship," in *England and the Continental Renaissance*, ed. E. Chaney and P. Mack, Woodbridge, 1990, pp. 165–75.

14 Cf. A. Pontremoli and P. La Rocca, *Il ballare lombardo: teoria e prassi coreutica nella festa di corte del XV secolo*, Milan, 1987; J. Nevile, *The Eloquent Body: Dance and Humanist Culture in Fifteenth-Century Italy*, Bloomington, 2004; J. Nevile, "The Early Dance Manuals and the Structure of Ballet: A Basis for

Italian, French and English Ballet," in *The Cambridge Companion to Ballet*, ed. M. Kant, Cambridge, 2007, pp. 9–18.

15 Cf. M. Nordera, "The Exchange of Dance Cultures in Renaissance Europe: Italy, France and Abroad," in *Cultural Exchange in Early Modern Europe*, ed. R. Muchembled, vol. 4, *Forging European Identities*, ed. H. Roodenburg, Cambridge, 2007, pp. 308–28.

16 Cf. I. Brainard, "L'arte del danzare in transizione: un documento tedesco sconosciuto sulla danza di corte," *La danza italiana*, 3 (1985), p. 77–89; I. Wetzel, ' "Hie innen sindt geschrieben die wellschen tennt': le otto danze italiane del manoscritto di Norimberga," in *Guglielmo Ebreo da Pesaro e la danza nelle corti italiane del XV secolo*, ed. M. Padovan, Pisa, 1990, pp. 321–43.

17 Cf. F. A. Gallo, "L'autobiografia artistica di Giovanni Ambrosio (Guglielmo Ebreo) da Pesaro," *Studi musicali*, 12 (1983), pp. 189–202; Nordera, "The Exchange of Dance Cultures." As pointed out by Katherine McGinnis (' "Your Most Humble Servant, Cesare Negri," ' in *Dance, Spectacle, and the Body Politick, 1250–1750*, ed. J. Nevile, Bloomington, 2008, pp. 211–28), Negri was also at the service of the King of France, but surprisingly neglected to mention such an important episode in his *curriculum vitae*, presumably due to the little convenience that it would pose in a Milan under Spanish rule.

18 Cf. B. Sparti, "La 'danza barocca' è soltanto francese?' " *Studi musicali*, 25 (1996), pp. 283–302. The fact contains something of a paradox if one considers – without wanting to revive parochial polemics that have been duly buried – that, according to a historiographic commonplace that could admittedly be reconsidered, 'French ballet' was introduced in Paris at the end of the sixteenth century by an Italian choreographer named Belgioioso.

19 Cf. B. Sparti, "Maestri di danza ebrei nel Rinascimento italiano: una danza ebraica?" in *Danza, cultura e società nel Rinascimento italiano*, ed. E. Casini Ropa and F. Bortoletti, Macerata, 2007, pp. 49–63. In addition, the contribution of the Jewish community is a motif that is found more frequently in the physical culture of Europe, and one which we have already found in the case of medieval German books on fencing.

20 On this, along with other themes mentioned here, see also my "Gioco e festa tra Rinascimento e Barocco," in L. L. Cavalli Sforza (dir.), *La cultura italiana*, vol. 6, *Cibo, gioco, festa, moda*, ed. C. Petrini and U. Volli, Turin, 2009, pp. 284–315.

21 L. Einstein, *The Italian Renaissance in England: Studies*, New York, 1902, pp. 69–73: 69.

22 *Ibid.*, p. 70.

23 Cf. J.-F. Dubost, *La France italienne: XVIe–XVIIe siècle*, Paris 1997, pp. 99–104 (*le spectacle italien*), 104–9 (*maîtres d'armes et voltigeurs*). The academy directed by Antoine de Pluvinel in Paris, in around 1600, took the Italian record in this area as so much for granted that it explicitly aimed to provide equestrian education to the French nobles while avoiding the need and inconvenience to travel in Italy: on this topic see now A. Bruschi, *Le accademie nobiliari francesi tra progetto e realtà (1570–1750)*, Milan, 2015.

24 A. Tuccaro, *Trois dialogues de l'exercice de sauter et voltiger en l'air*, Paris, 1599; cf. *Sport e giuochi*, vol. 1, pp. 28ff. (at p. 30). See now S. Schmidt, *Kopfübern und Luftspringen. Bewegung als Wissenschaft und Kunst in der Frühen Neuzeit*, Munich, 2008.

25 See *Réduire en art. La technologie de la Renaissance aux Lumières*, ed. P. Dubourg Glatigny and H. Vérin, Paris, 2008.

26 Cf. C. Bascetta, "Codes verbaux de jeu et littérature sportive italienne," in *Les jeux à la Renaissance*, ed. P. Ariès and J.-C. Margolin, Paris, 1982, pp. 95–107: 98–9.

27 Cf. Einstein, *The Italian Renaissance*, pp. 72, 70.

28 Cf. B. Sparti, "Isabella and the Dancing Este Brides, 1473–1514," in *Women's Work. Making Dance in Europe before 1800*, ed. L. Matluck Brooks, Madison, WI, 2008, pp. 19–48.

29 Echoing a felicitous expression of Curt Sachs – which drew inspiration from a form of dance that, with its endless variations ('mutanze'), dominated the halls of the time – a denomination in this sense for that season of Italian dance, which goes roughly from 1500 to 1650, was most recently revived by B. Sparti, "Historical Introduction," in E. Santucci Perugino, *Mastro da Ballo (1614)*, Hildesheim, 2004 (reproduction of the author's original manuscript), pp. 1–13.

30 On physical vigor and its manifestation as a sign of power (in France, at the dawn of the modern age) there is also the work of G. Vigarello, "S'exercer, jouer," in *Histoire du corps*, ed. A. Corbin, J.-J. Courtine, and G. Vigarello, vol. 1, *De la Renaissance aux Lumières*, ed. G. Vigarello, Paris, 2005, pp. 235–301.

31 I remit to the conclusions of A. Arcangeli, *Davide o Salomè? Il dibattito europeo sulla danza nella prima età moderna*, Rome, 2000, pp. 321–7; but one should also remember Anglo, *The Martial Arts*.

32 H. Roodenburg, "Dancing in the Dutch Republic: The Uses of Bodily Memory," in Roodenburg, ed., *Forging European Identities*, pp. 329–60: 359.

33 *Ibid.*, p. 330.

34 There is evidence offered for a variety of different interpretations on the nature of these themes and professional figures in the different contributions in the already cited volume *Danza, cultura e società*, ed. Casini Ropa and Bortoletti; this is found in detail in the above-mentioned section of *La cultura italiana* (see note 20).

19

WAR, ENTREPRENEURSHIP, AND POLITICS

Suzanne Sutherland

On 25 February 1634, the commander-in-chief of the imperial army, Albrecht Wallenstein, was assassinated with the approval of the Austrian Habsburg emperor, Ferdinand II (r. 1619–37). This notorious murder was organized by a group of Italian commanders, including Matthias Gallas, Rudolfo Colloredo, and Wallenstein's trusted subordinate, Ottavio Piccolomini (1599–1656). These men made their careers in Central Europe during the Thirty Years War (1618–48), but had emerged from the Italian *condottiere* tradition with its origins in the Renaissance. The assassination allowed Piccolomini and Gallas to move to the very top of the Austrian military hierarchy, an Italian coup that permitted them to promote their friends and followers more effectively.[1] Although he was not involved in the plot, Raimondo Montecuccoli (1609–80), a nobleman from Modena, would rely on Piccolomini, Gallas, and other Italians to propel his career in imperial service. He eventually became commander-in-chief of the Austrian army, President of the Imperial War Council, and a respected military theorist.[2]

This international group of plotters and assassins and their clients were military entrepreneurs. Military entrepreneurs exploited private wealth and credit to raise, maintain, and sometimes command soldiers in a contractual agreement with a prince, leading contemporaries to lament the "traffic or commerce" of war "in which he who has most money wins."[3] While military historians have become increasingly aware that military contracting continued to evolve in the seventeenth and early eighteenth centuries alongside the growth of global trade and credit markets, few examine its political consequences.[4] By contrast, in his iconic work on the Italian Renaissance, Jacob Burckhardt portrayed the *condottiere* as an independent, self-made man who used force and calculation to rise above his origins and create and defend a new kind of political legitimacy. He argued that the modern state, characterized by a centralized government, bureaucratic officials, and the complete sovereignty of the prince within his territory, emerged through this process.[5] Burckhardt's view of the state has been criticized for not capturing the complex, shifting, and pluralistic nature of early modern power, while his conception of the self-made man ignored the collectivist tendencies of Renaissance society.[6] Nevertheless, Burckhardt's perception of the significance of mercenaries for revealing patterns of political life that were intimately connected to other dynamic dimensions of the Renaissance – art, literature, personality, etc. – remains useful.[7]

For the seventeenth century, military men who moved back and forth between masters and ascended to power in distant hierarchies show the important role played by transregional networks in supplying the resources and expertise that built state power. At the same time, military entrepreneurs and their networks destabilized state authority since these men were semi-autonomous and might seek employment with more than one patron.[8] As a result, their loyalties – as Machiavelli lamented and Wallenstein's case showed – were questionable. Rather than condemn these paradoxical figures as disloyal, however, their careers provide ideal case studies for examining political strategies and conceptions of allegiance in an age more broadly characterized by "multiple loyalties."[9]

Italian military traditions and international networks

In the sixteenth and seventeenth centuries, many Italian elites embraced the noble call to arms. The fragmented peninsula, with its ceaseless fighting and political intrigue, as well as the financial resources of merchants and bankers, inspired the development of a robust mercenary tradition. The invasion of outside powers during the sixteenth-century Italian Wars militarized the Italian peninsula, turning it into a laboratory for testing out new technologies, tactics, and strategies, including the development of the *trace italienne*.[10] As Italians mastered the latest advancements in warfare and initiated proud family traditions of service, a Renaissance of war flowered, in which theorists and practitioners attempted to apply ancient military ideas to the present. With the conclusion of peace in 1559 and the domination of the peninsula by the Spanish Habsburgs, significant numbers of Italians took their military expertise and traditions abroad, serving in various – but mainly Habsburg – arenas of conflict.[11]

Prior to the Thirty Years War, the two most popular battlefield destinations were Flanders and Hungary, where Catholic supporters of the Habsburgs were pitted against Protestants and Muslims. The greatest commanders of the Spanish Army of Flanders, Alessandro Farnese and Ambrogio Spinola, were from Parma and Genoa, while as much as 10–20 percent of the entire army was composed of Italians. Spain employed a variety of strategies to encourage the service and loyalty of Italian princes and nobles, granting subsidies, revenues, titles, admission to military orders, and land as rewards.[12] In the Lombard Trotti and Visconti families, military careers in Spanish service evolved across multiple generations, elevating the family's status.[13] Many of those with experience in Flanders later fought in the Thirty Years War, such as the Neapolitan nobleman, Tommaso Caracciolo.[14]

While some Thirty Years War commanders started out in the War in Flanders, others had served in Hungary during the Long Turkish War.[15] Some of these noblemen maintained traditional feudal bonds to the Holy Roman Emperor – the most prestigious title that the Austrian Habsburg monarch held. Alleged to be the successor of the Roman Empire, the Holy Roman Empire had stretched into northern Italy at its medieval peak. The power of the Holy Roman Emperor was indirect, but conferred advantages upon petty princes and nobles bickering over status and position.[16] Many Italian families even claimed descent from medieval German warlords. Rambaldo Collato (1575–1630) came from a Venetian *terra firma* family that connected their territorial rights to Charlemagne. The Collalto family produced "men excellent and valorous in war" whose members served Venice, the Pope, the French king, and the Holy Roman Emperor.[17] Rambaldo pledged allegiance to Venice but later threw off Venetian ties to pursue a career under the Austrian Habsburgs. After serving in the Long Turkish War, he headed imperial forces in the War of the Mantuan Succession, became President of the Imperial War Council and a Knight of the Golden Fleece, and received Moravian estates.[18]

Marriage alliances also linked Italian noblemen to Central Europe. Emperors Ferdinand II and Ferdinand III each married a Gonzaga woman (both named Eleonora) in the effort to create a stable alliance with Mantua and to protect the military corridor that ran through northern Italy. These Gonzaga empresses promoted Italian musicians, artists, gardeners, and doctors, as well as military men, including at least two Imperial War Council Presidents: Collalto, a distant Gonzaga relative, and Annibale Gonzaga.[19] In 1656, the second Empress Eleonora co-founded a twelve-member Italian academy with Archduke Leopold Wilhelm that drew together an international cadre of military–diplomatic elites whose resources, expertise, and connections helped the Habsburgs assert and defend their interests across a wide swath of Europe.[20]

The War of the Mantuan Succession (1628–31), an episode of the Thirty Years War fought on Italian soil, tested the fraught relationships of the period. In 1627, Duke Vincenzo II of Mantua died without direct heirs and a French-born relative, Duke Charles of Nevers, took the helm of government. As Holy Roman Emperor, Ferdinand II had the right to confirm or deny Nevers' rule and Empress Eleonora hoped to entice Nevers into the imperial camp. However, Olivares, fearful of a potential French ally in Mantua, allowed Spanish-allied troops to invade the Mantuan dependency Monferrato and lay siege to Casale. This military move put an end to negotiations and set off a chain of events that drew aggressive reactions from both the French and Nevers. Ferdinand II protected his authority in the region by committing imperial forces as well.[21] Historians examining conflicts like the Mantuan Succession crisis tend to focus on the way the larger Habsburg–Bourbon rivalry played out at the expense of small Italian states. However, the activities of minor Italian actors impacted events.[22] One of the reasons that Ferdinand II had delayed in recognizing Nevers' claim and resolving the issue peacefully was that he needed to placate the Gonzaga military families allied to him by obtaining compensation from Nevers. Once Ferdinand II resolved to send imperial forces, many Italian noblemen – perhaps even some of those dissatisfied Gonzaga relatives – joined the army under Collalto, murderously sacking the city and ransacking the fabulous Gonzaga collections in 1630.[23] The Habsburgs needed the support of Italian noblemen, but these figures had their own familial goals that complicated wider relations.

Marriage alliances also deepened connections between Central Europe and Tuscany. Grand Duke Cosimo II's wife was Emperor Ferdinand II's sister, Maria Maddalena of Austria. During the Thirty Years War, Cosimo's sister, Claudia, and his daughter, Anna, both married Austrian archdukes, becoming Countesses of the Tyrol.[24] Two of Cosimo's sons, Mattias and Francesco, led troops during the Thirty Years War (Francesco fell ill and died in Central Europe). Mattias returned home to become Governor of Siena and head the Tuscan militia but maintained his Central European connections, using contacts in the imperial army to offer opportunities for Tuscans and to obtain specialized military services for his brother, Grand Duke Ferdinando II.[25]

The most illustrious Tuscan military career that flowered out of these ties belonged to Wallenstein's betrayer, Ottavio Piccolomini, who arrived in Central Europe with troops organized by Grand Duke Cosimo II to support the Austrian Habsburgs at the start of the Thirty Years War.[26] Piccolomini's father, Silvio, had fought in Flanders and Hungary, returning to Florence to become a Knight of Malta and Cosimo's Artillery General. Medici patronage extended to Silvio's son: when Ottavio headed to Central Europe, he carried letters of recommendation from Maria Maddalena.[27] Later, Piccolomini commanded a regiment at the Siege of Mantua and became a close confidant of Wallenstein's before orchestrating his assassination. Piccolomini was full of military ardor: as he gathered his troops during the retreat from the 1632 Battle of Lützen, three horses were shot out from under him and he was "grazed" by bullets seven times.[28]

Piccolomini's activities occurred within a broader military exchange between Tuscany and Central Europe. From 1560 to 1710, Siena and Florence appear to have supplied ninety-one officers to the Austrian army.[29] Florence became a stepping stone to Habsburg service for noblemen from other parts of the peninsula. Bartolomaio Strassoldo, who came from a region with feudal ties to the Holy Roman Emperor and a pattern of imperial military service, built connections in Florence at the start of his career. He served as a page to Grand Duke Ferdinando in 1636 before transferring to Piccolomini's regiment in 1640.[30] Strassoldo's case illustrates not only how dynastic alliances re-shaped feudal networks, but also how the reputations of individual military entrepreneurs generated new centers of gravity within these evolving sets of transregional relationships. Finally, the movements of soldiers were not unidirectional. Many commanders came back when military opportunities abroad dissipated or when conflicts erupted in the Italian peninsula. When Pope Urban VIII invaded the small central Italian Duchy of Castro, triggering the 1642–44 War of Castro, Italian rulers demanded that vassals serving abroad return home.[31] They may have hoped these vassals would bring troops with them or at least recruit new soldiers at short notice. In other cases, patrons at Italian courts might arrange for the transfer of military clients between two geographically distant nodes, playing a hand in the far-off movements of men.[32]

Access to troops and political influence abroad were two reasons that rulers encouraged their vassals to secure appointments in foreign armies and courts. These rulers understood the power military entrepreneurs exerted when they raised the capital and credit for the recruitment and funding of troops. The desire for the emperor's authority to exact contributions on imperial/Habsburg lands bound military entrepreneurs to Ferdinand II to some degree, but their regiments remained personal investments.[33] If military entrepreneurs were unsatisfied, there was a sense that they might take their troops (or at least their capital and credit) somewhere more profitable, a fact which even influenced official diplomatic negotiations. Peter Lindström and Svante Norrhem have analyzed the ways patron–client networks composed of "transnational families" provided France and Austria with critical military access and political influence abroad as they became great powers.[34] Transregional clientage networks were also tools of small-scale Italian rulers.[35]

Norbert Elias depicted the seventeenth-century court as a center of domestication of the nobility where unruly, warrior elites settled into a dependent relationship on the prince and either abandoned their arms for courtly display or were absorbed into a rigid military organization controlled by the monarch.[36] However, as Mantua and Florence reveal, courts were not self-contained – they were permeable and connected to other courts – nor were they necessarily the end points of careers.[37] Courtiers might chase marriage alliances or famous generals with the support of a local prince, moving within a political circuit that defied the parameters of the territorial state. Furthermore, the military opportunities that permitted much of this movement combined private and public elements of organization, allowing warriors to retain some autonomy. In the seventeenth century, both noblemen and common soldiers moved frequently and rapidly across Europe serving different generals and rulers, a testament to the fact that states, empires, and allegiances were in flux. Raimondo

Montecuccoli stepped into this context when he decided to take up the pike at age sixteen. He achieved remarkable success because of the way he understood his environment and took advantage of opportunities.

From Modena to Central Europe and back

Montecuccoli was born in a remote castle in the Appennine Mountains, but his ties to the Modenese court ruled by the Este family offered an entryway into a wider world. Montecuccoli's father, Galeotto, had served the Duke of Modena as a provincial governor. When Montecuccoli's mother moved the family to Modena after Galeotto's death, Duke Cesare's brother, Cardinal Alessandro, took Montecuccoli and his brother, Massimiliano, under his wing. From there, Raimondo and Massimiliano glided into a vibrant, cosmo-politan Catholic world in which courts, armies, and religious orders formed pathways for young nobles. Both boys, intending to pursue careers in the church, traveled with Cardinal Alessandro to Rome for the 1623 papal enclave that elected Urban VIII. Montecuccoli soon rejected the tonsure for the sword. He got his first glimpse of war after Collalto visited the Este court in 1625 and took Montecuccoli back to the imperial army. Massimiliano became a Jesuit in 1632 and traveled to Paraguay. Other members of the family would display strik-ing patterns of movement, taking up positions in Modena, Florence, the Tyrol, Vienna, and Flanders.[38]

Besides service to the Este family, the Montecuccoli clan boasted of long-standing imperial ties. In 1368, Emperor Charles IV confirmed the investiture of the Montecuccoli fiefs and permitted use of the imperial eagle in their coat of arms. In 1581, Emperor Rudolf II legiti-mized the birth of Montecuccoli's father, Galeotto. Galeotto had served in Habsburg con-flicts, but Montecuccoli's older relative, Ernesto, carved the most spectacular path.[39] Ernesto Montecuccoli fought in the regiment of Giorgio Basta during the Long Turkish War along-side another young recruit: Wallenstein. Ernesto remained close to Wallenstein throughout the Bohemian general's meteoric rise, eventually filling in for Wallenstein as commander-in-chief when Wallenstein fell ill during the Thirty Years War. Since older male relatives usually provided positions for younger relatives and regiments could be inherited, Ernesto's position was a windfall for young Raimondo.[40] Montecuccoli's real career began around 1629 as an ensign in the troops under Ernesto. Ernesto died in 1633 and Montecuccoli inherited his regiment in 1635, at which point he became a colonel and would have assumed the major responsibilities of a military entrepreneur: recruiting men, raising credit, and subcontracting to the captains of companies. Montecuccoli must have excelled at his duties: he commanded four regiments at the 1636 Battle of Wittstock.[41]

In 1644, Montecuccoli recited the sacrifices his family had made in imperial service:

> I don't speak of the Count Giovan Galeotto Montecuccoli, my father, who in his youth served and commanded three companies in the Hungarian wars, neither of Count Ernesto, my uncle, who died of three wounds as a prisoner of the Swedish in Colmar, nor of Count Girolamo my brother, who also died in imperial service, nor of my cousin killed, nor of my brother rendered lame in the Battle of Wittstock.[42]

With so many relatives serving – and some dying for – Habsburg causes, it became almost natural for an Italian family's loyalties and sense of purpose to be directed beyond the Alps in the late sixteenth and early seventeenth centuries. Perhaps this is why Montecuccoli wrote in a 1644 petition to Emperor Ferdinand II that the "fervor of devotion and faithfulness," which accompanied his desire for imperial military service, had been "absorbed with my milk."[43] Ideological and familial motivations for joining imperial service thus merged.

The transregional military alliances of these families grew richer and more complex as they pursued strategies of intermarriage much like emperors and princes. Both the Piccolomini and Montecuccoli families were related to the Caprara family. Enea Caprara, who was Ottavio Piccolomini's nephew, became Raimondo Montecuccoli's agent. The Caprara–Piccolomini alliance produced an impressive continuity of family ownership of a certain imperial regiment from its founding in the late 1620s to 1701.[44] In an effort to achieve a more secure power base in Central Europe, Italian families also married into Central European families. The Biglia, who were descendants of the Visconti and produced several imperial colonels, married into the Buquoy family, providing a genealogical link between the seventeenth-century German military contracting family and the great fifteenth-century Italian *condottieri*.[45] Piccolomini married the daughter of Duke Julius Heinrich of Sachsen-Lauenburg and Montecuccoli eventually married into the powerful Moravian Dietrichstein clan. Tracing the myriad interrelationships between the military elite that traversed the Italian peninsula and Central Europe would reveal dense, intersecting webs of private interest that both underpinned and undermined the activities of rulers.[46]

Throughout the first half of his Central European career, Montecuccoli remained close to his natural lord, Francesco I d'Este (r. 1629–58), sustaining a regular correspondence. Military historians have spent relatively little time closely analyzing the letters of early modern commanders: most studies focus on treatises, histories, and institutional records. While institutional records often reproduce the viewpoint of the ruler and can lead to an overemphasis on state power, treatises alone can be problematic because they represent ideals of military service that often contrasted to realities. Military entrepreneurship flourished during the Thirty Years War and some elements of proprietorship continued into the eighteenth century. However, the pervasive reality of entrepreneurial methods is all but ignored in contemporary treatises, which emphasize traditional noble values.[47] Letters, furthermore, provide insights into the still mysterious topic of what military men perceived and felt about their experiences, contributing the "human element" that is often missing from most studies of mercenaries.[48] An analysis of Montecuccoli's exchanges with Francesco provides insight into the ways that military entrepreneurs maneuvered politically and explained their activities.

Letters show that Francesco supported Montecuccoli's early career.[49] When Montecuccoli arranged for his brother, Galeotto, to join him in Central Europe in 1636, Montecuccoli reminded Francesco that "the exercise and the practice that he acquires of the art in military travails will be dedicated to Your Highness's service, which is the ultimate goal of us both."[50] A few months later, he assured Francesco that "there is no other interest in the world more primary to me than Your Most Serene Highness's service. As long as it is humanly possible, neither the length of the voyage nor the danger of the passage will ever keep me from it."[51] Francesco needed military expertise, but could not provide regular opportunities for gaining that expertise and lacked the resources necessary to maintain permanent forces. Furthermore, the near continuous fighting during the Thirty Years War created an environment in Central Europe that was similar to what Italians had experienced a century before during the Italian Wars. The 1630s saw the entry of one of the greatest military pioneers of the period into the war: Gustavus Adolphus of Sweden. Although Gustavus died at the 1632 Battle of Lützen, talented successors such as Johan Banér kept Habsburg generals busy. In 1635, Montecuccoli claimed that "nowadays, the true military discipline blooms in Central Europe."[52] Montecuccoli's military treatises – including a 1643 proposal for a Swedish-style militia for Francesco – captured the new tactics and strategies of the Thirty Years War, affirming the role played by such highly mobile warriors as "conduits" of military knowledge.[53]

Francesco's military needs were motivated by the goals of restoring lost Este properties (especially Ferrara, forfeited to Pope Clement VIII in 1597), incorporating new territories, and increasing his status within the contentious hierarchy of princes in the Italian peninsula.[54] Francesco was probably inspired by past dynastic achievements, including Este patronage of the illustrious Ferrarese Renaissance, when he started construction on the grandiose Palazzo Ducale in Modena in 1634. That year, Wallenstein's assassination opened up new possibilities for Italians in the Austrian army, which Francesco would try to exploit. When Francesco joined the alliance against Pope Urban VIII in the War of Castro with the principal intention of regaining Ferrara, he exploited connections to Central European commanders.[55]

During the War of Castro, Montecuccoli dutifully returned to the Italian peninsula and became Field Marshal of Francesco's forces – the highest position he had yet held. Francesco and Emperor Ferdinand III (r. 1637–57) had arranged his transfer after Francesco helped free Montecuccoli from an extended imprisonment by the Swedes.[56] Other Italians had assisted, including Francesco and Girolamo Montecuccoli, Mattias de Medici, and Ottavio Piccolomini.[57] Once Montecuccoli was released, Francesco demanded his swift return to Modena. "The reason for our haste," he wrote in August 1642, "is the imminent revolt of all the affairs of Italy."[58] He also asked Ferdinand III to allow Montecuccoli keep his regiment and raise more troops in Central Europe. After all, Francesco argued, "these states are Your Majesty's and to cooperate in their conservation will preserve that which is yours."[59]

Ferdinand III granted Montecuccoli a three-month leave to serve Francesco, but was reluctant to allow the use of imperial troops in Italy. The need for soldiers in the imperial army was too great, especially as the Thirty Years War continued to depopulate the empire.[60] Furthermore, Ferdinand did not wish to antagonize a pope already unfriendly to the Habsburgs. Francesco ultimately obtained 1,100 Swedish prisoners from the imperial army, as well as 300 Swiss mercenaries.[61] Montecuccoli and other returning Modenese lords also played a critical role ensuring compliance among the duchy's populations. The Montecuccoli family supplied 250 of their own subjects to Modenese forces and Raimondo exacted heavy punishments on individuals in contentious territories like Vignola who had accepted offices or patents of command from the enemy or were even suspected of disloyalty.[62] His reputation as an imperial officer must have made an impression on the villagers he encountered in the duchy's hills and plains, possibly encouraging some to join Francesco's effort since men preferred to fight for well-known generals.[63] Montecuccoli soon achieved a notable victory at the Battle of Nonantola in July 1643 against numerically superior forces, an outcome which he immediately reported to his old comrade-in-arms, Mattias de Medici, who headed allied Tuscan forces.[64]

Numerous other commanders from the imperial army joined the forces sparring in the War of Castro. Just prior to the victory at Nonantola, Francesco's secretary, Fulvio Testi, had reported the "most curious news" about one of Mattias de Medici and Montecuccoli's mutual acquaintances: Piccolomini. Testi asserted that Piccolomini had appeared in nearby Cento to pay his respects to the papal nephew, Antonio Barberini. Piccolomini sent a messenger to Montecuccoli requesting safe passage for one of his sisters. The Modenese, however, suspected that Piccolomini intended to serve the Pope and "had planned to spy on our arrangements." They cautiously detained the messenger.[65] Indeed, Urban VIII lobbied hard for Piccolomini's service, offering a cardinal's hat to both Piccolomini and his brother, cash prizes, and a generous stipend. Emperor Ferdinand III dissuaded Piccolomini from joining the war against Parma, Modena, Venice, and Tuscany because he did not want to strengthen Urban VIII's hand. Instead, Ferdinand arranged for Piccolomini to transfer to the Spanish Army of Flanders until he could be re-integrated into the imperial army.[66] However, the fact that Piccolomini nearly fought against his Medici lord and the forces led by his pro-tégé, Montecuccoli, shows the degree to which alliances fluctuated during the Thirty Years War. One can imagine Montecuccoli at the Modenese camp when Piccolomini's messenger arrived, sizing up the intentions of a purported ally who may have been abusing his trust to obtain information. Italians tended to agree about whose side they were on when fighting in Central Europe, but when conflict erupted in the Italian peninsula, friends easily became enemies.

Modenese agent and faithful Habsburg servant

Montecuccoli traveled to Vienna towards the end of the War of Castro to manage an inher-itance and never returned to lead Francesco's forces.[67] Nonetheless, he attempted to help Francesco from afar. In December 1643, he appealed to Ferdinand III, Archduke Leopold Wilhelm, and other members of the court to provide mediation in the War of Castro or else "soldiers and levies." Montecuccoli assured Francesco, "I explained with great humility what you commanded me and directed every argument at the goal that Your Highness perceive some effective help in these circumstances from the protection of the Emperor."[68] In early 1644, Montecuccoli was searching for a new General of Artillery to send to Modena. He also anticipated that an upcoming reform of imperial regiments would provide officers who would "voluntarily" transfer to the wars in Italy and bring troops with them.[69] A year and a half later he continued his efforts to levy troops for Francesco, writing that, despite obstacles, "I will nevertheless continue to toil."[70]

Over the next several years, Montecuccoli was the object of a political tug-of-war between the Duke of Modena and the Habsburg emperor, a position which he cleverly exploited. When Ferdinand III demanded that he return to the imperial army, Montecuccoli kept Francesco carefully apprised, explaining that "I do not deem anything in the world equal to the honor of your grace" and conveying the news that he had informed Ferdinand III that "I was not at my liberty and that I was obliged to serve Your Highness." The emperor reassured Montecuccoli that he would write to Francesco himself about the agreement. Montecuccoli begged to be allowed to return to Modena for a few weeks, but Ferdinand told him "that His Majesty's service would suffer no delay and gave me a decree in which I was ordered to be ready to depart anytime and to any place that His Majesty commands." As an incentive, Ferdinand offered Montecuccoli the first free regiment, advancement in office, and money.[71]

By 1645, Montecuccoli's military value to the Habsburgs was clear. As the imperial army rushed to head off Swedish forces, he confided to Francesco that Leopold Wilhelm, who was supreme commander, "has signified to me with favors of extreme confidence that he does not want to be served in this undertaking by any other generals except for Count Puchheim and me."[72] That same year, he secured court positions in Vienna as Councilor of War and Imperial Chamberlain. Montecuccoli told Francesco that Leopold Wilhelm was aware of Montecuccoli's obligation to return to Modenese service "anytime that Your Highness calls me" and mentioned that the archduke would write to Francesco.[73] In early January 1646,

Francesco remained convinced that Montecuccoli would return, urging that his "arrival must not be deferred much longer" and asking him to bring "one or two miners experienced in excavations."[74] A temporary lull in fighting had indeed convinced Leopold Wilhelm to grant Montecuccoli leave, but the archduke immediately revoked it when information about a new Swedish attack surfaced. When he reinstated Montecuccoli, Leopold Wilhelm offered him an attractive promotion to Cavalry General. Montecuccoli hoped Francesco would understand his desire to remain in the imperial army in such a position, writing of his "confidence" that "you will not deign to disapprove this delay on an occasion so grand."[75] This promotion opened up the possibility of greater influence over the circulation of troops, a fact which Francesco would have appreciated.

As it turned out, Francesco's latest bellicosity arose from his increasing dissatisfaction with the Spanish Habsburgs, whom Francesco accused of failing to provide adequate protection and rewards. Francesco had plunged headfirst into the calculating, manipulative world of Italian politics in pursuit of an alliance that could muscle papal and then Spanish hegemony out of the way. Soon Francesco would break his alliance with Spain and, in August 1647, stipulate a formal agreement with France. In 1648, Francesco headed a French assault on the Spanish-controlled fortress at Cremona in Milan, entering into combat against former allies.[76] Thus Montecuccoli's natural lord became an enemy of his new patrons, a political development that eventually toppled Montecuccoli's careful balancing act between Modena and Vienna. However, from 1645 to 1647 – up until the point when Francesco's treachery became clear – Montecuccoli continued to help his natural lord from afar, providing diplomatic and military services.

In late 1646, Francesco once again applied pressure on Montecuccoli to return to Modena. In December, Montecuccoli reported to Francesco that Leopold Wilhelm responded to his latest desire for leave with the promise of the official patent for General of Cavalry, a position he had held unofficially.[77] Once again, Montecuccoli's request for leave produced an important new reward. The patent for the General of Cavalry position, the original promotion to General of Cavalry, as well as other offers of regiments and awards all appeared as a result of conversations Montecuccoli had with his Habsburg patrons about returning to Modenese service. This pattern suggests that, despite Montecuccoli's proclamations of helplessness, he was not a simple pawn passed back and forth between rulers: Montecuccoli was an active agent who used his position between patrons to extract greater concessions from them.

Montecuccoli also sent a relative, Alfonso Montecuccoli, to Vienna to ask the emperor for leave. Alfonso was a Modenese diplomat who served on official missions while clearly also pursuing family interests, revealing how public and private goals blended in the careers of individuals.[78] Montecuccoli instructed him to report to Ferdinand III "the honors and benefits that the Lord Duke proposes to me" and the fact that "the fortune of these wars is very inconstant and my increasing age requires that I now establish some stable foundation."[79] In this way, Alfonso would carefully invite the emperor to make a more competitive offer. Montecuccoli sensed that the outcome of Alfonso's trip would render an important change in his life. He ordered Alfonso to begin looking for a wife from the Italian peninsula if the leave was accepted or Central Europe if the leave was denied. In case his leave was denied, he also wanted his "silver, jewelry, money, and credit bonds" transported to Venice "where I will always be able to obtain them with ease."[80] Montecuccoli may have feared serious repercussions for not reporting for service in Modena.[81]

Once again, Montecuccoli's leave was denied, but he continued to help Francesco.[82] From April to June 1647, Montecuccoli and Alfonso attempted to transport cavalry to Modena, but on 22 June Montecuccoli reported that "in leaving Silesia they had been encountered by an enemy party, which took them all prisoner besides two who were killed, together with the lieutenant who conducted them." He wanted to exchange them for prisoners held by the imperial army, but the enemy refused, demanding a huge ransom.[83] As he assisted in the conveyance of imperial troops in preparation for conflict against the Habsburgs, Alfonso was negotiating in Vienna on behalf of Francesco in a final attempt to avoid such a rupture.[84] Finally, from late August to early September, precisely when Francesco formalized his relationship to France, Raimondo sent a "qualified lieutenant" to Modena at Francesco's request.[85]

At about this time, Montecuccoli reported to Ferdinand III that Francesco had accepted command of French forces in Italy, with the stipulation that he not fight against imperial states.[86] Thus any military assistance Montecuccoli procured for the duke was intended for use against the Spanish in alliance with the French. If Montecuccoli had obtained leave, he would have fought against Spanish forces. Four days prior to formalizing the agreement with the French, Francesco sent Montecuccoli his final offer. His annoyance was evident. He told Montecuccoli, "I cannot believe anymore that the benignity of His Majesty has so long denied the requested leave to Your Lordship, who is my subject and feudatory." If Montecuccoli wanted to return to his service, Francesco believed that he could. He warned Montecuccoli "if Your Lordship does not come, do not think of ever having another place in my service and be certain that I will remain little satisfied with an improper and undue negative response."[87]

Montecuccoli responded to Francesco's persuasions and threats in typical fashion, emphasizing his ardent desire to return to Modena, but complaining that his hands were tied.[88] He claimed that Ferdinand III demanded "that I postpone every interest and desire of mine and everything else for His Imperial service and that I report to the army immediately and without another word, wherever he deems that I am necessary."[89] Montecuccoli exaggerated the emperor's power. Francesco was right: if Montecuccoli had wanted to leave imperial service, he could have. Montecuccoli decided to await the rewards promised by the emperor and forego Francesco's offers because he wanted to. In November, Francesco asked Montecuccoli to tell the emperor that he had agreed to marry Vittoria Farnese, solidifying a relationship to the French-allied Duchy of Parma.[90] After this exchange, there was a lull in their correspondence until Francesco reconciled with Spain in 1649.

Montecuccoli would have been relieved when Francesco decided to make peace with Spain; he even served as an intermediary, communicating Francesco's justifications to the emperor.[91] However, in the mid-1650s, Francesco re-aligned with the French, marrying Mazarin's niece, and fighting the Spanish again. These alliances with the French reverberated uncomfortably through Modenese kinship networks. For example, Montecuccoli was an imperial general and his cousin Andrea was a Spanish governor, but Alfonso fought under Francesco when he attempted to seize Cremona from the Spanish in 1648.[92] The same circumstances would have applied to multiple other Modenese families. When Francesco switched sides, he threw the international alliances of his vassals into disarray.

Of course, it was not unusual for common soldiers and officers to switch sides during the Thirty Years War. When Odoardo Farnese, Duke of Parma, put together an army to fight the Spanish Habsburgs in 1633, most of his experienced officers had come from armies that had fought for the Spanish Habsburgs, while hundreds of lower-ranking men from Spanish Habsburg territories enrolled.[93] However, the officers suffered from lack of continuity in their allegiances and networks. Fighting in alliance with the French directed some of them to careers in the French army, but many of these careers stalled once Odoardo signed a treaty with Spain.[94] The same officers would have had to start over in Spanish service.

For Montecuccoli, faithfulness, or at least its appearance, mattered. One of the reasons that Italians were so successful in imperial service was that so many members of their families fought on the same side of the war, in contrast to German families. Not only did their common allegiances create a more effective network, but Italians were perceived as particularly faithful by the Austrian Habsburg ruler. In 1656, Montecuccoli recounted a conversation with Count Schwartzenburg about Francesco's marriage to Mazarin's niece and how such a development would, Montecuccoli wrote, create an "impediment to my fortunes since [Habsburg patrons] would no longer trust me with important offices," an indication that serving multiple patrons was problematic in certain contexts.[95] The difficulty of establishing a reputation for faithfulness was acute in such an interconnected military and political environment. Time and again, Montecuccoli recounted his unswerving dedication to the emperor's service and reminded Ferdinand III that his brief period of fighting in Italy had been performed "not only with leave, but under Your Majesty's command."[96]

Perhaps fortunately for Montecuccoli, Francesco died during the hostilities in 1658, the same year that Leopold I (r. 1658–1705) was declared emperor.[97] Montecuccoli outlived Francesco by twenty-two years, during which time he ascended to a glorious career in Habsburg service under the new emperor. In 1656, he was included in Empress Eleonora's elite, twelve-member Italian academy and later became commander-in-chief of the army, President of the Imperial War Council, and a Knight of the Golden Fleece. Montecuccoli's military writings provided the blueprint for Eugene of Savoy's conquest of Eastern Europe and were admired by Frederick the Great, Napoleon, and Clausewitz. Montecuccoli was a close advisor to Leopold, who saw him as a trusted general who had served both his father and grandfather faithfully. In 1666, Leopold praised Montecuccoli's "excellent qualities" and record of "most submissive loyalty, enthusiasm, and devotion."[98]

A year after Montecuccoli's death, the Modenese historian Pietro Gazzotti produced an account in which he claimed that Spanish ministers had proposed that Ferdinand III confiscate the Duchy of Modena on account of Francesco's treason. One of the candidates they allegedly recommended to replace Francesco as duke was none other than Raimondo Montecuccoli.[99] Perhaps Gazzotti was simply airing the political fantasies of a later generation. Nonetheless, this account reveals an accurate picture of a military entrepreneur whose ultimate success in Habsburg service implied a betrayal of his natural lord and also paints Montecuccoli as a seventeenth-century Francesco Sforza. Decades earlier, Montecuccoli had recorded a series of "maxims" that he claimed to have learned from Piccolomini. "Politics," he asserted, "is the search for means in order to arrive at the stated goal; he who arrives there sooner is the better politician."[100] Francesco may not have arrived, but Montecuccoli certainly did. Such a feat required a powerful strain of Italian wisdom, one which originated in Machiavelli's Renaissance and continued to drive the careers of new generations of *condottieri*.

Conclusion

Charles Tilly called the Thirty Years War "a complex web of wars," an apt description that reflects the fact that these conflicts were acted out by webs of people.[101] Understanding the Thirty Years War entails examining many layers of convoluted and manipulative political relationships forged between small-scale actors – that is, between noblemen and between noblemen and minor princes – and between those actors and larger powers.[102] The Austrian Habsburg monarch – as well as the kings of Spain and France – groomed clients in northern Italy in order to protect the military corridor to Flanders and to gain access to men and money from the resource-rich peninsula. The Spanish and Austrian Habsburgs were more successful than the French at using clientage networks in the Italian peninsula.[103] Perhaps it is no surprise, then, that Austrian (rather than French) power eclipsed Spain in Italy by the end of the century. However, less is known about the strategies of Italian actors. Francesco I d'Este also attempted to control troops and contributed to the development of clientage networks. This behavior emerged seamlessly from the Renaissance *condottiere* tradition, in which rulers and nobles alike ensured their political survival by formulating military contracts (*condotte*) and switching allegiance when better military opportunities arose.[104] With few exceptions, the Italian peninsula had been pacified by the late sixteenth century. Commanders like Montecuccoli therefore used clientage networks to re-focus their careers on Central Europe with its regular opportunities for fighting and the system of rewards devised by the Austrian Habsburgs.

The clientage networks that facilitated a startling commerce in men during the period of the Thirty Years War therefore became tools not only of centralizing rulers, but also of a new aristocracy. Renaissance Italians understood particularly acutely that individuals were made by communities and that careers were collections of connections and associations, both formal and informal, which had to be used astutely for an individual to achieve power and autonomy.[105] No one assumed that such communities were curtailed by the borders of a territorial state, and certainly not the international contractors whose kinship and credit networks generated such a vast hemorrhage of war. The movements of vassal-entrepreneurs like Montecuccoli were widely supported by princes, but in the process of becoming more useful to his natural lord, Montecuccoli outgrew Modena. He became Francesco's Wallenstein: the central figure who could supply Modena with the military might its ruler coveted, but whose abilities, resources, and connections allowed him to operate autonomously and even treacherously. The fact that Montecuccoli chose his Habsburg patrons over his traditional lord affirms that political position derived from a relationship of mutual dependence.[106] Once it became clear that Francesco needed Montecuccoli more than Montecuccoli needed Francesco, Montecuccoli abandoned him.

Montecuccoli actively shaped his allegiances. As he eluded the demands of his natural lord, he claimed to be a subject of the Holy Roman Empire, rejecting the idea that as a "foreigner" he was ineligible for court positions in Vienna. In the early 1650s, when faced with this charge, two of his arguments for why he had been "naturalized" focused on the elements that had allowed him to leave the service of one lord for another: transregional family ties and military service. He emphasized that his ancestors had served the emperor for many generations and his relative, Girolamo, had served as Councilor of State.[107] Furthermore, he argued, if one made any distinction among aspirants, it ought to be based on "the merit of (that service)," adding, "there is a great difference between one and another type of service and that one thing is to serve in war and another is to serve at one's convenience and without ever risking either life, goods, or reputation."[108] The kinship ties and contracting practices that underlay Montecuccoli's military service – practices which required taking such extreme risks – were in fact highly ambiguous structural features of early modern political life. These features undermined Montecuccoli's relationship to his natural lord, allowing Montecuccoli to forge a career with a new patron. Machiavelli was right about mercenaries: their loyalties were unclear and potentially destabilizing.[109]

Montecuccoli's manipulation of his political status was only possible in a context in which political status was unclear. In particular, the distinction between subject and client was blurred. Feudal relationships maintained their hold and took on attributes of clientage. At the same time, clientage relationships were conceived of and justified in feudal terms.[110] Sharon Kettering and others laid the groundwork for understanding patron–client networks,[111] but little is known about the ongoing influence of feudal concepts and relationships as clientage evolved in the early modern period. As these interconnected communities grew, changed shape, and provided new opportunities, individuals like Montecuccoli succeeded by exploiting their inherent ambiguities. The independent, self-made man is a modern myth. However, if individuals are understood as products of their communities, then Montecuccoli and others like him were probably the closest thing to self-made men that the early modern period possessed.

Notes

1 A succinct account of the plot and its aftermath is Peter Wilson, *The Thirty Years War. Europe's Tragedy*, Cambridge, MA: The Belknap Press of Harvard University Press, 2009, pp. 535–42. A sympathetic yet compelling study of Wallenstein's life is Golo Mann, *Wallenstein, His Life Narrated*, New York: Holt, Rinehart and Winston, 1976. I would like to thank Corey Tazzara and William Caferro for reading and commenting on this chapter and Paula Findlen for shaping the project from its inception.

2 Thomas Barker, *The Military Intellectual and Battle. Raimondo Montecuccoli and the Thirty Years War*, Albany: State University of New York Press, 1975.

3 The Marquis of Aytona, quoted in Geoffrey Parker, *The Army of Flanders and the Spanish Road, 1567–1659: The Logistics of Spanish Victory and Defeat in the Low Countries' Wars*, Cambridge: Cambridge University Press, 1972, p. 18.

4 The most important recent work on early modern contracting is David Parrott, *The Business of War: Military Enterprise and Military Revolution in Early Modern* Europe, Cambridge: Cambridge University Press, 2012. See also Fritz Redlich, *The German Military Enterpriser and His Work Force: A Study in European Economic and Social History*, Wiesbaden: F. Steiner, 1964 and Jeff Fynn-Paul, ed., *War, Entrepreneurs, and the State in Europe and the Mediterranean, 1300–1800*, Leiden and Boston: Brill, 2014. For the broader influence of mercenaries in the fourteenth century, see William Caferro, *Mercenary Companies and the Decline of Siena*, Baltimore: Johns Hopkins University Press, 1998.

5 Jacob Burckhardt, *The Civilization of the Renaissance in Italy*, New York: Phaidon Press, 2006 (repr.).

6 For nuanced understandings of the Renaissance Italian state, see the essays in Julius Kirshner, ed., *The Origins of the State in Italy 1300–1600*, Chicago and London: University of Chicago Press, 1995.

7 For a multi-dimensional study of a late medieval mercenary see William Caferro, *John Hawkwood: An English Mercenary in Fourteenth-Century Italy*, Baltimore: Johns Hopkins University Press, 2006.

8 Janice E. Thomson, *Mercenaries, Pirates, and Sovereigns: State-Building and Extraterritorial Violence in Early Modern Europe*, Princeton, NJ: Princeton University Press, 1994.

9 Angelantonio Spagnoletti, *Stato, aristocrazie e ordine di Malta nell'Italia Moderna*, Rome: Ecole Française, 1988, p. 4.

10 Michael Mallett, *Mercenaries and their Masters: Warfare in Renaissance Italy*, Totowa, NJ: Rowman and Littlefield, 1974 and Michael Mallett and Christine Shaw, *The Italian Wars, 1494–1559: War, State and Society in Early Modern Europe*, Harlow: Pearson, 2012.

11 Gregory Hanlon, *The Twilight of a Military Tradition: Italian Aristocrats and European Conflicts, 1560–1800*, London: UCL Press, 1998, pp. 47–91, and Paola Bianchi, Davide Maffei, and Enrico Stumpo, eds., *Italiani al servizio straniero in età moderna*, Milan: FrancoAngeli, 2008.

12 See the essays in Thomas Dandelet and John A. Marino, eds., *Spain in Italy: Politics, Society, and Religion 1500–1700*, Leiden and Boston: Brill, 2007 and Aurelio Musi, ed., *Nel sistema imperiale. L'Italia Spagnola*, Naples: Edizioni Scientifiche Italiane, 1994 and Hanlon, *Twilight*, pp. 73–4.

13 Gianvittorio Signorotto, "Guerre spagnoli, ufficiali lombardi," in *I Farnese. Corti, guerra e nobiltà in antico regime. Atti del convegno di studi Piacenza, 24–26 novembre 1994*, ed. Antonella Bilotto, Pietro Del Negro, and Cesare Mozzarelli, Rome: Bulzoni editore, 1997, pp. 367–96.

14 Raffaele M. Filamondo, *Il genio bellicoso di Napoli, memorie istoriche d'alcuni capitani celebri napolitani: c'han militato per la Fede, per lo Re, per la Patria nel secolo trascorso raccolte*, Naples: D. A. Parrino, 1714, pp. 607–19. For Neapolitan examples, see Angelantonio Spagnoletti, "L'Aristocrazia napoletana nelle guerre del primo seicento: tra pratica delle armi e integrazione dinastica," in *I Farnese*, ed. Bilotto *et al.*, pp. 445–68.

15 Wilson, *Europe's Tragedy*, p. 83; Carl Max Kortepeter, *Ottoman Imperialism during the Reformation: Europe and the Caucasus*, New York: New York University Press, 1972, pp. 123–210.

16 On the Holy Roman Empire at the start of the early modern period, see Robert Von Friedeburg, "'Lands' and 'Fatherlands'. Changes in the Plurality of Allegiances in the Sixteenth-Century Holy Roman Empire," in *Networks, Regions and Nations: Shaping Identities in the Low Countries, 1300–1650*, ed. Judith Pollmann and Robert Stein, Leiden: Brill, 2010, pp. 266–7.

17 Galeazzo Gualdo Priorato, *Vite et azzioni di personaggi militari e politici*, Vienna: Appresso Michele Thurnmayer, 1673.

18 Collalto's patent for admission into the Moravian Land Diet can be found in Brno, Moravský zemský archiv (hereafter MZA), Rodinný Archiv Collaltů (hereafter RAC), značka 169G, k. č. 5, inv. č. 133, 1–13. Ferdinand II wrote to Cardinal Dietrichstein about his decision to admit Collalto in *Documenta Bohemica Bellum Tricennale Illustrantia*, vol. 3, Prague: Academia, 1971, no. 707. Collalto's sons were registered in the Golden Book of Venetian nobility. MZA, RAC, značka 169G, inv. č. 2455.

19 For a general study on these two empresses see Giambattista Intra, "Le due Eleonore Gonzaga Imperatrice," in *Atti e memorie della R. Accademia Virgiliana di Mantova, Biennio 1891–1892*, Mantua, 1893.

20 Herbet Seifert, "Akademien am Wiener Kaiserhof der Barockzeit," in *Akademie und Musik-Erscheinungsweisen und Wirkungen des Akademiegedankens in Kultur- und Musikgeschichte: Institutionem, Veranstaltungen, Schriften. Festschrift für Werner Braun zum 65. Geburtstag*, ed. Wolf Frobenius, Nicole Schwindt-Gross, and Thomas Sick, Saarbrücken: SDV, 1993, pp. 215–17. Notes from meetings of the academy can be found in Vienna, Österreichische Nationalbibliothek (hereafter ÖNB), Handschriften-Sammlung, Signatur 10108.

21 Wilson, *Europe's Tragedy*, pp. 438–40 and 443–6; J. H. Elliott, "Spain and the War," in *The Thirty Years' War*, ed. Geoffrey Parker, 2nd [rev.] edn., London: Routledge, 1997, pp. 95–8; and David Parrott, "A *prince souverain* and the French Crown: Charles de Nevers 1580–1637," in *Royal and Republican Sovereignty in Early Modern Europe: Essays in Memory of Ragnhild Hatton*, ed. Ragnhild Marie Hatton, Robert Oresko, G. C. Gibbs, and H. M. Scott, Cambridge: Cambridge University Press, 1997.

22 For this argument see David Parrott, "The Mantuan Succession, 1627–31," *English Historical Review* 117, 1997, 21–5.

23 Wilson, *Europe's Tragedy*, p. 444

24 Anna married Claudia's son in 1646. Gaetano Pieraccini, *La stirpe de' Medici di Cafaggiolo. Saggio di ricerche sulla transmissione ereditaria dei caratteri biologici*, Florence: Vallecchi, 1924, pp. 545–52.

25 Examples include: Walter Leslie to Mattias de Medici, Prague, 2 March, 1652, Florence, Archivio di stato di Firenze (hereafter ASF), Mediceo del Principato (hereafter MDP), 5450, fols. 265–6; Raimondo Montecuccoli to Mattias de Medici, Hohenegg, 31 July 1652, ASF, MDP, 5450, fol. 601; *ibid.*, Vienna, 29 August 1652, ASF, MDP, 5450, fol. 982; and *ibid.*, Regensburg, 16 June 1653, ASF, MDP, 5455, fol. 87. On Mattias' military career, and other Tuscans in Habsburg service, see Carla Sodini, *L'ercole tirreno. Guerra e dinastia medicea nella prima metà del '600*, Florence: Olschki, 2001, pp. 129–236.

26 On the Grand Duke's early contributions to the war see Sodini, *L'ercole tirreno*, pp. 64–7.

27 Maria Maddalena wrote to Emperor Ferdinand II on Piccolomini's behalf on 17 January 1620, *Documenta Bohemica*, vol. 2, no. 522. She wrote to the privy councilor Karl Harrach on 18 (?) January 1621, *ibid.*, vol. 3, no. 19. For similar recommendations, see Sodini, *L'ercole tirreno*, pp. 224–34.

28 C. V. Wedgwood, *The Thirty Years War*, Garden City, NY: Doubleday, 1961, p. 318. See also Thomas Barker "Ottavio Piccolomini (1599–1659): A Fair Historical Judgment?" in *Army, Aristocracy,*

Monarchy: Essays on War, Society, and Government in Austria, 1618–1780, Boulder, CO: Social Science Monographs, 1982, pp. 61–111.

29 Hanlon, *Twilight*, p. 243.
30 Corrado Argegni, *Condottieri, capitani, tribuni*, vol. 3, Milan: EBBI, Instituto editoriale italiano B. C. Tosi, 1936–7, p. 286. Examples of letters of recommendation from the Grand Dukes to Piccolomini can be found in Zámrsk, Státní oblastní archiv v Zámrsku (hereafter SOAZ), Rodinný archiv Piccolomini (hereafter RAP), inv. č. 11029–67.
31 Gregory Hanlon, "The Decline of a Provincial Military Aristocracy: Siena 1560–1740," *Past & Present*, no. 55, 1997, 86; Sodini, *L'ercole tirreno*, pp. 236–8.
32 For an example, see Sodini, *L'ercole tirreno*, pp. 234–5.
33 Parrott, *Business of War*, pp. 116–25.
34 Peter Lindström and Svante Norrhem, *Flattering Alliances: Scandinavia, Diplomacy, and the Austrian–French Balance of Power, 1648–1740*, trans. Charlotte Merton, Lund: Nordic Academic Press, 2013, especially pp. 7–26, 49–110, and 164–6.
35 For diplomatic networks, see Daniela Frigo, "'Small States': Mantua and Modena," in *Politics and Diplomacy in Early Modern Italy. The Structure of Diplomatic Practice, 1450–1800*, ed. Daniela Frigo, New York: Cambridge University Press, 2000, pp. 147–75.
36 Norbert Elias, *The Civilizing Process: Sociogenetic and Psychogenetic Investigations*, Malden, MA and Oxford: Blackwell Publishing, 2000.
37 On the court as a "contingent" or "open space," see Trevor Dean, "The Courts," in *The Origins of the State in Italy 1300–1600*, ed. Julius Kirshner, Chicago: University of Chicago Press, 1995, pp. 143–4.
38 Cesare Campori, *Raimondo Montecuccoli: la sua famiglia e i suoi tempi*, unabridged fac., Boston: Adamant Media Corp., 2006, pp. 1–38.
39 The Montecuccoli produced fourteenth-century *condottieri* such as Guidinello da Montecuccoli, who emerged from the internecine rivalries of the Frignano. Girolamo Tiraboschi, *Memorie storiche modenesi col codice diplomatico*, vol. 2, Modena, 1793. Hathi Trust Digital Library (http://babel.hathitrust.org/cgi/pt?id=uiuo.ark:/13960/t1qg01q83;view=1up;seq=6)), pp. 148, 189, 200.
40 Redlich, *German Military Enterpriser*, pp. 296–305. Duke Cesare d'Este also sent Ernesto recommendations for Guido Molza, Ercole Seghizzi, Bernardino Codebò, Alessandro Morano, Michele Cipriani, and Alfonso Mosti. Campori, *Raimondo Montecuccoli*, pp. 31–32.
41 Barker, *Military Intellectual*, p. 31. On Montecuccoli's earlier efforts to advance, see *ibid.*, pp. 22–7.
42 Luciano Tomassini, *Raimondo Montecuccoli. Capitano e scrittore*, Rome: Stato Maggiore dell'Esercito, Ufficio Storico, 1978, p. 15. On the service of Montecuccoli's family see also Campori, *Raimondo Montecuccoli*, pp. 21–2. Girolamo Montecuccoli started a court career in Florence before moving to the Tyrol to serve the Medici Archduchess Claudia and finally to Vienna.
43 Copy of Petition to Emperor Ferdinand III, 11 April 1644, Modena, Archivio di stato di Modena (hereafter ASMO), Ambasciatori Germania (hereafter AG), 96B.
44 Redlich, *German Military Enterpriser*, p. 299.
45 *Ibid.*, p. 303.
46 The general point about marriage alliances has been finely argued by Lindström and Norrhem, *Flattering Alliances*, pp. 193–4.
47 David Parrott, "Cultures of Combat in the Ancien Régime: Linear Warfare, Noble Values, and Entrepreneurship," *International History Review*, 27, 3, 2005, 518–33.
48 Caferro, *John Hawkwood*, p. 334.
49 Francesco d'Este wrote to Ernesto Montecuccoli in support of Raimondo. Campori, *Raimondo Montecuccoli*, pp. 40–1.
50 Raimondo Montecuccoli to Francesco I d'Este, Friedberg, 8 February 1636, ASMO, AG, 96B. At the start of his career in foreign service, Ernesto Montecuccoli expressed similar sentiments. Campori, *Raimondo Montecuccoli*, p. 23.
51 Raimondo Montecuccoli to Francesco I d'Este, near Aschersleben, 26 April 1636, ASMO, AG, 96B.
52 Raimondo Montecuccoli to Francesco I d'Este, Hagenau, 13 December 1635, ASMO, AG, 96B. Florentine records from 1624 show how much of the military experience of Tuscan captains, governors, and castellans was based on serving abroad. Sodini, *L'ercole tirreno*, pp. 219–21.
53 Caferro, *John Hawkwood*, p. 334. Several treatises and reports concerning the Swedish army can be found in Raimondo Montecuccoli, *Le opere di Raimondo Montecuccoli*, 2nd edn., vol. 3, ed. Andrea Testa, Rome: Stato maggiore dell'esercito, Ufficio storico, 2000.

54 Riccardo Rimondi, *Estensi: storia e leggende, personaggi e luoghi di una dinastia millenaria*, Ferrara: Cirelli & Zanirato, 2004, pp. 213–26, and Luciano Chiappini, *Gli Estensi: mille anni di storia*, Ferrara: Corbo, 2001, pp. 459–82.

55 On the ambitions and misfortunes of the Este family in the seventeenth century, see Frigo, "'Small States,'" pp. 165–70.

56 Barker, *Military Intellectual*, pp. 38–40.

57 Dispatches from Modena to Ottavio Bolognese, 20 June 1639, ASMO, AG, 94. In 1640, Montecuccoli wrote to Francesco thanking him for his help. Montecuccoli to Francesco I d'Este, Stettin, 8 March 1640, ASMO, AG, 87. See also Girolamo Graf Montecuccoli to Ottavio Bolognese, Innsbruck, 14 June 1639 and Francesco Montecuccoli to Ottavio Bolognese, Modena, 29 July 1639, ÖNB, *Autographen-Sammlung* (Autogr.), 27/66-1 and Campori, *Raimondo Montecuccoli*, pp. 118–20.

58 Francesco to Ottavio Bolognese, Modena, 28 August 1642. Fulvio Testi, *Lettere*, vol. 3, Bari: Laterza, 1967, no. 1568, p. 300.

59 Francesco I d'Este to Ferdinand III, Modena, 28 August 1642, *ibid.*, no. 1569, p. 302.

60 Davide Maffi, *Il baluardo della corona: Guerra, esercito, finanze e società nella Lombardia seicentesca (1630–1660)*, Florence: Le Monnier, 2007, pp. 103–4.

61 Campori, *Raimondo Montecuccoli*, pp. 138–9, 146. On the origins of soldiers in Italian armies, see Gregory Hanlon, *The Hero of Italy. Odoardo Farnese, Duke of Parma, His Soldiers, and His Subjects in the Thirty Years' War*, Oxford: Oxford University Press, 2014, p. 51 and Maffi, *Il baluardo*, pp. 92–152.

62 Campori, *Raimondo Montecuccoli*, pp. 160–1.

63 Caferro, *John Hawkwood*, p. 75.

64 Raimondo Montecuccoli to Mattias de Medici, from the camp at Modena, 22 July 1643. Cited in Campori, *Raimondo Montecuccoli*, p. 168.

65 Fulvio Testi to Cardinal Rinaldo d'Este, from the camp in Secco, 13 June 1643, Testi, *Lettere*, vol. 3, no. 1659, pp. 373–4.

66 Campori, *Raimondo Montecuccoli*, pp. 133–4. On the papacy's martial pursuits and relationships at this time see Giampiero Brunelli, *Soldati del Papa: politica militare e nobiltà nello stato della chiesa: 1560–1644*, Rome: Carocci, 2003, pp. 241–72.

67 Montecuccoli inherited Girolamo's properties after his wife's death. Francesco helped, writing to the Jesuit General in Rome to put pressure on the confessor of Girolamo's widow to favor Montecuccoli when she was on her deathbed. Francesco I d'Este to Muzio Vitelleschi, Modena, 16 December 1643, Testi, *Lettere*, no. 1737, pp. 428–9; Campori, *Raimondo Montecuccoli*, pp. 190–1.

68 See the letter and enclosed petition in Raimondo Montecuccoli to Francesco I d'Este, Vienna, 26 December 1643, ASMO, AG, 96B.

69 Raimondo Montecuccoli to Francesco I d'Este, Vienna, 2 January 1644, ASMO, AG, 96b and Campori, *Raimondo Montecuccoli*, pp. 192–3.

70 Raimondo Montecuccoli to Francesco I d'Este, from the camp at Teben, 27 August 1645, ASMO, AG, 96B.

71 Raimondo Montecuccoli to Francesco I d'Este, Vienna, 23 April 1644, ASMO, AG, 96B.

72 Raimondo Montecuccoli to Francesco I d'Este, Vienna, 22 July 1645, ASMO, AG, 96B.

73 Raimondo Montecuccoli to Francesco I d'Este, from the imperial camp at Teben in Hungary, 5 August 1645, ASMO, AG, 96B.

74 Minuti Ducale, Modena, 5 January 1646, ASMO, AG, 96B; Raimondo Montecuccoli to Francesco I d'Este, Modena, no date, 1646, ASMO, AG, 96B.

75 Raimondo Montecuccoli to Francesco I d'Este, Budweis, the Day of the Birth of Our Lord, 1645, ASMO, AG, 96B and Budweis, 10 January 1646, ASMO, AG, 96B.

76 Luigi Simeoni, *Francesco I d'Este e la politica italiana del Mazarino*, Bologna: N. Zanichelli, 1921, pp. 73–135.

77 Montecuccoli to Francesco, Freiberg, 24 December 1646, ASMO, AG, 96B.

78 On this general topic see Daniela Frigo, "Small States," pp. 152–3.

79 Montecuccoli copied the instructions in a letter to Francesco. Raimondo Montecuccoli to Francesco I d'Este, Freiberg, 24 December 1646, ASMO, AG, 96B.

80 *Ibid.* Montecuccoli achieved his marriage goals in 1657 when he married Margarethe Dietrichstein. I explore his quest for marriage and stability during the 1650s in Suzanne Sutherland, "From Battlefield to Court: Raimondo Montecuccoli's Diplomatic Mission to Queen Christina of Sweden after the Thirty Years War," *Sixteenth Century Journal*, forthcoming in 2017.

81 The Duke of Parma confiscated the properties of subjects who refused to join his war efforts against Spain in 1633. Hanlon, *Hero of Italy*, p. 52.

82 Campori, *Raimondo Montecuccoli*, pp. 250–1.

83 Raimondo Montecuccoli to Francesco I d'Este, Breßlau, 29 April 1647, ASMO, AG, 96B and Raimondo Montecuccoli to Francesco I d'Este, Baden, 22 June 1647, ASMO, AG, 96B.

84 Campori, *Raimondo Montecuccoli*, pp. 256–7.

85 Raimondo Montecuccoli to Francesco I d'Este, the imperial camp, 20 August 1647, ASMO, AG, 96B and Raimondo Montecuccoli to Francesco I d'Este, Pilsen, 5 September 1647, ASMO, AG, 96B.

86 Campori, *Raimondo Montecuccoli*, p. 263.

87 Minuti Ducale, Modena, 23 August 1647, ASMO, AG, 96B.

88 Raimondo Montecuccoli to Francesco I d'Este, Pilsen, 5 September 1647, ASMO, AG, 96B.

89 Raimondo Montecuccoli to Francesco I d'Este, Pilsen, 14 September 1647, ASMO, AG, 96B.

90 Francesco I d'Este to Raimondo Montecuccoli, Modena, 3 November 1647, ASMO, AG, 96B.

91 Campori, *Raimondo Montecuccoli*, pp. 279–80.

92 *Ibid.*, p. 264.

93 Hanlon, *Hero of Italy*, pp. 49, 66–8.

94 David Parrott, "Italian Soldiers in French Service, 1500–1700. The Collapse of a Military Tradition," in *Italiani al servizio straniero in età moderna*, ed. Paola Bianchi, Davide Maffei, and Enrico Stumpo, Milan: FrancoAngeli, 2008, p. 31; Hanlon, *Hero of Italy*, pp. 213–14.

95 Montecuccoli, *Le opere*, vol. 3, p. 355.

96 Copy of Petition to Emperor Ferdinand III, 11 April 1644, ASMO, AG, 96B.

97 Ferdinand III considered a military intervention against Francesco, but died in 1657. After his death, the Viennese court was preoccupied by Leopold I's election as emperor and the outbreak of the First Northern War. In 1658, Montecuccoli was appointed Field Marshal of the Habsburg auxiliary forces in that war, a position for which Leopold Wilhelm probably recommended him.

98 Raimondo Montecuccoli, *Ausgewaehlte Schriften des Raimund Fürsten Montecuccoli, General-Lieutenant und Feldmarschall*, vol. 3, ed. and trans. Alois Veltzé, Vienna: W. Braumüller, 1899, p. 319. For another duplicitous mercenary who later gained a reputation for honesty, see Caferro, *John Hawkwood*.

99 Campori, *Raimondo Montecuccoli*, p. 324.

100 Montecuccoli, *Le opere*, vol. 3, pp. 62–3.

101 Charles Tilly, *Coercion, Capital, and European States, AD 990–1992*, Malden, MA: Blackwell Publishing, 1992, p. 166.

102 Peter Wilson's erudite study of the Thirty Years War places political and military realities within a dense weave of alliances and motives, although for the most part does not include the Italian peninsula. Wilson, *Europe's Tragedy*.

103 Parrott, "Italian Soldiers," pp. 38–9.

104 Mallett and Shaw, *Italian Wars*, pp. 1–5.

105 Paul D. McLean, *The Art of the Network. Strategic Interaction and Patronage in Renaissance Florence*, Durham, NC and London: Duke University Press, 2007, pp. 1–34.

106 These relationships of mutual dependence were, of course, unequal. On these dynamics in trans-national context see Lindström and Norrhem, *Flattering Alliances*, p. 86. This insight is common to studies of absolutism.

107 A draft petition from 10 March 1651 can be found in SOAZ, RAP, inv. č. 12471, pp. 513–18.

108 *Ibid.*, p. 515.

109 However, it may have been the mercenary's familiarity with practices of deception on the battle-field – which Machiavelli advocated – that made him a particularly crafty politician. See Caferro, *John Hawkwood*, pp. 19–20.

110 Lindström and Norrhem point out that one ruler's subject was another ruler's client. This formulation makes sense in some cases, but in others it is hard to distinguish if someone was behaving as a subject or as a client. Lindström and Norrhem, *Flattering Alliances*, p. 202.

111 Sharon Kettering, "Patronage and Kinship in Early Modern France," *French Historical Studies*, 16, 2, 1989, 408–35.

Part IV

POWER AND REPRESENTATION

20

FROM FRONTIER PRINCIPALITY TO EARLY MODERN EMPIRE

Limitations and capabilities of Ottoman governance[1]

Kaya Şahin

During the Renaissance, and particularly in the *cinquecento*, the Ottoman Empire was universally seen as a powerful dynastic enterprise with seemingly limitless resources. Various observers and commentators, such as Niccolò Machiavelli (1469–1527), Francisco López de Gómara (ca. 1511–ca. 1566), Ogier Ghiselin de Busbecq (1522–92), several Venetian ambassadors in Istanbul, or the Safavid Shah Tahmasb (r. 1524–76), referred to the Ottoman ruler's political and ideological power, the military might of the empire, and its efficient administration.[2] Ottoman sources of the period, historical works and diplomatic writings alike, similarly propagated the image of a victorious polity that was well managed by the ruler and his obedient servants.[3]

In the modern period, this image has either been adopted too uncritically, or rejected altogether. Some scholars have presented the Ottoman "state" as the precursor of a modern Turkish/Muslim nation-state that acted as a regional and global power; this "state" has been portrayed as able in its bureaucratic capacity to manage its realm, and fair and tolerant in its application of justice and its treatment of religious difference. Other scholars, armed with Eurocentric and Weberian models, characterized Ottoman governance as a form of absolutism where the word of the ruler was synonymous with the law of the land; still others have seen in the Ottoman case a particularly inefficient and violent form of rule that was the result of intense elite factionalism.[4]

In this chapter, the aim is to revisit the emergence and development of Ottoman governance from the early fourteenth to the late sixteenth century, in the light of the historical record and documentary trail left behind by the Ottomans. The choice of this particular time span reflects the historical focus of this book, i.e., the Renaissance widely construed; this time span also corresponds with a period during which the Ottoman enterprise transformed itself from a frontier principality to an early modern empire. Instead of passing judgment on the bureaucratic capabilities of the Ottoman enterprise, or adopting a teleological approach that sees empire formation as a natural outcome, the chapter will discuss the composition and objectives of the Ottoman political center, the various methods it utilized, the records it kept, the interlocutors it addressed and created, the dynamism it displayed, and the limitations it faced. The term "governance" is privileged in the chapter over "state," since it is more conducive to a dynamic, multifaceted understanding of power. It is hoped that, at the end, the Ottoman case will look less arcane to an audience that is more familiar with similar issues from a European context.

The Ottoman enterprise began as a frontier principality in northwestern Anatolia, on the borders of the Byzantine Empire. The political and military core of the enterprise initially consisted of a charismatic tribal chieftain and his retinue, who mitigated their predatory raids against their neighbors with pragmatic alliances. The Ottoman political center needed, and eventually developed, better management techniques in order to muster natural and financial resources. The relative centralization of these resources helped transform the head of the Ottoman dynasty from a charismatic tribal chieftain to a princely figure, and then to an emperor living behind palace walls. By the middle of the sixteenth century, the Ottoman dynasty came to rule over a land-based early modern empire, whose economic and ecological dynamics were mostly tied to the Eurasian landmass and the Mediterranean basin. The empire's territories extended from Central Europe to western Iran, and from the northern shores of the Black Sea to North Africa and the Arabian Peninsula. In contrast to his nomadic ancestors' limited political claims, the Ottoman ruler was now presented to the empire's interlocutors in East and West as, alternatively, the last Roman emperor, the leader of the (Sunni) Muslim community, and the guarantor of justice and order on Earth.

This idealized image hides the fact that Ottoman rulers had to compete with entrenched interest groups in conquered territories, and the members of their own military-political elite (the *askeri* class, whose members were exempt from taxes, and received land grants and stipends from the ruler), for the control, use, and redistribution of available resources. Indeed, an important factor behind the expansion of Ottoman governance was the rulers' search for better control over the elite, while the large peasant population was kept in check through the management of taxes as well as the administration of justice. As a tool of control, conflict resolution, and legitimization, the administration of justice was a crucial component of Ottoman governance. Other ideological justifications were created and defended in Ottoman chancery documents, works of history, and writings of a religious nature, whose volume increased concomitantly with the expansion of Ottoman governance. In a society without a wide use of the printing press and the mass consumption of the written word, new public rituals helped bring together the elite with the members of the urban merchant and artisanal classes. In an early modern environment, even the most methodical administration saw its activities hampered, if not by fortune itself, then by the limitations imposed by the available technologies and the natural environment;[5] thus "the projection of power" through public rituals and other ceremonial forms offered another tool of governance, which was utilized to create consent among different constituencies.[6]

In the absence of documentary evidence, Ottoman governance in the fourteenth century can only be discussed through the lens of Ottoman chronicles, mostly composed in the second half of the fifteenth century.[7] Leaving aside the problem of chronological distance, we can extract from them the story of a tribal polity whose dynastic leadership incrementally distanced itself from the companions of yore (Muslim and Christian soldiers of fortune, low-level dervishes and tribal elements who lived and fought together with the leadership of the Ottoman tribe) by augmenting its political and economic power. These companions and their descendants retained a level of political and military power, however, and spearheaded Ottoman expansion into the Balkans and parts of Anatolia. They received land and other sources of revenue in return for their activities. The few surviving royal endowment deeds (*vakfiye*) from the first decades of the fourteenth century show that the dynasty sought to establish alliances with the dervish element through the redistribution of wealth garnered during military conquest. The endowment deeds became more detailed and sophisticated in style and content through time, under the impact of migrant learned men lending their services to the dynasty. The properties designated in the deeds increased in scope and number, and the endowments' charitable purposes included the creation and maintenance of building complexes in urban areas, with clear ritual and ideological functions. Members of prominent Muslim families in Anatolia also benefited from the mechanism of endowing properties to assert themselves within economic and urban life. The descendants of the soldiers of fortune, who spearheaded Ottoman military expansion and eventually established mini-dynasties on the Balkan frontier, secured their political and economic power in the Balkans through the use of endowments as well. The endowment, *vakıf*, thus emerged very early on as a major tool of governance that was utilized by the political center as well as other political and military actors.[8]

In Ottoman chronicles, taxes (some of which predated the Ottoman conquest) become more evident from the reign of Murad I (r. 1362–89) onwards. However, their imposition and collection cannot be assumed to have been regular or unchallenged. An important development was the emergence of the ruler's claim to one fifth of the slaves captured during raids (or one fifth of the nominal value of captured slaves in cash), under the name of *pencik*; this was legitimized, according to the chroniclers, with reference to the Islamic practice of ceding one fifth of the spoils of war to the leader of the Muslim community. Slaves collected through this form of taxation allowed the Ottoman ruler to create a fighting force loyal to him, the janissaries. By the end of the fourteenth century, the practice of *devşirme*, a related form of slavery-based military recruitment, seems to have been in place. Young boys were gathered from Christian families in the Balkans and Anatolia, at the rate of one from every forty households. They were raised as Muslims, to serve as janissaries, palace servants and, especially after the mid-fifteenth century, governors and viziers whose legal status as the slaves of the ruler bound them closely to the dynasty.[9] Military recruitment was conducted through other channels as well. Next to the raiders in frontier areas, troops supplied by vassals, nomadic-tribal cavalry units, and the janissaries, able-bodied men who typically worked the land in times of peace were drafted in infantry, cavalry, and auxiliary units in exchange for daily pay and tax exemptions.[10]

The fourteenth century also witnessed the Ottoman appropriation of a joint system of military recruitment and resource management that had been utilized, before the Ottomans, by various Islamic polities and the Byzantines. Particularly from Bayezid I (r. 1389–1402) onwards, the land revenue grant (*timar*) became more widespread.[11] Grants under the same name had been assigned to prominent military men and members of the ruler's retinue before Bayezid. *Timar* under Bayezid was given out in larger numbers, and smaller sizes, to lower-ranking military men and various associates and allies of the Ottoman enterprise, including some Christians in the Balkans. The revenue collected locally by the grantee (in the form of taxes and fines) usually matched his rank and function; in exchange, the grantees (called *sipahis*, "cavalrymen" in Ottoman usage) joined the army in campaign, in person or with small retinues; they were also expected to provide order and security in their designated areas.[12] Newly conquered lands were controlled through *timars* and tax farms, which not only increased the military and financial capabilities of the political center but also allowed the Ottomans to better incorporate these territories into their domains.[13] When annexation was not feasible, however, military power was used to secure vassalage relationships with local and regional dynasties in Anatolia and the Balkans, who paid tribute in the form of money and troops. Bayezid I's reign is also notable for attempts at increasing the ruler's political and cultural cachet. As a reaction, some Ottoman chroniclers, who sympathized with the polity's centrifugal elements, severely criticized Bayezid's various policies. In their accounts, Bayezid's rule is portrayed as a time when migrant secretaries from the Persianate East advised the ruler, and newly appointed judges abused their positions, while the increasingly distant Bayezid reveled in courtly pleasures in the company of his wife, a Serbian princess.[14]

By the time Bayezid I was defeated by Timur (r. 1370–1405) at the Battle of Ankara in 1402, there were diffuse yet recognizable practices and institutions, such as the *timar*, or the janissary army. There were three governorates-general (*beylerbeylik*), and their territories corresponded to the Balkan possessions, western and northwestern Anatolia, and north-central Anatolia, respectively. These were divided into provinces (*sancak*); medium-sized and small *timar*s, supporting members of the military-political elite with different ranks and functions, stemmed from them like bunches of grapes. There was a visible political center, where the ruler was supported by a small cadre of advisors/ministers (*vezir*); these advisors were not specialized administrators, and instead dealt with any problems as they came along. In rural areas, the subjects of the ruler experienced Ottoman rule, whenever they did, through the *sipahi*s, or the judges (*kadı*) found in townships. Urban areas, despite their long civic traditions, felt the Ottoman presence more heavily. Most of the existing local authorities resided in towns and cities; the ruler and the high-ranking members of his elite offered charity as well as better provisioning and security to urban dwellers. Law (as a set of rules that define property rights and the subjects' obligations, and maintain communal peace) was seen as an adaptable construct by the Ottoman conquerors, who accommodated the legal practices and cultures they encountered. The pre-existing legal discourses, and particularly the Sharia and customary law in the Muslim-dominated areas of Anatolia, offered both a challenge and a convenience to the new conquerors. Despite his growing political, financial and ideological power, the Ottoman ruler did not have much formal legal prerogative at the end of the fourteenth century.

Following the 1402–13 Interregnum, and particularly after the accession of Murad II (r. 1421–44, 1446–51), the main features of Ottoman governance become less blurred. Murad II's reign coincided with the rise of Hungary as the major competitor of the Ottomans in the Balkans, and witnessed a few crusading expeditions that shook the foundations of the Ottoman presence in the area.[15] Ottoman battle tactics and military logistics, which now relied on and supported a more intensive use of gunpowder weapons in offensive and defensive warfare, were accordingly transformed; as a result, from the first decades of the fifteenth century onwards, the business of war became more costly.[16] The Ottoman search for better control over land and resources led to a new level of sophistication in the administration of the provinces. The provinces continued to contribute to military recruitment through *timar*s. Larger grants that yielded more revenue, such as *zeamet* (assigned to mid-level officials), and *has* (typically assigned to provincial governors and governors-general), supported higher-ranking members of the Ottoman administration. The ruler received a share from provincial revenues through myriad sources bundled under the name of *havass-ı humayun*, i.e., imperial reserves.[17] His revenue sources included taxes from agricultural yields, levies from artisans and merchants, the poll tax collected from the non-Muslims, tax farms (*mukataa*), and taxes and other revenues in cash from mines, customs, salt works, mints, etc.[18]

The capture of Constantinople in 1453 by Mehmed II (r. 1444–46, 1451–81) signified an important turning point in the local and global reputation of the Ottoman dynasty, and the cultural (indeed religious) aura around the Ottoman rulers began to grow. While Bayezid I and Murad II had experimented with titles that emphasized the authority of the Ottoman ruler above the military-political elite, and over Anatolia and the Balkans, Mehmed II now became the ruler of "the two continents and the two seas," a claimant to the Roman/ Byzantine legacy, and a sultan who had realized an old prophecy about Constantinople's eventual conquest by the Muslims.[19] The geographical span of the enterprise was further enlarged under Mehmed II and, to a lesser extent, Bayezid II (r. 1481–1512). The level of cultural and military competition with regional rivals concomitantly increased. The Ottoman poltical center now preferred annexation over vassalage, and the smaller powers in Anatolia and the Balkans disappeared; the Ottoman–Hungarian competition intensified; the Ottomans increased their presence in the Eastern Mediterranean and competed with the Venetians; and most of the Black Sea shore entered Ottoman control. Further east, the Ottomans clashed with the Aqqoyunlu and the Mamluks over the control of eastern Anatolia. These developments required a better supervision of the available resources.

It is possible to follow the transformation of Ottoman governance from the first decades of the fifteenth century to the first decades of the sixteenth through secretarial recruitment, recording types and practices, and document content. The Ottoman political center had utilized as secretaries a composite group that included Muslim learned men who had migrated into Ottoman territories, secretaries who had been employed by Turko-Muslim polities taken over by the Ottomans, members of the "Byzantine scribal class," as well as "Hellenized south Slavic cadres." The local cadres, with their knowledge of the legal and administrative practices before the Ottoman conquest, and the linguistic ability to communicate with the local populations, worked in the preparation of land surveys (*tahrir*) that created Ottoman control over resources and fed members of the Ottoman military-political elite through revenue assignments. They also conducted the diplomatic correspondence of the ruler at a time when the Ottomans entered into more formal relations with various European powers.[20] Migrant secretaries from other Islamic polities made the Ottomans better acquainted with the administrative knowhow and techniques of Ilkhanid and Timurid polities to the East.[21] Ottoman secretaries could thus use Ilkhanid/Timurid tools (a Persian vocabulary and a chancery shorthand) to record the revenues of a Balkan province on the basis of information obtained by a local agent who may have been a Christian or a recent convert to Islam. In time, secretaries with more permanent positions and better-defined duties came to form an embryonic financial bureaucracy. Between the last decade of the fifteenth century and the second decade of the sixteenth, the numbers of secretaries working for the central treasury (*hzane-i amire*) fluctuated between fifteen and twenty. The palace gift registers where these numbers can be observed also record apprentices who received on-the-job training.[22] The financial secretaries encountered in these sources have titles that reflect a division of labor: they deal, alternatively, with daily revenue, expenses, revenues from tax farms, or revenues and expenses under a specific governorate-general. In contrast, even by the end of the fifteenth century, the chancery appears understaffed, and its workload undifferentiated.

The expansion in Ottoman governance is reflected in the growing number and types of records from this period. From Murad II onwards, the land survey register (*tahrir defteri*), which was used to assess revenue and distribute *tmar*, is encountered more frequently. These registers offer a practical as well as symbolic mapping of the Ottoman domains: they identify the sources of revenue, and the Ottoman subjects and officials in the provinces; they also extend a claim to sovereignty and control over specific lands, communities, and resources. There are nine extant registers from the reign of Murad II, and thirty-two from the time of Mehmed II.[23] From the reign of Mehmed II, we also have the earliest extant copies of the "detailed" (*mufassal*) registers. It is possible that there were other registers that disappeared, either for natural reasons or because they became redundant when a new survey was prepared. However, the surviving materials are representative enough of the aims, capabilities and challenges of the political center.

Some of these concerns and issues are illustrated in a land survey register from 1431–32. The register provides the overview of a *sancak* (literally "banner," a unit below the governorate-general) that covers most of the territory of today's Albania. In the register, the land is presented as a succession of *tımar* holdings; towns and villages, with estimates of their annual yields, are listed under these holdings, and the names of the individual grant holders are recorded. Some of the secretaries who worked in the survey are Christians; others are recent converts; all have a specific knowledge of the area's customs and languages. Some *tımar*-holders are Christians, but the highest-ranking recipients are all Muslim; some of the Muslim *tımar*-holders are listed as having been relocated to this frontier area from western Anatolia, where some of them were similarly holding *tımar*s. The register is an answer to the challenges of controlling the region and particularly its landed aristocrats, whose existence predated the fairly recent Ottoman conquest; it is also likely that the compilation of the register, which was seen as a further encroachment by the landed aristocrats, provided one of the reasons behind the Albanian rebellion of 1432. The element of discontent is obvious in the case of towns and villages whose representatives refused to meet the surveyors or provide estimates of their yearly yields.[24]

Related to the urge to secure revenues for an expanding central apparatus with ever-larger political ambitions, various forms of documentation about the palace household and financial management were produced in the second half of the fifteenth century. Five registers gathered in a single volume, from 1478 to 1480 CE (883–85 AH), portray a growing palace household that includes military men serving the ruler (different from the janissary army) as well as individuals assisting the day-to-day management of the palace household, from the kitchens to the gardens.[25] The financial imperative is seen in the ways in which the palace records the revenue in cash obtained from mines, salt works, marketplaces, and customs.[26] Two registers on the daily revenues and activities of the treasury, one from the time of Mehmed II and the other from Bayezid II, are further indications of a growing concern with revenue as well as record-keeping.[27] Another source of cash revenue is the poll tax imposed on non-Muslims, as recorded in five registers from ca. 1486 to 1510 CE (891–916 AH).[28] Next to military expenditures, these revenues are partly redistributed to the elite, as seen in records of salaries as well as a register that lists the contents and recipients of the ruler's largesse.[29] Other registers include records of salaries paid to troops manning fortresses in militarily important areas, such as the Adriatic and the northern Black Sea coast, and roll calls of infantrymen spread throughout the Anatolian provinces.[30]

Together with the financial bureaucracy, the imperial council (*divan*) slowly emerged as a locus of power. A register recording the council's decrees (*hükm*) to various officials between 8–17 June and 8–17 July 1501 offers a telling picture about the concerns, capabilities, and challenges of Ottoman governance.[31] The register is a testimony to the growing impact and workload of the council, whose existence became more formalized under Mehmed II with the participation of the viziers, the two military judges (*kazasker*) who helped manage the military-political elite, the treasurers (*defterdar*) of Rumeli and Anadolu, and the chancellor (*nişancı*). The transactions recorded in the register portray the council as a general supervisory body and a high court whose decision is sought in cases that are unresolved by local judges and authorities. The financial imperative is of primary importance, since the majority of the deliberations pertain to issues of taxation (including different forms of taxation, exceptions, refusal to pay taxes), and problems stemming from the assignment and exploitation of *tımar*s. The judges in the provinces appear as the most important supervisors, executors, and interlocutors of the center's decisions. The governors-general, various provincial governors, and the princes serving as provincial governors are the other major addressees of these decrees. If the number of dispatched decrees is an indicator of the level of control and the quality of communication, it then appears that the most connected geographical area is the governorate of Anadolu (in western and northwestern Anatolia), to which nearly half of the 479 decrees are addressed. Anadolu is followed by Rumeli (the Balkan possessions, 157 decrees), Rum (north-central Anatolia, 26 decrees), and Karaman (south-central Anatolia, 15 decrees). Several decrees address the case of the members of the military-political elite who clashed with other members of the elite over the use of assigned resources; these show both the level of tension within the elite, as well as the power of the council, which now intervenes in issues that would have been negotiated (and fought out) locally in previous eras.

In terms of regularity, the documentary evidence from this period is spotty at best. Documents and registers were prepared when the need presented itself, and their preservation was not always given the highest priority. At the same time, the vocabulary of Ottoman governance developed and spread around. The register (*defter*) started its rise to a ubiquitous presence in Ottoman administrative practice. The taxation and exploitation of the land was increasingly regulated through the preparation of diplomas (*berat*) and titles (*tapu*, which did not always give the right to sell or endow the property, but recognized the right of transfer). The number and size of endowments continued to increase, and the endowment solidified its function as a charitable/ideological institution, as well as a way to preserve individual/familial and communal wealth (for religious orders) by placing it under the protection of the Sharia. The struggle between the political center and various actors, over the control of land and its resources, is better observed in this period through the documentary evidence. While the political center advanced claims about the dynastic ownership of all land within the realm, various individuals and groups referred to privileges, stemming from the pre-Ottoman past or the earlier years of the Ottoman enterprise, to defend their rights either on the land itself or on its revenues.[32] The centrifugal elements that claimed historical and ancestral privileges included the descendants of the old companions in the Balkans, who continued to function as frontier commanders and competed with the political center over the use of resources available in the area. The strengthening of the janissaries and the palace troops in terms of effectives as well as matériel, facilitated by a better control over financial resources, helped counterbalance the frontier elements' military weight.

Another significant development of the period is the rise of the ruler's legal prerogative. Ottoman legal practice encompassed several historical and legal traditions. The Sharia offered rules for a social organization within which Muslims were placed above the non-Muslims from a legal and religious/cultural standpoint; it also underwrote a variety of claims to individual ownership rights that often posed a challenge to Ottoman attempts at financial control. The acts of Ottoman rulers and administrators, together with the rules and legislations of the territories they took over, contributed to a body of customary law that synthesized local tradition with present-day necessities. With Mehmed II and Bayezid II, we see the emergence of the first legal "texts" that brought together elements of these different legal practices. The first such text, following the conquest of Constantinople, offered a criminal code that was applicable to all subjects, Muslim and non-Muslim alike; it also contained several rules on taxation, but these treated Muslims and non-Muslims separately. A second legal text, originally prepared around 1476, placed the ruler atop a hierarchy of officials, and located the officials themselves within a detailed and hierarchical court protocol. Other legal documents from the time of Mehmed II include decrees on mines, coinage, and customs and monopolies. Under Bayezid II, the legal prerogative was deployed to address the realities of specific provinces, through rules and regulations placed at the beginning of land survey registers.

In these legal texts, the dynastic law, *kanun*, emerged as a source of law as well as an arbiter and a harmonizer. Moreover, they further distinguished the ruler from the elite, and the members of the military-political elite from the subject population at large.[33] While it often dealt with specific issues, *kanun* was a universal instrument, since it usually applied to Muslim and non-Muslim subjects alike. The spread of Ottoman law was made possible, in this period, by the expansion of the Ottoman legal network to the near-totality of the realm through the appointment of judges. The judges, together with *timar*-holders and provincial governors, more and more became the embodiments of an Ottoman financial-legal regime; they also contributed to the growing level of documentation by keeping court registers *sicil*. The rising numbers of these agents in the provinces increased the interactions between the local populations and the representatives of the political center, and helped "Ottomanize" (and sometimes further alienate) local groups and communities.

While the main directions and techniques of Ottoman governance had thus been laid out between the mid-fifteenth century and the first decade of the sixteenth, the reign of Süleyman (r. 1520–66) required a considerable expansion in governance, as an answer to the enlargement of the territories and population under Ottoman control, as well as the growing military and ideological competition with the Habsburgs in the West and the Safavids in the East. Selim I (r. 1512–20) had captured eastern Anatolia, Syria, and Egypt, acquiring control of the Holy Cities of Mecca and Medina in the process; Süleyman extended the empire further into the Mediterranean, Central and northeastern Europe, Iraq, and the Persian Gulf. Territorial expansion did not end with Süleyman, and the competition with the Habsburgs and the Safavids continued to determine Ottoman imperial policy.[34] These imperial struggles required novel administrative measures for a better supervision of land and resources, and the provisioning of the military forces whose sphere of action expanded considerably. The strong religious dimension of imperial conflict, particularly felt in the first half of the sixteenth century, pushed the Ottomans to paint themselves as advocates of Sunni Islam against what they initially termed as Safavid heresy, and later recognized as Twelver Shiism. The competition with the Habsburgs was not devoid of cultural tensions as well, as seen in both sides' claims to universal monarchy.[35] The universalist political ideologies of the period underwrote a specific vision of governance that began to look more like a "state." Despite the natural and structural barriers it faced, this early modern empire yearned to establish peace and security for its subjects while imposing perfect discipline on the members of its ruling elite. Dynastic law was promoted not only as a practical tool, but as an abstract ideal that contributed to a better management of the realm.

Under Süleyman, the political center expanded considerably, in terms of the individuals it employed, the documents it produced, and the sphere of action it claimed. The number and content of pre-existing forms of documentation increased; new forms of documentation and record-keeping (including a more careful approach to the preservation of older documents) came to the fore; the palace and the imperial council produced more documents; and the chancery and financial bureaucracies were increasingly distinguished from one another. The political center included different components, such as the imperial council, the ruler and the palace household, the office of the grand vizier, the chancery bureaucracy, the financial bureaucracy, and the legal-educational establishment. The constituents of these components did not always share the same views and visions, even though they ultimately constituted the empire's ruling elite, together with the *tımar*-holders in the provinces and the janissary army. The distinction among the men of the sword (*seyfiye*), the men of the pen (*kalemiye*, the secretaries), and the men of learning (*ilmiye*, the members of the legal-educational establishment) reflected an increased level of professional differentiation, as well as distinct and sometimes rival cultural identities.

One of the ways for the ruler to better supervise the empire and control the *tımar*-holders was to increase the number of land surveys (*tahrir*). In the areas of the empire where the *tımar* system was applied, the registers were drafted with more regularity, and the bulk of the nearly 2,000 *tahrir* registers that survive to this day date from the sixteenth century.[36] Between 1531 and 1536, Süleyman ensured through a series of decrees that *tımar*s beyond the introductory level would be granted with the ruler's approval.[37] The urge for information gathering and control is clearly seen in a unique group of registers from 1530, which together provide a panoramic vision of the empire's natural, economic and human resources.[38] Each register offers a "counting" (*muhasebe*) of a specific governorate-general: Rumeli (listed in two different registers, BOA TD 167 and 370), Anadolu (BOA TD 166 and 438), Karaman and Rum (BOA TD 387), and Diyarbekir-Arab-Zulkadriyye (the Levant and southeastern Anatolia, BOA TD 998). (Egypt, conquered in 1517, was not managed through the *tımar* system, and contributed annual payments to the treasury.)[39] These registers include the different levels and types of resources (land, mines, customs; *tımar, zeamet, has*) and the revenues these bring; they list the titles and effectives of Ottoman officials (governors, *tımar*-holders, fortress troops, judges, madrasa teachers); they collate the number of tax payers and those exempt from taxes; they enumerate towns and villages, with figures on the revenues they produce. Through the expansion of pre-existing registers, such as the *tımar ruznamçe*, or the introduction of new registers, such as the *rüus* (after 1546–47), the political center also strove to record the names of those who received *tımar*s and other appointments.[40] Finally, the *tımar* system, as before, helped manage the new territories added into the empire. By the end of Süleyman's rule, a list of governorates-general prepared by his longest-serving chancellor included the old Rumeli, Anadolu, Karaman, and Rum, and added units that came into being as the result of conquests by Selim (Aleppo, Damascus, Egypt, Zulkadriyye, Diyarbekr, and Kurdistan) and Süleyman (Cezair, i.e., the Mediterranean islands, Maghreb, Tripoli of Libya, Basra, Baghdad, Erzurum, Van, Luristan, Buda, Timisoara, Yemen).[41] Later conquests, such as the capture of Cyprus in 1571, further expanded this list; administrative reorganization added Bosnia in 1580; attempts at better controlling frontier areas led to the emergence of other governorates such as Eger and Kanizsa in the west, and Tbilisi and Tabriz in the east, some of which were short-lived.

These measures required the recruitment of more secretaries, and the expansion of the imperial council's scope. The imperial council, like other offices, had received a more formal definition under the rule of Mehmed II, as a managerial and advisory body that included specific officials such as the viziers, the two military judges, the treasurers of Rumeli and Anadolu, and the chancellor. The council not only symbolized the growing weight of government, but the distance between the ruler and his servants: the ruler would not attend the council meetings unless necessary, and the grand vizier would thus serve as a liaison between the council and the ruler. Under Süleyman, a new physical location was appointed for the council, and a more intense meeting schedule was adopted. The institution of the vizierate became more hierarchical, with the grand vizier being supported by the second, third, and fourth viziers. The figure of the grand vizier, as someone with executive prerogatives who could act as the ruler's surrogate, came to the fore particularly after the appointment of İbrahim Pasha in 1523. The commander of the janissaries, visiting governors-general, the admiral of the navy, and other officials could participate in the council meetings when required. The council became a locus for the coordination of different types of activity. These ranged from visibly important issues, such as the decision to go to war, to less visibly important issues that nevertheless fulfilled an important symbolic function, such as cases of personal grievance that found their way from different parts of the empire into the council.[42]

Both the treasury and the chancery began to employ secretaries in larger numbers in this period. From 1494–95 to 1527, the number of secretaries working for the chancery increased from five to eleven; it reached fifteen in 1531, and nineteen in 1548–49.[43] The individual in charge of the supervision of the land survey registers (*defter emini*) saw the growth of a bureau around himself, particularly after the decrees demanding central supervision over *tımar* grants. From a group of five, those working for the imperial registry (*defterhane-i amire*) increased to forty in the last decades of the sixteenth century. This bureau worked closely with the office of the chancellor, another position that rose to prominence under Süleyman.[44] The chancellor did not only supervise the functioning of the *tımar* system, however. In this period, he distinguished himself as an official who composed the ruler's decrees and correspondence (often with foreign rulers), and who contributed to the drafting of the ruler's law codes.[45] The secretaries working for the imperial council produced, every year, several thousand decrees whose contents are similar to the ones discussed above, in the case of a register from Bayezid II's reign.[46] The number of decrees increased nearly tenfold in this period, however. Perhaps more importantly, some of these decrees reflected a different notion of governance.

Individual decrees from earlier decades in the century, as well as the compilations of the council's decrees under the title of *mühimme* from the late 1550s, indicate the concerns of an early modern empire that is now interested more actively in the maintenance of "peace and security" (*emn u aman*), the compliance of its subjects, and the pursuit of deviance, either in the form of alternative religious beliefs or rebellious behavior. Also in this period, the symbiosis between the ruler and the secretaries became more pronounced. Through their drafting of the ruler's official correspondence and decrees, some of which were read publicly, the chancery secretaries developed a sophisticated official voice, one that reflected the level of ideological speculation around the figure of the ruler.[47] The ruler oftentimes saw the secretaries as instruments with which he could check the power of influential members of the military-political elite, since the secretaries ideally served the ruler by helping actualize the universal principles enshrined in Sharia and *kanun*. These ideals also led to tensions between the secretaries and the rulers: the secretaries developed a corresponding meritocratic narrative, and expected fair treatment in pay, appointments, and promotions. In the later decades of the century, their frustration found an outlet in the composition of critical treatises on the empire's decline.[48]

In the meantime, the offices and personnel under the treasury continued its growth. As discussed above, already in the late fifteenth century, the treasury employed more personnel with better-defined tasks compared to the chancery. There were two treasurers by the end of Mehmed II's reign, one for Rumeli and the other for Anadolu, both of whom resided in Istanbul as members of the imperial council. Selim's conquests in the East led to the creation of a treasurer for "*Arab ve Acem*," i.e., the lands of the Arabs and the Persians, who resided in Damascus and later in Aleppo. Early in Süleyman's reign, another treasurer resident in Istanbul, charged with the collection of revenues in and around the capital, was created, increasing the number of treasurers in the imperial council to three. From the 1540s onwards, we see the installation of treasurers of lower rank in major provinces of the empire. Throughout the sixteenth century, some twenty such positions emerged, some of which disappeared later.[49] Compared with the chancery, the treasury's agents had a more visible presence throughout the empire. Also, the financial career increasingly became more lucrative, and offered greater opportunities for promotion.[50] The number of treasury secretaries working in the capital increased from nearly twenty in the late fifteenth century to sixty-eight in 1574–75, and one hundred and eighty-three by 1592–93.[51]

Very much like the chancery, the workload of the treasury increased several-fold throughout the course of the sixteenth century, as shown by a series of registers that record various treasury transactions (*maliye ahkam defterleri*).[52] In these registers, the treasury is seen as functioning fairly independently; decisions on taxation and revenue-collection as well as some *tımar*-related questions are made under the treasurer's authority and relayed to the provinces. The ruler's properties and endowments occupy an important place in these transactions, together with taxes and revenues collected from tax farms, customs, animals, mines, fisheries, etc. Endowments continue to be an important source of revenue collection and redistribution for the members of the elite as well as for wealthy individuals. The territorial expansion of the first half of the century, the increased integration of the Ottoman economy with regional and global markets, and the growing need for cash to support the palace and the military establishment created both opportunities and challenges in the treasury's search for revenue. The business of government, or government as business, is a theme that crisscrosses the various documents and registers prepared by the treasury and its agents in this period.

Other components of Ottoman governance in the sixteenth century included the ruler and his household, and the network of courts and judges working for the ruler throughout the empire. The messianic persona adopted early on in Süleyman's reign gave the ruler a particular aura; later on, this messianic persona left its place to the figure of the ruler as the maker of dynastic law (*kanun*), which was described as a universal body of regulations that promised justice to the empire's subjects.[53] The palace household employed cooks, gardeners, artisans, and other officials; it also included several thousand military men distributed among different cavalry, infantry, and artillery units. The impact of the household in the empire's economy, mostly as a consumer and an agent of charitable redistribution, was considerable. Women, who were denied political roles in the Ottoman society at large, could become involved in household politics within the palace, and act as benefactors to the subject population through their charitable works.[54] The Ottoman courts brought together the rules and regulations sent from the center with the claims and problems of the subjects. The numerous court registers from the sixteenth century do not reflect the totality of attempts at problem solving, since some issues were resolved at the communal level; it is also obvious that Muslims used Ottoman courts more frequently than non-Muslims. Still, the court records give enough indications about the main dynamics of life in an early modern society that was more and more connected, internally and externally, with political and economic networks. In these registers, there is a society within which economic transactions, extending from the purchase and sale of immovable and movable property (most notably slaves) to cases related to taxation, rents, loans, and prices, inexorably connect Ottoman subjects from different backgrounds. Despite religious and cultural restrictions, women assert themselves in different ways; they are sometimes the objects and victims of male desire and violence; often, they also emerge as laborers, property owners, and, in general, claimants to an Ottoman/ dynastic justice that legitimized itself through its offer of protection.[55] The legal scholars and judges, men with madrasa backgrounds, increasingly came to the fore in this period, both as the formulators and interpreters of a new body of law that reflected Ottoman realities, and also as the supervisors of new forms of resource extraction and wealth accumulation.[56]

The features of Ottoman governance continued to change after Süleyman's reign ended in 1566, and these changes came, as before, as answers to challenges that stemmed from several directions: population growth and the concomitant pressure on land and resources; the "price revolution" and the globally high levels of inflation; the "military revolution," which led to a sharp rise in military expenditures; and the increasing impact of the "Little Ice Age," whose effect on agricultural productivity strained the empire's finances and further fed into social problems such as banditry and peasant flight.[57] Ottoman governance, as it had developed in the sixteenth century, was based on a working yet precarious collection of arrangements that reflected the empire's geographical and demographic diversity. At the turn of the sixteenth century, and throughout the seventeenth, the vulnerability of these arrangements to change was severely tested by the above-mentioned challenges.[58] The *tımar* system remained in place, but the amount of lands devoted to it decreased, being replaced by tax farms that allowed a better adaptation to increased monetization. Empire-wide surveys ended after the late sixteenth century, and new surveys were almost completely reserved for newly conquered territories or areas recovered from the enemy. *Avarız*, an extraordinary tax collected in kind and in cash, was administered with increasing frequency in the seventeenth century.[59] Factional struggles among the different constituents of the military-political elite increased, and the janissaries and the religious scholars distinguished themselves as particularly powerful interest groups within the empire's political life.[60] In a way, groups that were created and empowered by the Ottoman political center utilized the political arena to assert themselves, often making references to concepts such as law (*kanun* as well as Sharia) and justice that had been made a cornerstone of Ottoman governance from the mid-fifteenth century onwards.

Throughout the period discussed in this chapter, the Ottoman administration had to cope with a dynamic social panorama within which nomads, peasants, merchants, and members of the military-political elite pursued individual, local, and communal interests, trying to create and then supervise spaces of negotiation for various interests.[61] The growth of the early modern state, as a "coordinated and territorially bounded network of agents exercising political power," was an incremental and multifaceted process that resulted in the emergence of "a network of offices." The bureaucratic apparatus was small but, at the same time, it included relatively well-defined institutions with relatively well-defined purviews. Rulers had to take counsel and accept the placement of various constraints on their discretionary powers. In this context, beyond the individual rulers, legislation and the administration of justice became the purview of the central institutions.[62] The dawn of early modernity was a remarkable period with regard to the "increase of governance": relative administrative centralization was accompanied by the participation of individuals and groups at various levels, and the increase of governance led to the institutionalization of power relations via "a series of multilateral initiatives to be negotiated across space and through the social order."[63]

Early modern empires do not have to be judged according to whether they were precursors to the modern nation-state. At the same time, they cannot be easily dismissed as a loose form of organization that was particularly infested and incapacitated by patronage and factionalism; instead, they have to be evaluated as functional entities within their specific contexts.[64] In an early modern environment, power was exercised through networks, encounters, and interactions, as a dynamic practice; the intensity of power ebbed and flowed between naked aggression and paternalistic consolation; finally, the exercise of power in the early modern Ottoman society addressed several interlocutors and required their participation, rather than imposing a one-way relationship. In the Ottoman case, the natural barriers in front of intensive governance are obvious: the sheer size of the empire, and the variations in its geography, rendered quick communication and travel difficult. While the vocabulary of governance expanded, and the political center increased its claims to control, the military-political elite and the subject population had to rely on the power of wind, animals, and humans for travel, production, and resource extraction. When coercion did not or would not work, several compromises and exceptions were written into the body of Ottoman governance, ranging from the types and amounts of taxes collected in different areas to the level of political control exercised by the agents of the central government, and the level of freedom enjoyed by local notables.[65] Following Michael Mann, we can argue that the power exercised by the political center ranged between extensive and intensive, and authoritative and diffuse, depending on geographical distance, resource availability, and elite and popular consent/resistance.[66] Intensive and authoritative forms of power were easily exercised in close proximity to the political, military, ideological, and economic sources of control, but their range was limited. Perhaps the greatest achievement of the Ottoman political center was its creation of extensive forms of power, which allowed the establishment of a dialogue with individuals and communities from the center to the frontiers, and diffused forms of power, which led to a trickling down of the elite's cultural and political ideals.

Notes

1 I thank Nikolay Antov, Mehmet Beşikçi, William Caferro, Erdem Çıpa, Christopher Markiewicz, and Hendrik Spruyt for their comments.

   While the European authors of the Renaissance called the Ottomans "Turks," I prefer to use "Ottoman" as noun and adjective throughout this article since "Turk" now refers to a modern national and ethnic construct that did not exist as such in the early modern period. To make the chapter more accessible to non-Ottomanists I eschew the use of Ottoman-specific terminology as far as possible. All dates refer to the Common Era, even though the Ottomans used the Hicri (*Hijri* in Arabic) lunar calendar, which begins in 622 CE. For Ottoman Turkish (a language written in Arabic script), I follow the simpler modern Turkish orthography instead of a full transliteration with diacritical marks. Here is a simple pronunciation guide: c: "j" as in joy; ç: "ch" as in child; ğ: this letter lengthens the preceding vowel; ı: "e" as in open; i: "i" as in kid; ö: "u" as in turn; ş: "sh" as in sharp; ü: as the German letter "ü" in *über*. Vowels and consonants are not combined to form diphthongs or other sounds, and all the letters are meant to be pronounced.

2 Niccolò Machiavelli, *The Prince*, ed. and trans. David Wootton, Indianapolis: Hackett, 1995, p. 15. I am borrowing López de Gómara's remarks from Carmen Bernand & Serge Gruzinski, *Histoire du nouveau monde. De la découverte à la conquête*, Paris: Fayard, 1991, p. 242, n. 59. For Busbecq's views on the Ottomans see Kaya Şahin, "Political Pragmatism, Humanist Ideals and Early Modern Orientalism in Busbecq's *Turkish Letters*," forthcoming in Marcus Keller and Javier Irigoyen-García (eds.), *The Dialectics of Orientalism in Early Modern Europe*, New York: Palgrave Macmillan, 2016. For Shah Tahmasb's views, see *Tazkirah-i Shah Tahmasb*, ed. Karim Fayzi, Qum: Matbu'at-i Dini, 1383 [2004], pp. 80, 113, 122–4. For reports by Daniello de Ludovisi, Bernardo Navagero, and Domenico Trevisano see *Relazioni degli ambasciatori veneti al Senato*, series 3, vol. 1, ed. Eugenio Albèri, Florence: Società editrice fiorentina, 1840, pp. 1–32, 33–110, 111–92, respectively; for reports by Tommaso Contarini and Tommaso Mocenigo, see *ibid.*, vol. 14: *Costantinopoli: relazioni inediti (1512–1789)*, ed. Maria Pia Pedani-Fabris, Padua: Bottega d'Erasmo, 1996, pp. 33–9, 41–5 respectively.

3   For Ottoman secretaries' contributions to the management and legitimization of the empire, see Kaya Şahin, *Empire and Power in the Reign of Süleyman: Narrating the Sixteenth-Century Ottoman World*, New York: Cambridge University Press, 2013, pp. 214–42.

4   For a discussion and critique of these approaches, see *ibid.*, pp. 243–52.

5   For a discussion of these limitations see Jack A. Goldstone, "The Problem of the 'Early Modern' World," *Journal of the Economic and Social History of the Orient* 41, 3, 1998, pp. 249–84.

6   See Wayne E. Lee, "Projecting Power in the Early Modern World: The Spanish Model?" in Wayne E. Lee (ed.), *Empires and Indigenes: Intercultural Alliance, Imperial Expansion, and Warfare in the Early Modern World*, New York and London: New York University Press, 2011, pp. 1–2.

7   For a concise study of fourteenth-century Ottoman governance, see Linda Darling, "The Development of Ottoman Governmental Institutions in the Fourteenth Century: A Reconstruction," in Markus Koller and Vera Costantini (eds.), *Living in the Ottoman Ecumenical Community: Essays in Honour of Suraiya Faroqhi*, Leiden: Brill, 2008, pp. 15–34.

8   For endowments in Islamic and Ottoman history, see Amy Singer, "Devote the Fruits to Pious Purposes," ch. 1 in *Constructing Ottoman Beneficence: An Imperial Soup Kitchen in Jerusalem*, Albany: State University of New York Press, 2002, pp. 15–37. The Ottoman *vakıf* must have been influenced by Byzantine practices as well. For the earliest Ottoman endowments in the Balkans see M. Tayyib Gökbilgin, *XV. ve XVI. Asırlarda Edirne ve Paşa Livası: Vakıflar-Mülkler-Mukataalar*, İstanbul: İÜEF Yayınları, 1952, pp. 161–76.

9   See Colin Imber, *The Ottoman Empire, 1300–1650: The Structure of Power*, New York: Palgrave Macmillan, 2002, pp. 128–42.

10 For the Ottoman military in the early period, also see Pál Fodor, "Ottoman Warfare, 1300–1453," in Kate Fleet (ed.), *The Cambridge History of Turkey*, vol. 1, *Byzantium to Turkey, 1071–1453*, Cambridge: Cambridge University Press, 2009, pp. 192–226.

11 Direct evidence about the *tımar* under Bayezid is lacking. These conclusions are based on references made to Bayezid's rule in later documents. See Nicoara Beldiceanu, *Le tımar dans l'État ottoman (début XIVe–début XVIe siècle)*, Wiesbaden: Otto Harrassowitz, 1980, pp. 21–6. Some non-Ottoman Turko-Muslim entities in Anatolia had established similar practices, which the Ottomans usually recognized post-conquest. See *ibid.*, pp. 26–30.

12 For *tımar*, see Imber, *Ottoman Empire, 1300–1650*, pp. 193–206.

13 See Halil İnalcık, "Ottoman Methods of Conquest," *Studia Islamica* 2, 1954, pp. 103–29.

14 Cemal Kafadar, *Between Two Worlds: The Construction of the Ottoman State*, Berkeley and Los Angeles: University of California Press, 1995, p. 106.

15 Halil İnalcık, "The Struggle for the Balkans, 1421–1451," in Kenneth M. Setton (ed.), *A History of the Crusades*, vol. 6, *The Impact of the Crusades on Europe*, ed. Harry W. Hazard and Norman P. Zacour, Madison: University of Wisconsin Press, 1989, pp. 222–38.

16 Gábor Ágoston, *Guns for the Sultan: Military Power and the Weapons Industry in the Ottoman Empire*, Cambridge: Cambridge University Press, 2005, pp. 16–24.

17 For more details on Ottoman provincial administration, see I. Metin Kunt, *The Sultan's Servants: The Transformation of Ottoman Provincial Government, 1550–1650*, New York: Columbia University Press, 1983, pp. 9–29.

18 Halil İnalcık, *1300–1600*, vol. 1 in Halil İnalcık and Donald Quataert (eds.), *An Economic and Social History of the Ottoman Empire*, Cambridge: Cambridge University Press, 1994, pp. 55–75. While these sources of revenue become more visible in the documentary evidence in the fifteenth century, they were very likely exploited earlier than that.

19 Kaya Şahin, "Constantinople and the End Time: The Ottoman Conquest as a Portent of the Last Hour," *Journal of Early Modern History* 14, 2010, pp. 317–54.

20 Joel Shinder, "Early Ottoman Administration in the Wilderness: Some Limits on Comparison," *International Journal of Middle East Studies* 9, 4, November 1978, pp. 497–517.

21 For a study on a litterateur/secretary whose career spanned the Aqqoyunlu and Ottoman realms, see Christopher Markiewicz, "The Crisis of Rule in Late Medieval Islam: A Study of Idrīs Bidlīsī (861–926/1457–1520)," unpublished PhD dissertation, University of Chicago, 2015.

22 Cornell H. Fleischer, "Preliminaries to the Study of Ottoman Bureaucracy," *Journal of Turkish Studies* 10, 1986, p. 138; Rıfat Günalan, *Osmanlı İmparatorluğunda Defterdarlık Teşkilâtı ve Bürokrasi (XVI. Yüzyıl Maliye Ahkâm Defterleri)*, İstanbul: Kayıhan Yayınları, 2010, pp. 39–49.

23 For a listing of early registers see Beldiceanu, *Le tımar dans l'État ottoman*, pp. 99–102.

24 The register is published as Halil İnalcık, *Hicrî 835 Tarihli Sûret-i Defter-i Sancak-i Arvanid*, Ankara: Türk Tarih Kurumu Basımevi, 1954.

25 Bilgin Aydın and Rıfat Günalan, *XV.–XVI. Yüzyıllarda Osmanlı Maliyesi ve Defter Sistemi*, İstanbul: Yeditepe, 2008, pp. 34–7. For the growth of the palace household, see Rhoads Murphey, *Exploring Ottoman Sovereignty: Tradition, Image and Practice in the Ottoman Imperial Household, 1400–1800*, London and New York: Continuum, 2008, pp. 141–74.

26 Aydın and Günalan, *XV.–XVI. Yüzyıllarda Osmanlı Maliyesi*, pp. 120–2.

27 *Ibid.*, pp. 177–9, Also see a budget from the time of Bayezid II, in *ibid.*, p. 205.

28 *Ibid.*, p. 153.

29 *Ibid.*, p. 196.

30 *Ibid.*, pp. 92, 93–5, 106.

31 The register was published as İlhan Şahin and Feridun Emecen, *Osmanlılarda Divân-Bürokrasi-Ahkâm: II. Bâyezid Dönemine Ait 906/1501 Tarihli Ahkâm Defteri*, Istanbul: Türk Dünyası Araştırmaları Vakfı, 1994. There is a detailed discussion of the contents, pp. xvii–xxxv. Similar documents, from before the emergence of more regular registers of council decisions around the middle of the sixteenth century, are found in the Prime Ministry Archives in Istanbul. See, for instance, BOA (Prime Ministry Archives), A.DVN. 1, A.DVN. 2, A.NŞT. 1.

32 For a concise description of different types of land from an administrative-fiscal perspective, see İnalcık, *1300–1600*, pp. 139–41; for a longer discussion, see *ibid.*, pp. 103–31; cf. Oktay Özel, "Limits of the Almighty: Mehmed II's 'Land Reform' Revisited," *Journal of the Economic and Social History of the Orient* 42, 2 (1999), pp. 226–46.

33 For Ottoman legal thinking before the sixteenth century, see Snjezana Buzov, "The Lawgiver and His Lawmakers: The Role of Legal Discourse in the Change of Ottoman Imperial Culture," unpublished PhD dissertation, University of Chicago, 2005, pp. 116–23. Also see Halil İnalcık, *The Ottoman Empire: The Classical Age, 1300–1600*, London: Phoenix, 2000 (originally published in 1973), pp. 70–5; Imber, *Ottoman Empire, 1300–1650*, pp. 244–51.

34 For narratives of Ottoman history in this period see Şahin, *Empire and Power in the Reign of Süleyman*, pp. 23–149; Cornell H. Fleischer, *Bureaucrat and Intellectual in the Ottoman Empire: The Historian Mustafa Âli (1541–1600)*, Princeton, NJ: Princeton University Press, 1986, pp. 41–187.

35 Şahin, *Empire and Power in the Reign of Süleyman*, pp. 15–154.

36 For a list of the land survey registers housed at the Prime Ministry Archives in Istanbul and the National Land Registry in Ankara, see *Başbakanlık Osmanlı Arşivi Rehberi*, 3rd exp. edn., Istanbul: Başbakanlık Devlet Arşivleri Genel Müdürlüğü, 2010, pp. 100–37. Here, the registers are presented according to locality. While there are other registers at the Topkapı Palace, and in library collections in and outside of Turkey, this list represents the near-totality of the extant body.

37 Imber, *Ottoman Empire, 1300–1650*, pp. 200–3.

38 For the ideological link between universalist imperial ideologies and information-gathering, with a specific focus on intelligence collection, see Gábor Ágoston, "Information, Ideology, and Limits of Imperial Policy: Ottoman Grand Strategy in the Context of Ottoman-Habsburg Rivalry," in Virginia H. Aksan and Daniel Goffman (eds.), *The Early Modern Ottomans: Remapping the Empire*, New York: Cambridge University Press, 2007, pp. 75–103.

39 For a concise description of the difference between the governorates-general where the *timar* system prevailed and those that – ideally – remitted annual payments, see Gábor Ágoston, "A Flexible Empire: Authority and its Limits on the Ottoman Frontiers," *International Journal of Turkish Studies* 9, 2003, pp. 16–17.

40 Erhan Afyoncu, "Osmanlı Devlet Teşkilatında Defterhâne-i Âmire," unpublished PhD dissertation, Marmara University, 1997, pp. 27–30; Bilgin Aydın, "XVI. Yüzyıl Osmanlı Bürokrasisinde Tımar Tevcih Sistemi," *Journal of Ottoman Studies* 24, 2004, pp. 29–35.

41 Celalzade Mustafa, *Geschichte Sultan Süleymān Ḳānūnīs von 1520 bis 1557, oder, Ṭabaḳāt ül-Memālik ve Derecāt ül-Mesālik / von Celālzāde Muṣṭafā genannt Ḳoca Nişāncı*, ed. Petra Kappert, Wiesbaden: Steiner, 1981, p. 11b.

42 See Imber, *Ottoman Empire, 1300–1650*, pp. 154–76; Metin Kunt and Zeynep Yelçe, "Divân-ı Hümâyûn: le Conseil imperial ottoman et ses conseillers (1450–1580)," in Cédric Michon (ed.), *Conseils et conseillers dans l'europe de la Renaissance (v. 1450–v. 1550)*, Rennes: Presses Universitaires de Rennes; Tours: Presses Universitaires François Rabelais, 2012, pp. 299–339.

43 Şahin, *Empire and Power in the Reign of Süleyman*, p. 219. These numbers relate to the secretaries who were paid from the treasury, and do not reflect those who were paid via *timars*.

44 Afyoncu, "Osmanlı Devlet Teşkilatında Defterhâne-i Âmire," p. 9.

45 Şahin, *Empire and Power in the Reign of Süleyman*, pp. 220–30.

46 Christine Woodhead, "From Scribe to Litterateur: The Career of a Sixteenth Century Ottoman *Kātib*," *Bulletin of the British Society for Middle Eastern Studies* 9, 1, 1982, p. 61.

47 V. L. Ménage, "On the Constituent Elements of Certain Sixteenth-Century Ottoman Documents," *Bulletin of the School of Oriental and African Studies* 48, 1985, pp. 283–304.

48 Fleischer, *Bureaucrat and Intellectual in the Ottoman Empire*, pp. 224–31; Douglas Howard, "Genre and Myth in the Ottoman Advice for Kings Literature," in Aksan and Goffman, *Early Modern Ottomans*, pp. 137–66.

49 Fleischer, *Bureaucrat and Intellectual in the Ottoman Empire*, pp. 311–14; İnalcık, *1300–1600*, pp. 84–8; Linda T. Darling, *Revenue-Raising and Legitimacy: Tax Collection and Finance Administration in the Ottoman Empire, 1560–1660*, Leiden: Brill, 1996, pp. 53–67.

50 For the divergence of the chancery and financial careers, see Fleischer, *Bureaucrat and Intellectual in the Ottoman Empire*, pp. 218–23.

51 Darling, *Revenue-Raising*, p. 59.

52 Günalan, *Osmanlı İmparatorluğunda Defterdarlık Teşkilatı ve Bürokrasisi*, pp. 101–262.

53 Cornell H. Fleischer, "The Lawgiver as Messiah: The Making of the Imperial Image in the Reign of Süleymân," in Gilles Veinstein (ed.), *Soliman le magnifique et son temps*, Paris: La Documentation Française, 1992, pp. 159–77; Şahin, *Empire and Power in the Reign of Süleyman*, pp. 187–93.

54 İnalcık, *The Ottoman Empire: The Classical Age*, pp. 76–88; Baki Tezcan, *The Second Ottoman Empire: Political and Social Transformation in the Early Modern World*, New York: Cambridge University Press, 2010, pp. 93–108.

55 Yvonne J. Seng, "Invisible Women: Residents of Early Sixteenth-Century Istanbul," in Gavin R.G. Hambly (ed.), *Women in the Medieval Islamic World: Power, Patronage, and Piety*, New York: St. Martin's Press, 1998, pp. 241–68; Leslie P. Peirce, *Morality Tales: Law and Gender in the Ottoman Court of Aintab*, Berkeley: University of California Press, 2003.

56 For the first development, see Buzov, "The Lawgiver," pp. 135–89, and Guy Burak, *The Second Formation of Islamic Law: The Hanafi School in the Early Modern Ottoman Empire*, New York: Cambridge University Press, 2015; for the second, Tezcan, *Second Ottoman Empire*, pp. 30–43.

57 For a concise narrative of various challenges see Darling, *Revenue-Raising*, pp. 8–16, 35–47. Also see Oktay Özel, "Population Changes in Ottoman Anatolia during the 16th and 17th Centuries: The 'Demographic Crisis' Reconsidered," *International Journal of Middle East Studies* 36 (2004), pp. 183–205.

58 See Sam White, *The Climate of Rebellion in the Early Modern Ottoman Empire*, New York: Cambridge University Press, 2011; Oktay Özel, *The Collapse of Rural Order in Ottoman Anatolia: Amasya 1576–1643*, Leiden and Boston: Brill, 2016.

59 Darling, *Revenue-Raising*, pp. 81–212.

60 A discussion of these political transformations is in Tezcan, *Second Ottoman Empire*.

61 See Suraiya Faroqhi, "Politics and Socioeconomic Change in the Ottoman Empire in the Later Sixteenth Century," in I. Metin Kunt and Christine Woodhead (eds.), *Süleyman the Magnificent and His Age: The Ottoman Empire in the Early Modern World*, London and New York: Longman, 1995, pp. 91–113.

62 Michael J. Braddick, *State Formation in Early Modern England, c. 1550–1700*, Cambridge: Cambridge University Press, 2000, pp. 6, 20–7, 45–6.

63 Steve Hindle, *The State and Social Change in Early Modern England, c. 1550–1640*, Basingstoke: Macmillan; New York: St. Martin's Press, 2000, p. 23; also see *ibid.*, pp. 2–34.

64 Julius Kirshner (ed.), "Introduction," *The Origins of the State in Italy, 1300–1600*, Chicago: University of Chicago Press, 1996, pp. 1–10.

65 See Ágoston, "A Flexible Empire," pp. 15–31.

66 See Michael Mann, *The Sources of Social Power*, vol. 1, *A History of Power from the Beginning to AD 1760*, New York: Cambridge University Press, 1986, pp. 1–33.

21

COMMERCE AND CREDIT IN RENAISSANCE FLORENCE[1]

Paul D. McLean and John F. Padgett

Florence was the primary center of financial capital and one of the most important centers of international trade in Europe in the fourteenth and fifteenth centuries. Various Florentine individuals and families operated banks not only at home, but also in many major cities within Italy and across Western Europe: in Avignon, Barcelona, Bruges, London, Montpelier, Paris, Rome, Valencia, Venice, and more. During the fourteenth century, Florentine cloth manufacturers imported vast quantities of raw wool from England, turned it into fine textiles, sold some of those textiles to Florentine households, and exported a great quantity of the rest to destinations all over Europe – indeed, to such an extent that Florence was also one of the continent's leading manufacturing centers. That pattern continued into the 1400s, although under competition from English manufacturers, the industry shrank.[2] In the fifteenth century, luxury silk cloth production gradually supplanted woolen cloth production, encouraged and supported by the Florentine merchant-banking elite – an elite that was also the core of the city's political leadership.[3]

What organizational features and what institutional and cultural practices supported the exceptional vitality of economic activity in this city in the early 1400s? One element of the answer is that there emerged in late fourteenth-century Florence a number of technologies of business organization (notably, the partnership system) and accounting (notably, current accounts, and what we loosely refer to as double-entry bookkeeping) essential to modern financial management.[4] It would be difficult to coordinate relations within a complex and highly developed economy without such technologies.

An alternative explanation might stress the importance of a capitalist mentality. Werner Sombart proclaimed over a century ago that Florentine businessmen displayed noteworthy elements of a capitalist orientation, most notably with their frugal attitudes and their careful attention to bookkeeping.[5] The character Giannozzo Alberti in Leon Battista Alberti's dialogue *I libri della famiglia* famously considered it "a good sign if a merchant had ink-stained hands," indicative of his fastidiousness in noting all transactions meticulously.[6] The merchant Giovanni di Pagolo Morelli counselled scrupulous business conduct:

> Conduct your business with trustworthy people (*persone fidate*) who have a good reputation (*buona fama*) and ample credit (*che sieno creduti*) ... Don't let yourself be tricked by inflated offers, and always insist on contracts that have been carefully reviewed (*iscritte ispecchiate*).[7]

These two Florentine merchants were "attentive observers" of all elements of the economic environment in which they operated.[8]

However, the idea that Florentines exhibited a capitalist mindset has been disputed. In Sombart's own time, Max Weber famously argued that Florentines had developed some of the key "forms" of capitalism without exhibiting its spirit.[9] That is, they lacked the acquisitiveness and single-minded devotion to business – the "striving for profit" – that he regarded as essential to the spirit of capitalism. Consider the following preamble to a ledger of the company of Francesco and Niccolo Tornabuoni in 1425:

> In the name of God and His blessed mother the Madonna, St. Mary the Virgin, and the blessed St. John the Baptist, and the evangelists and the blessed apostles Saints Peter and Paul, and thus generally all the holy court of Paradise: that they grant profit to us, along with salvation of our souls.[10]

In this case, actually a typical one for Florentine company ledgers, the pursuit of profit was nested inside of fervently religious concerns.

Florentine economic historian Richard Goldthwaite has reflected, in addition, on "how seldom a competitive spirit comes into play in the relations among these merchants."[11] In fact, Florentine businessmen did pay meticulous attention to business, but without privileging the pursuit of profit over other aspects of life, including the pursuit of political office, the protection of their families and households, and the enjoyment of life on their country estates.

Above all, Florentines sought *connections* to each other and sought ways to maintain those connections, in economic life as in other social domains. Social historians have documented in detail the deeply personal character of Florentine social relationships,[12] as well as the ongoing importance of seemingly pre-modern mentalities to Florentines' organization of experience.[13] Business relations, too, were often deeply personal, not impersonal as economists presume they should be in capitalist markets. Florentine businessmen were as attentive to the persons with whom they did business as they were to the terms of the deals. A good reputation (*buona fama*) and credit-worthiness were vital concerns, as is evident in the passage above. Furthermore, a good reputation in business redounded into other domains, such as the fiscal domain, as Morelli also pointed out.[14] To put it succinctly, Florentine markets exemplified processes of social exchange as much as economic exchange.[15] And indeed, the social and the economic were interwoven in the very concept of credit they utilized, as we discuss below.

Careful techniques of accounting and attention to social relationships jointly highlight the importance of *circulation* in the Florentine economy.[16] An enormous part of this circulation was the input of raw materials into production, the flow of products into the market, and the circulation of currency and investment to aerate the system. But also crucial was the circulation of trust that allowed people to work together with confidence, and consequently invest in each other – especially when the recompense for that trust was not immediate.

We document these vital processes of circulation through an analysis of two disparate but complementary sources of data. First, we offer a qualitative analysis of business letters from the early 1400s. Florentine businessmen discursively maintained and managed commercial relationships through such letters. Woven into these texts were verbal statements of the standing of their accounts with each other, guidelines for offering credit to one another, and the expression of sentiments that framed their commercial interactions. Second, we present a quantitative analysis of the patterning of business credit and debt flows within and among several key industries – specifically international and domestic banking, the import/

export trade, wool production, silk production, and domestic cloth retail. These flows were summarized from merchants' account books and copied into the famous *Catasto* (household census) of 1427. We analyze this quantitative data using some of the principles of social network analysis, uncovering how patterns in the flow of commercial credit in the aggregate were deeply linked to other sorts of social network ties – especially families, neighborhoods, and membership in the political elite.

Our main goal is to show empirically that *both* careful accounting *and* the careful deployment and management of interpersonal relationships were essential to the operation of Florentine business. Indeed, sophisticated accounting and reliance on personal relationships were both utilized to the greatest extent in banking, the largest and most 'advanced' sector of the economy. Commercial transactions did not displace the oligarchic social networks of the time. Rather, they built upon and formalized these longstanding relationships into markets. Furthermore, from a methodological viewpoint, we demonstrate, by means of our synthetic approach, how important it is for historians today to integrate qualitative and quantitative methods to advance historical explanation.

The meaning of credit in Florence, and its treatment in business correspondence

When we talk about "credit," we may be tempted to focus strictly on economic resources: money lent, or collateral available. But even today, credit means not only credit scores and bond ratings, but also perceptions of the credit-worthiness of borrowers. In Italian, the term for credit is closely linked to the verb "*credere*": to believe, to have faith in.[17] For the Florentines, to offer someone credit meant having confidence in them, not only financially but also morally. In the passage from Morelli's *ricordi* quoted above, "*sieno creduti*" can loosely mean "they have credit," but more literally might be translated as "they are credited" or "they are believed (in)." Having credit was a sign that others trusted you to record your debts accurately and pay them promptly. It was also a sign that you were a person of character and honor, in more domains than just the economic.

This connotation of credit, in which considerations of economic solvency and moral worthiness were intermingled, infused the instruments Florentine businessmen used to communicate with one another. Their business correspondence provides insight into the discursive framings of credit which they brought to bear on their commercial operations. The volume of correspondence that Florentine businessmen exchanged must have been immense, but unfortunately, much of it has been lost. Here we examine some of the scant material that remains: published business letters to and from the Francesco Datini company in Milan,[18] and unpublished business letters of the Andrea de' Bardi company in Florence.[19] The Bardi letters are actually copies of letters sent to various corresponding banks abroad – copies kept for the home firm's own records to facilitate continuity of communication. Much of the content of these letters concerns flows into and out of accounts the various companies maintained with each other. For example, a letter from Andrea Bardi's company to Andrea de' Pazzi on 24 May 1405 starts off in a way that is quite typical, in both business correspondence and interpersonal correspondence: "For quite a while we have not had any letter from you, nor for our part have we written to you, there not having been any reason. And this letter is written to you for the reason I will tell you about below." Bardi proceeds to describe updates that must be made to different parties' accounts in light of the completion of a particular deal with the company of Giovanni di Andrea of Barcelona. Effectively, accounts and business letters worked in tandem: accounts distilled complex relationships into measurable, easily documented flows of resources, while letters often explained how and why those flows were occurring, providing a meaningful context for them.[20]

Before proceeding with our discussion of the content and tone of business letters, we should clarify what we mean by "accounts." Current accounts (*conti correnti*) and accounts of use (*conti di esercizio*) were the formal accounting vessels that contained and measured ongoing economic credit relationships among Florentine companies. Account relationships were best visualized using a bilateral format – a physical layout of the pages of a ledger often associated with (though not essential to) double-entry bookkeeping.[21] Bilateral format became widespread in merchant account books in the 1380s, precisely in conjunction with the invention and rapid diffusion of the partnership system (broadly speaking, holding company) mode of organization.[22] Simplifying a bit, to open up an account book in bilateral format was to place into clear sight the writer's economic relationship with a single person or company. Credits (both monetary amounts and descriptions of content) between the writer and that person or company would be listed on one side of the open ledger, and debts with that same person or company on the facing page. Such accounts usually were initiated with an opening deposit or a credit of some sort, but afterwards a whole series of transactions could ensue, with monies of account flowing both in and out.[23] Earlier more primitive single-entry account books, in contrast, were registers of the writer's transactions, ordered by date irrespective of the other party, each described in paragraphs with complicated schemes of cross-reference to determine whether the credit was ever repaid.[24] Simply put, the organizing unit of single-entry bookkeeping was the transaction, while the organizing unit of bilateral double-entry bookkeeping was the economic relationship.[25]

A fragment of the main ledger of the partnership of Francesco and Niccolò di Simone Tornabuoni from 1425 indicates that company's adoption of an accounts-centered organization of their books:

> This book is that of Francesco and Niccolo di Messer Simone Tornabuoni, residing in Florence, and it is called the large black ledger marked K, and in it we have recorded everyone who owes to us, or is owed by us … From page 2 to 200, we will write every account, to pay or to receive, debtors and creditors generated through mercantile trade, or which depend on merchandise. From page 200 to the end of the book we will record every debtor and creditor that depends on [that is, arising from] from money changing and from every other matter apart from merchandise.[26]

Via current accounts and accounts of use, paired companies maintained complementary 'bins' within each other into which their credits and debts could be transferred at each other's discretion on an ongoing basis. Such networks of open-ended credit linked legally separate branches of banks owned by the same holding company (as the famous Medici bank, for example, was organized); but they also linked completely separately owned companies who did frequent business with each other – so-called *corrispondenti*.

Corrispondenti relied on clear instructions from each other, as suggested by a letter written by Francesco Datini's associate in Milan, Tommaso di ser Giovanni, to Datini's assistant in Pisa:

You say you don't know why the report on prices from Barcelona is no good. I told you that it was all jumbled up and one thing was not specified from another, and similarly the merchandise ... One must furnish clear information and say, "Send me so much of this and so much of that, and here it costs this much." ... In any case, you must understand that, for me, it is not a nuisance but a pleasure to serve where I am obligated, and elsewhere, when I am ordered to do so; but I am careful to act so that no one suffers harm because of something I have done, and when I do something, I am careful not to be justifiably reproached by anyone.[27]

Corrispondenti also directed each other concerning the kinds of credit they would extend and to whom, as in this letter from Andrea de' Bardi to the Orlandini company in Bruges, April 6, 1405:

Anything that comes to you for us, you may commit to Paris or London, if it be to your own [company] there, to ours in Barcelona, in Lucca to Bartolomeo Belbani & Co., and in Venice to the Medici: continue in this way if no one instructs you otherwise. We do not wish you to exchange [*credere*] our money, nor the money of our company to any Venetian or Lombard, nor to Antonio Quarti & Co., nor to Niccolaio Tonghi, nor to Filippo Rapondi or others that might bring business to you from Dino Rapondi of Paris. Follow these instructions, and with the others [with whom you correspond] do as you wish and as if it were for yourself, having always due regard to lending well and, again, not to get yourself too indebted with anyone, and especially with Diamante degli Alberti & Co.[28]

Note that prohibited exchange is here specified more in terms of *people* than in terms of types of transactions. Bardi offered similar directives in a letter to Domenico and Poldeo Pazzi in Paris on 27 March 1405,[29] where he instructs them to honor bills of exchange for any amount with the Tornabuoni of Bruges, the Medici of Venice, and the Bardi companies of Barcelona and Florence, but imposes limits of 500 or 1,000 florins on exchanges involving certain other companies – notably, non-Florentines. Special caution was taken when fears arose about the solvency of particular companies:

You see how the money-changing activity is now. One had better have one's eyes open wide in exchange [*credere*], for every day new suspicions arise. Tell me how the firm of Diamante Alberti is managed and how you understand them to be doing business, because people have been speaking about them ... Do not exchange with them unless you hear otherwise from us, and make a note of it, that it does not slip your mind, so that we may in the end know how they are making out. Here they have plenty of possessions, but God knows if they are clear of obligations.[30]

Within such explicitly stated constraints, partners in *corrispondenti* relationships offered to do whatever each other requested, taking action on behalf of each other:

Of the affairs you still have to complete here, point yourself still towards Pisa with my company there, and also write often to me in Bruges, because I am going to live there ... With the grace of God I will stay there a little while, and if there is anything I can do for you, write to me of it and I will do it, for you and for your whole company, as if it were for myself alone.[31]

As a result of these routines of taking action on behalf of other companies, the expression, "pay it and post it to our account" (*pagate e ponete a nostro conto*) became a common feature of business correspondence from the 1390s on.[32]

While Florentine business letters focus overwhelmingly on the day-to-day details of transactions, spelling them out monotonously and repetitiously, it is also true that they are inflected with the rhetoric of fictive kinship and of friendship (*amicizia*) often enough to see these framings as constitutive of commercial interaction. Consider how Andrea de' Bardi mingled kinship, friendship, and business seamlessly in a letter written to Tommaso Sofia (*not* someone he knew well) on 1 April 1405:[33]

> Dearest brother [not an actual blood relation], we have concluded a purchase of a number of jewels from Bartolomeo del Nero ... As you must know, it is little my business, this work with jewels, but seeing the need the said Bartolomeo had, we decided to serve him, and hearing of your good reputation (*la vostra buona fama*) from the said Bartolomeo, and comforting ourselves, that, by your hands, we would be most well served and advantaged at the sale, we have decided and we are content, that by your assistance the sale of the rest of the jewels be brought to a conclusion.

Bardi went on to write that if some of the jewels remained unsold, he should give them to Bardi's *corrispondente*, Andrea de' Pazzi: "may it please you to consign [them] to the said Andrea in Barcelona, or, if he is away, consign them to whomever Andrea instructs you." He concluded: "May it please you, in the possession of these jewels, to promise to the said Andrea to do his will ... No more we have to say, except we recommend ourselves as obligated to you."

Note the multiple layers of trust and obligation operative here: Bardi expresses his desire to help a fellow Florentine businessman (del Nero); Tommaso enjoys a solid reputation with del Nero, which Bardi accepts at face value; Bardi trusts Andrea de' Pazzi to accept and account for the unsold merchandise; and Bardi defers to Pazzi's confidence in whomever he designates as his agent, should he be absent from Barcelona. We see clearly here traces of a network of cooperating enterprises.[34]

Another instance of the use of the rhetoric (and actuality) of kinship to grease the wheels of commerce appears in a letter Francesco Datini wrote to a new *corrispondente* in Milan, Giovanni da Pessano, in 1401.[35] Datini saluted da Pessano as "dearest like a brother," then proceeded to a recommendation of the banker Bindo Piaciti, "who is to me like a son, and equally he is the brother of my wife." Datini had previously advised Piaciti to look to da Pessano should he choose to get into the cotton trade; equally he now urged da Pessano to look to Piaciti for his money-changing needs in Venice:

> Above all, you may deal with him in everything as much as you want, I will hold it to be well done, for in him and in you I trust as my own self ... And in you I would trust as in a dear brother, inasmuch as Tommaso di Giovanni, my factor, has told me more than enough, and I offer such trust to the said Tommaso who is, as it were, a son to me, and so from now on may it be said forever that you make account of me like a dear brother, and thus I will do as regards you.

All ties within this mini-network of actual and proposed *corrispondenti* and employees were treated rhetorically as within-family relations.

The following excerpt makes clear the use of the language of friendship to frame commercial transactions:

> Your offer we accept like dear friends (*chari amici*), and we see that by your Tommaso you have written concerning our condition and company: this he did as a worthy (*valente*) person and out of courtesy ... And although you have many friends here who serve you, nonetheless we offer ourselves to all of your pleasures and, wanting advice concerning one thing or another, tell us and I will do it willingly (*faròllo volentieri*).[36]

Florentines saw no contradiction between friendship and making money. One purpose of helping each other was to make money, but also one purpose of making money was to make friends, through generosity in gifts.[37] Profit and friendship were paired concepts because both were facets of the same social-exchange mentality of constructing each other through reciprocity.

Many instances of the use of friendship language in business correspondence could be cited. One example is when Datini's agent in Milan wrote to the Datini company in Genova saying he had received their letter, and along with it, the letters of "many friends" (*più d'amici*) – meaning many other companies with which they conducted business.[38] Another intriguing one is a letter that Andrea de' Bardi wrote to the Orlandini company in Bruges on 26 March 1405. Concerning the adjudication of some dispute with a certain Bernardo, Andrea hoped that a resolution could be achieved *mercantivolemente* (in a merchant-like way) and *amichevolmente* (amiably, or in a friendly way).[39]

The language of goodwill and friendship in these passages may reflect contemporary theologians' concerns regarding usury.[40] Church doctrine held that the economy was constituted by a community of the faithful linked together in love. Legitimate transactions were supposed to be conducted in accordance with an unconditionally free will. But the language in these letters also recalls the language of patronage.[41] The final sentence of the Borromei letter at the top of this page is a common concluding element of much correspondence, but appears with particular regularity in patronage-related letters where writers assure recipients of their unconditional loyalty. Friendship commitments as they were expressed in the political patronage world occasionally bled over into commerce and finance.

Interpreting business relations as friendship occurred not only when business was going well, but also when business turned sour:

> We want only what is owed to us. May it please you also to want to proceed thus, and truly, for in good faith not a little have we discussed this dispute between us. May you or yours also wish to settle it as is done between friends.[42]

In practically identical terms, Bardi wrote to the Baldesi company in Bruges that "we have wanted, and still want, to settle this dispute as one must do between friends."[43] Several times in the same letter he claimed to have acted toward them "with love and faith, as one must do between friends." And according to another letter he wrote the same day to the Orlandini, he remarked that between friends "one may be more forthright in speech," commenting also that "we hold it dear that you have spoken from your heart at length."[44]

Framing business in terms of friendship and family obligation could be durable in the face of severe problems:

> I am advised by many letters that Basciano [da Pessina] is not there. You will have spoken with him about these blessed accounts that, by his shortcomings, are not settled, and truly it is a great wrong; this is not the friendship (*amicizia*) and brotherhood (*fratellanza*) that I had with him ... And I must observe that when he made accounts with me in Avignon, that amounted to 40,000 pounds or so, there was not even a penny missing, we had such a great relationship, so that one could go so far as to say that if I owed him 1,000 florins, I would approach him and say to him how I considered him more than a brother, and I still do. And despite what he has done to me, I will never forget the love and brotherhood that was between him and me.[45]

To summarize, although the social anchoring of credit relations in *actual* families and *actual* neighborhoods was crucial, as we will show below, invoking *fratellanza* (brotherhood) and *amicizia* (friendship) in business remained an important tool for negotiating empathetic understanding of each party's interests, and to coax each other's compliance.

Finally we turn to references to honor in these letters – less common than *amicizia*, but equally important for understanding the cultural context of Florentine commerce. We discern that discussions of honor arise most commonly in the context of economic troubles. For example, in a dispute concerning a thousand florins missing because of the actions of a certain Michele, Andrea de' Bardi wrote to both Antonio di Sandro Cittadini and Domenico de' Pazzi in May of 1405 that they should take action "for the honor of said Michele."[46] In a letter of 31 March 1404, Bardi wrote to Alberto Aldobrandini in Paris urging him to settle a particular deal because it redounded to both his honor (*onore*) and his advantage (*utile*).[47] And in the letter quoted above in which Datini fretted about his abandonment by Basciano da Pessina, he went on to assert that "I would come back a thousand miles to do my duty towards him and every other good affair; and it concerns his honor not to do likewise to me, even if I did not merit it."[48]

Honor typically communicated both an obligatory, internalized commitment and an expectation of assistance by others – a duality succinctly expressed by Bardi in a letter to Simone and Iacopo Covoni in the fall of 1404.[49] Here he both expressed his obligation to them, and urged them to honor their obligation to him: "as long as we both shall live I am certain you will do your duty." In this context, complimenting someone about their honor might gain overtones of a veiled threat about loss of that honor:

> Dearest friend ... When I was there I spoke to you many times about the money that you owe to the heirs of your partner Antonio di Tuccio Manetti. And now Andrea di Buonaventura has arrived there, who comes there for this reason and for other business of his, and he has begged me that I write to you concerning this matter, and that I pray of you that you should wish to act towards him as the worthy man that you are. And I am quite certain it need not be said to you, that you will pay your debt to him in this matter, both out of duty, and also to lighten the burden on your heart. And I pray of you that you should indeed wish to do this for them like the worthy man that you are.[50]

Indeed the question of honor was frequently tied, overtly or covertly, to the issue of reputation (*fama*) and reciprocity. *Fama* refers to other merchants' collective evaluation of one's character, and gossip was the mechanism through which such collective evaluations were made. Such gossip could help one:

> I, Andrea, have received letters from Ciandrello. I have told him so much about you, and that you have done him such honor, that if something pertained to you alone it would suffice [to obtain his help]. And if it were not already the case that I were obligated (*obrighato*) to you in every respect, now I am [obligated to you] that much more, and I thank you.[51]

Or such gossip could hurt you, as when Andrea de' Bardi wrote to one of his *corrispondenti* in Avignon that "we have heard via letters from Montpelier that this Guglielmo Pigniolo has lost the confidence of others (*avea perduto la fede*)."[52]

Mid-century businessman Tommaso Spinelli exemplifies the link between merchant gossip and personal anxiety about honor. In a letter to his friend Gherardo Maffei about the setbacks he received as a papal banker,[53] Spinelli referred to his honor half a dozen times, sometimes in salvific terms. He wrote that the Pope "has found out the truth and has recognized that I did my duty, and he has endorsed me as a faithful man and a good merchant … and thus he absolves me and imposes silence on whosoever would speak to the contrary." The absolution would clear his name "in the presence of merchants, and I greatly desire this strictly for honor's sake … I will have lost my [goods], but I will at least have conserved my honor." The language recalls the silk merchant Goro Dati's oft-quoted comment in his *libro segreto* [confidential company ledger] half a century earlier, in 1408, that, although his partner favored declaring bankruptcy to cut their losses, "I was resolved to face ruin rather than loss of honor."[54]

To conclude this part of the chapter: business letters blended economic and social concerns, as economic conduct was frequently framed in terms of social norms and objectives. Business was itself a vehicle for friendship and honor, even while flows of credits were meticulously recorded. Furthermore, a two-way causal relationship existed between language and social relations. On the one hand, linguistic expressions frequently referenced real social relationships and obligations in the writers' past experience. On the other hand, Florentine linguistic tropes and learned cognitive models, like *fratellanza* and *amicizia*, were extended far beyond their objective referents, as businessmen sought to frame and interpret each other's market actions in such terms, thereby forging new credit relations while also holding each other accountable.

With these ideas in mind about how business correspondence generated and maintained the circulation of goods and reputations, we proceed to a systematic examination of the circulation of credits, not between specific companies, but in the aggregate, at the level of the commercial credit *network* as a whole.

The network structure of Florentine commercial credit

Record-keeping was a widespread feature of Florentine society. Many Florentines wrote journals – commonly called *ricordi* or *ricordanze* – in which they recorded major life events, notably the births (and unfortunately, sometimes the deaths) of their children, marriages, the

345

occasions on which they served in communal office, and so on. Sometimes mixed into these memoirs are detailed (though sporadic) budget-like records of household expenses.

An important example of the Florentines' collective tendency towards detailed accounting and record-keeping is embodied in the 1427 *Catasto* – a document assembled by the commune which gathered together the tax 'returns' (or more precisely, property inventories and demographic information) of nearly 10,000 Florentine households, as well as the returns of many more households in the surrounding countryside and towns under Florentine control.[55] The *catasto* was a remarkable breakthrough in public finance, although modeled after a Venetian antecedent. Each household submitted a declaration – a *portata* – which the *catasto* officials distilled into a standardized format, called a *campione*. In order of topics covered, each *campione* identifies the location of the household, documents its agricultural assets, enumerates its shares of the public debt, describes members' participation in commercial activity (type of business, names of partners, start-up capital, and net revenues), lists all individuals and companies who were debtors or creditors of members of the household as of a single point in time (12 July 1427) along with the amount owed/owing, adumbrates certain expenses of the household, and specifies members of the household by name.

Although the *campioni* typically offer only a summary of the number of debtors and creditors a given company had, along with the aggregate value of the credits and debts it had amassed, one can frequently find in the surviving *portata* of the company's lead partner a summary version of his company's ledgers, called a *bilancio*. While the *bilancio* rarely includes much information about specific transactions, it does provide a list of a given company's (sometimes myriad) trading partners, and the balances owed or owing between them. That is, the *bilancio* provides a list of any given company's credit and debt ties to other companies. Taken collectively, these *bilanci* provide a high-resolution snapshot of the network of all credits and debts among Florentine banks, cloth manufacturers, and companies in a small number of other industries, at one specific, fleeting moment in time. Despite certain shortcomings – the content of ties is not systematically recorded, some *bilanci* are missing, information from one company's *bilancio* may not be corroborated in another's, and all of the network information comes from just one point in time – no comparably comprehensive data set about economic transactions exists for such an early period. It permits us to analyze patterns of economic activity that could not be measured systematically otherwise.[56]

The first step in our analysis of the 'networked' quality of the Florentine export-oriented economy is to assess the importance of credit from other companies as a source of any given company's operating capital, relative to the start-up capital provided by its own partners.[57] The larger the ratio between the amount of other people's money one uses to run a business, and the amount one supplies oneself as partner, the more vital is credit to its successful operation. Using a variety of measures of 'one's own money,' Table 21.1 shows that, across all the industries we studied, Florentine companies were highly dependent on the credit lent to them by others, although that dependence varied considerably by trade. To operate a business implied having enough of the confidence of others that they would lend you money or place their goods on consignment with you, trusting that they would be repaid.

Next we consider the flow of credits, first at the aggregate level, among industries, and subsequently at the disaggregated level of transactions and relations among companies. Figure 21.1 depicts the relative volumes of credit flowing among industries by comparing the

Table 21.1 Capital structure of 1427 *catasto* companies

A. *Average capital / corpo size of companies, in florins:*

	n	Corpo 1 = corpo only	Corpo 2 = corpo 1 + profit + sopraccorpo	Corpo 3 = corpo 2 + inventory
Merchant banks (international + Pisa)	23	5,080	5,751	6,973
Domestic merchant banks	24	6,375	9,941	10,119
Cloth retail	21	4,305	5,348	7,102
Silk manufacturing	25	3,568	3,928	4,851
Wool manufacturing (San Martino)	30	3,239	3,654	4,373
Wool manufacturing (other)	24	2,030	2,233	2,517
Cloth dyeing	8	1,095	1,195	1,595

B. *Average leverage* $= \sum_i$ *(total debt)* $/ \sum_i$ *(capital):*

	n	Corpo 1 = corpo only	Corpo 2 = corpo 1 + profit + sopraccorpo	Corpo 3 = corpo 2 + inventory
Merchant banks (international + Pisa)	12	5.42	4.98	3.62
Domestic merchant banks	14	4.93	3.29	3.20
Cloth retail	14	2.20	1.66	1.15
Silk manufacturing	19	0.94	0.86	0.66
Wool manufacturing (San Martino)	23	1.17	1.04	0.84
Wool manufacturing (other)	16	0.54	0.48	0.41
Cloth dyeing	7	2.27	2.03	1.44

Source. Originally coded by McLean from tax returns in 1427 Catasto (*campioni* version). To download the company-level data, disaggregated by specific company, see Padgett's webpage: home.uchicago.edu/jpadgett.

observed total number of credits flowing within and among industries to a statistical baseline of total number of credits expected on the basis of industry size alone. Note first that the volume of flows within and among the three banking industries (Florentine merchant banks abroad, Florentine trading companies located in Pisa, and Florentine domestic banks, or *tavole*) was enormous. Metaphorically speaking, the merchant-banking sector was a whirlwind of products, bills of exchange, and credits cycling around, hinted at through some of the letters we presented above. Banks constituted a critical engine of the entire economy. Moreover, as indicated by the volume and content of commercial correspondence discussed above, companies in this sector formed a cooperative banking and trading network *system*, with 'competing' merchant bankers providing much liquidity and business to each other. Second, woolen cloth of both high-end (San Martino) and more ordinary (Garbo) quality flowed more to local cloth retailers (*ritagliatori*) for local consumption than to merchant bankers for export. Third, the silk industry was strongly supported by investments and raw material inputs from domestic

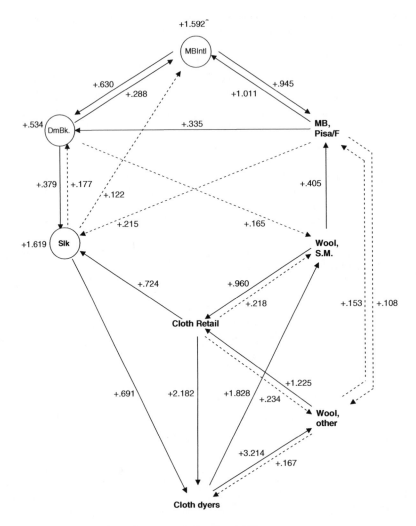

Figure 21.1 Flow of credits among industries, 1427.

Note: Aggregate input–output credits between industries: numbers report (observed # credits – statistically expected # credits)/expected # credits, when > .10. Dotted lines show weaker ratios.

bankers, and although it is not so easy to see here, the goods they produced flowed more to different kinds of export-oriented merchant bankers than to local cloth retailers. The latter two patterns hint at the shift of the Florentine economy away from wool and towards silk at this time, supported by the investments of the Florentine banking establishment. Considering further that two-thirds of bankers were from the leading political and social classes, while two-thirds of silk manufacturers were of middle- and lower-class background, this sponsorship of the silk industry takes on overtones of political patronage.

Now we proceed to consider the flow of credits among companies. Our analysis has two main parts. First we consider patterns in the *number* of credits between different companies – whether they had only one recorded credit relationship at a time, or multiple credits outstanding all at once. Generally speaking, banks probably handled one transaction (shipment) at a time with cloth manufacturers. For example, in the wool producer Parigi di Tommaso Corbinelli's *bilancio*, a credit he had with the bank of Zanobi di Gherardo Cortigiani and Company for 53 florins is crossed out and marked *pagato* on 20 May. Subsequently, he records a credit with the same company dated 14 November. We suspect such companies did repeat business with each other, even though our data from one point in time is unhelpful in discerning such a pattern. However, we do observe multiple simultaneous credits far more commonly among banks than between banks and cloth producers, indicating either the greater quantitative flow of credits between banks – imagine the constant succession of credits recorded with any given *corrispond-ente* spilling across multiple pages of the Tornabuoni ledger, discussed above – or a qualitative difference based on their maintenance of multiple accounts with each other (or both). Among banks and merchant-banks, 63 percent of the credits in our data were 'multiple' in one of the senses just mentioned. Between banks and cloth manufacturers, the rate of holding multiple accounts with each other or accumulating many simultaneous transactions was about half as great, and among cloth companies, it was lower still. In short, credit relations among banks were, more deeply relational and ongoing than any other sector of the economy.

The second and more substantial part of our analysis of credit flows examines how they were linked to other kinds of social relationships. Florence was not a large city by modern standards – in 1427 it had only 37,246 people.[58] Thus most Florentine businessmen would have known about each other, both in business and outside of business, minimally by reputation (*fama*). Furthermore, Florentine businessmen were not just businessmen, but also fathers, brothers, in-laws, neighbors, office-holders, adherents of factions, members of religious confraternities, and patrons of the arts, multiplying the domains in which they could have encountered one another. Analysis of guild records indicates that the average time span during which a Florentine banker was actually doing banking was only 8.2 years,[59] suggesting that success in business often was a stepping-stone toward other activities, like becoming a city councilor, a husband with connections, or an ambassador. The thick, overlapping texture of different domains of Florentine social life compels us to expect that economic activity was influenced by, and in turn affected, other aspects of personal biographies.

In this section, we analyze specific patterns: Which social networks were important for which commercial credit behaviors in which industries? We do this based on data collected over many years from primary and secondary sources on the patrilineages, marriages, neighborhoods of residence, personal wealth, political office-holding, social class membership, and factional affiliation of many thousands of fourteenth- and fifteenth-century Florentines.[60] Rather than discussing our findings exhaustively, including all of the statistical controls we used, we highlight our most significant findings – notably, the importance of family, of neighborhood, political participation, and the specific parts of the credit network in which those social ties were most important.[61] Statistically significant coefficients – broken down by markets between industries – were extracted from the full regressions, in order to highlight them in Table 21.2. Numbers in the table are coefficients indicating the strength of the association between this social relationship and credit flows. Degree of statistical significance is indicated by number of asterisks. We analyzed all credit flows within each market, then also distinguished those credits which are multiple and reciprocal (that is, deeply relational) from those which are not.

Table 21.2 Summary of significant coefficients from logit regressions conducted on company credit ties

A. All credits (dichotomous)

Market	Between partnership systems	Within partnership systems	Nuclear family	Patrilineage family	Parentado family	Gonfalone	Priorate	Scrutiny (1433)	Political factions
International merchant bank / silk				3.128**				.00225**	M: 5.943***
International merchant bank / wool			5.534***						A: 2.905***
International merchant bank		6.496***	3.662**	2.721***					M: 2.305***
Domestic merchant bank / International merchant bank		6.945**			1.822*	1.374***	2.118***		
Domestic merchant bank		5.291*	4.268*	1.974**		1.486***	1.471***		
Domestic merchant bank / wool						.635*		.00165**	
Domestic merchant bank / silk						1.071***			
Silk			5.571**						
Wool		13.726***	3.288*						
Ritagliatori / wool		15.455**							
Ritagliatori / silk									

B. Reciprocal credits

Market	Between partnership systems	Within partnership systems	Nuclear family	Patrilineage family	Parentado family	Gonfalone	Priorate	Scrutiny (1433)	Political factions
International merchant bank / silk				8.064**	2.559**				M: 6.380*
International merchant bank / wool			22.105***	14.774***	5.633**			.00817***	
International merchant bank		7.322***	5.937***	3.526*	2.542*	1.426**	2.547*	.00494**	A: 2.276*
Domestic merchant bank / International merchant bank		6.881***	3.202**						M: 3.793***

Market	Between partnership systems	Within partnership systems	Nuclear family	Patrilineage family	Parentado family	Gonfalone	Priorate	Scrutiny (1433)	Political factions
Dom. Merch-bank	1.110***	10.831**				1.801**			M: 4.351***
Domestic merchant bank / wool	12.763***				3.739*	2.266***	2.684**		
Domestic merchant bank / silk			13.902**			2.303***	2.969***		
Silk									
Wool			8.542**						
Ritagliatori / wool								.00357*	
Ritagliatori									
Ritagliatori / silk									

C. Non-reciprocal credits

Market	Between partnership systems	Within partnership systems	Nuclear family	Patrilineage family	Parentado family	Gonfalone	Priorate	Scrutiny (1433)	Political factions
International merchant bank / silk		9.182*	18.013*					.00213*	M: 6.084***
International merchant bank / wool						1.080**			A: 3.169***
International merchant bank									
Domestic merchant bank / International merchant bank			5.182**	2.148**		1.232**	1.796**		
Domestic merchant bank / wool						1.075**	1.861***	.00166**	
Domestic merchant bank / silk									A: 4.010*
Silk			5.942**						
Wool		14.484***	3.707*						
Ritagliatori / wool									
Ritagliatori									
Ritagliatori / silk									

Notes:
Asterisks indicate degree of statistical significance.
M = Mediceans
A = Anti-Mediceans
Source: Data originally coded by the authors from tax returns in 1427 *Catasto* (*campioni* version). See Padgett and McLean, "Economic Credit," for a more detailed analysis.

Family

When family relations among partners in different companies were present, they exerted a strong effect on those companies' credit behavior toward each other. Whichever way family is measured – at the nuclear-family level, at the level of patrilineage (shared surname), or in terms of marriage connections – across many markets within the Florentine economy, family ties commonly impelled companies to do business with each other. When family relations interpenetrated commercial relations, credit exchanges between companies clearly were as much social obligations as economic investments.

More strikingly, family was most frequently significant as a determinant of credit flows in markets involving international merchant bankers. What we term reciprocal credits in Table 21.2 is one (partial and imprecise) measure of the existence of those *correspondenti* relations discussed at length earlier in this chapter. When Florentine businessmen resided outside of their native soil, they relied on family even more than usual as the social scaffolding upon which they conducted their business. Thus, in their riskiest business endeavors, where financial accounting was most sophisticated, Florentines tended to close ranks within the most intimate social relations. Since Florentine families in international business were spread geographically all over Europe, some of the heaviest flow of international finance throughout Europe coursed through upper-class Florentine families' veins.

Neighborhoods

The social intimacy of Florentine neighborhoods has been documented extensively,[62] even though close interaction within neighborhoods could lead to hostility as readily as to friendship.[63] As indicated in Table 21.2, we found that basically all markets involving bankers residing in Florence relied to a significant extent on shared neighborhood affiliation to structure their commercial credit relations – this despite the fact that cloth manufacturers' plants were concentrated in particular zones in the city, as were the bankers' *tavole*, not distributed across geographic neighborhoods. So, whereas Florentine international merchant-banking business was organized substantially through family relations, Florentine domestic-banking business was organized substantially with neighbors and thus, presumably, trusted friends. This pattern perhaps helps to explain the predominance of 'friendship talk' in the business letters examined earlier, if the rhetoric of letters grew out of businessmen's practical experiences. Overall, it is remarkable that for an economy of such great reach, businessmen relied on such local identities to undergird credit ties.

Office-holding

The Italian word *onore* means both "honor" and "political office," reflecting the historical reality in Italian republics that it was a matter of considerable prestige to be elected to a public office (or more accurately, to be nominated and endorsed for inclusion in a pool of persons eligible to be selected for office by lot). Such selection meant that one's social superiors and peers felt one was worthy to be entrusted with leadership of the city. Ordinary respected and articulate citizens – not professional politicians – served two-month stints in office, taking unpaid time out from their routine pursuits.[64]

We found that when one or more partners in a domestic bank had served on the city's priorate (its most important political body), it was likely they would form credit ties to a company that likewise had partners with priorate experience. Unlike Florentine international merchant bankers who were scattered all over Europe, domestic bankers were more immersed in the volatile day-to-day politics of the city. Although the pattern we observe is based on concrete republican office-holding, we argue that what was at play was the social value of *onore*, a kind of political analogue of *buona fama*. Furthermore, civic involvement mattered to credit-tie formation as much or more than political partisanship did, measured by attachment to particular political factions.[65] Perhaps this was because civic involvement made one conspicuous and highly visible to tax officials, rendering more transparent one's financial situation as well as one's commitment to the commune.

Finally, as also reported in Table 21.2, not only did credit flow abundantly within companies that had adopted the partnership system structure, as one would expect, it flowed abundantly *between* independent banks that had adopted that structure. As we noted earlier, and as confirmed with our quantitative data, ostensibly competing banks were frequently *corrispondenti* cooperating with one another.

We have examined patterns of credit flow statistically, which is crucially important for assessing whether anecdotally reported cases are typical or atypical. But it also pays to consider the volume of effects for different types of social embeddedness. Family, for example, exerted a significant impact on companies' commercial credit relations with each other; but there are not enough brothers to go around to organize an entire credit market. That makes other kinds of social connections important, too. So, although the coefficients reported in Table 21.2 indicate that partnership systems and family had a stronger statistical effect on credit flows among domestic banks than neighborhood or politics, it remains the case that whereas 6.9 percent of credits among domestic banks were within-family ties, 30.4 percent were within neighborhood, and more than half were politically embedded via co-membership in the priorate or shared factional affiliation. And whereas 14.5 percent of domestic banks ties to international merchant banks were within partnership systems, and 11.5 percent were within family, 43.4 percent were within neighborhood, and almost three-quarters were politically embedded. Comparably, even though the social embedding of relations between banks and wool companies was negligible with respect to partnership systems and family, 14.9 percent of those ties were supported by shared political experiences. That last number is not statistically significant, but it is substantial and meaningful for an adequate understanding of the structure of the Florentine economy.

Conclusion

Although Florentine commercial credit markets in 1427 stood staunchly on the late-medieval social foundations of family and neighborhood, two Renaissance institutional innovations – partnership systems and the broadening of political eligibility to more upwardly mobile new men – pushed different families and neighborhoods into greater network connection with each other. The complementary consequences of this increased social-network connectivity were greater circulation of credit in markets, and greater city-wide elite cohesiveness in politics, buttressed by the circulation of reputations for honor. Those who had participated in communal government were nominated in the first place because they were deeply enmeshed in Florentine networks and institutions, including the economy – where, as we have suggested, notions of honor and credit-worthiness were not very distinct.

We close with a dramatic example of this two-way Florentine link between economic credit and republican election, from the *libro segreto* of Gregorio Dati. Dati was one of the successful new-man silk merchants in our 1427 data; but in 1408, he had veered very close to bankruptcy. As we noted earlier, he expressed to himself his intention of avoiding bankruptcy for the salvation of his honor. After four years of financial hardship, but also of demonstrable integrity, he remarked

> I was in debt for over 3,000 florins. That same year 1412, my name was drawn to be Standard-bearer of Justice, and I served in that office. That was the beginning of my recovery.[66]

Dati's perseverance as a businessman is probably what allowed him to receive forty positive votes in the 1411 scrutiny of potential office-holders – a number which still only placed him modestly in the top 2,400 vote-getters! Nevertheless, after his 1412 stint, he served again in 1421 and 1425. Reciprocally, his service in these offices probably helped his financial recovery: in 1427, Dati reported a taxable wealth of 3,368 florins, an amount which placed him among the wealthiest 7 percent of Florentine households.[67] In the 1433 scrutiny for potential office-holders, he received 243 positive votes, placing him among the top 600 vote-getters. His *buona fama* in both business and politics had resulted in successful upward mobility, perhaps confirmed by his late-life marriage into the prestigious Guicciardini family.

One common criticism of personal markets is that they are inherently self-limiting in extensibility and scale, compared to impersonal markets. This criticism has less force when discussing topologically open-ended social networks, like broad elites who take turns sharing political office, than it does when discussing topologically closed and fragmented social networks, such as are formed by autarkic, mutually isolated families. Florentine merchant-banking credit markets were very personalistic. Yet they geographically radiated all over Europe and brokered much of Europe's international trade. The organizational secret of the Florentines in their markets was their blending of multiple social networks into dense but socially open merchant-republican elites. Members of these overlapping elites reciprocally offered commercial credit to each other and to their clients, not as competitors, but as honorable men. Using gossip, ostracism, and reputation to discipline their wide extension of credit to each other, such men "kept everyone in line" through the same "dense and multi-textured social networks" that had created them in the first place.

Notes

1 This chapter is an abridged and substantially re-organized version of John F. Padgett and Paul D. McLean, "Economic Credit in Renaissance Florence," *Journal of Modern History* 83(1) (2011): 1–47. However, some new documentary evidence is introduced here.

2 See Franco Franceschi, *Oltre il "Tumulto": I lavoratori fiorentini dell'Arte della Lana fra Tre e Quattrocento*, Florence, 1993, p. 13; Hidetoshi Hoshino, *L'Arte della Lana in Firenze nel basso medioevo*, Florence, 1980, pp. 227–33; Sergio Tognetti, *Un'industria di lusso al servizio del grande commercio: il mercato dei drappi serici e della seta nella Firenze del Quattrocento*, Florence, 2002, p. 16; William Caferro, "The Silk Business of Tommaso Spinelli, Fifteenth-Century Florentine Merchant and Papal Banker," *Renaissance Studies* 10 (1996): 417–33.

3 Tognetti, *Un'industria di lusso*, p. 23.

4 Raymond de Roover, *The Rise and Decline of the Medici Bank, 1397–1494*, New York, 1966; Federigo Melis, "La grande conquista trecentesca del 'credito di esercizio' e la tipologia dei suoi strumenti sino al XVI secolo," in his *La Banca pisana e le origini della banca moderna*, ed. M. Spallanzani, Florence, 1987; John F. Padgett and Paul D. McLean, "Organizational Invention and Elite Transformation: The Birth of Partnership Systems in Renaissance Florence," *American Journal of Sociology* 111 (2006): 1463–568.

5 Werner Sombart, *The Quintessence of Capitalism: A Study of the History and Psychology of the Modern Business Man*, trans. M. Epstein, New York, 1915, pp. 126, 127, 132.

6 Leon Battista Alberti, *The Family in Renaissance Florence [I Libri della famiglia]*, trans. Renée Neu Watkins, Columbia, SC, 1969, p. 197.

7 Giovanni di Pagolo Morelli, *Ricordi*, in Vittore Branca, ed., *Mercanti scrittori: Ricordi nella Firenze tra Medioevo e Rinascimento*, Milan, 1986, p. 177.

8 Bruno Dini, "Produzioni e mercati nell'Occidente europeo," in his *Saggi su una economia-mondo*, Pisa, 1995, p. 137. Morelli advised, "See with your own eyes the countries, the lands, where you are thinking of trading." *Ricordi*, p. 177.

9 Max Weber, *The Protestant Ethic and the Spirit of Capitalism*, trans. Stephen Kalberg, Los Angeles, 2002, p. 34.

10 Florence, Archivio di stato di Firenze (hereafter ASF), *Mediceo avanti il Principato* (hereafter *MAP*) 84, fol. 9.

11 Richard A. Goldthwaite, "The Medici Bank and the World of Florentine Capitalism," *Past and Present* 114 (1987), p. 24.

12 For example, see Gene Brucker, *The Civic World of Early Renaissance Florence*, Princeton, NJ, 1977; Dale Kent, *The Rise of the Medici: Faction in Florence, 1426–1434*, Oxford, 1978; Paul D. McLean, *The Art of the Network: Strategic Interaction and Patronage in Renaissance Florence*, Chapel Hill, 2007.

13 Richard C. Trexler, *Public Life in Renaissance Florence*, Ithaca, NY, 1980; Ronald E. Weissman, *Ritual Brotherhood in Renaissance Florence*, New York, 1982.

14 "If you conduct business in anything, as has been said, offer proper contracts to everyone; and from this will redound to you a good reputation (*buona fama*), and you won't need to get rich quickly. You will not have such ravenous tax levies placed on you, and you will not develop a reputation as a usurer to visit upon your children. For you know, when it is said, 'He is, or was, a usurer,' everyone thinks they can harm him as they please." Morelli, *Ricordi*, p. 188.

15 Marcel Mauss, *The Gift: Forms and Functions of Exchange in Archaic Societies*, New York, [1925] 1967; Alvin Gouldner, "The Norm of Reciprocity," *American Sociological Review* 25 (1960): 161–78.

16 See Paul D. McLean and Neha Gondal, "The Circulation of Interpersonal Credit in Renaissance Florence," *European Journal of Sociology* 55 (2014): 135–76, for an examination of the circulation of personal loans and other kinds of non-commercial economic exchanges in the same time period as this chapter covers.

17 "Credito; 1) credit; reputation for solvency. 2) credit(s) (in bookkeeping)." Florence Edler, *A Glossary of Medieval Terms of Business. Italian Series, 1200–1600*, Cambridge, MA, 1934, p. 94.

18 Luciana Frangioni, ed., *Milano fine trecento: il carteggio Milanese dell'Archivio Datini di Prato*, Florence, 1994. Tens of thousands of business letters in the Datini archives remain unpublished.

19 ASF, *MAP* 87, fols. 335–53. The Pazzi letter quoted immediately below is from fol. 336r. Andrea de' Bardi was still actively in business in our 1427 credit data, discussed below.

20 Letters may have been utterly necessary, in fact, for reliably confirming deals. On 8 August 1395, Francesco Datini's agent in Milan, Tommaso di ser Giovanni, wrote concerning certain companies, "Letters in their hand I do not recognize," suggesting that handwriting provided corroboration for the authenticity of exchanges. Frangioni, *Carteggio Milanese*, letter #366.

21 Double-entry bookkeeping in its most developed form refers to an interplay among different ledgers, where debits flowing out in one ledger are recorded as credits flowing in to another ledger. This system of double recording of transactions does not interest us as much as the use of bilateral format per se.

22 Padgett and McLean, "Organizational Invention," pp. 1539–42.

23 In the 1416 founding contract of a company with partners Giovanni de' Medici, Benedetto and Larione de' Bardi, and Matteo di Andrea Barucci (ASF, *MAP* 94, fol. 116), Matteo promised "to keep good accounts, as if they were money in cash."

24 Raymond de Roover, "The Development of Accounting prior to Luca Pacioli according to the Account Books of Medieval Merchants," pp. 119–79 in his *Business, Banking, and Economic Thought in Late Medieval and Early Modern Europe*, ed. Julius Kirshner, Chicago, 1974. See especially pp. 121–5.

25 A third form of accounting collected credits in the first half of the ledger and debts in the second half, with elaborate cross-referencing. This form permitted double-entry profit calculations without making current accounts the fundamental unit of the system. A good example of this intermediate form is found in the Alberti *libri mastri* of 1348–59, published and analyzed in Richard A.

Goldthwaite, Enzo Settesoldi, and Marco Spallanzani, eds., *Due libri mastri degli Alberti: una grande compagnia di Calimala, 1348–1358*, Florence, 1995.

26 ASF, *MAP* 84, fol. 9.

27 Frangioni, *Carteggio Milanese*, letter #367: Tommaso di ser Giovanni in Milan to Stoldo di Lorenzo in Pisa, 23 August 1395.

28 ASF, *MAP* 87, fol. 341r. Instructions written in 1441 for Gerozzo de' Pilli, the Medici's partner in London (ASF, *MA*. 94, fol. 214ff.), remain substantially the same in form and spirit as those written around 1400.

29 *Ibid.*, fol. 352r.

30 *Ibid.*, fol. 353r., Francesco de' Bardi to Francesco Mannini in Bruges, 5 June 1405.

31 Frangioni, *Carteggio Milanese*, letter #657: Manno di ser Iacomo & Co. in Milan to the Datini company in Barcelona, 24 March 1397.

32 The earliest example we found in Datini's Milan correspondence appears in late 1383 (*ibid.*, letter #334). A variant of the expression appears in a letter of March 1387 from Lemo and Ghiselo and partners of Milan to the Datini company in Pisa (*ibid.*, letter #137), the first occasion we found between companies not tied by a shared partner.

33 ASF, *MAP* 87, fol. 339v.

34 Like Bardi, del Nero and Pazzi were active businessmen in our 1427 dataset.

35 Frangioni, *Carteggio Milanese*, appendix, letter #23, 7 December 1401.

36 Frangioni, *Carteggio Milanese*, letter #751: Giovanni Borromei to the Datini company in Barcelona, April 1400.

37 *The Albertis of Florence: Leon Battista Alberti's Libro della Famiglia*, ed. Guido Guarini, Lewisburg, PA, 1971, pp. 246ff.; Weissman, *Ritual Brotherhood*, 1982, pp. 36–41.

38 Frangioni, *Carteggio Milanese*, letter #454: Tommaso di ser Giovanni to Francesco di Marco and Andrea di Bonanno, 26 February 1396.

39 ASF, *MAP* 87, fol. 339r.

40 Odd Langholm, *The Legacy of Scholasticism in Economic Thought: Antecedents of Choice and Power*, Cambridge, 1998; Giacomo Todeschini, *I mercanti e il tempo: La società cristiana e il circolo virtuoso della ricchezza fra Medioevo ed età moderna*, Bologna, 2002; Giacomo Todeschini, "La riflessione etica sulle attività economiche," in Roberto Greci, Giuliano Pinto, and Giacomo Todeschini (eds.), *Economie urbane ed etica economia nell'Italia medievale*, Laterza, 2005.

41 McLean, *The Art of the Network*, ch. 4.

42 ASF, *MAP* 87, fol. 339r: Andrea de' Bardi to the Orlandini company in Bruges, 26 March 1405.

43 ASF, *MAP* 87, fol. 346r: 6 July 1405.

44 ASF, *MAP* 87, fol. 347v: 6 July 1405.

45 Frangioni, *Carteggio Milanese*, letter #8: Francesco Datini to Tieri di Benci in Avignon, 4 August 1392.

46 ASF, *MAP* 87, fols. 343r and 343v. Honor, he noted elsewhere (ASF, *MAP* 87, fol. 345v.), required that *corrispondenti* look out for each other's salvation (*salvezza*) as well as their own.

47 ASF, *MAP* 87, fol. 335v.

48 Frangioni, *Carteggio Milanese*, appendix, letter #8: Francesco Datini to Tieri di Benci in Avignon, 4 August 1392.

49 ASF, *MAP* 87, fol. 337v.

50 Frangioni, *Carteggio Milanese*, appendix, letter #18: Tommaso di ser Giovanni to Lorenzo di Tingo, 28 May 1400.

51 ASF, *MAP* 87, fol. 337r: Andrea de' Bardi to the Orlandini company in Bruges, 1 October 1404.

52 ASF, *MAP* 87, fol. 340r: Andrea de' Bardi to Lorenzo di Dinozzo & Co. in Avignon, 4 April 1405.

53 See Philip Jacks and William Caferro, *The Spinelli of Florence: Fortunes of a Renaissance Merchant Family*, University Park, PA, 2001, pp. 75–6 and 303–4. William Caferro, "L'Attività bancaria papale e la Firenze del Rinascimento. Il caso di Tommaso Spinelli," *Società e storia* 55 (1996), pp. 717–53. On the notion of *fama* in general, see the Introduction to Thelma Fenster and Daniel Lord Smail (eds.), *Fama: The Politics of Talk and Reputation in Medieval Europe*, Ithaca, NY, 2003, pp. 1–11.

54 Branca, *Mercanti scrittori*, p. 552. Similarly, Datini's associate, Tommaso di ser Giovanni, wrote to his boss, on 3 September 1396: "I think on doing that which is committed to me, and with the grace of God, I will achieve honor." Frangioni, *Carteggio Milanese*, letter #549.

55 See David Herlihy and Christiane Klapisch-Zuber, *Tuscans and their Families: A Study of the Florentine Catasto of 1427*, New Haven, 1985. The Herlihy–Klapisch data set is available online at www.stg.brown.edu/projects/catasto.

56 For more details on the comprehensiveness and reliability of the data, see Padgett and McLean, "Economic Credit," pp. 5–6. A full list of companies from which we gathered data may be found at http://home.uchicago.edu/~jpadgett.

57 This measure is comparable to the notion of leverage, the ratio of outstanding debt to assets, utilized in modern financial analysis.

58 Herlihy and Klapisch-Zuber, *Tuscans and their Families*, p. 56.

59 ASF, *Arte del Cambio* 11, 14.

60 For more detail on sources, see Padgett and McLean, "Economic Credit," pp. 20f. We also present a much more detailed analysis of credit flows there than space permits here.

61 William Caferro, "L'Attività bancaria papale," pp. 750–3.

62 For example, Samuel K. Cohn, *The Laboring Classes in Renaissance Florence*, New York, 1980; Christiane Klapisch-Zuber, "Kin, Friends and Neighbors: The Urban Territory of a Merchant Family in 1400," pp. 68–93 in her *Women, Family, and Ritual in Renaissance Italy*, Chicago, 1985; Nicholas A. Eckstein, *The District of the Green Dragon: Neighborhood Life and Social Change in Renaissance Florence*, Florence, 1995.

63 Gene A. Brucker, *Florentine Politics and Society, 1343–1378*, Princeton, NJ, 1962, pp. 126, 131. Kent, *Rise of the Medici*, pp. 68, 178.

64 John M. Najemy, *Corporatism and Consensus in Florentine Electoral Politics, 1280–1400*, Chapel Hill, NC, 1982; Nicolai Rubinstein, *The Government of Florence under the Medici, 1434 to 1494*, Oxford, 1966.

65 Sometimes factional affiliation is significant, but not in an obviously patterned way. A clearer argument for the importance of economic relations on factional politics in the 1430s can be found in Anthony Molho, *Florentine Public Finances in the early Renaissance, 1400–1433*, Cambridge, MA, 1971, pp. 166–82; and John F. Padgett and Christopher K. Ansell, "Robust Action and the Rise of the Medici, 1400–1434," *American Journal of Sociology* 98 (1993): 1259–319, especially pp. 1276–7, 1305–6.

66 Branca, *Mercanti scrittori*, p. 552.

67 ASF, *Catasto* 66, fol. 421ff.

22

AGAINST THE FISC AND JUSTICE

State formation, market development, and customs fraud

Corey Tazzara

In February 1636, Agostino Durante was investigated by Genoa's Casa di San Giorgio for an unusual incident. While serving aboard one of the vessels that patrolled Ligurian waters for customs violators, Durante and his fellow mariners refused their commander's order to pursue a particular ship – perhaps because they knew that the suspect ship was in possession of fraudulent grain, perhaps out of gross incompetence. In any case, Durante and his companions were lucky: rather than being condemned outright, they were released by San Giorgio on a surety of 50 *scudi*. Nor did they lose their jobs as enforcers of maritime customs.[1] A century later, in December of 1737, Antonio De Marchi was also hauled before the tribunal of San Giorgio. De Marchi had been caught smuggling cloth into the city of Genoa. Worse, while being pursued by customs agents De Marchi had sought "with weapon in hand to incite the people to his defense."[2] Evidently, the people did not answer De Marchi's call, and he was condemned to five months in prison.

These two episodes share a common protagonist: the Casa di San Giorgio. San Giorgio was the institution responsible for managing the Republic of Genoa's public debt, administering most of its revenues, and policing fiscal violations. It recorded its battle against customs fraud in a summary register maintained between 1630 and 1793. The tales of Durante and De Marchi come from this source. By revealing the modalities of customs fraud, the register makes it possible to explore the obstacles to economic and political integration in Liguria. But to understand why San Giorgio sought to clamp down on fraud during the middle decades of the seventeenth century, and why its efforts ultimately met with failure, we should begin by considering the peculiar heritage of the capital city, "Genoa the rich."[3]

Despite its fabled commercial success, Genoa was wracked with civil discord until late in the Renaissance. Andrea Doria (1466–1560) used his private fleet of galleys to impose a new order on Genoa in a coup in 1528, which cemented an alliance with Spain that endured for about a century.[4] The coup was associated with an important change in Genoa's constitution. As of 1528, most of the wealthy and influential citizens were admitted to the nobility under a new system of *alberghi*, or houses. By making the fictive house the basis for political rights, Doria and his allies hoped to eliminate conflict between nobles and commoners. Instead, a new division appeared between Old Nobles (*Vecchi*) and New Nobles (*Nuovi*). Old factions were not forgotten. New and old nobles practiced an impressive degree of group endogamy, and they often found themselves on opposite sides of the political aisle. Nevertheless, Doria's settlement inaugurated an era of civic peace, compromised only by a brief civil war in 1575.[5]

The Casa di San Giorgio seemed to tower like a serene bastion over the turmoil of the city. Machiavelli even claimed that the citizens of Genoa had transferred their "love" from a fractious republic to the efficient San Giorgio, creating something like a state within a state: "an example truly rare, never found by the philosophers in all the republics they have imagined and seen."[6] For some historians, these arrangements amounted to the alienation of the commonwealth to a consortium of private creditors.[7] Disputing the distinction between public and private, other observers see San Giorgio less as a separate institution than as an instrument in the ruling class's machinery of control, an integral part of the aristocratic republic. This revised view correctly identifies the role of the Genoese patriciate in staffing the institution and the socially regressive implications of the city's fiscal regime, but it exaggerates San Giorgio's capacity for exerting territorial control. Private lineage networks flourished throughout Liguria, unincorporated into the Genoese political system, while elites carved out vast pockets of formal and informal privilege. San Giorgio was too conditioned by the personal interests of its officials to serve as an effective arm of state power in the countryside.

San Giorgio's battle against fraud should also be viewed in the wider arc of Genoese economic history. During the Renaissance, Genoa was able to direct exchange within Liguria by delegating fiscal and political autonomy to the localities, which in turn routed their commerce through the Genoese entrepôt. Genoa also received monopoly rents from its network of trading enclaves scattered throughout the Mediterranean. Taxes on the city of Genoa's commerce and consumption supplied the lion's share of the Republic's revenues.[8] Political arrangements thus enabled Genoa to control certain economic flows within its realm. The Republic's tenuous hold over the territorial dominion as well its fiscal viability depended on its entrepôt.

As the Republic's long-distance trade collapsed, the city of Genoa was forced into the awkward predicament of having to cultivate a passive trade regime while maintaining a political structure inherited from the Renaissance. In seeking to entice merchants to bring their wares into port, rather than actively trading via a native merchant marine, Genoa had to forgo the intermediation profits that had made its citizens rich and had funded its government. Over the long term, the Republic "solved" these problems by extending the *porto franco* system and increasing consumption taxes in the city itself.[9] In the short term, however, the Republic sought to intensify direct impositions in the provinces. The project inevitably required greater territorial control. To regulate trade in the countryside, for instance, Genoa established a Magistrato dell'Abbondanza in 1564 for grain, a Magistrato dei Provveditori del vino in 1588 for wine, and a Magistrato dell'olio in 1595 for olive oil.[10] It also set in place a multitude of controls for policing the new order. The extension of power into the provinces provoked widespread evasion, however, and San Giorgio' efforts to repress fraud met with considerable opposition. Territorial integration in Liguria proved to be a dead-end.

There is something surprising about the Republic's inability to extend its fiscal reach. It had two immense assets in this endeavor: the fabulous wealth of the Genoese patriciate, probably the richest in Italy; and the stature of the Republic as the ultimate arbiter of judicial disputes within its territory. In addition, nearby Venice and Florence did achieve more substantial territorial and fiscal control over their countryside, in part to compensate for decline abroad. In the case of Venice, one might point to the transformation of the entrepôt into a hub for servicing its hinterland, or the opening of Venetian trade to its mainland subjects. For Florence, one might indicate the role of Medici grain policies in integrating the state, the spread of *mezzadria*, or the recruitment of provincials into the bureaucracy. These were signs of success that the Republic of Genoa failed to emulate, although elites were well aware of developments in neighboring states.

It is helpful to consider San Giorgio's inability to control the flow of goods as a kind of political failure, as the legacy of centuries of civic strife and delicate bargains. The more proximate obstacles San Giorgio encountered in policing commerce – the ecological "necessity" of Ligurians to trade, the strength of lineage networks in the countryside, the official complicity in fraud – were all conditioned by the political traditions of the Republic. I will consider in the conclusion whether such political failure did not bring some surprising economic benefits – if it was not, in other words, a strategy in its own right.

Fraud and the flow of resources

The town dominates the country. This axiom of historical sociology has found no more comfortable home than in Renaissance Italy. But the modality and the effects of town–country relations varied throughout the Italian peninsula. In subordinating regional exchange to their needs, some capital cities fostered economic integration within the bounds of the state.[11] By contrast, the Republic of Genoa conspicuously failed to organize local commercial life. Liguria remained poorly realized as an economic unit.[12] One of the primary weapons of any state in the sometimes conscious, sometimes unconscious process of region-building was fiscal control over the exchange of goods. A synoptic study of customs fraud over a long period enables us to explore why the Republic had difficulty controlling the movement of goods in its territory.

Customs fraud does not exist in a state of nature. The category of fraud is created by governments that seek to tax goods, regulate the flow of commerce, and prohibit certain kinds of exchange. For some commentators, "[t]axing what you need to survive and what you produce in exchange for it, even at such a low rate, has rightly been seen as essentially oppressive."[13] Whether just or unjust, San Giorgio's fiscal goals were certainly at odds with the exigencies of community survival. The inhabitants of Liguria were unable to produce nearly enough grain for their sustenance. They resorted to chestnuts and fruit to supplement their diets, exchanging olive oil or wine to get their proteins or carbohydrates. Seasonal emigration was employed for commercializing the region's labor, for converting labor into money and thence into food.[14] Yet it would be unwise to inscribe San Giorgio's failures into a universal history of the Mediterranean, in which state power clashed with an irrepressible need to trade.[15] Ecology conditioned the nature of the commerce that San Giorgio sought to control, but not the success or failure of its enterprise. After all, the Republic did channel exchange through its entrepôt during the Renaissance. The economic transformations that threatened its entrepôt also prompted a search for revenue in the countryside. Unfortunately, the arrangements on which its old system had rested handicapped its new fiscal ambitions.

To secure compliance with its dictates, San Giorgio imposed a multiplicity of controls on the movement of goods and people. It attempted to authenticate goods through paper stamps that recorded their movement and tax status. Goods were theoretically accompanied by a bill, marking their provenance, destination, ownership, and list of taxes paid. Some fraud cases involved the forgery of signatures or other forms of documentary skullduggery. For example, Francesco Marengo and his companions faked the hand of an official of the

Oleorum (oil tax).[16] But it was impossible to place regulators everywhere. San Giorgio concentrated officials in checkpoints at the city gates, in warehouses for high-value goods, and in the major maritime centers of Liguria. It also patrolled coastal waters for violators. It was much more common to evade or deceive officials than to manipulate customs documentation.[17]

San Giorgio's register offers a record of how its controls failed. Ideally, each entry contains the name of the suspect, a brief description of his crime, the particular tax defrauded, and the outcome of the case; sometimes, information about the origin of the individual, his occupation, or the location of the crime is also found.[18] Unfortunately, it is not certain how cases reached the Casa di San Giorgio in the first place. Some probably originated in anonymous denunciations; many, if not most, were probably rooted in animosities largely invisible in the register.[19] Nor is it clear whether the register contains all cases that came to San Giorgio's attention, or only those it chose to prosecute.[20] In any case, the register contains some 2,006 entries over this period. The average of thirteen cases per year is misleading, however. Most of the fight took place in the middle decades of the seventeenth century.

We can dispense with the idea that the effort to squelch fraud was in harmony with the real economy. The distribution of cases reveals a period of intense initial policing, a swift fall by 1640, a plateau between 1650 and 1700, and a terminal decline thereafter (Figure 22.1). Ship arrivals in Genoa provide the best index of economic life, since most shipping involved the transport of necessities for provisioning the city. The battle against fraud had little to do

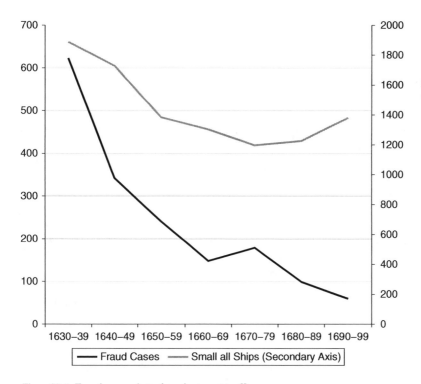

Figure 22.1 Fraud cases plotted against port traffic.

Sources: table 1 and Edoardo Grendi, "Traffico e navi nel porto di Genova fra 1500 e 1700," in *La repubblica aristocratica dei genovesi*, Bologna: Mulino, 1987, 309–64: 358–62

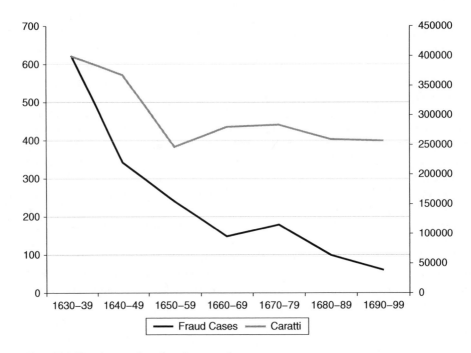

Figure 22.2 Fraud cases plotted against *caratti* revenue.
Sources: table 1 and Giulio Giacchero, *Il seicento e le compere di San Giorgio*, Genoa: Sagep, 1979, 679–81

with the vicissitudes of local life as revealed by the port traffic. Instead it provides a glimpse into the state's evolving capacity for policing commerce.

The fraud cases do track the curve for fiscal revenues such as the *caratti* (Figure 22.2). The *caratti* were customs duties on goods that arrived by sea, not only in Genoa, but all along the Ligurian coast. One might predict a direct correlation between state control and fiscal yields: a strong state is by definition one that can extract revenue from its subjects. And indeed, the decline in policing revealed by the customs fraud data corresponds to a decline in *caratti* revenues. The Genoese capacity to exact resources from its countryside was relatively intense in the early and mid-seventeenth century, but weaker thereafter. And this, not because the maritime economy was in trouble – the figures on port traffic suggest otherwise – but because Genoa's control over economic life in its provinces was increasingly relaxed.[21] A memorandum summarizing the laxity of tax enforcement along the Riviera admits as much.[22]

The machinery for governing town–country relations was intended to funnel goods from the localities into the capital city. Controlling this flow was essential, since substantial price differentials between town and country fostered arbitrage opportunities for those willing to smuggle goods into the city.[23] At least 356 cases occurred in the provinces: many of these were concentrated in the small towns near Genoa itself (Figure 22.3). Another 320 cases occurred at the city gates, offering further evidence of the capital's role in San Giorgio's scheme for combatting fraud. Yet the diffuseness of control in the localities was clearly a problem. What little power San Giorgio exerted was over provincial maritime traffic; the

Figure 22.3 Fraud cases in the provinces.
Source: ASG, CSG, 96. All cases taking place in the city of Genoa or at its gates were excluded from this map.

rocky hinterland seems to have been almost *terra incognita* to its customs agents. The map offers a telling morsel of evidence on this point: the concentration of crimes involving meat or cattle near the city of Genoa itself despite their near-total absence in the countryside.[24] This situation presumably reflects the hoof-mobility of this particular commodity. Cattle could reach Genoa by roads rather than by sea – when they reached Genoa at all, because they could also reach other destinations without embarking aboard a ship. Their presence in the provinces is therefore invisible.[25]

Policing efforts were concentrated overwhelmingly in the taxes on victuals – meat, grain, and wine gabelles (table 2).[26] Many of these cases involved smugglers, such as Ali, a slave belonging to Gasparo Franceschi, on whose behalf he attempted to smuggle meat into Genoa.[27] San Giorgio had good reason to focus on the movement of nutrients. Although Liguria had a highly specialized and commercialized economy, in the sense that much of its produce was oriented toward the market, regional trade was not highly monetized. Grain production in rocky Liguria was low relative to other regions in Italy, and most localities paid the bulk of their taxes in kind, often in olive oil and wine. Local producers also had to rely on these goods to purchase cattle from surrounding regions or grain shipped by sea. This was a system of "failed self-sufficiency" and "forced commercialization": since Liguria could not produce grain, it had no choice but to specialize in other commodities with which to purchase its foodstuffs.[28] No wonder San Giorgio tried to tax and control the exchange of food products.

A comparison with fraud in Genoa's bonded warehouses underscores the dominance of food products in provincial commerce. The vast majority of provincial cases involved meat, grain, and wine. Cases in the bonded warehouse almost always involved non-food items – cloth, spices, or dyes, and a few other goods (table 3). The form of customs control was thus differentiated by type of good. Of course, it is not surprising to find high-value, low-volume articles locked away in customs warehouses while bulkier goods traveled more plebeian paths of commerce. More surprising is the clear temporal disjunction between the two forms of control. Efforts to control the provinces were strongest in the earliest decades of the data set, in the 1630s and to a lesser extent the 1660s. While the Republic's grasp over its provinces slackened, customs agents intensified their control at the city gates and especially in the bonded warehouses (table 4). This shift occurred within the context of the declining trend in all fraud cases described above.

Nothing reveals the quotidian nature of customs fraud better than the frequency with which tax officials were assaulted or prevented from executing their tasks. Almost 15 percent of my cases were classified as instances of "obstruction" in which individuals refused to allow customs agents access to their goods or persons (table 5). A typical example is Pietro Maria Poliodoro, who refused to allow officials to inspect grain loaded aboard his vessel.[29] Most episodes categorized as "conflict" probably also originated in efforts to evade tax agents (13 percent). If so, over a quarter of all cases represent moments of obstruction. Many of these involved outright violence (37 percent).[30] One spectacular example is when Pellegro Molesino and a companion fired upon a patrol vessel near Portofino. They both were sent to the galleys "ob explosiones emissas."[31] Many men who shepherded goods between town and country carried weapons.[32] When Antonio De Marchi tried to incite "the people" against customs officials – to recall this article's opening anecdote – he had reason to hope that they would rush to his defense.

Fiscal pressure intensified between 1620 and 1640 as the Republic sought greater control over its region – in part to compensate for declining revenues from maritime trade, in part to exert political control over a wayward hinterland. A new tax on milling and a reformulated tax on assets were two tokens of this policy.[33] In addition, naval rearmament in these years was intended not only to promote long-distance commerce, but also to patrol coastal waters against corsairs and customs violators.[34] The spike in fraud cases at the beginning of my data series is an artifact of this moment of intense pressure from the center: that is probably why the register was maintained in the first place. Interestingly, the Republic also decided to record all bandits in its territory around the same time. The fight against banditry and that against fraud were two sides of the same coin. As one official observed about the inhabitants of Sturla: "they are divided among themselves into factions, but they are all for the most part against the Fisc and against Justice."[35]

In the face of difficulties in the direct administration of provincial tax revenues, after 1650 San Giorgio began sub-contracting more taxes to the localities. Presumably some of the decline in the provincial fraud cases owed to this mode of fiscal delegation. Nevertheless, the maneuver had the consequence of further attenuating the fiscal control exerted by the center over its peripheries. For example, the town of Celle Ligure collected six taxes on behalf of the capital city, such as the *pedaggio* on goods in transit. Local notables, including Genoese who owned property in the area, tended to be the main investors in such tax farms. It appears that this expedient did not solve the problem, however: these taxes were also liable to evasion and often failed to bring in sufficient revenue to meet obligations to San Giorgio.[36]

The fisc versus the family

Why did San Giorgio fail? Undoubtedly, the geographic and jurisdictional fragmentation of the state exacerbated the difficulties of territorial control. One thinks of the noble fiefs inside Liguria and at its borders, the mountains that harbored bandits, or the ready access among coastal communities to maritime networks. But the most pervasive obstacle to state power was the strength of lineage ties in Genoa and its hinterland. One frustrated official from Chiavari proposed dealing with refractory lineages by "starting to destroy their houses, to cut down their trees and vineyards ... without having any respect for *fedecommessi*, dowries, and creditors (often false)."[37] As much as some administrators might have fantasized about slash-and-burn governance, Genoa usually tried to negotiate to achieve its ends in Liguria. The Republic was the master of judicial arbitration in its territory. Juridical supremacy was no aid in the fight against customs fraud, however, or in the project of fiscal integration.

In the arena of customs fraud as in so many realms of life, private social networks lurk behind the bureaucratic order reflected in official documents. Confederates were mentioned in about 15 percent of all cases, often as siblings or fathers and sons.[38] For example: when the *Pedaggiorum* near the town of Rivarolo seized mules laden with rice belonging to Giovanni Maria Morassi, the man's sons attempted to rescue the animals from captivity.[39] Such filial piety was fairly common. When one of the secretaries of the *Carnium* was arrested for maladministration, his son did not hesitate to liberate him illegally from prison.[40] At just 15 percent, my estimate of cases involving confederates is conservative; the actual figure was probably much higher.[41] Lineages were by no means monolithic. The register records one case in which a man's dispute with his father-in-law landed him before San Giorgio's tribunal.[42] But everything we know about Liguria suggests that fraud was a family business.

Occupational information also suggests the relational nature of customs fraud in Liguria. Coachmen, slaves, and cooks of individual Genoese were identified in 8 percent of cases, as we saw earlier with the slave Ali. Most committed fraud at the behest of their patrician masters. One person was not even identified by name, but merely as the "cook of the most excellent Gasparo Donati."[43] In general, individuals in the transport industries and the victual trades appear often in the register (table 6). These people occupied key positions in exchange networks. Were their suppliers or customers involved in fraud as well?

Fraud was about movement and networks. The almost total absence in the register of the peasantry – of those who produced but did not supervise the movement of goods – is therefore no surprise.[44] More unexpected is the paucity of women in the register, who appeared as perpetrators in just ten cases, only three of which involved smuggling.[45] The rarity of women probably reflects a basic gender division of labor, in which females were not typically involved in the transport of goods. Women aided or abetted fraud in other ways, however, such as by proffering false testimony to defend their menfolk. And some women appeared in the document as victims rather than culprits. For instance, Francesco Lombruschino was stripped of his position as *famulus* for "an inappropriate demand made upon a married woman."[46]

Even data on outcomes suggests the social entanglements of customs fraud. The fraud register records conviction in 920 cases (46 percent of cases). Those convicted often had to pay a fine; sometimes they were subject to corporal punishment, galley service, or exile. One is struck by the mildness of punishments: the death penalty was levied in only 0.5 percent of convictions, the galley service in only 9 percent. Olaudah Equiano denounced the barbarity of the Genoese galleys when he passed through the city: the battle against customs fraud was not to blame.[47] Perhaps the reliance on fines reflects the "financialization" of the state embodied by San Giorgio. It also reflects the weakness of public power, which could not attack individuals too directly without meeting familial opposition. It is telling that San Giorgio did not always expect compliance with its writ and sometimes made provision *in casu innobservantiae*.[48] At least ten people were punished for violating the terms of their sentence, such as Michele Labono, who was exiled to Corsica after failing in his galley service.[49] And as for all those cases in which San Giorgio did not secure a conviction? It declined to prosecute in 302 instances (15 percent). A more common disposition was for an individual to be "relaxed" on surety – 545 cases (27 percent). Since surety often required family resources as well as guarantors, most of these matters further incorporated lineage networks into San Giorgio's catchment.[50]

Anecdotal evidence confirms that much of Ligurian society, from the highest nobility to the lowliest mule-driver, was involved in fraud. When Marietta Castella, an impoverished charwoman living in the Olivella quarter of Genoa, appeared around town in more expensive clothing, one of the neighborhood gossips had no trouble recognizing her as a counterfeiter: investigators later learned that Marietta had been taught how to counterfeit by an exiled priest from Rome and worked with a local goldsmith in converting her coin clippings into bullion. "I have always been fascinated and inspired by counterfeiting ever since I was a little girl," she admitted.[51] A notary who left a casuistic confession for having given bad advice or registered illegal contracts – "which I don't know for certain, but only by conjecture" – also noted that he had not always observed the tariffs on goods and had accepted gifts.[52] So inspired was the Genoese passion for fraud that it seems almost to have generated its own sector of professional consultants: one man was condemned for having advised a French merchant on how to defraud the local taxes – advice given in exchange for a payment, of course.[53]

Presumably, San Giorgio only learned about customs fraud when social relations had already broken down. We may surmise that personal hatreds, family vendettas, and factional loyalties played a role in generating criminal accusations. An illustrative case is Niccolò Alegretti, tax collector for the *Vinorum* working at the Porta S. Tommaso in Genoa. Alegretti first appears in the register in January of 1633 for assaulting a guard named Jacopo. The following year he was reported for maladministration. Was Jacopo trying to exact vengeance? Alegretti appeared twice more that same year. He did not lose his post as tax collector, however, perhaps because San Giorgio recognized the personal enmities that lay behind these accusations.[54] This example involves two officials. More often at play were relations between officials and those they were supposed to regulate. The nexus of personal ties does not point to the autonomy of the hinterland *vis-à-vis* the capital city, however. It indicates rather the unvanquished might of private power and the extent to which the Genoese elite was implicated in illicit exchange throughout Liguria. San Giorgio's battle against fraud was really a battle against itself.

The myth of Genoa

Whether one follows Machiavelli in treating San Giorgio as a kind of alternative commune, or whether one sees it as a precocious example of a joint-stock company, most commentators have celebrated its effectiveness as an organization.[55] Yet derelict officials were the deadliest threat to San Giorgio's efforts in the countryside and throughout the state. In over a quarter of *all* cases, criminals belonged to the regulatory apparatus itself (28 percent).[56] That statistic is probably the most reliable in the entire register. An individual's official status was recorded in a formulaic way throughout the register, which in other respects experienced many compositional vicissitudes over time. In addition, official fraud had a certain phraseology that coincided with the occupational data – for instance, terms like "maladministration" and the like served to confirm the occupational information. Given that most of these cases must have had non-official "companion" ones (i.e., the official and the smuggler he aided), the actual proportion of official involvement in customs fraud is much higher than the figure suggests. The extension of fiscal power into the countryside radically increased San Giorgio's remit while also unveiling the ongoing threat of elite opportunism.

Official fraud infected every branch of San Giorgio's administration, but it was especially prevalent in town–country relations. Commissaries and guards were the chief perpetrators (table 6). Guards served at the gates of the city, monitoring the flow of goods through the customs cordon that separated Genoa from its hinterland and from the sea.[57] Commissaries were those sent to supervise San Giorgio's operations in the localities; they had unparalleled opportunities to defraud the fisc with impunity. Some crimes by city officials were spectacular, such as when Andrea Pallavicino assaulted a notary in the Palazzo di San Giorgio.[58] More often, officials were involved in aiding smugglers (24 percent of official fraud) or accepting bribes for turning a blind eye to violators (5 percent). Many of the crimes termed "maladministration" probably also entailed aid to smugglers. If so, between 50 and 75 percent of official fraud pertained to the flow of real resources, rather than to outbursts of violence or to financial shenanigans.[59] Agostino Bracco, a guard in Genoa, was one such dishonest official: in exchange for a bribe he allowed a provincial butcher to slip through the Porta Fonte Amorosa without paying taxes on a cow.[60] Other modalities included allowing ships to unload wares without paying taxes, releasing captured items, or miscategorizing goods to reduce their tax burden – for instance, passing processed silk off as a raw material.[61] Such collusion was the most typical form of official fraud.[62] Giovanni Girolamo Gagiole must have been surprised when guards refused to accept his money for smuggling hides through Porta San Stefano.[63] Maybe Gagiole did not have the right connections.

The major point is clear. Genoese officials were charged with the task of controlling the flow of resources between town and country. Many abused their positions, either out of an entrepreneurial hunger for bribes, or because they had family interests in illicit exchange. Given the extent of Genoese ownership of country estates, the second possibility must have been common. The officials who staffed San Giorgio were not so much individuals as representatives of lineages, and they occupied positions that were eminently exploitable.

San Giorgio's struggle to control commerce reveals itself for what it was: a war waged against its own officials. If the Republic sought to impose elite power over the hinterlands and the shores, its aims were constantly frustrated by the very same elite. The end of the civil wars in 1576 did not inaugurate two centuries of elite consensus. Lineages paid lip service to the project of territorial unification while bucking it whenever possible. Under the fiction of a single corporate body, the Casa di San Giorgio, division flourished as rankly as ever. The inability to create a compelling civic order in Genoa during the Renaissance bequeathed a broken state apparatus to the seventeenth century. We might posit a kind of "myth of Genoa" – a republic rich but disunited, weak in civic spirit, privatizing everything centuries before the neoliberal turn. If the myth of Venice made extravagant claims for consensual rule, it did at least help secure compliance among citizens and subjects alike. That is one reason the Venetian state stood strong even amidst commercial decline. Genoa by contrast had few civic assets with which to meet its fiscal and political challenges.

Beyond state failure

By the late seventeenth century, San Giorgio was almost pleading with its citizens to pay their taxes. An edict against fraud from 1675 declared, "The collection of taxes is absolutely necessary ... for maintaining the most serene Republic and its liberty." It reminded citizens that Ligurian gabelles were "much more moderate in comparison to those paid in the states of many other princes."[64] This joint appeal to patriotism and self-interest fell on deaf ears. Liguria as an economic unit dissolved into a plurality of networks beyond the boundaries of the state. As a political force, the Genoese state could do little more than arbitrate disputes generated among the lineage networks that fell under its jurisdiction.

Endemic customs fraud points not only to the lack of economic integration in Liguria itself – it also points to changing patterns of commerce in the wider region. For example, from the late seventeenth century the town of Cervo converted much of its commercial activity from coral fishing to shipping activities throughout the Tyrrhenian region. As sailors the Cervesi participated in a capitalist mode of organization and in circuits of exchange far beyond the confines of their community.[65] Little of this commerce was mediated through the entrepôt of Genoa, as in a previous era it might have been. The roving ships of Celle Ligure, which frequently called as far away as Lisbon, offer another example of how local trading networks circumvented the capital city.[66] The growth after 1620 of a merchant class in the hinterland region of Fontanabuona was linked to the development of illegal exports of olive oil into Emilia and Lombardy. Those merchants were themselves intermediaries for landowners in Rapallo – local *borghesi* and rich Genoese citizens.[67]

The rise of Livorno and Marseilles as international centers of redistribution gave a fresh impetus to maritime fraud along the entire coastline, especially at the borderlands at either end of the Riviera.[68] One official, after explaining how ships from Livorno stopped outside of the port of Genoa and illegally loaded wares in plain sight of customs agents, wrote in breathless prose:

> One knows for sure that thousands of bales of Genoese paper arrive in Spain with scarcely the slightest payment ever being seen by the customs house, because at night they load them onto barks outside the ports of Voltri, Cogoletto, and Varazze. The aforementioned ships arrive in Flanders, England, and Spain with cargoes of rice that were loaded aboard ship by vessels in Voltri. A lot of fine merchandise and cloth from Piedmont are carried by those same vessels from Finale, navigating even by day, as they can come from Finale without the proper license; and if they meet any ships they say they are coming from Genoa. And in Sampierdarena, Cornigliano, and Fassolo they load a lot of very fine cloth from Germany.[69]

Many of these illicit networks of exchange stretched far beyond the coastal waters of Liguria or the Apennine mountains. After all, both Livorno and Marseille were well connected to ports much further afield. It is possible that the failure of integration within the bounds of the state facilitated Liguria's insertion into the evolving currents of international commerce.

San Giorgio's difficulties in the countryside were *not* a sign of systematic social failure. Far from imposing real suffering on the inhabitants of the localities, the weakness of fiscal control opened new opportunities for trade, making it possible to exchange local produce on the best terms possible. Perhaps it also helped support the resurgence of Ligurian fleets during the eighteenth century.[70] None of this would have been feasible had San Giorgio controlled exchange as it wished. And as for the Genoese elite? They too flourished long after Philip IV defaulted on their loans in 1627. Braudel reminds us that "Genoa created Italian unification," and it did so "for her own benefit."[71] The ruling class did not deliberately choose a strategy for Liguria based on fragmentation, diversification, and flexibility. It fell into it haphazardly and despite a common desire for greater unity. Ironically, this course was fully in keeping with the city's Renaissance traditions – which yet again steered Genoa through two centuries of uncertainties and travails.[72]

Notes

1 It was extremely common for officials to lose their posts after an investigation. Perhaps San Giorgio was satisfied with Durante's innocence or did not have the evidence necessary to convict him. Genoa, Archivio di Stato di Genova (ASG), Cancellieri di San Giorgio (CSG), 96, 2/7/1636, 9; Baptista Gaminaria, 2/7/1636, 42; Franciscus Carrega, 2/7/1636, 79; Sebastianus Laviosa, 2/7/1636, 222. Page numbers reflect my own count, since the folio numbers were not usually legible. In addition, I have sought to render names from Latin into Italian in the main body of my text; Latin is retained in the notes.

2 "… e armata manù concitando populum ad deffensam." *Ibid.*, 31; for a similar case, see *ibid.*, Jacobus De Ferrariis, 9/6/1740, 170.

3 Lewes Roberts, *The Marchants Mappe of Commerce*, London, 1638, 47.

4 See Steven A. Epstein, *Genoa and the Genoese, 958–1528*, Chapel Hill: University of North Carolina Press, 1996, 278, 309–18; Thomas Allison Kirk, *Genoa and the Sea: Policy and Power in an Early Modern Maritime Republic, 1559–1684*, Baltimore: Johns Hopkins University Press, 2005, 14–28, 46–50; and Céline Dauverd, *Imperial Ambition in the Early Modern Mediterranean. Genoese Merchants and the Spanish Crown*, Cambridge: Cambridge University Press, 2015, 55–80.

5 See Edoardo Grendi, "Profilo storico degli Alberghi genovesi," in *La repubblica aristocratica dei genovesi*, Bologna: Mulino, 1987, 49–102; and Edoardo Grendi, *I Balbi: una famiglia genovese fra Spagna e Impero*, Turin: G. Einaudi, 1997, 69–94; Kirk, *Genoa and the Sea*, 54–5.

6 Niccolò Machiavelli, *The Florentine Histories*, ed. Harvey C. Mansfield, Princeton, NJ: Princeton University Press, 1988, VIII:30.

7 Heinrich Sieveking, *Studio sulle finanze genovesi e in particolare sulla casa di San Giorgio*, Genoa: Tip. della Gioventù, 1905, 219–20; Claudio Costantini, *La repubblica di Genova*, Turin: UTET, 1978, 28–9; Grendi, "Traffico e navi," in *La repubblica aristocratica*, 351.

8 Frederic C. Lane, "Economic Consequences of Organized Violence," *Journal of Economic History* 18(4) (1958): 401–17; Avner Greif, "On the Political Foundations of the Late Medieval Commercial Revolution: Genoa during the Twelfth and Thirteenth Centuries," *Journal of Economic History* 54(2) (1994): 271–87; Epstein, *Genoa and the Genoese*, 133–5, 205–8; Jeffrey Miner, "Lest we break faith with our creditors: Public Debt and Civic Culture in Fourteenth-century Genoa," PhD dissertation (Stanford University, 2011), 103–33.

9 See Kirk, *Genoa and the Sea, passim*, esp. 194–5.

10 See Giulio Giacchero, *Il Seicento e le compere di San Giorgio*, Genoa: Sagep, 1979, 105–10, 573–80; Costantini, *La repubblica di Genova*, 173–84; Edoardo Grendi, *Il Cervo e la repubblica. Il modello ligure di antico regime*, Turin: Einaudi, 1993, 92–6.

11 See especially Stephan Epstein, "Cities, Regions and the Late Medieval Crisis: Sicily and Tuscany Compared," *Past and Present* 130 (1991): 3–50; Stephan Epstein, *Freedom and Growth. The Rise of States and Markets in Europe, 1300–1750*, London: Routledge, 2000. Among economists, market integration refers to the development of a marketplace in which price differentials reflect only differences in transport costs. Among historians, who have less access to price data, it refers to the concentration of commercial networks within the bounds of a certain state or region; as well as the insertion of such an area into supra-regional or supra-state networks of exchange.

12 Edoardo Grendi, *Introduzione alla storia moderna della Repubblica di Genova*, Genoa: Bozzi, 1976; Grendi, *La repubblica aristocratica*; Osvaldo Raggio, "Produzione olivicola, prelievo fiscale e circuiti di scambio in una comunità ligure del XVII secolo," *Atti della Società Ligure di Storia Patria* 22 (1982): 125–62; Osvaldo Raggio, *Faide e parentele: lo stato genovese visto dalla Fontanabuona*, Turin: Einaudi, 1990; and Osvaldo Raggio, "Social Relations and Control of Resources in an Area of Transit: Eastern Liguria, Sixteenth to Seventeenth Centuries," in *Domestic Strategies: Work and Family in France and Italy 1600–1800*, ed. Stuart Woolf, Cambridge: Cambridge University Press, 2003, 20–42.

13 Nicholas Purcell, "The Ancient Mediterranean: The View from the Customs House," in *Rethinking the Mediterranean*, ed. William V. Harris, Oxford: Oxford University Press, 2005, 200–32: 219.

14 Grendi, *Introduzione*, 15–40, 105–17, 133–68; Raggio, "Produzione olivicola," *passim*; and in general, Peregrine Horden and Nicholas Purcell, *The Corrupting Sea: A Study of Mediterranean History*, Malden, MA: Blackwell Publishers, 2000, *passim*, esp. 263–6. These ecological realities help account for the exceptional strength of lineage networks in Liguria: Giovanni Levi, "Famiglie contadine nella Liguria del Settecento," in *Centro e periferia di uno Stato assoluto: tre saggi su Piemonte e Liguria in età moderna*, Turin: Rosenberg & Sellier, 1985, 71–143.

15 Cf. Raggio, "Social Relations," 20 and 42.

16 ASG, CSG, 96, 12/28/1663, 86; other examples include Franciscus Gazius, 10/30/1643, 81; and Sargeus Antonius Gambarius, 1699, 26.

17 Cases of documentary fraud were rare in the register – at most ninety-eight instances or 5 percent including those categorized as account fraud, embezzlement, and false documents.

18 A fuller description may be found in the online appendix: http://community.scrippscollege.edu/ctazzara/.

19 See ASG, CSG, 96, Joannes Laurentius Sansalvator, 1639, 125; and Joannes Franciscus Basterius, 9/7/1644, 133. In general, see Edoardo Grendi, *Lettere orbe. Anonimato e poteri nel Seicento Genovese*, Palermo: Gelka, 1989.

20 A number of brief entries simply state that the "case was not pursued," but I suspect not all were reported.

21 Felloni presents fiscal snapshots in 1550, 1650, and 1750. Despite increased fiscal pressure on the countryside in the period 1550–1650, the fisc continued to depend primarily on taxes from the city of Genoa throughout the eighteenth century. Giuseppe Felloni, "Distribuzione territoriale della ricchezza e dei carichi fiscali nella repubblica di Genova (secoli XVI–XVIII)," in *Prodotto lordo e finanza pubblica secoli XIII–XIX*, Florence: Le Monnier, 1988, 766–803: 792–5.

22 Giacchero, *Il Seicento*, 616, n. 39.

23 *Ibid.*, 577.

24 Some seventy-two cases occurred in and around Genoa, but scarcely anywhere else.

25 Or to phrase this point differently: if control in the provinces had been intense, we would expect more cattle crimes in the hinterlands, since most cattle originated there. But cattle become "visible" in the register only when they approached the gates of Genoa.

26 Cf. Giacchero, *Il Seicento*, 697. Giacchero suggested that San Giorgio exerted its greatest control over maritime revenues such as the *caratti*. This and other tables are found in the online statistical appendix at http://community.scrippscollege.edu/ctazzara/.

27 ASG, CSG, 96, 5/21/1645, 14. No wonder so many of the violators identified as tradesmen were butchers (thirty-seven out of sixty-eight). Meat consumption was more of an urban than a rural privilege. Grendi, *Introduzione*, 35–6.

28 Grendi, *Cervo*, 78, 92–6, 192–3.

29 ASG, CSG, 96, 6/28/1630, p. 202.

30 This figure represents violence associated with obstruction and conflict episodes (196 cases out of 543).

31 ASG, CSG, 96, 6/21/1652, p. 207.

32 Contrabandists often had collusive relations with bandits, who provided armed escorts for them. Raggio, *Faida*, 13, 16, 145–6.

33 Grendi, *Cervo*, 5–6, 10.

34 Giacchero, *Il Seicento*, 373–4; Kirk, *Genoa and the Sea*, 134–8.

35 Raggio, *Faida*, 26–7; the quotation is on p. 28.

36 Paolo Calcagno, *"Nel bel mezzo del Dominio." La comunità di Celle Ligure nel Sei-Settecento*, Ventimiglia: Philobiblon, 2007, 92ff.

37 ASG, Acta Senatus, filza 512, quoted by Osvaldo Raggio, "La politica nella parentela. Conflitti locali e commissari in Liguria Orientale (secoli XVI–XVII)," *Quaderni storici* 63 (1986): 721–57: 738. A few cases in the register give hints of this violent enforcement of state aims: for instance, when the *cavaliere* Sebastianus Borrotus and his squad assaulted some millers around 1665 (p. 227). But can we be sure that private motives did not lie behind this use of public power?

38 This figure is based on a sample of 263 cases: all those whose first names began with "A."

39 ASG, CSG, 96, 7/23/1766, 172. Such rescue operations were by no means rare and often involved confederates, perhaps because they were difficult to pull off alone. Joannes Baptista Salutius, 8/30/1637, 121; Petrus Ferrus, 1/9/1645, 207; Petrus Capponus, 8/30/1637, 205.

40 *Ibid.*, Baptista Rezoalius, 11/26/1632, 38 and his son, Martinus Rezoalius, 11/26/1632, 184.

41 A detailed onomastic analysis would undoubtedly bring to light further examples of familial fraud, perhaps even intergenerational "dynasties" of criminals. A rough indication of the extent of family fraud: the register contains 2,005 cases, but only about 1,200 distinct surnames.

42 *Ibid.*, Salvator Franciscus, 2/14/1639, 94. I found this case difficult to decipher.

43 *Ibid.*, 1657, 65.

44 A point also made by Raggio, *Faida*, 144.

45 ASG, CSG, 96, Cecilia Villa, 6/20/1636, 61; see also Maria and Manuela Berrina's obstruction efforts in the late 1660s, p. 190.

46 *Ibid.*, 5/16/1725, p. 91. Salvator Lacumarinus, a guard at the Porta S. Tommaso, also extorted sex from women: 5/21/1685, p. 229.

47 Olaudah Equiano, *The Life of Olaudah Equiano*, Mineola, NY: Dover, 1999, 126–7.

48 See, for instance, the cases of Franciscus Gioellus in ASG, CSG, 96, 8/31/1648, 83; Thomas Cabella, 3/13/1634, 233; or Thomas Grondona, 1705, 235.

49 *Ibid.*, 4/23/1703, 191.

50 San Giorgio's extensive use of sureties allowed it to exercise clemency while retaining the capacity to intervene.

51 The anecdote and the quotation are in Edoardo Grendi, "Counterfeit Coins and Monetary Exchange Structures in the Republic of Genoa during the Sixteenth and Seventeenth Centuries," in *History from Crime*, ed. Edward Muir and Guido Ruggiero, Baltimore: Johns Hopkins University Press, 1994, 170–205: 192–3. This episode occurred in 1627.

52 Grendi, *Cervo*, 61.

53 ASG, CSG, 96, Joannes Antonius Petius, 4/10/1634, 109. An outsider such as a Frenchman could not draw upon familial resources for defrauding the fisc.

54 *Ibid.*, 1/13/1633, 2/17/1634, 9/20/1634, and 11/6/1634, pp. 193 and 194.

55 Carlo Taviani, "An Ancient Scheme: The Mississippi Company, Machiavelli, and the Casa di San Giorgio (1407–1720)," in *Chartering Capitalism: Organizing Markets, States, and Publics*, ed. Emily Erikson, Bingley, UK: Emerald Group Publishing, 2015, 239–56.

56 If only cases with known occupations are included, that figure soars to 62 percent. I explain in-text why I believe 28 percent is more accurate.

57 Some guards also served watch over the goods in Genoa's many bonded warehouses (twenty-three cases).

58 ASG, CSG, 96, 10/11/1645, p. 14. The notary was an official of the *caratti*.

59 The 75 percent figure includes "unknown" and "fraud" cases in the total, which probably also involved the flow of resources. The relative paucity of officials from the secretarial or administrative classes offers a further indication that the vast majority of official crime was about the flow of real resources rather than financial resources – despite the legendary fame of Genoese financial expertise.

60 ASG, CSG, 96, Andreas Fosinarius, 3/17/1631, pp. 3 and 4.

61 *Ibid.*, Petrus Joannes Lavagius and Bartholomeus Martinus, 1643, p. 206; Joannes Jacobus De Franchis, 1/7/1643, p. 127; Stephanus Cadamartori, 5/2/1680, p. 229.

62 The small number of extortion cases – only 5 percent of official fraud – underscores the complicitous rather than adversarial relations between officials and their clientele.

63 *Ibid.*, 7/14/1642, p. 122. Joannes Baptista Zoalius also tried to supply a bribe to a guard "ut moram traheret executionem sibi demandatam": 10/16/1634, p. 110.

64 Quoted in Giacchero, *Il Seicento*, 616.

65 Grendi, *Cervo*, 151–2, 182–93.

66 Calcagno, *"Nel bel mezzo del Dominio,"* 142–3.

67 Raggio, *Faida*, 136–7.

68 Finale, a Spanish fief near Savona that funneled goods and people into and out of Liguria and steadfastly resisted Genoese claims to its salt and *caratti* taxes: from the point of view of San Giorgio, Finale was like an engine for generating fraud. Giacchero, *Il Seicento*, 405–14. In addition,

Grendi, after celebrating the vibrancy of provincial ports in Liguria, notes that salt monopoly prices declined at the borders – in part to minimize fraud by competing with foreign prices. *Introduzione*, 136–7.

69 Quoted by Giacchero, *Il Seicento*, 460; see also *ibid.*, 580–1.

70 See, for instance, the role of Ligurian traders in the Kingdom of Naples: Annastella Carrino and Biagio Salvemini, "Porti di campagna, porti di città. Traffici e insediamenti del Regno di Napoli visti da Marsiglia (1710–1846)," *Quaderni storici* 121 (2006): 209–54: esp. 221ff.

71 Fernand Braudel, *Civilization and Capitalism, 15th–18th Century*, vol. 3, *The Perspective of the World*, Berkeley: University of California Press, 1984, 184 (quoting Carmelo Trasselli).

72 Finally, I would like to thank the following for their comments on drafts of this text: Naor Ben-Yehoyada, George Gorse, Daniel Hershenzon, Thomas A. Kirk, Jessica Marglin, Jeffrey Miner, Sophus Reinert, and Suzanne Sutherland.

23

REPRESENTATIONS OF THE FLORENTINE REPUBLIC AT THE ROYAL COURT IN THE KINGDOM OF HUNGARY[1]

Katalin Prajda

Frederick Antal (1884–1957), who started his career at the Museum of Fine Arts in Budapest, developed his most important scholarly concepts in his book entitled *Florentine Painting and its Social Background*, written between 1932 and 1938.[2] According to Antal, the "bourgeois republic" and the origins of the democratic system in Florence, can be traced back to the writing of the Florentine chancellor Coluccio Salutati. Antal emphasized the important role chancellors of the Republic played not only in the development of Florentine political thought, but also in establishing Florence's place in the context of European diplomacy as "defender of its own liberty."[3]

Thirty years later, William J. Bouwsma, in *Venice and the Defense of Republican Liberty*, proposed to assess the history of the Venetian Republic in terms of Renaissance studies by arguing against the predominance of Florence. In spite of this attempt, the first chapter of his book, dealing with "Renaissance Republicanism," was based primarily on Florentine political thought. However, Bouwsma mentioned only sporadically Salutati's activity, commonly associated with discourses on liberty.[4] Nevertheless, the subject of liberty had already entered political debates in Italy, even in Florence, by the time of Coluccio's chancery. In 1360, at the meetings of the most important city magistrates and politicians, a speaker stated that the "liberty of the commune" should be protected.[5] But it was Salutati's state letters that have provoked great admiration and were widely copied, to the extent that they provided ample ground for debate among contemporaries.[6]

Salutati believed that the Republic's liberty could be preserved by the establishment of amicable diplomatic relations with other European states. Such ties might help Florence protect her interests. As a result, the formation of a political alliance with the Guelf King of Hungary became an important objective of Florentine diplomacy in the pre-Medici period. The records of the Florentine chancery, which comprise state letters, public debates and embassies, are filled with references to the diplomatic exchanges with the Hungarian monarch.[7] This was not unique from the Florentine point of view, thanks to the richness of the Florentine National Archives, but the sources are remarkably diverse and extensive with respect to the availability of sources on the diplomacy of the Kingdom of Hungary.

The primary aim of this chapter is to provide an overview of the various forms of diplomatic representation of the Florentine Republic toward the King of Hungary in the pre-Medici period and to compare the Florentine case, to the extent possible, with other north Italian examples. The chapter looks at the language and the frequency of state letters which the Florentine chancery addressed to the Hungarian monarchs. It also analyzes the regularity and the composition of dispatching diplomatic contingents aimed at reaching the court while in Hungary. Finally, it intends to assess the relative importance of the Florentine community in Hungary, which represented the Republic on a permanent basis. Since the Kingdom of Hungary, indeed, became an important political ally to pre-Medici Florence, an analysis of the diplomatic relations between the two states might shed a new light on some aspects of Florentine diplomatic practices. Therefore, through the example of Hungary, the chapter also addresses more generalized questions regarding the pre-Medici diplomacy.[8]

Language of diplomacy

Scholars of Renaissance Italy have already dedicated a certain amount of literature to the philological aspects of diplomatic communication. William Caferro, in his monograph on the mercenary captain John Hawkwood, has emphasized the linguistic side of Hawkwood's letters as well as of written and oral diplomatic communication in fourteenth-century Italy.[9] Isabella Lazzarini's article on Rinaldo degli Albizzi's *Commissioni* (a documental unit produced during diplomatic missions) has analyzed the textual and linguistic skills of the Florentine ambassador in order to uncover the ways Florentines expressed emotions and argued in the context of international diplomacy.[10] Others, such as Ronald G. Witt, have been interested in defining the style applied by Salutati in his state letters in order to study the interpretative framework Renaissance humanists developed to justify Florence's maneuvers in the scene of international diplomacy.[11] Following this line of inquiry, state letters dispatched by the Florentine chancellery to the Hungarian monarch might mirror an image the *Signoria* wished to project about itself in relation to its corresponding partner. In this part, I shall look at the rhetoric and specifically the *salutatio* of the *missive* from this specific point of view.

The national archives of northern Italian states provide very limited possibilities for scholars who wish to study diplomacy with the Hungarian court. In Venice, for example, virtually no state letters have survived. In Mantua, fragments of correspondence kept with the royal chancellery testify to the continuous communication in written form starting from the 1340s.[12] Yet given their relatively small number and the greater consistency of the Florentine archival material, the importance of the Mantuan sources remains marginal to our subject.

In the Florentine Republic, the duty of maintaining correspondence with other European powers fell to the chancellor as head of the state bureaucracy. Thanks to their long office-holding, which might have spanned decades, they gained extensive knowledge of the diplomatic practices and history of the *Signoria*, developing as an expertise in international affairs. Letters composed by the chancellor or one of the other notaries of the Republic were supposed to be proof-read and approved by members of the government, and their content provided subjects for ample discussions at the meetings of the city councils, the *Consulte*, of which the chancellor was the main secretary. The chancellor's role in this regard was seemingly limited to the practical aspects of correspondence such as rhetoric, style, and registering and dispatching letters, though these details might have played a similarly important role in state-level communication. The letters and their registers, following the diplomatic line designed by the governing priors in cooperation with the political elite, also demonstrate a distinct pattern in handling diplomatic communication.

The period extending from the Black Death (1348) to Cosimo de'Medici's return to the city (1434) coincided with the reigns of Louis I (1342–1382), Mary (1382–1396), Charles of Durazzo (1386), and Sigismund of Luxembourg (1387–1437) and the chancelleries of five learned Florentine men. During the offices of ser Niccolò di Bonaventura Monachi (1348–1375), Coluccio di Piero Salutati (1375–1406), Benedetto di ser Lando Fortini (1376–1377, 1406), Piero di ser Mino (1406–1410), Leonardo Bruni (1410–1411, 1427–1444), and Paolo di ser Lando Fortini (1411–1427), the chancery adopted distinct measures in handling foreign affairs.[13] State letters were collected and copied into registers, kept very often by the chancellor himself. Most of them were produced during the chancellery of Monachi (six registers) and Salutati (twelve registers), while the chancelleries of Benedetto Fortini (one register), Piero di ser Mino (one register), Paolo Fortini (three registers), and Leonardo Bruni (four registers) have left us considerably smaller correspondences.[14]

Ronald G. Witt's hypothesis that the Florentine government would have relied significantly on state letters in diplomatic communication during Coluccio's time is also supported by the quantity and quality of *missive* sent to the King of Hungary.[15] According to the registers, before Coluccio entered into office, Niccolò Monachi addressed altogether three letters to Louis I.[16] At the same time, Coluccio's dispatches to Louis I, between 1375 and 1382, number twenty-three, almost eight times as many as in the previous period.[17] Following Louis I's death, his daughter, Queen Mary, received six letters from the chancery.[18] Besides her, Elisabeth and Charles of Durazzo (in his capacity as Hungarian king) were among the correspondents.[19] During Salutati's term, the chancery addressed ten letters to Sigismund of Luxembourg.[20] After Coluccio's time, the accuracy of record-keeping, the frequency of dispatching diplomatic correspondence, as well as their quality decline. In the following eighteen years, there are no traces of correspondence with the Hungarian royal court, and the remaining eight letters were written in a relatively short period of time, between 1424 and 1432.[21] Since the registers of the Florentine chancery seem to be consistent in this regard, we shall presume that besides the general decrease in the number of *missive*, record-keeping of the Florentine bureaucracy took a very inefficient and unsystematic form.

Not only the quantity but also the quality of the dispatches were improved with Coluccio's entrance into the Florentine bureaucracy. Ronald G. Witt has emphasized that the novelty of Coluccio Salutati's political writings lay in the fact that he developed a historical discourse, which made use of classical examples.[22] His writings remained in harmony with the *ars dictandi* and the *stilus altus* already adopted by his predecessors, at the same time, the salutations of Coluccio's state letters, addressed to greater powers, became elaborate, to the extent that sometimes they even reached exaggerated proportions.[23] The dispatches sent to the Hungarian ruler were seemingly no exception. Monachi's correspondence with the court contained short, straight-to-the point *missive*, and their *salutatio* was kept to the minimum, calling the Hungarian ruler "illustrious king and single lord" and "the most glorious and illustrious king."[24] Coluccio's letters, instead, were characterized by the extensive use of superlatives, in a similar way to other *missive* addressed to his correspondents of the same rank. The rhetoric Coluccio applied to his correspondence with the Hungarian monarch followed a pattern similar to that found in his letters to other monarchs, for example the French king.[25] Salutati's state letters had a tremendous effect at the French royal court, so we might expect the same reception in the *aula* in Hungary, which might also explain why Sigismund invited to Buda one of Salutati's followers, Pier Paolo Vergerio.[26] In Salutati's letters, both the Hungarian and the French sovereign were addressed as "our most serene Father and Lord," "Prince, our Father and Lord" and foremost "singular benefactor" of the Republic.[27] In a similar way, Witt has also noted, that while Niccolò Monachi made no distinction in his state letters between kings and queens, addressing them both as "Rex," Coluccio was sensitive to the issue.[28] In fact, when corresponding with queens, such as Mary of Hungary and Margaret of Naples, the female versions of these *salutatio* was used, such as "the most serene and glorious Queen" and "our most singular Mother and Dame."[29]

Besides the extensive use of "father–son," "lord–servant" paradigms, Coluccio also frequently recalled the past relations between the Hungarian monarchs and the Florentine government. In Mary's case, he mentioned the amicable contacts the *Signoria* maintained with her father; while the rhetorical setting of Sigismund's letters followed the same logic: the good contacts with Emperor Charles IV, father of Sigismund, would have provided, in his understanding, the basis for fruitful diplomatic contacts.[30] Coluccio's letters, in spite of their innovative nature, were standardized in their formalities, making no distinction between correspondents of the same rank, and were composed with little to no intention for personalization in their rhetoric. Rigorous record-keeping, eloquence in composing letters, and the emphasis on *missive* over embassies as means of diplomatic communication all indicate that during Coluccio's time, state letters stood as the most important tools for setting Florence in the context of international diplomacy. As part of this view, the amicable contacts with the Hungarian ruler remained an important factor in shaping the foreign affairs of the Republic. The value of Coluccio's activity as spokesman of the Florentine Republic lies not only in his innovative rhetoric when corresponding with foreign powers, but also in his activity as bureaucrat, his efficiency in record-keeping and organizing the Florentine chancery, responsible for international communication. This distinguishes him from all the other chancellors of the Republic during the period under consideration.

The remaining eight letters, written during the chancery of Paolo Fortini and Leonardo Bruni, show little novelty on the rhetorical level and testify to certain changes in the functioning of the chancery. Following Coluccio's time, state letters seem to have lost their importance in diplomatic communication, resulting in the fact that both Paolo Fortini and Leonardo Bruni put less emphasis on their improvement. State letters were consequently replaced by personal embassies assigned to foreign powers with a specific mandate.[31] One of the explanations might be, as Ronald Witt has pointed out, that this was a general tendency throughout Italy, which also led to the transformation of diplomatic practices. Ambassadors such as Rinaldo degli Albizzi proved to be more effective representatives of the *Signoria*'s interests abroad than state letters composed by Paolo Fortini.[32] The transformation of diplomatic practices would also explain Brian J. Maxson's argument that the *Signoria* tended to assign at least one learned man, preferably one versed in humanist studies, as a member of these embassies, who might have been able to deliver an oration in the foreign court.[33]

Diplomatic envoys and power representation

If we consider the records of the diplomatic contingents assigned to the court of the Hungarian king, we might find inequalities in the quality and the quantity of sources housed by some of the north Italian archives. The earliest information about a diplomatic contingent dispatched by the Florentine government to the King of Hungary dates back to 1347, and was recorded in the Chronicle of Giovanni Villani.[34] This date almost coincides with the earliest report about a Venetian embassy sent to the Kingdom of Hungary in 1348.[35]

It was not until 1376, just two months after Coluccio Salutati was nominated to the head of the chancery, that we receive a detailed account of a Florentine diplomatic contingent in Hungary.[36] Since most of the documentation produced by the Florentine chancery that deals with ambassadorships starts with his appointment, the number of Florentine diplomatic missions that precede this period is unclear. Ambassadorships, like state letters, were discussed at the meetings of the *Consulte* already in the 1350s. They address the issue of an embassy to Hungary. But there is no evidence that the priors had actually approved the proposals. Those dispatched to Hungary were designed according to the general protocol. Based on the advice of the most respected citizens at the *Consulte*, where names of possible ambassadors were proposed, the priors made the final decision. As the chancellor himself assisted with almost every meeting, his expertise in foreign policy-making enabled him to coordinate the trip of the ambassadors from the time of their election to the oral report they were supposed to deliver before the priors upon their return from their mission. By the time of their departure, the chancellor had given a detailed description of the ambassadors' task and was mediating during the entire time of the journey between the contingent and the *Signoria*. Documentation regarding the embassies sent to the royal court in Hungary consists mainly of this correspondence, but sometimes there are also personal accounts at our disposal, which allow us to reconstruct the personnel of these embassies. In spite of the fact that the corresponding registers of the Florentine chancellery starting from 1393 seem to be consistent, the total number of embassies to Sigismund's court remains low compared to the number of contingents which the *Signoria* sent to the neighboring Italian powers.[37] One very plausible explanation might be the considerable distance and difficulties of the journey between Florence and Buda, which also made the missions extremely expensive. During Coluccio's time two embassies were recorded. The chancery led by Paolo Fortini registered four diplomatic missions and consequently during Leonardo Bruni's chancery, three more. Among these, only six were heading directly to the Kingdom of Hungary.

In the first case, in 1376, the *Signoria* was seeking alliance with Louis I against Pope Gregory XI by sending one of the most influential politicians of his time, Simone di Rinieri Peruzzi. In 1396, the Florentine government dispatched another embassy in order to forge a marriage alliance between Sigismund and the house of Naples.[38] This happened the year after the Count of Mantua assigned his ambassadors to the royal court in Buda.[39] Nine years had passed since Sigismund's accession to the throne, without news about the sending of a diplomatic contingent from Florence. This is no wonder, since several sources underline that the Florentine political elite, during the struggle for the throne between Charles and Sigismund, was in favor of the former. In fact, in 1386, following the news of Charles of Durazzo's coronation as King of Hungary, Coluccio Salutati himself read aloud the letter of the newly made ruler and the Florentine government ordered public celebrations.[40] Instead, the Venetian *Serenissima* in 1387 decided to assign the Venetian nobleman Pantaleone Barbo to the court, accompanied by the notary Lorenzo Monaci, demonstrating their support for Sigismund.[41] By the Treaty of Turin (1381), once a year, a diplomatic contingent was dispatched from Venice to the royal court in order to hand over the 7,000 ducats the *Serenissima* was supposed to pay for the use of the Dalmatian ports.[42]

Florentine contingents were surely less frequent than that, at least in the decades preceding the 1420s, which is considered the most active period of Florentine diplomacy in relation to the Hungarian ruler, with four embassies following each other in the years 1424, 1426, 1427, and 1428.[43] In all these cases, the *Signoria* assigned its most influential politicians to the court. Among them were Biagio di Jacopo Guasconi (1424), Rinaldo di Maso degli Albizzi (1426), and Piero di messer Luigi Guicciardini (1427). In addition, learned men, such as the jurists Bene di Jacopo del Bene (1376), Nello di Giuliano Martini da San Gimignano (1426), and Luca di Maso degli Albizzi (1427), traveled with the embassies. In 1427, there was another additional member recorded, the notary ser Jacopo Riccardi, who served as the "chancellor" to the mission.[44] Thanks to the detailed and, from this point of view unique, diary and ledger kept by Luca degli Albizzi during his trip to Hungary, it is possible to reconstruct the costs of a journey of this kind. We learn, in fact, that the ambassadors set off from Florence with eighteen horses and probably with several servants. Luca surely had one employee traveling with him and he referred to three other persons in the capacity of servants. Because of the several stops they made and the unfavorable weather conditions, it took almost three weeks for them to reach the town of Segna (Senj, HR), Hungary's nearest port to Venice, commonly used by Florentine merchants. Because of Luca's illness, we do not know how much time the ambassadors spent on this particular occasion in Hungary. A year later, though, the same Piero di messer Luigi Guicciardini, fellow ambassador to Luca, served the *Signoria* for 108 days in the capacity of ambassador to Sigismund.[45] This would mean that he spent approximately two months at court, representing the Florentine state. Similarly, Rinaldo degli Albizzi and Nello Martini also had two months in Hungary, busy with traveling either in order to visit members of the court or to meet the king.[46]

In fact, Florentine ambassadors' duties also included visits to members of the *Curia*, barons, archbishops, and bishops, promoting in this way Florentine interests among the Hungarian elite. Gift giving, from both sides, was surely part of this protocol; some of them are recorded in the documents.[47] Interestingly, neither Rinaldo nor Luca degli Albizzi had ever mentioned the gifts they carried to the royal court. Luca, to cover his travel expenses, received 200 Florentine golden florins from the Dieci di Balìa, temporary governing body of the Florentine state.[48] From this sum, the ambassadors were expected to pay for their accommodation, meals, the salary of their servants, passage, supply for their horses, and for the smaller gifts they purchased for their hosts. Beyond this budget, upon their return to Florence, the ambassadors were entitled to get their salary, stipulated on the basis of the length of the mission.[49] In 1376, the heirs of Bene di Jacopo del Bene demanded his salary, which amounted to 3 florins, 19 soldi and 8 denari per day.[50] Fifty years later, in Piero di Luigi Guicciardini's case, this amount was 4 golden florins.

Usually, ambassadors traveling together did not receive the same salary from the Florentine government, yet, on the basis of the available information, we might stipulate the approximate costs of a journey of this kind, including the salary of the ambassadors, their servants, and a three-month-long trip. In the 1420s, the salary of the ambassadors alone might range between 270 and 360 florins per person and the daily expenses another 200 florins per person.[51] The costs of a diplomatic mission to a royal court, were, therefore, commensurate with the price of a nice house in the Florentine city center. These representative expenses in the 1420s, designed in order to maintain fruitful diplomatic relations with Sigismund of Luxemburg, might have far exceeded the amount the Florentine state might have dedicated to the issue during Coluccio Salutati's chancery.

Similarly, expenses might not have been insignificant when the Florentine government welcomed envoys on behalf of the Hungarian monarchs. The single detailed description of an event of this kind, which has survived from 1410, concerns the arrival at the city of an embassy led by the Florentine-born Hungarian baron Pippo Scolari.[52] The protocol, in this particular case, might have followed an unusual path, though it was not unique for diplomacy to rely on both sides on the service of Florentines.[53] Given the special guest, who provoked admiration among Florentine contemporaries, the *Signoria* honored Pippo with celebrations and with an official audience held in the presence of the priors and probably of the entire *Consulte*.[54]

Diplomacy and migration

In fact, the story of Pippo Scolari, who was raised to baronial rank by King Sigismund, and of his fellow Florentines who occupied secular or ecclesiastical offices, such as the archbishopric, bishopric, and city magistracy, is already well known.[55] His success in the Kingdom of Hungary, along with that of other Florentines, clearly shows the intensity of the diplomatic relations between the two states during the first decades of the fifteenth century and how effectively the Florentine *nazione* was represented in Hungary. Meanwhile, temporary ambassadorships resided in the proximity of the royal court only for a couple of weeks; the Florentine community and its members in Hungary served as permanent representatives of Florentines' interests. Population exchange and the temporary migration of a skilled labor force and especially long-distance-trade merchants and their role in domestic politics in the host country are considered as one of the main factors in measuring fruitful diplomatic relations.

Given the favorable political setting, it is natural that some merchants originating from Florence, because of their business activity, settled in Hungary. But it might be surprising to learn that during the same period, a few persons coming from the Kingdom of Hungary also made their way to Florentine political circles. That a foreigner would have been registered as a speaker in one of the volumes of the *Consulte* during the 180 years of its existence, happened only in one case, when a certain Johannes/Nanni Silvestri *unghero/ ungarus* appeared among those who were allowed to deliver a speech at the meetings. His name was recorded nine times, in the period between 1410 and 1415, when Sigismund fought his ongoing war with the Venetian *Serenissima*. We do not have any information about him, who he might be, or how he had obtained the privilege of intervening at the meetings, in which only city officers and other respected Florentine politicians were allowed to participate.[56] Johannes might have been knowledgeable in matters regarding the affairs of the Hungarian crown and the *Serenissima*, or he might have shared Florentine citizenship with those very few persons who were recorded in the tax registers as of "Hungarian" origin. Among them, we find a woman who claimed to be the widow of a certain Piero from Hungary, and her sons were probably a certain Niccolò di Piero d'Ungheria and Filippo di Piero d'Ungheria.[57] Two other "ungheri" appear in the 1427 census, both of them probably merchants.[58] As William Caferro has pointed out, since the last decades of the fourteenth century, several soldiers originating from Hungary had joined various military companies.[59] Therefore, it is no wonder, that the *condotta* or military contract from Pisa mentions two men in the service of the *Signoria*.[60]

The Florentine community in Hungary was more extensive than that, with some reaching the kingdom as early as the 1350s. Florentines seemingly outnumbered other Italian trading nations, such as the Genoese and Venetians.[61] Meanwhile, these first arrivals enjoyed special privileges thanks to Louis I. Besides members of the Sorba family, there is very little evidence of their presence in Hungary.[62] Only the Milanese ambassador, visiting the court in 1426, happened to be mentioned as having Genoese origins.[63] As the fragmentary documentation suggests, they might have lived mainly on the Dalmatian coastline, at such places as Zara, and not in the Hungarian hinterland. Since there has been no systematic research in the Genoese archives, we must presume that their number, in comparison to Florentines, was limited. Similarly, the Venetian community might have been more sizeable in Dalmatia, but not in other parts of the state. Though Hungarian sources occasionally mention locations which might indicate the intense presence of Venetian citizens in a particular town, this does not necessary imply that they were, in fact, filled with Venetians in a given period.[64] One of the possible explanations might be that the Venetian population, unlike the Florentine, was very heterogeneous in both origin and privilege, and many Dalmatians or even Florentines obtained Venetian citizenship, acquired the language, and moved to a particular town of the kingdom. Sporadic information about *cittadini originari* from Venice living in one of the free royal towns, such as Buda, Pressburg, or Gradec, during the reign of Sigismund does appear in sources.[65] One example from the 1390s shows that, like Florentines, they also cooperated with local citizens in selling their goods in Buda.[66]

Venice, however, in the last decades of the fourteenth century, already teemed with Florentines, both artisans and businessmen. Some developed tight contacts with other Florentines working in the Kingdom of Hungary. In spite of the protectionist legislation of the *Stato de Mar*, textiles produced in Florence had also reached its ports and there are signs that these measurements were softened from time to time, which allowed more space for Florentine merchants to market their domestic goods in and beyond Venice.[67] Some of these Florentines acquired citizenship in Venice early on, facilitating their involvement in international trade. In fact, an in-depth analysis of Venetian, Florentine, and Hungarian documents reveals that Florentines might have played an intermediary role in long-distance trade between the Venetian ports and the Kingdom of Hungary. The dense networks of Florentines, which had interwoven all important spheres of international trade, including transport, banking, insurance, and marketing, might have been the key to Florentines' success in the region. Furthermore, the amicable bilateral diplomatic relations also favored Florentine merchants, while the political tensions between the Hungarian crown and the Venetian *Serenissima* discouraged Venetian commerce in the kingdom.[68] Already in the 1390s, Florentine merchants' activity was framed by the existence of a joint organization in the town of Buda, headed back then by a consul of Paduan origins who later on was promoted to royal chamber master.[69] Already Louis I employed as mint master a Florentine named Francesco Bernardi.[70] Following this period, chambers and mines were run by Florentine officials, due to Pippo Scolari's influence over the industry. Thanks to the easy access to precious metal resources, as well as to salt, Florentines and other merchants from subject towns were heavily involved in their trade. Merchants from Prato, such as Tommaso di Piero Melanesi and Rinaldo di Diego Rinaldeschi, were employed in the copper mines, and traded regularly with them in Venice.[71] Since Pippo started his career as chamber master in Kremnica, the gold trade to Italy was seemingly in the hand of the Scolaris' employees. They obtained a certain interest in the silver trade, in cooperation with the Aretine nobleman Mariotto di Biagio Griffolini.[72] In addition, other members of his family, as well as several merchants from Arezzo, seem to have had commercial interest in Hungary.[73] Other Florentines, for example the Mannini brothers and Bernardo di Sandro Talani, gained access to salt deposits in the kingdom, another highly valued article on the domestic market.[74] Florentines occasionally also made their way onto city councils, for example in the free royal town of Gradec.[75] They also occupied church offices for certain periods, for instance the bishopric of Zagreb, the bishopric of Varadinum (Oradea, RO), and the archbishopric of Kalocsa.[76]

Conclusion

The sources, as we have seen, are exceptionally rich on the diplomatic relations between the Florentine Republic and the Kingdom of Hungary compared to other archives in northern Italy from the time of the Black Death (1348) to Cosimo de'Medici's (1433) return to the city. The communication between the ever-changing governments of a city-state, involving mainly merchants and the kings of a major European state, was characterized by unequal power relations. The Florentine *Signoria*, commensurate with its political weakness, tried to represent its interests in the Hungarian royal court, using as tools diplomatic letters composed by the head of the Florentine bureaucracy, contingents lead by influential members of the political elite, and the mediation of Florentine citizens who settled permanently or temporarily in the region. Despite their importance, the protocols of the bilateral relations, when dealing with the Hungarian ruler, probably followed a pattern similar to the cases of other European sovereigns. Even though the political discourse was filled with references to Hungary, the 1420s appear to have constituted the peak of these relations. The general Florentine political attitude toward the Hungarian ruler can best be described in the words of the politician Alessandro degli Albizzi, who said that "the benevolence of the king should be maintained in order to preserve the status of Florence as well."[77]

Notes

1 This study has benefited from the support of the "Lendület" Holy Crown of Hungary, Research Project (2012–2017) of the Institute of History, Research Centre for the Humanities, Hungarian Academy of Sciences. I am indebted to Ellen Petruzzella for revising the manuscript.

2 Frederick Antal, *Florentine Painting and Its Social Background. The Bourgeois Republic before Cosimo De'medici's Advent to Power, XIV and Early XV Centuries*, Cambridge, MA and London: Harvard University Press, 1986.

3 In his opinion, the period marked by the chancelleries of Leonardo Bruni and Poggio Bracciolini should be described as the highest forms of Florentine democracy. *Ibid.*, 53–7.

4 William J. Bouwsma, *Venice and the Defense of Republican Liberty: Renaissance Values in the Age of the Counter Reformation*, Berkeley and Los Angeles: University of California Press, 1968, 1–51. For the traditionalist literature on liberty see: Hans Baron, *The Crisis of the early Italian Renaissance: Civic Humanism and Republican Liberty in an Age of Classicism and Tyranny*, Princeton, NJ: Princeton University Press, 1955, 1–160.

5 For the earliest speech, in 1360, addressing the subject see: Florence, Archivio di Stato di Firenze (hereafter: ASF), Consulte e Pratiche 2. 190v. For later examples, in 1368 see: ASF, Consulte e Pratiche 10. 7r, 10.11r. Gene A. Brucker, *Florentine Politics and Society. 1343–1378*, Princeton, NJ: Princeton University Press, 1962, 73.

6 On the influence of Salutati's state letters see: Ronald G. Witt, *"In the Footsteps of the Ancients": The Origins of Humanism from Lovato to Bruni*, Leiden, Boston, and Cologne: Brill, 2000, 300–15. For his discussions about liberty see: Ronald G. Witt, *Coluccio Salutati and his Public Letters*, Geneva: Droz, 1976, 85–6.

7 For references see: Katalin Prajda, "Trade and Diplomacy in pre-Medici Florence: The Case of the Kingdom of Hungary (1349–1434)," in *Causa unioni, causa fidei, causa reformationis in capite et membris*, ed. Attila Bárány and László Pósán, Debrecen: Debrecen University Press, forthcoming

8 For a comprehensive history of Italian diplomacy see: Isabella Lazzarini, *Communication and Conflict: Italian Diplomacy in the Early Renaissance. 1350–1520*, Oxford: Oxford University Press, 2015. The book was not yet available at the time the manuscript of this chapter was being finalized.

9 William Caferro, *John Hawkwood: An English Mercenary in Fourteenth-Century Italy*, Baltimore: Johns Hopkins University Press, 2007, 4, 118–20, 141–3, 198–200, 217–20, 344–450.

10 Isabella Lazzarini, "Argument and Emotion in Italian Diplomacy in the early Fifteenth Century: The Case of Rinaldo degli Albizzi (Florence, 1399–1430)," in *The Languages of Political Society*,

Western Europe 14th–17th centuries, ed. Andrea Gamberini, Jean-Philippe Genet, and Andrea Zorzi, Rome: Viella, 2011, 339–63.

11 Witt, *"In the Footsteps of the Ancients,"* 300–15. David Peterson, "The War of the Eight Saints in Florentine Memory and Oblivion," in *Society and Individual in Renaissance Florence*, ed. William J. Connell, Berkeley: University of California Press, 2002, 190.

12 For letters sent by Louis I's chancery to Mantua see: Mantua, Archivio di Stato di Mantova (hereafter: ASMa), Archivio Gonzaga, busta 532. n. 1. (1347), n. 2. (1349), n. 3. (1376), n. 5. (1380), busta 2184. n. 614 (1370), n. 640 (1380). For the correspondence with the chancery of Sigismund see: ASMa, Archivio Gonzaga, busta 2185 (12/07/1404), For the Mantuan chancery see: Isabella Lazzarini, "'Peculiaris magistratus.' *La cancelleria gonzaghesca nel Quattrocento (1407–1478),*" in *Cancelleria e amministrazione negli stati italiani del Rinascimento*, ed. F. Leverotti, special issue of *Ricerche storiche* 24(2) (1994): 337–50.

13 For the history of the Florentine chancellery see: Demetrio Marzi, *La cancelleria della Repubblica fiorentina*, Rocca San Casciano: Cappelli, 1910.

14 For the registers see: Monachi: ASF, Signori, Missive, Cancelleria I, vols. 9–14. Salutati: Signori, Missive, Cancelleria I, vols. 15–24, 26. Benedetto Fortini: Signori, Missive, Cancelleria I, vol. 27. Piero di ser Mino: Signori, Missive, Cancelleria I, vol. 28. Paolo Fortini: Signori, Missive, I Cancelleria, vols. 29, 30, 31. Vols. 25 and 29 are mixed ones. Bruni: Signori, Missive, Cancelleria I, vols. 32–5. On Salutati's registers see: Hermann Langkabel, *Due Staatsbriefe Coluccio Salutatis*, Cologne and Vienna: Böhlau, 1981, 8–9.

15 Witt, *"In the Footsteps of the Ancients,"* 315.

16 ASF, Signori, Missive, I Cancelleria, 10.47r, 12.92r, 13.36v.

17 For the comprehensive list of missives sent by the Florentine chancery during Coluccio's office see: *Coluccio Salutati cancelliere della repubblica fiorentina. Carteggio pubblico 1375–1406. Indice onomastico e toponomastico*, ed. Roberto Cardini and Franek Sznura, Florence: Polistampa, 2013. For the missives sent to the Hungarian royal court see: ASF, Signori, Missive, I Cancelleria, 16.69r (02/05/1376); 17.11v (04/02/1376); 15.58r (04/26/1376); 17.21r (/04/29/1376); 17.23r (05/03/1376); 17.30v (05/27/1376); 17.52v (08/04/1376); 17.67v (09/28/1376); 17.99r (03/21/1377); 17.99r (03/23/1377); 17.123r (07/18/1377); 18.74v (10/17/1379); 18.81v (11/09/1379); 18.95r (12/30/1379); 18.135v (04/05/1380); 18.143v (04/16/1380); 19.42v (09/13/1380); 19.69r (10/29/1380); 19.80r (12/04/1380); 19.149v (07/10/1381); 19.175v (09/23/1381); 18.141r (s.d.); 18.141r (s.d.) Besides these letters, Armando Nuzzo also cites others for which there are no copies in the registers of the chancery already mentioned. Armando Nuzzo, "Coluccio Salutati e l'Ungheria," *Verbum* 11 (2005): 341–71.

18 ASF, Signori, Missive, I Cancelleria, 20.82v (03/15/1386); 20.12v (02/10/1388); 21.27v (05/16/1388); 21.41r (07/31/1388); 21.85v (03/06/1389); 24.110r (02/09/1395).

19 For a letter sent to the queen mother see: *ibid.*, 17.21r (04/29/1376).

20 *Ibid.*, 21.13r (02/10/1388); 21.39v (07/25/1388); 21.45r (08/17/1388); 21.131v (09/28/1389); 24.109v (02/09/1395); 24.121r (03/28/1395); 24.154r (09/12/1395); 26.28v (02/061404); 26.51v (07/11/1404); 26.136r (12/05/1405).

21 *Ibid.*, 32.65r–v (7/4/1429); 32.178v–179r (07/02/1430); 33.76r–78v (21/06/1432); 33.78v–80r (03/07/1432); 30.85v (30/10/1424); 30.104r (1426); 30.104v (1426); 30.114v–115r (24/05/1427).

22 Ronald G. Witt, "Florentine Politics and the Ruling Class, 1382–1407," *Journal of Medieval and Renaissance Studies* 6 (1976): 243–67.

23 On his style see: Daniela de Rosa, "Coluccio Salutati notaio e cancelliere," in *Coluccio Salutati e l'invenzione dell'Umanesimo*, ed. T. De Robertis, G. Tanturli, and S. Zamponi, Florence: Mandragora, 2008, 33–9. For an example of the salutatio in one of the letters addressed to the French king: "Serenissime atque gloriossime principium metuendissime domine nostrum ac populi Florentini columen et refugium singular," Witt, *Coluccio Salutati and his Public Letters*, 27–8.

24 "Regum illustris et domine," ASF, Signori, Missive, I Cancelleria, 10.47r; "Illustris rex et domine singularis," *ibid.*, 12.92r; "Gloriosissimo et illutris rex," *ibid.*, 13.36v.

25 For correspondence with the French king see: "Serenissime atque invictissime princeps," in *Coluccio Salutati, Political Writings*, ed. Stefano U. Baldassarri, Cambridge, MA: Harvard University Press, 2014, 16, 46. For other dispatches to the French king see: ASF, Signori, Missive, I Cancelleria, 20.30v; 19.97v; 21.44; 24.132v; 24. 93.

26 On the reception of Salutati's letters at the French court see: Ronald G. Witt, *Hercules at the Crossroads: The Life, Works, and Thought of Coluccio Salutati*, Durham, NC: Duke University Press, 1983, 125–6. For the letters in which Vergerio refers to Salutati as his master see: *Epistolario di Pier Paolo Vergerio*, ed. Leonardo Smith, Rome: Tipografia del Senato, 1934, 55, 33, 66.

27 For the letters addressed to Louis I see: "Serenissime et gloriosossimie princeps et benignissime pater et domine noster," ASF, Signori, Missive, I Cancelleria, 17.99r; 22.81v.

28 Witt, *Coluccio Salutati and his Public Letters*, ch. 3.

29 For a letter to Margaret see: ASF, Signori, Missive, I Cancelleria, 21.40. "Serenissima et gloriosissima regina," "singularissima mater et domina nostra." For a letter to Mary see: "Serenissima et gloriosissima regina," ASF, Signori, Missive, I Cancelleria, 21.26v.

30 ASF, Signori, Missive, I Cancelleria, 21.12r; 21.12v. Earlier, one of his letters addressed to Louis I recalled the memory of the king's great-grandfather, while praising the Angevins. Witt, *"In the Footsteps of the Ancients,"* 313.

31 De Rosa, in accordance with Ronald Witt, also emphasizes the inferiority of the style of Leonardo Bruni's state letters compared to Coluccio's. De Rosa, *Coluccio Salutati*, X–XI.

32 Witt, *Coluccio Salutati and his Public Letters*, 21–2.

33 For humanists' involvement in diplomatic embassies see: Brian J. Maxson, *The Humanist World of Renaissance Florence*, Cambridge: Cambridge University Press, 2013, ch. 6.

34 In this particular case, the embassy reached the King in Verona. *Cronaca di Giovanni Villani*, ed. Francesco Gherardi Dragomanni, Florence: Sansone-Coen, 1845, III.12.108, 161–2.

35 For a later copy of a register containing ambassadorships see: Venice, Archivio di Stato di Venezia (hereafter: ASV), Senato, Sindicati, Registri I.

36 For references regarding this particular ambassadorship see: Katalin Prajda, "Egy firenzei sírköve a középkori Budán: Bene di Jacopo del Bene szerencsétlenül végződött követjárása," in *És az oszlopok tetején liliomok formáltattak vala. Tanulmányok Bibó István tiszteletére*, ed. Áron Tóth, Budapest: CentrArt, 2011, 29–35. Prajda, "Trade and Diplomacy in pre-Medici Florence."

37 ASF, Signori, Legazioni e Commissarie, Missive e Responsive, vols. 1–10.

38 For the instructions to the ambassadors see: ASF, Dieci di Balia, Legazioni e Commissarie 2, 17r bis–18r. In response to this, the ambassadors, messer Gratia Castellani and messer Andrea Buondelmonti, prepared a written report about what they accomplished during they stay at the royal court. In the document, they give a detailed account to the *Signoria* of how they performed their task and represented the Florentine government at the royal court. ASF, Dieci di Balia, Relazioni di Ambasciatori 1, 20v–21r.

39 ASMa, Archivio Gonzaga, busta 533, n. 3, busta 531, n. 1. Lajos Thallóczy, *Mantovai követjárás Budán 1395*, Budapest: MTA, 1905.

40 Following the coronation, the news reached Florence by 20 January, when the standbearer, Dinozzo Stefani, suggested holding public celebrations in the city. ASF, Consulte e Pratiche 25.30r. For the diplomatic corresponndence see: ASF, Signori Missive I, Cancelleria 19. For the detailed description of the celebrations see: *Alle bocche della piazza. Diario di anonimo fiorentino (1382–1401)*, ed. Anthony Molho and Franek Sznura, Florence: Istituto Nazionale di Studi sul Rinascimento, 1986, 61.

41 The ambassador met Sigismund on 7 April 1387 at the palace in Buda. Sigismund proposed through the ambassador to Venice entering into alliance for the release of Queen Mary and Elisabeth. Péter E. Kovacs, "Mária királyné kiszabadítása: Magyar–velencei szövetség 1387-ben," *Századok* 140 (2006): 926–31.

42 Until 1400, they were sometimes the ambassadors who brought money to Buda or brokers of a local bank; Vieri de'Medici, e.g., took money to Hungary. For the payment in 1388 see: *Zsigmond-kori oklevéltár I–VII*, ed. Elemér Mályusz and Iván Borsa, Budapest: MOL, 1951–2001, vol. 1, 762, 882.

43 For these diplomatic contingents see: Katalin Prajda, "A Magyar Királyság és a Firenzei Köztásaság diplomáciai kapcsolatai a Zsigmond-korban," in *Causa unioni, causa fidei, causa reformationis in capite et membris. Tanulmányok a kosntanzi zsinat 600.évfordulója alkalmából*, ed. Attila Bárány and László Pósán, Debrecen: Debrecen University Press, 2014, 161–75. In 1428, the Venetian ambassador, Marco Dandolo visited the royal court. For a copy of a letter addressed to him see: ASMa, busta 2185.

44 For the edition of Luca di Maso degli Albizzi's diary see: Katalin Prajda, "Egy firenzei követjárás útinaplója.(1427)," in *Lymbus. Magyarságtudományi Forrásközlemények*, Budapest: MOL, 2012, 7–16.

For the ledger see: ASF, Signori, Diedi di Balìa, Otto di Pratica, Legazioni e Commissarie, Missive e Responsive 5.21r–25v. Similarly, also in 1426, a notary was traveling with the ambassadors.

45 ASF, Signori, Dieci di Balia, Otto di Pratica, Legazioni e Commissarie, Missive e Responsive 8.87v.

46 *Commissioni di Rinaldo degli Albizzi per il comune di Firenze dal 1399–1433*, ed. Cesare Guasti, Florence: Tipografia Cellini, 1869, vol. 2, 552–613.

47 On the gifts which Rinaldo and Nello received during their embassy see: *ibid.*, vol. 2, 580–1.

48 ASF, Signori, Dieci di Balìa, Otto di pratica, Legazioni e Commissarie, Missive e Responsive 5.21r.

49 It is not entirely clear if the budget they had received before their departure was part of their salary or not. Most probably it was not. For the register containing ambassadors' salary see: ASF, Signori, Dieci di Balìa, Otto di Pratica, Legazioni e Commissarie 8.

50 For documents regarding this embassy see: ASF, Del Bene 50.

51 One of the registers of the Dieci di Balìa, in fact, summarizes the expenses of some of the diplomatic missions executed on behalf of the Florentine state ASF, Signori, Signori, Dieci di Balìa, Otto di pratica, Legazioni e Commissarie, Missive e Responsive 8.

52 "Vita di messer Filippo Scolari cittadino fiorentino per sopranome chiamato Spano," in *Archivio Storico Italiano* 4 (1843): 180. "Diario Ferrarese dal 1409 al 1502," *Rerum Italicarum Scriptores*, ed. Ludovico Antonio Muratori, 24 (1738): 177–81. "Annales Estenses Jacobi de Delayto ... ab anno 1393 usque ad 1409," *Rerum Italicarum Scriptores*, ed. Ludovico Antonio Muratori, 18 (1731): 901–1096.

53 After Pippo's death, in 1427, the son of another influential member of the Florentine community in Hungary, Giovanni di Onofrio Bardi, visited Florence in the capacity of Sigismund's ambassador. ASF, Signori, Legazioni e Commissarie 7.76v.

54 For a description of his stay see: Bartolomeo di Michele del Corazza, *Diario fiorentino (1405–1439)*, ed. Roberta Gentile, Rome: De Rubeis, 1991. For the discussions at the *Consulte* following his hearing at the priors see: ASF, Consulte e Pratiche 40.180r–187r.

55 Katalin Prajda, "The Florentine Scolari Family at the Court of Sigismund of Luxemburg in Buda," *Journal of Early Modern History* 14 (2010): 513–33.

56 For his speeches see: ASF, Consulte e Pratiche 40.128v (1410); 41.71v (1412); 41.99r, 42.41r (1413); 42.48v, 42.106v, 43.39v (1415).

57 In 1427, she worked for the merchant Donato di Bartolomeo Barbadori. ASF, Catasto 21.446r. For his matriculation to the Por Santa Maria Guild see: ASF, Arte di Por Santa Maria o della Seta 7.69r. For his tax declaration see: ASF, Catasto 481.c. 387r.

58 For the tax declaration of Giorgio di Tommaso see: ASF, Catasto 37.648r. For Andrea di Michele's matriculation into the doctors' guild see: ASF, Arte dei Medici e Speziali 7.14v.

59 Caferro, *John Hawkwood*, 63–6, 237–9.

60 ASF, Mare 18.

61 There are only sporadic references to others coming from such places as, e.g., Verona. In 1433, Bernardo di Sandro Talani mentions in his tax declaration a merchant named Francesco di Pace da Verona who lived in Buda. ASF, Catasto 450.254v.

62 ASF, Signori, Missive, Cancelleria I, 13.36v.

63 Rinaldo degli Albizzi mentions Bartolomeo Mosca da Genova. *Commissioni di Rinaldo degli Albizzi*, vol. 2, 580.

64 For a reference to "Vico Venetiarum" in Varadinum (Oradea, RO) see: *Zsigmond-kori oklevéltár I–VII*, I.4222 (01/06/1396).

65 A tax declaration of the Melanesi mentions the house possessed previously by the Venetian Daniello Cini in Buda. ASF, Catasto 46.655v. In 1426, Rinaldo degli Albizzi refers to the factors of the Venetian Niccolò Sorger in Vienna. *Commissioni di Rinaldo degli Albizzi*, vol. 2, 579–80. On the basis of this, it is possible that Hans de Sorger, cited in a document issued by the city council of Pressburg, was also of Venetian origins. *Zsigmond-kori oklevéltár I–VII*, VII.1294. Similarly, two other Venetians, Luca di Giovanni Bomolo and Zacaria de Gangioni, are mentioned in the town of Zagreb. Kovács, "Mária királyné kiszabadítása," 934.

66 An example of Venetian textile trade to Hungary also suggests that Venetians might have used the same local brokers and retail cloth merchants in Buda as Florentines did. Michael Nadler, a German merchant and citizen of Buda, appears in Venetian sources in connection with textile trade: ASV, Giudici di Petizion 22.77r. At the same time, he is also listed as debtor of the Melanesi company in Buda: ASF, Catasto 46.654v.

67 For example, in 1393 Sigismund was allowed to export textiles from Florence to Hungary through Venice with the permission of the *Serenissima. Zsigmond-kori oklevéltár I–VII*, I.2765. According to an agreement of 1385, Florentine merchants were required to share their profits with Venice. For earlier scholarship on trade between Hungary and Venice see: Zsuzsa Teke, *Velencei-magyar kereskedelmi kapcsolatok a 13–15. században*, Budapest: Akaméiai Kiadó, 1979.

68 For the prohibition of trade with Venice see: *Zsigmond-kori oklevéltár I–VII*, VII.1275; VII.5472.

69 Katalin Prajda, "Justice in the Florentine Trading Community of Late Medieval Buda," *Mélanges de l'École française de Rome. Moyen-Âge* 127-2 (2015). Later on, in the 1430s, the Italian judge in Buda was first a Florentine then a Sienese.

70 Elemér Mályusz, "Az izmaelita pénzverőjegyek kérdéséhez," *Budapest Régiségei. A Budapesti Történeti Múzeum Évkönyvei* 18 (1958): 301–9.

71 Katalin Prajda, "Florentine Merchant Companies Established in Buda at the Beginning of the 15th Century," *Mélanges de l'Ecole française de Rome. Moyen-Âge* 125-2 (2013).

72 For the Griffolini family's trade in Hungary see: Robert Black, *Benedetto Accolti and the Florentine Renaissance*, Cambridge: Cambridge University Press, 1985, 7. In 1430, Mariotto appears as debtor of the company run by Antonio di Piero di Fronte and Pagolo di Berto Carnesecchi in Buda. ASF, Catasto 381.90v.

73 There were also Aretine merchants interested in the copper trade, such as a certain Agnolo: ASF, Catasto 450.254v. In 1431, a certain Niccolò and Antonio from Arezzo appear as creditors of messer Bartolomeo Panciatichi's company in Buda. ASF, Catasto 381.44v. The intense cooperation between these Aretine and Florentine networks is also well documented by the surviving account books of the Aretine Lazzaro di Giovanni Bracci. For examples see Lazzaro's book of creditors and debtors for the years 1404–1425. Arezzo, Archivio della Fraternità dei Laici di Arezzo, 3338–40.

74 For the Mannini family's involvement in the salt industry see: István Draskóczy, "Olaszok a 15.századi Erdélyben," in *Scripta manent: Ünnepi tanulmányok a 60. életévét betöltött Gerics József professzor tiszteletére*, ed. István Draskóczy, Budapest: ELTE Középkori és Koraújkori Történeti Tanszéke, 1994, 125–35. Talani also mentions in his tax declaration in 1433 that his salt in Hungary was confiscated. ASF, Catasto 450.254v.

75 Bruno Škreblin, "Ethnic Groups in Zagreb's Gradec in the Late Middle Ages," *Review of Croatian History* 9(1) (2013): 25–59.

76 The archbishop of Kalocsa earlier served as abbot of the Benedictine monastery in Pécsvárad and there were also other Florentines in the chapter of Varadinum. Katalin Prajda, "Trade and Diplomacy in pre-Medici Florence," (forthcoming).

77 "Quod benivolentia domini Regis tenaciter conservetur velut necessaria conservationi status comunis Florentie et quod in nullo a suis voluntatibus et consiliis discedatur". ASF, Consulte e Pratiche 9.59v. Brucker, *Florentine Politics and Society*, 241.

24

FROM THE PALAZZO TO THE STREETS

Women's agency and networks of exchange

Megan Moran

An expense made on the 16th of [September 1553] of 10 *lire* paid to Madonna Lucretia del Bene for part of the *libbre* of thick linen spun by her and brought by her servant Gostanza.

An expense made on the 20th of the said month [January 1553] to Madonna Oretta for 7 *lire* and 10 *soldi* for the part of 12 *libbre* of linen she spun and brought by her servant Sandra.

An expense made on the 24th of October 1555 to Nannina the *rivenditore* for 26 *lire* and 8 *soldi* for 24 *braccia* of lightweight cloth for a shirt.

From the account book, *Giornale e Ricordi*, of Maddalena Ricasoli (1553–1564)[1]

After the death of her first husband, Cosimo Acciauoli, in 1553, the Florentine patrician widow Maddalena Ricasoli kept a detailed account book to keep track of her financial situation. The handwritten book, labeled *Giornale e Ricordi di Maddalena Ricasoli*, noted large expenses such as the return of her dowry as well as the smaller day-to-day expenses incurred in the service of running a household.[2] Her participation in the wine and grain trade from the surrounding Tuscan countryside as well as her involvement in the consumption and sale of domestic goods such as cloth, clothing, and food reflects the integral role that patrician women played in the local Florentine economy. Maddalena's accounts and letters showcase the ways in which she formed commercial relationships with women in the Florentine community and smaller Tuscan towns in order to accomplish many of her financial and commercial activities. The entries from her account book above represent examples of female commercial relationships found throughout her financial records. While scholars have begun to examine the integral role *popolane* (lower-class) women played in the circulation of goods, there has been much less work on the ways in which patrician women participated in the Renaissance economy.[3] Instead of enclosing women from the outside world, the porous nature of the family palazzo or villa enabled women to engage in the economic life of the city. Patrician women in particular formed networks of commercial relationships with *popolane* women as a way to negotiate urban space and operate in economic activities in sixteenth-century Florence. The letters and account records found in family archives suggest that women from all social levels exerted their own agency to form complex networks of exchange.

The *"onore e utile"* (honor and profit) of the family name typically rested with the male head of the household in Renaissance Florence. Both individual and family reputation for men often depended on their ability and success in economic affairs.[4] The male-dominated guild system in Florence excluded women, and merchant companies formed by prominent men from patrician families controlled the large-scale international merchant and banking enterprises of the fifteenth and sixteenth centuries.[5] Scholars have pointed to lower-class women's involvement in the workforce in local industries. Judith Brown notes the presence of lower-class women in the wool and silk industries in Florence, while Christiane Klapisch-Zuber traces the lives of servants in Florence, and Monica Chojnacka documents the presence of women working in the streets and markets of early modern Venice, to name a few.[6] However, patrician women are still largely absent from studies of the Renaissance economy.[7] A recent essay by historian Joanne Ferraro poses the question: "How might we develop a gendered reading of Italy's economy?"[8] She suggests a systematic "questioning of such dichotomies as global versus local, urban versus rural, incorporated versus unincorporated labor, shop versus home production, paid versus unpaid work, agricultural versus non-agricultural labor, and production versus reproduction" in order to better understand the extent to which women participated in economic life in Renaissance Italy.[9] New work on shopping, consumer culture, and the movement of material goods has blurred the boundaries between production and consumption in ways that allow women a more visibly prominent role in economic activities.[10] Additionally, studies of economic life have increasingly highlighted the importance of social networks to see how family, friendship, and patronage influenced commercial transactions. Ann Matchette points out that "economic transactions cannot be seen as freed from the myriad social commitments that linked people to each other."[11] This focus on the role of social relationships provides room to explore the formal and informal exchanges that women engaged in on a daily basis to take part in economic activities. Breaking down the traditional boundaries of economic life reveals the ways in which patrician women constructed diverse networks of exchange to operate in commercial affairs in Florence.

The case study of Maddalena and the women she interacted with suggests that the domestic domain was, in fact, central to the operation of commercial life. Domesticity functioned as a more malleable concept tied less to the interior of the home than to the financial stability of the family unit. As a member of the Ricasoli household, Maddalena belonged to a prestigious family line whose origins dated back to the eleventh century.[12] The family owned lands in the Chianti countryside during the Middle Ages though they had long integrated into the mercantile elite of Florence through business associations, political ties, and marriage alliances by the sixteenth century. Maddalena married the Florentine patrician Cosimo Acciauoli in 1548 and after his death in 1553, she remarried another member of the patrician elite, Filippo Arrigucci, in 1558. When her second husband Filippo died in 1573, Maddalena, now a widow and childless after two marriages, returned to live with her brother Braccio, who emerged as the head of the family after the death of his brothers – Matteo and Raffaello – in 1566. Maddalena's letters throughout her second marriage as well as her widowhood reflect a familiarity with how to handle the flow of goods, prices for various food items, and the coordination of deliveries beyond a temporary involvement in such affairs. Her activities break down many of the dichotomies Ferraro identified: urban vs. rural, public vs. private, reproduction vs. production, and domestic household vs. commercial marketplace.

Prescriptive writers in Renaissance Italy often espoused the dangers that an independent woman in the public world might face with regard to her chaste reputation, and by extension, the reputation of her family. Leon Battista Alberti's character Giannozzo writes in his *Libri della Famiglia*, "it would hardly win us respect if our wife busied herself among the men in the marketplace, out in the public eye." The younger character Lionardo responds, "It is as though nature thus provided for our well-being, arranging for men to bring things home and for women to guard them."[13] Torquato Tasso's discussion of the female sex contends that "the woman's virtue is employed inside the house while that of the man is demonstrated outside."[14] These prescriptive works cautioned against women's involvement in commercial spaces of the city and advocated a separation of duties where women oversaw the domestic interior of the family home. Yet Maddalena's duties as wife and sister in a prominent family with landed estates required that she traveled outside the home regularly as she moved back and forth between Florence and the Tuscan countryside. As Cosimo Acciauoli's wife, Maddalena visited his lands in the Santo Marcellino region where she oversaw payments to farm workers and collected, then dispersed, the fruits of their labor.[15] She also aided her brothers in rebuilding the Ricasoli landholdings and collected profits from the goods produced on those lands.[16] This frequent travel challenged the image of women cooped up in the home and reflects a more flexible vision of domestic space for elite women. When she did express reservations about travel, her letters offered a simple explanation: she was too busy overseeing affairs in Florence or in Cacchiano to make any more trips. One letter to her brother explained how she left Florence eight days earlier to deal with some problems that arose with their farm laborers in the Chianti region. She left with such haste that she forgot to bring some items of clothing with her and asked her brother, Braccio, to send her *mantello*, or cloak, and a fleece hood to cover her hair from her wardrobe at the house in Florence.[17] Neither her own letters nor those of her brothers expressed any concern about her sexual reputation during their discussion of her movements. Maddalena's account records and letters reveal how she navigated the agricultural trade between the countryside and city, bridged boundaries between elite households and artisan communities through the purchase and sale of domestic goods, and operated out of the family home in ways that connected the domestic interior to the city streets and fields beyond.

The palazzo and villa: domestic and commercial space

Maddalena used her position as a wife, sister, and later widow to oversee the interior workings of the household; however, her duties did not end at the doors of the family palazzo. The palazzo served as a space to store goods such as wine, grain, and other foodstuffs delivered from the country estates for sale and consumption in Florence. Maddalena oversaw the movement of goods into the palazzo from outside the city and into storerooms before distribution back into the streets, shops, and homes of other patrician families. She took stock of which goods to keep for household consumption, which to give away to family and friends, and which would be marked for sale in Florence. Maddalena's correspondence details specific instructions on the precise location for the delivery and dispersal of agricultural goods.[18] In one letter to her brother, Braccio, in May 1553, Maddalena explained, "Dear brother, the bearer of this letter will be Francesco who will bring the eight barrels of wine, which are from me, from our house [the Acciauoli residence, her husband's house]. He [Francesco] wanted to help us and so he has taken care of these barrels of wine, which Cosimo [her husband] has then received. Do not forget this and thank him for the carriage."[19] Maddalena's home served as a place to collect and then sell farm products such as wine and grain; it also functioned as a space to collect payments for those goods sold on the market. Her brother,

Raffaello, wrote a letter to his sister on 15 January 1558 where he discussed the plans for their farm and the recent sale of grain. He wrote, "Dearest sister, I have your letter from the 12th of this present month regarding the business of the land … Matteo and Braccio will be together this Wednesday [in Cacchiano] where they will give the orders to start attending to the grain. They will send the money to you [for the grain], which has been sold for 89 *lire* and 5 *soldi*, in the hands of the farm worker who will deliver it to you."[20] Her brothers regularly conducted business with their sister out of her husband's palazzo. These transactions occurred during her first marriage to Cosimo Acciauoli, as seen in the 1553 letter, as well as her second marriage to Filippo Arrigucci, showcased in the 1558 letter. The palazzo itself may have belonged to her husband and his family lineage, but the business transactions fell within Maddalena's purview and she used the home, a domestic space, as the place to conduct her commercial affairs. Maddalena regularly wrote and received letters from family members, neighbors, and customers about the quantity and pricing of wine, grain, and other agricultural products over the years. A letter from Maddalena's neighbor, Diamante Antinori, addressed to her brother, Braccio's house in Florence, where she lived during her widowhood, requested: "Please send me 80 flasks of wine … and if it would please you to sell me another two, I would be in your debt."[21] Diamante knew that her home functioned as a space to store goods as they moved into and out of the city. As Alison Smith notes for sixteenth-century Verona, managing "these households required elite wives and widows to engage directly with their neighbors and local suppliers."[22]

Maddalena deliberately turned this domestic space into a commercial one in ways that belied traditional depictions of patrician women locked away in their homes. In particular, Maddalena's regular instructions to her female servant, Nastasia, related her intention to use the domestic interior of the palazzo as a central clearing house for the movement of goods from the family's landed estates. One letter explained, "Dearest Nastasia, there are 120 flasks of wine being sent from Cacchiano and you should wait to sell them for as long as possible. Remember to keep an eye on the house."[23] Maddalena relied on her female servants to coordinate deliveries, oversee the physical transaction of goods, and collect payments for the agricultural products as well as any household items purchased in Florence. One letter from Maddalena to Nastasia laid out very precise delivery instructions: "Dear Nastasia, this is in order to advise you how I am sending two *staia* of chestnuts to Pietro da Livorno and I would like you to bring one *staia* to the house of Diongi Carducci … if the carriage comes please then send us back the big mattress for the bed where Camilla sleeps … Also, please advise me if Madonna Lisabetta has remembered to send us the skein of wool and the quarter length of cloth that I asked for."[24] A postscript at the end noted, "And furthermore I will send one of the present carriages with the wood to the house of Diongi Carducci and they will send the rest of the goods ordered on to his sons."[25]

While Maddalena employed a number of female servants over the years (for longer or shorter periods of time), she formed a particularly close working relationship with Nastasia. They worked together for at least twenty years from the 1570s to 1590s.[26] Nastasia's letters to Maddalena are remarkable as examples of correspondence from lower-class servants, most of whom could not read and write. The extent to which Nastasia wrote her own letters is unclear; some reveal a very basic level of education with the large, sprawling letters across the page, numerous errors that are likely consistent with only partial literacy, and contain the signature "Io (na)stasia." Other letters were written in a much neater and tighter hand, which suggests that a more educated member of the household (possibly male servant, scribe, or even family member) wrote the letters for her.[27] Nastasia's reading level is also difficult to gauge. The letters often respond directly to Maddalena's own notes, which indicate that either she could partially read or another member of the household read the letters aloud to her. One note explained to her employer that she "has received the flour but without the wine" that was supposed to be on the carriage.[28] She urged Maddalena, "please send to me to say what you would want me to do."[29] The cooperation between servant and employer enabled Maddalena to maintain oversight of the movement of goods through the country lanes, urban streets, and into and out of her household.

The Renaissance villa also functioned as a location where women moved regularly between the interior of the home and the fields of their estates where they oversaw the production of agricultural goods. At the villa of Cacchiano, Maddalena's male stewards in charge of over-seeing the farm laborers regularly interacted with her personally to make decisions. A stew-ard named Alessandro Turilazzi wrote numerous letters to Maddalena's Florentine servant, Nastasia, with instructions he received directly from his female patron. One letter explained, "Dearest Nastasia, The farm is sending 120 flasks of wine and eleven of the cheeses from Bracciano [another Ricasoli farm]. Your *padrona* says you should wait to sell them and you should have care at the house. If the brother in law of the tailor brings money for the wine you should take it and make a good deal. You should see that he gives it for a sum of the 18 barrels of wine given from Cacchiano. Send a pair of shoes to Bindaccio and to Cosimo [Maddalena's nephews]."[30] Another steward named Filippo wrote to Nastasia: "this [letter] is in order to advise you how the *garzone* [servant] is sending a sack of flour that weighs 588 *libbre*. He is also sending two pigeons and a *staia* of nuts."[31] Maddalena followed up in her own handwriting at the bottom of the letter where she instructed: "please send us the green cloth for Cecia and the *camiciotto* made for Virginia from their wardrobe and chest" at the house.[32]

Maddalena engaged in activities that brought her into contact with the women and men working in the fields and moving through the streets of Florence on a regular basis. Her letters suggest that economic activities took women outside the home and simultaneously turned the domestic interior into a space used to facilitate commercial transactions. Though scholars have recently challenged gendered divisions of space as solely public or private in nature, these binary divisions remain difficult to dispel.[33] Elizabeth Cohen suggests an alter-native view where the "domestic" and "urban" (terms she sees more fitting than public and private) functioned as socially interactive spaces where men and women alike operated.[34] Maddalena Ricasoli's case study suggests that a more interactive, less binary, model of gen-dered space better fits the situation found in her letters where the domestic sphere remained deeply interconnected with the urban and rural commercial spaces surrounding the home.

Patrician wives, *popolane* women, and networks of exchange

Though Maddalena interacted with both male and female servants and workers, her cor-respondence particularly highlights how female networks proved useful to facilitate the exchange of commodities. As employers, patrician women assumed the authoritative posi-tion in the relationship. There was no question as to who was in charge; Maddalena often issued orders and instructions in her notes that she expected Nastasia to carry out. One letter noted:

> I am sending three sacks of flour: one sack weighs 205 *libbre*, the other 200, and the third is 192 for which the sum is 597 *libbre*. I am also sending 1 ½ barrels of olives,

which weigh 151 *libbre* and ten pieces of cheese in a sack, which weighs 11 *libbre*. I would like you to give three [of these] to Messer Ruberto [Pandolfini] [and] two to my niece Cassandra. Do not forget that in the other sack there are twenty-three pieces of cheese that weigh 26 *libbre* for which it would please me if you will sell the best pieces of those.[35]

She also asked that Nastasia give some of the goods to the nuns as a donation and then specified that she "should sell the rest."[36] Maddalena left the daily aspects of delivery involved with the circulation of goods to her lower-class servants. She kept careful track of what goods left her supervision and who oversaw those transactions. Maddalena often wanted to check the bills personally when she returned to Florence to make sure that there were no problems. In one letter she instructed: "Dearest Nastasia, first of all, I am sending you 120 flasks of wine and you should begin to sell them for me for a good price ... You should hold the bill until I arrive [in Florence] to make the payments for this week so that there will be no problems."[37] Nastasia replied several days later: "I have received 120 flasks of wine, fourteen cheeses, one flask of vinegar and one *staia* of nuts."[38] Their correspondence suggests a close working relationship where Maddalena relied on Nastasia's experience, expertise, and ability to move around the streets of Florence to act as her representative for the household in distributing goods, collecting payments, and making the physical purchase of clothing or other household items for the family.

The vertical networks between mistresses and servants aided patrician women who needed to bridge the gap between their elite circle of society and the artisans and laborers who operated in the Florentine economy. As a member of the lower class, Nastasia could move more easily through the public streets and city walls to engage with tradesmen. One of Maddalena's letters in September 1595 instructed Nastasia to collect money from the inn owners who bought wine from the Ricasoli vineyards. She wrote, "I would like you to find the owner of the inn at Castello who is the brother-in-law of our tailor; he will pay you for three amounts of the wine. Take the money and hold onto the receipt. You should make this service right away based on the letter I am sending you now."[39] Maddalena's letter reflected the trust she placed in Nastasia both as a member of the household and as a valued employee who performed her job well. Maddalena wrote a follow-up letter on 15 October 1595 where she checked in to see if Nastasia had followed these orders: "Dearest Nastasia, I would like to know if you have collected the money from the brother-in-law of our tailor from the inn at Castello for the eighteen barrels of wine I gave them and for the other two barrels of wine from the inn at Ponte a Ema."[40] She relied on Nastasia's abilities to deal directly with the inn owners in order to drop off shipments of wine and collect payments for these expenses. As a messenger and commercial courier for the family, Nastasia dealt with the artisans who sold cloth and other domestic goods regularly purchased by patrician households. One letter noted her customary receipt of the delivery from the countryside and then passed on several messages from a female spinner about some cloth that Maddalena ordered. Nastasia wrote, "I am sending you 4 pounds of linen which Mona Marietta has spun that are in the form of nine skeins of yarn and one skein of linen for Cassadrina [Maddalena's niece]. Moreover, I am sending 7 pounds of linen, which I have spun; there are twenty-eight skeins of yarn."[41] Another letter conveyed messages from the spinner and *petinatore* about the payment for clothing purchased by Maddalena for her nieces. Nastasia explained, "I will send you the black dress, which you ordered for Cecia and the cloak for Verginia [Maddalena's nieces] from the spinner ... and for both girls there are the two pairs of sleeves … I am sending you the letter from the *petinatore* who would like you to respond as soon as possible."[42] Nastasia's contact with these working women demonstrated the way in which she served as an intermediary between patrician and *popolane* circles in the commercial world of Renaissance Florence.

Maddalena also employed servants to keep her informed about affairs in the countryside when she traveled back to the Ricasoli palazzo in the city. In the 1580s, Maddalena's Tuscan counterpart to Nastasia was a servant named Maddalena, referred to as "the balia," or "the wet-nurse," who managed affairs at the villa of Cacchiano. Not much is known about her background other than that she married one of the stewards at Cacchiano, a man named Matteo, and worked as a wet-nurse for Braccio Ricasoli's young children. When the children outgrew the need for a wet-nurse she stayed on to work as a servant in the villa.[43] Maddalena "the balia" sent financial reports along with family news in her letters to Maddalena Ricasoli in a similar manner to Nastasia. One letter reported:

> To my dearest patron, Madonna Maddalena Ricasoli, on behalf of Simone di Sallo I have sent three *staia* of figs and several pears in a sack along with three *staia* of grain … I am also sending two letters from Signore Cavaliere who has remained with us here and a sack full of flour with some dry figs and onions … We recommend ourselves to you and send greetings from Signore Bindaccio and everyone else.[44]

In the 1590s, Maddalena corresponded with a servant named Camilla at Cacchiano who offered advice to her patron about the sale of goods from their estates. A letter written in July 1594 reported: "Dearest patron, Marco the *garzone* has brought the forty flasks of white wine and eighty flasks of red wine … These flasks will sell well for you because they are the better ones in the house. There are twenty-eight fresh eggs sent as well."[45] Camilla used her knowledge about the state of the vineyards to suggest that the new shipment of wine would sell better for the family. Another letter in August 1594 offered advice about how best to divide the livestock sent to Maddalena's relatives: "Dear patron, Pino the *garzone* is bringing the eighty flasks of wine and more than two pairs of chickens; one pair should go to Virginia and the other to Bindaccio and Cosimo. Please send my greetings to all of the children."[46] As with Nastasia, Maddalena Ricasoli trusted that her servants oversaw the deliveries and had knowledge of the best goods produced from the farms. Camilla's letters also show how she mediated economic transactions for Maddalena and local women in the Chianti area. One letter from Camilla in 1592 explained, "Dearest patron, Marco is bringing the 120 flasks of wine and seventeen bundles of cheese which weigh 18 *libbre* with the basket. The handkerchiefs are almost all spun and are white but the wet-nurse has still not brought them here."[47] Camilla used her own knowledge of women in the community surrounding Cacchiano, most likely from the nearby small town of Gaiole, to commission the purchase of handkerchiefs for Maddalena.

Though clearly not an equal partnership, female networks of exchange could prove advantageous to both patrician and *popolane* women. For instance, Maddalena used Nastasia's own expertise and initiative in many of her dealings, though she retained firm oversight of all financial activities. This was not always the case for domestic servants. Christiane Klapisch-Zuber notes how patrician wives often worried or complained about the unreliable and often peripatetic nature of their servants.[48] Yet Nastasia's case suggests that the relationship between patrician employer and servant could be mutually beneficial and long-lasting.

Nastasia benefited from the steady job as well as a specific expertise gained from her work. Maddalena gained a trusted employee and member of her household to aid in commercial affairs. As Raffaella Sarti notes, "in pre-industrial times the social identity of servants was quite ambiguous. Domestic service was at the same time an employment and a type of relationship."[49] As part of the household, servants acted as conduits for personal news, which they passed on to their patrons along with commercial goods. One letter asked Nastasia for family updates from Florence while Maddalena remained in Cacchaino: "please advise me if Cassandra [my niece] is in Florence and how Madonna Lisabetta is doing."[50] Nastasia often sent updates about the health of family members; one letter reported, "The present letter will be in order to advise you how by the grace of God we are all well and now to advise you how Madonna Cassandra is well and the same is true of her children ... Virginia also stays well."[51] Yet the affection their long-time collaboration produced for one another never overshadowed the employer–employee relationship. As Giovanna Bendusi points out, "this domestic and paternalist view of servant–mistress relations often contrasts with the more pragmatic behavior displayed by both employers and servants, who seemed to have viewed their relationships also in clear financial and labor terms."[52] One letter by Maddalena in February 1594 expressed concern for Nastasia's health: "Dearest Nastasia, I have heard from the servant of the Pandolfini that you were feeling badly, please advise me how you are doing."[53] Then, regardless of illness, Maddalena instructed: "please bring 20 *scudi* to Madonna Lisabetta and remember to write a receipt in the book and bring one *scudo* to Maria de Carducci."[54] Her concern for Nastasia's illness did not eclipse the importance of family business affairs.

While the liminal position as part family member and part wage earner could place female servants in a precarious position subject to potential exploitation by masters or mistresses, this role could also provide advantages for servants to form a variety of networks in the community. At times, letters suggest that *popolane* women overtly manipulated their position in elite households in order to pursue their own agendas. Patronage entailed a series of obligations and personal bonds where service and monetary ties blurred the lines between family, friendship, and employer–employee relationships. Maddalena "the balia" used the language of patronage when she asked Maddalena Ricasoli to reach out to her brother, Braccio, for a favor. She wanted Braccio to help her son receive a license to open a shop in Florence. She appealed to Maddalena, her employer, for help in this matter: "I ask you to please advise *il padrone* [Braccio Ricasoli] to see if he has it for him ... I ask that you perform this great charity for him [our son]."[55] Her appeal for help fused the language of patronage with charity (*carità*), a religious and civic practice of the elites where they donated funds for poor relief, to influence her employers. The outcome is unknown. Regardless, the fact that she made such a request suggests that *popolane* women had the ability to exert agency in their relationships with their employers in the service of their own interests.

There is evidence to suggest that servants successfully used patronage ties to pursue their own independent affairs, as patrician women took these requests seriously. Another Florentine patrician woman named Gostanza Ugolini wrote two letters to her brother, Benedetto Spinelli, a prosperous silk merchant and banker in Florence, where she asked him to employ the husband of her servant, Sandra, in his household as a favor to her. Gostanza wrote, "Honorable brother, the present [letter] is only in order to recommend to you a certain Mariotto who is the husband of my servant, Sandra. I recommend him to you for as much as you are able to help him."[56] When Sandra's husband died a year later in 1543, Gostanza wrote again to her brother to inquire about collecting Sandra's dowry money. She used the letter to provide an introduction for Sandra's mother, Piera, who would travel to Florence to collect her daughter's dowry. Gostanza explained, "the bearer of this letter will be Madonna Piera di Matteo, the mother of my servant Sandra, who comes [to you] in order to see about the dowry. I ask that out of your love [for me] you will grant all these favors and help as much as possible. She [Piera] is poor and has small grandchildren with no way to pay her expenses."[57] In the case of the servant Sandra, Gostanza emphasized the charitable aspect of helping this poor woman with dependants. She claimed both Piera and Sandra through their status as members of her household and then drew on family ties with her brother to transfer this obligation onto him. This agency was not just one-way; both Piera and Sandra actively drew on their mistresses' familial connections to aid their own family fortunes in a similar manner to Maddalena the wet-nurse's appeal to her Ricasoli patrons.

Much of the agency asserted by female servants occurred through their role as brokers for patrician families in the circulation of goods for the local economy. Service positions for *popolane* women at times enabled them to pursue more than one occupation and to potentially earn more profit for themselves and their families. *Popolane* women were often referred to as wet-nurse, spinner, laundress, or servant interchangeably in account records and letters. The occupational title varied depending on the service rendered and payment received. Maddalena Ricasoli regularly referred to her employees as a servant, wet-nurse, or spinner depending on the transaction under discussion. Maria Nobili Ricasoli, part of another branch of the Ricasoli family, kept a detailed account book of her expenses in the late sixteenth and early seventeenth century. She noted payments to several women – Cecia, Caterina di Casaillo, and Mona Gostanzia – whom she alternately referred to as wet-nurse, spinner, or servant depending on the specific payment incurred for services rendered at Broglio [a villa owned by another branch of the Ricasoli family].[58] Both women's records also note their interactions with various *rivenditori*, or sellers of used goods. These *rivenditori* were lower-class women who bought used domestic items and then resold the pieces in the marketplace.[59] Many *rivenditori* were men, but guild regulations at times also enabled women to work as used-goods dealers.[60] Patrician women's letters suggest that they dealt mostly with female resellers. Maddalena's niece, Cassandra, wrote a letter in 1593 where she told her aunt that the *riveditora* "says she will have a response for me tomorrow about the bed sheets. I am not sure about the velvet cloth but she says if we want it then she will bring it tomorrow."[61] Patrician women also used *rivenditori* to sell their own items on the market. Ann Matchette's work on used-goods dealers notes how "evidence from the supply side shows that women could also exercise a certain degree of agency over their own material possessions."[62] Another Florentine patrician named Maria Maddalena Peruzzi employed Nannina, identified as a *rivenditore*, to sell cloth from the household after her husband died in 1560. By working with a *rivenditore*, Maria Maddalena could cross class lines much easier to sell to other *popolane* women. For instance, she noted in 1566 that Madonna Nannina "sold 160 *braccia* of cloth to the wet-nurse of Madonna Margerita di Giovanni Altoviti."[63] Maria Maddalena's ties to the *rivenditore* made her work in the public spaces of the city more feasible than if she had tried to operate alone. Patrician women like Maria Maddalena Peruzzi, Maria Nobili, and Maddalena Ricasoli recognized the benefit of creating female networks that crossed class lines to work in the commercial spaces and streets of the city.

Conclusion

The economic networks formed between *popolane* women and their patrician employers required a continual negotiation of class and gender hierarchies in Florence. In order to manage Ricasoli financial affairs, Maddalena relied on building strong relationships with her female servants and other *popolane* women to coordinate deliveries and oversee the physical transaction of goods. These vertical relationships expanded the boundaries of gendered space as they enabled women to operate more extensively and move more freely between the palazzo and the streets. Maddalena did not passively await orders from her husband or brothers but rather initiated instructions and created her own networks to manage family financial affairs. At the same time, female servants demonstrated their knowledge of commercial life in the Florentine economy as they monitored the movement of goods and performed the physical deliveries for both the purchase and sale of commodities. The consumption of domestic goods such as clothing, shoes, handkerchiefs, bed linens, and more reached far beyond the interior of the family palazzo as these interactions required control over financial resources and interaction with artisans and tradesmen. Contrary to the image of patrician women shut into a world of domestic isolation, the activities of patrician women such as Maddalena Ricasoli instead reflect the central role that their activities in the home played in connecting to the streets of Florence and lands of the Tuscan *contado*. Their correspondence reflects their active involvement in commercial decisions where the home (city palazzo or country villa) served as a central point of production and consumption within the Florentine economy.

Additionally, Maddalena Ricasoli and her networks of exchange reflect the intrinsically linked nature of the urban and rural world for late sixteenth-century Florence. Her correspondence reflects the importance placed on the production and consumption of agricultural products for patrician families. Historians originally characterized the investment in landed estates in the sixteenth and early seventeenth century as a return to the land or a form of "refeudalization" moving away from the risky mercantile ventures characteristic of the fifteenth century.[64] More recently scholars have noted that landed estates played an important role in the financial life of patrician households.[65] Maddalena's account records and letters reflect the importance attributed to agricultural production in the urban economy of sixteenth-century Florence by women and men alike. Her authority reached beyond the doors of the palazzo or villa and onto the city streets and country lanes as she managed the sale and delivery of agricultural products such as wine, grain, and food all over Tuscany.

As a case study, Maddalena Ricasoli's actions in economic life offer both commonalities and exceptions as a model for the activities of other patrician women. While widowhood offered patrician women the most opportunities to exert autonomy in their own lives, particularly with regard to the control over financial resources, Maddalena's case suggests that patrician wives were incredibly active throughout their marriages in economic affairs. They only became more visible as they emerged in official household records as widows. Maddalena's letters and account books clearly demonstrate her active role in the circulation of goods and key involvement commercial transactions throughout her first marriage to Cosimo Acciauoli and her second marriage to Filippo Arrigucci. Her role increased even more dramatically once she moved back into her brother Braccio's house, as a widow, by the 1580s and 1590s. Maddalena's case is exceptional in that she had no children from either marriage; thus, she likely had more time to devote to overseeing the Ricasoli landed estates. Indeed letters from other family members, neighbors, and customers recognize her as a key point person to contact concerning their orders for Ricasoli agricultural products. At the same time, Maddalena's letters reflect her involvement in the lives of her nieces and nephews, particularly Braccio's daughter, Cassandra, to whom she acted almost as a surrogate mother after Braccio's first wife died and he subsequently remarried in 1581. There seems to be no comment on her lack of a reproductive role in family correspondence; her reputation appears only to have increased, not diminished, throughout her lifetime as a respected figure in the community and the local Florentine economy.

Maddalena's case study suggests that wives and widows based their sense of *"onore e utile"* beyond their reproductive role for the family unit. Instead, they conceived of a broader and more flexible definition of contribution to family life that included an active involvement in commercial affairs. Maddalena often asserted agency and independence in her economic activities on behalf of the financial health of her family and household. She formed her own networks of exchange in ways that crossed both class and gender lines. Maddalena's case represents the malleable nature of domestic life and the flexibility of family space for women as they crossed between the palazzo and the streets in Renaissance Florence and Tuscany.

Notes

1 Florence, Archivio di Stato di Firenze (hereafter: ASF), Ricasoli Parte Antica, Libri di amministrazione, Pezzo 270, *Giornale e Ricordi di Maddalena Ricasoli*, 1553–1564. "A spese alli 16 detto [luglio 1553] a Ma. Lucretia del Bene lire dieci per parte di libbre di coto di lino mi fa filare porta Ma. Gostanza serva." "A spese alli 20 detto [gennaio 1553] Ma. Oretta lire sette e soldi dieci per parte di libbre dodici di lino mi fa filare porto la sandra sua serva." "A spese ad 24 detto [ottobre 1555] a la Nannina rivenditora lire venti sei et soldi otto per braccia venti quattro di panno sottile per camice." The term *libbre* was a unit of weight and the term *braccia* was a unit of measure for cloth. The terms *lire* and *soldi* refer to monetary units used in sixteenth-century Florence.

2 Florentine men often kept *ricordi*, or journals, that contained a mixture of personal family news and account records. Scholars have found that women (often widows) also kept *ricordi* where they recorded account information for their households. There are five books related to Maddalena's financial records that range in date from 1553 (the death of her first husband) until 1614 (which falls after her own death in 1605). The last two books attributed to her name also contain accounts by family members dealing with her finances after her death. For more information on women's account books, see Giulia Calvi, "Maddalena Nerli and Cosimo Tornabuoni: A Couple's Narrative of Family History in Early Modern Florence," *Renaissance Quarterly* 45(2) (1992): 312–39.

3 Caroline Castiglione's recent book looks at the ways in which mothers managed family finances for their children in elite Roman families, such as the Barberini, in the seventeenth and eighteenth centuries. Caroline Castiglione, *Accounting for Affection, Mothering and Politics in Early Modern Rome*, New York: Palgrave Macmillan, 2015, 77. See also, Caroline Castiglione, "Accounting for Affection: Battles Between Aristocratic Mothers and Sons in Eighteenth Century Rome," *Journal of Family History* 25 (2000): 405–31.

4 John Day, "Money and Credit in Medieval and Renaissance Italy," in *The Medieval Market Economy*, Oxford: Basil Blackwell, 1987; Gunnar Dahl, *Trade, Trust, and Networks: Commercial Culture in Late Medieval Italy*, Lund, Sweden: Nordic Academic Press, 1998; Craig Muldrew, *The Economy of Obligation: The Culture of Credit and Social Relations in Early Modern England*, London: Macmillan, 1998; Alexandra Shepard, "Manhood, Credit, and Patriarchy in Early Modern England, c. 1580–1640," *Past and Present* 167 (2000): 75–106; Thomas Kuehn, *Heirs, Kin, and Creditors in Renaissance Florence*, Cambridge: Cambridge University Press, 2003; Paul McLean, "Economic Credit in Renaissance Florence," *Journal of Modern History* 83(1) (March 2011): 1–47.

5 David Herlihy, "Women's Work in the Towns of Traditional Europe," in *La Donna nell'economia, secc. XIII–XVIII*, ed. Simonetta Cavaciocchi, Florence: Le Monnier, 1989, 125. See also, Maryanne Kowaleski and Judith Bennett, "Crafts, Guilds and Women in the Middle Ages: Fifty Years after Marian K. Dale," in *Sisters and Workers in the Middle Ages*, ed. Judith Bennett, Elizabeth Clark, Jean O'Barr, B. Anne Vilen, and Sarah Westphal-Wihl, Chicago: University of Chicago Press, 1989, 12.

6 Judith Brown and Jordan Goodman, "Women and Industry in Florence," *Journal of Economic History* 40 (1980): 73–80. Brown and Goodman argue that the number of women working in industry in Florence stayed low during the fifteenth and sixteenth centuries and really only picked up during the seventeenth century. Judith Brown, "A Woman's Place Was in the Home: Women's Work in Renaissance Tuscany," in *Rewriting the Renaissance: The Discourses of Sexual Difference in Early Modern Europe*, ed. Margaret Ferguson, Maureen Quilligan, and Nancy Vickers, Chicago and London: University of Chicago Press, 1986, 209; Christiane Klapisch-Zuber, "Female Celibacy and Service in Florence in the Fifteenth Century," in *Women, Family, and Ritual in Renaissance Italy*, trans. Lydia Cochrane, Chicago: University of Chicago Press, 1985; Christiane Klapisch-Zuber, "Women Servants in Florence During the Fourteenth and Fifteenth Centuries," trans. Nancy Elizabeth Mitchell, in *Women and Work in Preindustrial Europe*, ed. Barbara Hanawalt, Bloomington: Indiana University Press, 1986; Sam Cohn, "Women and Work in Renaissance Italy," in *Gender and Society in Renaissance Italy*, ed. Judith Brown and Robert Davis, London and New York: Longman, 1998; Monica Chojnacka, *Working Women of Early Modern Venice*, Baltimore: Johns Hopkins University Press, 2001. For women's work in the countryside, see Gabriella Piccini, "Per uno studio del lavoro delle donne nelle campagne: considerazioni dall'Italia medievale," in *La donna nell'economica*, Cavaciocchi; M. Muzzarelli, P. Galeatti, and B. Andreolli, eds., *Donne e lavoro nell'Italia medievale*, Turin: Rosenberg and Sellier, 1991.
7 Joanne Ferraro notes the preoccupation with primarily lower-class women's activities in Italy's economic life. She encourages scholars to "know more about the roles of these patrician women – not just in Brescia but throughout early modern Italy, not just within the urban ruling class but also in convents with substantial real estate holdings – in economic investment and agricultural development." Joanne Ferraro, "Representing Women in Early Modern Italian Economic History," in *Structures and Subjectivities: Attending to Early Modern Women*, ed. Joan Hartman and Adele Seef, Newark: University of Delaware Press, 2007, 83.
8 Joanne Ferraro, "The Manufacture and Movement of Goods," in *The Renaissance World*, ed. John Jefferies Martin, New York: Routledge, 2007, 94.
9 *Ibid.*, 94–5.
10 Evelyn Welch's work on shopping and consumer culture argues that domestic production and market production "need to be understood as complementary rather than as competing forms of provisioning ensuring that the families of both well-off patricians and artisans alike had to make decisions as to who would take responsibility both for routine shopping and for special purchases." Evelyn Welch, *Shopping in the Renaissance: Consumer Cultures in Italy, 1400–1600*, New Haven: Yale University Press, 2009, 70. Welch notes that women did participate in consumption but she argues that men still oversaw their purchases. *Ibid.*, 223.
11 Ann Matchette, "Credit and Credibility: Used Goods and Social Relations in Sixteenth-Century Florence," in *The Material Renaissance*, ed. Michelle O'Malley and Evelyn Welch, Manchester: Manchester University Press, 2007, 225.
12 For general information on the Ricasoli family, see Luigi Passerini, *Genealogia e storia della famiglia Ricasoli*, Florence: Cellini, 1861.
13 Leon Battista Alberti, *I Libri della famiglia, Book 3*, trans. Renee Neu Watkins, Long Grove, IL: Waveland Press, 2004, 207.
14 Torquato Tasso, *Discorso della virtu feminile e donnesca*, ed. Maria Luisa Doglio, Palermo: Sellerio Editore, 1997, 56–7.
15 Cosimo specifically left the farm at Colle to her brothers (Matteo, Raffaello, and Braccio) when he died in 1573 without any children. Her account book showcases her management of the day-to-day activities at the farm. Records also indicate her eventual efforts to buy the farm outright from her brothers. She listed a payment of 323 florins paid to Braccio, Raffaello, and Matteo, "the heirs of Cosimo Acciaoli" for the farm at Colle. ASF, Ricasoli Parte Antica, Libbri di amministrazione, Pezzo 270, *Giornale e Ricordi di Maddalena Ricasoli*, 1553–1564, 21r.
16 The Ricasoli estates bordered Siena and Florence. They suffered damage after Duke Cosimo I's war with Siena in the 1550s and much of the sibling correspondence discussed how to restore the lands and rebuild profits for the estates.
17 Letter from Maddalena Ricasoli to her brother, Braccio Ricasoli, 17 [April] 1580. ASF, Ricasoli Parte Antica, Filza 41, Fascio II, Fascetto V, lettere n. 3.

18 Renée Baernstein notes how correspondence by patrician women was common by the middle of the sixteenth century and that "most family archives of merchants and nobility positively teemed with women's letters." Renée Baernstein, "'In My Own Hand': Costanza Colonna and the Art of the Letter in Sixteenth Century Italy," *Renaissance Quarterly* 66(1) (2013): 140.

19 Letter from Maddalena Ricasoli Acciauoli to her brother, Braccio Ricasoli, 13 May 1553. ASF, Ricasoli Parte Antica, Filza 32, Fascio II, Fascetto II. "Fratello carissimo, per la portatore di quest sarà è veturale di Francesco di ci non al quale darai barili 8 di avendo ne tue del me del nostro volendo ce ne accomodare l'avremo caro e darli ve ricevuto Cosimo a per manco servi di gratia a farai veturale e ne altro, dio guardi."

20 Letter from Raffaello Ricasoli to his sister, Maddalena Ricasoli, 16 January 1558. ASF, Ricasoli Parte Antica, Filza 32, Fascio II, Fascetto IV, lettere n. 2. "Carissima sorella, per loro tengo la tua di 12 di presente circa il negotio della terra ... per Matteo insieme con Braccio si trovono mercoldi si darà ordine di comincare attendere grano et ti si manderanno danari di mano i mano del grano del suo lavoratore ve ne è venduto per 89 lire 5 soldi che i danari pagahti per te." At the end of the letter he wrote, "ne altro saluta Filippo et la Maria a nome di nostro madre."

21 Letter from Diamante Antinore ne Ricasoli to Maddalena Ricasoli negli Arringhucci, August 1593. ASF, Ricasoli Parte Antica, Filza 49, Fascio I, Fascetto VI, lettere n. 41. "Per versi sicurta di V.S. [Vostra Signora] acciò la pigli di me di mandare 80 fiaschi di vino a vendere costi in casa V.S. ... li piacerà per questa volta farne vendere altre 2 some che era rimasta."

22 Alison Smith, "The Renaissance Household in Sixteenth Century Verona," in *Wives, Widows, Mistresses, and Nuns in Early Modern Italy*, ed. Katherine McIver, Burlington, VT: Ashgate Publishing, 2012, 149.

23 Letter from Maddalena to her servant Nastasia, 24 September 1595. ASF, Ricasoli Parte Antica, Filza 41, Fascio II, Fascetto IV, lettere n. 66. "Carissima Nastasia, Si manda vino fiaschi n. 120 di questo di Cacchiano, attenderai a vendere il più che sia possibile e habbi occhio alla casa."

24 Letter from Maddalena to her servant, Nastasia, 10 January 1594. ASF, Ricasoli Parte Antica, Filza 40, Fascio I, Fascetto, IV, lettere n. 6. "Carissima Nastasia (istasia) quell sia sarà per darti aviso chome per Pietro da Lornano io mando il staia due di maroni a qual vorrei che ne portasti il staia uno a casa [di] Messer Donigi Carducci e mi rachomandassi a loro ... e se vi viene il veturale mandaci una materassa di quelle grande del letto dove dormivà Mona Camilla ... e da ci aviso chome il sta Mona Lisabetta ricordati di ma[n]darci la materassa e il panno quarto prima."

25 *Ibid.* "E più mando legne la quale da porterai a casa Diongi che la mandino alle loro figliole."

26 The bulk of her letters with Maddalena are written in the 1590s. However, there are numerous references in Maddalena's letters throughout the 1570s and 1580s to Nastasia's activities. The letters of Cassandra Gualterotti, the mother of Braccio's first wife Costanza, also reflect her dealings with Nastasia throughout the 1570s. Cassandra helped with deliveries to the Ricasoli home in Florence when Maddalena and Costanza stayed out in Cacchiano for extended lengths of time Nastasia clearly served as the point person in the Florentine palazzo.

27 While much is known about Maddalena's background, Nastasia's life remains more hidden from the historical record. Legislation concerning domestic service, as well as last wills and testaments provide knowledge of the lives and choices of servants. Giovanna Bendusi, "Investing the Riches of the Poor: Servant Women and their Last Wills," *American Historical Review* 109(3) (June 2004): 808. Since Nastasia's own letters date from the 1590s (though evidence suggests that she worked for Maddalena since the 1570s) it is possible that she learned to write after her extensive service with the Ricasoli family, though there is no direct evidence to support this.

28 Letter from Nastasia to Maddalena Ricasoli, 3 [September?] 1597. ASF, Ricasoli Parte Antica, Filza 41, Fascio II, Fascetto IV, Lettere n. 131. "ho mi trovo scriva farina senza vino."

29 *Ibid.* "mandatemi a dire come voi volete."

30 Letter from Alessandro Turilazzi di Bracciano to Nastasia, October 1595, ASF, Filza 41, Fascio II, Fascetto IV, Lettere n. 68. "Si manda fiaschi 120 di vino e caci undici di questo di bracciano, si che dice la padrona che attendiate a vendere e habbiate cara alla casa se il cognate del sarto vi porta danari il vino pigliateli o tenetene buon conto e vedete che vi dia Osteria somma di barili diciotto di quell di Cachiano. Manderete un paio di scarpe a Bindaccio, e a Cosimo."

31 Letter from Filippo di Cacchiano to Nastasia, 19 May 1595. ASF, Ricasoli Parte Antica, Filza 41, Fascio II, Fascetto IV, Lettere n. 50. "Carissima Nastasia questa sarà per darti aviso chome per

giamino garzone si manda sacha di farina che pesano con le sacha libbre 588 e più si manda paia dua di piccioni e un staia di nocie."

32 *Ibid.* "e mandaci il verde della Cecia il camiciotto vergato della verginia sono ne loro armadio o nel cassone."

33 Dennis Romano notes that "the physical structures, the palaces themselves, often served as symbols of lineages or patrilines" even though "many of the activities carried out in houses were the special concern of women" as part of the domestic interior. Dennis Romano, "Gender and the Urban Geography of Renaissance Venice," *Journal of Social History* 23(2) (1989): 342. See also, Robert Davis, "The Geography of Gender in the Renaissance," in *Gender and Society in Renaissance Italy*, London and New York: Longman, 1998, 19–38; Laurie Nussdorfer, "The Politics of Space in Early Modern Rome," *Memoirs of the American Academy in Rome* 42 (1999): 162–4.

34 Elizabeth Cohen, "To Pray, To Work, To Hear, To Speak: Women in Roman Streets c. 1600," *Journal of Early Modern History* 12 (2008): 291.

35 Letter from Maddalena to her servant, Nastasia, 12 February 1595. ASF, Ricasoli Parte Antica, Filza 40, Fascio I, Fascetto IV. "Carissima Nastasia, si manda farina saccha tre, un saccho libbre 205, uno 200, il terzo 192 a tale che a la somma di libbre 597 di più si manda olio dua mezzi barili pesono libbre 151 con i vasi si manda caci dieci in un sachetto pesono libbre 11 de quali ne darei coppie tre a Messer Ruberto e dua alla Cassandra mia nipote e non manchare in un altro sacchetto sono caci venti tre pesono libbre 26 il quale ti piaceva venderlo il meglio."

36 *Ibid.* "e il resto gli venderai."

37 Letter from Maddalena Ricasoli to her servant, Nastasia in Florence, 23 June 1594. ASF, Ricasoli Parte Antica, Filza 40, Fascio I, Fascetto IV, Lettere n. 5. "si manda fiaschi centro venti di vino il quale lo comincerai a vendere metti il prezzo a uno giusto il mancho di manda Messer Ruberto se glie bene mettela più e tiene conto che non vadia male tanto che io vengha dice farò costi questa settimana che viene."

38 Letter from Nastasia to her employer, Maddalena Ricasoli, 20 May 1595. ASF, Ricasoli Parte Antica, Filza 40, Fascio I, Fascetto IV, Lettere n. 17. "Honorada padrona, ho ricevuto per lo sgerra n. 120 fiaschi di vino, 14 caci e uno fiasco d'agresto, e uno staia di noce."

39 Letter from Maddalena to her servant, Nastasia, 24 September 1595. ASF, Ricasoli Parte Antica, Filza 41, Fascio II, Fascetto IV, Lettere n. 66. "Carissima Nastasia, Si manda vino fiaschi n. 120 di questo di Cacchiano, attenderai a vendere il più che sia possibile e habbi occhio alla casa penso ti vorra a trovare l'hoste da Castello cogniato del sarto il quale ti pagherà tre some di vino piglia danari e tiene buon conto, farai il servizio delle lettere che ti mando quanto prima."

40 Letter from Maddalena Ricasoli to her servant, Nastasia, 15 October 1595. ASF, Parte Antica Ricasoli, Filza 41, Fascio II, Fascetto IV, Lettere n. 71. "Carissima Nastasia, Vorrei sapere se tu hai mai ricosso i danari dal cognate del sarto hoste al Castello di barili diciotto di vino datoli e di più barili dua di vino dall' hoste dal Ponte a Ema."

41 Letter from Nastasia to Maddalena Ricasoli, 14 February 1595. ASF, Parte Antica Ricasoli, Filza 41, Fascio II, Fascetto IV, Lettere n. 78. "vi mando libbre 4 di lino di quello che a filato Mona Marietta che sono matasse 9 che ve ne una matassa di lino Cassandrina e più vi mando libbre 7 di lino di quello che o filato che sono matasse n. 28."

42 Letter from Nastasia to her employer, Maddalena Ricasoli, 20 May 1595. ASF, Ricasoli Parte Antica, Filza 40, Fascio I, Fascetto IV, Lettere n. 17. "vi mando la vesta nera della ceca … e quello della Verginia il vostra mantello di filatrice … e fra anni de fanciulli e 2 paia di manice galle … vorrebbe la risposta di quella lettere e vi mando una lettera del petinatore e dice che avrebbe caro che voi gli risponderei quarto prima."

43 Her husband, Matteo, likely wrote the letters as the handwriting looks remarkably similar to his own correspondence. He often attached messages regarding the estates to the bottom of her letters.

44 Letter from Maddalena the balia to her employer, Maddalena Ricasoli, 24 March 1589. ASF, Ricasoli Parte Antica, Filza 46, Fascio I, Fascetto III, Lettere n. 6. "Carissima padrona per Simone di Sallo si manda staia 3 di fiachi sechi 2 corbelli di pere o branche libbre 34 dice se che con l'sachetto e un paniere carne secche preso libbre 27 et staia 3 d grano … e servo si manda 2 lettere de Signore Cavaliere ci rimandarete quell l'saccha che si la farina e i fichi sechi l'altra volta e le cipolle il sacho … E a il Signore Bindaccio et a tutti ne altro di vi guardi di male."

45 Letter from Mona Cammilla to Maddalena Ricasoli, 19 July 1594. ASF, Parte Antica Ricasoli, Filza 41, Fascio II, Fascetto IV, Lettere n. 12. "si manda fiaschi 40 di vino biancho et fiaschi 80 di vino rosso … le venderete per che ve ne de che meglio voi in casa e più si manda 28 uove fresche ne altro rachomandatimi a quelli bambini e dio vi guardi di male. Io Mona Cammilla vostra a Cacchiano."

46 Letter from Cammilla a Cacchiano to Maddalena Ricasoli, 2 August 1594. ASF, Parte Antica Ricasoli, Filza 41, Fascio II, Fascetto IV, Lettere n. 15. "si manda fiaschi 80 di vino e più paia dua di pollastre un paio in darete a la Verginia et a paio a Bindaccio e Cosimo rachomandatimi a tutti questi bambini et a voi sopra a tutto ne altro dio vi guardi di male. Io Mona Cammilla a Cacchiano."

47 Letter from Cammilla a Cacchiano to Maddalena Ricasoli, 26 July 1592. ASF, Parte Antica Ricasoli, Filza 41, Fascio II, Fascetto IV, Lettere n. 13. "si manda fiaschi 120 di vino et coppia 17 di cacio che pasa libbre 18 con il paniere … e fazoletti sono quasi tutti il filo indente a bianco ma la balia non la anchora recato."

48 Zuber, "Women Servants in Florence," 61–2. Dennis Romano also looks at the importance of loyalty in the relationship between masters and servants in Renaissance Venice. Dennis Romano, *Housecraft and Statecraft, Domestic Service in Renaissance Venice, 1400–1600*, Baltimore: Johns Hopkins University Press, 1996, 191–226. For more about the relationship between masters and servants, see Piero Guarducci and Valeria Ottanelli, *I servitori domestici della casa Borghese Toscana nel basso medioevo*, Florence: Salimbeni, 1982; Sarah Maza, *Servants and Masters in Eighteenth-Century France: The Uses of Loyalty*, Princeton, NJ: Princeton University Press, 1983; Cissie Fairchilds, *Domestic Enemies: Servants and Their Masters in Old Regime France*, Baltimore: Johns Hopkins University Press, 1984.

49 Raffaella Sarti, "Who are Servants? Defining Domestic Service in Western Europe (16th-21st centuries)," in *Proceedings of the "Servant Project"*, ed. S. Pasleau and I. Schopp, vol. 2, Liège: Éditions de l'Université de Liège, 2005, 6. The language of Nastasia and Maddalena's letters certainly reflected this as Nastasia began her letters, "Carissima padrona Madonna Maddalena" and Maddalena Ricasoli often ended her letters with "tua padrona, Maddalena."

50 Letter from Nastasia to Maddalena Ricasoli, 17 January 1594. ASF, Ricasoli Parte Antica, Filza 40, Fascio I, Fascetto IV, Lettere n. 7. "da mi aviso se la Cassandra e ne in Firenze e come stanno Madonna Lisabetta."

51 Letter from Nastasia to Maddalena Ricasoli, 18 October 1595. ASF, Ricasoli Parte Antica, Filza 40, Fascio I, Fascetto IV, Lettere n. 26. "La presente sarà per avisarano come per quasi il dio siamo tutti sani e simile sentitramo che sia li voi ora aviso come Madonna Cassandra e sta bene e cosi li figliole … la Verginia sta bene."

52 Bendusi, "Investing the Riches of the Poor," 815.

53 Letter from Maddalena to her servant, Nastasia, 9 February 1594. ASF, Ricasoli Parte Antica, Filza 40, Fascio I, Fascetto IV, Lettere n. 10. "Carissimo Nastasia da il garzone del Pandolfino inteso li sentivi male avisa come stai."

54 *Ibid.* "portassi scudi venti a Madonna Lisabetta deva lita roti che facessi fare la ricevuta in libro e uno scudo portassi alla Maria de Carducci."

55 Letter from Maddalena "the balia" to Maddalena Ricasoli, 9 April 1590. ASF, Ricasoli Parte Antica, Filza 46, Fascio I, Fascetto III, Lettere n. 7. "Pero prego V.S. che avvisi il suo padrone che se fa per lui lo tenga … prego V.S. che di gratia facci questa carità."

56 Yale University, Beinecke Rare Book and Manuscript Library (hereafter, BRML), Box #129, Folder #2698, Spinelli Family Papers I. "Honorado fratello la presenta sia sola per raccomandarvi costui un certo Mariotto il quale e marito della Sandra mia serva … e per tanto vi si raccomando di quanto voi possete aiutarlo senza vostre charico sempre la volta prima l'onore vostro e di poi l'aiuto di questo povedretto."

57 *Ibid.* "della presente Ma. Piera di Matteo madre della Sandra mia serva che viene costi per vedere di risquotere non so che selva che dice essere della dote sua pregovi quanto posso il più che per amore nostro le facciate tutto quell favore et aiuto che e possible per che desidereri per essere quella poveretta et ha qua certi nipoti picchole a quale non ha il modo a fare le spese."

58 ASF, Ricasoli Parte Antica Libri di Amministrazione, Pezzo 304, *Entrate e Uscite di Maria Nobili Ricasoli*, cominciato 25 settembre 1602.

59 For information on the second-hand goods trade, see Patricia Allerston, "Reconstructing the Second Hand Clothes Trade in Sixteenth- and Seventeenth-Century Venice," *Costume* 33 (1999): 46–56;

Jacqueline Musacchio, *Art, Marriage, and Family in the Florentine Renaissance Palace*, New Haven: Yale University Press, 2009, 254.

60 Judith Brown, "A Woman's Place Was in the Home," 213.

61 Letter from Cassandra Ricasoli Tornabuoni to her aunt, Maddalena Ricasoli, 1593. ASF, Ricasoli Parte Antica, Filza 41, Fascio III, Fascetto V, Lettere n. 31. "la riveditora ieri mi porto 38 de padiglione la tela aveva la risposta domatina del lenzuola no[n] so tal nullo del' veluto dice ch' lo vuole portare domani."

62 Matchette, "Credit and Credibility," 233.

63 BRML, Box #22, Folder #528, Spinelli Family Papers I, 5r. "et più tempo fa vende una tela la balia di Madonna Margherita di Giovanni Altoviti di braccia 160 di panno da camice."

64 Robert Lopez and Harry Miskimin, "The Economic Depression of the Renaissance," *Economic History Review* 14 (1962): 408–9; Harry Miskimin, *The Economy of Early Renaissance Europe, 1300–1460*, Englewood Cliffs, NJ: Prentice Hall, 1969; Harry Miskimin, *The Economy of Late Renaissance Europe, 1460–1600*, New York: Cambridge University Press, 1977.

65 Salvatore Ciriacono, "'Protoindustria, lavoro a domicilio e sviluppo economico nelle champagne venete in epoca moderna," *Quaderni Storici* 52 (1983): 59–62; David Herlihy, "City and Countryside in Renaissance Tuscany," and "The Problem of the 'Return to the Land' in Tuscan Economic History of the Fourteenth and Fifteenth Centuries," in *Women, Family, and Society in Medieval Europe, Historical Essays, 1978–1991*, Oxford: Berghahn Books, 1995; Domenico Sella, *Italy in the Seventeenth Century*, London: Longman, 1997; Salvatore Ciriacono, "Economie urbane e industria rurale nell'Italia del Cinque e Seicento. Riconversione o stagnazione?" *Rivista storica italiana* 113 (2001): 7–8; Ferraro, "Representing Women," 84.

FURTHER READING

Alam, Muzaffar and Sanjay Subrahmanyam, eds. *The Mughal State, 1526–1750* (Delhi: Oxford University Press, 1998).

Bouwsma, William J. *A Usable Past: Essays in European Cultural History* (Berkeley and Los Angeles: University of California Press, 1990).

Brown, Alison. *The Renaissance* (London: Longman Publishing, 1999).

Burckhardt, Jacob. *The Civilization of the Renaissance in Italy*, trans. S. G. C. Middlemore and introduced by Peter Gay (New York: Penguin Books, 1982, originally published in 1860).

Burke, Peter. *The European Renaissance: Centres and Peripheries* (Oxford and Malden, MA: Blackwell, 1998).

———. *The Renaissance Sense of the Past* (New York: St. Martin's Press, 1969).

Caferro, William. *Contesting the Renaissance* (Oxford and Malden, MA: Wiley-Blackwell, 2011).

Celenza, Christopher S. *The Lost Italian Renaissance: Humanists, Historians and Latin's Legacy* (Baltimore: Johns Hopkins University Press, 2004).

Certeau, Michel de. *The Writing of History*, trans. Tom Conley (New York: Columbia University Press, 1988).

Dannenfeldt, Karl H., ed. *The Renaissance: Medieval or Modern?* (Boston: D. C. Heath and Company, 1959).

Eisenstein, Elizabeth L. *The Printing Press as an Agent of Change*, 2 vols. (Cambridge: Cambridge University Press, 1979).

Ferguson, Wallace K. *The Renaissance in Historical Thought: Five Centuries of Interpretation* (Cambridge, MA: Houghton Mifflin, 1948).

Findlen, Paula. *Early Modern Things: Objects and their Histories, 1500–1800* (London: Routledge, 2012).

Foucault, Michel. *The Order of Things: An Archeology of the Human Sciences* (New York: Pantheon, 1970).

Frazier, Alison Knowles. *Possible Lives: Authors and Saints in Renaissance Italy* (New York: Columbia University Press, 2004).

Gossman, Lionel. *Basel in the Age of Burckhardt: A Study of Unseasonable Ideas* (Chicago: University of Chicago Press, 2000).

Grafton, Anthony. *Commerce with the Classics* (Ann Arbor: University of Michigan Press, 1997).

Greenblatt, Stephen. *Marvelous Possessions: The Wonder of the New World* (Chicago: University of Chicago Press, 1991).

———. *Renaissance Self-Fashioning: From More to Shakespeare* (Chicago: University of Chicago Press, 1980).

Grendler, Paul F. *The European Renaissance in American Life* (Westport, CT: Greenwood Publishing, 2006).

Hale, John R. *The Civilization of Europe in the Renaissance* (New York: Harper, 2005).

Hay, Denys, ed. *The Renaissance Debate* (New York and London: Holt, Rinehart & Winston, 1965).

Huizinga, Johan. *The Autumn of the Middle Ages*, trans. Rodney J. Payton and Ulrich Mammitzsch (Chicago: University of Chicago Press, 1996, originally published in 1919).

Hunt, Lynn. *Writing History in a Global Age* (New York: Norton, 2014).

Jardine, Lisa and Jerry Brotton, *Global Interests: Renaissance Art between East and West* (London: Reaktion Books, 2000).

Kelly, Joan. "Did Women have a Renaissance," in Renate Bridenthal and Claudia Koonz, eds. *Becoming Visible: Women in European History* (Boston: Houghton Mifflin, 1977): 137–64.

King, Margaret L. *The Renaissance in Europe* (London: Laurence King, 2003).

Kirkpatrick, Robin. *The European Renaissance, 1400–1600* (London: Longman, 2002).

Kraye, Jill, ed. *A Companion to Renaissance Humanism* (Cambridge: University Press, 1997).

Law, John E. and Lene Østermark-Johansen, eds. *Victorian and Edwardian Responses to the Italian Renaissance* (Aldershot: Ashgate, 2005).

MacLean, Gerald, ed. *Re-Orienting the Renaissance: Cultural Exchanges with the East* (Basingstoke: Palgrave Macmillan, 2005).

Martin, John J., ed. *The Renaissance World* (New York: Routledge, 2007).

Meserve, Margaret. *Empires of Islam in Renaissance Historical Thought* (Cambridge, MA: Harvard University Press, 2008).

Molho, Anthony. "The Italian Renaissance, Made in the USA," in Anthony Mohlo and Gordon S. Wood, eds. *Imagined Histories, American Historians Interpret the Past* (Princeton, NJ: Princeton University Press, 1997): 264–7.

Muir, Edward. "The Italian Renaissance in America," *American Historical Review* 100(4) (October 1995): 1107–8.

Murphey, Rhoads. *Exploring Ottoman Sovereignty: Tradition, Image and Practice in the Ottoman Imperial Household, 1400–1800* (London and New York: Continuum, 2008).

Najemy, John M., ed. *Italy in the Age of the Renaissance* (Oxford: Oxford University Press, 2004).

Pagden, Anthony. *European Encounters in the New World* (New Haven and London: Yale University Press, 1993).

———. *The Fall of Natural Man: The American Indian and the Origins of Comparative Ethnology* (New York: Cambridge University Press, 1982).

Panofsky, Erwin. "Renaissance and Renascenses," *Kenyon Review* 6 (1944): 201–36 [Reprinted in *Renaissance and Renascences in Western Art* (Boulder, CO: Westview Press, 1972)].

Ray, Meredith. *Daughters of Alchemy: Women and Scientific Culture in Early Modern Italy* (Cambridge, MA: Harvard University Press, 2015).

Ruggiero, Guido. *The Renaissance in Italy: A Social and Cultural History of the Rinascimento* (Cambridge: Cambridge University Press, 2014).

Ruggiero, Guido, ed. *A Companion to the Worlds of the Renaissance* (Oxford and Malden, MA: Blackwell, 2002).

Şahin, Kaya and Julia Schleck. "Courtly Connections: Anthony Sherley's *Relation of his Travels into Persia* (1613) in a Global Context," *Renaissance Quarterly*, 69(1) (2016): 80–115.

Sider, Sandra. *Handbook to Life in the Renaissance* (Oxford: Oxford University Press, 2005).

Singh, Jyotsna G. *A Companion to the Global Renaissance* (Oxford and Malden, MA: Wiley-Blackwell, 2013).

Smith, Pamela H. *The Body of the Artisan: Art and Experience in the Scientific Revolution* (Chicago: University of Chicago Press, 2004).

Spiegel, Gabrielle. "The Task of the Historian," *American Historical Review* 114(1) (February 2009): 1–15.

Starn, Randolph. "A Postmodern Renaissance?" *Renaissance Quarterly* 60(1) (2007): 1–24.

Subrahmanyam, Sanjay. *Explorations in Connected History: From Tagus to the Ganges* (Oxford: Oxford University Press, 2004).

Terpstra, Nicholas and Colin Rose, eds. *Mapping Space, Sense, and Movement in Florence: Historical GIS and the Early Modern City* (New York: Routledge, 2016).

Welch, Evelyn. *Shopping in the Renaissance: Consumer Cultures in Italy, 1400–1600* (New Haven: Yale University Press, 2005).

Woolfson, Jonathan, ed. *Palgrave Advances in Renaissance Historiography* (New York: Palgrave Macmillan, 2005).

Wyatt, Michael, ed. *The Cambridge Companion to the Italian Renaissance* (Cambridge: Cambridge University Press, 2014).

INDEX